First published in the Isle of Man in 2015,
this edition 2020

Distributed by G2 Entertainment www.G2books.co.uk

Printed and bound in Europe
ISBN 9781782815808

Cover photos and image

Front cover image:
The Ferrari 340MM of Hans Ruesch and the Jaguar C Type of Stirling Moss at Parkfield in the 1953 British Empire Trophy Race. Painting by Peter Hearsey.

Rear cover photos:
(Top left): The Honourable Charles Rolls driving his Wolseley at Cronk-ny-Mona in the 1905 Gordon Bennett Trial. He won the 1906 Tourist Trophy Race driving an early Rolls-Royce.
(Top right): A.J. Hancock was a member of the Vauxhall team in the 1914 Tourist Trophy. Pictured at Ramsey's Parliament Square, he later crashed and over-turned on the Mountain road.
(Bottom left): Hugh Hamilton (MG Magnette K3) in Bucks Road, Douglas, between Princes Street and Tynwald Street, in the 1933 Mannin Beg Race. He retired after setting the fastest lap.
(Bottom right): Reg Parnell's Nash-Healey at Governor's Bridge in the 1951 British Empire Trophy Race, the first for production sports cars rather than racing cars. He retired when his gear lever broke.

EXTENDED SECOND EDITION

ISLE *of* MAN CAR RACES 1904 - 1953

Neil Hanson

This page: In the 1933 Mannin Beg race passing St. Thomas' Church, with the Manx Museum on the hill in the background, the MG Magnette K3 of Kaye Don (18) leads the similar car of Hugh Hamilton (16) from Church Road Marina into Finch Road. Don retired with camshaft drive failure and Hamilton suffered rear axle failure. [Magna Press]

Previous page: In the 1950 British Empire Trophy race Reg Parnell in his Scuderia Ambrosiana Maserati applies opposite lock outside the Isle of Man Bank on the exit from Manx Arms corner in Onchan Village. He finished sixth, a lap behind Bob Gerard's winning E.R.A. He had led the race but was delayed by a slipping clutch. Later the clutch started to grip and he set a new lap record. [Manx National Heritage]

CONTENTS

ACKNOWLEDGEMENTS

A BOOK such as this cannot be researched and written without considerable assistance. This is gratefully acknowledged by the author. Particularly so is the advice and help received from Robert Kelly, Ron Brew, the late George Bridge, Malcolm Buckler, Norman Caley, Les Clarke, Eric Corkish, Geoff Duke OBE, Richard Evans, Ian Harrison, Neville Hay, Stan Hughes, Peter Kelly CP, the late Brian Mylchreest LVO, OBE, TD, JP, David Mylchreest, Mylchreests Group, Eve Park, Billy Skelly, Ray Stanfield, Barbara Thorn and the Librarians and staff members of the Douglas Borough Library, the Leece Museum of Peel, the Manx National Heritage Manx Museum Library and i Museum, Murray's Motorcycle Museum, National Motor Museum Beaulieu and Onchan District Commissioners.

In the production of this book the help, advice and professionalism of Peter Duke of Duke Marketing Ltd, Jules Gammond and Ian Mackenzie of G2 Entertainment Ltd., Adrian Hatherall of Jellyfish Solutions Ltd, and Ruth Sutherland were greatly appreciated

Illustrations have been sourced as indicated.

In the 1933 Mannin Moar, race winner Brian Lewis takes Onchan Hairpin in his Alfa Romeo. He led from lap 7 to the finish, taking the first of his three Mannin Moar victories. [Ron Brew collection]

DEDICATION

The author wishes to dedicate this publication to the undying memory of Linda and Robert Kelly in appreciation of all their help, support and encouragement

FOREWORD

BY NIGEL MANSELL, CBE

As I lived on the Isle of Man for much of my time as a Grand Prix Driver, reading Neil Hanson's Isle of Man Car Races 1904 – 1953 brought back happy memories of the Island and its rich motor racing heritage.

By 1907, the year of the first of the Isle of Man TT motorcycle races which have become world-famous and also the year when the first car races in England were held on the newly-opened Brooklands circuit, the Island had already hosted two Gordon Bennett Trials and the first two RAC car TT races. With the aid of many evocative photographs, Neil's book gives a comprehensive and extensively researched account of the Island's car racing story from those early days of races, on roads no better than cart tracks, and brave and skilful pioneers like Clifford Earp and Charles Rolls to the street races in Douglas between the wars and the arrival of Stirling Moss and Mike Hawthorn on the post-war Douglas circuit.

I thoroughly enjoyed reading the book and hope it will bring pleasure to all who have an interest in the first fifty years of motor racing.

Nigel Mansell, CBE

PREFACE

I WAS seven years old when cars last raced on the Isle of Man's roads. I never saw a race or even a practice although my father was a Steward for all the British Empire Trophy Races from 1947 to 1953. However we lived very close to the TT Grandstand area where the races were based and the sight and sound of race cars on their way to and from the Paddock aroused an early interest in this alternative to the TT and Manx Grand Prix motorcycle races which were so much more popular at the time.

I gradually found out more about the Island's car races – that there had been two TT races for cars before the first motorcycle TT, that the car TT had been lost to Northern Ireland in 1928 and never brought back to the Island despite opportunities to do so, that cars had raced in the streets of Douglas in the thirties and that an initially promising post-war revival in 1947 had faltered in the face of local political opposition before being abandoned in favour of a poorly supported TT Sidecar race.

Although there was a lack of books on the subject (apart from Richard Hough's Tourist Trophy, published in 1957) my knowledge of the races gradually increased with a growing collection of magazine race reports and articles, postcards and photographs. Assisting leading Manx Author Robert Kelly with his book TT Pioneers (published in 1996) which covered the early races to 1922 generated my ambition to write a book about the later races between 1933 and 1953. My retirement in 2011 gave me time to research and to write the book which I extended to cover the entire period of Isle of Man car races from 1904 to 1953. The book was first published in 2015 after my first book of car race photographs from the Keig photographic collection, published in 2013.

At an early stage I discussed my project with a gifted and highly respected motoring writer. He asked me whether I was writing a motoring history or a local history. I said I thought it would be both. I have tried to write it in this way and both the text and the choice of photographs are aimed at illustrating not only the races but also the Isle of Man as it was in the first half of the twentieth century. I hope the book will be of interest both to motorsport enthusiasts and to all who have an interest in the Island's rich and varied history.

Neil Hanson.

In the 1914 Tourist Trophy, A.J. Hancock's Vauxhall is pictured in Queen's Pier Road, Ramsey, approaching Cruickshank's corner. Later he crashed on the approach to the Bungalow and his mechanic George Gibbs was critically injured. [Les Clarke collection]

INTRODUCTION

On behalf of the Mylchreests Group, and indeed the Mylchreest family I am delighted to provide sponsorship for Neil Hanson's book entitled "Isle of Man Car Races 1904 - 1953", and to have been given the opportunity to write this short foreword. I am only sorry that my late Father Brian Mylchreest did not quite live to see the fruits of Neil's hard work, although he had talked to Neil about the book during its gestation.

Those who know Neil Hanson will agree that anything he puts his mind to will be executed in a thorough and professional way and most of all you will know that every single detail will have been thought through carefully and the end product will be as accurate as it's possible to be. Neil's passion for cars and motor racing, and especially when related to his native Isle of Man, is legendary.

The Mylchreest association with motor cars, motor sport and of course through the Mylchreests Dealerships, selling and repairing cars is, I think, synonymous with the Isle of Man. In the pioneering days of motoring my Grandfather and his brother set up the first "Mylchreest" garage, in Athol Street, Douglas, and this was to be the start of the Family's involvement in all things motoring. We like to think that we were the pioneers of the Manx motor trade really! We have represented and continue to represent many of the leading car manufacturers, including such famous names as Riley, Rover, Wolseley, Austin, Morris, Triumph, Daimler, Jaguar, MG, Vauxhall, Land Rover, Mitsubishi, Volvo, Subaru, Rolls-Royce and Bentley. Some of these are of course just memories now!

My Family's connection with Manx motor racing, in both two and four wheeled guises probably goes back to the very beginning of the sport. We have been providing and driving the official course cars for almost all of the motor sport events ever held on the Isle of Man! We have wonderful family photographs of my Grandfather opening the roads exactly 100 years ago, in his own Bentley and in a Crossley, and of my Father in Nancy Mitchell's "Works" Mille Miglia MGA leaping over Ballaugh Bridge over 60 years ago! This is a tradition that is still proudly in place today, with both me and my Son James, the third & fourth generations of the Mylchreest family competing in various disciplines of this wonderful sport and of course still driving the official cars for the TT, Manx Grand Prix and Southern 100 motorcycle races.

My late Father was himself passionate about Manx History, and especially Manx motoring history. As you read through this book you will see a number of photographs from his large "collection", and he would have been delighted that Neil has chosen them to be featured in this wonderful book. Of course my Father had been involved himself as an Official for the British Empire Trophy Races, he was the Clerk of the Course's official driver, and this involved driving the Clerk of the Course out to incidents on the course – during the races themselves! I can recall him telling me that at times that job was almost as exciting as the actual racing, it certainly was for him!

David Mylchreest
January 2020

THE EPIC ERA 1904 - 1922

Campbell Muir's Wolseley "beetle" is pictured on Douglas Promenade during the one kilometer standing start speed test which followed the 1904 Gordon Bennett Trial. He retired on lap 1 of the Trial with a broken spring but was sixth in the one kilometer speed test and fifth in the hill-climb at Port-e-Vullen. [Brian Mylchreest collection]

1900-1903 Gordon Bennett Races

As well as providing a name which became an exclamation of shock or surprise, James Gordon Bennett, proprietor of the *New York Herald*, founded a series of early motor races which led directly to the establishment of motor sport on the Island.

In the earliest times, from the Paris-Rouen Trial of 1894, inter-city motor races were very much a French monopoly, both in organisation and in successes of car manufacturers. James Gordon Bennett believed a prestigious trophy for competition between national teams would encourage manufacturers of different nationalities to compete in an effort to end the French domination of the sport. In 1899 he wrote to national automobile clubs offering a trophy for annual competition, to be called the *Coupe Internationale* (although, against his wishes, it became known as the Gordon Bennett Cup). He specified that the first race should be run in France by the Automobile Club de France. Then the winning country's national automobile club would be responsible for organizing the next race but, if that proved impossible, the race would be run in France by the Automobile Club de France.

After an inauspicious start in 1900, when two French cars were the only finishers, and in 1901, when the only team was French, the races started to be taken seriously. In the 1902 race, combined with the Paris-Vienna race but finishing at Innsbruck, the only starters to challenge the French were the British team consisting of Selwyn Edge's Napier and Montague Grahame-White's Wolseley. After a heroic drive, Edge won the Cup for Great Britain. That meant the Automobile Club of Great Britain and Ireland had the obligation of organising the 1903 race. As it was legally impossible to race on closed public roads on the United Kingdom mainland and as there was no chance of persuading Parliament to alter the legislation, the Automobile Club decided to organise the race in Ireland, where it was possible to change the law. The chosen course was a figure-of-eight closed circuit at Athy in County Kildare, the race distance being 327.5 miles.

The Automobile Club held "eliminating trials" in order to decide the team. The trials consisted of flying kilometre and standing mile speed tests on the Duke of Portland's estate at Welbeck Abbey and three climbs of Dashwood Hill, near High Wycombe. The hill climbs took place in early morning, illegally and secretly, on a public highway. These trials were hardly satisfactory and clearly something better would be needed for 1904.

After the 1903 race – won for Germany by the Belgian driver Camille Jenatzy in a Mercedes, with France second, third and fourth and Edge placed fifth but later disqualified for receiving assistance – the thoughts of the Automobile Club pondered how and where to arrange better eliminating trials for 1904.

1904 Gordon Bennett Eliminating Trial

Planning

After the Automobile Club had considered the Ardennes Circuit in Belgium as a possible venue for the 1904 trial, and rejected it because of the Belgians' excessive financial demands, Club Secretary Julian Orde had an inspiration. His cousin, Lord Raglan, who until 1902 had been UK Under-Secretary of State for War, was now Lieutenant-Governor for the Isle of Man. Orde thought that the Island might readily welcome motor racing and that Tynwald, the Island's Parliament, might be willing to pass a Bill to make it possible. After deciding to approach his cousin, Orde arrived in Douglas in February 1904. He was enthusiastically received by Raglan, who immediately became the driving force in the introduction of motor racing to the Isle of Man.

Raglan acted quickly. Douglas Town Council met on 9th March to appoint a Committee to assist in arranging the trial. On 15th March Raglan introduced in the Legislative Council (the Upper House of Tynwald, the Island's Parliament) "The Highways (Light Locomotives) Bill, 1904". Based partly on the Bill drafted by Lord Montagu to permit the Irish Gordon Bennett Race of 1903, the Manx Bill gave the Highway Board, with the consent of the Governor, the power to order that public roads on the Island could be used for races with "light locomotives". The Board would have power to suspend and regulate other traffic for the safety of the public and to restrict speed in "populous places". The Bill also provided that laws restricting speed or imposing penalties for furious driving would not apply to light locomotives or drivers engaged in races. The powers given to the Board were limited to 1904 and exercisable only for three weekdays.

The Legislative Council gave the Bill its formal first reading without even seeing it. It was still with the printers.

Later a copy of the Bill arrived from the printers and the Council rushed through the second and third readings, passed the Bill and sent it downstairs to the House of Keys (the Lower House of Tynwald). After criticism of the way in which they were being asked to rush through a Bill giving the Highway Board unprecedented powers (and, some said, unlimited powers to endanger the public), the House agreed to consider the Bill. After discussions, the Keys passed the Bill and it was formally signed by members of the Council and Keys in early evening. It was then sent to London for Royal Assent, which was eventually granted. All new Acts of Tynwald were required to be promulgated at the annual open air parliamentary sitting held in July on Tynwald Hill, a circular tiered "wedding cake" mound of turf in the village of St. John's. This involved the public reading, in English and Manx, of the short title and the purpose of every Act passed during the year. Clearly July would be too late – the trial was scheduled to take place on 10th May – so a special sitting was held at St. John's on 5th May when the Act finally took effect after a minor embarrassment as Julian Orde's Wolseley, carrying Lord Raglan to St. John's, broke down at Braddan Bridge, less than two miles out of Douglas. Orde quickly solved the problem and the Governor arrived punctually at St. John's.

Arrangements started as soon as Tynwald had passed the Bill. On 23rd March, Highway Board members met Raglan and Orde to inspect the course and discuss required road improvements. The Highway Board approved a draft Order to close the roads for the trial. As the Advertising Board had no funds to assist with costs in connection with the trial, the Mayor of Douglas and a sub-committee raised a fund to meet half of the estimated £425 required to cover policing, signalling, printing and other expenses. The Isle of Man Steam Packet Company designed special frames for lifting cars on and off its ships.

While planning the course, accompanied on his Wolseley by Lord Raglan, Deemster Kneen (the Island's senior Judge) and Chief Constable Freeth, Orde was surprised when the steering wheel came off in his hands. He swiftly replaced it and none of his passengers appeared to notice!

The course originally proposed by Orde was quickly abandoned. The route went in an anti-clockwise direction north from Douglas by way of the coast road through Laxey to Ramsey. Passing through the centre of Ramsey via Waterloo Road, the course travelled south via Kirk Michael and Ballacraine to Ballasalla before returning to Douglas. This course was considered unacceptable because of disruption to the shopping centre of Ramsey and the mining industry of Laxey. The quickly planned replacement took a clockwise direction, starting outside Douglas and travelling south via Ballasalla to the outskirts of Castletown. It then turned north, via Ballacraine and Kirk Michael to Ballaugh. There, instead of continuing through Sulby to Ramsey in the reverse direction of the original course, a detour was included by Orde to provide extra mileage, taking the course to Ramsey via Ballaugh Old Church, Sandygate and St.Jude's. From Ramsey, instead of returning to Douglas via the Laxey coast road, the course climbed the

Above left: The Trial meant the arrival of racing cars on the Island for the first time. The photograph shows the unloading of a Napier from an Isle of Man Steam Packet Company ship at the Battery Pier, Douglas. [Keig collection]

Left: Automobile Club Secretary Julian Orde inspected the course at the wheel of his Wolseley, accompanied by Lieutenant Governor Lord Raglan, First Deemster Thomas Kneen and Chief Constable Col. Freeth. They are pictured with George Drinkwater, President of the Manx Automobile Club. [Keig collection]

Officials at the Ballasalla control await the arrival of the first car. The control marked the start of a neutral zone which extended through Ballasalla along the main road to Castletown and round the outskirts of the town to another control where timing resumed. [Ray Stanfield collection]

Snaefell Mountain Road for the return. The total lap distance was 52.125 miles and six laps were to be completed.

Alfred "Toby" Rawlinson, Managing Director of the Darracq importers, arrived in Douglas with a 40hp Darracq, one of the first racing cars to be seen on the Island. He said "I fancy it would be impossible to obtain a course more suited to test cars and drivers".

Entries

In April, the Automobile Club required intending entrants to present their cars at the Club's garage in Down Street, Mayfair, where they were weighed. Five Napiers came from the company's nearby factory in Lambeth. There was a 100hp model to be driven by Mark Mayhew, a 90hp car of Selwyn Edge, two 65hp versions for John Hargreaves and Clifford Earp and "the little 55hp job" of Jack Stocks. Three racing green Wolseleys, for Campbell Muir, Sidney Girling and Charles Jarrott, were brought from Birmingham. Muir and Jarrott were to drive "beetles" or "cockroaches" which had pointed nose cones formed by fairings in front of the radiators while Girling's car had a more conventional flat-fronted radiator. Finally, after a long delay, the scrutineers were about to leave when the three 100hp cars of the Darracq team of Rawlinson, Edmond and Victor Hemery arrived, having been brought by train from the Glasgow factory of G. & J. Weir Ltd. The reason was that, to comply with the Gordon Bennett rules, these French cars had been assembled by G & J Weir in Glasgow using drawings received only ten weeks earlier. For the same reason, Michelin sent a tyre assembly plant to England. The Darracqs were scarcely finished, unpainted and short of tyres. In addition to the three teams which attended, three Huttons had been expected but failed to appear and were deemed to have been withdrawn. Some cars were over-weight and needed further work before being brought to the Island.

Preparation

As soon as the course was finalised Douglas Corporation agreed to build a wooden grandstand with a capacity of one thousand seats, in a field on Quarterbridge Road where there would also be a tented refreshment area. In Ramsey, while inspecting the course, Orde was button-holed by the Town Commissioners, who wanted the trial to start and finish in the Town. Instead, they were offered a depot in Queen's Pier Road, between Parliament Square and the start of the Mountain climb, where trial competitors could take on fuel, oil and water, and a hill-climb at Port-e-Vullen, two miles outside the town, on the day after the main trial.

In the interest of safety, for drivers and for the public, Julian Orde provided five "Control Zones" in populated areas. These were neutral sections where drivers would be given a generous time allowance between stopping points at the beginning and end of each zone. The zones were from the entrance to the village of Ballasalla to the far side of Castletown (1.375 miles to be covered in 4 minutes), at Foxdale (a stop and re-start to neutralize a

Above: In Parliament Square, a car approaches the time control in Queen's Pier Road at the end of the Ramsey neutral zone. The uphill bend leading into Cruickshank's corner and May Hill can be seen in the distance. [Manx National Heritage]

Above right: Jack Stocks stops his Napier at the Foxdale control. This was a simple stop and restart in order to limit the speed of competitors on the dangerous double bend under the Foxdale Railway Bridge. Stocks finished fourth in the Trial. He was selected as a reserve for the British team in the Gordon Bennett Race. [John Watterson collection]

dangerous narrow S-bend between the stone pillars of a railway bridge), at Kirk Michael (where "Lace's Control" was used to neutralize a half mile section starting outside the house of Lace the Shoemaker in Kirk Michael village with a two minutes allowance), at Ramsey (a half mile section through the outskirts of the town, for which two minutes were allowed), and finally the 1.5 miles stretch from Willaston Corner on the outskirts of Douglas to the Start/Finish at Quarterbridge, to be covered in three minutes. Time allowances for the competitive parts of the course were:

Quarterbridge – Ballasalla 8 miles – 10 minutes including acceleration tests from the start-line on each lap.

Castletown – Kirk Michael 16 miles – 22 minutes including the Foxdale Control and a stop-start test.

Kirk Michael – Ramsey 11.25 miles – 15 minutes including the 0.5 mile speed test from a point one mile past Ballaugh Old Church.

Ramsey – Willaston Corner, Douglas 13 miles – 18 minutes including a 2.5 miles hill-climb speed test on the Mountain road, starting from the Ramsey control.

The course included four Isle of Man Railway level crossings, at Quarterbridge, Ballasalla, Ballacraine, and Ballaugh and also the Snaefell Mountain Railway crossing at the Bungalow. Isle of Man Railway services were therefore suspended during the event but the Snaefell Mountain Railway continued, with trams stopping just below the road crossing and passengers using a short pedestrian tunnel under the road.

Racing cars driven on the Island before 10th May were required to be fitted with efficient silencers. They were allowed to be driven on the roads only between daybreak and 7am and not at all on Sundays, under threat of disqualification.

The Automobile Club was anxious that the trial should not be described as a race. The Regulations emphasised that it was intended to be "a high speed reliability trial including speed tests against time over half a mile on the flat in each circuit, speed tests against time in climbing a hill in each circuit, acceleration tests from rest and stopping observations, observation of the skill and suitability of the driver and examination of condition of cars at termination of trial". It also stated in the regulations for the trial that (as in today's rallies) there would be no bonus marks for taking less than the scheduled minimum time. The reason given for the Club's avoidance of the word "race" was that it wanted to avoid being committed in the selection of the British team by the results of a race alone. The need for reliability was stressed. Another possible reason was the need to appease public opposition to the event – even the

Marshals for the Trial were required to appear before Justices of the Peace to take the oath of Special Constables, giving them the legal power of Police Officers to enforce the closure of the roads. Marshals at Foxdale were sworn-in at Foxdale Mines by Mines Captain William Kitto J.P. [Keig collection]

King telegraphed the Club Chairman to urge that everything possible should be done to ensure the safety of competitors and spectators. There was nervousness about the possibility of fatal accidents with the disastrous Paris-Madrid Race of 1903, which had claimed the lives of at least five drivers and mechanics as well as several spectators, still fresh in everyone's memory. Alarmists predicted "a large crop of broken necks and heads" while *The Motor* said the Island's course was "a nasty, twisty course, full of death-traps and if there were a horrible accident in tomorrow's race there would be an end to motor sport events in the kingdom".

Confusion was rife, in the minds of the public, the Government, and even the Club itself, as to whether the event was a race or not. In reply to a spectator who asked who had won, senior Automobile Club official Earl Russell replied "It isn't a race, it isn't over, and, as in Alice in Wonderland they have all won". However, a lady's souvenir cotton headscarf was embroidered with a car and the words "Manx Car Race 1904", while the Act of Tynwald which made the event possible referred to "races with light locomotives", the Highway Board's Road Closing Order stated that the roads would remain closed "until the termination of the race", and the Club's official car, which followed the last car in order to re-open the roads to public use, carried a "Race Finished" sign!

Competitors also were dis-satisfied with the ambiguity. Under the leadership of Darracq Team Manager "Toby" Rawlinson, with the support of the Napier and Wolseley drivers, they wrote to the Automobile Club saying that they wanted a race, pure and simple, with no speed restrictions. One of the drivers alleged to *The Motor* that the letter included an ultimatum to the Club that if their demand for a proper race was not met there would be no trial under the Club's control but instead a privately-organised race. This is highly unlikely because there could have been no British Team in the Gordon Bennett Race unless selected by the Automobile Club. Nevertheless, in a meeting which started at 5pm on the Sunday evening before the trial, adjourned for dinner at 8pm, and then resumed and continued until a late hour, Club officials produced a compromise. The event would not be a race, in that no driver would be allowed to complete the 49.25 miles of competitive sections of the course in less than 65 minutes (a time which nobody was likely to achieve), but there would be an additional speed test over a stretch of three miles on the Ballamodha Straight between the third and sixth milestones on the road between Castletown and Foxdale, and minimum times allowed between control zones would be reduced. This included a reduction of the minimum time for the 13 miles section between Ramsey and Willaston Corner on the outskirts of Douglas from 18 minutes to 13 minutes.

The compromise was grudgingly accepted by the drivers, who felt that their point had been made. Charles Jarrott later commented: "For some reason best known to themselves the Committee of the Automobile Club wished to obscure the fact that the trial was really a race, the selection of cars remaining in their hands, regardless of what the results of the trial were. In similar vein, Selwyn Edge said in his *Motoring Reminiscences*: "It was emphasised that it would be nothing more than a trial and not a race but subsequent events proved that it was far more a race than a trial". He added "Exactly why the Automobile Club was so anxious to disguise the contest as a trial I never understood, for the selection of drivers to represent this country in the Gordon-Bennett Trophy race rested entirely with the racing committee, irrespective of who put up the best performance".

Practice

Informal practising on the course was permitted on weekdays only, between dawn and 7am. The course was open to normal traffic and unmarshalled, apart from a few volunteers who opened the gates across the Snaefell mountain road as cars approached. There were various incidents. Mark Mayhew, after a "sideslip", collided with an embankment and a tree, breaking his front axle. He sent a request to the Napier factory for a replacement car and remained resolute in the face of pressure from his wife not to compete. There was no replacement car. Instead, the axle was hammered straight but unfortunately re-fitted the wrong way round. Earp's Napier hit a house adjoining the Whitestone Inn in Ballasalla at 5.40am whereupon the driver elected to walk the eight miles back to Douglas with the mechanic rather than wait for the 8am train. Hemery's Darracq hit a cow, resulting in "hysterics and nervous shock" – to the cow, according to a Darracq team bulletin! Charles Jarrott, after his serious accident in the 1903 Gordon Bennett Race in Ireland, worried that "nerves" were inevitable. He recalled "I feared that in some indefinable manner, when I came to drive a car in a race, all that dash which is necessary to race successfully would be lacking. I had never known what nerves meant, and any sense of danger when racing was foreign to me. It can therefore be understood that I was somewhat anxious to know whether I had changed".

Unsurprisingly, early morning practising gave rise to complaints. *The Automotor Journal* reported as early as 9th April "Already there appears to be some inconsiderate driving taking place on the Isle of Man, and the complaints which naturally follow these ill-advised proceedings are finding their way into the local press".

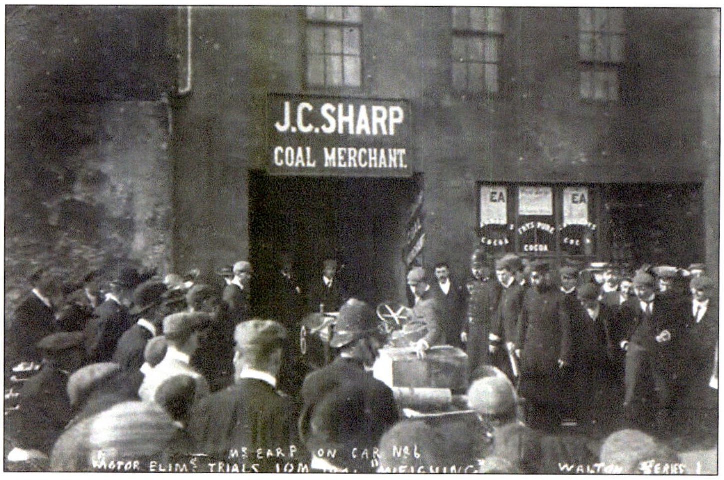

Above: J.C. Sharp's coal yard on North Quay, Douglas was the venue for the pre-Trial weighing of the cars. Clifford Earp's Napier is pictured at the entrance. [R and L Kelly collection]

Below: In this photograph of the Wolseley garage the three cars of Charles Jarrott (12), Campbell Muir (7) and Sidney Girling (10) are worked on by mechanics. The cars of Jarrott and Muir were pointed-nosed "beetles" but Girling had a more conventional car with a flat-fronted radiator. [Brian Mylchreest collection]

On Monday 9th May the pre-race weighing-in took place in a coal-hole, according to *The Motor*. This was a shed at J.C. Sharp's coal and coke yard "in a rather unsavoury quarter of the North Quay" at Douglas, where cars were weighed by Mr Sharp under the watchful eye of Worby Beaumont of the Automobile Club. The Napiers were all well within the weight limit and were quickly passed. Due, perhaps, to accumulations of mud and grease during practising, others had difficulty in getting under the weight limit of 1,000kg (2,240lbs), despite having met the limit when weighed in London. Drastic measures were needed. The Wolseleys of Campbell Muir and Charles Jarrott were about 18lbs over weight and Muir's car had its front wings removed although both had been nearly 50lbs under when weighed in London, and although Girling's Wolseley passed without modification. The Darracq team was in real trouble, being forced to remove bonnets, silencers, cushions, brackets, battery boxes, magneto covers and even floor boards in its efforts to discard some 60lbs of excess weight. Even then, Rawlinson's car was still over weight at 10pm and had to be re-checked the following morning while Edmond's car received a concession of 6lbs for grease in order to achieve the limit. It was later alleged that one of the Darracqs had arrived at the start line on the next day minus its rear brake shoes!

A well-known motoring correspondent wrote before the trial "We have only one wish left, and that is that the hotel keepers of the Isle of Man will prove themselves as modest as their confreres in the Emerald Isle showed themselves exorbitant in their charges!" His wish was granted for *The Motor* reported that on the eve of the trial: "Douglas was found in a kind of ferment…there is the

same enthusiastic welcome as found in Ireland in 1903…", but "…in every direction one obtains evidence of the desire of the inhabitants to cater for their visitors as fully as they can, and to do the thing at a moderate figure. To the islanders, the motor invasion is something to marvel at". The report continued "The Island is wild with enthusiasm and without any attempt to go the whole hog and overdo matters as they did in Ireland, ample preparations are being made for a great day tomorrow".

1904 Gordon Bennett Eliminating Trial

All 11 remaining entries assembled at the starting point on the Castletown road near to the Quarterbridge Hotel early on Tuesday 10th May. There were the Napiers (Nos.1, 3, 6, 9 and 14) of Jack Stocks, John Hargreaves, Clifford Earp, Selwyn Edge and Mark Mayhew, the Darracqs (Nos. 2, 4, and 11) of Edmond, Victor Hemery and "Toby" Rawlinson and the Wolseleys (Nos. 7, 10 and 12) of Campbell Muir, Sidney Girling and Charles Jarrott. The missing numbers (5, 8 and 13) had been allocated to the Hutton team which had been scratched after failing to attend the London inspection. The starter was Major (later Colonel) Lindsay Lloyd, who later became well-known as Clerk of the Course at the Brooklands Track. He stood behind the cars and, when he dropped his flag, the signal was replicated by Professor Vernon Boys who stood 200 yards along the course to conduct the standing start acceleration test. The dropping of Boys' flag was the signal for the driver to start. Cars were to be started at five minutes intervals.

The first starter, at 9am, was Jack Stocks with the "little" 55hp Napier. Edmond's Darracq should have started next, but water had been found in his fuel and his tank was being drained. The second starter, therefore, was the 65hp Napier of John Hargreaves, Master of Foxhounds, "as cool as a cucumber and clad in a well-worn slip-on and a cap with a most pronounced and horsey-looking peak", according to the fashion-conscious reporter for *The Autocar*. The next in starting order was Hemery with the second Darracq but, as he also was absent, Hargreaves was followed by the 65hp Napier of Clifford Earp who "looked very workmanlike in a marvellous Norfolk suit of white rubber" and the Wolseley of Campbell Muir who "had a hearty farewell from the crowd, who openly admired his athletic frame, which towered above the bucket seat in a way which showed unmistakably how finely developed a man he was". At this point, according to *Motoring Illustrated*, Hemery "made a sensational entry on the scene, the engine of his Darracq banging like a volley of salute guns". Edge, whose 90hp Napier was now next in line to start, asked Colonel Lloyd "He won't start before me, will he?" and Hemery was waved away to await his turn. Edge was "a most striking figure, with blue skull cap and a white rubber poncho; in fact, the car and its crew looked most motoristic, as the mechanician was dressed to match the hawk-eyed occupant of the driver's bucket". After Edge came the Wolseleys of Girling and Jarrott, whose first speed gear wheel broke on the line. This left him worrying that the broken parts inside the gearbox would jam the other gears and wreck the car. Then Hemery, described by *The Autocar* as "a picture of listless, self-confident dirtiness for he was in truth far from well groomed" suddenly appeared with flames spouting from the Darracq's exhaust pipes and surrounded by a cloud of blue smoke. He caused consternation (and threats of disqualification) by charging away from the line without waiting for the start signal, apparently due to language difficulties. He was followed by Edmond, who had replaced

Above: On the first lap the Napier of John Hargreaves was first to reach the Ramsey control on the outskirts of the town at St. Olave's, where Jurby Road joins Bowring Road. Competitors were allowed two minutes to drive through the town to Queen's Pier Road, where they were re-started for the Mountain climb. [Stan Hughes collection]

Left: Charles Jarrott's Wolseley is pictured at the Ballasalla control near the Whitestone Inn. This marked the start of the neutral section which extended to the far side of Castletown. Jarrott was fifth fastest overall but set the second fastest lap time, only thirty seconds slower than team-mate Sidney Girling. [Brian Mylchreest collection]

On the first lap in Parliament Square, close to the Ramsey control, the Wolseleys of Sidney Girling (10) and Campbell Muir (7) receive attention. Muir had already had tyre trouble and his gear lever had broken. After stopping in Ramsey for three hours, he retired at the end of the lap with a broken spring. [R and L Kelly collection]

his contaminated fuel. Mark Mayhew, delayed on his way to the Start by a collision with a frightened pony, was the next starter at 10.11. Rawlinson, his Darracq also delayed by water in the fuel, was the final starter at 10.58, after some had started on the second lap. Typically of the Darracq team's numerous problems, Rawlinson said that he got an electric shock every time he pulled the clutch out.

The *Isle of Man Examiner* observed that "The three Darracq cars, which had been hastily flung together and brought to the Island in a very raw state, were the terror of the countryside during practising and they provided sensations of a spectacular kind on race day. Stripped of their bonnets to comply with weight conditions, they snorted and spewed forth smoke, and with engines banging like a volley of salute-guns they were the real villains of the drama. 'Toby' Rawlinson, or 'Brimfire Jack', as he was temporarily called by the Manx people by reason of the daring way in which he tore over the course in his flame-producing Darracq, simply screamed up to the starting line, while spectators and officials scattered in all directions.

"As the word was given for him to go, he supplied all the elements of a first-class thunder-storm – heavy peals, lightning, clouds and the smell of burnt rubber – and when the storm cleared 'Toby' had disappeared, leaving trifling bits of mechanism spread about the road. Very shortly after, however, the mighty engine was struck dumb, and the driver leisurely took the first exit to the left and made an inglorious exit – within a few seconds of quitting the starting point!" The universal joint on his propeller shaft had sheared.

Hargreaves covered the eight miles from the start to the Ballasalla control in seven and a half minutes, while Hemery was only a half a minute slower. As ten minutes was the minimum time allowed, both risked disqualification! Hargreaves was first to reach Ramsey, arriving at 10am, and stopped to tighten his clutch spring. He had caught and passed Stocks, who had been delayed with valve trouble and arrived at 10.10, stopping to repair the driver's seat and a water leak. Earp arrived two minutes later, followed at 10.19 by Edge who removed his exhaust pipe and reported that Muir had stopped at Kirk Michael with tyre trouble. Soon afterwards, Edge himself was reported to have stopped twice on the mountain climb with punctures and to have driven seven miles on a flat tyre. Girling arrived at 10.24 and replaced an inlet valve. He was followed by Jarrott at 10.30, the latter reporting that Muir's gear lever had broken. Jarrott then stopped to fish the fragments of both first and reverse

Selwyn Edge's Napier crosses Quarterbridge to complete a lap. His was the third fastest time for the five laps, Clifford Earp's Napier and Sidney Girling's Wolseley both being faster, although he had no problems other than a stop at Ramsey on the first lap to remove his exhaust pipe. [Manx National Heritage]

The Darracq driven by the French driver Edmond is pictured at the foot of Bray Hill on the first lap. Edmond arrived at the end of the lap smothered in oil from a burst pipe and without any effective brakes. The car was then withdrawn in the interests of safety as was the sister car of Hemery which also had brake failure. [Peter Kelly collection]

gear wheels out of the box before continuing. Muir arrived at 10.49, continuing after three hours but retired at the end of the lap with a broken spring after overcoming problems with run big-ends (according to *The Car Illustrated*) or a broken change-speed-lever (according to *The Automotor Journal*). He took six hours to complete the lap. Edmond's Darracq arrived with driver and mechanic smothered in oil which spurted from a broken pipe and, although Hemery was going well, both Darracq drivers soon had brake trouble.

Hargreaves was the first to complete the lap, two minutes ahead of Stocks, and was ready to start the second lap at 10.31. Stocks re-started seven minutes later, followed by Earp (10.42), Edge (10.46) and Jarrott (10.55), three minutes before the hapless Rawlinson made his abortive start. Both the other Darracqs completed the first lap without brakes. Hemery, who had ignored a signal to stop at Ballasalla due to his false start, was again signalled to stop by Major Lloyd, who had to run for his life as he was almost pinned to the wall when the Darracq's brakes failed. Although Hemery was keen to continue, Rawlinson withdrew both cars in the interests of safety, perhaps anticipating similar action by Major Lloyd! Girling changed a tyre at the end of the lap, Stocks adjusted his commutator and Mayhew's brakes were adjusted. The latter arrived at 12.14, after a lap of 2 hours 3 minutes.

On the second lap, one of Edge's tyre covers flew off and lodged in a tree. Hargreaves also stopped with tyre trouble and Stocks again led on the road at Ramsey despite stops at Castletown (adjustment to commutator chain) and Kirk Michael (fixing regulator levers with wire). Earp and Edge both arrived in Ramsey at five minute intervals, with Hargreaves 15 minutes later after a delay at Castletown when first gear would not engage. They were followed by Jarrott, Girling and Mayhew, the latter being "disappointingly slow but I know that he has domestic worries on his mind", wrote *The Motor* reporter.

Stocks kept the lead on the third lap although Hargreaves speeded up (despite a stop at Kirk Michael to adjust his clutch) while Edge overtook Earp, and Girling overtook Jarrott, who stopped at Kirk Michael to fit a new inlet valve and to make the first of two plug changes. The fourth lap was comparatively uneventful, although both Edge and Jarrott had punctures. This was the first of Edge's problems. Officials decided to reduce the trial from six laps to five as it would have been impossible to complete six laps within the eight hours maximum allowed. On the fifth and final lap Hargreaves and Jarrott had new tyres fitted at Castletown, while Stocks stopped at Kirk Michael to repair his seat for the second time. Girling also stopped at Kirk Michael, to fit a new chain. Edge had to fight two fires caused by fuel from a puncture in his carburettor float igniting on the exhaust pipe.

When overall times were adjusted by subtraction of times spent in control areas, Earp was the "winner" for Napier in a time for the five laps of 7 hours 26.5 minutes, with Girling's Wolseley second in 7 hours 30 minutes. Third and fourth were the Napiers of Edge and Stocks in times of 7 hours 35.5 minutes and 7 hours 46.5 minutes respectively, while Jarrott was the fifth and final finisher in 7 hours 52 minutes. Hargreaves was not classified as he completed the final lap 57 minutes outside the eight hours limit. Girling set the fastest lap in 1 hour 16 minutes 30 seconds (41 mph), only 30 seconds faster than Jarrott.

The day was an undoubted success, not least because it had been free of accidents, despite gloomy pre-event predictions. While large crowds had been attracted to the course, the *Isle of Man Examiner* was unenthusiastic. "From a spectacular point of view the trials were not over-successful", said the paper. "Ploughing matches are perhaps the dullest form of sport imaginable but in point of interest and excitement they closely resemble motor trials conducted under conditions as they obtained on Tuesday. Really there was nothing of the nature of racing connected with them. They were well called the Eliminating Trials for the Autoclub took particular care to eliminate from them all the elements of racing".

Port-e-Vullen Hill-climb

On Wednesday 11th May, in magnificent weather, large crowds travelled by train, Manx Electric Railway tram, and car to Ramsey for the hill-climb trial at Port-e-Vullen, approximately two miles outside the town, where the Automobile Club had selected a half mile course on the road from Ramsey to Maughold village. With the event scheduled to start at 3pm, spectators gathered outside the Mitre Hotel in Ramsey's Parliament Street, the Club's headquarters for the day, where they could see the competing cars marshalled behind the railings which surrounded the Courthouse. Later, the crowds travelled by electric tram to Port-e-Vullen where, according to the *Isle of Man Examiner*, "Enterprising farmers, whose property bordered the road and who had vehemently denounced motor-racing during the early morning practising, were now insisting that the trial were a great boon to the Island – they were charging sixpence a head to those who wished to view the races from their plantations and fields!"

The cars were not the sole source of entertainment. There was a mixture of cheers, jeers and laughter from spectators when "someone had got into someone else's garden, and there were visions from the swaying crowd of angry, gesticulating females verging on a fight – a most unedifying scene which all the biased wisdom of the local 'bobby', who most unfairly took the part of she who trespassed, could not obliterate". Earl Russell, one of the senior Automobile Club officials, supported the householder, offering her both encouragement and advice on her property rights. The matter got totally out of hand when one of the trespassers deliberately trampled some garden plants underfoot, so much provoking the householder that she broke free from the constable's restraining grasp and hit him full in the face with a well-aimed clod of earth.

The Darracqs were absent, as was Mark Mayhew's Napier, reducing the field to four Napiers and three Wolseleys. After a half hour delay caused by the late arrival

The Napiers of Jack Stocks (1), John Hargreaves (3), Clifford Earp (6) and Selwyn Edge (9) line up for the hill-climb at Port-e-Vullen on the day following the Trial, followed by the Wolseley of Sidney Girling (10). Edge was fastest at 47mph, followed by Earp (42.1mph) and Girling (41.4mph). [National Motor Museum]

Above left: Charles Jarrott in his Wolseley awaits the start of the hill climb at Port-e-Vullen. His best time of 47.4 seconds was the fourth fastest time of the day. [Brian Mylchreest collection]

Left: Charles Jarrott drives his Wolseley back to the Start line of the hill-climb at Port-e-Vullen after a run up the hill towards Maughold village. His first run of 47.4secs was the fourth fastest. [Ray Stanfield collection]

Above: At Port-e-Vullen hill-climb, Selwyn Edge (Napier) and Sidney Girling (Wolseley) return down the hill after one of their runs. On the first of his three runs Edge set the fastest time of the day in 38.4 seconds. Girling, on his third run, set the third fastest time of 43.0 seconds. [Eric Corkish collection]

of the Wolseleys, competitors were started at intervals of three minutes and each had a practice run and three timed runs. Edge was fastest with a time of 38.4 seconds (47mph), followed by Earp in 42.8 seconds (42.1mph) and Girling in 43 seconds (41.4mph). The aggregate times of the three runs were Edge (117.2 seconds), Earp (130.4 seconds) and Girling (131.6 seconds).

Although "Regrets were universal at the absence of the Darracqs", *Motoring Illustrated* reported that "the run was splendidly stage-managed and, beyond the delay in starting, everything passed off in grand style. The spectators were delighted at seeing racing cars breast the hill at nearly 50 mph and some of them had never seen cars before. Their first impressions were of the liveliest satisfaction." *The Motor* was somewhat less enthusiastic with its comment that the event was staged "as a sideshow and as a sop to the Manx people for giving up their rights on the highway".

Douglas Promenade Acceleration and Speed Test

The final event was a one kilometre standing start acceleration and speed test on Douglas Promenade. The course started outside the Villa Marina, near the foot of Broadway and extended north to Palace Terrace. In addition to the four Napiers and three Wolseleys which had contested the hill-climb, Rawlinson (Darracq) and Muir (Wolseley) also took part.

The event started at noon. Conditions were not ideal, with intermittent showers and a thick sea mist. After a practice run, each competitor was to have three timed runs. The drivers were held at the north end of the course until all had completed their first timed run, and were then instructed to return in convoy to the start for the second run. All went well until the second run had been completed but, on the return to the start, an impromptu "race" took place. This resulted in a serious incident when Clifford Earp seemed to realise that his speed was dangerously fast in relation to the small braking distance available. He applied his hand-brake, whereupon the car slid. He tried to regain control by releasing the brake, but was unable to do so. The car continued to slide for some 65 yards, hit a wall and rebounded. The car was badly damaged, a man who had "eluded the vigilance of the police" was slightly injured, and Earp and his brother (variously referred to as "Arthur" and "Walter") were thrown out. Clifford Earp was knocked out but soon recovered consciousness and was taken to hospital with his brother and the injured spectator. No one was seriously hurt but the event was immediately stopped.

Clifford Earp later explained that his brake lever

catch had broken earlier and that he had repaired it with wire. The sudden strain when he had applied the brake had caused the wire to snap. This meant that he was unable to dis-engage the catch from the notches in order to release the brake. This accident gave rise to the racing "fly-off" handbrake, released simply by letting go of the lever.

Edge was fastest on both runs with identical times of 39 seconds (57.50 mph). Earp was second in 42 seconds (53.20 mph). Rawlinson managed 42.6 seconds on his second run, faster than Girling (43 seconds) and Jarrott (45.4 seconds).

1904 Gordon Bennett Eliminating Trial Results

Tuesday 10th May 1904. Start 9.00am.
5 laps of 51.1 miles course, total distance 255.5 miles.
11 starters 5 finishers.

1 Clifford Earp (Napier), 7hrs 26mins 30secs
2 Sidney Girling (Wolseley), 7hrs 30mins
3 Selwyn Edge (Napier), 7hrs 33mins 40secs
4 Jack Stocks (Napier), 7hrs 46mins 40secs
5 Charles Jarrott (Wolseley), 7hrs 52mins 10secs

Fastest lap:
Sidney Girling (Napier), 1hr 16mins 30secs (41.00mph)
Completed the course, but out of time:
John Hargreaves (Napier), 7hrs 57mins
Retirements:
Lap 1:
A. ("Toby") Rawlinson (Darracq), broken universal joint.
Edmond (Darracq), brake problems.
Campbell Muir (Wolseley), broken spring.
Lap 2:
Victor Hemery (Darracq), brake problems
Lap 4:
Mark Mayhew (Napier), ignition problems.
Ballaugh flying half mile speed test

1. Selwyn Edge (Napier), 73.0 mph.
2. Sidney Girling (Wolseley), 65.5 mph.
3. John Hargreaves (Napier), 64.5mph.

Port-e-Vullen Hill-climb, Wednesday 11th May 1904

Name	*First run*	*Second run*	*Third run*
Selwyn Edge (Napier)	38.4secs	39.2secs	39.6secs
Clifford Earp (Napier)	44.4secs	42.8secs	43.8secs
Sidney Girling (Wolseley)	44secs	44.6secs	43secs
Charles Jarrott (Wolseley)	47.4secs	48.2secs	51.6secs
Campbell Muir (Wolseley)	49.6secs	51.4secs	50secs
John Hargreaves (Napier)	51secs	52secs	51secs
Jack Stocks (Napier)	57.6secs	57.2secs	55.2secs

Douglas Promenade 1 kilometer Standing Start Speed Trial, Thursday 12th May 1904

	First run	Second run
1 Selwyn Edge (Napier)	39secs (57.32mph)	39secs (57.32mph)
2 Clifford Earp (Napier)	42secs (53.22mph)	42.4secs (52.72mph)
3 A. ("Toby") Rawlinson (Darracq)	46.6secs (47.97mph)	42.6sec (52.47mph)
4 Sidney Girling (Wolseley)	44.8secs (49.89mph)	43secs (51.99mph)
5 Charles Jarrott (Wolseley)	45.4secs (49.24mph)	45.4secs (49.24mph)
6 Campbell Muir (Wolseley)	47secs (47.56mph)	47secs (47.56mph)
7 Jack Stocks (Napier)	47.2secs (47.36mph)	48.2secs (46.37mph)
8 John Hargreaves (Napier)	49.6secs (45.07mph)	47.6secs (46.96mph)

Team Selection

Shortly after the finish of the speed tests the Automobile Club announced the team which would represent Great Britain in the 1904 Gordon Bennett Race. The selected team was 1. Edge (Napier), 2. Girling (Wolseley) and 3. Jarrott (Wolseley). Stocks (Napier) and Hargreaves (Napier) were nominated as reserves. Surprisingly and, perhaps, unwisely the Club also announced that Earp would have been given second place in the team but for his accident.

Selwyn Edge was enraged by the Club's treatment of Earp. He immediately lodged a protest against the decision and, on returning to London, entered into acrimonious correspondence with Automobile Club Secretary Julian Orde. The Club, apparently, had based its decision on the assumption that neither car nor driver would be fit to compete in the race in Germany on 17th June. In fact, Edge and the Napier mechanics had been able to tow the car away, with replacement front wheels fitted, within an hour of the crash and had predicted that the car would be roadworthy within a week or two. In fact the car was driven by Earp at a Nottingham Automobile Club hill-climb on 27th May and had set a time only 4.8 seconds slower than Edge on his 80 hp Gordon Bennett car. Against this, it could be argued that the regulations for the trial stated that selection would be based on the condition of the cars at the end of the trial, when Earp's car was clearly not roadworthy. *The Motor* remarked: "Mr. Edge would be ill-advised in persisting in his attitude, because the judges were right in regarding Earp and his car as hors de combat when the moment came for selecting the team".

In his *Motoring Reminiscences*, however, Edge quoted his letter to the Club, in which he pointed out that the purpose of the trial was to select the best possible team to represent Great Britain, that Earp's driving had proved that Earp and his Napier were the second best combination (as the Club itself had admitted), that the accident had not occurred during the trial, that both would be fit to race on 17th June and that Earp had been eliminated through what appeared to be a panic decision.

It was rumoured at the time that Edge had gone much further, with an ultimatum to the Club that he would withdraw from the team if Earp were not reinstated. Edge twice denied this strongly in *My Motoring Reminiscences* but Lord Montagu wrote in The Gordon Bennett Races that Edge had asked the Automobile Club that: "As a record of my sporting disapproval of a decision given in contradiction to actual proved results, I would prefer that your Committee should relieve me of the honour of representing the English Club in the International Gordon Bennett race". Going even further, according to Lord Montagu, Edge descended to cheap gibes against Wolseley by telling Julian Orde that it was "most unwise" to select cars which were not capable of 80mph. This brought Campbell Muir into the fray, with the comment that "Most people say that Earp drove the best but it is all very well to say this when one has no trouble". *The Autocar*, after initially supporting Edge, made the comment that "we cannot see anything sporting in Edge's attitude". The decision stood.

The 1904 Gordon Bennett Race, on the Homburg circuit in Germany, was won by the French driver Leon Thery, driving a Richard-Brasier. Girling finished 9th and Jarrott 12th and last, but Edge retired on the last lap when his engine seized. It was to be his last long-distance road race. His reasons for this decision, he wrote, were his dissatisfaction with the manner in which the Automobile Club had handled his protest on behalf of Earp, innuendoes and criticism, the testing advantages which lack of speed restrictions gave to continental rivals, the professional element which was creeping into the sport, the cheating which had been allowed in the Gordon Bennett race in Ireland in 1903 and lack of time for racing due to business commitments.

1905 Gordon Bennett Eliminating Trial

Planning

The 1904 Trial aroused considerable interest on the Island and led directly to the formation of the Manx Automobile Club by the Island's first motorist George Gillmore, George Drinkwater of Kirby, and *Isle of Man Times* Editor George Brown. Although it attracted fewer tourists than expected (between 1,000 and 2,000) it brought the

Pictured at the wheel of his Wolseley outside the race headquarters at the Peveril Hotel in Douglas, Automobile Club Secretary Julian Orde was the kingpin of the organisation of the two Gordon Bennett Trials and six Tourist Trophy races which the Club organised on the Island. [Author's collection]

Island welcome publicity, and the authorities thought it worthwhile to repeat the 1904 experiment. Clearly The Automobile Club of Great Britain and Ireland needed a course for a trial to select the British team for the 1905 Gordon Bennett Race in France, and Lord Raglan's invitation to return to the Island was promptly accepted.

Meanwhile another idea was forming. *Motoring Illustrated* saw little financial point in developing large noisy racing cars and wanted to see the development of quiet well-built touring cars. Claude Johnson, Starter at the Ramsey Control for the 1904 Trial and a partner in Rolls-Royce, believed that the British motor industry, then in its infancy with numerous manufacturers competing for business, needed an effective test for its products. Recognising the publicity value of public competition, he proposed that an international race for "tourist" (touring) cars should be held on the Island, over the Gordon Bennett Trial course. He even suggested a name for the race – The Tourist Trophy. Enthused, Rolls offered to enter two Minervas, an Orleans and two Rolls-Royces, one of which he would drive himself. The Automobile Club started drawing up regulations in November 1904.

In March 1905, Lord Raglan persuaded Tynwald to renew the road closing legislation without the previous one-year limit. The road closure power was extended to six days per year, to allow for the Gordon Bennett Trials and the new Tourist Trophy Race in September. Power to close roads for motorcycle races was included because the Auto-Cycle Club (the motorcycling branch of the Automobile Club) wanted to hold an eliminating trial to choose a British team for the International Motorcycle Cup (sometimes known as "the motorcycling Gordon Bennett" although it had no connection with James Gordon Bennett). Planning for both

Harry Goodwin's Star is pictured at the start of the 2.5 miles speed test on the Ballamodha straight between Castletown and Foxdale. The fastest three were Napiers – Arthur Macdonald (81.20mph) followed by John Hargreaves (70.10mph) and Cecil Edge (69.50mph). [Author's collection]

the motorcycle trial and the Tourist Trophy then took place together, with the motorcycle trial scheduled to take place over three laps of the course in the early morning of the day after the Gordon Bennett Trial.

Arrangements for the Gordon Bennett Trial took into account a number of lessons from 1904. Entries were restricted to British nationals on the Automobile Club register and, in the light of the Darracq experience in 1904, silencers were required on all cars. Cars which failed to meet the maximum weight limit would be allowed three attempts to comply, after which they would be disqualified, due to concerns in 1904 that excessive lightening had made cars unsafe. The Trial would consist of six laps (approximately 310 miles) of the 1904 course but without a hill-climb at Maughold and a speed test on Douglas Promenade. The official reason was the limited number of days available for road closures but the more likely reason was fear of serious accidents in events which were really only "sideshows". The Ballamodha speed test was reduced from 3 miles to 2.5 miles but the flying half mile test at Ballaugh and the timed hill-climb on the Mountain road were retained. Controls were again sited at Ballasalla, Foxdale, Kirk Michael, Ramsey and Douglas. A proposal to omit the southern loop of the course was deferred.

Travel arrangements were improved, with special trains to carry cars to Liverpool from Coventry (Siddeley), Birmingham (Wolseley), Wolverhampton (Star) and London (Napier), and a special train for Automobile Club members and their friends from London Euston to Liverpool. There were still complaints – there was no buffet car on the special train, and the Isle of Man Steam Packet Company's oldest and slowest ship suffered a bearing failure during the voyage causing a long delay in heavy seas and prompting a passenger to remark "More carburettor troubles, I suppose". *The Automotor Journal* commented that if the races were to become annual, better arrangements for travel to the Island were essential.

Entries

There were only ten entries, one less than in 1904. Two Island favourites from 1904 were missing, Selwyn Edge and Charles Jarrott having retired at the ages of 37 and 28 respectively. Newcomers were the two red-painted Stars, built in Wolverhampton and driven by the Goodwin brothers, Harry and Fred. They brought their sister Victoria, described as "the famous lady motor expert" who "drove about the Island bringing grace and fashion" to the Island's motoring scene and did much to improve the public image of motoring. Algernon Lee Guinness brought his own re-built 1904 Darracq, re-named as a Weir Darracq, altered in appearance and with various new parts. Cecil Bianchi (Charles Jarrott's mechanic in 1904) and newcomer Charles Rolls had 96hp Wolseleys. Rolls' father Baron Llangattock was a friend of Lord Raglan, who had known Charles since he was a boy. Sidney Girling's 100hp Siddeley was a newcomer to the Island. It had been built at the Wolseley

The Stars of the Goodwin brothers, Harry and Fred, are pictured on the quayside at Douglas after unloading. Harry's car is on the right. [Ray Stanfield collection]

Clifford Earp's Napier is pictured outside the Douglas Bay Hotel, the Napier headquarters for the event. The hotel quickly became a traditional base for both car and motorcycle racing teams due to the ample garaging available in its stables. [Manx National Heritage]

factory at Birmingham (control of Siddley having passed to Wolseley) to the order of Lionel de Rothschild and had originally been entered by him but de Rothschild had to withdraw as entrant due to family mourning for his uncle Baron Alphonse de Rothschild. J.D. Siddeley then took over as entrant. Completing the field were four Napiers. There were three 80hp cars, to be driven by John Hargreaves (the only driver other than Guinness who owned his car), Clifford Earp (whose car had been driven by in 1904 by Mark Mayhew, who had since retired) and Island newcomer Cecil Edge (whose car had been driven by his cousin Selwyn Edge in 1904). Cecil had been mechanic to Selwyn in the 1902 Gordon Bennett Race. The fourth Napier was the spectacular looking 90hp "Samson" to be driven by Arthur Macdonald, who had been Selwyn Edge's mechanic in 1904. In January 1905 Macdonald had set six world land speed records with this car at Daytona Beach, Florida, including the flying mile record at 104.65 mph, beaten later by Victor Hemery's Darracq at 109.65 mph. Samson arrived on artillery wheels, which were changed to lighter but stronger Rudge-Whitworth wire spoked wheels for the race.

Preparations for the race included the laying by the Highway Board of a dust-laying compound known as *Dustroyd*, produced by R.S. Clare & Co. of Birkenhead. This was not entirely successful. Due to lack of funds the Highway Board could do very little preparation work on

John Hargreaves' Napier stands on Douglas pier outside Imperial Buildings (formerly the Imperial Hotel), headquarters of the Isle of Man Steam Packet Company for many years. [Ray Stanfield collection]

In order to prevent loss of drivers' visibility in dense clouds of dust the course was sprayed with the dust-laying compound "Dustroyd". This was pumped from a barrel to two hand-held hoses with spray nozzles, as illustrated in this photograph on Hillberry straight. One barrel was sufficient to treat the surface from the point where a man is standing in the middle of the road. [Peter Kelly collection]

Photographs taken on Hillberry straight were used to advertise the efficacy of the dust-laying compound "Dustroyd" by comparing the difference between treated and untreated parts of the road. The driver is Sidney Girling (Siddeley). [R and L Kelly collection]

Pre-event weighing and technical inspection took place at Douglas Corporation's weighbridge and yard in Lake Road, said to have been a great improvement on the North Quay coal yard used in 1904. Fred Goodwin's Star is pictured undergoing inspection among horse-drawn carts. [Manx National Heritage]

the roads, in contrast to 1904 when a great deal had been done. This resulted in a comment that the roads were "fifty per cent worse" than in the previous year and Bianchi said that there was only one good piece of road on the entire course – a half mile stretch near Ballaugh.

Weighing of the ten cars took place on the day before the trial at the Douglas Corporation weighbridge in Lake Road. There were fewer problems than in 1904, although initially the Stars were well over the limit and needed hard

The Napier of John Hargreaves is pictured at the Douglas Corporation weighbridge in Lake Road, Douglas, where pre-event weighing and technical inspection took place. Due to problems with clutch, brakes and plugs, Hargreaves completed only one lap in the Trial but was selected as a reserve for the British team in the Gordon Bennett Race. [John Watterson collection]

During early morning practices drivers sometimes took their wives for a drive round the course, allowing their mechanics to have a lie-in – a custom which continued for the Tourist Trophy races. Here John Hargreaves is pictured with his wife aboard his Napier, at Hillberry. [Author's collection]

Algernon Lee Guinness, pictured on Ballanard Road, made his Isle of Man debut at the wheel of his own Darracq, one of the 1904 cars which he had acquired and partly re-built. Despite his comment that it was "a very big car for a real beginner to handle" he was first to complete the first lap, passing both Stars, but retired on the second lap. As well as the 1905 Trial, he competed in every Isle of Man TT, the only driver to do so. [R and L Kelly collection]

work with tin-snips to reduce their weight sufficiently, while Girling simply fitted well-worn tyres in order to bring his Siddeley down to the stipulated weight.

Practice

Practising on open roads was allowed between 4am and 7am on weekdays during the two weeks prior to the event. Cecil Bianchi, however, had to make do with only three morning practices. He had been given a one month suspension by the Automobile Club after receiving a fine for speeding while testing his Wolseley in the New Forest. The Stars also lost practice time due to lack of testing time before being brought to the Island and the need to run-in their engines. Nevertheless, Harry Goodwin managed an unofficial practice lap in 59 minutes. Algernon Lee Guinness found his Weir Darracq "a very big car for a real beginner to handle". The only real incident reported during practising involved Cecil Edge. Blinded by dust at the left hander between Cronk-ny-Mona and Cronk-y-Berry on the outskirts of Douglas, he crashed into a sod hedge and landed, with his mechanic, in "a friendly gorse bush". One of the wheels had to be dug out of the hedge with a spade. The crash occurred on the Saturday ten days before the trial and the car, having arrived back at the Napier factory in London on the following day, was rebuilt and back on the Island by the following Thursday. The corner was then named "Edge's", the first corner on an Isle of Man race circuit to be named after a competitor. The name was used during the RAC TT Races up to and including 1914, and was still in use when the corner formed part of the British Empire Trophy Race circuit between 1947 and 1953, the motorcycle TT Clypse Circuit between 1954 and 1959, and the Willaston Circuit used for the Manx Classic pursuit sprint organised by the Manx Motor Racing Club from 1989 to 2000, although on the later (post 1914) circuits the direction of travel was reversed.

1905 Gordon Bennett Eliminating Trial

With the trial scheduled to start at 9am on Tuesday 30th May, an official course inspection crew was surprised to find a lone spectator on a wall at 2am. He had confused the start time of the motorcycle trial (3am on Wednesday) with that of the car trial (9am on Tuesday) and was expecting the first car to arrive shortly after 3am!

The 9am start, in brilliant sunshine under a cloudless sky, was orderly, with none of the late arrivals and dramas which made the 1904 start so chaotic. Drivers were again started at intervals of five minutes, with the Stars of the Goodwin brothers leading the field away from Quarterbridge. The Darracq of Algernon Lee Guinness and the Wolseley of Cecil Bianchi started at 3 and 4 respectively, the Wolseley appearing powerful and making a quick getaway. They were followed by the three 80hp Napiers of Cecil Edge, Clifford Earp and John Hargreaves. Edge and his mechanic "clad in white, with a white drill cap and little rolls to protect the ears…looked like business, and they vanished up the hill at high speed", reported *The Autocar*. Earp's car carried a white handkerchief attached to the radiator funnel at the request of a lady admirer, to enable her to identify him as he approached. Like Edge, he made a fast start but Hargreaves appeared to have clutch trouble. The Napiers were numbered 6, 7 and 9 as numbers 5 and 8 were not allocated, in order to avoid possible confusion with number 3. The remainder of the field consisted of Sidney Girling's Siddeley (10), Charles Rolls' Wolseley (11) and finally Macdonald's Napier (12). The *Isle of Man Examiner* commented "One of the most noticeable features of the trials was the great improvement in the cars on the previous year. The engines ran more smoothly and regularly, and there was none of the difficulty in starting the cars that had been experienced in the first car race on the Island".

On the flying half-mile at Ballaugh, Macdonald was

Arthur Macdonald's streamlined Napier is pictured at the end of the long straight to Hillberry. This new six cylinder car established six world speed records at Daytona Beach, Florida in January 1905. It was less successful in the Isle of Man, crashing at Cruickshank's corner in Ramsey on the third lap. [Peter Kelly collection]

John Hargreaves (Napier) is pictured at the Castletown control. This marked the end of the neutral section which started near the Whitestone Inn in Ballasalla and extended to the outskirts of Castletown, for which four minutes were allowed. [Stenlake Publishing]

Sidney Girling crashed his Siddeley at St. Jude's crossroads on the second lap. His steering appeared to fail but the real cause may have been badly worn tyres. He hit the wall of a cottage causing extensive damage but his only injury was a broken finger and his mechanic escaped unhurt. He was second fastest in the half mile speed test and in the hill climb. [Author's collection]

decisively fastest at 88.20mph, followed by Girling (79.80mph) and Edge (79.97mph). Earp, who had been going well, could manage only 76.40mph. Harry Goodwin's Star, which had made an unimpressive start, had leaking water jackets and the second Star was very slow, achieving less than 50mph.

Guinness was the first driver to complete the lap, in 1 hour 19 minutes, including time spent in control zones. He was followed twelve minutes later by Harry Goodwin who lapped faster than two of the Napiers – a creditable effort by a newcomer to racing, driving an untried car. All drivers completed the first lap, the fastest being Edge in 1 hour 16 minutes, averaging close to 40 mph. His driving was, according to *The Automotor Journal*, "a trifle rash". Rolls, however, had already started to encounter problems. At Cronk-ny-Mona, "at a terrible rate", he swerved into a gutter to avoid a dog, mounted a grass footpath, grazed a sod hedge, broke two spokes and travelled at a 45 degree angle for an estimated ten yards before landing in the middle of the road and continuing. "Dumb struck" spectators recovered enough to raise a cheer for Rolls' quick, humane and skilful reaction.

Other drivers with problems were Macdonald (broken oil pump chain), Hargreaves, who had to change all four plugs, and Fred Goodwin (suspension).

The second lap was more eventful. Guinness, slowed by inexperience, the need to conserve his tyres and the handling of the big Darracq, retired with a broken piston and a run big-end. At St.Jude's, after the Ballaugh speed test, Girling had a lucky escape when his steering appeared to fail, although it was suggested that the problem was due to his decision to start with badly worn tyres. The car hit a kerb, lost a wheel and continued on three wheels for about 70 yards before crashing into the wall of "Master" Cain's cottage near St. Jude's with such force that the car "crumpled up like matchwood". The impact knocked bricks out of the gable wall, demolished the doorstep, broke most of the windows and forced open the front door. Both driver and mechanic were thrown clear, hitting the ground and appearing to bounce. One of the eye-witnesses, a doctor, believed both were dead, but their injuries were minor. Girling had scratches, a bruised chest caused by the steering wheel and a broken finger, but they hitched a lift to Ramsey where, according to *The Car Illustrated* "they were lunching at the Mitre Hotel not so very long after the mishap". Both Edge and Hargreaves had brake trouble. Earp was fastest on this lap, in a time of 1 hour 8mins 30secs with Bianchi only 6 minutes slower.

On lap 2, Macdonald's gear lever had kept sticking because of a broken tooth. It could be moved only with a hammer wielded by the mechanic who, on one occasion, hit Macdonald's foot instead of the gear lever. Eventually, constant hammering made the lever so loose that

At the Ramsey Control Clifford Earp's Napier (7) and Fred Goodwin's Star (2) await the re-start after the neutral section through the built-up part of the town. Earp completed the Trial in the shortest time and set the fastest lap (45 mph). Goodwin retired with a broken rear spring on lap 4. [National Motor Museum]

Cecil Bianchi poses in his Wolseley. The location is believed to be Cronk-ny-Mona. In the Trial Bianchi finished second on aggregate time to Clifford Earp and was selected for the British team in the Gordon Bennett race together with Earp and Charles Rolls. [R and L Kelly collection]

Macdonald had to hold it in position with his right hand while steering with his left hand. On lap 3, he lost control on Queen's Pier Road on the way out of Ramsey. The car slid on loose stones and collided with the garden wall of High Bailiff Cruickshank's house at the foot of May Hill. Macdonald was unhurt but the front nearside wheel was badly buckled, having taken the force of the impact with the wall. The incident proved the strength of wire-spoked wheels compared with artillery wheels but this did not help Macdonald – he was out of the race.

Also on lap 3, Edge was slowed by coil trouble and failed to complete lap 4 within the time limit. Fred Goodwin's Star was "merely touring" and retired at the end of the lap with a broken rear spring, and Hargreaves was still suffering from the clutch problem noted at the Start. Selwyn Edge quickly found and fixed the problem but Hargreaves also failed to complete lap 4 within the time limit. Harry Goodwin's Star continued to Ramsey on lap 5 where he was stopped at the expiration of the time limit.

Charles Rolls' troubles continued. On a bad bump, his mechanic accidentally kicked four low tension wires off the commutator, causing a delay while the wires were traced and re-connected. He also had to stop to make a temporary repair to a fractured oil pipe. Then a second dog slowed him on the timed hill-climb and finally he was delayed by over-zealous marshals who flagged him down unnecessarily when Edge stopped on the Mountain section, many miles ahead. His combined delays meant that he could complete only five laps within the time limit.

Making his first Isle of Man appearance, the Hon. Charles Rolls drives his Wolseley through Ramsey with Albert Road School in the background. He was back later in the year with a Rolls-Royce for a very brief appearance in the first Tourist Trophy, and again in 1906 for his famous TT victory. [Stenlake Publishing]

The only drivers to complete six laps were Clifford Earp (6 hours 4mins) and Cecil Bianchi (6 hours 16mins). Charles Rolls completed five laps in 6 hours 21mins 30secs. Earp, Rolls and Bianchi were then chosen as the British team for the Gordon Bennett Race at Clermont-Ferrand in Auvergne, with Edge (who had done the fastest lap before retiring) and Hargreaves (who had completed only one lap) as reserves. The selection again provoked controversy as it was argued that Rolls, who completed only five laps, should not have been given second place in the team in preference to Bianchi, who had completed six laps. The Automobile Club defended its decision by explaining that, fine though Bianchi's performance had been, other factors (including incidents during the trial and technical problems which had been overcome) had been taken into account which made Rolls' performance intrinsically better. The Club also pointed out that Rolls had set a better time than Bianchi on the hill-climb. In the Gordon Bennett Race, Rolls was the highest finisher of the British team, in eighth position. Earp finished ninth but he and his brother Arthur were nearly blinded by a dust-laying compound called *Pulveranto* and "had to be led about in bandages". Bianchi finished eleventh. The race was again won by the French driver Leon Thery, driving a Richard-Brasier. This was the last Gordon Bennett race for cars – the world had changed since the inception of the Cup in 1899, motoring competition was no longer a pastime for wealthy amateurs but had become a championship for constructors and national clubs had lost interest. James Gordon Bennett himself was sickened by commercialization of car racing and decided that the 1906 Gordon Bennett race would be "a great aeronautical contest on somewhat similar lines to those in accordance with which the Gordon Bennett automobile races were originally organised". The Gordon Bennett Aeronautical Cup, for balloons, continued from 1906 to 1929 and the Gordon Bennett Aviation Cup, for aeroplanes, was run from 1909 to 1920 (both excluding 1914 to 1919).

1905 Gordon Bennett Eliminating Trial Results

Tuesday 30th May 1905. Start 9.00am.
6 laps of 51.1 miles circuit, total distance 306.6 miles.
10 starters, 3 finishers.

1. Clifford Earp (Napier), 6 laps, 6hrs 4mins
2. Cecil Bianchi (Wolseley), 6 laps, 6hrs 16mins
3. Hon. Charles Rolls (Wolseley), 5 laps, 6hrs 21mins 30secs

Fastest lap:
Clifford Earp (Napier), 1hr 8mins 30secs (45.00mph)
Retirements:
Lap 2:
John Hargreaves (Napier), clutch problems, out of time
Sidney Girling (Siddeley), crash at St. Jude's due to broken steering
Algernon Lee Guinness (Darracq), run big end and broken piston
Lap 3:
Arthur E. Macdonald (Napier), crash at Cruickshank's Corner, Ramsey
Lap 4:
F.R. Goodwin (Star), broken rear spring
Cecil Edge (Napier), out of time
Lap 5:
H.G. Goodwin (Star), out of time

2.5 miles speed test:

1. Arthur E. Macdonald (Napier), 81.20mph.
2. John Hargreaves (Napier), 70.10mph.
3. Cecil Edge (Napier) 69.50mph.

Half mile speed test:

1. Arthur E. Macdonald (Napier), 88.20mph.
2. Sidney Girling (Siddeley), 79.80mph.
3. Cecil Edge (Napier), 79.70mph.

Hill climb:

1. Arthur E. Macdonald (Napier), 32.30mph.
2. Sidney Girling (Siddeley), 31.60mph.
3. Cecil Edge (Napier), 31.40mph.

The International Motorcycle Cup Eliminating Trial

Although it was sensible to run the motorcycle trial on the morning after the car trial, with all the course and organisation arrangements in place, the event was rather an anti-climax. The intention was to use the same circuit as the cars but for only three laps (approximately 155 miles), starting at 3am and finishing no later than 8am, but with the difference that this was to be a true race, without the controls and special tests of the car trial. Out of seventeen entries received, only eleven appeared for the weighing-in and only seven started, with only two finishers. The northern part of the course was abandoned due to a prior accident on the mountain climb and the inability of the motorcycles to climb the mountain road. The shortened course turned right at Ballacraine and returned along the main Peel to Douglas road to the Start at Quarterbridge. While local opinions of the event varied between a non-event and a fiasco, it was the Island's introduction to racing motorcycles and led directly to the inception of the motorcycle Tourist Trophy Race two years later.

GORDON BENNETT TRIALS "WINNER" 1904-1905 – CLIFFORD EARP

Although the trials were not races in the strict sense, it was clear that Clifford Earp was the best overall performer in both events. It was most unfortunate that he was not to be selected for the British team due to his crash when returning to the start-line after a timed run in the Douglas Promenade speed test in 1904.

One of the pioneer British racing drivers, Earp was born in Lambeth in 1879. He was a protégé of Selwyn Edge who objected vociferously to his controversial non-selection after the 1904 trial. Selected in 1905, Earp was the second-placed British finisher in the Gordon Bennett Race on the Auvergne circuit in France, being placed eighth overall. In 1905 he set a time of 23 seconds for the flying start kilometre at the first Brighton Speed Trials and, in 1906, he broke the World Land Speed Record over 100 miles at Daytona beach Florida, driving a 90hp Napier. He shed his rear tyre at around the 35 miles point and completed the run on the rim. He also set four new world records (50 miles, 150 miles, one hour and two hours) at Brooklands in 1907, driving a 60hp Thames.

1905 Tourist Trophy – Arrol-Johnston Beats Rolls-Royce

Planning

After the Gordon Bennett Trial, attention turned to the first Tourist Trophy Race on Thursday 14th September 1905. Charles Rolls and others believed that the days of "pure" motor racing with expensive specially-built cars were over, as it was not worthwhile for manufacturers to spend vast sums building special racing cars which would be of no further use. The future was in touring cars, with manufacturers incurring much less expense in preparing production cars for racing and obtaining significant development from testing them over the demanding Isle of Man course in competition with their rivals, while gaining valuable publicity from doing so. *The Autocar* said the TT was "the most interesting race of 1905" and Selwyn Edge said the TT was "in many ways the most useful and valuable experience to manufacturers". These views, however, were not universal and the initial reception was lukewarm. Some said the race would be "tame" while John Hargreaves, Master of Foxhounds and Napier driver in the 1904 and 1905 Gordon Bennett Trials, called the TT "a race for donkeys".

It was always going to be difficult to define a "touring car". The Automobile Club announced that the race would be for four-wheeled touring cars with four seats and would be held over four laps of the Gordon Bennett Trials course, a total distance of 208.5 miles. Fuel tanks were to be of 12 gallons capacity but the maximum allowance was 8.5 gallons, supplied by the Club. This was calculated to provide one gallon for each 25 miles of a dry average road, being the road from London to Oxford via Uxbridge, High Wycombe and Stokenchurch. (As a precaution against cheating, official cars would patrol the course to supervise the breaking of seals in cases of fuel feed or carburettor problems). Chassis weight was to be 1,300-1,600lbs and chassis load was to be a minimum of 950lbs of which 660lbs was to consist of driver, mechanic and loose ballast (bags filled with sand in the rear of the body) to represent two passengers. The minimum wheelbase was 7 feet 6 inches. Car bodies had to be "of the ordinary touring type, properly upholstered, comfortably seated for driver and three passengers facing forwards, two in front side by side and two behind side by side". Seats had to be nearly three feet from the ground. Bodies also had to be easily removable for weighing. Every entrant had to declare the manufacturer's selling price with the entry and provide a manufacturer's written guarantee to accept at that price all orders received for exact duplicates of the car within one month of the race. The entry fee was £20 per car with each manufacturer limited to two entries.

Perhaps unsurprisingly, there was criticism that manufacturers were being asked to build special cars to meet the conditions – the very thing that the Club had wanted to avoid. For instance, it was said that the minimum chassis load and wheelbase meant that some manufacturers would have to build special bodies. There were examples of the use of rags as axle caps, cardboard bonnets and steps, and removal of spring leaves.

The Isle of Man Railway Company had been unhappy about interference with trains during the Gordon Bennett Trials. There were four railway crossings on the course, at Quarterbridge, Ballasalla, Ballacraine and Ballaugh, and the Company was reluctant to suspend its services during the race. The Automobile Club therefore decided to issue competitors with railway timetables (to be fixed to their dashboards) and to place red flags at crossings. The Railway Company arranged to run trains with an extra locomotive to ensure punctuality and to limit the closure of crossing gates against the course to 30 seconds at stated times when cars were not expected and provided no cars were in sight! In addition, on the insistence of local authorities, 10 mph speed limits were imposed in towns and villages on the course where red flag zones were established with large banners across the roads. This caused controversy, as drivers thought such limitations were inappropriate in a race and unenforceable in cases of cheating. Selwyn Edge protested on behalf of the drivers that "if 10 mph is necessary in the various villages it should be definitely adhered to by having proper time controls. If this is not done it appears to me that, with the best intentions, one will either render oneself liable to disqualification or put oneself at a disadvantage with some of the other competitors". It followed that the winner could be a cheat and it was not worthwhile for honest drivers to compete. The Club's response was that overtaking would be permitted only where the car being passed was in obvious difficulty or going at such speed as to hinder other cars unreasonably. Any car which stopped was required to pull in to the left. Observers would be placed in the red flag zones to ensure consistent enforcement of the rules. Competitors were not required to stop at any point and there was no designated pit area.

The start line was moved from the Quarterbridge location used for the Gordon Bennett Trials to Alexander Drive. This road joined the course on Quarterbridge Road, some 200 yards before Quarterbridge. The start line was about 150 yards before the junction outside the house known, then and now, as "Woodlands". On starting, drivers could save fuel by coasting down a gradient (known as Brown's Hill after the owner of "Woodlands") to the junction with Quarterbridge Road and continue coasting before engaging gear on reaching Quarterbridge.

A race paddock and parc ferme was set up in a field adjoining "Woodlands", where two large marquees, adorned with flags and bunting, and many tents were erected. Here pre-race scrutineering of cars, weighing and fuelling was to take place. The finish line was located on Quarterbridge Road, a short distance before the Alexander Drive junction, overlooked by the Club enclosure. This contained a grandstand, huts, tents and a scoreboard 12 feet high. Spectator arrangements included information blackboards on Douglas Road in Castletown opposite the entrance to King William's College, at the North Star Inn in Kirk Michael, at the Bungalow and at Hillberry. Footbridges with advertising banners for *Westrumite* dust laying compound were erected at Castletown, Ballacraine and Ramsey, and a walkway was constructed under the Quarterbridge. In Ramsey, the arrival of cars was to be signalled by the whistle of a railway locomotive in the nearby station.

Entries

By mid-August, 58 entries of 39 different makes (£20 per car) were received, including almost every British manufacturer and Continentals such as Fiat, Leon Bollee, Mercedes and Mors. Unfortunately, some declined to enter or withdrew. Mors could not meet the weight limit. The Managing Director said there was no chance of success for standard touring cars and nearly all TT cars would be unsuitable for touring unless considerably strengthened. Mors entered the only lady competitor, Dorothy Levitt. After being changed from the latest Mors touring car to a 1903 car fitted with smaller wheels and aluminium wings, the entry was withdrawn because Miss Levitt was ill, with the company forced to deny that the car was uncompetitive. Bristol could not meet the weight limit. Duryea said it could, but was not prepared to compete against "cars of a freak nature" which would be sold to the public. Other withdrawals were two Daimlers, two Renaults, two Crossleys, a Deasy, a Germain, a Royal Enfield, one of two Stars, and a Spyker. Turner Meiss had a problem with weight and a greater problem with the requirement that the fuel should be petrol, as their steam cars burned paraffin to generate steam, but the Automobile Club refused to change the regulation.

Fuel was not a problem for the £600 White steam cars from Cleveland, Ohio. Two were entered, with burners adapted to operate in "a slightly different manner". They produced 15hp at 900 rpm and, as a White had broken the world one mile track record at 74.07 mph, they could be a threat if they could control fuel consumption.

One of the first cars to arrive on the Island was one of two £395 Belgian Minervas, entered by the British agent C.S. Rolls & Co. Their four-cylinder engines produced 16hp at 1,200 rpm, higher revving than all TT cars except the Speedwells at 1,250 rpm but with 4hp less. The cars were said to be good for 47 mph in third gear. The drivers were Rolls' Manager E.H. Arnott and W.C. Holloway.

C.S. Rolls & Co. of Manchester was the first manufacturer to enter, after Rolls had been encouraged by wealthy Yorkshireman Arthur Harry Briggs, the owner of the first "Heavy Twenty" Rolls-Royce to be sold. The company entered two four-cylinder 20hp £600 (chassis only) Rolls-Royces, one to be driven by Rolls himself and the other by Percy Northey. The cars had been tested over 500 miles from Manchester to Scotland and back with fuel consumption well within the limit. Charles Rolls, who drove in the 1905 Gordon Bennett trial, visited the Island with a car as early as Easter, to determine the most suitable gear ratios. Known as the "Light Twenty", the cars were lightened by use of nickel steel in the chassis and front axle. Their engines were so quiet that many who equated noise with speed did not expect them to be competitive. Northey's engine had smaller diameter cylinder bores than that of Rolls and developed 18hp. The cars had four forward gears, with the direct third gear being used for normal running and fourth being an overdrive or, in the terminology of the time, a "sprinting gear" which saved fuel consumption and gave effortless performance. The Minervas had a similar gear. Rolls, always conscious of publicity, lent a 30hp Rolls-Royce to the Automobile Club for use as an official car during the race period.

The two Arrol-Johnstons, built in Glasgow, were particularly interesting. Their engines were horizontally opposed flat twins with two pistons per cylinder. They produced 18hp at only 800 rpm and were fast, economical and reliable but relatively expensive at £750. Low-slung, rakish and fitted with Rudge-Whitworth wire wheels they looked like "tourist racers" according to a critic but complied with the regulations. One had won a reliability trial in Scotland and recorded the lowest fuel consumption. Their latest "upgrade" for the TT was a special carburettor, said to be "wonderfully economical". The drivers were the company's Chief Engineer and Designer, John S. Napier and E.J. Cyril Roberts.

Argyll Motors Ltd of Glasgow entered two four-cylinder De Dion engined 14hp £460 cars to be driven by W. Parker Thomas and John Downie. During the practice period, while Parker Thomas was standing by his car extolling its virtues to an admiring spectator as the engine ticked over, the crankshaft broke. He wired immediately to Paris for a replacement which was delivered two days later by special messenger.

A famous make with a humble beginning was Cadillac of Detroit. The single cylinder car, the lowest powered (9hp at 900 rpm) and cheapest (£250) in the race, was one of the first American cars exported to Britain. The only difference between the TT version and the standard touring version was the forward re location of the front axle by a foot to meet the wheelbase requirement. The driver, F.S. Bennett, a well-known hill-climb and reliability trial driver, bought the car in New York.

The French Darracq company entered two twin cylinder 10hp £265 cars, the cheapest in the race apart from the Cadillac. The drivers were Algernon Lee Guinness, who had driven in the Gordon Bennett trial in May and would drive in all the Isle of Man TT races, and another Gordon Bennett Trials driver, Alfred "Toby" Rawlinson.

Other twin-cylinder entries were a 10-12hp £350 Peugeot driven by Charles Friswell and a 14hp £450 Wolseley driven by James Hadley.

Dennis Bros of Guildford started business in 1895 as bicycle makers. Three years later John Dennis was charged with furious driving of a motorised tricycle, whereupon the brothers proudly advertised the fact that their machines could "climb Guildford High Street at 16 mph on the sworn testimony of a police constable". Later famous as commercial vehicle manufacturers, the company's main business in 1905 was manufacture of touring cars and town carriages. They made their first commercial vehicle, a 15cwt box van for Harrods, in 1904 and obtained the most orders of any exhibitor at the Crystal Palace Motor Show. For the TT, the company entered two 14hp cars of different specifications, weighing 17cwt. One was a £400 twin cylinder car and the other was a £500 four cylinder version, the drivers being designer John Dennis (whose mechanic was his sister, the only woman in the race) and R. Downing. John Dennis had to drill his flywheel arms in order to comply with the weight limit.

Humber cars competed in more Isle of Man TT Races that any other make, missing only 1922. Two four-cylinder 16-20hp £450 cars were entered as Beeston Humbers, built at the Beeston factory rather than at Coventry. The cars were standard, except for a special carburettor, and very close to the maximum weight limit. The drivers were James Reid and C.H. Cooper.

A late entry came from James and Browne Ltd. of Hammersmith, London for C.L. Cattell. The company had decided not to enter as they were preparing a van for a Light Delivery Van Trial. The Trial was cancelled only four weeks before the TT, whereupon the company submitted an entry and took a four-cylinder 14-16hp £525 landaulette out of stock. It was the first chain-driven car to be equipped with Rudge-Whitworth wire wheels, fitted only for the race and only on the front axle, with artillery wheels on the rear. Only three other TT cars had Rudge-Whitworth wheels – the two Arrol-Johnstons and the Simms-Welbeck. Although all others continued to use wooden artillery wheels, Selwyn Edge warned that they were not entirely reliable in all conditions.

Two four-cylinder Napiers were entered for Isle of Man "veteran" Clifford Earp and Frank Cundy. These were 18hp cars. Like the Thornycrofts, their fuel tanks were vertical cylinders behind the seats - to provide ease of fuelling and to ensure that the last drop of fuel could reach the engines. The cost was £650 (chassis only).

Rover of Coventry had two four-cylinder 16-20hp £375 cars, the drivers of which were Ernest Courtis and Edmund W. Lewis.

There were two three-cylinder engine cars: the 15hp £450 Ryknield, driven by Arthur J. Clay and the 12-14hp £340 Vauxhall driven by A.J. Hancock. The latter had overdrive ("sprinting gear") on all three forward gears and on reverse.

The four-cylinder 14hp £465 Scout, to be driven by Percy Dean, was built by Dean and Burden Bros. Ltd. of Salisbury in a matter of days after their original TT car was damaged in an accident near the Wiltshire factory.

Isle of Man "veteran" Sidney Girling's twin-cylinder 18hp £650 Coventry built Siddeley was said to have completed 50,000 trouble-free miles before the TT. Unfortunately it was not trouble-free during the race.

The Simms Manufacturing Co. Ltd. of Kilburn, London entered a £525 four-cylinder 20hp Simms-Welbeck, fitted with pneumatic front bumpers which were intended to protect the car in frontal collisions. The driver was Richard Lascelles.

Speedwell of Reading produced three cars with the intention of using the two which proved best in practice. There were two high-revving (1,250 rpm) four-cylinder cars, one of 14hp and the other of 12hp, and one twin-cylinder. The drivers were W.J. Warren and A.J. Dew.

The Standard Motor Co. of Coventry entered a four-cylinder 20hp car. It had a weight problem, solved by reducing the weight of the chassis and substitution of smaller wheels. The car had a "sprinting gear". The driver was R.W. Maudslay.

Thornycroft entered two four-cylinder cars, one of 14hp and the other 20hp, priced at £425 (chassis only). They had rope brakes on the prop-shaft drum. The standard fuel tanks were replaced by gravity-feed tanks resembling milk churns, which were placed behind the front seats. These led to the cars being known as "the milk carts". The drivers were Tom Thornycroft and Guy Baxendale.

The London built Whitlock-Aster, driven by Claude Clench, had a four-cylinder 12-14hp Aster engine, an Aster chassis and a Whitlock body.

Other entries included a four-cylinder 14hp Clement built in France and driven by the English agent E.H. Lancaster, a four-cylinder 14hp £475 Dixi from Eisenach, Germany (Karl Beireiz), a four-cylinder 14hp Gladiator from France (priced at £425 for the chassis only) for Arthur McCormack, a four-cylinder 20hp Maudslay from Coventry with a "sprinting gear" (W.H. Cox), two completely standard four-cylinder 15hp £500 Orleans built in Twickenham, fitted with special flat fuel tanks behind the front seats (W.H. Astell and Thomas Jenner), a 18hp £450 Star, two four-cylinder 16hp Swifts driven by Harvey du Cros Junior (Managing Director of the Swift Motor Company and son of the Chairman of Dunlop) and Ernest de Wilton and a French four-cylinder 14hp £420 Vinot-Deguingand driven by Norman Littlejohn.

According to Isle of Man Steam Packet Company sources, the total insured value of cars brought to the Island was £50,000. This included some cars brought by officials and spectators which were valued at £1,250 to £1,500.

Practice

Practice was permitted, with the roads open to the public, from dawn to 7am in the two weeks before race day. Dawn was, of course, much later in mid-September than in May when the Gordon Bennett Trials had been held. This meant much less time for legal daylight practice. Inevitably, therefore, practice became an all-day affair with the police turning a blind eye. Local people were at first tolerant of "scorching", as high speed driving came to be known. Even Lord Raglan, the Lieutenant Governor whose foresight had allowed the introduction of motor racing to the Island, was alleged to have been a "scorcher". Away from the course, drivers on Douglas Promenade ignored the 14mph speed limit and exceeded 40mph.

As time passed and excesses of speed increased, there were complaints from farmers. As in Ireland before the 1903 Gordon Bennett Race, many hens were slain and, in one case, a driver paid four shillings (20p) as the extortionate compensation demanded by an angry farmer. Another driver was accused of continuing "at a furious pace" after killing a dog. Practising disrupted the harvest and gates on the Snaefell Mountain road were left open or even removed from their hinges, allowing sheep to wander. Rolls, Bianchi and Algernon Lee Guinness gave their names to gates with which they collided.

Illegal practice on Sundays caused complaints both of danger to church-goers and violation of the Sabbath. The Vicar of Kirk Michael, where disruption of church services was particularly serious, called a protest meeting at the ancient Parish cross and publicly accused Lord Raglan of being one of the offenders. In the face of protests in the Press and a unanimous resolution in the House of Keys that motor racing should not be allowed on Sundays, Lord Raglan threatened that unless the Automobile Club gave an assurance that competitors would conduct themselves better in future there would be no more TT Races, as he would refuse to sign the necessary Road Closing Order for 1906.

Despite the complaints, however, *The Motor* reported that "the voice of the complainer is, to a large extent, drowned in the general chorus of approval. That the Isle of Man has materially benefited by the advent of the motorcar is universally admitted. The Tourist Trophy race has actually prolonged the season here for a fortnight and at the moment the hotels and boarding-houses, instead of showing a pronounced tendency towards emptying, are quite full of a nice class of people. As to the closing of the roads and the reduction of the train service, Mr Orde, the secretary of the Automobile Club, is minimising the inconvenience by every available means".

Practice was hectic, with numerous incidents reported. It was a busy time for Ramsey Engineer Percy Brooke, the Automobile Club's official repairer, whose premises at the junction of Parliament Street and West Street received a steady stream of horse-drawn carts carrying damaged TT cars. On the Mountain road Arthur McCormack had to brake so violently to avoid a herd of cattle that his Gladiator "nearly shook itself to pieces". The knuckle joint

W.J. Warren's Speedwell is weighed on the Automobile Club machine, described by Richard Hough in Tourist Trophy *as "an instrument of vast proportions and dreadful inaccuracy". The bodies were lifted from the chassis to ascertain weights separately. The scales at each corner were borrowed from the Island's railway stations. [Stenlake Publishing]*

The Swift of Harvey du Cros Junior leads the Siddeley of Sidney Girling at Cronk-ny-Mona. Du Cros finished sixth but Girling retired on the last lap with his radiator cracked. In early races the course turned right at Cronk-ny-Mona, continuing via Willaston to Bray Hill. In 1922 this section was replaced by the new section via Signpost Corner, Governor's Bridge and Glencrutchery Road to Bray Hill. [R and L Kelly collection]

from the expanding brake from the gear box was broken and could not be repaired, putting him out of the race. Ernest de Wilton's Swift hit a wall but was rebuilt in time, while an Argyll hit a house, a White Steam Car went through a wall, and a Wolseley ploughed a field. Percy Dean's Scout also had an accident but was expected to be repaired in time for the race. Collisions were not confined to the Island – en route to the Island, Lancaster crashed through an unlit railway crossing gate while driving his Clement through the night from Paris to Boulogne to catch a cross-channel ferry. Despite bending the front axle, he pressed on to Liverpool where he found Isle of Man sailings suspended for three days due to storms. He arrived in time for the race, but too late to practise.

Some drivers adopted a methodical approach. Charles

On the day before the race the cars were required to be taken to a marquee at the Automobile Club's enclosure near to the start line for fuelling and technical inspection and were then kept there overnight before being pulled to the start line by horses on the morning of the race. The Argyll of W. Parker Thomas is seen undergoing its inspection. [Author's collection]

Rolls filled many notebooks with details of stones and potholes as well as noting advertisement signs which could be used as braking or gear-change points (the fore-runners of the "pace notes" used in rallies today). Tom Thornycroft was seen walking along the course "with a very serious face", carefully measuring gradients with a handkerchief.

Although there was no official timing for the practices, unofficial timing and fuel consumption revealed the favourites. Charles Rolls lapped at 33 mph with a fuel consumption of 26 mpg, while John Napier's Arrol-Johnston lapped in 1 hour 39mins, an average of 31.50 mph. In 1955 Fred Bennett made an impressive, albeit surprising, claim that he had done a 33 mph practice lap on his Cadillac.

At the end of the practice period, there was concern that the race might have to be postponed. The mid-September date had been chosen to allow time for harvesting to be completed, but flooding caused by two days of heavy rain at the end of August had delayed the harvest so much that there were doubts whether the farmers could stand the disruption which race day would cause. Also, could farmers spare enough horses to pull the 14 carts needed to cover the course with 10,000 gallons of the dust-laying compound *Westrumite*, (which replaced the *Dustroyd* used for the Gordon Bennett Trial) diluted by 80,000 gallons of water? To everyone's relief, they could and it was decided that the race would go ahead.

The pre-race examination and weighing of the cars took place at the Automobile Club enclosure. The cars, without fuel, oil and grease, were pushed onto a rig with scales for each wheel. The bodies were then lifted from the chassis, which were then weighed separately. The bodies were then replaced and the totals re-checked. The first car took 1 hour 45 minutes. Great efforts were put into lightening cars by scraping mud from the chassis, stripping and drilling.

Fuel tanks were another issue. Two cars were found to have concealed tanks. The vertical gravity feed tanks fitted to the Thornycrofts and the Napiers were rejected as not being touring car fitments. These tanks had to be re-located below the front seats, where the standard Napier Tanks were normally fitted.

In a practice crash on the downhill S-bend approaching the Fairy Bridge at Ballalonna on the Castletown road, Ernest de Wilton's Swift hit a stone wall and was reduced to "match-stick timber". A team of mechanics was sent from Coventry and carried out a complete re-build but this left de Wilton short of time to make final adjustments before weighing-in. A senior official of the Automobile Club verbally granted an extension of time, and de Wilton submitted the car on the following day in reliance on the verbal concession only to be disqualified for being too late. This disqualification reduced the starters to 42 cars of 29 different makes, with 28 British and 14 foreign drivers.

This view of the interior of the marquee in the official enclosure shows Charles Rolls' Rolls-Royce (1), the Speedwells of W.J. Warren (6) and A.J. Dew (7), W.H.Astell's Orleans (8), C.L.Cattell's James and Browne (19), A.J. Hancock's Vauxhall (23) and the White Steam cars of A.C. Kent (28) and Frederic Coleman (29). [Author's collection]

The second Swift, driven by Harvey du Cros Junior, was also in trouble. When weighed on Coventry Council's scales it had been 12lbs within the weight limit. When weighed by the Automobile Club it was 14.5lbs over weight. When du Cros queried whether the Automobile Club's scales (brought from London due to doubts about the Douglas coal merchant's scales used for weighing the Gordon Bennett Trials cars) had been tested he was told that they had not, as they had been correct when they left London. On suggesting that the scales should be tested, du Cros was told that they would be if he obtained the necessary weights. On producing certified weights supplied by the local Inspector of Weights and Measures, the Clerk of the Scales refused to test the scales until all cars had been weighed, saying that he would assume that they were accurate until proved otherwise. Du Cros then removed 13lbs of his car's weight, and submitted the car for re-weighing, when it was found to be 5lbs under the maximum weight. This meant that the first official weight was 6.5lbs wrong if the second was correct!

After weighing-in, the cars were drawn by horses into a marquee, where they remained under police guard until the morning of race day. After a last-minute concession, the fuel allowance was increased from 8.5 to 9.5 gallons to allow for 22.5 mpg rather than 25 mpg, the cars were fuelled under official supervision and the tanks were sealed.

1905 Tourist Trophy Race

Race day was a public holiday. The weather was warm and sunny and so many spectators crowded the course that, bearing in mind the custom of Manx country folk to leave doors unlocked, there were fears of houses in the country being burgled while the occupants were out watching the race and the police were on duty on the course.

A cavalcade of seven official course cars left the start. There were two White Steamers, an Orleans, a Martini, a Dixi, a Rolls-Royce lent by Charles Rolls and Julian Orde's Daimler.

The 42 competing cars were pulled by horses from the marquee to the Alexander Drive start line, where they were to be started at 9am, at one minute intervals. This following a sensible last-minute decision by the Club to change the intended interval of two minutes which would have seen the early starters on lap 2 before the later runners were on the course. Many cars were decorated with sprigs of white heather. Richard Lascelles, driving the New Simms-Welbeck, "a bit of a wag" according to the *Isle of Man Times*, wore a large fluffy coat and had a curious doll mascot attached to his car. "Toby" Rawlinson had his pipe, a pouch of tobacco and a raw potato stowed beneath his Darracq's seat cushion. He was reticent about his purpose in carrying the potato but Edmund Lewis was more forthcoming about the basket of raw potatoes in his Rover – they were for throwing at other competitors who failed to move over to let him pass!

Charles Rolls was first away, coasting down Brown's Hill to save fuel. His engine was heard to fire and the first Tourist Trophy Race was under way. He crossed Quarterbridge, where Lord Raglan gave him a wave of encouragement, and turned into the Castletown Road. As he approached the railway crossing, he attempted to engage third gear, failed, tried to engage his "sprinting gear", failed and then tried third again. This time there was a dreadful noise as the gears were stripped and Rolls coasted to a halt. His race was over with less than a mile completed. Perhaps hastily, Rolls alleged sabotage. The police had been guarding the marquee overnight and they maintained that nobody could have gained access to the cars. Nevertheless Rolls said that he found a number of broken loose nuts at the bottom of the gearbox, which must have been inserted through a hole at the top. These, he said, clearly had jammed the gears and stripped the teeth. The nuts were never produced for official examination as Rolls quickly had the car removed to the Isle of Man Steam Packet Company warehouse to await its return to the factory. It had to be said that it was not at that time recommended practice to engage a gear while coasting.

The first lap became even more eventful. At Ballasalla, John Downie's Argyll failed to take the corner at the Whitestone Inn, almost making an early visit to the bar.

On the morning of race day a "hay motor" pulls the Orleans of Thomas Jenner out of the marquee where the cars were secured overnight, on the way to the start line. In a successful race for Orleans, Jenner was ninth of the 18 finishers while the other Orleans, driven by W.H. Astell, was seventh. [The Bystander]

A large crowd assembled outside (and on top of) the gate of "Woodlands" on Brown's Hill for the start. After about 100 yards the hill joined the course at Quarterbridge Road and the finish line was on Quarterbridge Road about 200 yards before the junction. The race consisted of four laps of 52 miles. [National Motor Museum]

W.H. Astell, pictured at the start line with his Orleans, finished seventh after a steady and uneventful race. [John Watterson collection]

Despite breaking a wheel, he was able to continue, only to run out of petrol later. James Hadley's Wolseley went up a bank at "Post Box corner" (believed to be between Sandygate and St. Jude's, at the junction with the Summerhill Road). The rear of the car partly blocked the road and was hit by Tom Thornycroft who continued with a bent axle and a wobbly wheel. Meanwhile Hadley also had a bent axle, which he took to the local smithy, within a mile. The blacksmith straightened the axle and Hadley and his mechanic replaced it and continued in the race. His first lap took 4 hours 46mins.

Fred "Reliability" Bennett's Cadillac was going well, passing six cars on the Mountain until, coasting rather too

The Rolls-Royce of Charles Rolls and the Napier of Clifford Earp are lined up for the start of the first TT outside "Woodlands" on Brown's Hill, Alexander Drive Douglas. Rolls coasted down the hill to conserve fuel but when he tried to engage a gear he could not do so. There was a dreadful noise from the gearbox and Rolls had to retire less than a mile from the start. Although he suspected sabotage nothing was proved. [National Motor Museum]

John Downie, photographed at the Bungalow, was involved in one of the first incidents of the race when he crashed into the wall of the Whitestone Inn at Ballasalla on lap 1. He continued after repairing one of his Argyll's wheels but was the second driver to run out of fuel, on the Mountain on the third lap, with sixty miles still to run. [Author's collection]

James Hadley's Wolseley is pictured at the start line on Brown's Hill on Alexander Drive, Douglas. After running up the bank on the first lap at Post Box Corner, between Sandygate and St. Judes, he had his bent front axle straightened by the local blacksmith but took nearly five hours to complete the lap and was out of time. [John Watterson collection]

Fifty years on, in a unique ceremony in Crosby during the Veteran Car Club's Isle of Man TT Golden Jubilee Rally, F.S. Bennett (then VCC President) was presented with part of a wheel of the Cadillac which he drove in the 1905 race. This had been recovered by a young boy from the site of Bennett's crash below Keppel Gate. [George Gelling collection]

fast below Keppel Gate, he lost control when the ballast in the back of his car moved on a sharp corner. "We'll not make it!" shouted the mechanic. He was right – the car hit the garden wall of a cottage, the wheels collapsed, the car ended up on its side and the mechanic was thrown over the stone wall. He was not seriously hurt. Bennett himself was unhurt in the accident but was still nursing a sprained ankle which had been strapped up after a fall on a banana skin outside his hotel. After his mechanic had been taken for treatment, Bennett attended to his car and then walked back along the course to the Bungalow, a distance of about three miles. There he caught a Snaefell Mountain Railway tram to Laxey and became involved in the first serious tramway accident since the opening of the Mountain Railway in 1895. The railway had been running a shuttle service for race spectators when an ascending tram had stalled at Lhergy Veg due to a motor fault or loss of wire contact, and the third of three trams descending on the same track, unable to stop in time, had run into the back of the second tram. Race ambulance staff from the Bungalow attended. Although passengers suffered cuts, bruises and shock, and four needed hospital treatment, there were no serious injuries. The scene of Bennett's crash then became known as "Bennett's Corner", but the name did not survive.

Bennett's accident had a remarkable sequel 50 years later when, as President of the Veteran Car Club of Great Britain, he was on the Island with his Cadillac, taking part in the Club's TT Golden Anniversary Rally. After the accident John Mylroie, a young boy from Laxey spectating at the scene, had grabbed a piece of a wooden spoke and a bolt as a souvenir. These relics were mounted and presented to Fred who said "In the long history of motoring there has never been such a unique presentation".

Warren's Speedwell retired with a broken wheel, as did Rawlinson's Darracq at Ramsey. Tom Thornycroft cut Hillberry corner very fine, thought that he had nipped his tyre on the step of the cottage, changed it, nipped it again and then realised that the problem was the wheel wobbling after the collision with Hadley's Wolseley. Arnott's Minerva stopped with gear trouble but continued.

At Ballacraine, John Napier took to a ditch in his Arrol-Johnston after a violent swerve to avoid "big and playful" dogs which, according to *The Motor*, had been a problem during practice. He managed to keep going.

Clifford Earp's Napier was surprisingly slow, being passed by a number of cars before Ramsey. The problem was excessive fuel consumption and Earp was driving to finish.

The first cars to pass Ramsey Hairpin at the start of the Mountain climb, watched by an estimated crowd of 500,

In this Ramsey street scene Charles Friswell's Peugeot passes under the temporary footbridge where Bowring Road joins Parliament Square. The northern loop, taking competitors from Ballaugh to Ramsey via Sandygate and St. Jude's, was used only for the Gordon Bennett Trials of 1904 and 1905 and the TT of 1905. [Stenlake Publishing]

were the two Orleans of Jenner and Astell. They had been the sixth and seventh starters and still led on the road at the end of the lap, followed by the wobbly-wheeled Thornycroft. Lanchester's Clement came next, with Kent's White Steamer attempting to pass, with much waving and shouting by the driver. Kent thrilled the spectators on the grandstand when he managed to squeeze past in front of them, putting two wheels on the footpath in the process. Meanwhile Northey's Rolls-Royce, the two Arrol Johnstons, and the Vinot were obviously fast.

On corrected time, Napier's Arrol-Johnston led at the end of the lap, in a time of 1 hour 32mins 36.4secs (33.64 mph), from Percy Northey's Rolls-Royce (1 hour 34mins 0.2secs – 33.03mph), Norman Littlejohn's Vinot (1 hour 34mins 30.4secs – 33.72 mph), the second Arrol-Johnston of Cyril Roberts (1 hour 36mins 46secs – 32.45

W. Parker Thomas takes his Argyll along Jurby Road on the northern outskirts of Ramsey. The 1905 TT was the only one to use the 52 miles course which took in the northern loop from Ballaugh to Ramsey via The Cronk, Sandygate and St.Jude's. Thomas finished eighth of the 18 finishers. [Stenlake Publishing]

John Napier climbs the first part of the Mountain Road between Ramsey Hairpin and Waterworks on his way to becoming the first TT winner. He beat runner-up Percy Northey's Rolls-Royce by 2mins 9secs. [The Bystander]

Guy Baxendale passes Bungalow Bridge, where the Leslie Graham Memorial now stands. He retired his Thornycroft after completing two laps, with broken springs and a deflated tyre. Team owner Tom Thornycroft fared no better, retiring on the third lap with rear axle damage. [Author's collection]

mph) and Ernest Courtis' Rover (1 hour 38mins 47.6secs – 31.58 mph).

Both the Whites retired on lap 2: Kent at Castletown Corner with a broken wheel and Coleman with a choked vaporiser and broken pipe. Arnott, who had been in trouble on the first lap, retired his Minerva with ignition and carburettor problems and a loose camshaft. A.J. Hancock skidded into a ditch a mile out of Kirk Michael, crossed the road and crashed his Vauxhall into a tree, breaking a wheel, and Algernon Lee Guinness cornered too fast at Hillberry and hit the steps of a cottage. The steps were known as "Guinness' steps" until they were demolished before the 1908 TT. By the end of the lap, the leaders on the road were catching the last starters on lap 1. The Rolls-Royce led on the road, followed by the two Orleans but Napier's Arrol-Johnston came through fourth. Napier had started 41st and had therefore overtaken 37 cars in two laps. On aggregate time, the Arrol-Johnston still led at the end of the second lap (3 hours 4mins 38.8secs) from the Rolls-Royce (3 hours 7mins 32.4secs) with the Vinot still third (3 hours 8mins 32.4secs). The Rover, after lapping in 1 hour 33mins 19secs, was now fourth with an aggregate time of 3 hours 12mins 06.6secs, with the second Arrol-Johnston fifth with an aggregate time of 3 hours 14mins. Guy Baxendale retired his Thornycroft at the end of the lap, with a broken spring and deflated tyre and Cooper retired his Beeston Humber with a broken front spring.

The third lap saw the retirement of Tom Thornycroft below Keppel Gate, with the final collapse of his back axle after the collision with the Wolseley on the first lap. The Wolseley also retired on its third lap, out of time after its long stop on lap 1. The Dixi of Karl Beireiz stopped at Ramsey – the first car to run out of petrol, soon followed by John Downie's Argyll. Napier's time for three laps was 4 hours 37mins 47.2secs. Northey was still second (4 hours 39mins 14.2secs), Littlejohn third (4 hours 41mins 56.8secs), and Roberts fourth (4 hours 52mins 56secs).

John Napier went past the enclosure to start his last lap with his exhaust pipe and silencer trailing on the ground, due to a broken mounting bracket, and held on only by a strap. He stopped about a hundred yards beyond the enclosure to re-attach the pipe with wire, and was away after some three minutes, enough to give Percy Northey the lead and to set up a tense finish.

Retirements continued on the final lap – Dew's Speedwell (on the instructions of the judges, with trouble with a valve cotter and a nut on the differential brake), Sidney Girling's Siddeley (cracked radiator and choked water system), Claude Clench's Whitlock-Aster (three punctures but only two spare tubes), and Holloway's Minerva with an ignition coil trembler problem. Cattell's James and Browne, James Reid's Beeston Humber, Cox's Maudslay, Percy Dean's Scout, and Lancaster's Clement all ran out of petrol. Reid and Lancaster both ran out "near Kirk Michael, conveniently outside of a place where liquid refreshment of a consoling nature could be obtained" according to *The Motor.*

Percy Northey was the first driver to complete the race. The approach of his Rolls-Royce could be heard long before it was seen, due to a siren fitted to the car to facilitate passing. He crossed the finish line to great applause, as if the crowd thought he had won, but the difference in start times between Northey (no.22) and Napier (no.53) had to be taken into account. Napier threw caution to the winds with the fastest lap of the race (1 hour 31mins 9.6secs – 34.20 mph) and the Arrol Johnston crossed the line to complete the race in a time 2mins 8.4secs inside the time taken by the Rolls-Royce, a

With the retirement of Charles Rolls less than a mile from the start, his team-mate Percy Northey was left with a heavy responsibility. Seen here at Ballasalla, he finished second to John Napier's Arrol Johnston by 2mins 9secs and could have won after Napier was delayed when his exhaust system came adrift. [Ron Brew collection]

John Napier, winner of the first TT, drives his Arrol-Johnston past the Bungalow. He averaged 33.90 mph, with a fastest lap of 34.30 mph. His aggregate time of 6hrs 9mins 14secs was 2mins 9secs less than that of runner-up Percy Northey's Rolls-Royce, despite a stop due to a broken bracket which left his silencer trailing on the ground. [R and L Kelly collection]

Arthur J. Clay's Ryknield crosses the finish line outside "Meersbrook" on Quarterbridge Road. He finished fourteenth. [R and L Kelly collection]

total time of 6 hours 9mins 14.6secs (33.90mph) compared with Northey's time of 6 hours 11mins 23secs (33.60mph). Napier had 8.3 pints of fuel left, having consumed 25.4 mpg, while Northey had 6.8 pints left (24.8 mpg). Norman Littlejohn's Vinot-Deguingand came in third in 6 hours 14mins 35secs. The second Arrol-Johnston of Cyril Roberts was fourth, the Rover of Ernest Courtis was fifth, and the Swift of Harvey du Cros was sixth with the second best fuel consumption (26.9 mpg).

While Northey was philosophical, Rolls was bitterly disappointed and amply demonstrated the fact by following up his earlier allegation of sabotage by submitting an official protest against Arrol Johnston, on the grounds that Napier had illegally gained a power advantage through the loss of his silencer. He even alleged that driving with the silencer dragging on the ground had been dangerous and went as far as to suggest that this had been a deliberate act. The protest was summarily rejected by the Stewards, Napier having responded that he had stopped promptly to fix the silencer, he had been hindered by loss of power (since the exhaust system had been designed to enhance power output) and by the silencer dragging on the ground. He also pointed out that there were no race regulations governing the fitting and use of silencers. Perhaps surprisingly, the Stewards must have found some merit in Rolls' protest because they refunded his protest fee. It would have been normal for the fee to be forfeited when a protest was rejected as being unjustified. On the other hand, the Stewards may have wished to avoid aggravating the situation after the dispute between the Automobile Club and Rolls after the Gordon Bennett Trials of the previous year!

The best fuel economy was achieved by Robert Downing with his Dennis, the 18th and last to finish, in a time of 9 hours 5mins 48.8secs, an average speed of 23 mph and a consumption of 27.2 mpg, with 12.7 pints still in his tank. Clifford Earp balanced speed and fuel consumption to perfection, finishing tenth at 28 mph with

Clifford Earp is pictured on Ballanard Road, between Willaston and Bray Hill. As his Napier's fuel consumption was heavy he decided to drive to finish, which he did to perfection. He finished tenth averaging 28 mph and 22.5 mpg and, at the finish, his tank was completely empty. [Author's collection]

22.5 mpg and no fuel left in his tank. Richard Lascelles (New Simms Welbeck) also finished with 22.5 mpg and no fuel left but he averaged only 23.7 mph and finished 17th.

The beautiful weather of race day quickly changed, forcing the cancellation of the Graphic Challenge Trophy hill-climb scheduled for the following day on the section of the TT Course from Ramsey Hairpin to the Bungalow. The event attracted limited public interest and only twelve entries. When competitors arrived at Ramsey for the start Julian Orde, having just driven over the course, announced that low cloud on the mountain meant that it would be unsafe to hold the event. After a half-hour delay there was no improvement and the event was postponed to 7 am on the next day (Saturday) but later cancelled when it appeared that most competitors would have left the Island by then or would be about to do so.

1905 Tourist Trophy Race Results

Thursday 14th September 1905. Start 9.00am. 4 laps of 52miles circuit, total distance 208miles. 42 starters, 18 finishers.

1. John S. Napier (Arrol-Johnston), 6hrs 9mins 14.6secs (33.90mph) 8.3 pints left, 25.4 mpg
2. Percy Northey (Rolls-Royce), 6hrs 11mins 23secs (33.60mph) 6.8 pints left, 24.8 mpg
3. Norman Littlejohn (Vinot), 6hhs 14mins 35.4secs (33.40mph) 2.6 pints left, 23.3 mpg
4. Cyril Roberts (Arrol-Johnston), 6hrs 36mins 58.6secs (31.7mph) 6.2 pints left, 24.6 mpg
5. Ernest Courtis (Rover), 6hrs 43mins 53.6secs (31.00mph) 8.5 pints left, 25.5 mpg
6. Harvey du Cros (Swift), 7hrs 1min 12.4secs, (29.70mph) 11.9 pints left, 26.9 mpg
7. W.H. Astell (Orleans), 7hrs 7mins 42.2secs, (29.20mph) 11.25 pints left, 26.6 mpg
8. W. Parker Thomas (Argyll), (7hrs 10mins 25secs (29.00mph) 6.25 pints left, 24.6 mpg
9. Thomas Jenner (Orleans), 7hrs 19mins 32.4secs (28.50mph) 9.45 pints left, 25.9 mpg
10. Clifford Earp (Napier), 7hrs 27mins 44.6secs (28.00mph) nil fuel left, 22.5 mpg
11. R.W. Maudslay (Standard), 7hrs 28mins 2.4secs (27.9mph) 1.3 pints left, 22.9 mpg
12. Edmund W. Lewis (Rover), 7hrs 41mins 23.6secs (27.10mph) 8.7 pints left, 25.5 mpg
13. Charles Friswell (Peugeot), 7hrs 58mins 54.4secs (26.20mph) 10 pints left, 26.0 mpg
14. Arthur J. Clay (Ryknield), 8hrs 11mins 44.2secs (25.40mph) 2.6 pints left, 23.3 mpg
15. Frank G. Cundy (Napier), 8hrs 17mins 10.4secs (25.20mph) 6.4 pints left, 24.6 mpg
16. John Dennis (Dennis), 8hrs 26mins 43.6secs (24.7mph) 6.1 pints left, 24.5 mpg
17. Richard Lascelles (Simms-Welbeck), 8hrs 49mins 8secs (23.70mph) nil left, 22.5 mpg
18 Robert Downing (Dennis), 9hrs 5mins 48.8secs (23.00mph) 12.7 pints left, 27.2 mpg

Fastest lap: John S. Napier (Arrol-Johnston) 1hr 31mins 9.6secs (34.20mph).

Cars which ran out of fuel, and miles completed:
C. L. Cattell (James and Browne), 203.5 miles
James Reid (BeestonHumber), 187.5 miles
W.H. Cox (Maudslay), 186.9 miles
Percy Dean (Scout), 185.4 miles
E.H. Lancaster (Clement), 181.7 miles
John Downie (Argyll), 148.4 miles
Karl Beireiz (Dixi), 141 miles

Retired:

Lap 1:
Hon. C.S. Rolls (Rolls-Royce), gearbox problems
W.J. Warren (Speedwell), broken wheel
F.S. Bennett (Cadillac), crash at Keppel Gate
A. ("Toby") Rawlinson (Darracq), broken wheel

Lap 2:
A.J. Hancock (Vauxhall), crash near Kirk Michael
A.C. Kent (White Steam Car), broken wheel at Castletown corner
Frederic Coleman (White Steam Car), vaporiser choked, broken pipe
E.H.Arnott (Minerva), ignition and carburettor problems, also loose camshaft
Algernon Lee Guinness (Darracq), crash at Hillberry

Lap 3:
Tom Thornycroft (Thornycroft), damaged rear axle
C.H. Cooper (Beeston Humber), broken spring due to accident
Guy Baxendale (Thornycroft), broken springs

Lap 4:
A.J. Dew (Speedwell), damaged propeller shaft coupling
Sidney Girling (Siddeley), cracked radiator
Claude Clench (Whitlock-Aster), three punctures but only two spare tubes
W.C. Holloway (Minerva), trembler coil problem

Out of time: James Hadley (Wolseley), due to lengthy repairs after accident.

Reaction

The race results had huge significance for the future of both Arrol-Johnston and Rolls Royce. Encouraged by John Napier's efforts as Chief Engineer as well as the TT victory, in 1906 The Mo-Car Syndicate Ltd. of Glasgow changed its name to The New Arrol-Johnston Car Company Ltd. and increased its capital to £100,000. The company focussed its efforts on the construction and marketing of a 12hp side entrance tonneau, powered by the TT engine and priced at £400. For Rolls-Royce, despite Charles Rolls' personal disappointment, the TT result was a turning point in the evolution both of the car and of the company. A failure in the TT might have discouraged potential financial backers but Arthur Briggs (who had been sufficiently convinced of the value of racing in improving cars and in marketing them to the public to suggest to Rolls that he should enter for the TT) now encouraged a combination of C.S. Rolls & Co. and Royce Ltd. The new company, named Rolls-Royce Ltd., was formed on 16th March 1906 with F.H. Royce, Charles Rolls, Claude Johnson and A.H. Briggs as Directors. The race also demonstrated the value of the "sprinting gear" which became standard on the 1906 Rolls-Royces.

To prove that the TT had been a fair test of fuel consumption and that its results had been an accurate indication of what the ordinary motorist could expect; Charles Rolls tested the two TT cars on the London-Oxford road. With two Press representatives as passengers and observers, Rolls drove his TT car and Claude Johnson drove Percy Northey's car. Each car carried extra weight to simulate a third passenger. They started at the tenth milestone out of London and drove several miles apart to a point beyond the 52nd milestone. There, fuel consumption was checked prior to the return journey. Rolls' car did 24.7mpg on the outward journey and 22mpg on the return, a mean of 23.3mpg while Johnson's car did 25.1mpg on the outward trip and 24.6mpg on the return, a mean of 24.9mpg. In the TT Race, Northey's car did 24.8mpg.

Reflecting on the first TT, *The Automotor Journal* said that "Unmistakeably, the unanimous opinion of those who attended the race – public, manufacturer and competitor alike – was that it had proved a thorough success and that this new type of contest for touring cars had justified in practice the hopes of its most ardent supporters". *The Autocar* thought "There is no doubt that the Tourist Trophy Race last week was the most interesting competition which has ever been held in the automobile field. It was an honest attempt to frame regulations which should make the employment of monstrous cars impossible, and also prevent the employment of machines of the exact opposite".

1906 Tourist Trophy – Rolls Wins On New Course.

Planning

Within a few days of the 1905 race, 16 manufacturers had followed Charles Rolls in sending enquiries for the 1906 event to the Automobile Club although regulations had not been considered and a date had not been fixed. It was not even certain that there would be a race, due to the Church's opposition to Sunday practising and the farmers' concerns about disruption of the harvest. They were not against racing per se, but wanted a spring or early summer date. Both groups had substantial political influence.

Lord Raglan placated the Church with the assurance that he would not sign a Road Closing Order unless the Automobile Club satisfied him that there would be no disturbance of the Sabbath, while the Highway Board took the initiative over the date by informing the Automobile Club that a September date would be "inconvenient". The Club then asked for October but the Board refused that also, as the harvest could still be affected and the tourist season would have ended. At a meeting on 23rd February, the Club agreed to a May or June date from 1907 but persisted with a request for 27th September 1906, as there would be new technical regulations and entrants would need time to prepare. The Board accepted this for one year only. The farmers were not happy but the national interest prevailed, not least because of financial considerations. In 1905, one team's expenditure on the Island during the race period was said to have been £300 (the equivalent of over £44,000 today).

Details of the new technical regulations were soon revealed. The minimum wheelbase was increased from 7 feet 6 inches to 8 feet. The fuel allowance remained at 25 mpg but an increase in minimum weight from 950lbs to 1,125lbs would increase consumption. The "sprinting gears" which had been popular in 1905 were regarded by the Club as not being normal touring car equipment and the regulations were aimed, unsuccessfully, at eliminating them. Cars would have to be able to stop and re-start with a full load on a gradient of 1 in 6 and would also have to be capable of travelling at 12 mph in top gear on a level road.

Rolls lost no time in checking whether his 1905 cars could meet the new requirements. Early one morning he and Claude Johnson tested the cars in top gear over a measured half mile in The Mall in London when one car travelled at 9.04 mph and the other at 8.31 mph, doing 195 and 180 revolutions per minute respectively. They then went to a 1 in 6 incline in Jasper Road, Sydenham where both cars stopped and re-started easily with 6 passengers and a total weight 279lbs more than the Automobile Club requirement. The test was repeated with nine passengers of 13 stone each and again the cars passed. A hill in Kent with a gradient of 1 in 4.8 was suggested, and easily climbed by a Rolls-Royce with four passengers.

Then there came the surprise revelation of a new course. Unfortunately the first that the Highway Board heard of the Club's intentions came as late as August and not from the Club but from a Manx journalist acting on behalf of *The Autocar*. This was not, in the Board's view, "the proper channel". After appropriate apologies, ruffled feathers were smoothed and an agreement reached, after Julian Orde undertook that Sunday practice would be prohibited and that punitive action would be taken against any offenders. The reason for changing the course was, according to the Club, inconvenience to the Isle of Man Railway's level crossings at Quarterbridge, Ballasalla, Ballacraine and Ballaugh. The solution was to remove the southern loop, re-routing the course along the central valley from Quarterbridge via Union Mills and Crosby to cross the 1905 course at Ballacraine before continuing on a new loop through St.John's to Peel. The course would travel through the town from Tynwald Road via Albany Road, across Derby Road to Church Street and leave the town via Peveril Road to head north along the coast road re-joining the 1905 course at Kirk Michael. At Ballaugh, instead of taking the northern loop via Ballaugh Old Church, Sandygate and St. Jude's to Ramsey, the new course would take the more direct route to Ramsey, via Sulby and Lezayre. This would remove four railway crossings but add a new one where the Ramsey line crossed the coast road several miles north of Peel at St. German's. No trains would run on this line on race day. The changes would reduce the lap distance by about 25%, from 52 miles to 40.28 miles. The Start was to remain in its 1905 position but the finish on Quarterbridge Road was to be moved a short distance because two houses had been built on part of the site of the 1905 race enclosure.

Orde then had to meet the Peel Town Commissioners to obtain their agreement for the race to go through the town. This was given unanimously after Orde agreed that the Club would pay the cost of filling in gutters with tarmac to make the roads level with the pavements, and the cost of reinstatement after the race. Also a lamp-post at the junction of Derby Road and Church Street would be removed and the Club would provide a race progress board there for spectators.

To facilitate travel to the Island, the Automobile Association opened new agencies between Coventry and Liverpool and the Midland Railway offered to transport cars between London St.Pancras and Liverpool, and onward to the Island by Isle of Man Steam Packet Company ferries at a cost of £6.19s (£6.95p) at owner's risk, or £8.13s 9d (£8.69p) at company's risk.

Entries

In total 49 entries were received. Two 1905 entrants, Orleans and Ryknield, were absent. Arrol-Johnston, Rolls-Royce, Argyll, Thornycroft and Humber were all regarded as possible winners.

The 1905 winner, Arrol-Johnston, had two £590 cars, to be driven by John Napier and Campbell Muir. Almost identical in appearance, they produced 18hp but Napier's car had direct drive on fourth gear, Muir's car on third.

Rolls-Royce had two cars ready in April and both Rolls and Northey were on the Island in July. The cars had slightly larger engines than in 1905, producing 22hp at 1,000 rpm and costing £735. Royce wanted wire wheels but was unsure whether the company could afford them. He mentioned this to Claude Johnson, adding that the wheels could save half a minute a lap, whereupon Johnson readily accepted the cost of £40.

The two £500 Argylls were similar in design to Argyll production cars and were fitted with wire wheels. They had four cylinder 16hp engines and four forward gears, with direct drive on top gear. The drivers were W. Parker Thomas and A.E. George.

Tom Thornycroft entered one of his 14hp £650 cars and there were two Humbers, one from Beeston and one from Coventry, to be driven by their designers Thomas Pullinger and the Parisian Louis Coatalen respectively. Pullinger's car was a 16/20hp which had been lightened while Coatalen's was a 20hp model, apparently similar to a production car introduced in 1907, and substantially overweight. To avoid fuel starvation on the Mountain climb, the cars had pressurised systems. The cars were priced at £495 and £800 respectively.

The 14hp Academy, to be driven by Turberville Smith, could not be accused of being a "freak" touring car. One of the smallest-engined and quietest cars in the race, it had a 14hp White and Poppe engine with a newly-patented carburettor. Its three-speed gearbox and self-lubricating universal joint were both invented by West. The frame was ash, reinforced top and bottom with steel flitch plates, rather than pressed steel. Priced at £375, it was the cheapest car entered, £20 cheaper than the 10hp Peugeot of Charles Friswell. Built by E.J. West Ltd. of Coventry to the specification of the Motor Academy of Notting Hill Gate, London, it was fitted with dual controls for clutch and brake. It was a true touring car but, if reliability was a key feature, fuel efficiency certainly was not – it would cover only 131 miles before coming to a halt on lap 4.

One of the most revolutionary cars was the £450 Armadale, built in Northwood, London. It had a 16hp four-cylinder engine and a variable friction gear which would deliver any speed between 11.5 and 36 mph at normal engine speed. The driver was W.G. Batchelor.

The two 22hp French Berliets (£600 for chassis only – no price complete with body was quoted) were to be driven by Ernest Hutton and Paul Bablot. They had hand levers which could alter the richness of the fuel mixture while running, which was expected to assist fuel economy. They were said to be one of the few genuine touring cars in the race. Also built in France were the S.C.A.R., an 18hp four-cylinder car priced at £500, in the hands of H.A. Bate, a 20hp £600 Clement entered for Georges Braud (said to be a genuine touring car), a 20hp Gladiator priced at £600 entered by Arthur McCormack, and a 16hp £575 Vinot to be driven by Norman Littlejohn

The Climax Motor Co. of Coventry entered two different 14hp cars. One, for E.W. Leather, had an Aster engine, while the other, for Thomas Watson, was powered by White and Poppe. The cars were priced at £425 and £485 respectively.

Two four-cylinder 15hp Darracqs, priced at £490, were entered for experienced Isle of Man drivers Algernon Lee Guinness and Sidney Girling. The seats were so low that driver and mechanic were almost sitting on the floor.

A pair of £525 Coventry-built 24hp Deasys were to be driven by R.A. Bell and J.W.F. Crouch. A little-known make was a 25hp Hardman, entered and driven by W.L. Hardman. Its quoted price was £650.

A new James and Browne from London, with a four-cylinder 20hp engine and priced at £565, was completed just 13 weeks from the start of design work. It had a James and Browne patent metal-to-metal cone clutch. The driver was C.L. Cattell.

Two Minervas with four-cylinder 22hp engines were to be driven by Warwick Wright and M. Ross Browne. They cost £485 and were intended to be fitted with wick carburettors designed by Wright. These were lost in transit to the Island, forcing a reversion to normal carburation. The cars were too high for fast cornering. A 28hp Pipe, expensively priced at £750 and said to be one the best Belgian cars, was to be driven by Georges Dumont and a 24hp Metallurgique priced at £650 was entered for Oscar Cupper.

A four-cylinder 20hp Rapid, built in Turin and priced at £650, was to be driven by G.W. Roberts. Other Italian entries were the 16hp £650 Bianchi from Milan, entered and driven by H.P. McConnell, (also the entrant of the Rapid), and an 18hp Florentia from Florence, entered and driven by Lieut. J. Lesmoir Gordon.

Two Rovers, 16hp four-cylinder engine cars priced at £450, were said to have undisclosed modifications from the 1905 car. The drivers were Ernest Courtis and John Kemp Starley II, son of Rover's founder.

Percy Dean entered one of his 17hp Scouts, built in Salisbury and priced at £500, and R. Every was the driver of a 16hp Swift built in Coventry.

The two 18hp Siddeleys, designed by A.A. Remington of Wolseley and priced at £600, were reckoned to be the smartest cars in the race. The drivers were Montague Grahame Wright and A.E. Crowdy.

Two 18hp Wolverhampton-built Stars priced at £500 were entered for G.F. Prew and J. Lisle.

The Vici, built in West Kilburn, London, had a 12/16hp four-cylinder engine, a three speed gearbox and shaft drive. The company said that its future production cars would be all-British, although some foreign parts had been used in order to complete the TT car in time. In fact the TT car was probably the only one made.

Withdrawals before the race were two Aries, a 20hp Brown (driver Albert Brown), a 10hp Peugeot (Charles Friswell), an18hp Speedwell (M.L. Braithwaite) and two 12hp Straker-Squires (Sidney Straker and L.R.L.Squire).

Practice

Despite the Automobile Club appealing for caution, there were numerous complaints of dangerously fast driving. In Peel particularly, competitors took full advantage of the filling-in of gutters by driving on pavements, "straight-lining" the corners and hugging walls, disregarding the safety of pedestrians. Some, practising after the 7 am deadline, endangered children walking to school. The removal of the lamp-post at the junction of Derby Road and Church Street was delayed but clearly did not deter the drivers, leading a reporter to suggest that there was no need to remove it for the race as competitors would surely do so themselves! Competitors, however, were not the only source of danger. A Daimler owner took to driving his car on the course in the opposite direction during practice periods. As the roads were not closed, he was entitled to do so, but was begged by competitors to desist. Apparently this was successful as no head-on collisions were reported.

Percy Northey said "The mortality in chickens before the race must have been immense" and the *Isle of Man Times* warned of possible price rises due to shortages. There had been problems in 1904 and 1905 (as in Ireland before the 1903 Gordon Bennett Race). Rolls accounted for a rooster, and one driver killed so many chickens that he called on householders to admit his guilt and pay his dues, the going rate being three shillings (15p) per bird. A farmer's wife in Ballaugh fastened the corpse of a hen on a pole and waved this at every passing competitor. At the discounted rate of half a crown (12.5p) she recovered the chicken's value many times over before talk among drivers brought her fowl trick to light.

Rolls was clearly very determined and it was rumoured that he planned to do the fastest possible race lap regardless of fuel consumption, and leave Northey to take the win. The rooster was not his only victim – accompanied by a reporter on a practice lap, Rolls slowed for a barking sheep dog in the middle of the road but,

Hugh McConnell (Bianchi) was one of the more unlucky drivers. After two practice crashes at Sulby Bridge (and a dislocated shoulder) he found his fuel system blocked by oil just before the start. He had to use part of his fuel allowance to clear the blockage, which meant he would inevitably run out of fuel, which he did – inevitably at Sulby Bridge! [R and L Kelly collection]

J.W.F. Crouch attempted to take Hillberry too fast on the last practice morning and crashed his Deasy into the stone steps of a cottage. Although he was unhurt the mechanic suffered a fracture to the base of his skull. A replacement car was sent from Coventry but was not raced, the driver being "unnerved" by the crash. [Author's collection]

encountering the same dog on the next lap, kept his foot firmly down, sending the dog "swirling around, head over heels, legs and tail every way". The dog survived but thereafter howled dolefully and ran for miles whenever it caught a whiff of petrol. Rolls and Northey found it helpful to travel as passenger with each other, but at Ballaugh one morning, Northey frightened Rolls by taking the hump-backed bridge flat-out. In doing so, he jumped 18 inches into the air and, crossing the bridge diagonally, grazed the walls on both sides.

There were numerous crashes, and gates on the Mountain road were again smashed by the Thornycroft and one of the Humbers. Hugh McConnell, London motor dealer and later Royal Automobile Club Consultant Engineer, was practising with his Bianchi one morning when, at 80mph on the approach to the right hand corner over Sulby Bridge, one of his rear tyres burst and the Bianchi (with McConnell and the *Isle of Man Times* reporter accompanying him) went through the stone wall and landed on the bank of the Sulby River, ten feet below road level. McConnell suffered a dislocated shoulder, sent the Bianchi to a Ramsey garage for repair and wired to London for a replacement practice car. The replacement was a rolling chassis but, sitting on a box and driving one-handed, the intrepid McConnell resumed practice. Then, stranded at Ballaugh with a wheel problem, he gratefully accepted a lift on a Minerva. Soon, he again found himself on the bank of the Sulby River – to the consternation of the local constable who enquired "'Ello, 'ello, 'ello, are you over here again?" "Oh no", replied McConnell, "We were simply trying to see if we could go over in safety. Now we find we can." Several days later he threw his mechanic off the car at the foot of Bray Hill, prompting the suggestion that he might carry a few spares and speculation that the throwing out of the mechanic might be considered as shedding ballast, contrary to the rules!

Hillberry was the scene of two alarming incidents. When Starley's Rover skidded and spun, the company's head foreman, William Riley, was thrown from a back seat and landed in a field, suffering a life-threatening fracture to the base of his skull. Neither Starley nor his mechanic noticed that he was missing until several miles down the road. They turned back and found Riley, "barely sensible". The other Hillberry incident, during the final practice, involved J.W.F. Crouch who tried to take the corner too fast and crashed his Deasy into the stone steps of a cottage. The mechanic, Hinds, like Riley, sustained a fracture to the base of the skull. After first aid by a medical student spectator, he was rushed unconscious to hospital by the next competitor to arrive. He awoke to find himself in the next bed to Riley, with whom he had worked some time previously. For a time his condition caused enough concern for his relatives to be summoned by telegram, but he recovered. The Deasy also had a passenger, the wife of Edmund Lewis, designer of the car. She was neither injured nor unnerved and was soon on the course again in other cars.

The two Hillberry incidents prompted the *Isle of Man Times* to warn that "back seats are absolutely unsafe in racing cars".

Competitors blamed the road surface for the incidents but the Automobile Club rejected this, saying that the roads were no worse than in 1905, their condition was to be expected after heavy summer traffic and touring cars should be able to cope with them. Nevertheless the Highway Board did level ruts where possible.

Sunday practising was still a major embarrassment to the Club after three complaints prompted Lord Raglan to threaten to stop the race. Julian Orde threatened instant disqualification for any further offenders. Then, arising

On the day before the race drivers had to take a slow running test on Douglas Promenade, to prove that their cars could be driven on a level road at 12 mph on top gear. The cars were taken in an official convoy from the Automobile Club enclosure to the Promenade and are seen here in Broadway. [Peter Hearsey collection]

early on the next Sunday, he went to Braddan Old Church at 5am and hid behind a gravestone overlooking the course. After a time, Norman Littlejohn's Vinot appeared. Orde emerged and stared at the driver. The driver stared back. Neither spoke but, as the car passed, Orde noted that the driver was not Littlejohn but his mechanic. Spoken to later, Littlejohn said that he had been asleep, unwell, in his hotel room at the time of the offence and claimed that the mechanic's early morning lap had been unauthorised. He pleaded for leniency, as did a representative of the manufacturer. Nevertheless, the entrant and driver were responsible for their mechanic and an example had to be made as a deterrent to others. The disqualification stood.

By the Monday night before the race, eight cars had withdrawn (Brown, Pipe, two Aries, Speedwell, two Straker-Squires and Florentia). Littlejohn's Vinot was disqualified, Crouch's Deasy was withdrawn due to the Hillberry crash (although a replacement car sent from Coventry had arrived on the Island in time, the driver was considered unnerved by the accident), Muir's Arrol-Johnston broke its crankshaft and the Rapid was withdrawn. This left 37 of the original 49 cars. On Tuesday morning, two days before the race, the remaining competitors were required to assemble at the Club enclosure by 10am, prior to being taken in convoy to the Promenade for the slow speed test and then to Bank Hill, outside Douglas Railway Station, for the hill stop and re start test. At 8am, when the enclosure gates were opened, only one car was present. A steady stream started to arrive at 9.30am but a number were missing when the gate was closed. *The Motor* reported that Orde waited until after 10am and then sent two men up the road to see whether any cars were coming. Only then was the gate closed but, shortly afterwards, the two Rovers and the Armadale arrived, followed by the Metallurgique (15 minutes late) and the Gladiator (30 minutes late). In accordance with the regulations, which were very clear, all were disqualified for late arrival, despite various excuses. The Rover mechanic had cleaned out the carburettors and had emptied the fuel tank, forgetting that storage of petrol in the stable was forbidden and that the nearest supply was half a mile away. The time taken in obtaining petrol, re-fuelling and driving to the enclosure meant that the cars arrived three minutes late. Both the Metallurgique and the Gladiator had been delayed by punctures during morning practice and the Armadale mechanic had been working on the car single-handed as the driver was ill and was unable to complete the work in time. Thus five more cars were out of the race due to

The pre-race hill climbing test was held on Bank Hill, adjacent to Douglas Railway Station. With the Railway Hotel and a large crowd in the background and a dog alongside, the well-loaded Rolls-Royce of Charles Rolls ascends the hill. [Manx National Heritage]

The Rolls-Royces of Charles Rolls (4) and Percy Northey (5) are seen alongside the fuelling rig during pre-race technical examination in the Automobile Club enclosure near to the start line in Alexander Drive Douglas. [Manx National Heritage]

misfortune and what some might have regarded as a harsh decision by the Club, as fines might have been more appropriate than disqualifications. Nevertheless the Club had decided to take a tough line after problems with late arrivals for technical examination in 1905 and requests to punctual competitors to sign a petition for the reinstatement of the late-comers were unsuccessful. With the withdrawal of Watson's Climax, which unluckily broke its change-speed lever on the way to the enclosure, the field was now reduced to 31. Watson then took over Leather's Climax (No.35).

After being marshalled in numerical order, the cars were led by one of the six official White Steamers (with the other five accompanying the convoy) via Broadway to Central Promenade for the slow speed test. Each car had an observer on board to ensure that the car was in top gear when it crossed the line and that the driver did not touch the clutch. "It was a brutal test", said *The Motor*, "but one that was considered necessary for reducing the speed of the cars in the race. Without this test, and the next, that of climbing a hill with a gradient of 1 in 6, the gearings would have been much higher all-round, with the result of increased speed of car". *The Autocar* commented "This was a very difficult test for the highly geared cars, and most of them bumped and thumped along in rather a painful manner; the drivers were

Sidney Girling (Darracq, 3) and Thomas Sopwith (Peugeot, 22) are pictured on Quarterbridge Road, Douglas during practice. The Peugeot, originally entered by Guy Lewin to be driven by Charles Friswell and only recently sold to Sopwith, had to be withdrawn as it was over the permitted length. Girling ran out of fuel after 145 miles of the race. [Author's collection]

nervous, and several utterly failed on the first trial, but on the second essay all managed to do the trick except No. 11 (Argyll), which failed by a narrow margin". In fact, eight cars had to re-take the test in the afternoon, including Napier's Arrol-Johnston, and all passed except the Argyll of Parker Thomas. Now there were 30, after a test which was stressful and embarrassing for drivers and incomprehensible to spectators – a complete antithesis of racing. After completing the test, the cars were driven to Bank Hill for the 1 in 6 stop and restart test which failed, thankfully, to eliminate anyone else. Then the cars returned to the enclosure for weighing and examination. The weighing machine was described as "a great advance on last year's apparatus". Most problems arising from the examination were resolved but Friswell's Peugeot had to be withdrawn because its frame was six inches short. This meant that there would be only 29 starters.

1906 Tourist Trophy Race

Race day was warm and dry. Effective coating of the roads with *Westrumite* had ensured that the cars would raise no dust, but race officials were faced with an immediate problem in Peel. During the night a water main in Albany Road had burst, flooding the course. It would be impossible to repair the main before the race and any repair would have left the road surface in an unsafe condition. The only possible solution, to which the Peel Waterworks Company agreed, was to cut off the supply to the area until after the race. Apparently there were no complaints, probably due to the entire town being affected by what the local newspaper, the *Peel City Guardian*, called "motoritis". Shops closed for the day and the talk of the town was the race and the qualities of cars and drivers. The focal point was the junction outside the Court House where the course left Albany Road, crossed Derby Road and entered Church Street. Here, Julian Orde had thoughtfully provided a race progress board and there was an official timekeeper on a roof.

Drivers also had problems. Tom Thornycroft had dislocated his right knee, not in a practice crash but in a fall from a wall while trying to see a tailless Manx cat. He intended to drive with his right leg strapped in a sling on the side of the car, with his mechanic operating the clutch pedal with his right foot. Siddeley drivers Montague Grahame-White and A.E. Crowdy were worried about their radius rods. Due to fears that excessive lightening at the factory had left the road dangerously weak, replacements had been sent to the Island but these had not been fitted as the originals had stood up to the rigours of practising: a controversial decision. Hugh McConnell had lost fuel pressure. Although the system had been cleaned out with petrol, he found that it was blocked with clean oil. He had to flush the system on the last minutes, using part of his petrol allowance for the race. John Napier made a last minute change of mechanic, taking his unlucky team-mate Campbell Muir who would have been driving the other Arrol-Johnston but for its crankshaft failure.

With four Dunlop promotional balloons overhead, equipped with viewing baskets and inflated with town gas from the Douglas gas works, the cars were lined up for the 9am start. The start was at intervals of 1 minute 30 seconds, extended by 30 seconds from 1905. John Napier started first with Rolls starting at number 4, with shouts from the crowd of "better luck this time". While the start was uneventful, the first lap was not. First, news was received that Percy Northey's Rolls-Royce had stopped at Sulby Bridge with a broken front spring. This deprived the team of the rumoured strategy of relying on Northey to win the race while Rolls concentrated on speed. Northey toured back to Douglas, taking 1 hour 5mins 51secs for the lap. Then Bell's Deasy retired at Ramsey with gearbox failure and Warrick Wright's Minerva retired on the Mountain climb with its clutch leather burnt out. At Keppel Gate, Richard Lascelles suffered a steering failure due to breakage of the coupling securing the steering gear to the chassis of his Vici. The failure, apparently due to a practice collision with a gate, caused the Vici to mount a bank, career from side to side and crash into an embankment, all without injury.

John Napier was the first to complete the lap, followed by Charles Rolls who had gained nearly three minutes on him, having caught and passed both Darracqs. Rolls therefore led on corrected time, lapping in 1hr 0mins 13.6secs. Second was the Argyll of A.E. George, described by *The Autocar* as "one of the most earnest and fearless

Percy Northey took second place for Rolls-Royce in 1905 after Charles Rolls' very early retirement but the positions were reversed in 1906 with Rolls winning while Northey retired with a broken spring at Sulby Bridge on the first lap. He is pictured at Douglas Road Corner, Kirk Michael. [Manx National Heritage]

Arthur George approaches the Bungalow at the wheel of his Argyll. One of the fastest and most determined drivers, he was unlucky in 1906 (when loss of compulsory ballast due to broken floorboards while second brought disqualification) and in 1908 (when a carburettor fire on the last lap demoted him from first to third. [Author's collection]

men in the race". Like Earp in the Gordon Bennett Trial of the previous year, he had attached a handkerchief to his radiator funnel at the request of "a fair lady", he said, "so I had to imagine myself the modern knight doing his unworthy devoir". His time was 1hr 1min 17.4secs. Napier's Arrol-Johnston was third (1hr 3mins 2.6secs). They were followed by Ross Browne's Minerva, Paul Bablot's Berliet and Sidney Girling's Darracq. Louis Coatalen had caught his Humber team-mate Thomas Pullinger, and Crowdy, driving the second Siddeley, had caught Grahame-White.

On lap 2, as on the first lap, Sulby Bridge provided the main drama with the news that the Arrol-Johnston had stopped nearby. The off-side rear tyre had been punctured by a nail. This was followed by a second puncture. Napier had two more tube failures, one caused by the tube being nipped during a change and the other by a burst due to the tube being too small. The delays, during which 17 cars passed the Arrol-Johnston, resulted in a second lap time nearly 75 minutes longer than the first lap (Napier completed his second lap 12 minutes after Rolls completed his third) and deprived him of a possible second TT victory. Grahame-White's concern about radius rods proved to be justified when his chain jumped the sprocket and bent the rod, which broke when he tried to straighten it with a hammer. His race ended only 20 yards past the

The Siddeleys of Montague Grahame White (24) and A.E. Crowdy (25) are pictured in Quarterbridge Road, near the finish line. Grahame-White retired after two laps with a broken radius rod but Crowdy overcame a similar problem and finished eighth. [Author's collection]

timekeepers' box. Crowdy had a similar problem on the same lap when a stone buckled the radius rod, which stood up to being hammered straight on a door-step. He lost approximately 50 minutes and two places in the finishing order. Also on the second lap, Watson retired at Peel when the crankshaft of the Climax broke and Every's Swift retired with a seized gearbox. Tom Thornycroft was slowed by pre-ignition which caused the plugs to overheat and burst. He had to stop 15 times during the race. Percy Dean stopped his Scout near Ramsey with a choked carburettor but was able to continue. Rolls still led at the end of the lap (2hrs 1min 0.4secs) with George 1min 52.8secs in arrears and already looking safe in second place, although there were doubts whether his fuel would last. Ross Browne was a further 14 minutes back. Bablot was fourth, Girling fifth and Braud's Clement sixth.

When George completed his second lap (18 seconds slower than his first) the mudguards of his Argyll were obviously damaged. An official car found a bag of ballast, marked with the Argyll's number, on the road. Later a lamp, floorboards, more ballast, a torn rug, tools and other debris were also found lying on the road. The floorboards, only 3/8 inch thick, had given way and, together with the contents of the tonneau, had fallen into the road. The rug and some spare coats had then fouled the prop-shaft and brought the car to a halt. The loss of ballast meant inevitable disqualification, as the race regulations required ballast to be carried throughout the race and to be produced with the car at the post-race scrutineering.

On the third lap, Ross Browne's Minerva retired with a broken clutch at St.John's, at a time when George's impending disqualification would have given him second place. Tom Thornycroft was still running although only on three cylinders, having run out of plugs. Although the Arrol-Johnston was faster on the level, the Rolls-Royce was faster on the Mountain at 26mph compared with 25.1mph for the Arrol-Johnston. As in 1905, this was the lap when the thirstier cars began to run out of fuel. First to stop was Cattell's James and Browne, near Kirk Michael. This car had stopped earlier due to loss of coolant caused by a cracked cylinder jacket, but continued after taking on water from a roadside horse trough near Ramsey. Lisle's Star stopped near Ballaugh but Prew's similar car reached Ramsey. McConnell's Bianchi was also one of the first cars to run out of fuel. Given his practice problems, the scene of his race retirement just had to be Sulby Bridge – and it was! Bate's S.C.A.R. managed 108 miles before stopping at the Bungalow. Rolls' time for three laps was 3hrs 2mins 24.6secs. His lead over George was 11 minutes but this was only a technicality as George was officially no longer in the race, having ignored Julian Orde's signal to stop on completing lap 3. Therefore Rolls' nearest effective challenger was Bablot, 23 minutes 7 seconds behind. Braud was third, almost 11 minutes back and going well despite a brief stop in Peel when his mechanic fell off the

In 1906 and 1907 the course passed through the streets of Peel. This 1906 photograph shows the race progress board at the junction of Albany Road, Derby Road and Church Street with Georges Braud's Clement heading down Church Street after crossing Derby Road from Albany Road. He finished fourth. [Leece Museum, Peel]

Joseph Lisle's Star begins the climb from the dip at Glen Wyllin to Douglas Road Corner, Kirk Michael. The Ballacraine – St.John's – Peel – Kirk Michael loop was used only in 1906 and 1907. Of eleven drivers who ran out of petrol, Lisle was the second. He completed only 98 miles before retiring near Ballaugh on the third lap. [Stan Hughes collection]

car. He was followed by the Darracqs of Girling and Guinness and the Humbers of Pullinger and Coatalen.

Only 15 cars remained to attempt the final lap, which was long and tedious for spectators. Charles Rolls completed the race in a time of 4hrs 6mins 0.6secs (40.10mph). The runner-up was Paul Bablot (Berliet) in 4hrs 32mins 58.2 secs, followed by Guinness' Darracq in 4hrs 42mins 48.6secs. Braud brought the Clement home fourth with a time of 4hrs 47mins 20secs and he was followed by the Beeston and Coventry Humbers of Thomas Pullinger (4hrs 56mins 1.2secs) and Louis Coatalen (5hrs 0mins 52.6secs) respectively. The two Humbers, each driven by its designer, had circulated in close company throughout the race and were the only team of two cars to finish. Pullinger's Beeston Humber was also the first all-British car to finish, as the Rolls-Royce had a foreign-made magneto. John Napier finished seventh in an aggregate time of 5hrs 22mins 1sec. Without the stoppages on his second lap, which had lost him 75 minutes, and assuming that he had completed his second lap in the same time as his first, he would have finished second, 1 minute 33 seconds behind Rolls. His final lap was 0.4 of a second slower that Rolls' first lap, which was the fastest lap of the race. Of course, in a race-long battle, both could have gone faster, and either or both could have run out of petrol. Crowdy's Siddeley was eighth in 5 hours 47mins 19secs and Percy Dean's Scout brought up the rear with a time of 6hrs 57mins 18.2secs. The final lap saw six cars run out of fuel. They were Turberville Smith (Academy) beyond Peel, W.L. Hardman (Hardman) at Ballaugh, Sidney Girling (Darracq) before the Bungalow, Gordon Usmar (Vinot) and Tom Thornycroft (Thornycroft) near Ramsey, together with Ernest Hutton (Berliet), whose tank ran dry less than one mile from the finish, so close that he could hear the band playing in the Automobile Club enclosure.

Paul Bablot's Berliet approaches the bottom of Church Street prior to turning right into Peveril Road and heading for Kirk Michael. Fifth at the end of the first lap, the French driver took advantage of retirements and George's disqualification to finish second, 27 minutes behind Charles Rolls. [Leece Museum, Peel]

With Peel Hill in the background, A.E. Crowdy turns his Siddeley from Tynwald Road into Albany Road, Peel. He finished eighth after being delayed for fifty minutes by a broken radius rod. His team-mate Montagu Grahame-White retired with a similar problem, due to excessive lightening at the factory. [Leece Museum, Peel]

After the race the Automobile Club issued a statement regarding George's Argyll as follows: "Having ascertained that car No. 12 was running without its ballast and some of the contents of the tonneau, the committee have resolved that no circuit of this car can be officially recorded". Although not officially disclosed, it was unofficially stated that his total time was 4hrs 28 mins, easily the second fastest, despite the delay in freeing his propshaft. George explained after the race that his troubles had started with a broken rear spring. This meant that the car body hit the differential casing with such force that the boards were knocked out and the body was forced away from its fixings, being held only by the fuel tank. He had damaged the near side of the car when he grazed a bank and had removed the rear nearside wing when passing another car.

Arthur George's Argyll is pictured in Albany Road, Peel. Second to Charles Rolls for the first two laps, he was disqualified because some of the obligatory ballast fell from his car when the floorboards gave way. He was third in 1908, driving a Darracq. [Leece Museum, Peel]

Advertising by Argyll Motors Limited after the race caused trouble with the Automobile Club. The company claimed in an *Evening Standard* advertisement, repeated in *The Motor*, that George's car "finished second in the second fastest time". This resulted in a telegram warning from Julian Orde to the company not to repeat the statement which was not correct, as the car was not even placed, and requiring a satisfactory explanation; failing which, the company and its cars might be debarred from further competitions held under the Club's rules. Argyll Managing Director Alec Govan responded that the wording was not produced by the company but by the publications concerned. The only wording which he had produced, he said, was "Argyll finished second, but unfortunately was disqualified through the floorboards breaking and losing ballast". He apologised and asked for permission to use the amended wording. *The Motor* later said that its advertisement had been produced by the company, but the matter seems not to have been followed up except by a Club requirement that future advertisements of TT performances should be subject to prior approval by the Club.

Interviewed by *The Motor*, Charles Rolls said, pointing to his car's engine, "I had nothing to do but sit there and steer. It was this that won the race". He was also generous in his praise of Henry Royce's engineering design, saying that the credit was "obviously due to Mr Royce, the designer and builder" of the car. He added that he had no "narrow shaves" during the race except that he had nearly killed a cat. The only really exciting incident had taken place while he was trying to overtake Hugh McConnell's Bianchi, which took 18 miles. The shower of stones thrown up by the Bianchi had been so great that a stone had broken the glass in his goggles and cut his face, and Eric Platford, his mechanic, had to hand him a spare pair of goggles. Rolls confirmed that Rolls-Royce Ltd. was in a position to take full advantage of the commercial value of the win but confirmed that development of the business would be "gradual and certain", with Royce's rigorous training programme which guaranteed that the quality of the cars would be maintained.

The "Graphic" Trophy

The "Graphic" race, cancelled due to bad weather in 1905, was held on the day following the TT Race. This, *The Motor* felt, was two days too late – many visitors had returned home on Friday morning's boats, the event inevitably suffered and would have been better if held on Wednesday afternoon. The course was the first 4.25 miles of the Gordon Bennett Trials course from Quarterbridge on the outskirts of Douglas to the fifth milestone on the Castletown Road, near to the Brown Cow Inn at Santon, and including a long climb from the start followed by the steep ascent of Richmond Hill. There were 11 entries, the first starter being C.H. Cooper's 60hp six-cylinder Humber. Cars were started singly, with only one car on the course at a time. In addition to the Humber, there was a 50hp Napier driven by C.A. Glentworth (reputedly aged only 18), two Daimlers (George S. Barwick and Albert Farnell) two Berliets (William Watson and Paul Bablot), an Isotta-Fraschini (H.O. Hall), a Sorex (Anthony), a Rapid (G.W. Roberts), a S.C.A.R. (H.A. Bate) and an Ariel-Simplex (J. Ernest Hutton). The latter was the strong favourite which performed impressively in practice but failed to finish due to a broken cylinder within sight of the finish because of a lack of water in the evaporiser. The Napier won in a time of 4mins 39.8secs (an average of almost 60mph), followed by Barwick's Daimler (5mins 3secs) and Watson's Berliet (5mins 7.4secs).

1906 Tourist Trophy Race Results

Thursday 27th September 1906. Start 9.00am. 4 laps of 40.25 miles circuit, total distance 161 miles. 29 starters, 9 finishers.

1. Hon. Charles Rolls (Rolls-Royce), 4hrs 6mins 0.6secs (39.60mph)
2. Paul Bablot (Berliet), 4hrs 32mins 58.2secs (35.40mph)
3. Algernon Lee Guinness (Darracq), 4hrs 42mins 48.2secs (34.20mph)
4. Georges Braud (Clement), 4hrs 47mins 48.2secs (33.60mph)
5. Thomas Pullinger (Beeston-Humber), 4hrs 56mins 1.2secs (32.60mph)
6. Louis Coatalen (Coventry-Humber), 5hrs 0min 52.8secs (32.10mph)
7. John Napier (Arrol-Johnston), 5hrs 22mins 1sec (30.00mph)
8. A.E. Crowdy (Siddeley), 5hrs 47mins 19secs (27.80mph)
9. Percy Dean (Scout), 6hrs 57mins 18.2secs (23.20mph)

Fastest lap: Hon. Charles Rolls (Rolls-Royce), 1hr 0min 13.6secs (39.90mph)

Cars which ran out of fuel, and miles completed:

Ernest Hutton (Berliet), 160.14 miles
Tom Thornycroft (Thornycroft), 148.35 miles
Gordon Usmar (Vinot), 146.85 miles
Sidney Girling (Darracq), 145.85 miles
W.L. Hardman (Hardman), 138.85 miles
Turberville Smith (Academy), 131.85 miles
H.A. Bate (S.C.A.R.), 108.07 miles
G.F. Prew (Star), 104.57 miles
Hugh McConnell (Bianchi), 101.57 miles

Joseph Lisle (Star), 98.57 miles
C.L. Cattell (James and Browne), 95.57 miles
Retirements:
Lap 1:
Percy Northey (Rolls-Royce), broken front spring
Warwick Wright (Minerva), burnt clutch
R.A. Bell (Deasy), broken gear
Richard Lascelles (Vici), broken steering gear
Lap 2:
Grahame Wright (Siddeley), broken radius rod
T. Watson (Climax), broken crankshaft
R. Every (Swift), broken gear
Lap 3:
M. Ross Browne (Minerva), broken clutch

Disqualified for loss of ballast: A.E. George (Argyll), who completed the course in 4hrs 27mins 53secs.

Reaction

The TT race came under attack from *The Times* of London for its commercialism after Rolls and others had sought to capitalise on their successes. The newspaper pointed out that mechanics had been thrown from their cars and, whether they lived or died, the public would be inclined to think that "a contest not entirely free from the suspicion of commercialism, the preparation of which involves so much risk, ought not to be sanctioned… The Club organises the competitions with a view to the improvement of motor cars which is a good object. The motives of the entrants may not be entirely divorced from the spirit of sport but they are certainly not devoid of the desire for gain. That desire is not, of course, bad in itself but it is not a feeling commending itself to all so strongly as the feeling of honourable rivalry". *The Autocar* said that car racing as represented by the TT was an early phase in the evolution of the motor car. It was carried out in a spirit of fairness and mutual regard which was called sportsmanship. "We cannot understand the carping critics who belittle the race because of its commercial aspect ("taint" they would term it) and we should be sorry to see it degenerate into a mere sporting event where it had no utilitarian purpose to serve".

The Automotor Journal commented: "Looking back calmly on the events of last week on the Isle of Man, one cannot avoid a thrill of genuine pleasure at the unquestionable success which has been scored by the A.C.G.B.I. with their essentially British racing contest" while *The Motor* Special Correspondent said "In my opinion (and I am usually considered an exacting critic) the Club managed the race very well. That is to say that out of a thousand details only three or four could have been improved upon".

1907 Tourist Trophy – A New Race For Heavy Touring Cars

Planning

Discussions within the Automobile Club and at a meeting of Club officials and competitors in the autumn of 1906 resulted in revised regulations for the 1907 race. The fuel allowance remained as one gallon per 25 miles. The race distance was initially announced as not less than 150 miles and not more than 300 miles, which (on the 1906 course) could be anything from four laps (161 miles) to seven laps (281.75 miles). In fact the distance was increased from four laps to six laps (241.5 miles). The chassis load was a minimum of 1,400lbs (1,125lbs in 1906 and 950lbs in 1905) but the increased weight now included spare parts, spare tyres, tools, luggage and provisions, removing temptation for drivers to leave necessary spares behind. Cars would have to carry ballast as necessary but, instead of the sandbags which had caused so much trouble in 1906 , it was to be lead, securely fixed to the floor and back seat boards of the cars with 140lbs on the back seat boards (to simulate an average passenger). There was no minimum chassis weight. Although diagrams were not yet provided, bodies were required to be of a type fit for everyday use. To facilitate weighing, bodies had to be easily removable by undoing not more than six bolts or hinges and without disconnection of ignition apparatus, lubricator and fuel pipe connections. Mudguards were to be wider, but less wide than those of normal production cars. The specific gravity of the fuel was increased to a range of 0.715 to 0.725 at 60 degrees Fahrenheit, compared with 0.695 to 0.705 previously. This heavier fuel, with a higher calorific value, was in general use and would mean increased performance, needed in view of the weight increase. Cars were allowed a maximum of four speeds forward and reverse, except in the case of a variable speed gear. The tests of ability, to drive for a half mile at 12mph on top gear without use of the clutch and to stop and re-start on and ascend a hill with a gradient of "about 1 in 6" on a forward gear, were retained. As before, two entries per manufacturer were allowed. The starting order would be in order of receipt of entries.

The Autocar pointed out that a comparison of chassis loads and fuel allowances showed that the petrol allowance per ton mile had been reduced year by year, from .105 gallon in 1905 to .079 gallon in 1906 and, in 1907, 0.064 gallon for touring cars and 0.0625 gallon for heavy touring cars.

In addition to the technical changes, the regulations reflected concerns about practising in 1906. Practising on a Sunday would result in instant disqualification of car and driver. Drivers would be allowed to practise on the 14 weekdays prior to the week of the race from daylight to 7.30am, after which no car entered for the race would be allowed on the course or any part of it. No competitor would be allowed to drive or be driven in any car after 7.30am on a weekday or on any Sunday. A first offence would mean a fine not exceeding £20 and a second would mean disqualification. It was unclear how the restrictions affected the Beeston Humber team which was based on the course at Kirk Michael or how a car unable to complete a lap by 7.30am would be affected.

The Club announced that it had met the Society of Motor Manufacturers and Traders to discuss the possibility of another class for cars of a heavier type, and regulations had been drafted for consideration by the Club Committee. This was welcomed by *The Autocar* which had advocated classes both for heavier (large) and for lighter (small) cars, in addition to the existing race for "medium" cars.

Later, the Club announced that there would be an International Heavy Touring Car Race for larger, more powerful and much more heavily loaded cars. The fuel allowance would be 16mpg compared with 25mpg for the TT cars and the minimum chassis load would be 2,240lbs (1 ton), compared with 1,400lbs for the TT cars. The heavy cars would be required to carry a vertical wooden screen behind the front seats, 8 feet high from the ground and 5 feet 3 inches wide, to simulate the body of a closed car. Two holes had to be provided for visibility. The race distance would be not less than 250 miles and not more than 400 miles which (on the 1906 course) meant between seven and nine laps. The chosen distance was seven laps (281.75 miles). Increased dimensions effectively meant that wheelbase would be six inches longer.

In February 1907 the King granted the Club permission to use in its name the prefix "Royal", so that the Club became known as "The Royal Automobile Club" or "RAC."

Despite concerns about the condition of the course, the Highway Board had no money for improvements. In an effort to help, the RAC offered a steam-powered road roller for use not only on the TT Course but also on other Island roads. The Manx Automobile Club was delighted but, embarrassingly, the Highway Board declined the offer, saying that the two rollers which it already possessed were enough for its needs. The true reason was that the Board could not afford the cost of operating a third roller. The problem was resolved by Julian Orde, a supreme diplomat, who offered the grateful Board a donation by the RAC of £200 towards costs of road maintenance with the promise of further annual sums as long as the RAC continued to organise the TT on the Island. This had an immediate result in the widening of a corner on the Mountain section and the clearing of verges.

The RAC made a request to Peel Town Commissioners for road improvements within the town, only two weeks before the start of the practice period. Peel residents queried whether the Commissioners had power to fill in gutters, to incorporate pavements into the roads, as they had done in 1906. The Commissioners were satisfied that they had the power but the objection and lateness of the Club's request enabled the Commissioners to impose a condition which the Club had to accept. This was the positioning of Club officials at street corners within the town from 5am to 7am each practice morning, to report competitors driving at excessive speeds. Two officials were stationed at Albany Road, one at Church Street and one at Walpole Road.

To ease the dangers of practising on open roads, a competitor suggested that flagmen should be stationed at danger points. The RAC accepted the suggestion and the Dunlop Tyre Company undertook to recruit marshals and to provide them with white coats and three flags – white for all clear, another for caution and a yellow flag for danger.

In view of a disappointing number of entries the RAC decided to run the two races concurrently on Thursday 30th May rather than on separate days as originally planned, with roads closed from 9am to 6pm. This left Tuesday 28th May free for the first motorcycle Tourist Trophy Race on the 15.81 miles St. John's circuit; an anti-clockwise, triangular circuit, starting at St. John's and continuing via Ballacraine to Kirk Michael. There the course turned left onto the coast road and continued through Peel before returning to St. John's. In view of the proximity of the two events, the RAC and the Auto Cycle Club agreed to share expenses such as the swearing-in of marshals for both events.

Entries

Entries received were 31 touring cars (later reduced to 22) and 16 heavy touring cars (later reduced to nine).

In the touring car class, Rolls announced his entry in October 1906 but, in April 1907 *The Autocar* announced that Rolls-Royce was then making six-cylinder models only and its participation in the TT was in doubt. In May, Rolls withdrew because the company could no longer supply duplicates of their 20hp model for sale. Other withdrawals were Aries, Daimler-Mercedes, two Gregoires (too busy selling touring cars), James and Browne (who could not stock TT type cars), one of two Metallurgiques and Vici.

Arrol-Johnston entered two 25hp £560 cars to be driven by John Napier and Cyril Roberts. Two Berliets were entered for Jean Porporato and Ernest Hutton and two 18hp £485 Darracqs for the Guinness brothers. There were two 20hp Humbers, the Coventry model of W.G. Tuck and the Beeston model of James Reid. The driver of the remaining 24-28hp £625 Metallurgique, the most powerful car in the race, was Oscar Cupper.

Rover entered two 20hp £450 cars for Ernest Courtis and E.R. Folker. These were similar to the 1906 cars except for substitution of the company's own wire wheels and re-positioning of the fuel tank above the engine. Their cream and green bodies were particularly smart compared with the drab lead paint finish of some cars.

There were two 18hp £300 Stars for Harry Goodwin and G. Prew and two 16-20hp £575 West-Asters (Dick Collier and Percy Lamb) complete with wick carburettors which had been lost in 1906.

A 20hp £800 Hillman-Coatalen, the fastest car in the race, was entered by Louis Coatalen, who later married one of William Hillman's six daughters. Coatalen's mechanic was Jim Broadbent from Onchan, Isle of Man, who became a full-time employee of Hillman and drove in the 1908 2,000 miles Scottish reliability trial.

There were single entries of an 18hp £600 Clement (Georges Braud), an 18hp £600 Gladiator (M. Ross Browne), a 17-20hp £500 Scout (Percy Dean), a 14hp £625 Thornycroft (Tom Thornycroft), and a 20hp £475 Vulcan (Thomas Rimmer). The 10-12hp Leader, also known as New Leader, had the smallest engine of any car in the race. Its driver was R. Goodenough. A 24hp £675 Vinot driven by Norman Littlejohn was the second most powerful car in the entry.

No Argyll was entered, perhaps due to the advertising controversy in 1906, but the company gained publicity by lending one of its cars to the *Tatler* representative at the event. The magazine then published photographs of the Argyll at various points on the course.

In the heavy touring car class, withdrawals of an Aries, two Armstrong-Whitworths, one of two Berliets, one of two Gladiators and two Siddeleys reduced the entries to only nine. There were two 45hp £770 Ariel Simplex cars, drivers of which were Charles Sangster and A.E. Harrison, and two 30hp £525 Beeston Humbers (C.H. Cooper and George Mills). Single entries consisted of a 40hp £850 Arrol-Johnston (E.H. Arnott), an £820 Berliet (William Watson), a 25hp £745 Gladiator (Graeme Fenton), a 25-30hp £700 Straker-Squire (L.R.L. Squire), and a 30hp £725 Thornycroft (H. Niblett).

Practice

Although 14 weekdays were allowed for practice, only 15 TT and 6 Heavy Touring Car drivers had arrived and registered with five days left. The weather made the change of date from early autumn to late spring look unwise with muddy, slippery roads causing many crashes. Drivers hastily contrived under-shields and obtained thicker coats to combat the rain and high winds. Heavy rain on the final Monday night made the course particularly slippery between Douglas and Peel and at Keppel Gate. Speeds were therefore low on Tuesday morning but conditions were better on Wednesday, although still treacherous in patches and with mist on the Mountain section.

The Autocar expected, however, that speeds would be higher than in 1906 and thought that some cars might lap inside the hour. Despite the additional weight to be carried, some drivers were getting within the fuel allowance. Others, however, were not. Light cars were having difficulty while the heavy cars were very slow and had difficulty in achieving the minimum weight, resorting to lead sheets on floor and seat boards, and even one inch cast iron footboards.

The Autocar offered the following insight into the way the cars were treated: "In the course of practice they are run at speeds well exceeding sixty miles per hour, they are wrenched, twisted and skidded as found best round the corners, the brakes are jammed on without respect for tyres or mechanism, clutches are let in with a fearful bang, whilst closed to open throttle and retarded to advanced ignition is performed with the rapidity that no private owner would dream of employing in everyday use. The race is really one to destruction of the parts of the car if it is at all possible to destroy them".

Dick Collier's West-Aster arrived on the Island on Tuesday 21st May. On its first outing the following morning, the car crashed on Sulby Bridge. The mechanic, George Perkins, suffered serious leg injuries, the front part of the car was wrecked and half of the bridge wall was demolished. Other incidents involved damage to Napier's Arrol-Johnston which collided with a loose horse on the Peel road, James Reid's Beeston Humber which crashed at Kerroomoar, and Folker's Rover which broke a wheel at Sulby Bridge. Tom Thornycroft crashed twice – once between the Devil's Elbow and Kirk Michael when an offside tyre burst causing a collision with a wall (he had been using tyres left over from 1906!), and again on the Mountain. Thomas Rimmer's Vulcan hit Guinness' steps at Hillberry, and Ernest Hutton was side-lined when the bottom fell out of his Berliet's fuel tank.

Despite magneto trouble, one of the fastest cars was the Hillman-Coatalen which was reported to have lapped in 57 minutes and to have climbed the Mountain at over 25mph. After Napier's Arrol-Johnston lapped in 66 minutes *The Motor* commented "John Napier is undoubtedly a fine driver and he is here to win". Cyril Roberts with the other Arrol-Johnston was reported to have lapped in 62 minutes.

It was clear from practice times that the "Heavies" would be unable to complete the race within the road closing time and the competitors therefore successfully petitioned

Dick Collier crashed his West-Aster at Sulby Bridge during practice, demolishing part of the bridge wall. His mechanic suffered serious leg injuries. In the race, the car overturned near Keppel gate on the third lap and two wheels were broken. [R and L Kelly collection]

James Reid crashed his Beeston-Humber at Kerroomoar during practice. The car was repaired and he finished second in the race, just under twelve minutes behind the winning Rover of Ernest Courtis. They were the only finishers in the Tourist Trophy. [R and L Kelly collection]

the RAC for a reduction of the race distance from seven laps to five (201.25 miles). This decision was announced on the Monday of race week at the same time as the locations of the hill-climb and slow-running tests. These locations were kept secret until the last moments to avoid public disturbance by practising. This had not been successful, however, because competitors had guessed that Crellin's Hill, the steepest in town, would be used and had practised there, even on Sundays during services at St. Thomas' Church at the foot of the hill. The hill finally selected was Brown's Hill on Alexander Drive, the site of the race start line. In response to competitors' requests for a more private venue, the test of the cars' ability to complete a half-mile at 12mph in top gear was moved from the 1906 location on the Promenade to the straight section of the Peel road between Quarterbridge and Braddan Bridge.

Competitors were required to produce their cars at the RAC enclosure on Tuesday morning between 8am and 10am. After the 1906 debacle, when a number of cars were excluded for late arrival, nobody took any chances. The Club issued written reminders and obtained written acknowledgments and even stipulated that the "official time" was that shown on a specified chronometer in Douglas. First to arrive, ten minutes early, were the Rovers, still smarting from their 1906 exclusion but smart enough to gain publicity with a photograph titled "Last in 1906; first in 1907". How right they would prove to be! The Humbers were also early and the Metallurgique was the last to enter before the gate was closed at 10am. Despite the warnings, someone had to be late, and it was the inappropriately named Leader of R. Goodenough. He was duly excluded and, reportedly on the verge of a nervous breakdown after the hard work and strain of the previous few weeks, was ordered to bed by his Doctor. All the remaining cars then passed scrutineering.

Tom Thornycroft crashed his Thornycroft twice during practice. His first crash, between Devil's Elbow and Kirk Michael, was caused by the off-side front tyre bursting – he was using tyres left over from the 1906 TT! His second crash was on the Mountain. In the race he ran out of fuel after passing through Ramsey on the last lap. [Manx National Heritage]

1907 Tourist Trophy Race

After two bitterly cold days and a night of continuous rain, Thursday dawned with heavy rain, low cloud and

As part of the pre-race checks, competitors were required to take a test on the straight section of road between Quarterbridge and Braddan Bridge, to prove that their cars could be driven for half a mile at 12 mph on top gear. The photograph shows the scene at Quarterbridge. [National Motor Museum]

such strong winds that the morning steamer to Liverpool was delayed. Early in the morning the RAC announced that non-skid tyres with metal studs would be allowed and increased the fuel allowance for Heavy Touring Cars by 1 gallon 5 pints to 14 gallons 2 pints, equating to 14.135 mpg. This concession was controversial as it was said that the smaller of the Beeston Humber cars could have completed the race on the original allowance. The allowance for the Touring Cars remained at 9 gallons 6 pints, which equated to 25mpg. The driver of an official car reported that pre-race conditions on the Mountain were very bad, with extremely poor visibility, but that less rain between Peel and Ballaugh meant that the roads in that area were better than on the rest of the course.

After some hesitation, RAC officials eventually decided that postponement was impossible and cancellation unthinkable and the race started 11 minutes late, with cars started at intervals of 30 seconds.

Louis Coatalen knew before he started that his chances of winning had evaporated with the two gallons of fuel which had leaked from the fuel gauge of his Hillman-Coatalen overnight. With topping-up forbidden, he was forced to start the race with no possible chance of finishing. All he could do was to try for the fastest lap.

By Ramsey on the first lap, James Reid's Beeston Humber had passed 9 cars but Coatalen (the twentieth to start) had passed 13! On the Mountain, Reid passed Algernon Lee Guinness' Darracq to take the lead but Coatalen was flying. He passed Reid before the Bungalow and gained five minutes on the descent, completing the lap in 1 hour 4mins 39.8secs (37.50mph).

Second at the end of the first lap was James Reid (1 hour 13mins 52.2secs), followed by Norman Littlejohn's Vinot (1 hour 16mins 53.4secs). The next three were John Napier (Arrol-Johnston), Oscar Cupper (Metallurgique) and W.G. Tuck (Coventry Humber). Guinness was seventh and Courtis (Rover) eighth. Roberts stopped for about four minutes beyond Quarterbridge when his Arrol-Johnston's engine stopped and later he had to replace a broken inlet valve at Peel. Percy Dean's Scout had trouble with water in the magneto, stopping at Peel and elsewhere. The Berliets of Jean Porporato and Ernest Hutton were soon in trouble – they had discarded their under-shields to reduce weight and their gears were clogged with mud. Tom Thornycroft had a puncture at Sulby. There were, however, no retirements among the TT cars on the first lap.

In the Heavy Touring Car Race the two Ariel-Simplex cars led with Charles Sangster lapping in 1 hour 13mins 59secs and Harrison 18.2secs back. Third was Cooper's Beeston Humber. The only retirement was Arnott's Arrol-Johnston, at Peel, due to a bent front axle.

Less than a mile into lap 2, Coatalen skidded at Quarterbridge and hit a kerb. He had to replace a tyre which had been forced off the wheel, losing at least 15 minutes during which he was passed by Reid, Littlejohn, Napier, Cupper, Tuck and Algernon Lee Guinness. Also at

Starting the race short of fuel after an overnight leakage, Louis Coatalen (pictured at the Start) had no chance of completing the race. Instead he opted for speed. Although delayed by a burst tyre and the broken spring which caused his retirement, he completed the second lap only 16 seconds behind the leader. He was credited with the fastest lap, at 37.50 mph. [Author's collection]

G.F. Prew retired his Star on the second lap after hitting the wall at Quarterbridge, breaking both the offside front wheel and the front axle of his Star. His mechanic received a knee injury. This was Prew's second TT – in 1906, also driving a Star, he ran out of fuel. [Author's collection]

Quarterbridge, Prew took the corner too fast, skidded, hit the wall and was forced to retire his Star with a broken wheel and axle. His mechanic suffered a knee injury.

Reid led at the end of lap 2, lapping in 1 hour 14mins 29.4secs. Coatalen was only 14.2 seconds behind him on corrected time but had to retire at the end of the lap with a broken hanger to the off side rear spring. This had happened during his fast descent from the Mountain. He had lapped in just under 1 hour 24 mins, including his 15 minutes stop at Quarterbridge. The order behind Reid was then Napier, Cupper, Tuck and Guinness. Littlejohn's Vinot was next with the Rover of Courtis seventh. In the "Heavies" class, Harrison's Ariel led with Cooper's Beeston Humber second, Watson's Berliet third and Sangster's Ariel now down to fourth.

At the end of the third lap Napier led Reid by 23 seconds, with Cupper third, followed by Tuck, Littlejohn, Guinness and Courtis. During this lap Hutton retired with his gearbox hopelessly clogged by mud. Porporato was still struggling on with the other Berliet, using a spare axle spring to force his gears in and out of mesh. Other lap three retirements were Kenelm Lee Guinness (the bevel pinion driving his differential gear having broken three miles above Ramsey) and both West-Asters. Dick Collier's car overturned near the second gate on the Mountain and, although he and his mechanic were unhurt, two wheels were broken. Percy Lamb retired the other West-Aster at the end of the lap owing to mud clogging the gear gate selector bars, which were exposed owing to the dust shield having been removed. There were 16 TT cars still running. Charles Sangster was back in front in the Heavy Car Race, with a lead of nine minutes over Watson's Berliet. The Beeston Humbers, Cooper and Mills, were third and fourth. All eight heavy cars which had completed the first lap were still running.

Napier's chances of a second TT win disappeared on the fourth lap when he arrived at Hillberry with his engine misfiring badly. He stopped just beyond the corner and

Ramsey photographer G.B. Cowen took this photograph of 1905 TT winner John Napier driving his Arrol-Johnston in very wet conditions in Sulby Village. Napier had various delays and finally ran out of fuel at Sulby, 18 miles from the finish. [R and L Kelly collection]

At Ballaugh, a rare location for an early TT photograph, Kenelm Lee Guinness is pictured driving his Darracq over the bridge. He retired at Ramsey on the third lap of the race with rear axle damage. His brother Algernon, driving the other Darracq, was leading when he ran out of fuel at Hillberry on the lap lap. [Manx National Heritage]

On Quarterbridge Road M. Ross Browne's Gladiator (21) and Charles Sangster's Ariel-Simplex (6 in the Heavy Touring Car class) pass the finish line. Ross Browne was stopped, out of time, after five laps and Sangster set the fastest lap in his class but ran out of petrol on his final lap. [Author's collection]

William Watson, 1908 TT winner, drove a Berliet in the 1907 Heavy Touring Car Race. Seen cornering at the junction of Ballanard Road with Bray Hill, he ran out of petrol on the final lap, as did four other cars in his class. He was only twelve miles from the finish. [R and L Kelly collection]

Pictured at the Finish, racing cyclist George Mills won the "heavies" race with his Beeston Humber, averaging 28.8 mph. With this win and James Reid's second place in the Tourist Trophy Race, it was a very successful year for Beeston Humber. [Author's collection]

lost an hour in clearing the fuel pipe to the carburettor, which had become clogged. He lost a nut but was lucky enough to find a suitable replacement which had earlier been in a spectator's pocket! He had unavoidably lost a quantity of fuel and, with it, his chance of victory. At the end of the lap Humbers were first and second, Tuck having overtaken Cupper who was now third ahead of Littlejohn, with Courtis' Rover fifth and Guinness' Darracq sixth. Percy Dean's Scout retired with water on the magneto, leaving 15 cars still in the race. Sangster still led the "Heavies" with Harrison second again and Mill's Beeston Humber third. The other Beeston Humber of Cooper retired with a broken coil, leaving seven runners.

Lap 5 was the penultimate lap of the TT Race and the final lap of the Heavy Touring Car Race. Tuck retired with a burst tyre and broken wheel while Reid failed to appear when he was due. Cupper's Metallurgique therefore led by four minutes at the end of the lap but was running badly. Guinness' Darracq was second, going well. Then Reid appeared, 22 seconds behind Guinness, after being delayed by water and mud on his magneto and not going well. Roberts' Arrol-Johnston arrived next, "going great guns", with Courtis next, leading Roberts by nearly two minutes and only 16 seconds behind Reid on corrected time. Napier was sixth, "travelling grandly". During the lap Littlejohn's Vinot ran out of fuel. At the end of the lap, Porporato's Berliet, Rimmer's Vulcan, Ross Browne's Gladiator, Goodwin's Star and Folker's Rover were officially stopped. Browne had enough fuel left to have finished the race had he not run out of time – his pace had been too conservative. Eight survivors then attempted the last lap. Meanwhile five of the remaining seven Heavy Touring Cars ran out of fuel on the last lap of their race. They were the Straker-Squire driven by L.Squire, Watson's Berliet, Niblett's Thornycroft and the Ariels of Sangster and Harrison. This left just two finishers, with the Beeston Humber of George Mills taking the flag over 20 minutes ahead of the Gladiator of Graeme Fenton.

There was even greater attrition on the dramatic final

In the Heavy Touring Car Race, as in the Tourist Trophy, only two cars finished. Illustrated is the winning Beeston Humber of George Mills who averaged 28.7 mph for the five laps and finished twenty minutes ahead of second placed Grahame Fenton's Gladiator. [National Motor Museum]

lap of the Tourist Trophy. Braud's Clement ran out of fuel at Peel, as did Cupper's Metallurgique, which had led at the start of the lap. This left Guinness in the lead, pursued by Reid, Courtis and the Arrol-Johnstons. When Guinness was reported through the Bungalow he seemed to have the race in his pocket but then came a report that he was out of fuel at Hillberry, less than two miles from the finish. Then Roberts became the favourite as he was going faster than anyone else and had been within two minutes of Reid and Courtis at the end of the previous lap. Roberts actually overtook both, but then, with enough fuel left, stopped with a broken universal joint. Napier's Arrol-Johnston and the Thornycroft both ran out of fuel near Ramsey and, with Reid slowing, Courtis became the likely winner if he could only keep going. He could, and won the Tourist Trophy in a time of 8 hours 23mins 27secs, a margin of 11 minutes 50.2secs ahead of James Reid and with nearly two pints of fuel left. They were the only finishers.

The "Graphic" Trophy

The "Graphic Trophy" event took the form of a hill-climb on the Ramsey to Douglas coast road. Starting at Ballure Bridge and finishing at the Rest and be Thankful Inn, it covered a distance of 2,550 yards with a rise of 425 feet and a maximum gradient of 1 in 12, and was held on Friday 31st May. Praised by the Automotor Journal as a pure and simple race in which the fastest driver was the winner and with simple rules easily understood by the public, the race was open to touring cars of up to 60hp, built for the driver and three passengers, costing £300 to £1,000 and equipped with lamps, mudguards and proper bodies.

Fourteen entries were received. Of these, a Gracile never arrived on the Island, Napier's Arrol-Johnston was a non-starter due to damage in the TT, and Barwick's Daimler had crashed during practising. A Napier, to be driven by Cundy, was also damaged in a practice crash and, although repaired, broke its propeller shaft just before starting. The second Napier, entered by Selwyn Edge to be driven by Paul, was the subject of a protest by Ernest Hutton and Capt. Owen, alleging that it was not a true touring car due to the chassis and front axle being drilled for lightness. The RAC upheld the protest and excluded the car, causing some ill-feeling, as many 1906 and several 1907 TT cars had been similarly drilled. Moreover, Paul had spent some time practising and reportedly had easily

Despite crashing his Beeston Humber at Kerroomoar during practice, James Reid, pictured at Willaston corner, drove a well-judged race while others ran out of fuel. He finished second to Ernest Courtis' Rover. [National Motor Museum]

On the day after the Tourist Trophy, the Graphic Trophy Hill Climb was held on a course of 1.5 miles on the Ramsey to Douglas coast road from Ballure Bridge to the Rest and Be Thankful inn. The photograph shows the start area, with a Manx Electric Railway tram in the background. [R and L Kelly collection]

An Ariel-Simplex driven by Charles Sangster in the Heavy Touring Car Race was then driven by A.E. Harrison in the Graphic Trophy. The car crashed at a difficult corner where a Daimler and a Napier had already crashed during unofficial practice. The winner was Ernest Hutton's Berliet. [R and L Kelly collection]

covered the course in 2mins 45secs – much faster than anyone achieved in the event. The nine remaining entries consisted of the Berliets of Ernest Hutton (60hp), Jean Porporato and William Watson (both 40hp) together with the 35hp Daimlers of Thomas Henshaw, and Francis Bolton, a 20hp Hillman-Coatalen (Louis Coatalen), a 40hp Junior (Capt. W.E.D. Owen) and the two Ariel-Simplex entries of Charles Sangster and A.E. Harrison.

There were two crashes during the event. Both occurred at the corner (described by *The Motor* as "wicked") which had claimed the Daimler and the Napier in practice. Harrison's Ariel-Simplex was completely wrecked. The driver was cut and dazed, and one of the passengers (a Manxman) fell on the mechanic (who had jumped from the car). Both rolled in the mud and escaped with a shaking. Worst injured was the third passenger, named Anderson, who suffered severe contusions to his back, scalp wounds and shock. The other crash involved Francis Bolton's Daimler, which almost turned over and shed its chain, which prevented it from continuing.

The winner was Ernest Hutton in a time of 3mins 40.4secs followed by William Watson (3mins 45.6secs) with Thomas Henshaw third in 3mins 54.6secs. Henshaw's third place was very creditable as he completed the climb with his Daimler's near-side front tyre flat. The event was a great success for the Berliet team, with their cars finishing first, second and sixth.

1907 Tourist Trophy Race Results

Tourist Trophy Race

Thursday 30th May 1907. Start 9.11am.6 laps of 40.25 miles circuit, total distance 241.50 miles. 22 starters, 2 finishers.

1. Ernest Courtis (Rover) 8hrs 23mins 27secs (28.80mph)
2. James Reid (Beeston Humber) 8hrs 35mins 17secs (28.10mph)

Fastest lap: Louis Coatalen (Hilllman-Coatalen) 1hr 4mins 39secs (37.5mph).

Cars which ran out of fuel, and miles completed:

Algernon Lee Guinness (Darracq), 240 miles
Tom Thornycroft (Thornycroft), 229.5 miles
John Napier (Arrol-Johnston), 223.5 miles
Georges Braud (Clement), 211 miles
Oscar Cupper (Metallurgique), 210.5 miles
Norman Littlejohn (Vinot), 181 miles

Officially stopped on lap 5:

Thomas Rimmer (Vulcan)
M. Ross Browne (Gladiator)
H. Goodwin (Star)
E.R. Folker (Rover)
Jean Porporato (Berliet)

Retirements:

Lap 2: G.F. Prew (Star), collision with Quarterbridge
Lap 3: Kenelm Lee Guinness (Darracq), damaged rear axle;
Ernest Hutton (Berliet), jammed gear change;
R.H. Collier (West-Aster), overturned on Mountain Road;
P.R.Lamb (West-Aster), carburettor and clutch problems;
Louis Coatalen (Hillman-Coatalen), broken front spring;
Lap 4: Percy Dean (Scout), water in magneto.
Lap 5: W.G. Tuck (Beeston Humber), broken wheel
Lap 6: Cyril Roberts (Arrol-Johnston), broken universal joint.

Heavy Touring Car Race

Thursday 30th May 1907, 5 laps of 40.25 miles circuit, total distance 201.25 miles. 9 starters, 2 finishers.

1. George Mills (Beeston Humber) 7hrs 11mins 0secs (28.70mph)
2. Graeme Fenton (Gladiator) 7hrs 31mins 35secs (26.70mph)

Fastest lap: Charles Sangster (Ariel) 1hr 12mins 0.2secs (33.54mph)

Cars which ran out of fuel, and miles completed:

H. Niblett (Thornycroft), 193 miles

W. Watson (Berliet), 189 miles

A.E. Harrison (Ariel), 187 miles

Charles Sangster (Ariel), 186 miles

L. Squire (Straker-Squire), 182 miles

Retirements:

Lap 1: E.H. Arnott (Arrol-Johnston), broken front wheel

Lap 4: C.H. Cooper (Beeston Humber), broken coil.

"Graphic" Trophy

1. Ernest Hutton (Berliet) 3mins 40.4secs
2. William Watson (Berliet) 3mins 45.6secs
3. Thomas Henshaw (Daimler) 3mins 54.6secs
4. Capt. W.E.D. Owen (Junior) 4mins 10secs
5. Charles Sangster (Ariel-Simplex) 4mins 13.4secs
6. Jean Porporato (Berliet) 4mins 31.8secs
7. Louis Coatalen (Hillman-Coatalen) 4mins 37.8secs

Retirements:

A.E. Harrison (Ariel-Simplex)

Francis Bolton (Daimler)

Reaction

Courtis' win was a popular one, with Rover and Beeston Humber providing a double victory for the British motor industry, and a happy day for Courtis himself in view of the previous year's exclusion. For the Rover company its success, according to The *Tatler*, "could not have been of more value to any other competing firm". The company recognised Courtis' achievement with a dinner at the King's Head Hotel in Coventry, the presentation of a gold watch and an extra week's holiday.

Post-race comments were mixed. *The Car Illustrated* said that the races "have proved at once the most puzzling and the most striking, the most drastic and the most impressive, automobile events of first class importance which have ever been witnessed since the inception of the movement". *The Motor* thought that "The race for the Tourist Trophy was the most exciting motor contest that has ever been held" and elaborated by commenting that usually one car gets the lead and keeps it whereas the TT had been anybody's from beginning to end, with positions constantly changing and suspense continuing right to the finish. Speculating on the chances of the race being run in 1908, *The Motor* remarked that consideration shown by drivers combined with respect for the Sabbath and limitation of practice time had overcome all previous grounds for public complaint, and also that there was a growing public awareness of the economic benefits of racing. The manufacturers welcomed the races as good advertisements, although they were tired of complicated rules and would welcome something simpler.

Pointing out that there are usually lessons to be learnt, *The Automotor Journal* felt that a poor impression was given to the general public, many of whom would feel that there is a serious flaw if bad weather essentially prevents the majority of cars from finishing. The real lesson, therefore, was that drivers were mostly in the dark as to how much fuel was in their tanks and therefore has no means of estimating the speeds at which they should drive. "Needless to say", said the magazine, "if there is one thing which the Tourist Trophy principle is intended to avoid, it is that the contest should partake in any shape or form the nature of a guessing competition between the drivers. Its very merit is that it demonstrates the true relative merits of the competing cars". The conclusion was that an efficient fuel gauge was needed for races and that this would also be warmly welcomed by thousands of motorists for their own cars – another example of the adage that "racing improves the breed".

The *Isle of Man Times* commented that the majority of cars, although in touring car specification, had been unable to finish. Although the conditions had been exceptional and fine weather and normal road conditions would have made a difference to the whole race and, perhaps, its conclusion, the general opinion was that strict limitation of fuel had served every useful purpose and that it was time for a change.

1908 Tourist Trophy – Watson Wins On "Isle of Manslaughter"

Planning

It was plain after the 1907 TT that a radical re-think was needed. Only two cars had finished in each race, no less than eleven had run out of fuel and five had been flagged off without the opportunity of attempting the last lap. After three "fuel limit" races it was time to look again at the whole basis of the Tourist Trophy. This the RAC did, but the ultimately successful solution adopted by the Club caused so much controversy that it almost led to the abandonment of the event for 1908 and, perhaps, for ever.

The solution, announced in November 1907, was abandonment of the fuel limit, its rationale that the previous formula had served its purpose in giving the manufacturers the chance to amass data to facilitate development of their cars. The new TT formula was intentionally simple. It would be a single race for medium weight cars not exceeding 1,600lbs including driver, mechanic, fuel, oil, water, spare parts, spare tyres and tools. Bodywork restrictions were abolished. Instead of limiting power output by limiting fuel consumption there would be a simple limit. The diameter of the cylinders in inches, squared and multiplied by the number of cylinders was not to exceed 64. This meant that the cylinder bore diameter could not exceed four inches in a four cylinder engine or the equivalent in a six cylinder engine. This limit, according to RAC calculations, would limit horse power to 25.6, a reasonable output for an average touring car and only a little more than some of the 1907 TT cars. Only a few racing cars of the time had a cylinder diameter as small as four inches and the only smaller one was the 1907 four cylinder La Buire (98mm). Cylinders of six, seven or even eight inches were in use, and the 1908 Grand Prix Austin had six cylinders of five inch diameter.

There had been no serious accidents in the three previous TT Races or in the supporting Graphic hill-climbs, and the new formula was expected to add no more than ten to fifteen miles per hour to maximum speeds. Nevertheless, concern turned into furore when Napier built a 5.8 litre engine car with the brand name of Hutton after Napier's sole London agent. This car, named "Little Dorrit", achieved a speed of 83mph at the new Brooklands Track at Weybridge. To compensate for the limited bore, Napier and other manufacturers lengthened the stroke, producing engines of much greater power than the RAC had expected. The Hutton had an eight inch stroke and piston speed approaching 2,700ft/min at 2,000rpm. With total disregard of fuel consumption now possible, high compression, complicated manifolds, improved lubrication and valve design increased both power output and reliability. Instead of the expected 25hp, some engines attained 70hp or more. Nevertheless, as *The Motor* pointed out, the expected power outputs and speeds were nothing new on the Island. In the 1905 Gordon Bennett Trials, Macdonald's Napier had produced 90hp and had been officially timed at 89mph. Other Napiers were rated at 85hp, the Wolseleys and the Siddeley at 96hp and the Darracqs at 80hp, with the Siddeley and the smaller Napiers being officially timed at 80mph.

In July, while opposition mounted, the RAC met the Highway Board and agreed that the date of the race would be Thursday 24th September. The Club had earlier proposed early October but this had been opposed as being outside the summer season. The Club also requested a new course. After the 1907 TT it had wanted to delete the section through Peel's narrow streets, the one remaining level crossing and the notorious Devil's Elbow, and to revert to using the southern loop taking in Ballasalla, Castletown and Foxdale as used in 1905. Now, however, the Club wanted to delete the Peel section without reinstating the southern loop. This would mean a course of 37.5 miles, turning north at Ballacraine and continuing via Ballig Bridge through Glen Helen to Kirk Michael and Ramsey before returning to Douglas over the Mountain road. This course, initially named "The Four Inch Course", would be used for the motorcycle TT Races from 1911. It forked right at Cronk-ny-Mona and continued via Willaston to the top of Bray Hill and (for 1908 only) the start/finish was moved to the straight approaching Hillberry. With minor changes, including the replacement of the Willaston section by the Signpost Corner, Governor's Bridge and Glencrutchery Road section, it became "The TT Mountain Course" used for the motorcycle TT races to this day. The race, by far the longest TT yet, was to be run over nine laps, 337.5 miles.

The people of Castletown were unhappy at the decision not to reinstate the southern loop. To placate them, the RAC offered to run the Graphic Trophy speed trial between the third and sixth milestones from Castletown on the Foxdale road on the morning of the day before the race. This event and the Henry Edmunds Trophy hill-climb over three miles of the Mountain Road scheduled for the afternoon of the same day were cancelled due to lack of competitor interest – drivers did not want to risk their cars in minor events on the eve of the race.

The RAC also asked for an extension in morning practice to 8am but this was refused. Several weeks later Julian Orde arrived on the Island with a cheque for a £200 contribution to the cost of road improvements and a list of demands. The Club wanted to lay tarmac on the approach to Sulby Bridge, to employ sweepers on the road between Douglas and Ramsey to clear mud and dust (brushes to be supplied by the Club), to lay *Akonia* (a dust-laying compound similar to the *Dustroyd* and *Westrumite* products used previously) and to erect footbridges over the course. Orde also repeated the request for extension of practice time to 8am and produced a new request – for the practice period to be increased to three weeks in order to give drivers more time to learn the course. All were agreed except the three weeks' practising. After a heated discussion the Highway Board was split, with three in favour and three against. The Chairman, Colonel William Anderson, had to use his casting vote. He rejected the easy way of voting for the status quo, accepted the RAC arguments, and agreed to three weeks' practising. He may have thought the question was academic, as there was a good chance that the TT would be cancelled due to public opposition in England!

Among the English Press, The *Times* led the opposition. It suggested that the RAC was showing great temerity in proceeding with the race. "It is difficult to imagine any more audacious flouting of public opinion" it thundered. It forecast that the race was likely to cost several lives. At the worst time for the RAC a Mercedes caught fire at Brooklands Track, both the driver and mechanic were thrown into a river and the mechanic died.

There were even doubts from within the racing community. Humber's Thomas Pullinger was quoted as saying that some TT cars would be capable of averaging more than 60mph. Passing would be difficult on the Island's narrow roads. Cars would be "on top of each other" on the first lap and drivers would take risks in trying to get away from each other. Bends would be regarded as opportunities to gain on opponents and crashes would result. This, he thought, could harm the automobile movement. Even Selwyn Edge announced his intention of withdrawing Napier cars from all dangerous competitions in deference to the public feeling against dangerous racing according to *The Autocar*, which said that although Edge had not defined "dangerous" it presumed "he would call the Four Inch Race dangerous on the Isle of Man course though not so on Brooklands".

Other national newspapers and English Members of Parliament jumped on the bandwagon. The Island was even dubbed "The Isle of Manslaughter" and the campaign gained such momentum in England that the RAC held two meetings to consider whether the event should be cancelled. At the second meeting, chaired by Prince Francis of Teck, Club Chairman, and a brother of the future Queen Mary, it was decided by 24 votes to 9 to proceed with the race. The RAC then issued a statement that it was satisfied that every reasonable precaution had been or would be made to prevent accidents to the public and competitors. Nevertheless several manufacturers withdrew in apparent deference to public opinion.

Meanwhile Governor Raglan and Highway Board Chairman Colonel Anderson apparently believed that the TT had been cancelled. Without reference to anyone, even by Raglan to his cousin Julian Orde, they signed an Order rescinding the Road Closing Order. This was kept quiet and others in Government decided to check the position, only to be told by Orde that there had never been any doubt but that the race would go ahead. The "lugubrious lucubrations" of *The Times* would be falsified, he said.

Support for the RAC came from veteran Island driver "Toby" Rawlinson who said that the race would be "the finest race ever organised" and "infinitely the most sporting event in racing history".

The decision made, efforts to improve safety were re-doubled. To facilitate overtaking, drivers were advised to fit exhaust whistles, to wear caps with ear rolls to enable them to hear approaching cars and to carry several spare pairs of goggles. The use of goggles in bad weather was prohibited. At Sulby Bridge, in addition to tarring the approach, a dummy hedge was built to save drivers from possible confusion about whether to turn right or left. At Hillberry the banking was reversed to assist rather than to hinder the drivers, "Guinness' steps" were removed and a ruined cottage was demolished with the owner seeking no compensation and the contractor accepting a gold sovereign. A ditch at Willaston was filled in, footbridges were built, and ambulance positions arranged at mile intervals and the entire course was swept and treated with *Akonia*. All side roads were to be barricaded and warning banners were to be erected twenty feet above the course before significant corners with white-coated Dunlop flagmen placed in advance of danger points. Eyesight checks were introduced, with drivers required to drive an obstacle course with first one and then the other eye covered. Their hearing was also tested. Marshals were briefed by Lord Raglan that drivers knew and accepted the risks they took but that the greatest care should be taken to ensure the safety of spectators.

Chief Constable Col. Freeth swore in 610 Special Constables as marshals, almost one per hundred yards. The course was divided into 21 sections, each with its own Clerk of the Course and a car ready to carry a doctor to any emergency. In addition, there were 10 ambulance stations with stretcher parties, 37 ambulance posts, 11 telephone posts, 8 telegraph stations and 9 points at which messengers and cycle messengers were stationed.

The abolition of the fuel limit brought the need for re-fuelling facilities. Two areas were provided, one at Ballacraine and the other at Ramsey, both being designated as tyre depots. The Ramsey area on land adjoining Albert Road School was the main service area and popular with spectators. Here, local builders James Callow and Son built "pens" or "pits" with manufacturers' names painted in red, blue and black letters on boards erected at right angles to the road so as to be easily visible to approaching drivers. Behind the pens were tents in which drivers' teams and supporters could prepare refreshments but were prohibited from working on the cars. All re-fuelling, tyre changing and repairs had to be carried out by drivers and mechanics only. The use of oxygen, acetylene and other aids to combustion was not allowed.

While *The Times* fought on with a fatuous compromise proposal that cars should be fitted with screens to slow them down, despite the dangerous instability caused by screens on Heavy Touring Cars in 1907, local reaction was positive. The *Isle of Man Examiner* said that past experience had shown no danger in motor racing on the Island. If the new cars threatened any section of the community in early practising the RAC could be given notice to quit but the *Examiner* thought this unlikely. It commented: "Puritanism may be predominant in the Island but Manx Puritans are keen sportsmen and are in no way ashamed to proclaim a fondness for pure sport".

Entries

The RAC received 38 entries of 17 different makes.

Arrol-Johnston, 1905 winner, was not to be under-rated. There were three cars, to be driven by Cyril Roberts who had driven in 1905 and 1907, Dario Resta and Geoffrey Moss who was a private entrant of his own car. The cars were finished in white and were regarded as "artistic" in appearance apart from a shield in front of the fuel tank. The carburettor had been re-designed and the gearbox had three speeds, third being direct. The claimed power output was 60hp. Roberts' car was named "White Heather".

The two Calthorpes built in Birmingham had a wheelbase of 8 feet 4 inches, the second shortest in the race, and standard chassis. They had no shock absorbers as their suspension seemed better suited to Manx roads without them. They had two sparking plugs per cylinder and four speed gearboxes, third being direct. Their drivers were Leslie Porter from Ireland and Henry Robinson. *The Autocar* believed they were potential winners.

Among the favourites were the three Darracqs from France, the drivers being Algernon Lee Guinness, Arthur George and "Toby" Rawlinson. All were very experienced on the Island and their cars were very advanced, fast, well prepared and looked dashing with their low lines. They were standard cars except for specially designed engines and were fitted with quick-release fuel tank caps, Rudge-Whitworth wheels, and "monocle" windscreens mounted on the steering columns.

The two Deasys from Coventry, to be driven by designer Edmund Lewis and Philip Graham (with a lady mechanic), had still not been assembled at the beginning of September. Said to be standard, the cars had small valves of only 1.375 inches compared with the three inch valves of the Hillman-Coatalens. The four cylinders were cast en bloc with water jackets and valve pockets complete, both the cylinders and upper part of the crank chamber being one piece. They had a new three-speed gearbox with direct drive on top. The fuel tank doubled as a spare tyre carrier, a feature which also appeared on the Vinots.

The sole De Dion Bouton built in France and entered by London agent Jack Stocks was huge, with a wheel-base of 10 feet 5 inches compared with the Huttons' 9 feet 6 inches. It weighed 3,057lbs compared with Thomas Rimmer's Vulcan, the lightest car in the race at 1,742lbs but Stocks was unconcerned, believing that the weight would aid road-holding. The De Dion's chassis was compared to that of a motor 'bus and *The Motor* commented that many weaker front axles had been seen on two ton vans. Competitors, worried about the space the De Dion would take up on narrow roads and the possible difficulties of passing it, were unwise enough to call on Stocks to voice their concerns. His replies, reputedly, were short and to the point. The car had broken a number of records at Brooklands earlier in the year and had been fitted with a larger fuel tank, two seats and smaller Rudge-Whitworth wheels to reduce the gearing. It was said to develop 70hp at 2,300rpm.

Hillman-Coatalen of Coventry entered cars for Louis Coatalen and Kenelm Lee Guinness. Coatalen's

Leading Irish driver Leslie Porter, pictured at Cronk-ny-Mona, drove his Calthorpe to a fine fourth place behind the Hutton of William Watson and the Darracqs of Algernon Lee Guinness and Arthur George. [Manx National Heritage]

"Toby" Rawlinson in his Darracq and Louis Coatalen in his Hillman-Coatalen are pictured at Cronk-ny-Mona after a morning practice. Drivers normally stopped and left the course there at the end of practice sessions, making it a popular venue for talking to other drivers and posing for photographers. In the race, Rawlinson drove car 30 and Algernon Lee Guinness took over number 4. [Manx National Heritage]

Jack Stocks and his mechanic pose with the huge De Dion Bouton at Cronk-ny-Mona after a morning practice. This was the largest car in the race, with a wheelbase 11 inches longer than that of the Huttons. Drivers who complained to Stocks that his car would be difficult to pass received short shrift! [John Watterson collection]

Kenelm Lee Guinness is pictured at the wheel of his Hillman-Coatalen. He retired at the Bungalow on lap 5 when his frame broke. [John Watterson collection]

The Beeston Humber team was based at Kirk Michael where this photograph of James Reid is believed to have been taken. The flimsy "bonnet", consisting of a wire mesh cage known as a "meat safe" can be clearly seen. Reid crashed in Kirk Michael on the eighth lap. [Brian Mylchreest collection]

mechanic, as in 1907, was factory foreman Jim Broadbent from Onchan. The cars had three-speed gearboxes with direct drive on third. A distinctive feature was four separate exhaust pipes leading to an exhaust box outside the frame. Power output was 63hp at 2,200rpm.

Two 60hp Beeston Humbers, to be driven by James Reid and W.G. Tuck, were said to be "very whippy". They were unlike any previous Humber, with different radiators mounted in Renault style behind the engine, overhead valves, overhead camshaft with skew gears and vertical shaft drive at the front of the engine. The engine itself, exposed to the elements, was protected by a wire-mesh cage known as a meat safe. The bodies consisted of two seats and a platform for the fuel tank. The steering columns were raked. The cars were fitted with Humber-designed quickly detachable centre-lock wire wheels and their general appearance was much "racier" than Humber's previous rather staid designs. There was also a Coventry Humber (named "Manxman") for G.W.A. Brown, the designer of the car. Although producing 67hp, it proved to be much slower than the Beeston cars. It had a four-speed gearbox with direct drive on third.

"Of the three Hutton cars very few facts have been allowed to be made known" reported *The Motor*. The cars were modified Napiers, which Napier of London had specially designed and built for the race, in contrast to many cars described as "practically standard". "Little Dorrit" (named, presumably, after the eponymous character in the Charles Dickens novel) was to be driven by its owner William Watson, although entered by Selwyn Edge. The other Huttons were entered by their owners, Ernest Hutton and P.D. Stirling, the latter's car being named "Dolly Varden" (presumably after the character of that name in Dickens' novel Barnaby Rudge). Hutton's car had a special engine and was more or less a Grand Prix car. The Huttons were said to be "Hot 'uns".

The Metallurgiques were fancied as possible winners. Their drivers were Warwick Wright, the rather wild Oscar Cupper from Germany and J.T.C. Moore-Brabazon (1907 Circuit des Ardennes winner, later to become Lord Brabazon of Tara, a well-known early aviator who was responsible over forty years later for introducing Geoff Duke to car racing). Said to be capable of reaching 60mph from a standing start in 100 yards, the cars reputedly produced 103hp at 2,400rpm. The three drivers had formed a company, Warwick Wright Ltd of Marylebone, to act as British concessionaire.

A single wooden-wheeled Piccard Pictet (or "Pic-Pic") came from Geneva, Switzerland. Designed by Marc Birkigt, the Swiss designer of the first Hispano-Suiza, the cars were known by some as "the Swiss Rolls-Royce". The driver was Andre Debuissey.

The 1907 winning Rover, now a private entry driven by H.B. Browning, was, according to tradition, listed to start first. It was a standard touring model and, as it had not been the fastest car in 1907 and definitely was not in

1908, Browning was later relegated "by mutual agreement" to last in the starting order.

Three S.C.A.T.s built in Turin had four-speed gearboxes and a wheelbase of only 8 feet 6 inches. At 120mm, their stroke was one third less than that of the Metallurgiques. The drivers were R.O. Harper, Fred Ward and Harold S. Buckley.

Thornycroft was fancied. The three cars, built in Chiswick, were to be driven by Tom Thornycroft, who had driven in all three previous TT Races, Guy Baxendale and D.S. Hodge who was a newcomer to the Island. Thornycroft's car was practically the same as his 2,000 Miles Trial car except that the engine had been modified for the race. His gearbox had four indirect speeds while the other Thornycrofts had direct drive on one gear. The cars were painted green instead of their usual red.

The three 42hp Vinots from France were said to have the longest stroke engines in the race, at 5.125 inches. The drivers were M. Ross Browne, Rowland Outhwaite and Leon Molon. A flat platform behind the seats carried the fuel tank within the spare tyres.

The Vulcan, built in Southport, was to be driven by Thomas Rimmer. It had a standard carburettor and a three-speed gearbox with direct drive on third, an unusually low chassis and Rudge-Whitworth wheels. The popularity of these wheels among competitors was shown when the manufacturers announced that they had supplied no less than 317 wheels and rims for use in the race, including spares carried on cars and at depots. The wheels were used on 22 of the competing cars.

The two Westinghouses, built in Le Havre, were to be driven by J. Gall and A.L. Hartridge. They were practically standard, apart from racing bodies and detachable rims, and were claimed to be the most expensive in the race,

Although Rover had won the previous year's TT their 1908 car driven by H.B. Browning, pictured at Cronk-ny-Mona, was the slowest car in the race. As the Trophy holder, the car was allocated number 1 but was transferred to the back of the field "by mutual agreement". After a first lap of 90 minutes the car was stopped, out of time, after five laps. [Ray Stanfield collection]

costing £590. The cars made history, not because of their performance but because of Gall's superstitious nature. He was given number 13 but, after several practice sessions, complained about bad luck and changed the number to 12A. Then he exchanged cars with his team-mate Hartridge who took over 12A, giving Gall number 26. The Auto-Cycle Union later stopped allocating 13 in the motorcycle TT Races and the RAC followed suit when the TT moved to Ards in 1928. The Manx Motor Cycle Club also eventually dropped 13 in the Manx Grand Prix motorcycle races.

Also entered, but withdrawn at the last minute, were two Berliets, one of which was to have been driven by the Italian national but French resident Jean Porporato who had driven a Berliet to victory in the Targa Bologna. The French company had always been opposed to racing but their attitude had softened with Porporato's success, only to harden again in the face of U.K. public opinion.

The withdrawal of the Berliets reduced the entry to 36, of which 16 were of foreign manufacture. *The Automotor Journal* said there was "no attempt whatever to form a competition between touring cars" and that the cars were "as racy in their design as the Gordon Bennett flyers of old".

Practice

Either despite the extra week of practising or, perhaps, because of it, there were relatively few problems and no serious ones. There were complaints about noise and about speeding in Kirk Michael and Ramsey which the RAC addressed on 9th September by instructing competitors to fit silencers and by imposing 14mph speed limits in those areas. There were, however, no serious complaints or public protests about "scorching" as in 1906 and no complaints about breaches of the ban on practising on Sundays.

Practice was allowed from first light on weekdays but no car was permitted to start a lap at Quarterbridge after 7.15am except at a speed not exceeding 14mph and cars arriving at Hillberry after 8am were subject to the same speed limit. These concessions were to allow cars to be driven back to their garages only. They were not allowed on the course at other times.

On the first practice morning, Thursday 3rd September, all the cars then on the Island turned out, with Fred Ward's S.C.A.T being first away. One of the Darracqs damaged a wheel and axle but all cars except the S.C.A.T. completed two laps. Friday was cold, with wet and greasy roads. Geoffrey Moss overturned his Arrol-Johnston at the right hand corner from Ballanard Road onto Bray Hill but the car was quickly righted and, after checking it over, Moss continued on his way. Fred Ward was unable to stop his S.C.A.T. at Sulby Bridge and hit a Dunlop advertising board, broke four spokes and bent his front axle. Saturday morning was fine with dry roads, all drivers were out and the fastest lap was thought to have been done by George's Darracq, at about 50mph.

On Monday 7th September everyone was out except the Darracqs of Rawlinson and George. The weather was fine but there was mist on the Mountain. G.W.A. Brown's Coventry Humber skidded at Kerroomoar, hit a tree and overturned but the crew were unhurt and the car was undamaged. At Cronk-y-Voddy, after cresting a blind brow, Cyril Roberts encountered a herd of cattle being driven onto the road by a farmer. A collision was unavoidable, two calves were killed, another suffered a broken leg and the Arrol-Johnston hit the hedge. The grim task of clearing up the scene had been completed before the next car arrived and, no doubt after suitable compensation had changed hands, the farmer was unperturbed and Roberts and his mechanic were found in the farmhouse enjoying boiled eggs and buttered toast.

Most mornings were wet, cold and misty, although spectators were undeterred and, reportedly, enthusiastic. The conditions resulted in many skids but no serious accidents. On Wednesday, Gordon Usmar's Vinot broke a wheel on the corner at Creg-ny-Baa, hit the hedge and overturned. Usmar suffered an internal injury which, combined with a touch of bronchitis, led to his car being taken over by Ross Browne. The mechanic was unhurt. Friday morning was fine and warm, with many spectators round the course. Watson lapped in about 45mins on his Hutton, the consistent Calthorpes managed about 49mins and Stocks' De Dion about 50mins. Times, of course, were entirely unofficial and there were suggestions that some drivers were "sandbagging" – giving a false impression of the speed of their cars by stopping or slowing down during fast laps or by doing fast laps from (say) Sulby to Sulby. The only incident of the morning occurred when one of the S.C.A.T. team broke a wooden wheel on the Mountain but nobody was hurt.

On Monday 14th September, 19 cars were out and, according to *The Autocar*, Stirling's Hutton "encountered a horse on the road to Glen Helen" not far from the scene of Roberts' bovine encounter on the previous Monday, but no further details are known.

On Tuesday 15th September, 21 cars practised. Brown had his second accident with his Coventry Humber when he skidded on Ballanard Road, between Willaston and Bray Hill. His car hit the footpath on the right, went across the road, hit the hedge and re-crossed the road. Brown and his mechanic, Howarth from Coventry, were thrown out and Howarth was unconscious for a short time but was up and walking by the time a cyclist had summoned Doctor Marshall. Howarth was severely shocked and had a small cut on his leg but Brown was unhurt. The car had a broken axle and twisted chassis and had to be returned to Coventry for urgent repairs.

On Wednesday, Leslie Porter attempted Hillberry too fast and hit the hedge, damaging his rear axle and body. The damage was quickly repaired and the car was out again the next day. Various cars had mechanical problems. Thursday was wet and so misty that some drivers complained that they could not see the length of their cars.

On Friday morning, in fine weather with dry roads, 23 cars were on the course and potentially the most serious of the crashes occurred when Oscar Cupper overturned his Metallurgique at Edge's Corner, the left hander between Cronk-ny-Mona and Cronk-y-Berry. Both the driver and his mechanic Emile Brandt were trapped under the car. A *Mona's Herald* reporter was spectating at the scene with Harry Bregazzi, a member of a Douglas art dealing and picture framing family. They were unable to

Cyril Roberts collided with a herd of cows near Glen Helen during an early morning practice. Despite the damage, both to car and cows, the matter was amicably resolved and the farmer's wife provided Roberts and his mechanic with breakfast while they awaited recovery of the car. [R and L Kelly collection]

After a wheel collapsed on the corner at Creg-na-Baa during practice, Gordon Usmar's Vinot crashed and overturned. The driver was taken to hospital with an internal injury and M. Ross Browne took over the car for the race, finishing sixth. [R and L Kelly collection]

G.W.A. Brown crashed his Coventry Humber (named "The Manxman") on Ballanard Road, between Willaston and Bray Hill, during practice. The car, which he designed, had to be sent to Coventry for urgent repairs. This was Brown's second practice crash – the first, at Kerroomoar, caused no damage. [Author's collection]

Oscar Cupper crashed his Metallurgique at Edge's Corner, between Cronk-ny-Mona and Willaston, during practice and the crew had to be extricated from underneath the overturned car. First on the scene to help was G.W.A. Brown, who himself had two practice crashes. Both drivers retired on lap 6 of the race. [Author's collection]

free Cupper (although Brandt got out easily) and were at risk themselves – a Darracq passed without slowing and one of its wheels tore the trailing tail of Bregazzi's coat as he lay on the ground trying to reach Cupper. Then the Coventry Humber of G.W.A. Brown arrived and stopped. Mrs Brown, who was enjoying a morning spin with her husband and his mechanic (and, perhaps, exerting a calming influence after her husband's two crashes) went back up the road to warn oncoming drivers while the others, joined by Dunlop flagmen, extricated Cupper and Brandt. Cupper was shocked but his only injury was a scratch above the left eye. Brandt, however, was taken to hospital for treatment to two broken ribs and cuts to the head but was released, swathed in bandages, in time to watch the race from a table at the Ramsey pits. Cupper, meanwhile, resumed practising with a repaired car, a new mechanic, and a new driving style which involved "treating the corners with great respect" according to the special representative of *The Motor*.

On Saturday, Molon was out with his Vinot for the first time. There were 26 cars on the course for an uneventful session.

Monday morning's practising was uneventful, again with 26 cars out in misty conditions. Stocks took a lady round the course in place of his mechanics. The final practice on Tuesday saw only 17 cars with no serious attempts at fast laps.

On Wednesday afternoon, after a final road test, Tom Thornycroft was returning with his race car on the coast road from Douglas to his Ramsey base when he was met at Dhoon by a Westinghouse, driving in the opposite direction. The Westinghouse, driven by Hartridge (formerly number 13 but now ironically now re-numbered as 12A), was on the wrong side of the road, according to Thornycroft. Both cars swerved but the rear wheel of the Westinghouse caught the front wheel and axle of the Thornycroft, removing the wheel and damaging the axle. There was not enough time to repair the Thornycroft before the following day's race but Guy Baxendale gave up his car to his brother-in-law for the race, moving Thornycroft up the starting order from number 35 to 9 and reducing the number of starters to 35. There was also a re-shuffle of start numbers in the Darracq team. Algie Guinness, originally 17, took Rawlinson's car (4) while George, allocated 30, took Guinness' car and Rawlinson took 30. This, presumably, was a team tactic so that their faster drivers would have less of the slower cars to pass.

1908 Tourist Trophy Race

The practice period ended with relief that there had been no disasters as predicted by the English newspapers. The general impression was that some drivers had been cautious, particularly as the weather had been generally poor; although there was no doubt that some were much faster than their lap times suggested. Also, as always, there was an element of luck – some of the accidents could have had much more serious consequences.

When the Chairman of the RAC, His Serene Highness Prince Francis of Teck, arrived in Douglas with the First Lord of the Admiralty on the Mona's Queen on the afternoon before the race, he found an atmosphere of cautious optimism. Race day, a public holiday, dawned still and warm and Douglas was packed. The *Mona's Herald* said that the Island had never seen as much money, or as much spending. An estimated 3,000 day trippers (including 200 from the Vulcan works in Southport) joined the crowds already on the Island and spending per head was unusually high. The course was in good condition after being entirely hand-swept to remove loose stones, nails and other debris, *Akonia* had been spread to lay the dust and some corners had been banked.

At the new start/finish point at Hillberry there was a

huge crowd of spectators and the atmosphere was tense. It was a fashionable social occasion. Governor Raglan accompanied Prince Francis. Many ladies were present and Lady Raglan's black hat with white feathers attracted the attention of The *Tatler* photographer. An iron grandstand had been erected on one side of the road with the Club enclosure in a field on the other. A large scoreboard was topped by a clock, and live music was provided throughout the day by a military band composed of members of the Isle of Man Volunteers. There was a "Special Information" blackboard on the front of the Timekeepers' box, on which news was chalked throughout the race, and Julian Orde gave a regular megaphone commentary as in previous races. A useful result of the English Press campaign of opposition, apart from the extra publicity for the race which doubtless increased visitor numbers substantially, was the presence on a packed Press grandstand of some hundred English journalists with representatives from European and even American newspapers. There was a telephone link from the pits at Ramsey, by which a constant flow of information would be sent to the Press enclosure during the race. Two telegraph wires had been fed to the site for Press use during the race and there were fifteen Post Office Operators on duty from 9am to 6pm. There was also a direct link to the RAC London headquarters where members relaxing in the smoking room of the Club's opulent premises received a stream of race information constantly updated on a huge white screen. The *Isle of Man Examiner* remarked: "The agitation which has been worked up so bitterly and freely in a section of the English Press so advertised the competition that even had torrential rain prevailed there would have been a large assemblage to witness the so-called dangerous trials of speed".

In an incident reported by the *Isle of Man Examiner*, horses drawing a wagonette containing English reporters were startled when overtaken by the Darracq team of Algie Guinness, Arthur George and "Toby" Rawlinson. The reporter from *The Times* jumped from the wagonette, hurt his leg, and limped for the rest of the day, and the Automotor Journal photographer also injured a leg. After they resumed the journey, the horses were again startled but this time all the reporters jumped off and refused to take their seats until the horses were calmed. The irony of the incident was not lost on the *Examiner* which remarked drily: "Probably the predictions of catastrophe indulged in so freely by some of the newspapers they represented reacted on their nerves". Be that as it may, the news received during the race did nothing to confirm the gloomy prophesies of the English Press. As *The Motor* put it "The absence of blood-curdling news was visibly depressing the spirits of those pressmen who had been instructed by their journals to smother the course with blood and strew the hedges with smashed-up cars and mangled corpses".

An altercation between two visiting Press representatives prompted the *Isle of Man Times* to comment; "I am reminded that among the soi-disant press men which motorism calls into evidence there are some who certainly are not gentlemen".

Around the course an estimated 20,000 spectators awaited the 9am start. There had been complaints from drivers that this was too late and would not allow enough time for slower cars to complete the full distance, given the length of the race and the fact that the roads had to be re-opened by 6pm. The drivers asked for a 7am start but this was refused. The drivers were also unhappy at the reduced starting interval of 30 seconds which they considered to be unsafe. They wanted the normal minute intervals to be reinstated but this, too, was refused.

With a brief hesitation, William Watson's Hutton led the 35 starters away. The first incident was at Ballacraine when Stirling's Hutton hit a wall. Nobody was hurt but the car was too badly damaged to continue. Then "Toby" Rawlinson overturned his Darracq at Ramsey. The crew were uninjured and the car was put back on its wheels and continued after a half hour delay for repairs.

At the end of the lap Watson led on the road but was sixth on corrected time, having lapped in 45mins 45secs. The leader on time was Arthur George with a lap of 44mins 57secs (50mph), during which he had passed 13 cars despite predictions that overtaking would be impossibly dangerous. Next were the Beeston Humbers of Tuck and James Reid (45mins 04secs and 45mins 36secs respectively). He was followed by the Darracq of Algie Guinness, who had passed seven cars, and the Arrol-Johnston of Cyril Roberts (both 45mins 40secs). At the

While William Watson took first place with his Hutton "Little Dorrit" his team-mate P.D. Stirling was less successful, crashing his Hutton "Dolly Varden" into a wall near Ballacraine on the first lap, fortunately without injury. The third Hutton, driven by Ernest Hutton, crashed at Ramsey on lap 5. [Ray Stanfield collection]

completion of the lap, Geoffrey Moss retired his Arrol-Johnston with three broken tappets. Browning, starting last in his hopelessly outclassed Rover, took 90 minutes to complete his first lap.

Just into lap two, Andre Debuissey's Piccard-Pictet bent a wheel at Quarterbridge but changed it and continued. Otherwise the lap was uneventful but Ernest Hutton stopped for tyres on this and every lap. His Hutton, more powerful than Watson's car, was wearing out tyres much more quickly. At the end of the lap George, averaging 51.5mph, had increased his lead over Tuck to 28 seconds. George's growing time was 1hr 28mins 43secs. Guinness was third, 39 seconds behind Tuck, while Watson was up to fourth, Roberts fifth, and Warwick Wright's Metallurgique sixth.

On the third lap Wright retired at Ramsey with a timing gear problem, and Gall retired his Westinghouse with magneto trouble. Fred Ward lost over seven minutes cleaning a fuel filter on his S.C.A.T. and both the Hillman-Coatalens were delayed – Kenelm Lee Guinness for more than 10 minutes and Louis Coatalen for nearly 30 minutes. George completed the lap in a growing time of 2hrs 12mins 10secs and led Tuck by 1min 27secs. Guinness was catching Tuck, gaining 22 seconds on the lap. Watson was still fourth, 1min 12secs behind Guinness with Reid up to fifth and Roberts sixth.

The fourth lap brought more misfortunes. Dario Resta retired at Union Mills when his Arrol-Johnston's clutch broke while Jack Stocks' De Dion went out with a sheared pin in the timing gear. Moore Brabazon lost 90 minutes with an exhaust valve problem, which later led to the retirement of his Metallurgique in an unfortunate misunderstanding, and George had the first of several problems when he attempted to take Creg-ny-Baa too fast. He hit a bank, distorting the frame of the Darracq. Grabbing two fence posts, driver and mechanic quickly straightened the frame and were away in hardly more than a minute. At the end of the lap his growing time was 2hrs 56mins 32secs and he now led Guinness, who had displaced Tuck from second place, by 1min 21secs. Tuck was now third, 43seconds behind Guinness with Watson now only 28 seconds behind Tuck. Reid and Roberts were still fifth and sixth with lengthening gaps. This was the first lap on which George had not been fastest – he lapped in 44mins 21secs compared with Guinness' time of 43mins 59secs. The pace of the leading group is illustrated by the fact that when Watson completed four laps, eight cars had still not completed three laps.

Lap 5 was rather more eventful. Ernest Hutton retired at Ramsey Hairpin after skidding into a wall, bursting a front tyre, buckling a rear wheel and bending his front axle. Edmund Lewis retired at Sulby Bridge when his Deasy

The Hutton driven by Ernest Hutton is pictured after its crash at Ramsey Hairpin on lap 5, caused by a burst tyre. The front axle was bent and a rear wheel was buckled. [John Watterson collection]

suffered a crankshaft failure but he and his mechanic removed the broken pieces and later drove the car back to Douglas on two cylinders. Kenelm Lee Guinness retired when his Hillman-Coatalen's chassis broke on a bump near the Bungalow. Cupper's Metallurgique was delayed with an ignition problem and Rawlinson hit a wall near Glen Helen, losing "four inches of wheelbase and twelve feet of lock". He continued, although Ramsey Hairpin proved to be quite a problem! Also on this lap Philip Graham crashed his Deasy (named "The Pimpernel") between Kirk Michael and Ballaugh without injury. Harper's S.C.A.T. retired with broken timing gear, Molon's Vinot was delayed for ten minutes with valve trouble, Ward's S.C.A.T. retired and Tuck's Beeston Humber was delayed.

The other Beeston Humber, driven by James Reid, was also in trouble, with a broken steering arm which was repaired at Ramsey. He rushed into the Ramsey depot where, according to *The Motor*, "Little stoves were glowing and kettles boiling, while jellies, beef tea, chickens and sandwiches appeared from some mysterious source like

Pictured with his Deasy "The Pimpernel" and his lady mechanic, Philip Graham retired after an accident on lap 5 between Kirk Michael and Ballaugh. Nobody was injured. [John Watterson collection]

the contents of a magician's hat". But a steering arm was what Reid needed and a steering arm was what he got. Thomas Pullinger, Humber designer and former race driver who was in charge of the Humber depot, took his own car, dashed round the corner to Ramsey quay where the reserve Humber awaited shipment, removed its steering arm and dashed back to the depot. In twenty minutes the replacement had been fitted and Reid was away to the accompaniment of cheers from rivals. Sadly, a worse problem awaited the gallant team.

A serious accident, rather played down by contemporary reports in the Technical Press, occurred when Henry Robinson lost control of his Calthorpe on Quarterbridge Road, between the junctions of Brunswick Road and Selborne Road, close to the finishing point of previous TT Races. At over 60mph he went into a ditch on the left, scraped the hedge, and knocked a woman spectator off the top. He then veered across the road, hit the opposite hedge, ran along it with the front of his car five feet in the air and then overturned in the centre of the road. The mechanic was thrown clear but Robinson was trapped under the car with his clothing entangled in the wreckage. Miraculously neither suffered more than cuts and bruises. The spectator, Mrs Lena Lace who was the wife of Joseph Lace, a local carter and manager of a boarding house, suffered severe bruising of the right ankle, cuts and bruises to the left leg from ankle to knee, facial cuts and shock.

Mrs Lace sued the Calthorpe Motor Co. for damages in the Isle of Man High Court in a case which went on for some four years. She claimed damages not exceeding £200 for her injuries plus 11 guineas for medical expenses, £10 for help to conduct her business while incapacitated and £30 for loss of business. She alleged negligent and unskilful driving by Robinson and also that there had been an ineffective attempt at Ramsey to repair

Henry Robinson crashed his Calthorpe at high speed on Quarterbridge Road on lap six of the race. The driver was trapped under the car with his clothing entangled in the wreckage but the mechanic was thrown clear. Both escaped with cuts and bruises but a lady spectator was injured. [Stan Hughes collection]

damage suffered earlier in the race, resulting in the steering being erratic. Initially Calthorpe raised an objection to the jurisdiction of the Isle of Man Court. This objection was over-ruled in February 1911, and eventually the case was listed for hearing in April 1912, but a settlement was reached and the case was formally dismissed without going to trial.

During lap 5, although Guinness was now second on time he was behind Watson on the road due to having started a minute later. Watson, in third place, was therefore delaying Guinness in his pursuit of George. Watson was driving a cautious race, no faster than necessary and never pressing the Hutton beyond 70mph, but he was anxious not to let Guinness past. Watson said later that several times Guinness had blown his exhaust whistle and he had pulled over but at the same time accelerated, and the power of the Hutton had enabled him to pull away just enough to prevent Guinness from passing. It was chiefly down the Mountain that Guinness had been able to gain on him.

At Ramsey, Guinness stopped at the depot just after Watson but, thanks to the Darracq's quick-release fuel tank cap and an extra-large funnel, he completed his re-fuelling more quickly that the Hutton crew and got away 90 seconds before them. At the end of the lap Guinness led on the road for the first time, but Watson managed to re-pass him.

George, meanwhile, had been flying, completing the fastest lap of the race in 43mins 15secs (52mph), giving him a time for the five laps of 3hrs 39mins 48secs. This left him with a substantial lead of 4mins 36secs over Watson, whose fifth lap took 47mins 20secs. Guinness was third, 11 seconds back after a lap of 46mins 41secs. Tuck was down to fourth, 8mins 8secs behind Guinness.

Browning's Rover was officially stopped at the end of the fifth lap. On the sixth lap Brown retired his Coventry Humber, which had trouble with the bevel pinion in the live axle, and Leslie Porter's Calthorpe passed through the start/finish area with a spare tyre hanging from the rear strap, dragging on the road and stirring up clouds of dust. It was still there a lap later. Oscar Cupper had a long stop in Ramsey with plug problems on his Metallurgique – an experiment with new plugs was proving unsuccessful. He was stopped for over two hours and eventually retired with valve trouble at the end of his sixth lap after eight cars had finished the race.

On lap 6 George stopped at Ramsey to re-fuel. "How am I going?" he asked as fuel splashed around. "Am I" he said, when told he was leading. Throwing an empty fuel can on the road he swallowed several oysters, seized his mechanic by the scruff of the neck and went on his way.

Despite his stop for fuel and oysters, George

completed his sixth lap in 43mins 17secs, only 2 seconds slower than his fastest lap. With an aggregate time of 4hrs 23mins 05secs he now led Guinness by 6mins 21secs, the latter having lapped in 44mins 51secs. Watson's lap was quicker by over a minute than Guinness' and he was now only 43 seconds behind Guinness on corrected time. Tuck was still fourth, nearly seven minutes back. George seemed to be unbeatable.

At the start of lap 7, the unlucky Moore-Brabazon retired his Metallurgique with a broken exhaust valve. He had been on the road for six hours and completed six laps. After his valve replacement he had done two laps in just over 46 minutes for each lap. Stopping the Club enclosure, he asked whether he had time to finish. He was told that he had 2 hours 15 minutes before all cars would be stopped. This meant that he had to do his seventh and eighth laps and start his final lap within the time but he thought it meant that he had to complete all three laps in 2 hours and 15 minutes. Due to this misunderstanding, he retired although he might well have finished.

During lap 7, Hartridge's Westinghouse (the notorious 12A) retired after hitting a hedge at Glen Helen and breaking a wooden wheel. The road was blocked for a time and Watson was delayed. Tuck retired his Beeston Humber with ignition problems while fourth, Debuissey's "Pic-Pic", retired at Quarterbridge with a water circulation problem, and Rawlinson's Darracq skidded at Glen Helen, demolished a wall, but continued to set its fastest lap of the race.

Lap 7 also brought the most serious accident of the race when Reid's Beeston Humber arrived in Kirk Michael, where the team was based at the Mitre Hotel. Entering the village to cheers from supporters, Reid lost control when the steering gear again failed. The car hit a stone wall on which two women and several children were sitting. All were thrown off the hedge, while the car crossed the road,

The Watson and Guinness battle at Ramsey Hairpin. They were fighting for second until Arthur George retired his Darracq at Glen Helen on the last lap. Many times Guinness tried to pass but found it impossible due to the Hutton's superior acceleration, although Guinness was faster on the descent from the Mountain. [Ron Brew collection]

Approaching Cruickshank's corner at the top of Queen's Pier Road in Ramsey, William Watson's winning Hutton is pressed by Algernon Lee Guinness' second placed Darracq. The pits and the tented enclosure behind can be seen in the distance. [Brian Mylchreest collection]

James Reid crashed his Beeston Humber at high speed in Kirk Michael on the seventh lap. The cause was steering failure. Reid was badly shaken and his mechanic was seriously injured, but recovered. Two women and several children were thrown off the wall at the crash site, but escaped unhurt. [Author's collection]

demolished six feet of the wall and finished in the centre of the road. Gutteridge the mechanic lay unconscious in the wreckage with his right thumb almost severed. Fortunately none of the women and children was injured and Reid was badly shaken but uninjured. An ambulance party took Gutteridge to hospital where he was placed in intensive care on the instructions of Julian Orde of the RAC. He later developed double pneumonia, his condition became critical and his parents came to the Island. Happily, he recovered.

On completion of the lap, George still led but by a margin reduced from 6mins 21secs to 1min 49secs after a stop at Ballacraine when he changed all four wheels. His growing time was 5hrs 12mins 17secs, with Watson now second having gained 5mins 26secs from George by virtue of lapping only a second slower than his previous lap of 43mins 45secs. Guinness, lapping a minute slower than Watson, was back to third, 12 seconds adrift of Watson. Following Tuck's retirement, Porter was now fourth, 22mins 45secs back. At the end of the lap 14 cars were still running.

Harold Buckley's S.C.A.T., with a timing problem, was the only retirement on the eighth lap, but Cyril Roberts (Arrol-Johnston, delayed by radiator problems) and Roland Outhwaite (Vinot, delayed by seized exhaust valves) were both officially stopped on completion of their seventh laps. At the end of lap 8, George had increased his lead over Watson by 13 seconds to 2 minutes 2 seconds. His aggregate time was 5hrs 56mins 2secs. Guinness was 3mins 35secs behind Watson after a lap of 47mins 30secs. Porter was 24mins 26secs behind Guinness with Thornycroft fifth, a further 24 ½ minutes back. The sixth driver, Ross Browne was nearly 23 minutes behind Thornycroft. After completing eight laps, Leon Molon's Vinot was officially stopped after being delayed by seized exhaust valves, the same problem as had delayed his team-mate Outhwaite.

Although much of George's lead had evaporated with his tyre change at Ballacraine on lap 7, his lead of over two minutes at the start of the final lap should have been enough. In motor racing, however, the unexpected is a certainty and, less than thirty miles from the finish, George's race unravelled. Two nuts securing the inlet

In a rural scene at Douglas Road Corner, Kirk Michael, the Thornycroft of D.S. Hodge (22) is chased by the Vinot of Rowland Outhwaite. Hodge, in his first Isle of Man race, finished tenth and last while Outhwaite was stopped, out of time, after completing seven laps. [National Motor Museum]

Tom Thornycroft and his mechanic replenish their Thornycroft car at Ramsey pits in Queen's Pier Road. This was the first TT race in which pits were provided. Thornycroft finished fifth with an average speed of 44 mph for the nine laps of the race. [National Motor Museum]

manifold to the cylinder head had been gradually loosened by vibration and, at Glen Helen, escaping fuel vapour was ignited by heat from the exhaust. Seeing a flash of frame, George stopped, his mechanic lifted the bonnet and a fire was revealed. George quickly smothered the fire with a spectator's overcoat which he begged, borrowed or stole (it was never clear which but George said later that the spectator was "pretty sporting"). Although George's prompt action prevented serious damage to the car, two fire-damaged plugs had to be replaced before the Darracq was mobile again. Six minutes had been lost and, with them, the race.

At Hillberry, a crowd six deep lined the road awaiting the winner, unaware as yet of what had happened to George. Watson, visible in the distance by his white coat, took the flag in a time of 6hrs 43mins 5.6secs (50.25mph), to resounding cheers. Algie Guinness crossed the line 2mins 15.4secs later, after a fine drive during which he had taken what he described as "very extreme risks", but there was no sign of George and, as the seconds ticked away, there was a gasp "He's lost!" Eventually George came into view to take third place after a fine drive during which he had led on every lap except the last. He finished 5mins 21secs behind Watson and 3mins 15secs behind Guinness with a final lap of 52mins 34secs, including his stop of over six minutes. At least he had the compensation of the fastest lap and Darracq was the only team to finish. Porter brought his Calthorpe home fourth, in a time of 7hrs 14mins 19secs, a triumph for a £450 standard touring car of only 25hp which had been beaten only by three out-and-out racing cars. Calthorpe promptly promised that deliveries of their 1909 model, an exact replica of the TT car, would be available from 1st December. Fifth was Tom Thornycroft, 25 minutes behind the Calthorpe, with Ross Browne's Vinot 28 minutes further back. Of the 35 starters, only 10 completed the course, 21 retired and 4 were officially stopped as being out of time.

After the race there was profound relief that, despite the dramas and incidents, there had been no really serious accidents of the kind predicted in the press and only one person was in hospital. The relief was clear at the prize presentation in the Palace Ballroom at Douglas when Prince Francis asked the crowd of 7,000 to open Hymns Ancient and Modern and sing hymn number 379: "Now Thank We All Our God".

1908 Tourist Trophy Race Results

Thursday 24th September 1908. Start 9.00am.9 laps of 37.5 miles circuit, total distance 337.5 miles. 35 starters, 10 finishers.

1. William Watson (Hutton), 6hrs 43mins 5.6secs (50.25mph)
2. Algernon Lee Guinness (Darracq), 6hrs 45mins 21secs (50.00mph)
3. Arthur George (Darracq), 6hrs 48mins 36.6secs (48.00mph)
4. Leslie Porter (Calthorpe), 7hrs 14mins 19secs (47.00mph)
5. Tom Thornycroft (Thornycroft), 7hrs 39mins 15.4secs (44.00mph)
6. M. Ross Browne (Vinot), 8hrs 7mins 52.4secs (41.50mph)
7. Alfred ("Toby") Rawlinson (Darracq), 8hrs 11mins 51.8secs (41.25mph)
8. Thomas Rimmer (Vulcan), 8hrs 14mins 29.2secs (41.00mph)
9. Louis Coatalen (Hillman-Coatalen), 8hrs 20mins 35.2secs (40.50mph)
10. D.S. Hodge (Thornycroft), 8hrs 56mins 10secs (37.75mph)

Fastest lap: Arthur George (Darracq), 43mins 15secs (52.00mph)

Stopped on expiry of time limit for the race at 5.15pm:

Leon Molon (Vinot), 8 laps completed
Cyril Roberts (Arrol-Johnston), 7 laps completed
Roland Outhwaite (Vinot) 7 laps completed
H.B. Browning (Rover), 5 laps completed

Retirements:

Lap 1:
P.D. Stirling (Hutton), hit wall at Ballacraine

Lap 2:
Geoffrey Moss (Arrol-Johnston), broken tappets

Lap 3:
J. Gall (Westinghouse), faulty magneto
Warwick Wright (Metallurgique), timing gear problems

Lap 4:
Dario Resta (Arrol-Johnston), broken clutch at Union

Mills
Jack Stocks (De Dion), sheared pin in timing gear
Lap 5:
Philip Graham (Deasy), accident between Kirk Michael and Ballaugh
R.O. Harper (S.C.A.T.), broken timing gear
Ernest Hutton (Hutton), Hit wall at Ramsey Hairpin, bending front axle, and buckling rear wheel, after tyre burst
Kenelm Lee Guinness (Hillman-Coatalen), broken frame at Bungalow
Henry Robinson (Calthorpe), crash on Quarterbridge Road
Edmund Lewis (Deasy), broken crankshaft at Sulby Bridge
F. Ward (S.C.A.T.)
Lap 6:
G.W.A. Brown (Coventry Humber), bevel pinion in live axle
Oscar Cupper (Metallurgique), valve problem
Lap 7:
A. Hartridge (Westinghouse), broken wheel
James Reid (Beeston Humber), crash at Kirk Michael
J.T.C. Moore-Brabazon (Metallurgique), broken exhaust valve
W.G. Tuck (Beeston Humber), ignition problem
Andre Debuissey (Picard), water circulation problems and buckled wheel after crash at Quarterbridge on lap 1
Lap 8:
Harold S. Buckley (S.C.A.T.), timing gear problem.

Reaction

The Motoring Press was enthusiastic and its comments were favourable. Pre-race, on the last day of practising *The Motor* had proclaimed "That the event is going to be a success there is not the slightest doubt; in fact it will be, provided the weather is favourable, the finest race that has ever been contested in the British Isles". Post-race, *The Motor* headed its review "The Finest and Most Successful Motor Race Ever Held". *The Autocar* described the race as "a Grand Prix in miniature" and *The Automotor Journal* thought "...it was a good race, and that is, as often as not, just what a motor contest of this description utterly fails to provide". The Special Correspondent of *The Car Illustrated* said "That this is a trying course no one for a moment will deny, embracing as it does up and down gradients of 1 in 10. Taking it on the whole the surface of the roads is good. At any rate, it may be said that it is fairly typical of ordinary British roads. Considering the climate which prevails in Manxland, I must confess that as far as road surface is concerned I was very agreeably surprised". There were also tributes to Secretary of the Meeting Julian Orde for "his excellent management of a difficult event".

Clearly the critics had been confounded and were reduced, as *The Motor* pointed out, to condemning "the utter uselessness of the race and its lack of instructive lessons". This was unjustified because the race had taught useful lessons, not least of which was that extreme tests of cars were still needed.

Nevertheless, the RAC had been fortunate – crashes both in practising and during the race could easily have had much more serious consequences and even the Motoring Press had reservations. *The Car Illustrated* said "The RAC must cease for the moment to emphasize speed and cultivate instead other qualities for the modern motor car" while *The Motor* said "Whether it be expedient to promote any more races is another matter, one that may safely be left to the Royal Automobile Club to decide".

After four successful events in four years, justified hopes of another TT Race in 1909 were dashed in May when the *Mona's Herald* announced that the Manx Automobile Club was endeavouring to get the RAC to organise another race on the Island but success was very doubtful as the King, Patron of the RAC, had "expressed himself very strongly against road racing by motors". It appeared that regardless of any royal influence the motor industry – probably influenced by Napier's decision to withdraw – was not in favour of a TT in 1909.

In 1910 a local Committee was set up with a view to a race in 1911, to mark the 50th anniversary of the Douglas municipal authority. Following the death of King Edward VII the idea was extended to take in a celebration of the Coronation of King George V. A "Three Inch" race was proposed but, after consultation with the industry, the RAC said that it could not organise a race in 1911 and would not issue a permit for a race to be organised by others, although the Island could do so itself if it wished to take sole responsibility. The Committee, with dynamic *Isle of Man Times* Editor George Brown as Secretary, decided to organise a "Three Inch" race and an open handicap race for amateurs and, supported by the Town Clerk of Douglas, approached the Highway Board for a Road Closing Order. Incredibly, bearing in mind the importance of racing to the tourist industry and the Board's willingness to agree to increased road closures for the motorcycle TT to transfer to the "Four Inch" course, the Board, after meeting the Committee and Lord Raglan, said that it had agreed with the Governor that permission "could not be accorded". No reason was given and, after being asked for its reasons, the Board refused. George Brown then asked for the decision to be reconsidered but this was also refused.

It might have been suspected, bearing in mind that the

start of racing in the Island had resulted from a request by Julian Orde to his cousin Lord Raglan, that a similar request had caused the stoppage. Had the RAC been "warned off" racing by its Patron and communicated this through Orde to Lord Raglan?

Any suspicion soon gained credence. The Committee made discreet off-the-record enquiries which led them to the conclusion that the new King and new RAC Patron, George V, was opposed to car racing. This obviously left the RAC unable to organise a race or to issue a permit for one, especially as part of the Coronation celebrations, and Lord Raglan's hands were also tied.

Brown's next step was a telegram to Buckingham Palace. As Editor of the *Isle of Man Times* he said that an influential committee wished to celebrate His Majesty's Coronation with a car race but had been refused an Order to close the Island's roads. It had been stated unofficially that the reason was His Majesty's disapproval of racing. The telegram ended "Inhabitants much disappointed. Please say if His Majesty has expressed disapproval of this race".

The reply from the King's Secretary confirmed the suspicions – "His Majesty was not even aware of the proposed motor car races". As the reason for the refusal had been exposed as a fabrication, Brown maintained that the matter should be reconsidered. Again the Highway Board was challenged to give its reasons for refusal and again it refused. It was suggested that trade influence was the real reason. Alternatively the RAC may have decided that it had been very lucky that there had been no deaths in the 1908 race and that it would be unwise to risk another race in case its luck ran out. Nothing more was heard until 1913.

1914 Tourist Trophy – "Bill" Guinness Wins Longest Isle of Man TT Race

Planning

After four years without a TT, the RAC decided that it was possible to organise a race in 1913. Public opinion towards motor cars had changed appreciably since 1908 – car ownership was no longer restricted to the very wealthy and the fact that many newspaper readers now owned cars like the Standard 9, priced at £195, meant that an anti-racing campaign as waged by *The Times* and other national dailies in 1908 would no longer sell papers. Motor Racing was more respectable and attracted positive publicity. Also, there was a patriotic element because the absence of endurance racing on public roads, as organised in continental Europe, deprived British manufacturers of development opportunities available to continental manufacturers.

The Society of Motor Manufacturers and Traders rejected the idea of a race in 1913 as there would be insufficient time to design and build "real racing cars". The RAC then proposed a race for production cars which would not need to be designed and built from scratch but the SMMT also rejected this proposal, forcing the RAC to delay the race for a year. An application to the Highway Board for a date in July 1914 was refused as being too near the peak of the holiday season but after discussion a race over two days, Wednesday 10th and Thursday 11th June, was agreed. This was three weeks after the motorcycle TT, allowing sharing with the Auto-Cycle Union of the costs of swearing-in marshals, grandstands and other items, as in 1907. There was also discussion over road closing times, with the RAC asking for 9.00am to 4.30pm but settling for 8.45am to 4.00pm, after the Board insisted that the roads must be opened by 4.00pm. Previously the RAC had donated £200 towards the cost of road improvements but Governor Raglan now made this a condition of the Road Closing Order.

The race was to be longer than any previous TT, with a distance of 16 laps (8 laps per day) of the "Four Inch" course, a total of 600 miles. Cars would start on the second day in the classification order at the end of the first day. The Start was to be at the top of Bray Hill with the Finish on Ballanard Road. The formula was again simple – engine size was limited to 3,310cc, the minimum weight was 21.5 hundredweight and fuel of any type could be used provided a sample was submitted to the RAC two weeks before the race. For the first time there would be cash awards – the winner would receive £1,000 donated by the Daily Telegraph, the runner-up £250 and the winning team £300. The Henry Edmunds Trophy was resurrected as an award for the fastest aggregate time for the 16 ascents of a 6.5 miles stretch of the Mountain Road between Ramsey and the Bungalow.

Entries

The RAC received 26 entries, reduced to 23 by the withdrawal of three Pipes from Belgium, substantially less than for the four previous TTs but of high quality with technical interest and a strong international flavour. Substantial development in car design since 1908 meant the exciting prospect of what the Press called a "titanic struggle".

The Sunbeam team were clear pre-race favourites. The drivers were the Guinness brothers and Dario Resta, Italian born but London resident from the age of two, who had driven an Arrol-Johnston in the 1908 TT. He won the Indianapolis 500 in 1916 and became one of the most famous drivers of his time. The cars, designed by

Louis Coatalen who had left Hillman in 1909 to join Sunbeam's racing campaign, had overhead valve, twin camshaft engines with four valves per cylinder. Weight distribution, suspension and braking had received careful attention and, after testing at Brooklands, had been adjusted in the light of the drivers' advice. The braking system was described as "top hole". The brake shoes were very light and the foot brakes were on the back wheels for better cooling than if mounted at the rear of the gearbox. The handbrakes had "fly-off" operation, with the ratchet disengaged unless brought into operation by a knob on top of the lever. It was alleged that the cars were copies of the 1913 racing Peugeot, Coatalen having obtained a Peugeot, taken it to his home in Wolverhampton, dismantled it in his drawing room, and had drawings made of the entire car. The team's base in Douglas was the Fort Anne Hotel, in a garage used by previous TT competitors and still containing benches and lockers on which "C.S. Rolls" was painted. As Kenelm Lee Guinness had failed to finish in the 1907 and 1908 TT races while driving light green cars he regarded this colour as unlucky, so Coatalen had the team cars painted in what he called a dark shade of green. Some later described it as a purplish blue and the Daily Telegraph called it purple.

Sunbeam's main challenger was the Vauxhall team with black ultra-light, rakish twin overhead camshaft 3,308cc cars, designed by Chief Designer Laurence Pomeroy, identical to the Vauxhall Grand Prix cars except for smaller engines to comply with TT regulations. Pomeroy predicted crankshaft speeds of 5,000rpm and said that his were already achieving 4,500rpm. Instead of the time-honoured method of saving weight by drilling holes wherever possible, he had dispensed with the under-frame and passed the springs through the axles. After Vauxhall had decided seven months earlier to produce new cars for the TT and the French Grand Prix Pomeroy, in conjunction with the company's chief draughtsman, had produced plans within weeks. Construction however was delayed. Vauxhall's workforce was a tenth the size of Sunbeam's and the cars were completed only two weeks before the TT, did not arrive on the Island until 1st June, and were inadequately prepared, with "bad tempered" and poorly tuned engines. Modifications were essential – for example one of the drivers could not reach the brake pedal. Number one driver, 1908 winner William Watson, was backed up by leading amateur and Shelsley Walsh hill-climb record holder Joseph Higginson and Vauxhall Director and 1905 Vauxhall TT veteran A.J. Hancock, now an established Brooklands driver and holder of eleven world records set at Brooklands in a "Prince Henry" Vauxhall.

The Humber team was based at the Mitre Hotel at Kirk Michael. The photograph shows the team cars of Burgess (2), Tuck (13) and Wright (20) outside the hotel with supporters including a German waiter who, having returned home, reputedly returned soon as a prisoner in Knockaloe internment camp. [Paul Cashin collection]

Tenth at the end of the first day, Frank Clement retired his Straker-Squire at Ramsey on the tenth lap with a broken piston. His new friendship with W.O. Bentley led to a drive in the Bentley team for the 1922 TT when he finished second to Jean Chassagne's Sunbeam. [Brian Mylchreest collection]

Humber, the only company to have entered every previous TT, produced a team of three pure racing cars which reputedly cost £15,000. Specially designed "from starting handle to back axle" said *The Motor*, the stone-grey cars had 16 valve twin camshaft 3,295cc engines which delivered 100hp at 3,200rpm. The design, like that of the Sunbeams, closely followed the design of the racing Peugeots. The chassis weight of the cars was the heaviest in the race. The drivers were designer Fred Burgess, soon to be working on aero-engines with W.O. Bentley, together with Fred Tuck and Sam Wright, a hill-climber who had ridden Humbers in the 1910, 1911 and 1913 motorcycle TT races.

The two bright red Stars from Wolverhampton with standard sporting chassis were alleged to be capable of reaching 96mph at 3,000rpm. They had extra-large brakes on the rear wheels. Their drivers were Richard Lisle and Robert Crossman, both newcomers to the TT.

Straker-Squire of Bristol entered two blue 3,260cc cars with overhead camshaft engines developing over 80hp at 3,200rpm. The engines, with the shortest stroke of all in the race, were designed by Roy Fedden who was soon to become an aero-engine designer. The cars had a very short wheelbase and were very light. The drivers were R.S. ("Dick") Witchell, later Works Manager at Bentley Motors, and Star's head tester Frank Clement, a former road tester for Vauxhall and later a Bentley driver in the 1922 TT. The team had no practice car and, rather than risk the race cars, the drivers took to the course on Clement's Rudge motorcycle with the owner driving and Witchell on a "flapper bracket".

The other British entry was a dark green 3,273cc Crossley for Cecil Bianchi, making his first TT appearance, although he had driven a Wolseley in the 1905 Gordon Bennett Trial. The car had an ordinary engine, an almost standard chassis and an air-cooled oil tank between the dumb-irons.

Notable among foreign challengers were three yellow Minervas from Antwerp. The cars were technically interesting for their Knight sleeve-valve engines which caused controversy, with dense trails of oil smoke caused by the auxiliary exhaust ports at the bottom of the cylinders. Their drivers were Jean Porporato who had driven a Berliet in the 1907 TT, Leon Molon who had driven a Vinot in 1908 and Island newcomer C. Riecken.

Also from Antwerp came an almost standard light green sports model S.A.V.A. for French speaking Swiss driver Rene Berger from Lausanne. The 3,267cc engine was said to produce 70hp. Due to its continental successes, Louis Coatalen regarded the car with concern before the race.

There was an impressive team of three Adlers built in Frankfurt and driven by Otto Goebel, Joseph Rutsch and Hugo Wilhelm. Although unknown in the British Isles,

The Straker-Squire team consisting of Dick Witchell (3) and Frank Clement (14) had its headquarters at the Railway Hotel, Kirk Michael, near the Humber base at the Mitre Hotel. Witchell finished fourth, only 30 seconds after Leon Molon's Minerva, but Clement retired on lap 10 with a broken piston. [Stan Hughes collection]

Cecil Bianchi's Crossley receives attention at Cronk-ny-Mona after a morning practice. In the race he was thirteenth and last at the end of the first day and retired on the second day, on lap 12. He drove a Wolseley in the 1905 Gordon Bennett Trial but 1914 was his first TT. [Ron Brew collection]

Wilhelm was said to be Germany's top driver. The cars were specially built racing cars and looked highly efficient in a colour scheme of white with red stripes with, it was said "the best finished upholstery that is to be found in any of the cars". The bodies had huge tails which *The Autocar* compared to "an elongated half egg". The engine, "a typically German job" according to *The Autocar*, had a very long stroke of 3,308cc, considered equal to that of the Minervas and Vauxhalls, and a magneto driving-gear across the end of the crankshaft operating two magnetos. Technical information was difficult to obtain and there was much speculation about gear ratios. Like the Sunbeams, the cars had fly-off handbrakes.

One of the most popular drivers in the race, perhaps because he raced in the motorcycle TT in 1909 and 1910, was Walter Owen Bentley, in his first road race in a car. His motorcycle TT experience would be of limited use as prior to 1911 the motorcycles had used the short St. John's circuit which included less than seven miles of the Four Inch course, between Ballacraine and Kirk Michael. He entered a small dark red 2,000cc D.F.P., a French car for which his company was the British concessionaire – a "very plucky" entry, thought *The Motor*. The car was clearly under-powered compared with cars of 3,300cc but had completed ten laps of Brooklands at 81.98mph with a flying lap of 89.7mph. Meticulously prepared by Bentley, who regarded the TT as a prime opportunity to demonstrate of the car in tough competition against much more powerful cars, the D.F.P. was standard except for axles and some detailed modifications to deal with race stresses and extract maximum power from the small engine. It had aluminium pistons, lightened reciprocating parts and a high compression ratio. There were two fuel tanks, one at the front and one at the rear, and the body had a rounded tail, hinged for access to the spare wheels. This was removed for the TT. Asked what the letters D.F.P. stood for, Bentley replied "Deserves First Place". There were other suggestions but in fact the letters represented the constructors, Doriot, Flandrin et Parant of Courbevoie, Seine. Parant had visited Brooklands and been amazed at the performance of his little family car and Doriot came to the Island to watch the car in the TT,

Minerva of Belgium entered a team of three cars, pictured in Peveril Square beside the Douglas Sea Terminal building. The drivers were C. Riecken, Leon Molon and Jean Porporato, and they finished second, third and fifth respectively, winning the team prize. [Manx National Heritage]

The Adler team from Germany was based at Creg-na-Baa Hotel where Otto Goebel and his mechanic (car 18) are pictured in front of Joseph Rutsch's similar car (23). Goebel retired on lap 2 with gearbox trouble and Rutsch on lap 11 with engine trouble. Their team-mate Philip Stapp also retired with engine trouble, on lap 2. [R and L Kelly collection]

Adler reserve driver Philip Stapp and his mechanic pose with their car outside the team headquarters, the Creg-na-Baa Hotel. They retired on the second lap of the race with engine trouble. [John Watterson collection]

Based at the Athol Motor Garage in Hill Street, Douglas, W.O. Bentley's French D.F.P. had a two litre engine while every other engine in the race was over three litres. Nevertheless Bentley's preparation was meticulous and he finished sixth and last after an excellent drive. [R and L Kelly collection]

W.O. Bentley, with his French mechanic Jean Leroux, rounds Ramsey Hairpin during his determined and creditable drive in his D.F.P. Sadly Leroux, a French Army reservist, was killed in Lorraine only 65 days after the race. [Ian Harrison collection]

accompanied by a French mechanic, Jean Leroux.

"Toby" Rawlinson, a 1904 Gordon Bennett Trial veteran and by far the oldest driver in the race, entered a silver American Hudson, a standard touring car except for a reserve oil tank. Some considered him a dark horse, which he perhaps encouraged by stopping during practice laps to observe other drivers. Unfortunately he was a non-starter in the race. Soon he would be in charge of the air defence of London.

Alfred "Toby" Rawlinson, a veteran of the 1904 Gordon Bennett Trial, entered an American Hudson. Seen at Quarterbridge before a sunny morning practice, the car suffered persistent engine trouble during practice and was a last-minute non-starter when it failed to climb Bray Hill en route to the Start on race day. [Ron Brew collection]

Practice

There was an unreal atmosphere as competitors, mechanics, officials and spectators assembled in Douglas. It was very much business as usual – a normal holiday season, a normal TT race and the normal high spirits typical of summer in Douglas but tinged with a hedonistic, "live for the day" attitude. According to an RAC official there was a sense of Utopia and yet only 55 days were to pass between the race and the declaration of the First World War, which would change a secure and happy world forever and would result in some of the Island's June visitors never seeing another race – indeed W.O. Bentley's DFP mechanic Jean Leroux, a French Army reservist, was killed in Lorraine on 15th August, only 65 days after the race.

For the first time, racing cars were required to be licensed, presumably because they were being driven on open roads during practising. Previously officials had turned a blind eye. It was not usually necessary for racing cars to be licensed for road use, although the Humbers arrived with English number plates, and the DFP, the Sunbeams, the Straker-Squires, the Crossley, the Stars and the Vauxhalls all had to be licensed by the Highway Board and fitted with Manx number plates before practising.

Practice was allowed between dawn and 7.00am, except that drivers were not permitted to pass Quarterbridge on a new lap after 6.15am unless they were returning to bases at Glen Helen or Kirk Michael (where the Humber and Straker-Squire teams were based), in which case they were subject to a 20mph speed limit. They were not allowed on the course at any other time, even on foot, on bicycles or as passengers, under threat of a fine for a first offence or disqualification for a subsequent offence. An additional restriction for 1914, introduced because of reckless driving of motorcycles during their TT period which had disturbed church services and made people frightened to walk on streets and roads, was a complete ban on the use of motor vehicles on Sundays except with a permit issued by the Chief Constable who would not issue any permit without being satisfied that there was good reason. This ban confined drivers to their hotels where they were forced to invent various indoor entertainments such as singing, dancing and three-legged races and gave rise to the expression "sad Sundays".

The first practice, on Monday 25th May, brought appalling conditions with low cloud, rain and even snow on the Mountain. Only the three Sunbeams, the three Humbers and Clement's Straker-Squire were out. On Tuesday and Wednesday the weather was bright and warm. The Guinness brothers both lapped in 40 minutes with Tuck's Humber two minutes slower and Resta and Clement both on 43 minutes. The fastest motorcycle TT lap had been 42 minutes 16 seconds (53.50mph). A large variation became apparent between the Humber drivers. Fred Tuck was fastest by far – so much so that Bill Guinness said in a postcard "Straker-Squire and one Humber also very hot stuff" – with Fred Burgess slowest to the extent of facing possible replacement, and Sam Wright improving steadily.

The RAC encountered a potentially serious problem on 26th May in the form of a complaint from James Murray Cruickshank, High Bailiff (Stipendiary Magistrate) of Ramsey, who lived on the corner at the junction of Queen's Pier Road and May Hill where the course left Ramsey. The noise of the cars taking the corner (known to this day as "Cruickshank's") was making sleep impossible, he said. The RAC then ordered the fitting of silencers but some teams objected that they did not have silencers and would have to have them made, which could disrupt practising. Having made his point, the High Bailiff relented to the extent that he would withdraw his complaint provided silencers were fitted when available. Then, according to the Daily Telegraph, "like a good sportsman" he retired to a family home in Peel for the duration.

The Minerva team caused a major controversy with their sleeve-valve oil smoke, which brought complaints from other drivers that visibility was affected so badly as to make overtaking impossible. W.O. Bentley recalled more than forty years later "the grey cloudy streaks of smoke that were almost impenetrable when driving into the low sun at dawn towards St. Johns". His memory of the smoke was obviously clearer than his memory of the course as St. John's is the most westerly point – he probably meant Sulby! Complaints were made and the Minerva team made adjustments but these were ineffectual, whereupon Humber Ltd. made an official protest, seeking to have the Minervas excluded. This resulted in Riecken making two demonstration runs up Bray Hill, observed by David Citroen the Managing Director of the English concessionaire for Minerva, Professor C.Y. Knight the sleeve-valve designer and Julian Orde with other RAC officials. Smoke emissions were slight and did not justify exclusion but the complainants maintained that this was because the engine was cold at the time of the test and that emissions were much greater when the engines were hot. *The Autocar* believed that Minerva were experimenting with different plugs, a suspicion supported by the fact that emissions varied from appalling to slight at the same point on the course, prompting Kenelm Lee Guinness (known as "Bill") to opine that Minerva engineers would eventually succeed in reducing emissions to "normal exhaustiness". Also, each car had a different make of carburettor. To appease the complainants the RAC warned the Minerva mechanics" to keep a sharp look-out by eye and ear" for drivers trying to pass, although how the Minerva mechanics would be able to see through the smoke behind them any better that following drivers could see through the smoke in front of them was not explained. The result was that two days before the race there were still complaints of "a blue film clean across the Mountain from one horizon to the other", although few were fast enough to be in a position to overtake the Minervas and those who were reported that the Minerva drivers readily gave way.

Adler erected their own "secret signs" measuring 12 inches x 4 inches, yellow painted with circles or arrows pointing to right or left, at various points on the course. In what may have been an indication of anti-German feeling some signs were altered while others were

The Minerva of Claude Riecken enters Parliament Square, Ramsey. Other teams complained about the smoke trail, evident in the photograph, which was emitted by all three Minervas, due to their sleeve-valve engines. After an excellent drive, Riecken finished second but twenty minutes behind Kenelm Lee Guinness. [Brian Mylchreest collection]

obliterated or disappeared. None lasted long.

There were various practice incidents. The Vauxhalls were leaping over Ballaugh Bridge. Cecil Bianchi, dazzled by the rising sun, spun his Crossley through 720 degrees at Sulby Bridge before continuing unscathed, while Dick Witchell had a similar spin on a wet patch at Greeba Castle in his Straker-Squire, travelling some 70 yards, grazing a stone wall and twisting his front axle. Resta took a piece out of the wall at Sulby Bridge but avoided a serious crash. S.A.V.A. driver Rene Berger, who was based with the company's works manager at Ballamoar, Jurby, then the home of a Belgian banker, found the course dangerous, but his worst experience was caused by a blackbird which hit him in the face near Kirk Michael, smashing his goggles which cut his face. He avoided crashing but, despite medical treatment, his eyes were sore and inflamed for a long time.

The worst practice incident occurred on Friday 5th June at Waterworks corner on the climb up the Mountain from Ramsey when Adler driver Hugo Wilhelm, blinded by a dust cloud from another car, charged a stone wall at 55mph and overturned. Both Wilhelm and his mechanic H. Roth were trapped under the car and the sole spectator at the scene, 14 years old Arthur Hibbert of Ramsey, jumped off the hedge and ran back along the road to warn two oncoming drivers, Frank Clement (Straker-Squire) and "Toby" Rawlinson (Hudson). With their mechanics, they ran to the scene and released Wilhelm and his mechanic, both of whom were taken to hospital. Wilhelm had a fractured rib and Roth had head injuries and concussion. Wilhelm was passed fit to race by a local doctor but, on instructions from Germany, Team Manager Max Meyer withdrew him from the race and substituted reserve driver Philip Stapp with the spare car. Arthur Hibbert later received a gold medal, awarded by the German tyre company Continental and presented by Lord Raglan.

Bill Guinness and Dario Resta decided to undertake destruction testing of the Sunbeam team's spare car with the mutual challenge "let's go and try to do in the spare!" which at least preserved their race cars. Guinness was the winner when he bent both frame and axle in a crash on the Mountain but his mechanic, with blow-torch and lever, restored mobility.

Dario Resta had a wild reputation but he was also crafty. Coatalen had told his drivers not to exceed 3,000rpm (good for 90mph) during practice but said "They are all bad boys and like to do 97 when they can". How right he was – although initially he was pleasantly surprised to find that the "tell-tale" (an extra needle showing the maximum revs reached) on Resta's rev-counter never passed 2,800rpm, he later discovered that Resta had been disconnecting the drive to the instrument as soon as he was out of sight and re-connecting it at the last corner before the end of the lap. "Oh, he is a bad boy, that Resta, but a grand driver", he said.

Despite the dangers of the course, both Mrs Resta and Mrs Coatalen enjoyed practice laps with their husbands, and various journalists were also taken for rides by competitors, giving mechanics the chance of extra hours in bed before a day's work on their teams' cars. *The Motor* representative described a lap with Resta as "a harrowing experience" but managed to comply with Coatalen's instruction to take care not to be thrown out.

Practice produced a problem common to all the competitors. This was the constant failure of their porcelain sparking plugs which they had to change continually. This led to a comment in the Daily Telegraph that "A fortune awaits the successful inventor of a sparking plug that can stand the intense heat of the modern racing engine". Louis Coatalen then suggested to Bill Guinness that he should develop a new plug. This was the K.L.G. plug which was used by almost every car in the 1922 TT.

There were a few problems before and during the weighing-in of cars at Lewin's weighbridge in Lake Road. Witchell's Straker Squire had a patched-up front axle while the team awaited a replacement from Bristol which would be fitted before the race. Burgess' Humber had ended up in a ditch during a test run, bending a dumb-iron and an extension of time for weighing-in was agreed. Cathie's Star had a broken crankshaft but, when he tried the spare car which he was to drive in the race, he found he was unable to reach the pedals. He therefore had to be substituted by Robert Crossman, the reserve driver. The Vauxhalls were under the minimum weight by up to 56lbs and, while a temporary solution was a sack of stones, properly secured ballast had to be carried in the race. Algie Guinness' Sunbeam would also have to carry ballast

The Vauxhall of A.J. Hancock is weighed at the weighbridge in Lake Road, Douglas, where the pre-race technical inspections were carried out. [Ron Brew collection]

Dick Witchell's Straker-Squire stands on the weighbridge at Lake Road Douglas. Witchell may have been emulating a ploy adopted by Sidney Girling at the 1905 Gordon Bennett Trial – bringing the car to the weighbridge on worn tyres in order to get within the weight limit! [Stan Hughes collection]

In early morning sunlight William Watson awaits the start of practice in his Vauxhall. The winner of the 1908 TT in a Hutton, his defence of his title sadly ended at Union Mills, only two miles into the first lap of the race, when his crankshaft broke. [R and L Kelly collection]

– 20lbs in his case, as would the spare Star. While Joseph Higginson's Vauxhall was being warmed up, only 24 hours before the start of the race, a connecting rod had gone through the crankcase and he was a doubtful starter.

1914 Tourist Trophy Race – The First Day

At first the weather was very poor, with mist, heavy rain and strong winds on the Mountain. Fortunately there was rapid improvement. After a course inspection with Campbell Muir in a Cadillac, Chief Constable Madoc said at 7.30am that it was still misty on the Mountain but clear enough. This seemed to be confirmed by the fact that Muir had allegedly lapped at well over 40mph! Later, Madoc wrote in his diary that "the day was grand".

By the time of the 9.00am start the sun was breaking through the clouds but the roads were still wet and muddy, especially under trees. Most cars had non-skid tyres and many were hastily fitted with makeshift light mudguards to protect drivers concerned not only about mud, but also about risks to their eyes due to the 75 tons of *Akonia* which had been spread on the course in order to lay the dust! As it was a Bank Holiday on the Isle of Man (not for the race but in honour of the King's birthday), crowds of spectators were described as "moderately good" especially at Hillberry and Creg-ny-Baa, while at the Bungalow "a few hundred" reportedly walked on the course and crossed at will but quickly moved when the first cars appeared. A similar problem was reported at Hillberry.

The Vauxhalls made the start only after their mechanics had worked all night by candle-light and, in the words of designer Laurence Pomeroy, "well knowing that their cars were the worst prepared in the event". There was only one non-starter – "Toby" Rawlinson's Hudson. This car had given trouble during practice and the engine was an amalgam of its original race engine and an old engine from a Hudson touring car. Finding that the car would not go up Bray Hill to the Start without being pushed, Rawlinson had no hesitation in withdrawing it. The cause was suspected to be a faulty piston.

The first car, Jean Porporato's Minerva, was started promptly at 9.00am, with the others following at intervals of 90 seconds. In 1908 there had been complaints that 30 seconds intervals were unsafe and the RAC had reverted to one minute for 1914 but changed to 90 seconds at the suggestion of *The Motor*.

The first lap brought dramatic news. First, the 1908 winner William Watson failed to appear at Ballacraine and it was soon announced that he had completed only two miles before retiring at Union Mills with his Vauxhall's crankshaft broken. Worse was to come. Dario Resta, a potential winner, retired at Ramsey with a broken big-end bolt and Joseph Higginson's Vauxhall retired at the Bungalow having lost all the oil from the crankcase due to a stripped thread on an oil pipe, over-tightened by one of the tired mechanics who had worked through the night. Also in trouble and late at Ballacraine was Richard Lisle's Star, with a slipping clutch which later required a pit-stop.

Already the pattern of the race was clear. The two surviving Sunbeams were flying – Kenelm Lee Guinness had passed both Burgess' Humber and Witchell's Straker-Squire by Ramsey, while Algie passed no less than six cars before the end of the lap. Rene Berger's fancied S.A.V.A. had passed Bentley's DFP. First to complete the lap was Porporato's Minerva, followed by Bill Guinness, Burgess and Witchell. The Sunbeams were decisively fastest, with Bill lapping in 38mins 14secs and Algie in 40mins 21secs. Next fastest was Porporato (42mins 18secs), followed by the Straker-Squires of Clement (42mins 49secs) and

"Bill" Guinness and his mechanic are pictured in discussion as they pass through Parliament Square in Ramsey. There was probably not too much to talk about as they had a trouble-free run with the Sunbeam apart from the brakes not releasing properly on the first day. [Brian Mylchreest collection]

Witchell (43mins 22secs), and the Minervas of Molon (43mins 47secs) and Riecken (43mins 53secs). Obviously predictions during practising of the superiority of the Sunbeams, Minervas and Straker Squires were correct.

Lap 2 saw the retirement of the Adlers of Philip Stapp and Otto Goebel at Creg-ny-Baa where the team was based. Both had big-end problems which had been caused by a change of engine oil. Consumption of the light oil used during practising had been very heavy – as much as five litres per lap. This oil was replaced for the race by a heavier type of oil which did not circulate adequately. The only other retirement on this lap was Tuck's Humber, at Ramsey, with a broken valve. At the end of the lap the first three were unchanged. Bill Guinness' elapsed time of 1 hour 16mins 09secs meant a second lap time of 37mins 55secs (59.34mph), the fastest lap of the race but slower than his unofficial fastest practice lap of 36mins 45secs (61.50mph). This increased Bill's lead on Algie (1 hour 19mins 58secs) who in turn increased his lead on Porporato (1 hour 24mins 35secs). Witchell took fourth place from Clement with a time of 1 hour 24mins 58secs, 22 seconds ahead of Clement. Riecken was now sixth (1hour 26mins 6secs) with Molon seventh, 1 min 34secs back.

Kenelm Lee Guinness and his mechanic, Harold Cook, had a fright on the hump-backed bridge at Ballaugh. Guinness later said "The most exciting – and amusing – incident I met with was due to my mechanic and right-hand man Cook. He is a splendid racing mechanic and also an excellent worker when work has to be done. Well, for some reason even unknown to himself, friend Cook took it into his head to get out of his seat to have a look at the back tyre on my side, choosing the approach to Ballaugh Bridge for his inspection. Well, we were on the

Algernon Lee Guinness' Sunbeam passes a Snaefell Mountain Railway tram at the Bungalow. During racing the service to the summit of Snaefell was suspended and trams bringing spectators from Laxey stopped below the crossing, allowing passengers to alight and cross the road by means of a pedestrian tunnel. [John Watterson collection]

Winner Kenelm Lee Guinness takes Ramsey Hairpin. His was the only Sunbeam to finish but he drove a dominant race, finishing 20 minutes ahead of Riecken's second- placed Minerva. [Ian Harrison collection]

bridge before I had a chance to do anything. He shot clean up in the air and I thought it was all up with him. However, I had momentarily forgotten Newton's laws of motion. He landed back with his nose first – on my head – luckily only a glancing blow. I won easily and poor Cook got a nasty bump. However, he managed to get himself back into the car again and soon made light of his harrowing experience. He said it was a good omen, as we had drawn first blood!"

On lap 3, Berger's S.A.V.A., which had worried Coatalen during practising, retired at Ramsey. Julian Orde, multi-tasking as Commentator as well as Clerk of the Course and Secretary of the Meeting, made a megaphone announcement of the retirement but was unable to state the cause. "The only news we have", he said, "is that the driver and mechanic are basking in the sun". The problem was later reported as a broken crankshaft. This lap saw no change among the leaders. The Guinness brothers sped up with growing times of 1hour 55mins 33secs and 1hour 59mins 13secs. Bill Guinness had lapped in 39mins 24secs. Algie Guinness now led Porporato by 7mins 3secs. Witchell was 20secs down on Porporato and 26secs up on Clement, whose lead over Riecken was 47 seconds. At the pits there were various stoppages, and spectators on the grandstand were also entertained when Bill Guinness overshot the right turn from Ballanard Road into Bray Hill and had to continue into the mouth of Ballaquayle Road.

By 1pm, with half the day's distance completed, there had been seven retirements. Witchell had now taken third place from Porporato by six seconds. Bill Guinness (2hours 33mins 36secs) led his brother by 5mins 4secs. Algie led Witchell by 8mins 49secs. Fourth placed Porporato was only 39secs ahead of Clement, who led Riecken by 2mins 36secs.

Lap 5 saw Robert Crossman retire his Star at the pits with a water leak. Bill Guinness completed the lap in a cumulative time of 3 hours 12mins 32secs. His brother's time of 3 hours 18mins 20secs was 9mins 50secs faster than Witchell who now led Porporato by nine seconds. Porporato now led fifth-placed Riecken by 3mins 30secs and Molon was sixth, 4mims 48secs back. Clement was now down to seventh after a pit stop due to a broken tappet finger.

On lap 6 the leader continued to extend his lead. His growing time of 3 hours 52mins 10secs gave him a lead of 7mins 56secs over the second Sunbeam. Porporato had now regained third with a time of 4 hours 9mins 9secs, a margin of 9mins 3secs behind Algie Guinness. Dick Witchell was back to fourth, 41 seconds in arrears but leading Riecken by 2mins 39secs. Molon was still sixth, 5mins 16secs behind Riecken.

Lap 7 brought the only non-technical retirement of the day when Richard Lisle's Star collided with Ballaugh Bridge, without injury to driver or mechanic. *The Daily Telegraph* suggested that he had been trying to lap faster than anyone else. Bill Guinness slowed. His elapsed time was 4 hours 35mins 57secs compared with Algie's time of 4 hours 39mins 33secs. Algie's lead on Porporato, whose time was 4hours 50mins 17secs, was now 10mins 44secs. Witchell was still fourth with a growing time of 4 hours 52mins 24secs, 16 seconds ahead of Riecken. Molon was still sixth but 7mins 2secs behind Riecken.

At 2.00pm Rutsch's Adler made a surprise appearance at the pits after an off-course absence of an hour at the team's base at Creg-ny-Baa. Although there was talk of exclusion, presumably due to suspicion of outside assistance, no action was taken. Twenty minutes later, Bill Guinness' Sunbeam completed the final lap of the day with an elapsed time of 5 hours 15mins 47secs. He was followed only 3mins 10secs later by Algie whose lead over Porporato was a healthy 12mins 12secs. Riecken, Witchell and Molon finished fourth fifth and sixth. With no more retirements, thirteen cars survived the day's racing.

After completing the final lap, the cars were required to be kept overnight under parc ferme conditions in a marquee in the RAC enclosure, guarded by police. No access was permitted until the cars were taken to the start line on Thursday morning and any necessary repairs, re-fuelling etc had to be done at the pits, after the re-start. This caused a problem for the Sunbeam team particularly, as both cars had experienced problems with seizing brakes and Bill had had to rely on his handbrake for much of the day.

The RAC and the Chief Constable also had a problem. The Road Closing Order required the roads to be re-opened to the public by 4pm but, due to the race taking longer than anticipated, it became clear that this would be

Sir Algernon Lee Guinness, pictured at Hillberry, had a successful first day in his Sunbeam, finishing three minutes behind his younger brother Kenelm. He was unlucky on the second day when his rear universal joint seized, forcing his retirement. [Stan Hughes collection]

Jean Porporato accelerates out of the Gooseneck, with his Minerva trailing the smoke cloud which was a characteristic of the make throughout the event. He finished fifth, the least successful of the team, with team-mates Riecken and Molon second and third respectively. [Ian Harrison collection]

impossible unless some drivers were flagged off before completion of the full distance. If this happened the already severely reduced field would be even more depleted for the second day, but if slower drivers were not flagged off the race would have to continue on roads which were illegally closed or unsafely opened. Examination of the results shows that Frank Clement completed his eighth lap at 3.39pm but Joseph Rutsch, A.J. Hancock and Cecil Bianchi were still racing at 4.00pm and for some time after that. The possible solution was that the roads opening car started to lap the course before 4pm, as soon as the last car had started its eighth lap although the entire course was not open at 4pm. Nobody seemed to mind, however, and Chief Constable Madoc fudged the issue in his daily log by recording "We kept the roads closed as long as possible and opened them at 4pm" and commenting that the day's racing went "very well".

Interim Classification at the End of the First Day.

1. Kenelm Lee Guinness (Sunbeam), 5hrs 15mins 47secs (57.00mph)
2. Algernon Lee Guinness (Sunbeam), 5hrs 18mins 57secs (56.44mph)
3. Jean Porporato (Minerva), 5hrs 31mins 9secs (54.36mph)
4. C. Riecken (Minerva), 5hrs 32mins 28secs (54.14mph)
5. R.S. ("Dick") Witchell (Straker-Squire), 5hrs 33mins 57secs (53.90mph)
6. Leon Molon (Minerva) (Minerva), 5hrs 41mins 51secs (52.65mph)
7. Sam Wright (Humber), 6hrs 6mins 39secs (49.09mph)
8. F.T. Burgess (Humber), 6hrs 7mins 3secs (49.04mph)
9. W.O. Bentley (D.F.P.), 6hrs 13mins 20secs (48.21mph)
10. Frank Clement (Straker-Squire), 6hrs 19mins 25secs (47.44mph)
11. Joseph Rutsch (Adler), 6hrs 42mins 59secs (44.07mph)
12. A.J. Hancock (Vauxhall), 7hrs 3mins 53secs (42.46mph)
13. Cecil Bianchi Crossley), 7hrs 18mins 14secs (41.07mph).

1914 Tourist TrophyRace – The Second Day

The weather was again good and there were even bigger crowds than on Wednesday. After a 7.15am course inspection, the re-start took place at 9.00am. The cars were started in the order of classification at the end of the first day and, again at the suggestion of *The Motor*, the starting interval was increased to three minutes to take account of the fact that almost half of the field had retired. After being given the starting signal, every crew pushed its car to its pit to take on fuel, oil and water and to carry out repairs. Although pushing of cars was prohibited by the regulations, a blind eye appears to have been taken. The cars remained at their pits for times varying from 3mins 21secs (Witchell's Straker-Squire) to 53mins 49secs (Hancock's Vauxhall). Hancock and his mechanic had to fit a new water manifold, a new carburettor, new plugs, and a new magneto after which the car left the pit with a misfire. Bill Guinness took 6mins 9secs at his pit while Algie took 6mins 45secs. Both their Sunbeams had problems with their brakes which were not releasing properly as the fulcrum pin was over-tight. The solution was to fit each car with a cable and pulley assembly to enable the mechanics to pull on the lever when required. Bill Guinness thought that this was "quite brainy" but later agreed with *The Motor* that it did

With Kate's Cottage in the background, A.J. Hancock's Vauxhall negotiates the corner at Creg-na-Baa. Poor preparation meant a difficult race for the Vauxhall team with 1908 TT winner William Watson and Joseph Higginson both retiring on lap 1 and Hancock crashing near the Bungalow during the final lap. [National Motor Museum]

not work well. The Minervas all took on 10 gallons of oil, causing *The Autocar* to express "astonishment on finding our wildest estimates exceeded". There was also trouble in the Minerva team when Riecken announced at the last moment his intention to push his car to its limit despite all hazards and despite the rest of the team wanting all three cars to finish. After much discussion, Porporato's tact and diplomacy resolved the difficulty.

Bill Guinness completed lap 9 with a lap of 45mins 48secs, including his pit stop, while Clement (who had a bad double skid on the corner from Ballanard Road onto Bray Hill) and Hancock were still at their pits, the latter now over three hours behind the leading Sunbeam. Bill's growing time of 6 hours 1min 35secs gave him a lead of 4mins 35secs over his brother Algie who had lapped in 47mins 23secs before stopping at his pit to loosen hisbrakes and take on oil. During this lap Porporato dropped from third to fifth with a 49mins 12secs lap giving a growing time of 6 hours 20mins 21secs. Riecken was up to third (6 hours 19mins 33secs) and Witchell to fourth (6hours 19mins 47secs). Molon remained sixth, ten minutes behind Porporato.

On lap 10, Clement retired his Straker-Squire at Ramsey with a piston through the cylinder head. At the end of the lap, the order was unchanged. The times of the Guinness brothers were 6 hours 39mins 51secs and 6 hours 47mins 22secs respectively but Riecken and Witchell were tied for third place, sharing a cumulative time of 6 hours 59mins 37secs. Witchell gained 1min 19secs on Porporato. Algie Guinness stopped again at his pit on completing the lap.

Lap 11 brought two more retirements. Burgess' Humber had a seized piston at Sulby Bridge and Rutsch's Adler blew a cylinder at Union Mills. The Guinness brothers were still

Passing Kate's Cottage, Frank Clement's Straker Squire descends the hill towards Creg-na-Baa. He retired at Ramsey on lap 10 with a broken piston. [John Watterson collection]

The Humber of F.T. Burgess turns out of Johnny Watterson's Lane into Ballanard Road at Willaston corner, followed by Dick Witchell's Straker-Squire. Burgess retired at Sulby Bridge on lap 11 with a seized piston and Witchell went on to finish fourth. [National Motor Museum]

first and second, with times of 7 hours 18mins 18secs and 7 hours 28mins 57secs. With a growing time of 7 hours 38mins 52secs, Riecken moved ahead of Witchell by 11 seconds but otherwise the order was unchanged.

On lap 12, Bianchi retired his Crossley, leaving nine cars still running. After completing the lap Witchell's engine died about 400 yards past the pits. He stopped, found that the fuel pipe was broken, and sent his mechanic back on foot to the pit for a replacement. There was no spare but Louis Coatalen sportingly (if illegally) supplied a pipe and some wire from the Sunbeam pit, enabling Witchell to continue. At three-quarters distance, the Sunbeams were still first and second. Kenelm Lee Guinness' time was 7 hours 57mins 6secs and he led his brother Algernon by 12mins 33secs. Riecken's Minerva was still third, a further 8mins 2secs back and now leading Witchell's Straker-Squire by 2mins 9secs. The other Minervas of Porporato and Molon were fifth and sixth, with Porporato 42secs behind Witchell and 18mins 3secs ahead of Molon. Wright's Humber, Bentley's DFP and Hancock's Vauxhall occupied the final three places.

Algie Guinness stopped at Ballacraine for over five minutes on lap 13. He then continued, now relying solely on his handbrake, but made the fastest Mountain climb of the entire race, in a time of 7mins 3.2secs (55.28mph), compared with his brother's fastest time of 7mins 10secs (55.10mph) on the previous day. Soon afterwards his universal joint finally seized on the approach to Creg-ny-Baa. He managed to take the corner with a piece of superb driving, steering one-handed while pulling on the cord

Cecil Bianchi, a veteran of the 1905 Gordon Bennett Trial, made his first TT appearance in 1914 at the wheel of the sole Crossley in the race which had a virtually standard engine and chassis. He retired on lap 12. [Brian Mylchreest collection]

The Sunbeam of Sir Algernon Lee Guinness passes Ballacraine Farm, the appearance of which has changed surprisingly little in 100 years. Second to his younger brother Kenelm at the end of the first day, he retired on lap 13 at Hillberry with a seized universal joint. [Stan Hughes collection]

After a troubled race, due to poor preparation affecting all three Vauxhalls, Hancock's car finally came right and he decided to show what it could do. Sadly, due to weakened dampers causing excessive roll, the car went off the road approaching the Bungalow and overturned. Mechanic George Gibbs was critically injured but recovered. [Brian Mylchreest collection]

connected to the foot brake on his side in order to get braking action on one wheel. He then coasted to Hillberry to retire after a fantastic drive in which he had held second place for more than three-quarters of the race.

Lap 13 also saw the second and more serious crash of the race. After suffering various problems and stopping to change a magneto, A.J. Hancock was driving his Vauxhall very hard in an effort to break the lap record. Nearing the Bungalow, he lost control of the car due to weakening dampers which caused the car to roll excessively. The car mounted the grass verge, broke through the roadside fence and overturned several times on the mountainside. A doctor was sent from the Bungalow and reported that Hancock was not seriously injured but that the condition of mechanic George Gibbs was critical. He had head injuries and fractures of the jaw and one leg. A car was sent from Ramsey with a doctor and stretcher party to take Gibbs and Hancock to hospital in Douglas, and marshals flagged down Dick Witchell, who had to stay behind the doctor's car until it reached the crash site. This delayed Witchell for some six minutes, costing him third place. On completion of the lap, Bill Guinness' cumulative time was 8 hours 36mins 40secs. Riecken was second, 19mins 19secs back following Algie Guinness' retirement and Porporato moved up to third, 3mins 43secs behind his team-mate. Molon was now fourth, 20mins 8secs behind the second Minerva and Witchell was down to fifth, 45 seconds behind Molon after his delay. Sam Wright's Humber was sixth and Bentley seventh.

Wright retired at Quarterbridge on lap 14. His was the final retirement, leaving the first five in the same order as at the end of lap 13 with Bentley's DFP sixth and last. Guinness, with an aggregate time of 9 hours 17mins 31secs, now led Riecken by 17mins 58secs with Porporato 4mins 45secs further back, and leading Molon by 20mins 51secs. Molon in turn was 32 seconds ahead of Witchell, with Bentley trailing by a further 50mins 10secs. The order was now settled, barring problems, with huge gaps between the first three, and the only real question was whether Witchell could re-pass Molon.

The order remained unchanged at the end of the penultimate lap. Guinness (9 hours 57mins 12secs) had a comfortable lead of 18mins 47secs over Riecken, who stopped for 2 minutes to change a rear tyre. Porporato was now slowing with engine trouble and was 19mins 39secs behind Riecken. Molon was a further 7mins 15secs back and his lead over Witchell was now down to 6 seconds. As Guinness passed the grandstand to start his last lap, a spectator shouted "You have nothing to do but win now".

The 16th and final lap was uneventful except for the enthusiastic cheering of the winner everywhere on the

Spectators cheer Kenelm Lee Guinness as he passes the Bungalow on his victorious last lap. He led on every lap of the 16 lap race but his was the only Sunbeam to finish with Dario Resta retiring at Ramsey with a big end problem on the first lap and Algernon Lee Guinness retiring at Hillberry on lap 13 with a seized universal joint. [John Watterson collection]

Dick Witchell's Straker-Squire passes through Kirk Michael village. Driving one of the fastest cars, he was third and challenging Riecken's Minerva for second going into the last lap. Then, reduced to a crawl on the Mountain behind a doctor's car going to Hancock's crash, he lost his place to Molon's Minerva – by thirty seconds. [National Motor Museum]

course. Slowed by brake problems, Kenelm Lee Guinness took the flag at 2.22pm, after leading on every lap, in a time of 10 hours 37mins 49secs (56.44mph). Riecken brought the first Minerva home 19mins 49.2secs later with his team-mate Leon Molon third, 24mins 41.8secs behind. Dick Witchell slowed but finished only 30.4secs behind Molon. He was desperately unlucky to lose third by such a small margin after being baulked by another driver on the first lap, the delay with the broken fuel pipe and the further delay due to Hancock's accident. Porporato was fifth, finishing 17mins 54.2secs after Witchell, on three cylinders with a broken oil pipe. Bentley's superb drive in the little DFP brought him the final place with a very creditable average of 48.38mph but, as he later remarked, the irony of his effort was that the outbreak of war deprived him of the benefit of the sales which would otherwise have followed his success. Minerva, the only team to finish intact, won the team prize after an impressive display of speed and reliability. In the whole of

Kenelm Lee Guinness' Sunbeam is seen turning from Ballaquayle Road into Somerset Road on the way from the finish line to the enclosure. [John Watterson collection]

the six hundred miles the team stopped only once for replenishments. The Sunbeams stopped twice and others more than twice.

The Sunbeam team was welcomed back to the Fort Anne Hotel with a three gun salute and celebrated their victory with an impromptu dinner given by Louis Coatalen at the hotel, prior to the prize presentation at the Palace Ballroom on Douglas Promenade. Kenelm Lee Guinness drove along the Promenade in his winning car, draped with Union Flags and heliotrope ribbons, and with the six team mechanics sitting on the bonnet. At the gates of the Palace, Guinness was garlanded before being carried shoulder-high into the ballroom which was packed with 5,000 fans who sang "For He's a Jolly Good Fellow". Guinness said "I think it's the most glorious day I have ever had" and, referring to the Sunbeam, "It is a real pleasure to drive such a car. It is a wonderful production".

1914 Tourist Trophy Race Results

Wednesday/Thursday 10th/11th June 1914. Start 9.00am.16 laps of 37.5 miles circuit, total distance 600 miles. 22 starters, 6 finishers.

1. Kenelm Lee Guinness (Sunbeam) 10hrs 37mins 49secs (56.44mph)
2. C. Riecken (Minerva) 10hrs 57mins 38.2secs (54.74mph)
3. Leon Molon (Minerva) 11hrs 22mins 20secs (52.76mph)
4. R.S. ("Dick") Witchell (Straker-Squire) 11hrs 22mins 50.4secs (52.75mph)
5. Jean Porporato (Minerva) 11hrs 40mins 44.6secs (51.37mph)
6. W.O. Bentley (DFP) 12hrs 24mins 1.2secs (48.38mph)

Fastest lap:
Kenelm Lee Guinness (Sunbeam) 37mins 55secs (59.34mph)
Team Award: Minerva

Henry Edmunds Trophy (fastest average speed on the 16 ascents of the Mountain road): Kenelm Lee Guinness (Sunbeam) 53.43mph

Retirements:
Lap 1:
William Watson (Vauxhall) broken crankshaft, Crosby
Joseph Higginson (Vauxhall), stripped oil pipe union, Lezayre
Dario Resta (Sunbeam), sheared big end bolt, Ramsey
Lap 2:
W.G. Tuck (Humber) broken valve, Ramsey
Otto Goebel (Adler) gear trouble, Creg-ny-Baa
Philip Stapp (Adler) engine trouble, Creg-ny-Baa
Lap 3:
Rene Berger (S.A.V.A.) broken crankshaft, Ramsey
Lap 5:
Robert Crossman (Star), water leak
Lap 7:
Richard Lisle (Star), crash at Ballaugh Bridge
Lap 10:
Frank Clement (Straker-Squire) broken piston, Ramsey
Sam Wright (Humber) broken valve, Quarterbridge
Lap 11:
F.T. Burgess (Humber) seized piston, Sulby Bridge
Joseph Rutsch (Adler) cylinder blown out, Union Mills
Lap 12:
Cecil Bianchi (Crossley)
Lap 13:
A.J. Hancock (Vauxhall) crash near Bungalow
Algernon Lee Guinness (Sunbeam) broken universal joint, Hillberry

Reaction

The Hon. Harry Lawson MP, Editor of the Daily Telegraph, made a speech at the prize presentation thanking the Manx people for their hospitality, their welcoming attitude to motorists, and the Island's contribution to British services. He said that the race was the first real road race in the British Isles for real racing machines and naturally it had improved the breed and strengthened the make. There had been a great deal of splendid progress and he congratulated the drivers on their magnificent skill, nerve and endurance.

There was no doubt that the race had been successful. It had attracted a great deal of positive publicity in contrast to the controversy of 1908, and the Daily Telegraph sponsorship brought unparalleled national newspaper coverage. Many technical lessons would benefit the motor industry to a much greater extent than the previous TT races had done and would also prove beneficial to the forthcoming war effort.

Immediately after the race the Daily Telegraph proposed a TT in 1915 with a 2,000cc capacity limit. *The Autocar* praised the RAC "for its courage in having given the British public a frank road race for motor cars without blinking the fact and one the quality of which has not been exceeded elsewhere" and echoed the Telegraph suggestion of a 2,000cc TT in 1915 but went further by proposing a three days marathon of nine laps per day with a total distance of 1,012.5 miles.

The Isle of Man Government quickly revoked the ban on Sunday motoring during TT periods, resolving a row with the Auto-Cycle Union, which had been so incensed over the issue that it had threatened to take the motorcycle TT to Ireland but now announced that it would organise its 1915 event on the Island. The A-CU also confirmed an earlier report that on 24th September 1914 it would organise a new International Cyclecar TT for three and four wheeled light cars of up to 1,100cc and 385lbs minimum weight, on the 15.8 miles St. John's circuit used for the motorcycle TT races from 1907 to 1910. The RAC was less quick off the mark – on 6th August 1914, two days after Britain declared war on Germany, The Auto-Motor Journal announced that it had decided not to hold the TT on the Island in 1915.

In early September the A-CU announced the postponement of the Cyclecar TT but said it intended to hold the race as soon as possible. Sadly, the war was not "all over by Christmas" as some optimists predicted, the Cyclecar TT was the TT that never was, there was no more TT racing until the motorcycle TT resumed in 1920 and no TT for motorcars until 1922.

1922 Tourist Trophy – Chassagne's "Nightmare In A Sea Of Mud"

Planning

After the end of the Great War in November 1918, recession and reconstruction inevitably delayed the resumption of motorsport. There was little activity until 1920 when Brooklands re-opened after war-time damage had been repaired. 1920 also saw the first post-war motorcycle TT and the opening of the Le Mans circuit, which was to stage the 1921 French Grand Prix and its first 24 hours race in 1923.

In April 1921 the RAC applied to the Highway Board for a Road Closing Order for a TT Race over three days in June 1922. The Board was unhappy about road closures on three consecutive days and suggested two days (a Tuesday and a Thursday) in June 1922 and a further day for a race for light cars in September 1922. The RAC did not consider a light car race practicable but accepted the two days in June. This renewed pre-war tensions between the A-CU and the Isle of Man Government, with the A-CU believing that the RAC was being given preference and considering taking its TT to Belgium. It was not practicable for motorcycles to race on the course after cars because of ruts and other damage which the cars would cause. Therefore the A-CU, faced with completing practising and racing before the end of May when daylight for morning practices would be limited, asked for the car TT to be held one week later. With neither party entirely happy, it was agreed that the final motorcycle race would be on 2nd June and the car race on 20th and 22nd June. The RAC also agreed to a course variation involving the deletion of the section from Cronk-ny-Mona via Edge's Corner, Cronk-y-Berry, Willaston and Ballanard Road to Bray Hill and the substitution of a new section from Cronk-ny-Mona via Signpost Corner, Governor's Bridge and Glencrutchery Road to Bray Hill. This would involve moving the start/finish and pits from the 1914 site at the crossroads at the top of Bray Hill to an area on Glencrutchery Road alongside the Douglas Borough Cemetery where the A-CU had established a new start/finish, grandstand, pits and scoreboard in 1921. The variation increased the lap distance to 37.75 miles. The Highway Board agreed to carry out extensive road repairs, especially between Ramsey and the Bungalow.

The RAC decided on a three litres limit with a minimum weight of 1,600lbs. The capacity limit was surprising not only because of the 1914 proposal to reduce it to two litres for 1915 but also because the Grand Prix formula had been reduced from three litres to two litres for 1922. What was not surprising was that the race did not attract many entries, with three cars each from only three manufacturers – Bentley, Sunbeam and Vauxhall. It was suggested that the RAC had not realised that the formula had been changed for 1922 and it appeared also that the Vauxhalls had been built under the misapprehension that the three litres formula had another year to run. Sunbeam still had their 1921 Grand Prix cars and W.O. Bentley had his experimental prototype three litre touring cars.

Obviously only nine cars would provide a poor spectacle and the RAC proposed two additional races. One was a Light Car Race to be run concurrently with the eight lap TT race but over six laps and open to cars of up to 1,500cc with a minimum weight of 1,000lbs. The other race, to be run separately, would be a "Sportsman's Cup" over five laps for bona fide amateurs driving their own three or four wheeled cars of up to 1,600cc, with amateur mechanics. The Highway Board approved both races, as did the local motorcycling community, represented by the Manx Motor Cycle Club. This was where Manx politics came into play. The MMCC supported the amateur car race because it wanted to organise its own Amateur TT motorcycle race over the Mountain Course in September 1922. The A-CU had refused to grant a permit for such a race because it disliked the idea of the TT title being attached to an amateur race organised by a Manx club and saw the race as a potential threat to the A-CU TT. The local farming community was also opposed to a September race, as in the early days of the RAC TT. Because of the farmers' opposition to the amateur motorcycle race, Lieutenant-Governor Sir William Fry refused to approve the amateur car race because he knew that if he approved an amateur race for cars he could hardly refuse an amateur race for motorcycles.

Fry's refusal caused consternation and a threat of

resignation by the Highway Board. It was unfortunate for Julian Orde (now Sir Julian) that Lord Raglan's days as Governor had ended in 1919 and, although he rushed to the Island to meet his cousin's successor, he could not persuade Fry to change his mind.

Media criticism was immediate and strident. The *Isle of Man Times* – its Editor George Brown being a leading light in the Manx Motor Cycle Club – said that the Sportsman's Cup could attain a greater importance than the TT itself and that the race could go to Ireland if the Isle of Man did not support it. He accused the Governor of "a huge tactical blunder" and of unwarranted interference. The *Isle of Man Examiner* accused the Governor of "taking a step which was virtually a veto on an important decision of the Legislature" and pointed out, prophetically, that the RAC had just returned the car TT to the Island and, if the Government was disagreeable and dictatorial, it might not come back. Finally, at a meeting of his Executive Council on 21st May, the Governor relented and a majority voted in favour of the race although they still opposed the September motorcycle race, which Tynwald rejected in July.

After all the controversy, the Sportsman's Cup did not attract support from competitors, perhaps due to shortness of preparation time or expense, and was cancelled. The RAC then reduced the event to one day, Thursday 22nd June, when the TT and the International 1,500cc Trophy Race would be run concurrently over eight laps and six laps respectively. A hill-climb from Hillberry to Kepple Gate, which the Manx Automobile Club proposed to run on Friday 23rd June, was also cancelled when only seven entries were received by the closing date.

The return of car racing attracted some opposition, principally from Sir Hall Caine, the leading Victorian author whose home was on the course, at Greeba Castle. He loved cars but deplored racing and questioned the power of the legislature to deny public access to the roads.

Practising was to take place over two weeks from 4.30am to 7.00am on weekdays and, for the first time, the roads were to be closed for practices as well as races. Cars were to leave the course at Hillberry, after which they were subject to a 20mph speed limit when driven on the open roads.

In obtaining road closures for practising, the RAC was ahead of the A-CU which was unable to achieve this until 1928, after Archie Birkin (brother of racing driver Sir Henry "Tim" Birkin) was killed in an early morning practice in 1927 when he fell from his motorcycle at Rhencullen while swerving to avoid a collision with a fish van travelling in the opposite direction. In other respects, however, contemporary comparisons of the respective organisations were unfavourable to the RAC. The *Isle of Man Times* commented: "One missed the military precision of the A-C.U." Although motorcycle practising still took place on open roads the circuit was always well marshalled and controlled, while car practice arrangements were allegedly haphazard, with drivers allowed to start and finish wherever they wished. For example, the Bentley team was based at the Prince of Wales Hotel on Ramsey's South Promenade and started from the town, while the Vauxhall team could start from their base at White House, Kirk Michael.

In apparent acceptance of deficiencies in their practice arrangements, which consisted of little more than telephone links to Post Offices on the course and supervision by occasional police officers, the RAC turned to the Manx Motor Cycle Club, which organised the marshalling of the motorcycle TT, with a request for the Club to organise marshalling for the car TT also. The MMCC readily agreed to work with the Manx Automobile Club as agents of the RAC on a joint rota for both practices and race day, but the RAC felt unable to agree that the MMCC should have total control over competitors when organising the practices, as was the case when the MMCC organised practices for the A-CU. This created an impasse and the event was the loser.

Yet further tensions emerged when the RAC declined to accept corner warning signs erected by the A-CU, although most car drivers preferred these to the 1914 RAC overhead banners, and insisted that the A-CU signs be taken down and the old banners re-erected. The reason given was that the overhead banners would be clear of dust clouds but a critic said "They are by no means as effective and moreover are exceedingly dangerous if they fall down or blow down or disappear altogether as they have in the past".

Entries

Soon after the end of the war W.O. Bentley began to prepare for the manufacture of his own cars, with the intention of racing in the TT as soon as it resumed. He assembled a team of skilled engineers and drivers. These included Fred Burgess, the designer of the 1914 TT Humber which closely resembled the 1913 Peugeot Grand Prix car, as would the dimensions of the first Bentley chassis. The 1914 TT Straker-Squire drivers Frank Clement (a war-time aero engine tester) and Dick Witchell (a friend of Bentley at Clifton College) became Development Manager and Works Manager respectively. Roy Fedden, another of Bentley's Clifton friends who had built aero engines during the war, was engaged to manufacture parts much more quickly than others could offer. On the workshop wall there was a D.F.P. advertising poster depicting "W.O." driving his DFP on the Mountain road during the 1914 TT and Leslie Pennal, a young mechanic who had worked for Bentley & Bentley and aspired to be a riding mechanic, evoked the team spirit when he recalled "I used to look at this picture and dream – how wonderful it would be, if it ever came to that...I suppose it was part of that dream that made me so enthusiastic to stay overtime and work at every opportunity".

Bentley made ambitious plans to enter a car in the 1922 Indianapolis 500 race in the U.S.A. and three cars in the TT. Bentley and Clement were to drive in the TT and their riding mechanics were to be Leslie Pennal, living the dream inspired by the DFP poster, and Arthur Saunders respectively. Douglas Hawkes was to drive at Indianapolis with Bertie Browning as mechanic and also drive the third TT car if he were able to return from the U.S.A. in time. The possibility that they might not be back in time prompted Bentley to seek a reserve driver. Initially he nominated Arthur Hillstead, but this upset others who felt they had a prior claim whereupon Bentley decided to seek the best possible driver. He deputed Frank Clement to undertake the embarrassing task of approaching Malcolm Campbell who, while "quite nice about it" as Clement recalled, made it clear that he would accept a definite drive or no drive. Fortunately, Hawkes and Browning, having finished 13th and last at Indianapolis, were back in Liverpool two days after the start of practice and on the Island in time to take part. The cars were almost standard touring cars with four cylinder 2,996cc engines with four valves per cylinder but had special carburettors, high compression pistons, smaller and flatter radiators than the touring cars and outside exhaust systems. The total cost of the modifications was £25 per car. The bodies were special two-seaters with streamlined tails, like the Indianapolis car. A major disadvantage was that the cars had only rear wheel brakes whereas the Sunbeams and Vauxhalls had brakes on all four wheels.

After testing at Brooklands the team cars were painted cream with scarlet chassis. The cream paint, applied two days before leaving for the Island, failed to dry and was cleaned off with petrol and undercoated, with the top coat applied on the Island. There was also a practice car, EXP2, which could be cannibalised for spares as required.

The blue-grey (described as "dreadnought grey" in the Isle of Man Highway Board registration records) 1921 Sunbeam Grand Prix cars were the clear favourites. They had straight-eight engines with four valves per cylinder, designed by Louis Coatalen. The drivers were 1914 TT winner Kenelm Lee Guinness, Parisian born and Wolverhampton resident Jean Chassagne and Major Henry Segrave. The team also had the use of a new 1922 four-cylinder two litre Grand Prix car which Chassagne was to drive in the French Grand Prix at Strasbourg. The cars had three layers of spring steel round the spokes of the steering wheels to cushion the drivers' hands from road shock and the mechanics had small floor-mounted levers to adjust the front and rear brakes.

The vivid scarlet (initially light green) Vauxhalls, designed by chief designer C.E. King, had four cylinder double overhead camshaft engines designed by Harry Ricardo with four valves per cylinder and a claimed power output of 110bhp at 4,500rpm running on a petrol and alcohol mixture which emitted a distinctive aroma. The brakes were actuated by compressed air. In testing at Brooklands, 100mph had been achieved. The drivers, all 1914 TT riding mechanics, were repair shop foreman Matthew Park, finished vehicles foreman Oswald Payne and road test department foreman Ernest Swain. TT veteran driver A.J. Hancock was in charge of the team and clearly lessons had been learnt from 1914 when poor race preparation had ruined the team's chances. This time

Both Henry Segrave (left) and Kenelm Lee Guinness were unfortunate in being unable to take advantage of their Sunbeams' superiority. Segrave retired on lap five after leading for the first three laps while Guinness was a last minute non-starter with clutch slip. [Brian Mylchreest collection]

Pre-race "weighing in" and technical inspections took place in Lake Road, Douglas. The Vauxhall team is depicted outside the Railway Hotel, awaiting their turn. The drivers were Oswald Payne (5), Matthew Park (2) and Ernest Swain (8). [Ray Stanfield collection]

they arrived early with well-prepared cars, a spare car, a lorry, a road car and a motorcycle.

There were 11 entries for the 1500cc Trophy Race. Talbot-Darracq, Bugatti and Aston Martin each entered three cars while Hillman and Enfield-Allday each entered one.

The blue Talbot-Darracqs, similar to the pre-war Darracqs and, like the Sunbeams, designed by Louis Coatalen were to be driven by Sir Algernon Guinness (replacing Rene Thomas), Albert Divo (a war-time pilot in the French Air Force) and Jean Moriceau. Said to be tricky to handle and called "roller skates" by some, the cars had very noisy exhausts but they had four wheel brakes and Algie Guinness reached 90mph at 4,000rpm on Sulby straight.

The yellow Bugattis, 2cwt lighter than the Talbot-Darracqs but with two wheel brakes, were sometimes called Crossley-Bugattis (and were so registered with the Isle of Man Highway Board), as Ettore Bugatti had arranged for Crossley Motors Ltd of Manchester to build 16-valve cars under licence. A later suggestion that there would not have been time for Crossley to have produced the cars which were raced in the Island, and that actually these cars were built at the Bugatti factory in Molsheim, is confirmed by a contemporary report in the *Mona's Herald* of 21st June 1922 that the cars were sent direct to the Island from France. They were registered on the Island

Quarterbridge was a popular meeting place for hot drinks, photographs and autographs at the end of morning practices. The Talbot-Darracq team of Albert Divo (31) Sir Algernon Lee Guinness (24) and Jean Moriceau (28) pose with the TT Sunbeams of Kenelm Lee Guinness and Henry Segrave visible behind. [Stenlake Publishing]

This early morning Quarterbridge photograph shows the Bugatti team of Mones Maury (27), Bertram Marshall (30) and Pierre de Vizcaya (22) alongside an ambulance. [Stenlake Publishing]

on 15th June 1922, not having been registered in England. The original nominated drivers were E. Frederich, Pierre de Vizcaya and Bertram Marshall. Later, the Marquis de Casca Maury (known as Mones Maury), a Spanish nobleman who had enlisted in the Royal Flying Corps on the outbreak of war, was nominated in place of Frederich, but there was doubt until the last minutes whether de Vizcaya and Maury would both come to the Island as one or both might have to stay in France to prepare for the French Grand Prix. Leon Cushman was therefore nominated as a replacement and actually practised but de Vizcaya and Maury both arrived and raced, with Maury replacing Cushman after the latter crashed at The Nook during practice.

The three light green Aston Martins were to be driven by Count Louis Zborowski, Kensington Moir and Clive Gallop. In fact the TT cars were not ready and only "Bertie" Moir arrived, with his old Brooklands racing car known as "Bunny".

The single bright peacock blue Enfield-Allday for A.C. Bertelli was said to have been built specially for the TT. It had an overhead valve engine and four wheel brakes, although the front brakes were removed on the last day of practice. It was regarded as a dark horse.

George Bedford's Hillman, known as "Heluva 1", with polished aluminium finish was expected to perform well and appeared to have been well prepared.

The Sunbeams, Talbot Darracqs, Crossley-Bugattis and the Enfield-Allday were all registered with the Isle of Man Highway Board.

Practice

Most, but not all, teams were based in Douglas. Sunbeam headquarters were at the Fort Anne Hotel as in 1914. Talbot-Darracq was also based there but there was insufficient garage accommodation for both, which meant that the team had to use a shed behind the hotel, fronting on Douglas Head Road, where their activities were open to scrutiny by passers-by and overnight security was a major concern. Bugatti was based at the Falcon Cliff hotel in Douglas and Hillman and Enfield-Allday had sheds in the town.

The Bentley headquarters was the Prince of Wales Hotel on the South Promenade in Ramsey, where mechanics returning late from nights out with local girls slept in W.O. Bentley's road car which was parked outside, sharing the car with W.O.'s pet Blenheim spaniel. The race cars were garaged in a coach-house close to the harbour, near to which Aston Martin had a shed.

The Vauxhall team was comfortably accommodated at the White House, a country mansion at Kirk Michael which was the home of Joseph Mylchreest, who was in partnership with his brother Harold at the Athol Motor Garage in Douglas. The Mylchreest brothers were sons of Joseph Mylchreest, known as "the Diamond King" due to his mining career in South Africa. They had assisted W.O. Bentley with his DFP in 1914 and drove Bentley's practice car as the official roads opening car in 1922. The team

The Bentley team headquarters was the Prince of Wales Hotel on Ramsey's South Promenade. Left to right are W.O. Bentley's touring car, W.O. Bentley and mechanic Leslie Pennal (9), Douglas Hawkes and mechanic Bert Browning (6), Frank Clement and mechanic Arthur Saunders (3) and the team's practice car Exp. No. 2. [Brian Mylchreest collection]

Race day photographs show drivers taking Ramsey Hairpin slowly and carefully in the atrocious conditions but in this practice picture, taken in dry and dusty conditions, Frank Clement applies opposite lock as his Bentley slides dramatically. [R and L Kelly collection]

flew the Vauxhall Griffin flag from the White House flag pole and, according to *The Autocar*, the drivers spent their spare time shooting rooks in the estate rookery, accounting for over fifty by the end of their stay.

The weather for practising was mostly dry, sunny and windy. The bumpy condition of the course caused problems for most teams. Bentley had to strengthen everything and replaced rivets with bolts with castellated nuts and split pins. When a clutch seized, W.O. ordered the removal of all of them for adjustment. The Bugattis were ill-prepared, ill-equipped and had not been properly tested. Their brakes did not suit the course and there was a nasty incident at The Nook, above Governor's Bridge, when Cushman rolled his Bugatti and was trapped underneath with his mechanic. He said that a tyre had burst but disagreed with witnesses as to whether this was the cause or the result of his loss of control. The mechanic suffered head injuries. Bertram Marshall showed de Vizcaya and Maury the way round the course, but both lost their way on the next lap. Nevertheless, de Vizcaya managed a lap in forty minutes. Segrave bent one of his Sunbeam's wheels, and Vauxhalls suffered a damaged front wheel at Governor's Bridge and a bent rear axle near Ramsey.

There was no official timing during practising and there were many rumours of lap times as low as 28 minutes! Segrave, driving a Sunbeam which was higher geared than the others, was more credibly said to have done the fastest practice lap of some 35 minutes, with Vauxhalls achieving 37 minutes and Bentleys 39 minutes. Concerned at his cars' speed disadvantage, Bentley sent to London for larger fuel tanks with the intention of completing the race without a re-fuelling stop. The fastest 1,500cc lap was reputedly set by Algie Guinness' Talbot-Darracq in 39 minutes. Bedford's Hillman, with no differential, was said to be one of the best cornering cars and to have managed a forty-minute lap. There was unofficial timing at Quarterbridge by courtesy of the *Isle of Man Times* and, because of this but more importantly because of an endless supply of hot drinks from the Quarterbridge Hotel by courtesy of Dunlop, Quarterbridge became the popular after-practice meeting point for drivers, teams, reporters and spectators, there being no facilities at the official start/finish area on Glencrutchery Road.

While there was discontent at the lack of official timing, there was a more serious complaint arising from the handling of Cushman's accident at The Nook. A motorcycle TT rider injured in a crash at the same corner had received attention within two minutes, whereas the release of Cushman and his mechanic took much longer, and the arrival of medical assistance was even further delayed. There was no marshal at the corner, but only a flagman who was not a first-aider. The nearest police officer was at Governor's Bridge but he had no first aid equipment. There was a telephone at Governor's Bridge but nobody to use it and a motorcycle TT marshal who happened to be there telephoned for assistance. While there was an ambulance at Quarterbridge there was no doctor and, when attempts were made to contact Quarterbridge, it was found that calls had to be passed through the timekeepers' box at the Grandstand where there was one telephone upstairs and one downstairs, but the official upstairs could not guarantee hearing the ring of the unmanned telephone downstairs. This episode caused embarrassment to the RAC when its organisation was unfavourably compared with the A-CU/MMCC organisation of the motorcycle practices. Shortly after this, the RAC ordered the re-erection of the A-CU warning signs, explaining that there was less dust because the roads had been tarred and sprayed with *Westrumite*.

Unusually in TT practising, but perhaps because the roads were legally closed for the first time, there were no reported incidents involving animals, although *The Autocar* reported: "Manx cats are unpopular, for somehow they are all out at 4am, and a Manx cat looks all wrong at that hour."

"Long Tom", a bookmaker well known at Brooklands who set up a stand in the TT paddock, offered 2 to 1 on Segrave to win. Other odds were 4 to 1 Chassagne and Clement, 8 to 1 Bentley and Park and 10 to 1 others. In the 1,500cc race Algie Guinness was 2 to 1, 4 to 1 Divo, 8 to 1 Bedford and Moir and 10 to 1 others. Despite being warned off by police, "Long Tom" was not averse to risk. He stayed at his post and no action was taken.

At the pre-race weighing-in all the cars were over the minimum weight. The regulations also required all drivers and mechanics to weigh at least 140lbs. All did, with the exception of Mones Maury (119lbs) and his mechanic (120lbs) so their Bugatti had to carry ballast to make up the difference.

1922 Tourist Trophy Race

The morning of race day brought the first rain for days, with wet and misty conditions reminiscent of 1907. After a course inspection at 8am the decision was made to start the race on schedule but the Sunbeam team caused consternation by arriving only ten minutes before the 9.30am start, without Kenelm Lee Guinness who was declared a non-starter. After an oil joint broke during practice, two big-end bearings were run and it was decided to change his engine. This work was completed in time, after an all-night effort but, when the engine was started on the morning of the race, the clutch was slipping badly, forcing him to withdraw. A similar problem had affected the practice car and, as with Rolls in 1905, there was a suggestion of sabotage but there was no evidence and, unlike Rolls, Guinness was not reported to have voiced any suspicions publicly.

Teams were unprepared for the conditions, and makeshift mudguards or "splash boards" were hastily made and fitted. On most cars these were on the driver's side only, leaving the mechanics unprotected from rain and mud, but the Vauxhalls had more substantial mudguards on both sides as well as rudimentary windscreen wipers, lever-operated by the mechanics. Tyre changes were hastily carried out with the Bentley team fitting steel-studded covers on the off-side front wheels of Frank Clement's and W.O. Bentley's cars but running out of time to fit them to Douglas Hawkes' car. Jean Chassagne changed ribbed tyres for a new "traction-tread" type of Dunlop Cord with skew notches on the tread, and was balancing his front wheels only ten minutes before he was due to start. Drivers also were unprepared, with

Henry Segrave is pictured on the starting grid in his Sunbeam. In the worst conditions his first lap was fastest of the race, 57.3 mph, and he led by two minutes. He stopped at Ramsey on lap five with magneto trouble. He re-started but, unable to climb the Mountain with only one magneto working, stopped finally above the Gooseneck. [Brian Mylchreest collection]

inadequate wet weather protection. Bentley did not even have a cap and found that mechanic Leslie Pennal's cap was much too small.

Cars were started at intervals of one minute, with the 3 litre TT cars starting before the 1,500cc Trophy entries. In Guinness' absence, Park led the field away from the start. In dreadful conditions: "The first two laps frightened me stiff", said Frank Clement later, Segrave passed both Clement and Park by Sulby and averaged 70mph to Ramsey. The Sunbeams' superiority was emphasised when Segrave completed the lap in 39mins 15secs (57.70mph), the fastest lap of the race and 2mins 10secs faster than Chassagne. The latter, however, was only 28secs faster than Bentley. Park was fourth with a time of 42mins 38secs but stopped at his pit for three minutes with his Vauxhall's engine sounding unhealthy. The order of the remaining cars was Clement (43mins 32secs), Payne

This picture of the rain-soaked starting grid shows the Vauxhalls of Matthew Park (2) and Oswald Payne (5) and the Bentleys of Frank Clement (3) and Walter Bentley (9). Park retired but Clement finished second, Payne third and Bentley fourth. [Brian Mylchreest collection]

Walter Owen Bentley, the sixth and final finisher in the 1914 TT in a D.F.P., returned with his own team in 1922. Finishing second (Frank Clement), fourth (W.O. Bentley) and fifth (Douglas Hawkes), the team won the team prize. [Brian Mylchreest collection]

(43mins 55secs), Hawkes (44mins 45secs) and Swain (45mins 33secs).

On lap 2, with wind and rain increasing, Park's Vauxhall retired at Ballig with engine trouble and Swain nearly ditched his Vauxhall at the Gooseneck. Hawkes was also in trouble when his radiator plug detached itself and his radiator lost all its coolant. After stopping on the Mountain he was able to return slowly to the pits, shouting "I want water!" "Nobody else wanted it – we were all wet through", the *Isle of Man Times* reporter commented drily. A replacement plug could not be found and, after more than twenty minutes, Hawkes continued with an improvised plug consisting of a beer cork, plasticine and insulating tape. A spare plug was found after he had gone. At the end of the lap Segrave still led with a growing time of 1 hour 19mins 24secs but with his lead over Chassagne reduced to 1min 49secs. Bentley was still third but his growing time of 1 hour 25mins 9secs was almost four minutes behind Chassagne. He led Clement by 16 seconds with the two remaining Vauxhalls of Swain and Payne respectively 3mins 30secs and 6mins 57secs further back. Hawkes, after his long stops, was still running but over 21 minutes behind Segrave.

The weather improved slightly on the third lap, with the ridges on the northern hills becoming visible from the Grandstand. Segrave finished the lap with a cumulative time of 1 hour 59mins 21secs, increasing his lead to 2mins 50secs. Segrave speeded up slightly but Chassagne's lap time of 40mins 58secs was 1min 10secs slower than his previous lap. Having passed Clement, Chassagne became involved in a duel with him as they passed and re-passed each other, with Chassagne having a slight advantage in speed and a great advantage in braking but with Clement cornering better. Bentley slowed, giving third place to Clement, and became involved in a battle with Swain, who had speeded up. Clement's growing time was 2 hours 6mins 28secs, 4mins 17secs behind Chassagne. Bentley was 3mins 23secs back, with Swain 12 seconds behind him. Payne was over five minutes behind Swain, with Hawkes 36 minutes further back.

On lap 4, said *The Autocar*, "the conditions touched the zenith of misery". Segrave was reported to have approached the Gooseneck at a crawl, unable to see where the corner was. During the lap he had to stop near Ballacraine for a wheel change due to a puncture and he stopped at his pit at the end of the lap to refuel, take on oil and water and substitute a new spare wheel for the one with the punctured tyre. His stop took 37 seconds. On completion of half the race distance, Chassagne led with a growing time of 2 hours 42mins 18secs, 44 seconds ahead of Segrave. Clement was still third, 4mins 20secs behind Segrave and 3mins 32secs ahead of Swain, who had passed

Approaching the Gooseneck in his Talbot-Darracq, Sir Algernon Lee Guinness is shown a warning flag, perhaps because of the obstruction caused by Segrave's Sunbeam which had retired a short distance above the corner. [Stan Hughes collection]

Bentley and led him by 3mins 49secs. Payne was still going, still sixth and 3mins 25secs behind Bentley. Hawkes was 39 minutes behind Payne.

On the fifth lap, with the rain clearing and visibility improving, Segrave stopped in Ramsey when one of his two four-cylinder magnetos cut out, the contact breaker having completely broken up. He re-started with four cylinders running off the other magneto but finally stopped on the Mountain climb where the gradient was too steep for his reduced power. Had he been able to reach the top, he could probably have driven slowly to the pits, fitted a new magneto and resumed the chase. His stationary car was narrowly missed by Clement, who was now second but seven minutes behind Chassagne. Then Clement found himself stuck behind one of the 1,500cc Bugattis. He said later "Two of the Bugs gave me no trouble but the third I followed for miles and the blessed mechanic wouldn't once look round. Mile after mile I tried to get by, and I felt round for a heavy spanner to throw at them but couldn't find anything likely to hurt enough. And there I was on half throttle with only Chassagne in front of me". Also on this lap Swain retired at Ballacraine with engine trouble, after an excellent drive which could have made him a challenger for second, leaving only five cars running, of which Payne's was the sole Vauxhall. Chassagne's growing time for five laps was 3 hours 21mins 47secs and his lead over Clement was 6mins 43secs. Bentley was back in third place from fifth, with a time of 3 hours 37mins 59secs. With a lead over Payne of nearly two minutes, Bentley was vulnerable, having discarded the sloping floorboard in front of the pedals, which had worked loose and was obstructing the pedals. This meant that he had to rest his feet on the pedals which soon caused cramp. A two gallon can of petrol had been attached to the board, and Pennal had to take the can between his knees. Bentley also lost his exhaust pipe, causing Pennal to be covered with soot and endangered by flashes of flame

W.O. Bentley passes the Central Hotel at the entrance to Ramsey's Parliament Square. "W.O." finished fourth and, with team-mates Frank Clement second and Douglas Hawkes fifth, Bentley Motors won the team prize and priceless publicity for the company. [R and L Kelly collection]

uncomfortably close to the two gallon petrol can! Hawkes was still running but well out of contention.

Chassagne made an excitable pit stop of almost three minutes at the start of lap 6, over-shooting the pit and having to push the car back, in marked contrast to Segrave's precise braking for his earlier stop. Water and fuel splashed everywhere, with Chassagne "talking volubly and gesticulating all the time". Coatalen warned him to take to take it easy but Clement had passed the troublesome Bugatti at last, had been signalled by his pit to hurry up, and was a possible threat. At the end of the lap Chassagne led on time by 4mins 15secs, with a growing time of 4 hours 4mins 48secs and, as Clement had started four minutes earlier, they were again in sight of each other at times and even passing and re-passing. Bentley held third, 11mins 36secs behind Clement and only 51 seconds ahead of Payne, while Hawkes was still last. The rain had stopped, the roads were drying, dust was becoming a problem and calcium chloride was affecting drivers' eyes. The Bentleys discarded their mudguards.

The order was unchanged at the end of lap 7. Chassagne's growing time was 4 hours 44mins 44secs and his lead over Clement was 4mins 30secs. Bentley was still ahead of Payne, but by only 32secs and, with Hawkes still running, the Bentley team was still complete.

Jean Chassagne completed his eighth and final lap in a time of 5 hours 24mins 50secs but, due to confusion, failed to stop. The original plan had been that the end of race flag would be yellow. This was later changed to blue but either Chassagne had not been told or there was a language problem. He was eventually stopped at Ballacraine, but continued to complete his ninth lap. After his fastest lap of the race, Frank Clement finished second, 4mins 9.6 seconds behind. In a magnificent effort, after being signalled to speed up, Clement had completed the last four laps in 54.4 seconds less than Chassagne, in improving conditions, driving a touring car in pursuit of a racing car. Oswald Payne was third, 14mins 45.6secs behind Clement and only six seconds ahead of Bentley, having gained 38 seconds on the last lap which, for both Payne and Bentley, was the fastest lap of the race. Bentley was unfortunate, as cramp in his legs must have made the last three laps particularly painful. Hawkes finished fifth, also setting his fastest lap but nearly 45 minutes behind Bentley, to secure the team prize for

Jean Chassagne's Sunbeam passes a flagman and two marshals at Hillberry during an early morning practice. In appalling race day conditions he was the winner of the last RAC Isle of Man Tourist Trophy race, beating Frank Clement's Bentley by more than four minutes. [Stan Hughes collection]

Oswald Payne takes a tight line at a wet and muddy Ramsey Hairpin. Payne finished third, splitting the Bentleys of Frank Clement and Walter Bentley. He was the only finisher in the Vauxhall team. [Stenlake Publishing]

Bentley Motors. This necessitated a quick visit by RAC officials to a Douglas jeweller's shop to obtain a team prize. They found a suitable trophy, intended for use as a cattle award at an agricultural show, and persuaded the jeweller to sell it. It is not known how it was inscribed but W.O. Bentley was happy to receive it.

Henry Segrave won the cup for fastest lap, presented by Birmingham motor agent Percy Evans.

Interviewed by *The Autocar* after the race, Jean Chassagne recalled his experience as "A nightmare in a sea of mud and most unpleasant rain". His success, he told *The Motor*, was due to "The car, its brakes – wonderful, wonderful! With good brakes you can take risks. Front wheel brakes are absolutely necessary. And servo brakes are even better. If the three-litre cars had been fitted with servo brakes they would have been two minutes per lap faster. I always start slowly and after a few laps do what is necessary".

1922 1,500cc Trophy Race

The 1500cc cars and drivers were no better prepared for the conditions than their TT counterparts. The Talbot-Darracqs had wire windscreens and tiny mudguards, only 12 x 6 inches, fixed to the off-side scuttles. Marshall's Bugatti had neither mudguards nor windscreens while the other team cars of de Vizcaya and Mones Maury at least had windscreens. Bertelli's Enfield-Allday and Moir's Aston Martin had no mudguards and the Aston Martin had smooth rear tyres. Moriceau changed his ribbed covers for a set with rubber studs and checked his front wheels' balance carefully.

The nine starters were reduced to six on the first lap. Kensington Moir, the first starter, retired his Aston Martin at Glen Helen with a broken inlet valve. Also at Glen Helen, Jean Moriceau caught Mones Maury's Bugatti but, in attempting to overtake at the top of the hill, his Talbot-Darracq slid in the mud. Almost simultaneously a tyre deflated, the car swung round and overturned. Three wheels were buckled, the car was out of the race and Talbot-Darracq was out of contention for the team prize. Luckily, Moriceau suffered only a few bruises and a cut lip and his mechanic was unhurt. Near Keppel Gate there was another lucky escape when George Bedford crashed his Hillman "Heluva 1" at about 80mph. Blinded by mud, he shouted to his mechanic to remove his goggles but with a wheel in a ditch, a tyre came off, the car went 200 yards down the hillside, broke a spring and lost its sump on a boulder before ending up on its wheels beside a stream. The mechanic, Bottrill, suffered a sprained ankle but Bedford escaped unhurt.

Earlier, Bedford's Hillman, Bertelli's Enfield-Allday and Algie Guinness' Talbot-Darracq were all reported to have caught Pierre de Vizcaya's Bugatti by Ramsey although the Bugatti had started one minute before Bedford, two minutes before Guinness and three minutes before Bertelli. Bertram Marshall, in the third Bugatti, was having trouble with a misfire. He had had an engine change on the previous day.

Guinness was the leader at the end of the lap, with a time of 41mins 35secs, and Albert Divo in the other surviving Talbot-Darracq was only ten seconds behind. Of the TT competitors, only the Grand Prix Sunbeams of Segrave and Chassagne were quicker than Guinness and Divo on that lap and Chassagne was only ten seconds faster than Guinness! The two Talbot Darracqs were followed by the Bugattis of Maury and de Vizcaya (44mins 16secs and 44mins 36secs respectively) and Bertelli's Enfield-Allday (46mins 48secs). Marshall, delayed by his misfire was last, nearly six minutes behind Bertelli.

On the second lap, Divo, half-blinded by mud and rain, had a serious skid at the Gooseneck but took the lead on corrected time when Guinness was slowed by a puncture on the Mountain. Bertelli stopped the Enfield-Allday at his pit to adjust his brakes, taking 30 seconds. On completion of the lap, Divo's growing time was 1 hour 23mins 35secs and he led Guinness by 3mins 40secs. Although he had been the last starter he was now third on the road, having passed everyone except Guinness and de Vizcaya, who was third on corrected time, only five seconds behind Guinness. He had great difficulty in passing de Vizcaya and almost crashed at Hillberry when he swerved from side to side in an unsuccessful attempt, throwing up his arms in despair. Eventually he succeeded but where and how is not recorded. Maury was fourth, 2mins 14secs behind de Vizcaya and 6mins 11secs ahead of fifth placed Bertelli. Marshall, still misfiring, was out of contention, 25 minutes behind the leader.

Divo slightly increased his lead over Guinness during lap 3 as the weather improved slightly. Marshall had a short stop below Creg-ny-Baa and Bertelli overshot at Signpost Corner, went up the escape road towards Onchan and reversed to re-join the course. Divo's time at half-distance was 2 hours 6mins 7secs, giving him a lead over Guinness of 4mins 1sec. Guinness had extended his lead over de Vizcaya to 55 seconds. Maury had fallen back to 4mins 24secs behind de Vizcaya, with Bertelli now 10mins 16secs further back and Marshall still last, over 35 minutes behind the leader.

Lap 4 saw Guinness regain the lead, with Divo experiencing pressure problems. After surviving a lurid four wheel skid at Signpost, de Vizcaya stopped at the beginning of the lap to take on oil. He was driving very hard, as were Guinness, Divo and Maury but was soon to experience problems which would ruin his chances of finishing in the top three. Completing the lap, Guinness led Divo by 28 seconds with a growing time of 2 hours 52mins 22secs. Divo led de Vizcaya by 3mins 52secs with

A.C. Bertelli drove the sole Enfield-Allday in the International 1,500cc Trophy Race, finishing fifth behind two Talbot-Darracqs and two Bugattis. [Author's collection]

Maury 4mins 48secs back. Bertelli lost a further 1min 2secs on Maury with Marshall still running but losing further time.

Quickly improving conditions on lap 5 produced heroic driving. After driving for 151 miles in appalling conditions, Guinness lapped in an incredible 41mins 4secs which was 21 seconds faster than Chassagne's first lap. Divo lapped in 36 seconds slower than Guinness while de Vizcaya had another big skid, this time at Quarterbridge where he could not avoid hitting the bridge. A rear tyre burst but it is not clear whether this was cause or effect. He continued and regained some of the lost time. Going into the final lap, Guinness' growing time was 3 hours 33mins 26secs and he led Divo by 1min 4secs. De Vizcaya was now 9mins 21secs down on Divo but had increased his lead over Maury to 5mins 36secs. Bertelli and Marshall were still going, but well out of contention.

On the final lap Guinness slowed, but only marginally. He seemed assured of victory when he reached the Bungalow just before Divo reached Ramsey, but he must have remembered 1907 when he had run out of petrol at Hillberry with a big lead and within two miles of the finish. This time, however, he took the flag in a time for the six

One of the Bugattis passes two groups of sodden spectators at the Creg-na-Baa Hotel. The Bugatti team of Pierre de Vizcaya, Mones Maury and Bertram Marshall was the only team in the 1,500 race to finish intact. [National Motor Museum]

Sir Algernon Lee Guinness celebrates his victory with his riding mechanic. He finished nearly two minutes ahead of his Talbot-Darracq team-mate Albert Divo and over 22 minutes ahead of third placed Mones Maury's Bugatti. He had competed in every Isle of Man event since his debut in the 1905 Gordon Bennett Trial. [National Motor Museum]

laps of 4 hours 14mins 56.4secs and the countdown began. To beat him, Divo had to finish less than the starting difference of seven minutes after Guinness. In fact he arrived 2 minutes 41.6 seconds too late and Guinness was the winner. Guinness' final lap time was 41mins 30.4secs, his second fastest lap, whereas Divo's last lap of 43mins 8secs had been his next to slowest. On the final lap, after a heroic drive, Pierre de Vizcaya lost third place to Mones Maury after a series of punctures. Maury finished 19mins 34secs behind Divo and 10mins 30secs ahead of de Vizcaya. Bertelli came in fifth, 3mins 43.2secs in arrears and Marshall, who started his last lap just after Divo finished the race, completed the course almost 21 minutes after Bertelli, enabling Bugatti to win the team prize. With a good engine, he would have finished much higher.

The race confirmed the superiority of the Talbot-Darracqs in 1,500cc racing and Algie Lee Guinness' victory was well deserved and popular after his years of bad luck in the Isle of Man races. He told *The Autocar* that during the race there was not the slightest suspicion of trouble with the Talbot-Darracq's engine; never did it seem to flag, and the only doubtful moment – a very brief one – was due to a small carburettor trouble when the engine was running at high speed against little throttle on the Keppel Gate – Governor's Bridge section during the last two rounds. The Talbot-Darracqs' nickname was emphasised when a roller skate was found parked alongside his car outside the Fort Anne Hotel!

1922 Tourist Trophy Race Results

Tourist Trophy Race

Thursday 22nd June 1922. Start 9.30am. 8 laps of 37.75 miles circuit, total distance 302 miles. 8 starters, 5 finishers.

1. Jean Chassagne (Sunbeam), 5hrs 24mins 50secs (55.78mph)
2. Frank Clement (Bentley), 5hrs 28mins 59.6secs (55.21mph)
3. Oswald Payne (Vauxhall), 5hrs 43mins 45.2secs (52.71mph)
4. W.O. Bentley (Bentley), 5hrs 43mins 51.2secs (52.69mph)
5. Douglas Hawkes (Bentley), 6hrs 28mins 41secs (46.61mph)

Fastest lap: Major Henry Segrave (Sunbeam) 39mins 15sesc (57.70mph)

Team Prize: Bentley

Retirements:

Lap 2:

Matthew Park (Vauxhall), engine trouble, Ballig Bridge

Lap 5: Major Henry Segrave (Sunbeam), magneto trouble, Ramsey

Ernest Swain (Vauxhall) engine trouble, Ballacraine. .

International 1,500cc Trophy Race

Thursday 22nd June 1922. 6 laps of 37.75 miles circuit, total distance 226.5 miles. 9 starters, 6 finishers.

1. Sir Algernon Lee Guinness (Talbot-Darracq), 4hrs 14mins 56.4secs (53.30mph)
2. Albert Divo (Talbot-Darracq), 4hrs 17mins 38secs (52.75mph)
3. Mones Maury (Bugatti), 4hrs 37mins 12secs (47.23mph)
4. Pierre de Vizcaya (Bugatti), 4hrs 47mins 42secs (47.23mph)
5. A.C. Bertelli (Enfield-Allday), 4hrs 51mins 25.2secs (46.63mph)
6. Bertram Marshall (Bugatti), 5hrs 12mins (43.55mph)

Fastest Lap:

Sir Algernon Lee Guinness (Talbot-Darracq), 41mins 4secs (55.15mph)

Retirements:

Lap 1:

Jean Moriceau (Talbot-Darracq), front tyre burst while trying to overtake Maury near Glen Helen

H. Kensington Moir (Aston Martin), valve trouble near

Glen Helen

G. Bedford (Hillman), off road near Keppel Gate.

Reaction

The race report in *The Motor* was positive: "During the last two weeks the Isle of Man has been the scene of the greatest excitement; practically everyone who is anybody in the automobile industry crossed over to Douglas for the two races, and there is no doubt that so far as the trade is concerned they were a great success. Public interest perhaps was not as pronounced as it was in the case of the motorcycle races which, by reason of their annual continuity, have become very classic events." However an editorial in the same magazine told a rather different story. While allowing for the low state of the industry, the bad weather and the expense of transporting cars to the Island, the writer complained of a lack of publicity, drive and showmanship and said that unless the races "are carried out more energetically they are not likely to be repeated. Compared with the motorcycle races a few weeks earlier, there was practically no interest taken in the car races in the Island",

The race day weather was certainly depressing and the reduced number of entries compared with the earlier car TT races (due, apparently to the RAC decision to run to an out-dated formula) must have affected public and press interest and resulted in spectator numbers which compared very poorly with those of previous years and with the motorcycle TT of a few weeks before. Nevertheless the *Isle of Man Times* reported that there was a very large crowd at Hillberry and that the hedges were crowded from Governor's Bridge up to Keppel Gate. Clearly the "atmosphere" failed to recapture the pre-war excitement and happy-go-lucky spirit of adventure which had prevailed in 1914 and earlier years and which, but for the outbreak of war, could well have been built on in 1915. The RAC TT might then have achieved the kind of continuity and established place in Island life which, despite having started two years after the RAC TT, the motorcycle TT was already enjoying and which enabled it to continue into its second century.

1905 – 1922 RAC TOURIST TROPHY RACE WINNERS

John S. Napier, Arrol-Johnston – 1905

The winner of the first Tourist Trophy Race was responsible for the design and production of his winning car. John Napier joined the Mo-Car Syndicate (later to become The New Arrol-Johnston Car Co.) in 1903, as Chief Engineer/ Managing Director. He led on each of the first three laps of the race but lost time when his exhaust and silencer fell onto the road. On the last lap, however, he re-passed the Rolls-Royce of Percy Northey to win by 2mins 9secs. He defended his title in 1906, when he was second fastest to Rolls of the first lap but lost time on the second lap due to three successive punctures, eventually finishing seventh of nine finishers. Returning in 1907, he ran out of fuel 18 miles from the finish.

Hon. Charles S. Rolls, Rolls-Royce – 1906

A founder of Rolls-Royce, Charles Rolls was, with the Hon. John Scott-Montagu, the first British driver to race on the Continent. They drove a Panhard in the Paris-Ostend and Paris-Boulogne races in 1899. Rolls himself was the best British finisher (eighth) in the Gordon Bennett Cup Race of 1905, driving a Wolseley. After the disappointment of his early retirement from the 1905 TT, his decisive 1906 victory was particularly gratifying and provided an early example of the commercial potential of racing success. Rolls entered for the 1907 TT, but withdrew, saying that the company did not have a car which complied with the race regulations. He later turned to aviation and lost his life in a flying accident in 1910.

Ernest Courtis, Rover – 1907 Tourist Trophy Race

Aged 31 at the time of his win, Ernest Courtis started work as a signal fitter on the Brighton and South Coast Railway. After acting as a mechanic to Mr. E.J. Pennington, he worked in the fitting shops of the British Motor Co., the Motor Manufacturing Co., Wolseley, Pollock Engineering Co., Humber, Beeston and Daimler before becoming chief of the fitting department of Rover, with responsibility for inspecting every car before leaving the factory. After finishing fifth in the 1905 TT he had been confident of victory in 1906 but suffered the disappointment of not being allowed to start due to late arrival at the enclosure. He found the 1907 race "...the hardest I have ever experienced in my life. The roads were like ploughed fields after the third round, and it was positively awesome to come down the mountain, where we could not see a telegraph pole's length ahead". He said he had had no trouble with his car and had fully expected to win from the start.

George P. Mills, Beeston-Humber – 1907 Heavy Touring Car Race

George Mills started his racing career as a cyclist. In 1885 he captured 24 hours records on an old high bicycle and won the Land's End to John O' Groats bicycle and tricycle records. In 1907 he was Thomas Pullinger's Assistant Manager at Beeston-Humber, having recently joined the company after many years as works manager and designer at Raleigh cycles. The 1907 TT was his first motor race. He had no problems with his car apart from an air lock at Hillberry but found that the weight of his car (2.5 tons) and the handicap of the windscreen meant that driving was a considerable physical effort. He had been confident that he could complete the race without running out of fuel but had doubted that he could beat the Ariel-Simplex cars of Sangster and Harrison on speed.

William Watson, Hutton – 1908

William Watson was born in Liverpool. Like Selwyn Edge, Charles Jarrott and George Mills he was a champion cyclist in his youth. He founded W. Watson & Co., a cycle and motor car manufacturer in 1901 and built the business into the largest car distributorship in the north-west of England, concentrating on Rolls-Royce and Morris. He bought the Hutton, named Little Dorrit, from Selwyn Edge after being impressed with its success at Brooklands. His only problem during the race was the need to change the coil and he said afterwards that the car ran "like a poem throughout". He also raced Berliets and Vauxhalls but retired in the 1907 TT when his Berliet ran out of fuel and also in 1914 when his Vauxhall broke its crankshaft on the first lap.

Kenelm Lee Guinness, Sunbeam – 1914

After starting in motor racing as riding mechanic to his elder brother Algernon, Kenelm Lee Guinness (known as "Bill") turned to driving, joining the Sunbeam factory team in 1913 and continuing with the Sunbeam Talbot-Darracq team after the Great War. He raced Sunbeams at Brooklands and claimed the last World Land Speed Record to be established there, at 133.75mph over a kilometre. He drove a Darracq in the 1907 Touring Car TT, and a Hillman-Coatalen in 1908, retiring with rear axle damage in 1907 and with a broken frame in 1908, but his 1914 TT win was free of problems except for sticking brakes on the first day. In his business life, Guinness was the founder of the K.L.G. sparking plug company.

Jean Chassagne, Sunbeam – 1922 Tourist Trophy Race

French driver Jean Chassagne was the first foreign winner of a TT race. Prior to the Great War (in which he served as a pilot in the French Air Force) he finished third in the 1913 French Grand Prix in a Sunbeam and took pole position in the 1914 Indianapolis 500, in which he finished 29th. He returned to racing after the war, still driving for Sunbeam, and finished 7th at Indianapolis in 1902 and 18th in 1921. He famously described the conditions in the 1922 TT as "a nightmare in a sea of mud". He became a friend of the "Bentley Boys" with whom he shared an adventurous, carefree approach to life.

Algernon Lee Guinness, Talbot-Darracq – 1922 1,500cc Trophy Race

The elder of the Guinness brothers drove a Darracq in the 1905 Gordon Bennett trial and was the only driver to take part in all the Isle of Man TT races, always driving Darracqs. He crashed in 1905, finished third in 1906, ran out of fuel in 1907, was runner-up in 1908, retired in 1914 after holding second place for three-quarters of the race, and finally won the 1,500cc Trophy in 1922. He was particularly unfortunate in 1907 to run out of fuel while leading, less than two miles from the finish. He drove a V-8 200hp Darracq at Saltburn Sands and at Brooklands. After retirement he remained active in the sport as an official and returned to the Isle of Man in 1952 as RAC Steward at the British Empire Trophy Race.

Interlude 1923-1932

There was no RAC TT in 1923 because manufacturer support was lacking and the Society of Motor Manufacturers and Traders opposed proposals for another 1500cc race due to motor industry conditions. A Manx Motor Cycle Club proposal to organise a car race on the TT Course met a similar reaction, and therefore a refusal by the RAC (as governing body of motor sport) to grant a permit, although in 1923 the Manx Motor Cycle Club's perseverance secured its amateur motorcycle race on the TT course – an event which survived to achieve continuity like the motorcycle TT and celebrated its 90th anniversary in 2013.

In December 1927 Douglas Town Council approached the RAC to organise a race on the TT Course in 1928. The RAC had also received an approach from the Ulster Automobile Club to organise a race in Northern Ireland and responded that, although no definite decision had been made, it favoured Northern Ireland and had given provisional acceptance to the Ulster A.C. proposal because Northern Ireland's inducements were more acceptable than those offered by the Isle of Man.

A week later the *Isle of Man Times* informed its readers that, despite what the RAC said, there would be a race in Northern Ireland in 1928. Quoting a Northern Ireland newspaper, the Times said that a 24 hours race would be held on 18th August, the Northern Ireland Government having offered a prize fund of £2,000, a grandstand for 3,000 people and the attendance of 500 police. In a strange contradiction, the Times said that the race distance would be 400 miles. Probably the original proposal was for a 24 hours race like Le Mans but the Northern Ireland Government refused this.

Commenting on the report, the Times said it was "not quite certain that the RAC have played the game with the Island". The RAC had not said what they wanted but the Island would have met any conditions required. There were "enormous influences" in Northern Ireland and the Island had been to sleep. *The Times* recalled how, when the Auto-Cycle Union had wanted to take the motorcycle TT to Belgium, the Manx Motor Cycle Club had fought the A-CU and the TT had remained on the Island. It was a pity that the Manx Automobile Club had not done the same with the RAC.

In February, the *Isle of Man Times* reported that it appeared from *The Autocar* that money for the proposed 1928 TT was difficult to find. The large capital expenditure required would not provide a return for a number of years. *The Times* predicted "Ulster would probably find the RAC not as dependable as could be desired. They organise a race this year but goodness only knows if they will organise one next year or within the next ten years and Ulster is hesitating to spend this money for one year".

Nevertheless the RAC soon confirmed that although the TT would be revived in 1928 it would not be on the Isle of Man course but on the 13.7 miles Ards circuit in Northern Ireland.

Despite this disastrous blow, the Manx authorities continued their overtures to the RAC In August 1929 the Governor appointed a delegation to meet RAC representatives with a view to a race in 1930. Amid renewed interest, representatives of both the *Isle of Man Times* and the *Isle of Man Examiner* visited Ards to observe the 1929 TT. This led to critical reports in both newspapers of the Ards course and its facilities, causing a strong rebuttal in the *Belfast Evening Telegraph* and complaints from Belfast of "spies" from the Isle of Man. Despite its criticisms, however, the Times thought that it would be very difficult for the Isle of Man to get the TT back, as Northern Ireland had a strong hold and great political influence. *The Times* suggested attempting to secure a completely different type of race and suggested two shorter alternatives to the TT Course. The first choice would start at Quarterbridge on the outskirts of Douglas, take the main road south to Ballasalla and continue through the village to Cross Four Ways. There it would turn right and continue via Foxdale and Ballacraine to return to Quarterbridge. This would give a lap distance of about 20 miles. It was almost identical to the course used for the 1905 eliminating trials for the International Motorcycle Cup. *The Times*' other alternative was the St. John's – Ballacraine – Kirk Michael – Peel – St. John's circuit used for the motorcycle TT from 1907 to 1910 inclusive, with a lap distance of 15.8 miles.

The Isle of Man delegation visited the RAC in December 1929 but the RAC was already committed to Ards for 1929 and 1930 and ruled out a return to the Island on the grounds that the Island's course although "a magnificent test of a driver's skill and a car's reliability" was less well surfaced that Ards and no longer really suitable for car racing.

In June 1930 the motorcycle TT newspaper, *TT Special*, took up the point that the TT Course was no longer suitable for car racing. Two alternative courses had been suggested, it said. The preferred alternative was in the north of the Island. Covering about 11.5 miles, it ran in a westerly direction from Ramsey, through Lezayre to Sulby. It then went northwards towards Andreas and from Andreas Village south-east back to Ramsey. This course could be extended north east from Andreas to Bride and then south to Ramsey, extending its length to 16-17 miles. Much road widening would be required, it said, but the Manx authorities were prepared to do this. The RAC was diffident about leaving Ards, which had become well-known and there was a larger public in Northern Ireland. The *TT Special* article did not give details of the alternative course but *Mona's Herald* revealed details of a course in the south of the Island which it claimed was the preferred choice. This course would start on the main Douglas Castletown road between the Mount Murray Hotel and the Lancashire Inn. From there it would continue south to Castletown via Ballasalla before turning north on Malew Road. Passing Cross Four Ways, it would continue via Ballamodha to Foxdale and turn east past Foxdale Church and Braaid crossroads to the Plains of Heaven where it would turn right to return to the Castletown road.

August 1930 brought a flurry of activity. The *Isle of Man Examiner* said that the proposed course in the north of the Island, 16 miles from Douglas, was too remote and suggested a 6-7 miles course in the Douglas area. This was a vague and unrealistic proposal, using a two miles section of the existing TT Course from the start to Braddan or Union Mills before taking a non-existent road to link up with the TT course between Hillberry and Governor's Bridge.

Representatives of Manx newspapers visited Ards to observe the TT. The *Examiner* reported press comment that Manxmen were trying to steal the TT, while the *Mona's Herald* said that the Irish authorities were apprehensive. The Isle of Man could not attract more than a tenth of the crowd at Ards, which the *Examiner* estimated at 500,000. The event used 1,200 police and far less would be sufficient, the *Mona's Herald* thought. Isle of Man TT marshalling and control was vastly superior to that of Ards and there was a lack of news for press representatives during the race. *The Times* thought that it would be very difficult to recover the TT for the Isle of Man but that no effort should be spared. At a banquet, Northern Ireland's Prime Minister, Viscount Craigavon, had promised the RAC whatever they wanted and Colonel Lindsay Lloyd of the RAC had said that it would take a "devil of a big bribe" to persuade the RAC to change the venue and that they had not yet been offered that bribe. Commenting on this, the Times said that Ulster must be beaten and the bribe must be paid, whether it was £1,000, £2000 or £3,000. The Island must make it clear that it would do anything in its power to recover the TT, including meeting financial requirements and putting roads in order. A new race would be no good – the TT must be brought home to the Island.

Then there was a significant development in the Island's favour. Reporting that two RAC representatives had visited the Senior Manx Grand Prix motorcycle race and had paid particular attention to policing and marshalling arrangements, the *Isle of Man Examiner* of 12th September said that this was directly connected to the Island's bid to win back the TT and that the prospects of another TT in Northern Ireland were "rather remote". Instead, it said, the RAC was considering the possibility of staging the race on the Island or in the Irish Free State.

The *Isle of Man Weekly Times* of 13th September contained an article by the Motoring Correspondent of the *Irish Independent* who had been present at the banquet at which Viscount Craigavon had offered the RAC whatever it wanted. The chief impression that he had gained from Viscount Craigavon's speech, he said, was that the Prime Minister was "most apprehensive lest the RAC should forsake Ards for some other course outside Northern Ireland and that he was really anxious to retain it". Colonel Lindsay Lloyd's reference to a big bribe was "an unfortunate expression", he thought, but the position and attitude of the RAC was clear – the race would be given to the highest bidder. While the Isle of Man had claimed that Northern Ireland had stolen the TT, this was incorrect. The old TT had died in 1922 and the Isle of Man had made no effort to resuscitate it or to provide an alternative, whereas the Ulster people had persuaded the RAC to organise a modern TT race which had no similarity to the Isle of Man races and had made a success of it. The article concluded that it had been said unofficially that the Isle of Man was prepared to spend £20,000 to regain the TT and that Northern Ireland would have to go one better in order to succeed.

Captain Phillips came to the Isle of Man in February 1931 to inspect courses which had been suggested as suitable for the TT. Reporting this, the *Mona's Herald* quoted an article in the *Sporting Life* which alleged that £1,500 prize money for the Ulster TT had not been forthcoming from the usual source, a National newspaper. Therefore, it said, Ulster must raise £1,500 or lose the race.

On 3rd March the *Mona's Herald* reported that if the TT were to return to the Island, it would be held on a course of about nine miles near Ramsey. The start would be on the Jurby Road, at Mr Criggal's residence. From there it would enter Ramsey via Bowring Road, pass the Central Hotel and continue along Lezayre Road to Sulby Bridge and St. Jude's, to return along the Jurby Road to the start. Plans had also been made for the siting of a grandstand and for access to the grandstand via Mooragh Park.

In a strange development in April, two Island newspapers quoted a *News Chronicle* article alleging that talks were taking place about a British Grand Prix for cars, to be held in early August 1932 on a 12 miles course between Ramsey, Sulby, St. Jude's and Ramsey. According to the paper the Manx Government was willing to spend up to £10,000 on road widening and improvements but the *Mona's Herald* said that this was not so and that there was no need to spend anything like as much. As the *News Chronicle* said that Ulster would use every endeavour to keep the races, the reference to a British Grand Prix rather than the TT is puzzling.

Nevertheless, in June two Island newspapers, again quoting a *News Chronicle* report, revealed that all arrangements had been made for the British Grand Prix to be held on 21st August 1932, on a class handicap basis closely following the basis of the race held in Ulster for the three previous years. There had been a choice of three courses. One was the Ramsey course of 11 miles, described as starting about a mile outside Ramsey and continuing through Ramsey via an acute corner at the Station. Then it went four miles to Sulby Bridge, continued on a 1.5 mile straight to Sandygate and a one mile stretch to St. Judes, followed by a two mile straight back to the start. This differed from the course described in the *Mona's Herald* in March which took a different route in Ramsey and did not include Sandygate. Also considered had been a course of 30 miles, near Castletown, and one of nine miles outside Douglas including part of the TT Course. The RAC preferred the Ramsey course, which contained four straights allowing a maximum speed of 130mph.

On 26th June the *Ramsey Courier* quoted an article in the *Belfast News Letter* which said that some people were taking it for granted that the TT would be moved to the Isle of Man but that there was no evidence to justify this. The RAC was not committed. The Star however had claimed: "Big Race Auctioned – RAC Event to be transferred from Ulster to Isle of Man" and alleged that there had been "a spirited auction" at which the Isle of Man had offered such inducements that Ulster had been outbid and the Manx offer accepted subject to a suitable course which had been found and approved – the 11 mile course outside Ramsey.

The RAC denied that any decision had been made. It said that it had not yet decided to hold a race in 1932. It resented the suggestion of an auction. Courses had been inspected but the RAC was always open to doing this as a matter of courtesy if for no other reason. If the TT were held in 1932 it could be on either course, the RAC said, but it would need, before abandoning Ards, to be satisfied that the race would benefit by the change. The priorities were suitability and safety. Then, all being equal, the RAC might consider inducements.

In August the Manx newspapers reported that the Island was making a very strong bid and that a deputation had visited Ards to witness the TT. RAC Secretary, Commander Armstrong, and Competitions Committee Chairman, Colonel Lindsay Lloyd, had visited the Island and inspected the proposed course. Strong inducements had been offered in the shape of guarantees and the odds were in favour of the Island.

Shortly afterwards the *Daily Mail* reported that only swift action by Ulster would prevent the transfer of the TT to the Isle of Man, which had made a concrete proposal to the RAC. Ulster had not yet made a proposal but would do so in the next few days. There had been considerable speculation resulting from the visit of RAC officials to the Island, which had caused concern in Ulster and from a statement by Lindsay Lloyd that there was doubt whether the race would be held at all. Northern Ireland Government co-operation, however, was expected to secure the race.

In the first week of September, English National newspapers reported that the Isle of Man had secured the TT. The *Mona's Herald*, however, said that no information had been received by the Manx authorities and that it believed that there would be no decision for a month. "Everything points to the race coming here", it said, "but it is yet too soon to shout."

On 12th September, the *Peel City Guardian* quoted a *Daily Herald* article of 8th September stating that Ulster had lost the TT. Secret conferences and private preparations had resulted in victory for the Island. Ulster had only just been able to meet the expenses of the TT each year and the prize fund of £1,500 (paid by the *Daily Mail* in the first three years) had been guaranteed from private resources (Sir Charles Wakefield in 1931). The Isle of Man, the *Herald* said, had already raised a guarantee fund of £3,500 and the Manx Government was prepared to spend £5,000 on roads and to guarantee the prize fund. Agreements with landowners for grandstands at Ramsey and for parking were already in place.

All then went quiet until December. The *Mona's Herald* of 8th December reported a short but devastating announcement in the *Daily Express* of 4th December that the 1932 TT would be held at Ards on 20th August. The *Ramsey Courier*, quoting the *Daily Herald*, said that it was expected that the Isle of Man would continue its campaign and would also seek to organise its own car race. The *Daily Herald* also revealed that Lady Houston had agreed to provide the £1,500 prize money to enable the Ards race to take place. Later, in an effort to balance the books, the Northern Ireland Government introduced legislation to allow half a crown (12 ½ p) to be taken from every car entering the area of the course on race day. This, it was said, raised several thousand half crowns and lost many thousands of spectators.

In a leader on 12th December, the *Isle of Man Times* expressed the disappointment felt on the Isle of Man. It described the alternative courses which had been offered by the Isle of Man. *The Times* also pointed out that the Isle of Man offer had included a guarantee of over £2,000. The Belfast offer was nothing like as substantial and therefore the political pull of Ulster must have been much greater. It was evident that the Island had lost the TT car races for all time. It would now be most undignified for the Island to approach the RAC again. The Island had offered everything that had been asked for and the offer had been turned down. It left a nasty taste in one's mouth – a feeling that the Island had been used as a lever to get better terms from Ulster. This bargaining was undignified and had left a certain amount of feeling in Ulster against the Isle of Man which was not quite fair to the Island. The Island's course was equal to Ards, many Island facilities were better, a guarantee against loss of £2,000 had been offered to the RAC and yet the Island had lost the races.

Manx persistence was to pay off with an alternative event, however. Although it made it clear that the return of the TT (albeit on a shorter course) was its preference, the Manx Government sought a compromise in two possible formats.

The first alternative was a race for light cars on the TT Course or some other course. In January 1932 the *Isle of Man Examiner* reported that MG's Managing Director Cecil Kimber had proposed that three separate races should be held on the TT Course for light cars of 750cc, 1,100cc and 1,500cc capacities. His company had already achieved racing successes including victories in the RAC TT at Ards. The RAC responded that it would not organise such a race because the Trade did not want it, but that any application from a responsible club for an organising permit for such a race would be carefully considered. *The Motor*'s columnist "Grande Vitesse" thought the proposal was not practicable. To increase National prestige, foreign entries would be needed and Kimber's proposal was likely to attract only British entries (Austin and M.G. in the 750cc class, M.G. and Riley in the 1,100c class with Aston Martin, Frazer Nash and perhaps Alvis contesting the 1,500cc class).

Kimber persisted. He wrote to the Auto-Cycle Union to seek its approval for a demonstration lap on the TT Course by two MG Midgets. The drivers were to be two TT riders, Norman Black and Syd Crabtree. Kimber wanted the demonstration to take place immediately before the 1932 Senior TT. While the A-CU did not agree to this, Kimber sent a racing MG Midget to the Isle of Man for use on the TT course as an official car during the 1932 motorcycle races.

The second alternative was a "Round the Houses" race, modelled on the Monaco Grand Prix which had been introduced successfully in 1929. One feature of this type of racing was the fact that cars rarely had much chance to reach maximum speeds. Reliability, braking power, acceleration and driving skills mattered more than sheer speed. The RAC opted for this idea, deciding to organise two races of equal importance on a street circuit in Douglas, in an event which would be unique in the British Isles and which would give British drivers experience of Continental type racing.

ROUND THE HOUSES 1933 - 1937

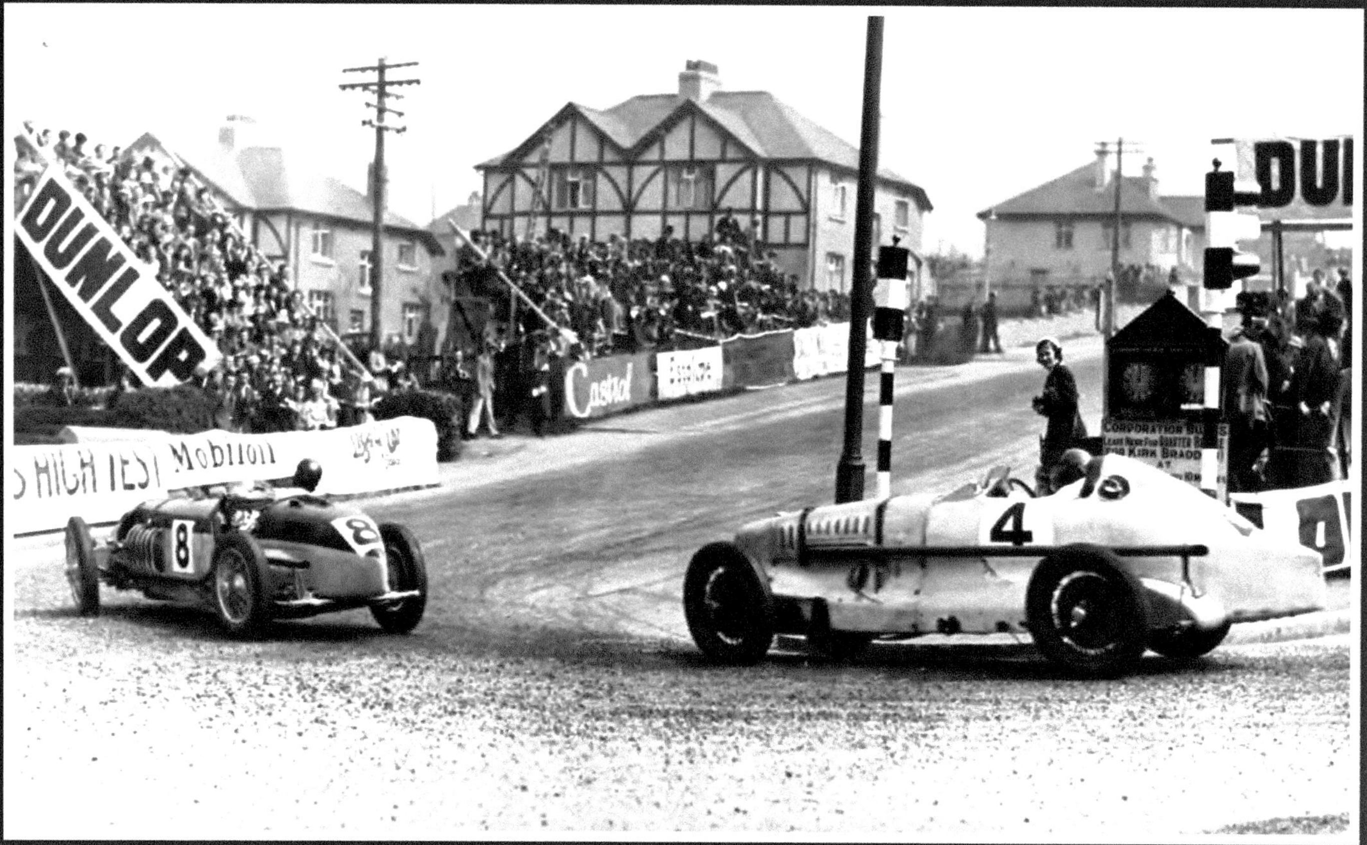

At Bray Hill Hairpin during the 1934 Mannin Beg race, George Eyston's special bodied MG Magnette K3 (known as EX135) is pursued by another special bodied Magnette, driven by Hugh Hamilton. Eyston finished third but Hamilton crashed into a telegraph pole on Bray Hill and retired. A lady appears to be waiting to cross the road! [Magna Press]

1933 Mannin Beg And Mannin Moar – Wins For Dixon And Lewis

Planning

In July 1932 British Racing Drivers' Club officials met the RAC Competitions Committee to discuss the proposals. On the Isle of Man a Race Committee was appointed, consisting of seven members of the Town Council and five non-members with well-known organising capabilities. The concept of a Monaco-style race was regarded as "thrilling." It would show the world that the British Isles still had the finest drivers and cars and could produce one of the finest road circuits, considered to be superior to that in Monaco. Douglas Corporation agreed to ask the Lieutenant-Governor, Sir Claude Hill, to arrange with the RAC for a race in Douglas in July or September 1933, preferably in July, and Sir Claude arranged to meet the RAC.

Promotional work was deferred, however, pending a meeting in Douglas of Race Committee and RAC representatives, leading to complaints of "exaggerated secrecy." Leaked information worried MG's Managing Director Cecil Kimber, who wanted separate races for different classes of cars to suit his 750cc MGs. It was pointed out, however, that there were only three English manufacturers who competed regularly. This meant that the larger classes would still be "a gift to the foreigners" as there were no English cars capable of competing with large capacity foreign cars. Nevertheless, it was decided that two races would be run, on Wednesday and Friday 12th and 14th July, with roads closing at 8.30am and each race of 50 laps (230 miles) starting at 9.30am. Practices would take place on Thursday, Friday and Monday, 6th, 7th and 10th July from 10.30am to 12 noon with roads closing at 9.30am. The first race (to be called the "Mannin Beg", which was Manx for "Little Man") would be for supercharged 1,100cc and unsupercharged 1,500cc cars. The second race (to be called the "Mannin Moar", Manx for "Big Man") would be for supercharged cars of 1,500cc and unsupercharged cars over 1,500cc. According to *The Autocar* Manx titles were chosen after Colonel Lindsay Lloyd of the RAC asked why the Manx people always used other people's language for the names of their races.

The formulae meant that foreign, and some British, entries would be discouraged as 1,500cc supercharged cars would be forced to compete against cars of unlimited capacity in the Mannin Moar. Moreover, riding mechanics were required to accompany all drivers which automatically debarred single seat racing cars from both races. There were predictions that there would be poor entries for both races. Indeed, Earl Howe, who was one of Britain's leading drivers, prophesied in a letter to *The Motor* that the races would be "second rate affairs."

There was uncertainty over the proposed course. The first proposal was a course that started at an undefined point on the Promenade, turned into Broadway and continued via Victoria Road to Governor's Bridge and thence to Onchan Village. A right turn into Royal Avenue would take the course back to the Promenade via Port Jack and King Edward Road.

The second proposal involved a start on Glencrutchery Road, running north via Governor's Bridge to Onchan, down the steep Summer Hill and along the entire Promenade, turning up Victoria Street at the south end of the Promenade and through the town via Buck's Road and Woodbourne Road to Glencrutchery Road.

The third and fourth proposals amended the second plan by moving the start from Glencrutchery Road to an undefined point on the Promenade and suggested a possible substitution of the Governor's Road, Onchan hairpin and Summer Hill Road section by a shorter descent from Governor's Bridge to the Promenade via Blackberry Lane.

By late November the Society of Motor Manufacturers and Traders had given approval and arrangements on the Island were well under way. Chief Constable Henry Madoc, one of the leaders, arranged for support from Manx Automobile Club members who had helped with the Gordon Bennett Trials and TT car races.

In mid-December Madoc met Captain A. W. Phillips, the Assistant Clerk of the Course and later revealed that Phillips had scrapped the proposed course as it would be too fast for small-engined cars and contained "some element of danger". He thought the start should be in front of the Villa Marina on Douglas promenade and outlined a new course of 4 miles 1,056 yards (4.6 miles). This would take the cars up Church Road Marina, past St Thomas' Church, up Finch Road, past Government Office, up Buck's Road and Woodbourne Road to Laureston, turning right at St. Ninian's Road (skirting the playing fields) and thence via Upper Duke's Road and Falcon Cliff Terrace to Victoria Road and Cunningham's Holiday Camp. From there the route would go via Governor's Road to Onchan Village, returning by

Summer Hill Road to the Promenade. Madoc recorded: "I thought it would do A1."

Officials were unsure about possible speeds but thought the fastest cars might achieve 110 mph. on the Promenade and perhaps over 100mph. on the straight up Woodbourne Road. Estimates of lap speeds varied between 50 mph. and 75 mph. with the probability was that speeds would be nearer the higher figure than the lower.

Road surfaces added to the hazards, particularly at Dukes Road, on Woodbourne Road between Avondale Corner and Laureston Corner and more especially on Summer Hill, where the present surface meant that fast driving could be undertaken only with extreme danger. Remedial work could be undertaken in places but, as long as the races were experimental and there was no commitment to a long-term series, it was unlikely that a major financial investment could be justified. Sand bagging the whole course, for example, would be impossible. Road widening, however, was carried out in Upper Duke's Road. At least there was one positive safety factor – nearly all parts of the course could be reached from within the circuit, simplifying the provision of break-down and other rescue vehicles.

Two major trophies were donated – the Wakefield Trophy presented by Lord Wakefield of Hythe for the Mannin Beg, and the MG Trophy presented by the MG Car Company for the Mannin Moar. Smaller trophies for fastest laps and best teams were also forthcoming.

Some thought Tynwald (the Isle of Man Parliament) should finance prize money and organisational expenses, as for the TT motorcycle races, but a Guarantee Fund of £4,000 was established by local tradesmen and businesses with the Town Council contributing £1,000, to guarantee organisers against loss. A similar fund had financed the early car races.

Clearly the races would cause disruption. The Mayor admitted "No great event like this could take place without inconvenience." He was convinced, however, that "what these races will do for the Island will, in every way, compensate the general public for that inconvenience." The Mayor thought that other seaside towns would dearly like to emulate the Island, particularly Brighton. "The races will provide the greatest spectacular thrill of our time" he said, "and will be watched with interest and envy by our competitors round the British Isles." The world-wide publicity for the Island would be difficult to estimate. The Mayor agreed that, at first sight, the plans might seem rather alarming but he believed that marshalling and sand-bagging would reduce the potential dangers.

The Highway Board agreed to the road closures and times on 3rd May. Meanwhile, there was concern about the safety of spectators on the grassed areas on the seaward side of the promenade, the wide footpath beyond and also the foreshore, particularly near the foot of Summer Hill. It was felt that a car could get out of control on the steep descent and cross the grass area and footpath, endangering spectators on the foreshore. The result was legislation empowering Douglas Corporation to close the foreshore to the public during race periods.

This prohibition raised the question whether there would be sufficient safe areas within the course to accommodate the expected large numbers of spectators. Madoc calculated this finely, even to available space on grandstands – three persons for every 60 inches. Spectators would be prepared to pay an admission fee, he reckoned, provided the charges were not extortionate.

Madoc's final estimate was that there was viewing space for 31,400. This included 5,300 at side roads and 4,700 on three covered Corporation grandstands. One, with 1,300 seats, would be at the Villa Marina facing the Scoreboard and Pits. The second with 1,400 seats, at the junction of the Promenade with Church Road Marina (Greensill's Corner), would give a clear view of the start and the first and second corners. The third and largest (2,000 seats) would be at Queen's Promenade, with a view of cars on the fast descent of Summer Hill and the dash along the Promenade to the start/finish. Windows of Promenade hotels and boarding houses were estimated to provide viewing for a further 6,400. St Ninian's Church grounds could accommodate 1,000 with a further 3,000 along the walls of the adjoining Noble's Park recreation ground and 4,000 more in the grounds of Cunningham's Holiday Camp, if available. Shops and houses on Woodbourne Road offered possible viewing areas for 1,500. The remainder was accounted for by small numbers like 50 at the Gaiety Theatre, perhaps 100 at buildings near Government Office and 150 in Somerset Road. An Information Bureau at the Victoria Pier would open early on practice and race days. Madoc arranged also for the distribution of circulars and maps aboard Isle of Man Steam Packet Co. vessels. These gave details of grandstands and coupons for advance booking of seats.

Motorists wishing to bring their cars to the Island could book their passage through the RAC. If there were sufficient bookings, a special boat would be provided. Another plan was to divide shipping of cars between passenger and cargo vessels. A new crane, supplied by the Leeds firm Thomas Smith and Sons (Rodley) Ltd., was provided at the Victoria Pier to ease lifting on and off of cars.

Madoc reckoned that between 300 and 500 Special Constables would have to be enrolled for spectator control. This led to the Mayor of Douglas calling on employers to release appropriate staff if required. *Isle of Man Times* Editor, George Brown, added the suggestion that perhaps people who had homes or shops around the course might agree to marshal outside them.

There would be 35 flag stations manned by the Manx Automobile Club, sited in such a way that each Flagman could always see one other on each side of him. Every Flagman would have an assistant and it would be his responsibility to look after any car involved in a crash and to get competitors out of a crashed car. Other helpers, to control the crowds and the course, would be Special Constables and would be given different armlets to indicate this. Transport would be arranged to bring "Specials" into Douglas from other parts of the Island. In total, 540 were enrolled.

There were 3 first aid posts per mile, 12 temporary hospitals (including one at Government House, offered by Sir Claude and Lady Hill), 6 mobile fire stations, 19 telephone points and 10 breakdown crews (each consisting of a leader and 10 men).

The clearing of the roads on race days would have to start from about 8am. This would be undertaken by a team of Special Constables on motorcycles, followed by "Specials" in cars and then cyclists who would undertake the final "sweep up."

Another problem was school children. The Matriculation Examinations at secondary schools close to or on the course coincided with the race days. Such a noisy environment was considered unacceptable and the examinations were transferred to a quieter location.

The Education Authority also decided that the elementary schools in Douglas and Onchan should be closed on race days and that, on practice days, morning school should be from 9.30am to 12.30pm so that children would be kept in school until the roads were opened after the practices.

Now drivers came to see the course. Towards the end of May, whilst the MG he intended to race – in which he had come second in the International Trophy at Brooklands – was being prepared, Eddie Hall brought a 1,087cc supercharged MG Magnette on a Saturday, tested it over the course in normal traffic conditions and then left on the Sunday. Whilst on the Island he acquired an old converted stable and arranged for its renovation as a garage for his use. This included installation of electric light and a zinc-sheeted work bench. Good work could not be done, he said, except in good surroundings. Hall also photographed every corner on the course, and compiled an album with notes, one of the most thorough preparations ever for a British race. He thought the tramlines on the promenade would play havoc with tyres.

Other drivers departed with grimmer sentiments. They told veteran RAC, TT and Gordon Bennett Trials organiser Colonel Lindsay Lloyd, who was helping in the organising of the races, that the course was a horribly dangerous one. They doubted whether they could complete 50 laps without an accident. This resulted in a relatively high insurance premium payable by competitors, who were deemed to be responsible for any damage caused by them. That meant that of the entry fee of £15 10s, £5 was allocated for third party insurance. Attention to safety became increasingly paramount – for example, granite chippings were laid on road surfaces, to provide a non-skid surface. Fencing in Onchan, in the interests of safety, was also agreed at the request of the Chief Constable.

Entries closed on 15th May. Drivers were required to complete a minimum of five practice laps, all within the permitted hours. Practising at other times would lead to exclusion. Three attendants were allowed in each pit but only as helpers. Repair work during the races was restricted to the driver and mechanic and had to be undertaken only at the pits. All competitors were required to be in position 30 minutes before the start. They could warm up their engines prior to the race but engines had to be stopped at least 15 minutes before the start.

Rules of overtaking required that the mechanic of a pursuing car should raise his hand if his driver wanted to overtake a car in front. The mechanic of the latter should then wave him on.

The first car to complete 50 laps would be the winner, and would be shown the chequered flag. Drivers who had been lapped would be allowed to continue after the winner had finished the race but all cars would be stopped 15 minutes after the winner crossed the line, irrespective of the number of laps completed.

Mannin Beg Entries

The Mannin Beg attracted an all-British entry of twenty cars, of which twelve were supercharged MGs. These consisted of eight Magnette K3 models (six-cylinder 1,087cc) and four Midgets (four-cylinder 747cc). The Magnettes were to be driven by Robin Mere (K3009), Eddie Hall (K3006), Ronald Yallop (K3752), George Eyston (K3003, the Mille Miglia car which he had shared with Count Lurani), Hugh Hamilton (K3008), Kaye Don (K3002, the Birkin/Rubin Mille Miglia car), Earl Howe (K3001) and Whitney Straight (K3011). Driving in his first major event, as was Yallop, Mere was so full of enthusiasm that he bought a Bentley to tow his MG to Liverpool and to use as a tender on the Island. He had all his tools cellulosed in yellow, as a precaution against theft. He was the first driver to arrive. Eyston was to drive the car in which he had won the 1,100cc class in the Mille Miglia three months earlier and Howe was to drive the car in which he had finished second in class with Hamilton as co-driver. Hall's car had finished second in the

International Trophy at Brooklands. Owing to the death of Sir Henry Birkin, Kaye Don was to drive Bernard Rubin's Magnette, which Rubin and Sir Henry had driven in the Mille Miglia. Don was already known on the Isle of Man as a representative for Avon Tyres and was destined to achieve notoriety in 1934. Whitney Straight was another non-starter on medical grounds.

The MG Midget drivers entered were Dennis Mansell (son of the Managing Director of Norton Motorcycles) and J. Ludovic Ford (who entered the car which he had driven at Le Mans with his reserve driver M.H. Baumer – they towed the chassis to the MG factory at Abingdon on the day before they sailed to the Island in order to have the rebuilt Le Mans engine fitted overnight, prior to driving to Liverpool to catch the Isle of Man ferry the next day). The other two Midget drivers were E.L. Gardner and TT motorcycle rider Syd Crabtree, who both entered the cars which they had driven at Brooklands. Crabtree's reserve driver was Walter Handley, already famous as the winner of four motorcycle TT Races.

One of the four Riley entries was that of Freddie Dixon, described by *The Light Car* as "a meteoric driver who can be counted on for thrills." He was already very popular on the Island as winner of the 1923 Sidecar TT on the famous Douglas outfit which had a lever-operated banking mechanism for the sidecar. This ingenious invention had caused a sensation. Dixon had also won the 1927 Junior TT on an H.R.D.-J.A.P. machine. The Mannin Beg would be his 21st Isle of Man race; his car an all-black, unsupercharged TT car. Victor Gillow, a London car dealer, Raymond Mays and Humphrey W. Cook were the other Riley drivers. Dixon and Gillow had entered four-cylinder 1,100cc cars while Mays and Cook entered six-cylinder 1,500cc models.

A four-cylinder Frazer Nash was entered by London-resident Manx driver T.G. ("Tom") Moore, owner of the Billown Estate in the south of the Island and one-time Proprietor of *Motor Sport* magazine. A six-cylinder car of the same make was entered by C.M. Needham. W. Sullivan entered his Morris Minor Sullivan Special.

The only foreign car was French - a supercharged Salmson - entered by famous British comedian Jimmy Nervo of the music hall act of Nervo and Knox. The entrant came from a circus family. He was in a high wire act with his brothers by the time he was eight years old and was a music hall juggler when he was sixteen. With Knox, he was part of the Crazy Gang. His interest in motor racing included ownership of an Aston Martin. The driver, J.H. Bartlett, was well known at Brooklands.

Mannin Moar Entries

The Mannin Moar attracted only fifteen entries of which only nine were starters. The only British car to start was the unsupercharged low chassis 4.5 litre Alpine Trial Invicta, entered by Manxman Alfred (also referred to in the press as "Arthur") Lace, the General Manager of Invicta Cars. The remainder of the starters consisted of Alfa Romeos and Bugattis.

George Eyston's Alfa Romeo was painted in British Racing Green, rather than Italian Racing Red. This was Bernard Rubin's car, in which Eyston had finished third in the French Grand Prix at Montlhery. It had been driven in the Monaco Grand Prix by the late Sir Henry Birkin who, but for his untimely death, would have driven it at Douglas. Brian Lewis was to drive a similar car, but painted red, owned by Noel Rees. Lewis had won the Junior Car Club International Trophy at Brooklands in this car. A third Alfa Romeo, to be driven by Kaye Don, had been driven to second place in the 1931 TT at Ards by Baconin Borzacchini.

A further Alfa Romeo was entered by motorcycle racer Walter Handley with Syd Crabtree as reserve driver. Behind this entry there was an interesting story, revealed by Walter's nephew John Handley in his 2012 biography *None More Brave*. Handley had an ambition to try car racing but his approaches to various manufacturers came to nothing. Then Giorgio Parodi, son of the President of the Moto Guzzi motorcycle company for which Handley was riding, spoke to Count Carlo Felice Trossi, President of the Scuderia Ferrari and a current driver of the team's Alfa Romeo racing cars. This resulted in Handley meeting Count Trossi and Enzo Ferrari in Milan in May. He told them of the forthcoming Isle of Man "round the houses" race and asked for the loan of an Alfa Romeo. With Ferrari showing no enthusiasm, Trossi offered Handley his own 2.3 litre Alfa Romeo. On Tuesday 4th July, Handley again went to Milan, only to be told that the team was short of cars due to crashes and that Trossi's car was therefore no longer available. After discussion, Ferrari agreed to prepare a 2.6 litre Alfa Romeo, which would have to arrive on the Island on Monday 10th July in time to take part in the last practice session for the race on Friday 14th July. The car would therefore have to be shipped from Liverpool at midnight on Sunday, a very ambitious time-scale. Then, only a week before the race, to his great disappointment Handley received a telegram informing him that the car could not be prepared in time. Naturally this was a severe embarrassment to Handley – the entry of the 2.3 litre car was in the Race Programme and had generated considerable publicity.

Five Bugattis were on the entry list. Richard Shuttleworth's car was a twin camshaft model, which had been driven by Louis Chiron in the Monaco Grand Prix. His reserve driver was Charles Brackenbury, who had never driven in a road race. Tim Rose-Richards had been Brian Lewis' co-driver at Le Mans. The other Bugatti drivers were Lindsay Eccles, T.A.S.O. Mathieson and Tim Fothringham, the latter in the car in which Sir Malcolm Campbell won the 1927 Junior Car Club 200 mile race at Brooklands. Mathieson had a two litre model, the others being 2.3 litre cars.

Other entries were Whitney Straight (Maserati), Raymond Mays (Riley), Edmund Harker (Harker Special) and C.M. Needham (Frazer Nash).

C.M. Needham entered his six-cylinder Frazer Nash for both races. The car did not appear in the first two practises and although reserve driver N.A. Berry drove the car in the third session on its Mannin Moar number as pictured, it was a non-starter for both races. [Ray Stanfield collection]

Practices

Douglas was a divided town. Part of the population wanted to welcome the racing fraternity; part did not.

"One would like to say that the town is alive with excitement and that for the past week nothing has been the topic of conversation but the forthcoming races and the chances of the drivers" wrote a correspondent for *The Autocar* immediately ahead of race week. "But something is lacking. . ."

That "something" was the traditional thrilling atmosphere that was experienced during the TT motorcycle races.

Whilst the Island had proved itself to be a lover of racing, what angered the opposition group was the disruption this type of racing was going to cause in the heart of town at the peak of the season.

Bus services in the town and to other parts of the Island were totally disrupted; all pedestrian traffic in the course area prohibited as from 10am on practice days and 9am on race days.

A large section of the town was shut off, observed *The Autocar*. "Inhabitants must stop indoors or escape from the race area before nine o'clock in the morning."

Douglas Gas Light Company was one of the welcoming groups. Its shop window was given over to a relief map of the course with toy cars, propelled by gas, which moved up and down the Promenade.

Elsewhere the vibes were different. "We were not wanted by the islanders or their usual July guests" observed *The Autocar* later. The sorts of visitors that were on the Island knew they could never afford to buy a car, it said, so to them private cars were just "a darned nuisance." The Island's traditional holidaymakers from Lancashire and Yorkshire seemed to resent the invasion of racing motorists.

What upset people particularly was a large notice on the foreshore which prohibited its use. Matters were aggravated by its remaining there even when the beach was not closed.

Even before the start of practice, the entry list was reduced by withdrawals. In the Mannin Beg, the two Riley six-cylinder models of Raymond Mays and Humphrey Cook and the Frazer Nash of C.M. Needham (also entered in the Mannin Moar) were not ready. Earl Howe had suffered an eye injury in the French Grand Prix at Montlhery and rumours that his MG Magnette might be driven by Stanley Woods (already the winner of six motorcycle TT races) proved to be unfounded. Whitney Straight, who had entered a Magnette in the Mannin Beg and a Maserati in the Mannin Moar, was also unfit to drive having sustained a burn to one of his feet while racing in France. Also in the Mannin Moar, the Alfa Romeo entered by motorcycle racer Walter Handley failed to arrive, as did the Riley of Raymond Mays. Edmund Harker, who had entered a Harker Special in the Mannin Moar, decided, wisely according to *The Light Car*, that his car was unsuitable.

One important fact emerged during practising. Power alone was not sufficient to ensure that a car would lead the pack. The skill of the driver and the technical ability to last the distance mattered equally as much.

In Monaco, said George Eyston later, it was possible to use top gear only for two brief periods. On the Manx circuit there were only "a few stretches" where a car could be worked up to its highest speed. Because of this, Eyston reckoned that Round the Houses racing was not as dangerous as it appeared. By imposing demands on driving skill, meanwhile, it helped to increase the ability of competitors.

Freddie Dixon described the course as "the trickiest I have ever driven on." It could be improved, he thought, by removing the section from St. Ninian's Church alongside the Playing Fields via St. Ninian's Road, Upper Duke's Road, Falcon Cliff Terrace and Victoria Road to Governor's Bridge. Instead, he suggested continuing up

Ballaquayle Road to Glencrutchery Road and past the TT Grandstand to Governor's Bridge, round the Governor's Bridge old road (to slow the cars on the fast straight from St. Ninian's to Onchan) and thence to Onchan Hairpin. Dixon said that he was reaching 106mph on the Promenade. He had no problem with the tramlines and the bumps. "I can sit back on the Promenade and drive with one hand!"

Brian Lewis found the course "very amusing" but thought that the surface was not too good for racing. There was too much loose gravel. He also asked for a directional arrow to be placed at the junction of Upper Duke's Road and Falcon Cliff Terrace where he had overshot the tight right-angled turn.

Tim Rose-Richards said it was "a very sporting course" and found many bumps.

Kaye Don, who was the first driver to take to the course in the first session, completed only one lap. He described the course as "very difficult."

The Mannin Beg and Mannin Moar cars practised together in all three sessions, which saved time and added to the spectacle. Although the Official Programme stated that practice times would determine the starting order in each race, confusion emerged in contemporary reports as to whether this was actually the case or whether grid positions were determined by drawing lots. *The Motor* stated in its 11th July report that practice times were used but a week later stated that lots were drawn. *Motor Sport*, the *Isle of Man Examiner* and *Mona's Herald* all stated that practice times were used, while *The Light Car*'s report referred to lots. Comparison of the grids with photographs and reported practice times confirms that the grids were indeed in order of practice times. This was novel. The first Grand Prix at which this system was used was at Monaco earlier in the 1933 season.

In the first practice, E.L. Gardner skidded in Church Road, mounted the pavement and buckled a wheel. He recovered and pressed on, only to be black-flagged and stopped after reports from marshals that the wheel was obviously unsafe. In the second session, at exactly the same place, he stopped with a big-end failure.

There was an interesting innovation in the first practice when Fronteras, the reserve driver of Yallop's MG Magnette, experimented with shoulder straps in an effort to prevent him from being thrown around violently while cornering at speed. He abandoned the straps after only one lap.

Victor Gillow had a torrid second session. He passed on the wrong side of the sandbags at Greensill's Corner, swerved at the end of Castle Street, in Finch Road and at Government Buildings and hit the bags at Onchan Hairpin. He also lost his radiator cap which he replaced with the top of a cigarette tin. On his last lap he hit the wall of St. Thomas Church, proceeded, but stopped at Prospect Hill with a buckled wheel. He complained of dogs on the course and said he had "nearly got one." Actually some of the Stewards expressed regret that he had not quite succeeded!

Dogs were a serious problem, as might be expected on a "Round the Houses" course. There were additional reports in the second practice of a dog at the pits and a terrier which approached the course from Bray Hill but was chased away. Both The *Isle of Man Times* and *Mona's Herald* reported a terrier going under Freddie Dixon's front wheel at Falcon Cliff Terrace and, surviving this encounter undeterred, attacking George Eyston's MG Magnette, which missed the dog "by a hair's breadth." This may have been a case of a reporter confusing the identities of the two Riley drivers because George Eyston, in an obvious reference to the incident at a dinner given by the Mayor of Douglas, suggested that an Act should be passed to prohibit mad dogs from the course. "One had gone straight for Mr. Gillow" he said, "but was flattened out and when it got up it was without its tail."

In a further incident, a stray Airedale, caught and secured by a breakdown crew with rope and grappling iron, escaped by chewing through the rope! It returned to the course before marshals chased it away. The Stewards issued a public appeal for dogs to be kept indoors but, in the third session, Tom Moore's Frazer Nash was reported as having nearly hit a Pomeranian dog at Christian Road and another dog (breed unspecified) at Duke's Road.

Among Mannin Moar drivers in the first session, Tim Fothringham hit a kerb at the junction of Woodbourne Road and Albany Road, ricocheted across the road and hit the wall of a house on the opposite side. His car was badly damaged, but the driver escaped with a grazed chin. Lindsay Eccles' Bugatti was sidelined by a broken conrod which penetrated the cylinder. Brian Lewis overshot the turn from the Promenade into Church Road and used the Castle Street run-off. In the second session, he was reported as driving "a snake-like" course in Woodbourne Road and was on the pavement at the Playing Fields, nearly hitting a house. In the third session there was a near-collision between Moore's Frazer Nash and Lewis' Alfa Romeo. Manxman Alfred Lace's four-seat standard unsupercharged Invicta impressed spectators with its silence and fast cornering but was considered uncompetitive with its supercharged rivals. He completed a total of eleven practice laps in all, more than any other driver except Freddie Dixon who completed twelve laps.

During the second practice session an *Isle of Man Times* reporter was taken on a lap of the course in the MG Midget of Syd Crabtree, described in the report as "the originator of the races." The reporter gave readers a vivid account, including "holding on for grim death" at Onchan Hairpin. He credited Crabtree with "judgment beyond belief."

Before the last practice session, Kaye Don was the beneficiary of a very sporting gesture. After completing only one lap in the first session, his Mannin Moar Alfa Romeo had suffered a serious loss of oil pressure which could not be rectified on the Island. His car had to be sent back to England for repair which meant that he could not practise in the remaining sessions. That made him an inevitable non-starter. Learning of this, Noel Rees lent him the spare car which he had brought to the Island for Brian Lewis, although Don was one of Lewis' main rivals. This enabled Don to complete four more laps in the final practice session in order to qualify. He changed back to his own car (by then returned from London after repair) for the race.

Throughout the practices, MG drivers had problems. Hall encountered an unexpected fault with a new sump, fitted with cooling fins, which had been designed for the engines of road racing MG Magnettes. It was so new that none was available when the Magnettes were shipped to the Island. Hall had one flown to the Island but, on fitting it to his MG in time for the practices, he discovered that oil, picked up by the big-ends, was contaminating the sparking plugs. When he cornered, meanwhile, oil was lost from the filler-cap at the rate of a quart per lap. Despite seven attempts to remedy the problem through the fixing of baffles to control the oil, the new sump was replaced by a slightly modified old one.

Hamilton found his Magnette's brakes "spongy" and had difficulty with carburation and an oiled plug. Meanwhile, the shaft of the supercharger of Mansell's Midget broke, necessitating an all-night session by the MG mechanics.

Kaye Don's problem was more serious. He became a possible non-starter in the Mannin Beg when his MG Magnette was towed from the course towards the end of the last practice session. The problem was reputedly a broken back axle. In fact, the half-shafts were twisted and the differential had been damaged. Don's chief mechanic, Donald Finlayson, was unable to locate suitable spares. The MG Competitions Department had brought a large amount of spares to the Island but had not anticipated this sort of problem. The only solution to avoid the car having to be scratched, decided Finlayson, was to find a privately-owned MG on the Island whose owner would be prepared for the vital parts to be removed. He hurried round hotels, car parks and garages and eventually discovered a Magnette which, while not a racing model, had a rear axle identical to that fitted to Don's car. Fortunately, the owner was an old friend of both Kaye Don and Sir Henry Birkin, and he willingly came to Don's rescue. He delivered the MG into Finlayson's custody and told him to strip whatever was necessary.

The fastest practice times were set by Freddie Dixon's Riley in the Mannin Beg at 4min 36secs (60.00mph) and by Brian Lewis' Alfa Romeo in the Mannin Moar at 4min 17secs (64.43mph). The maximum speed reached was said to be 114-115mph, much more than anticipated. These speeds made the Douglas circuit faster than Monaco, where the average speed of Varzi's Bugatti in the 1933 Grand Prix was 57.04mph.

1933 Mannin Beg Race – Dixon Wins Race of Attrition

Fourteen cars lined up for the start of the Mannin Beg at 9.30am on Wednesday 12th July. All were British – ten MGs, two Rileys, one Frazer Nash and the Morris Minor Sullivan Special. Bartlett's Salmson was missing, having dropped a valve in practice. The cars were arranged in alternate rows of four and three. It had been cloudy and there had been light rain as the course closing car made its lap. "Not altogether bad" reckoned *The Autocar*. The rain would help lay the dust and bind the granite chippings. Then, shortly before the start, the sun began to break through, drying the road surfaces and rendering hastily-contrived mudguards unnecessary. Drivers were relieved for some were still worried about the tramlines. Practising had been conducted in dry weather so no one had had experience as yet of negotiating the lines when they were wet.

Most cars had been stripped of all non-essentials to lighten them. During practising some drivers had risked driving without any tools, a risk which the Ford/Baumer team had regretted when their MG Midget had been stuck on the course with ignition problems and no tools

Hugh Hamilton, MG Magnette driver, is introduced to Lieutenant Governor Sir Montagu Butler at the pits on Douglas Promenade before the start of the race. [Magna Press]

to undertake the necessary work. Now, most competitors carried some tools but only those which they regarded as essential. All except Hall discarded their spare tyres, reckoning that the course was so short that the cars could be driven on wheel rims to the pits if necessary. Hall disagreed. He carried a spare wheel, a copper wheel hammer and a jack. He preferred the handicap of the extra weight to the prospect of a slow drive on a wheel rim to the pits.

British Broadcasting Corporation North Regional provided a live radio commentary on the race but not on Friday's Mannin Moar race.

On the front row of the starting grid were Freddie Dixon's Riley (4mins 36secs) and three MG Magnettes driven by George Eyston (4mins 42secs), Hugh Hamilton (4mins 44secs) and Robin Mere (4mins 48secs). The second row was composed of the Magnettes of Ronald Yallop (4mins 48secs) and Kaye Don (4mins 49secs), with Syd Crabtree's MG Midget (also 4mins 49secs). On the third row were Victor Gillow's Riley (4mins 56secs), Eddie Hall's Magnette (4mins 58secs), Tom Moore's Frazer Nash (5mins 07secs) and Gardner's Midget (5mins 14secs). The MG Midgets of Dennis Mansell (5mins 14secs) and Ludovic Ford (5mins 15secs) together with Sullivan in his Morris Minor Sullivan Special (5mins 19secs) brought up the rear. The count-down was given by holding up boards at five minutes and then four, three, two, and finally one, whereupon Chief Timekeeper A.V. "Ebbie" Ebblewhite started the race by lowering a Manx flag. As the RAC recognised the Union Flag as the official starting flag for British events this must have been a gesture much appreciated by Manx people.

The start came with "an ear-splitting roar." Drivers jockeyed for position as they raced to the first corner just 200 yards away. Kaye Don shot forward into the lead in his MG Magnette, passing Hamilton on one side while Crabtree passed Hamilton on the other side. Don was then closely followed into Church Road by Crabtree, Hamilton and Dixon. After several attempts, Hamilton managed to pass Crabtree coming onto the Promenade at the end of the lap, and on lap 3 he passed Don in Finch Road to take the lead. Meanwhile, Hall, who had already made a pit stop at the end of lap 2 to discard a makeshift mudguard and make a plug change, provided the first crash. He skidded in Church Road, hit the kerb and bent the front axle of his MG Magnette. According to *Motor Sport*, a front tyre had deflated after being cut by a tramline. As the only driver who had taken the precaution of carrying a spare wheel, it was ironic that now that he faced a burst, a wheel change would not be sufficient to get him going again, due to the axle damage. Other early retirements were Gillow, who stopped at the pits at the end of lap 3 with valve trouble, and Moore at Church Road on lap 4 with big end bearing trouble.

In the 1933 Mannin Beg race passing St. Thomas' Church, with the Manx Museum on the hill in the background, the MG Magnette K3 of Kaye Don (18) leads the similar car of Hugh Hamilton (16) from Church Road Marina into Finch Road. Don retired with camshaft drive failure and Hamilton suffered rear axle failure. [Magna Press]

On the third lap Eddie Hall's MG Magnette K3 punctured a tyre, probably on a tram line, skidded and hit the kerb on the exit from Greensill's corner into Church Road. The deflated tyre and the damaged wheel and bent axle caused by impact with the kerb are apparent in the photograph. [National Motor Museum]

After five laps, Hamilton led at an average speed of 57.76mph, closely followed by Don (57.30mph) Crabtree (57.10mph), Dixon (57.08mph), Eyston (57.06mph) and Yallop (55.57mph). At this point, 18 seconds covered the first four drivers. Crabtree was particularly impressive in hanging on to the six-cylinder 1087cc Magnettes in his four-cylinder 747cc Midget.

On the sixth lap, Eyston was reported to have retired at the junction of Woodbourne Road and York Road, with a broken camshaft drive. This promoted Yallop to 5th place and Gardner to 6th. This was the order after ten laps with Hamilton now averaging 58.82mph and increasing his lead over Don (57.70mph)Freddie Dixon, still in fourth place at the end of lap 10, had a nasty moment when he appeared to overshoot the turn from the Promenade into Church Road and stopped in the escape road (Marina Road). In fact, a binding universal joint had forced him to take this action. While his mechanic grabbed a piece of timber from behind the Riley's seat squab, Dixon lifted the rear end of the car. The mechanic then used the timber as a jack to prop the car before running back to the pits, about 200 yards away, for tools and oil. On establishing the problem, Dixon emptied a tin of oil over the joint. The mechanic then said he thought that one of the brakes was binding. Dixon spat on the brake drum and, when it did not sizzle, announced to those who were watching, "They're all right. That's how my wife tests her flat-iron." Secret signallers based in a Promenade hotel indicated to him that he had been lapped twice by now. He had to go "all out" to make up the lost time. Freddie accelerated so hard at times that his car no longer seemed steady. It tended to shake when crossing the tramlines on the Promenade.

After 15 laps, Hamilton's average was 58.16mph and on lap 15 he did the fastest lap of the race (4mins 41secs, 58.93mph, which was still slower than Dixon's fastest practice lap of 60.00mph). Don and Crabtree were still

In a race of attrition, only three of fourteen starters were running at the end. Hugh Hamilton, seen at the junction of Woodbourne Road and Ballaquayle Road in Upper Douglas, led the race from lap 3 until his retirement on lap 36. None of the six MG Magnette K3s finished and three, including Hamilton's, had rear axle failure. [Magna Press]

Syd Crabtree's "C" type MG Midget (19) leads Freddie Dixon's winning Riley (7) past Finch Hill Church in Buck's Road with a large congregation looking on. Crabtree, like Dixon, was a motorcycle TT competitor. In a fine drive, he held third place from the start until lap 17, when he retired after crashing in Onchan. [National Motor Museum]

second and third, (57.78mph and 57.56mph respectively).Yallop, Gardner and Ford made up the first six. During lap 15, Sullivan had retired at Falcon Cliff Terrace with a supercharger problem and Mere had retired at St. Ninians with rear axle failure. He had earlier been delayed with misfiring caused by plug trouble and had pitted several times but, after this had been resolved, he had shown his true potential by equalling Hamilton's lap time on the previous lap.

Crabtree, meanwhile, had problems. During lap 5 he had found that he had no brakes but had managed to continue and to hold on to third place. Now, eleven laps later, on his 16th lap, he hit sandbags at Onchan hairpin. With the supercharger damaged and a wheel buckled, he could only limp to the pits to retire. Sadly, he would crash fatally on the first lap of the 1934 Lightweight motorcycle TT.

Entering St. Ninian's Road from Ballaquayle Road, the supercharged MG Midget "C" type of Syd Crabtree (19) is followed by the Riley of race winner Freddie Dixon (7). Crabtree was third from the start until his retirement on lap 17 after hitting the sandbags in Onchan Village. [Magna Press]

At Avondale crossroads in Woodbourne Road, George Eyston parked his MG Magnette K3 (15) in the mouth of York Road., Like Kaye Don, his problem was camshaft drive failure. Robin Mere passes in his Magnette (1), which was later side-lined with rear axle failure. [Magna Press]

By lap 20, the duelling Hamilton (averaging 58.10mph) and Don (57.80mph) were more than two minutes ahead of their nearest rival, Yallop in the third MG Magnette. Baumer was now fourth, Gardner fifth and Mansell sixth. Then, on lap 24, dramatically, Don retired. His MG was brought to a halt at the corner of Hill Street with Buck's Road with a broken camshaft drive – the identical fault to that which had earlier side-lined Eyston. This left Hamilton well out in front. He had a nasty moment on Buck's Road when he had to brake hard to avoid a dog which had strayed on to the course but his lead rose even so, to 2 minutes 22 seconds. On the same lap, Gardner retired at the pits. Different reasons were given – plug trouble, big end failure and that he "fell off the track".

This Victoria Road view shows the MG Midget "C" type of E.L. Gardner (21) followed by the Magnette K3 prototype of Ronald Yallop (14). Gardner retired with plug trouble and Yallop with the K3's major weakness, rear axle failure. [Magna Press]

It seemed that all Hamilton had to do was keep going and he was sure of victory. At only half distance, with 25 laps to go, there were only five cars left in the race and none of them posed a serious challenge to Hamilton. Yallop was now second averaging 56.82mph compared with Hamilton's 57.96mph and the Riley of a relaxed Freddie Dixon was now 3rd at 53.06mph. The others were the Ford/Baumer team with Baumer now driving their MG Midget (4th but 15 minutes 6 seconds behind Hamilton) and Dennis Mansell (5th and last in another Midget, 15 minutes 19 seconds down on Hamilton). Dixon's chances of catching Hamilton seemed impossible.

Freddie Dixon is pictured during his stop in Marina Road, outside Greensill's Chemist shop, to pour oil on a binding universal joint. [Murray's Motorcycle Museum]

Kaye Don passes Government Office on the corner of Finch Road and Bucks Road. On lap 25 of the race he retired just round the corner, in Buck's Road, with camshaft drive failure. He led for the first two laps and held second place behind Hugh Hamilton until his retirement. [National Motor Museum]

He was eleven minutes behind. In the next laps he managed to narrow the gap by half a minute, increasing his average to 53.80mph by lap 30 (with the order remaining unchanged) and to 54.20mph by lap 35, but this was insignificant given the size of Hamilton's lead.

Dixon had contented himself from the start to let others set the pace. Personally he had doubted if he could manage to play a "waiting game" but he had managed to restrain himself, not once pushing his personally-tuned Riley to the sorts of speeds it had achieved in practising. Other competitors had lapped him. It seemed at one stage that he was out of the running altogether. His tactic, however, was to last out and that was what he did. Now his patience was to be rewarded.

First Yallop, who had a bad slide at Church Road, retired at St. Ninians on lap 31 with rear axle failure (as Mere had done on lap15).Now Dixon was second, gaining on Hamilton. We will never know whether he could have caught Hamilton, because, on lap 36, after leading since lap 3, Hamilton retired because of a broken rear axle at Governor's Bridge – the third Magnette to retire with a similar failure to that suffered by Kaye Don in practice. Sympathetic cheers greeted him when he arrived back at the pits on foot. Dixon was now one of only three left in the race and comfortably ahead of the others. At 40 laps, Baumer's MG Midget lay 10 minutes 41 seconds behind. Mansell's MG Midget was 12 minutes 15 seconds in arrears.

On lap 25 Kaye Don retired his MG Magnette K3 with camshaft drive failure opposite Government Office in Buck's Road, parking the car in the mouth of Hill Street. George Eyston's Magnette retired with a similar problem. Dennis Mansell passes in his MG Midget. [Murray's Motorcycle Museum]

Freddie Dixon's Riley passes Kaye Don's stricken MG Magnette, parked in Buck's Road opposite the Legislative Buildings where Don was to stand trial in 1934 for the manslaughter of MG mechanic Frankie Tayler in a pre-race crash while testing his race car on open roads. [Murray's Motorcycle Museum]

The Ford/Baumer partnership had adopted a policy of restraint similar to Dixon's - to hold a steady speed that was within the powers of their MG Midget. This had been rewarded by its survival but they did not get the second placing that once had seemed so secure. Their lead of 1 minute 34 seconds over Mansell's Midget was wiped out on lap 42 when Maurice Baumer was brought to a halt at Governor's Bridge when the under-bonnet wiring came loose because of vibration. He was stuck there for five minutes faced with a mass of tangled wires, which included the lighting circuit fitted for the Le Mans race, endeavouring by trial and error to establish which of the many wires would complete the ignition circuit. It seemed that he might have to retire. Indeed, it was announced prematurely at the pits that he had done so. Then his co-driver, Ford, tried the starter-button and the engine fired and he was able to restart. Arriving at the pits for a

Freddie Dixon has taken the first corner from the Promenade past the Collinson's Café and Greensill's Chemist building on the right and passes the hotels of Church Road Marina, lining up his Riley for the left turn into Finch Road, at St. Thomas' Church. [Murray's Motorcycle Museum]

Ronald Yallop, driving the second prototype MG Magnette K3, exits Onchan Hairpin from Governor's Road into Summerhill Road and the descent to Douglas Promenade. His car, like the similar cars of Mere and Hamilton, succumbed to rear axle failure, completing 31 laps before retirement. [National Motor Museum]

In an MG Midget battle, Dennis Mansell's J4 (4) leads while his mechanic looks back to check the position of the Ludovic Ford/ Maurice Baumer "C" type (12) as they pass St. Thomas' Church in Finch Road. They finished second and third respectively. [National Motor Museum]

change of plugs, he lost so much time that everyone began to agonise over whether he had enough time remaining to him in which to finish the race. By now he was 24 minutes 32 seconds behind Dixon.

Troubles with an over-heating gearbox meant that Dixon was restricted to third and top gears for most of the last laps. First gear could be engaged only when the gearbox cooled. When his speed rose, his pit staff, worried about his speed, waved frantically for him to slow down. When a "Go slow" sign went unheeded they amended it to "Please do go slow." Still it went unheeded.

Dennis Mansell's MG Midget J4 is seen outside the Isle of Man Prison in Victoria Road. He finished second to Freddie Dixon's Riley. They were the only drivers to complete the full 50 laps although the Ludovic Ford/Maurice Baumer "C" type Midget, which completed 49 laps, was credited with third place. [Magna Press]

The pit manager then descended to threats and rude remarks, according to *Daily Express* reporter, Harold Pemberton. "I have never seen in any race such fervent signals given to a driver to go slow ... but there has never been a race in which only two out of fifteen cars finished" he wrote. It transpired later that Dixon had misinterpreted the excitement of his pit attendants as being indicative of a need to go faster.

Eventually spectators began to wonder if anyone would finish. Even if the cars were still roadworthy they could run out of time. Eventually Dixon, too, must have wondered whether he could finish. Whilst victory was his for the taking, to keep going was no easy undertaking. On the last lap his Riley ran out of oil. Slowly he eased the car to the finish - and it expired when its engine seized a little more than a hundred yards after crossing the finish line. Crowds of spectators mobbed Dixon as he stopped and the police and race officials had problems in holding back the crowds to keep the course clear for Mansell and Baumer, both of whom were still very much racing, against the clock, in the hope of completing the full race distance of 50 laps within the cut-off time of fifteen minutes after Dixon's finish. If they failed, they would be flagged off, and would be non-finishers. In anticipation of this, the signallers in the pits of both drivers had instructed them to go faster.

Thus was achieved an incredible Manx motor sport first. Freddie had won Manx races on two wheels and three - in the motorcycle TT races for solo machines and

Race winner Freddie Dixon and his mechanic enjoy refreshing drinks after the finish. Dixon inherited the lead on lap 36, when Hugh Hamilton retired after leading from lap 3, and kept his Riley going to the end. Only Dixon and Dennis Mansell completed the full 50 laps. [Peter Kelly collection]

Runner-up Dennis Mansell and his mechanic relax after a gruelling race. In a supercharged MG Midget J4 Mansell finished 15 minutes after Freddie Dixon and a lap ahead of the supercharged MG Midget "C" type of Ludovic Ford and Maurice Baumer. [Peter Kelly collection]

sidecars. Now his Mannin Beg victory meant he had won also on four wheels and his unsupercharged four-cylinder Riley had defeated six of the six-cylinder supercharged Magnettes. After wiping grime from his eyes, Freddie celebrated with a glass of champagne and then was mobbed by autograph hunters. The *Isle of Man Times* said "Never has a winner had a more enthusiastic reception, never has there been a more popular win." Dixon himself, perhaps conscious that his win owed much to Hamilton's misfortune, said "I should never have won. Why, I did 60mph in the practices."

With approximately ten minutes in which to complete his final two laps, Mansell scraped home in time to clinch second position in his first road race. The flag was showing, however, to denote the end of the race before Baumer could start his final lap. Out of time, he was stopped. After consultations with the Stewards and with the approval of the Island's Lieutenant-Governor, however, and after the final result had been hoisted onto the scoreboards at the Start, officials decided that Ford and Baumer's performance merited acknowledgement. Their car had at least kept going when others had failed. Because of this, Ford and Baumer were credited with third place, and the prize money of £100.

It had been a thrilling, amazing race. The *Isle of Man Times* enthused "It had much to commend it – such as some of England's finest drivers, England's finest cars and time and time again the gigantic crowds at every vantage point were thrilled with exhibitions of magnificently daring and yet controlled driving." The retirement rate (bearing in mind that there were only two crashes) had been huge; the retirement of all six MG Magnettes with three suffering rear axle failure and two camshaft drive failures, completely unexpected, given their previous successes.

The Magnettes had been fastest, with Hamilton's fastest lap of 58.93mph, although Dixon's 60mph practice lap had been unmatched in the race. However, as *The Autocar* observed: A race in which there were an estimated 1,100 gear changes "and heaven knows how much brake effort" did not always go to the fastest. MG had learned important lessons at the cost of its failures. Five of the six Magnettes which had failed to finish had done so because of faults revealed by the stresses of the race, particularly the hard acceleration and braking. Whilst the pre-selector gearboxes had made gear-changing quicker and easier by enabling drivers to change gear without needing to match the car's speed with the engine speed and this had given much enhanced braking power, these advantages had come at a high price. They had imposed excessive stresses on the gearboxes and all parts of the transmissions of the K3

The MG Midget "C" type shared by Ludovic Ford and Maurice Baumer rounds Onchan hairpin from Governor's Road into Summerhill Road. In a valiant effort, they completed 49 laps of the 50 lap race and, although strictly out of time, were credited with third place. [Magna Press]

Magnettes, resulting in one failure in practice (Don) and three more in the race (Mere, Yallop and Hamilton). This problem would be cured by replacement of two-star differential wheels with a four-star version, in the K3 racing models immediately and in production Magnettes in 1934. Kaye Don and George Eyston had been stopped by the shearing of a spindle which provided the drive between the dynamo and the overhead camshaft. Cracks had developed because of a latent defect. The spindles had been bored too close to their shoulders by the dynamo manufacturers and the spindles had cracked at this point. Thus, out of disappointment came simple improvements which would enable the K3 to regain its former dominance.

The Mannin Beg had proved to be an important testing ground for MG. It had confirmed the old adage that the stresses of racing provide improvements for production cars.

At the prize presentation in the Villa Marina grounds, Freddie Dixon received the Wakefield Trophy and a cheque for £200. His victory was acclaimed by a crowd of 3,000 who cheered him to the echo while some of his TT friends, according to the *Isle of Man Examiner*, sang the anthem "Why was he born so beautiful, why was he born at all?"

1933 Mannin Beg Race Results

Wednesday 12th July 1933. Start 9.30am. 50 laps of 4.6 miles circuit, total distance 230 miles. 14 starters, 3 finishers.

1. Freddie Dixon (1,089cc Riley) 4hrs 13mins 35secs (54.40mph)
2. Dennis Mansell (747cc MG Midget) 4hrs 28mins 30secs (51.40mph)

Failed to complete required 50 laps:

3. J. Ludovic Ford/Maurice Baumer (747cc MG Midget) 49 laps, 4hrs 34mins 9secs (49.33 mph)

Fastest lap, Hugh Hamilton (1,087cc MG Magnette) on lap 15, 4min 41secs (58.93mph)

Retirements:

Lap 3:

E. R. Hall (1,087cc) MG Magnette, burst tyre, hit kerb, bent front axle, Church Road

Victor Gillow (1,086cc Riley), valve spring problems, pits.

Lap 4:

T. G. (Tom) Moore (1,496cc Frazer Nash), big end problems at Church Road

Lap 6:

George Eyston (1,087cc MG Magnette), broken camshaft drive at Woodbourne Road junction with York Road

Lap 15:

W. Sullivan (732cc Morris Minor Sullivan Special), supercharger trouble at Falcon Cliff Terrace

R. M. Mere (1,087cc.MG Magnette), rear axle failure at St Ninian's

Lap 16:

S. A. Crabtree (747cc.MG Midget) following crash into sandbags at Onchan Hairpin

Lap 24:

Kaye Don (1,087cc MG Magnette), broken camshaft drive at Hill Street junction with Buck's Road

E. L. Gardner (747cc MG Midget), plug trouble at the pits

Lap 31:

R. A. Yallop (1,087cc MG Magnette), rear axle failure at St Ninian's

Lap 36:

Hugh Hamilton (1,087cc MG Magnette), rear axle failure, Governor's Bridge.

1933 Mannin Moar Race – Lewis Wins After Terrific Fight

For the Mannin Moar on Friday 14th July, there were just nine starters out of an entry of 15. It might have been worse but for some quick repair work. Tim Fothringham's Bugatti which had crashed during practising had been repaired in time only by flying in spare parts from Brooklands.

The only British car, and the only unsupercharged, was the four-seat standard Invicta of Manxman Alfred Lace. It had performed well in practices but was still outmatched by the three Alfa Romeos and five Bugattis. The only drivers who had competed in Wednesday's Mannin Beg were George Eyston and Kaye Don, both driving Alfa Romeos.

Lack of numbers led to speculation, in the light of what had happened in the Mannin Beg, as to whether there would be any finishers. This helped to irritate even more the already vocal race critics. Was all the inconvenience to be in aid of just a fiasco? *The Autocar* referred to "a certain unpleasantness generally" and said "it was stated on no very certain grounds that mass meetings of irate citizens had condemned the races roundly." It claimed that one man was heard to say that the Douglas horse trams were fast enough for anyone. Another allegation was that a man had almost attacked a press photographer, apparently holding him responsible for "this murderous business." *The Motor*, however, contained no such reports.

Pre-race rumours suggested that several drivers were so anxious for a finish that they were considering the adoption by them of trials procedures. This included unofficial check points around the course with target times in which to reach them.

Douglas woke up to heavy rain which quickly cleared

Brian Lewis (bare arms) and George Eyston (white overalls) chat on the starting grid between their Alfa Romeos. They finished first and third respectively with the Bugatti of Tim Rose-Richards second. [Stenlake Publishing]

and the roads were drying as competitors made their way to the start. Spectators were slow to appear and many of the grandstands had empty seats. These contributed to a somewhat gloomy atmosphere, although the race proved to be full of excitement.

The front row of the starting grid contained the Alfa Romeos of Brian Lewis (4mins 17secs, 64.43mph) and George Eyston (4mins 21secs), and the Bugattis of Charles Brackenbury (shared with Richard Shuttleworth) and Tim Rose-Richards (both 4mins 27secs). The second row was formed by the Bugattis of Lindsay Eccles (4mins 32secs), Mathieson (4mins 37secs) and Tim Fothringham (4mins 48secs), with Alfred Lace's Invicta (4mins 49secs) and Kaye Don's Alfa Romeo (4mins 56secs) on the back row.

Brackenbury led into Church Road, but first Eyston and then both Lewis and Rose-Richards passed him on the first lap. Eyston led at the end of the lap, averaging 60.21mph from a standing start, followed by Lewis, Rose-Richards, Brackenbury, Fothringham, Don and Mathieson, with Lace last.

Eccles was the first to retire. Having pitted at the end of lap 3 because of a gearbox problem, he rejoined the race some five laps behind the leaders. Busily pumping up fuel pressure, he let his attention wander from the road ahead. A wall appeared directly in front at Duke's Road. Try as he would, he was unable to avoid it. The resultant impact broke a front spring, putting him out of the race.

After five laps Eyston still led, averaging 62.73mph, but his brakes appeared to be deteriorating. The order behind him remained as at the end of the first lap (except that Eccles was out) but with Lewis and Rose-Richards both gaining ground. The latter was credited with the fastest lap, at 63.94mph.

On lap 7, at his third attempt, Lewis passed Eyston on Buck's Road, and on lap 9, Rose-Richards took second place from Eyston. At the end of lap 9, Mathieson, already two laps behind, rejoined the race after a lengthy pit stop making carburettor adjustments. At 10 laps, the order was Lewis (63.47mph), Rose-Richards, Eyston, with the remainder unchanged, except that Don had passed Fothringham who retired after 11 laps, having stopped earlier to cure a water leak. During the previous lap spectators had seen smoke coming from the car. He had stopped in Finch Road to investigate. Now he arrived at Greensill's Corner with so much smoke coming from the car that everyone thought it had caught fire. Again he stopped in Finch Road, just past the bottom of Crellin's Hill, and established that lack of lubrication due to a burst oil pipe had caused a connecting rod to hole the crankcase. Despite the frustration of his retirement, however, Fothringham was sufficiently good-natured to sign a boy's autograph album.

After 12 laps, Lewis caught and lapped Don. Three laps later, Lewis' average was 63.75mph. He was followed by Rose-Richards, Eyston, Brackenbury, Don, Lace and Mathieson. On lap 17, when Lewis set a new fastest lap at 65.19mph, there was an interesting development. Brackenbury had hit a kerb at St. Ninian's on lap 13, prompting the marshals to report that his cornering

Lindsay Eccles turns his Bugatti from Falcon Cliff Terrace into Victoria Road. After only three laps, he stopped at the pits with gearbox trouble. Continuing, he stopped again at St. Ninian's and restarted again only to retire after crashing into a wall at the Playing Fields, a short distance further along St. Ninian's Road. [National Motor Museum]

"seemed to indicate that he is excited." Indeed he was, because on lap 17, swerving on the Promenade tramlines, he equalled Lewis' fastest lap. Now, the spectators also were excited, looking out for him and shouting "here he comes!" when he approached.

At 20 laps, Lewis still led (64.10mph), with Rose-Richards 13 seconds in arrears and Eyston a further 39 seconds back, followed by Brackenbury, Don and Lace. The refuelling stops then became critical for Rose-Richards and Brackenbury. Rose-Richards came in first, at the end of lap 24. Fifteen gallons were taken aboard in 37 seconds as a seated Rose-Richards was covered in a special hood to protect him from possible splashes from the fuel. While he was in the pits, Eyston took second place before his refuelling stop at the end of lap 25. He took 40 seconds at his pit to take aboard 20 gallons, some of it slopping over the car, while Rose-Richards re-took second place. At the end of lap 28, after setting a new fastest lap on lap 24 at 65.45mph and increasing his average to 64.24mph, Lewis stopped and took aboard the same amount of fuel and had his shock absorbers adjusted in

Brian Lewis' Alfa Romeo (6) overtakes Alfred Lace's Invicta (1) in Finch Road. Behind them, T.S. Fothringham's Bugatti is parked on the pavement beside St. Thomas' Church where it had expired in clouds of smoke after a connecting rod failed. [National Motor Museum]

Brian Lewis takes the corner from Finch Road into Buck's Road, passing St. Andrew's Church on his left and Government Office on his right. The 1933 Mannin Moar was the first of his three Isle of Man victories. [Manx Motor Racing Club]

just 30 seconds - "a wonderful piece of trained organisation," said *The Autocar*.

In sharp contrast, when Brackenbury arrived at the pits in his Bugatti at the end of lap 25, a member of the pit team sprayed the car with fire extinguisher powder and then held the extinguisher to the head of one of the crew. There was an explosion of language among the mechanics as most were blinded. Shuttleworth, who was about to take the wheel, was similarly affected. On getting behind the wheel, meanwhile, he revved the engine and let in the clutch so violently, said *The Autocar*, that Brackenbury had to make a frantic leap to prevent being run over. This stop took 1 minute 42 seconds.

Whilst most competitors, and particularly Lewis, amazed spectators over the control they had of their cars, Shuttleworth was not so proficient. He was also a risk-taker. According to the *News Chronicle*, he missed death only by a miracle, coming within inches of walls, garden hedges and grass banks. At one point, when travelling at an estimated 140mph, his car leapt three feet into the air but landed safely. There was nearly a major incident when he had to use Marina Road as an escape road.

On lap 28, Rose-Richards was on a charge, setting a new fastest lap at 65.98mph, but unfortunately ran over and killed a cat at Burnside Terrace on lap 29. The positions after 30 laps were Lewis (63.92mph), Rose-Richards, Eyston, Shuttleworth, Don and Lace. On the next three laps, Lewis led by 10 seconds (reduced from 14 seconds), 5 seconds and then 6 seconds. By the end of lap 35 his lead was 8 seconds. Lewis responded to the challenge with a fastest lap of 66.24mph (4minutes 10 seconds).

After 35 laps, meanwhile, Shuttleworth's erratic progress reached even greater heights, "indulging in fireworks and sensations... and generally giving an impression of *joie de vivre* without commensurate increase in speed, but greatly to the joy of the spectators..."

Tim Rose-Richards was second to Brian Lewis from lap 7 until the finish, apart from a brief period after his re-fuelling stop. In mid-race he was as close as five seconds behind Lewis until his Bugatti was slowed by a misfire and loss of third gear. He finished two minutes behind. [Ray Stanfield collection]

according to *The Autocar*. After hitting a black cat and speeding between cheering crowds on the Promenade, Shuttleworth misjudged his approach to the pits. To compensate, he hauled on his handbrake. The Bugatti spun round in a circle and its rear end crashed into the four-inch stanchions of two pits. The off-side rear tyre was burst and partially wrenched off the wheel in the process and the front axle was broken.

A split-second reaction by the representative of a lubricating oil company probably saved a woman from almost certain death, according to the *News Chronicle*. Mrs Percy Butler, wife of a Surrey businessman, was standing nearby. The oil man ran to her, picked her up and threw her to safety along the footway behind the pits. She recalled later: "Somebody gripped me by the nape of the neck. I was lifted up bodily and slung to safety." In that same moment, pieces of the wooden pits, fuel churns, spare wheels and other equipment flew in all directions. Four pits were destroyed.

Freddie Dixon, who was seated on a pit counter, was seen to be thrown to the ground with "a terrific wump" and then be hit by a balk of timber which gave him a nasty cut on the shin. A Dunlop pit attendant was hit in the thigh.

That no one was seriously hurt was considered miraculous. In fact, many who were in the danger area were able to leap clear because the pits were open at the back. Shuttleworth was hit on the shoulder by a plank of wood but, according to *The Autocar*, "seemed to regard the whole thing as the world's greatest joke." His mechanic, however, did not think it was so funny. Using awful language, said *The Autocar*, he changed out of his overalls and apparently resigned on the spot!

A skid created an equally dramatic exit from the race for Manx driver Alfred Lace in his Invicta. Earlier he had

On lap 35 Richard Shuttleworth misjudged his speed on approaching the pits. He grabbed his handbrake and spun the car, causing its rear end to hit a pits stanchion and collapse the structure. People in the pits were lucky to escape serious injury. Shuttleworth was much amused but his mechanic resigned immediately, with a stream of foul language. [Stan Hughes collection]

survived an encounter with a dog at Rosemount and lost upwards of five minutes in the pits whilst he had adjusted his increasingly inefficient brakes. Now, after stopping in Onchan on his 38th lap to make further brake adjustments, he skidded on the fast descent of Summer Hill. The Invicta hit and demolished a telegraph pole and brought down telephone wires. These were draped across the road but were quickly cleared by a breakdown gang, just a few seconds before Don appeared on the scene. Lace and his mechanic escaped injury but the Invicta suffered badly, particularly in the front. Lace said later that he had had no brakes for the previous 15 laps, but as the only driver of an English car, he had felt an obligation to continue.

After 40 laps, Lewis had overcome Rose-Richards' challenge. Rose-Richards' engine developed a misfire and he lost third gear. This had enabled Lewis to increase his lead to 53 seconds, his average 64.27mph. By the end of lap 45 the lead was 1minute 26 seconds.

At the back of the field, after spending a long time in the pits, "Taso" Mathieson was having a difficult race, including a spin on the left hand corner at St. Thomas' Church, when he shot up Crellin's Hill. Fortunately no other car was near, and he re-joined the race safely without hitting anything. He was not so fortunate turning off the Promenade into Church Road at Greensill's Corner, when the foot brake of his Bugatti failed at an estimated 110mph on his 43rd lap. One report suggested that the brake pedal had snapped. Steering with one hand, he hauled on the handbrake, locked the rear wheels and then turned into Marina Road which had been designated as an escape road and had been used as such already. Unfortunately, the slip road was clear for only about 100 yards. A barrier had been placed across it there and at least 50 spectators were standing behind it. According to the *News Chronicle* there were about 400. Apparently they were unperturbed by his approach for they did not attempt to run.

Mathieson engaged third gear. The car skidded. A near-side rear wheel hit a kerb and the car was thrown into the centre of the road. Fighting to reduce speed, "Taso" forced the gear lever into second and then bottom, burning a leg on the gearbox casing. Screeching tyres and the black rubber skid marks on the road testified to its effect but it was not enough. Having spun twice, "Taso" knew now that he had only one solution to avoid hitting the crowd. That was to deliberately crash into a building. *The Light Car* said later that with amazing pluck, and surely knowing that he risked his own life and that of his mechanic, he swung the steering wheel, mounted a kerb and cannoned off the wall between Modes Ltd. (a milliner's shop) and Taylor's chip shop. According to *The Motor* he just missed the window of the milliner's shop. Part of a drain pipe came crashing down and splinters of the shop front flew in all directions. Then, in a half circular skid, the tail of the Bugatti hit the barrier.

Four people, including a woman, were knocked over and hurt sufficiently for them to be taken to hospital for treatment. They included three holidaymakers from Leigh in Lancashire - Miss Emma Risley, her fiancé Robert Evans and his sister Miss Florence Evans - who were reported to have arrived at the shop door at the time of the accident. Their injuries were initially reported not to be serious – Miss Risley had suffered back injuries, Mr Evans had suffered a fractured bone in one of his feet and Miss Evans had suffered shock. Later it was reported that Miss Risley

Alfred Lace in his Invicta exits the corner from Upper Duke's Road into Falcon Cliff Terrace, past an under-populated grandstand. He pressed on doggedly with deteriorating brakes until a complete failure on Summerhill caused a crash into a telegraph pole and forced retirement, fortunately without injury. [National Motor Museum]

had suffered a spinal fracture necessitating a plaster cast.

In fact, the situation could have been much worse. Earlier that day someone had moved the barrier forward but Captain Phillips, the Assistant Clerk of the Course, had had it returned to its original position. Had that not been done Mathieson would have had significantly less distance in which to manoeuvre and more people would probably have been hurt.

Lewis reeled off the remaining laps, finishing just over two minutes in front of Rose-Richards, with Eyston third, only 17 seconds later. The fourth man, Don, was still running, but was flagged off at the end of the fifteen minute allowance after the winner finished, having completed only 49 laps. Like Ford in the Mannin Beg, he was treated as a finisher.

The race had produced plenty of excitement and, as was to be expected, higher speeds than the Mannin Beg. Lewis' fastest lap was over 7mph faster than Dixon's fastest lap in the Mannin Beg and the winning average nearly 10mph faster. This made the outright lap record 9mph faster than that of the Monaco circuit, which was less than two miles in length and lacked a long straight where cars could reach the very high speeds attained on Douglas Promenade.

1933 Mannin Moar Race Results

Friday 14th July 1933. Start 9.30am.

50 laps of 4.6 miles circuit, total distance 230 miles. 9 satrters, 4 finishers.

1. The Honourable Brian Lewis (2,336cc Alfa Romeo) 3hrs 34min 52secs (64.20mph)
2. Tim Rose-Richards (2,263cc Bugatti) 3hrs 36min 57secs (63.61mph)
3. George Eyston (2,336cc Alfa Romeo) 3hrs 38min 57secs (63.05mph)

Failed to complete required 50 laps:

4. Kaye Don (2,336cc Alfa Romeo), 49 laps, 3hrs 57min 4secs (57.04mph)

Fastest lap, The Honourable Brian Lewis (2,336cc Alfa Romeo) 4min 10secs (66.24mph)

Retirements:

Lap 4:

A.H. Lindsay Eccles (2,263cc Bugatti), broken front spring – crash at Duke's Road

Lap 12:

T.S. Fothringham (2,263cc Bugatti), broken con-rod, Finch Road

Lap 36:

R.O. Shuttleworth (2,300cc Bugatti), crash at pits

Lap 38:

A.C. Lace (4,467cc Invicta), crash into telegraph pole, Summer Hill

Lap 44:

T.A.S.O. Mathieson (1,998cc Bugatti), crash, Marina Road.

Reaction

According to *The Autocar* the Mannin Beg was "a flop" with grandstands half empty, but the Mannin Moar was "a great race". *The Motor* suggested that, because of the number of retirements, the races could not be considered "an unqualified success."

The Light Car saw the events, as "two classic events well worthy of taking their place on the International Calendar and deserving next year of a far bigger entry." While admitting that there were critics on the Island the magazine made the astonishing claim that "at least 100,000 folk followed every minute and move" of the races.

Certainly, mistakes had been many and public irritation was widespread. A reader's letter to The *Isle of Man Examiner* complained that the town had been shut up for three days, with "Hitler-like prohibitions" and stoppage of trade. The balanced *Examiner* leader stated that no event in the British Isles would get a better Press and no sporting contest could produce a greater thrill than the Mannin Moar. Was the cost worthwhile? In terms of visitors the events were a failure, the shore being closed on five mornings out of nine. In any poll of the Town, the overwhelming majority would be against, but no hasty decision should be made. A long view should be taken, allowing an experiment for a year or two, but there should be changes. The closure of the shore and disruption of trade should be reduced with practices held in early mornings and completed by 7.30am or 8.00am. The races should be held in June or September (preferably immediately after the motorcycle TT) and race days should be Friday and Monday to avoid affecting the same visitors twice.

Isle of Man Times Editor, George Brown, urged forgiveness. Mistakes were lessons which should be digested, and faults should be looked for and remedied for another year. There were unnecessary restrictions, particularly the closure of the foreshore and placing of some barriers further from the course than necessary. Crowd control had been excessive as there was a "tradition of obedience" among Manx people well used to motorcycle races. He thought that practices should be held in early mornings and it was unnecessary to close the roads as early as one hour before the start of racing. Despite his criticisms, however, he demonstrated his continued support for the races by notifying the Town Clerk that if the races continued the Times was prepared to double its contribution to the Guarantee Fund. That was how much faith the Times had in the races, he said.

It was reported later that the races had cost £3,400,

which meant that the full amount of the Guarantee Fund (£3,235) would be required. Of 240 Guarantors, 200 had paid by 3rd November, with the majority of them paying cheerfully and saying "carry on." Most of the few who had not paid were said to be away on holiday.

In the first week of November, two Manx newspapers reported a threatened boycott of Island races by British drivers. A statement issued by the Secretary of the British Racing Drivers' Club complained that "Taso" Mathieson, a Club member, had been threatened by Manx officials with arrest and imprisonment as a result of injuries suffered by spectators when he crashed in Marina Road during the Mannin Moar race. As all drivers were insured by the RAC against liability for claims by third parties this action, even if legal, was unreasonable and unwarranted, and the BRDC would ask members to refrain from entering for Manx races unless and until the RAC informed the Club that there would be no danger of repetition. The statement is difficult to understand and the BRDC may have misunderstood the legal position.

No more was heard of the threatened drivers' strike, but Miss Risley made a claim for damages against Mathieson and the RAC. At a three-day trial in Douglas in June 1934 the jury exonerated Mathieson from liability but decided that the RAC was negligent as the slip road was not long enough and the barrier should have been stronger. The jury awarded Miss Risley damages totalling £1,190, payable by the RAC.

One month later, however, when the case came before the Court again for judgement to be granted to Miss Risley, the RAC Advocate applied for the verdict to be set aside, claiming that the RAC had not been negligent. The Highway Board was responsible for the erection of barriers in positions indicated by the Chief Constable. The RAC, through Captain Phillips, had merely approved the positioning of the barrier and Phillips, finding that the barrier had been moved nearer to the course, had moved it back to the position fixed by the Chief Constable.

In October 1934 the Judge, Deemster Farrant, accepted the RAC's argument and set aside the jury's verdict, leaving Miss Risley without compensation but with the option of a claim against the Highway Board.

In a leader headed "Justice must be done" the *Isle of Man Examiner* suggested that the Government should make an ex gratia payment to Miss Risley or a grant from public funds. National prestige was involved, and a fight to the finish would probably result in a payment out of public funds by the Highway Board. Nothing more was heard until 1st March 1935 when the *Examiner* reported that Miss Risley's claim had been settled. Neither the payer nor the settlement terms were disclosed but a representative of the RAC's insurers had been on the Island during the week of the report.

1934 Mannin Beg And Mannin Moar – Wins For Black And Lewis

Planning

A week after the 1933 event the *Isle of Man Examiner* quoted a Sunday Dispatch claim that the Mannin Races would be repeated in 1934. Island authorities were taking steps to meet all reasonable causes for complaint, the Dispatch said. The races would be held in May, June or September, with early morning practices. The foreshore would remain open and footbridges would be erected over roadways. It was alleged that some tradesmen had reported increased trade during the 1933 race period. Those who had reported losses had agreed that the new proposals would alter the position.

The *Examiner* pointed out that no definite decision would be made until the 1933 event had been reviewed. Nevertheless, it felt that the Dispatch article was substantially correct and hoped that the premature

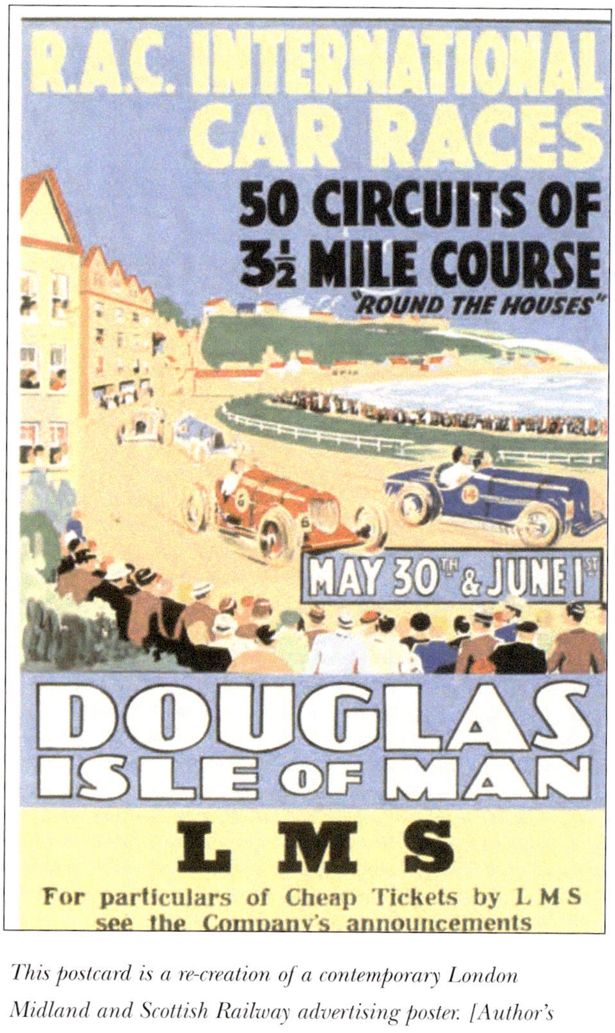

This postcard is a re-creation of a contemporary London Midland and Scottish Railway advertising poster. [Author's collection]

Charlie Martin's MG Magnette K3 is parked at the temporary pits on Douglas sea front. In 1935, with unusually high tides during both races, the pits became flooded and mechanics were drenched by spray. [Magna Press]

announcement would be confirmed by events.

In October 1933, Tynwald agreed to contribute £5,000 towards the cost of the TT motorcycle races and the Mannin car races in 1934. Later, it was decided that the car races would receive £1,500 towards a total cost of £3,500.

On 1st December 1933 the *Examiner* reported that a Manx delegation had met RAC representatives Colonel Lindsay Lloyd and Captain Phillips in London. Objections from the 1933 races were considered, particularly the questions of free access to the foreshore and erection of footbridges. The Mathieson incident during the Mannin Moar race was also discussed.

A shorter, less twisty, course of 3.658 miles was proposed, reducing the total distance of the races, over 50 laps, from 230 miles to 182.9 miles. The start would be moved north along the Promenade from the Villa Marina to the Crescent Cinema. A covered grandstand would be erected in an open area in front of the cinema and the pits would be opposite, on the seaward side of the road, set back, to keep the roadway clear for the cars. Douglas Corporation later undertook levelling of the the pavement area to make this possible.

The proposed course turned right at Broadway, forked left into York Road and went from there via Stony Hill to the foot of Bray Hill. There it took a hairpin right turn up the famous hill to a long straight into Glencrutchery Road, past the TT grandstand and on to Governor's Bridge and Main Road, Onchan, following the 1933 course. A hairpin bend there (known locally as "the lazy corner") turned the course into Hague Road. This bend became known to competitors as "Hong Kong," the latter, presumably, sounding like Onchan. From here the course descended Summer Hill to the Promenade.

The new course reduced the number of acute bends from twelve to three. Longer straights provided better passing opportunities so, whilst braking and acceleration

The tail end of the field turns from the Promenade into Broadway on the first lap of the race. [Stan Hughes collection]

would still be important, really high speed would count for infinitely more than in 1933. A lap speed of 80mph was believed to be "not improbable." The organisers thought this would make the Mannin Races resemble far more closely a continental Grand Prix.

In December 1933 the *Examiner* reported lack of liaison between the RAC and the ACU. The proposed dates for the 1934 Mannin Beg and Mannin Moar were Wednesday 30th May and Friday 1st June respectively, while the motorcycle TT practices were scheduled to start on Thursday 31st May and to continue daily until the following Saturday week. This, it was said, would mean the loss of TT practices on 31st May and 1st June. The matter was resolved by the loss of one TT practice, on the day of the Mannin Moar.

The *Isle of Man Times* of 13th January 1934 announced the adoption of the proposed course as discussed at the London meeting. It commented that the course would avoid a large portion of the business area of the town and that the foreshore would be kept open with footbridge access. It also reported that riding mechanics would no longer be carried in competing cars. Later, it was confirmed that single-seat racing cars would be accepted.

In February *Mona's Herald* reported that the cost of the 1934 races was estimated at £3,500. It was agreed that the Isle of Man Government and Douglas Corporation would each contribute £1,500, with the balance of £500 to be raised by public subscription. The Government and the Corporation agreed to share equally a deficit of £1,100 from 1933.

While visiting the Island, Captain Phillips was interviewed by Manx newspapers. He confirmed that practices would take place from 6.30am to 7.30am (later altered by the Highway Board to 5.00am to 7.00am) on Monday and Tuesday 28th and 29th May, with races taking place between 10am and 1pm on Wednesday 30th May and Friday 1st June. The foreshore would remain open. Drivers had been consulted and were strongly in favour of the new, faster course. Approximately 50 entries in total were expected for the two races – about 20 for the Mannin Moar and 25-30 for the Mannin Beg. Unfortunately, however, the Mannin Beg was still limited to supercharged 1,100cc and unsupercharged 1,500cc cars, again forcing supercharged 1,500cc cars to compete in the Mannin Moar against cars of unlimited capacity.

A problem arose over vehicle registration. Racing cars were not registered or licensed in England which meant they were unable to comply with Manx registration requirements. It was therefore agreed by the Highway Board that racing cars could be registered on the Island according to their RAC race numbers and exempted from payment of any Manx registration fees.

Mannin Beg Entries

MGs in various forms, but principally Magnettes, accounted for 15 of the 25 entries in the Mannin Beg. They included two teams of three Magnettes, one team entered by entrant and driver George Eyston and the other by another entrant and driver, the former motorcycle TT rider and 1931 RAC TT winner Norman Black. Other members of Eyston's team were two TT motorcycle race winners, Walter Handley and Charlie Dodson, both of whom would be staying on the Island after the Mannin Beg to ride the TT. The Mannin Beg was to be Dodson's first road race for cars but, in September1934, he would win the car TT at Ards driving an unsupercharged MG Magnette. Therefore, with Freddie Dixon also competing, there would be two current and two former motorcycle TT riders in the race.

While Handley and Dodson would drive the latest light-bodied K3 Magnettes (K3026 and K3020 respectively), Eyston had an entirely different car (K3023), which would make its first public appearance on the Isle of Man. He had ordered the car in the autumn of 1933. Based on the new K3 design, it was known as EX 135. It had two interchangeable bodies: one extremely streamlined with a wedge-shaped front to reduce drag, for attempts on track records; the other useable for road races such as the Mannin Beg. The car was actually "tailor-made" to fit Eyston. The cream and brown liveried record-breaking body would become known as the "Humbug." The road-racing body, which featured a larger, open cockpit for the driver, would be nicknamed the "Coal Scuttle".

Norman Black's team consisted of himself (driving K3024), A.P. Hamilton (K3022) and the outstanding Kaye Don (K3021). Roy Eccles (cousin of Mannin Moar driver Lindsay Eccles) entered two cars, to be driven by himself (K3027) and Charlie Martin (K3025). Other Magnettes were entered by their drivers, Ron Horton the holder of numerous international records (K3007), P.L. Donkin (K3013), Eddie Hall the winner of the Instone Trophy for the best performance at Brooklands in 1933 (K3006), Geoffrey "Jock" Manby-Colegrave (K3004) and Hugh Hamilton (K3009). The latter was an Irish-born 29 years old salesman with University Motors, the London MG distributors. He had led the 1933 Mannin Beg for 33 laps and, driving a J4 Midget in the 1933 TT, had finished only 40 seconds behind Nuvolari's winning K3 Magnette despite a disastrous seven minute pit stop. Two MG Midgets were entered, to be driven by Bill Everitt (QA0251) and F. Allen (J4004).

The challengers to the 15 MGs included the new, and subsequently withdrawn, ERA and six Rileys. Three of the latter were prepared and entered by Freddie Dixon. He intended to drive one of two six-cylinder 1,485cc versions, with the other being driven by Cyril Paul. After the race, the engines of both cars would be exchanged for 1,807cc engines and raced in the Mannin Moar. A four cylinder 1,089cc version was entrusted to Dixon's "apprentice", 26-year-old Liverpool-born but South African-raised Pat Fairfield, otherwise known as "Skidder" Fairfield because of his driving style. Other four-cylinder cars were entered by Victor Gillow, E.K. "Teddy" Rayson and Bobby Baird.

The three remaining entries were a Singer entered by Arthur Fox, to be driven by The Honourable Brian Lewis, the McEvoy Special of H. Laird (a bored-out Wolseley Hornet with a modified chassis) and the supercharged two-stroke Jameson Special of Dudley Froy.

Mannin Moar Entries

In March 1934 a new and exciting British racing car was revealed. Soon it would be tested on the Isle of Man.

During 1933 a 1,500cc six-cylinder Riley, known as the "White Riley," had been supercharged for hill-climbing by the British racing driver and ex-Grenadier Guardsman Raymond Mays. This car had achieved such notable success that it had inspired the formation of English Racing Automobiles Limited, a company based in Bourne, Lincolnshire, to produce racing cars based on its design, to be known as ERAs.

Here, it was believed, was the British racing car that would stop all the racing honours going to continental Europeans. The brainchild of Mays was resourced by wealthy 1920s hill climber, sprinter and Brooklands racer, Humphrey Cook.

Car designer and engineer, Peter Berthon, who had worked on other cars for Mays, had collaborated in its production with engine designer, Murray Jamieson, and Reid Railton of the Brooklands-based Thomson and Taylor Limited. Railton had been responsible for the chassis. Subsequently he would be involved in the production of cars for Sir Malcolm Campbell and John Cobb in their attempts on the world land speed record.

Two versions in light green livery, likened to giant roller skates with drivers, were the result in the late spring of 1934 – the R2A, a six-cylinder supercharged 1,091cc model entered for the 1934 Mannin Beg and the R1A, a six-cylinder supercharged 1,488cc car entered for the Mannin Moar. Humphrey Cook entered them both and, eager to test-drive the cars personally in race conditions on public roads, listed himself and Mays as their drivers. Cook was the first-named driver for the Mannin Beg, with Mays as "reserve." For the Mannin Moar the roles were reversed.

Considering that work on preparing the cars was still underway, the submission of entries was optimistic. Indeed, the R2A had to be scratched. It was not even brought to the Island. The R1A, meanwhile, was completed only a week before the Mannin Moar. It was given a half-hour test at Brooklands and then shipped to the Island. Any technical problems, therefore, were left to reveal themselves during the two short practice sessions.

A particularly exciting entry for the Mannin Moar came from Noel Rees and Arthur Fox. Rees had hired a Grand Prix monoposto (single-seater) twin-supercharged 2.6 litre eight-cylinder Alfa Romeo Type B (P3) from the Scuderia Ferrari for The Honourable Brian Lewis to drive. A team of 2.6 litre P3 cars had been raced in Europe by the Alfa Romeo factory in 1932, the drivers being Nuvolari, Borzacchini and Carracciola. This particular car had reputedly been driven by Nuvolari. For economic reasons, Alfa Romeo announced their withdrawal from Grand Prix racing before the 1933 season. Although Enzo Ferrari had previously organised the racing team for Alfa Romeo, he was not allowed to race the P3s independently in 1933, but only the earlier "Monza" models. During the season, however, the Monzas proved to be uncompetitive with the Maseratis and the P3s were released to Ferrari. Meanwhile Alfa Romeo continued with development.

In view of Ferrari's difficulties in obtaining the P3 cars in 1933, Noel Rees' success in obtaining one in 1934 was amazing. Behind this success there was a story of great persistence. It had been made known that new P3s would be available for sale to private entrants in 1934. Following this, *The Motor* reported that in November 1933 Rees had attempted to place an order for a new P3 with a deposit but, after a quick about-turn, Rees' order was politely rejected. Undaunted, Rees and Lewis went to the Alfa Romeo factory in Milan, where they pleaded with the Racing Manager, Signor Gobbato. Rejected again, they went to Modena to meet Enzo Ferrari, with the same result. Returning to Milan, they resorted to "supercharged pleading, supplication and threatening" when Gobbato eventually relented, wept, gave way and agreed to the hire of the car. The hire fee was undisclosed but a deposit of £2,500 (equal to £155,875 in 2015) was paid to Gobbato, to be held by him to prevent any dispute between Ferrari and Rees. The car was to be insured for £3,500 (equal to £218,226 in 2015) and the transport costs would amount to £250. It was alleged that Lewis' father, Lord Essendon, had used his influence and even that the Italian faschist dictator Benito Mussolini had been involved in the arrangement. The terms of the deal, according to Motoring Journalist Rodney Walkerley, were that Lewis would drive the car carefully, win the race and send the car straight back to Italy. This would be the first occasion when a P3 had been raced as a private entry and the first appearance of a P3 in the British Isles. Rees also had a

Tim Rose-Richards' Bugatti is unloaded at the pier at Douglas. Over the thirty years since the first Gordon Bennett Trial, racing cars had developed at a much greater pace than the Douglas harbour facilities! [Peter Kelly collection]

Maserati available for Lewis to drive if the Alfa Romeo failed to materialise.

With the Alfa came two mechanics, nicknamed by Lewis in a process of anglicising their names, as "Robinson Crusoe" and "Matilda." They were jealous guardians of the Alfa's secrets, reputedly reluctant to lift the bonnet when anyone was near and might see what lay inside. One unusual technical feature was the use of two propeller shafts to the back axle. This allowed a lower seating position and, with the differential attached to the back of the gearbox, a lighter rear axle. The car proudly carried the prancing horse badge of Scuderia Ferrari.

Other Alfa Romeos were entered by Kaye Don, Portugese champion Vasco Sameiro (the only foreign driver) and John Cobb, a future Land Speed Record holder and, in 1947, the first man to exceed 400mph on land.

Bugattis were entered by four of the previous year's drivers of the marque: "Taso" Mathieson, 1933 runner-up Tim Rose-Richards, Lindsay Eccles, and Richard Shuttleworth whose memorable 1933 race had famously ended in the demolition of several pits.

The 1933 Mannin Beg winner Freddie Dixon entered two six-cylinder 1,807cc Rileys, one of which he would drive and the other to be driven by Cyril Paul. These were the same cars as Dixon entered, with 1,485cc engines, for the Mannin Beg. Dixon had bought the two TT cars from the Riley factory at the end of the 1933 season and had carried out extensive improvements to them, or, in the language of the time, had *Dixonised* the cars.

Completing the entry list of twelve was a Maserati entered by Whitney Straight, to be driven by jazz musician R. ("Buddy") Featherstonhaugh.

Practices

Out of 25 entries for the Mannin Beg, 20 arrived for practice. The non-arrivals were the ERA of Humphrey Cook, Rayson's Riley, Allen's MG Midget J4, Froy's Jameson Special and Manby-Colegrave's MG Magnette. In all cases the reason for absence was that the cars were not ready.

Only one of the 12 Mannin Moar entries failed to arrive. This was Whitney Straight's Maserati, which was to have been driven by "Buddy" Featherstonhaugh. Again, the car was not ready. "Taso" Mathieson's Bugatti entry was taken over by the aviator Flight Lieutenant Chris Staniland, a member of the record-breaking British Schneider Trophy team.

For the first practice session, the weather was dull but dry. As in 1933, drivers in both races practised together, witnessed, it was reported, by thousands of spectators all round the course.

At the foot of Bray Hill, Freddie Dixon twice missed the corner, skidding each time and rotating completely on the second occasion. The morning's major incident, however, occurred on the bump at the top of Bray Hill when Horton's MG Magnette jumped one foot in the air and landed heavily, breaking a stub axle. The driver managed to keep the car on the road, sliding for some 80 yards trailing sparks. Interestingly, when Ettore Bugatti had seen the second K3 prototype in Italy in 1933 when it was used as the MG team's Mille Miglia practice car, he had immediately said that the front axle was not strong enough. The MG designers had then ordered a batch of stronger axles and Horton was the only customer who refused the modified axle.

Another bump, at Governor's Bridge, caused Staniland to take flight at some 100mph. He said that he reached a height at which cows grazing in the adjoining field could be seen over the hedge. On landing, he went into a terrific skid, but regained control.

In a gloomy morning practice at the foot of Bray Hill, Kaye Don's Alfa Romeo (10) leads Tim Rose-Richards' Bugatti (2) and Brian Lewis' Alfa Romeo (4). In the race Don was a non-starter, Rose-Richards retired and Lewis was the winner. [Isle of Man Times]

The bend at the junction of Ballaquayle Road and York Road caused problems due to loose gravel and a bump. Several drivers were reported to have missed a pillar box by inches. Loose gravel peppered it like machine gun bullets every time a car passed. Walter Handley's MG had engine trouble at Broadway, where Vasco Sameiro overshot the corner.

In the first session, the fastest Mannin Moar driver was Staniland in 2mins 49secs, a speed of 77.92mph. He was followed by Lewis (77.01mph), Rose-Richards (76.56mph) and Eccles (73.98mph). Among Mannin Beg drivers, Dixon was fastest in 2mins 58.secs (73.98mph). Other fast laps were those of Dodson (71.97mph), with Hugh Hamilton and Eyston both lapping at 71.58mph.

After Monday's practice, John Cobb returned to London due to the serious illness of his brother. It was announced that Charlie Dodson would drive Cobb's Alfa Romeo in the Mannin Moar.

An atmosphere of gloom over-shadowed Tuesday morning's practice session, with the tragic news that Kaye Don had crashed his MG Magnette late in the previous evening. The crash had occurred on open roads while Don was testing the car. In the collision, with a taxi travelling in the opposite direction, Don's mechanic, Frank Tayler, had suffered injuries which later proved to be fatal. Don had also been injured and had been detained in hospital.

Due to Don's injuries, A.P. Hamilton drove Don's Alfa Romeo in the Mannin Moar and Ron Gibson took over Hamilton's MG Magnette in the Mannin Beg.

Tuesday's practice was less spectacular than Monday's, although speeds were faster. At Broadway, two of the Rileys had problems. Paul overshot the corner and Fairfield, with a flat tyre, took the corner but mounted the pavement outside the Central Hotel. Shuttleworth also skidded at this point.

Speeds were much faster. The RAC had predicted that the 80.30mph maximum allowed for in the Official Programme's Speed Table would be exceeded and Lewis and Dixon were fastest in 2min 44sec, 80.30mph exactly! The next fastest in the Mannin Moar were Rose-Richards (78.86mph), Sameiro (77.46mph) and Dodson (77.01mph). In the Mannin Beg, fastest was Handley in 2min 56sec (74.82mph), followed by Hugh Hamilton (73.57mph) and Eyston (72.36mph), with Lewis and Everitt both lapping at 71.58mph.

Mona's Herald commented that Freddie Dixon in his "Silver Bullet" Riley had electrified spectators during practice by reeling off lap after lap at amazing speeds, and the paper regarded him as the hot favourite for both races. Certainly it was no mean feat for Dixon's 1,800cc unsupercharged Riley to equal the best time of Lewis' twin-supercharged 2,600cc Alfa Romeo, although it was said that Lewis could not use full throttle on the section from the top of Bray Hill to Onchan. Also, Lewis might have been holding back.

For Raymond Mays and Humphrey Cook, practising with their one remaining ERA yielded disappointment. Mays proved that it had enormous power. He even delivered a lap speed of 72.76mph, taking it up to 7,000rpm but it was all over the road and Mays was not happy about the prospect of racing the car in its condition. Tim Rose-Richards was then asked to try the car and he confirmed Mays' opinion. Achieving what Mays did was attributed by *The Light Car* to his pluck and ability. Adjustments to tyre pressures and shock absorbers made no difference and Mays attributed the handling problems to excessively stiff springing while the designer, Peter Berthon, believed the problem was with the lay-out of the steering. A great deal of work was undertaken in conjunction with Reid Railton in an effort to make the car race-worthy and another team even provided assistance. However, the available resources were too limited to achieve significant improvements. On the eve of the race, Mays, Cook and Berthon assessed what had been achieved and finally accepted Railton's advice that chassis modifications were needed which could be done only at the Thomson and Taylor works.

Because of this, the car was withdrawn from the race and returned to England. *The Motor* said that he had no wish for it to make a poor showing in its first race but added that, when the car's chassis had been modified "we shall see fireworks". *The Autocar* thought that Cook's decision was a wise one. The ERA was too new to have been tested, it said, and was unusually difficult to handle.

1934 Mannin Beg Race – Black Leads MG Revival.

A heat haze hung over Douglas on race day. The sun struggled to get through and eventually did so, but not until the race was well under way. *The Motor* commented "it was an ideal setting for what approximates to Britain's Grand Prix".

Media coverage of the event was augmented by the BBC's North Region providing live outside broadcasts of both races. There were two commentary points. Major Vernon Brook, a car racing authority, was at the Start. Victor Smythe, the BBC's official representative for all North Regional outside broadcasts, was at the TT Grandstand. Later the *Isle of Man Times* would say that the background roar of the cars, the cheering of the crowds and even the sound of an aeroplane overhead, had made the commentaries realistic. One of the commentators even said that the Isle of Man was the original home of racing and had mentioned that the Island was the original home of the Derby before it was moved to Epsom Downs.

There were 19 starters. Early race day rumours suggested that Freddie Dixon would have to withdraw because his car had suffered a cracked cylinder head, but his low-slung Riley appeared on the front row nevertheless. Dixon joined some others in making last minute adjustments. His engine had a misfire and he did not expect to go the distance.

Handley (2mins 56secs), Dixon (2mins 58secs), Hamilton (2mins 59secs) and Eyston (3mins 02secs) formed the front row of the starting grid, with Dodson (3mins 03secs) Everitt (3mins 04secs) and Black (3mins 05secs) on the second row.

After practising, Norman Black reckoned that there were four or, possibly, five cars which were definitely faster than his MG Magnette. For him to try to keep pace with them would mean either taking too many risks at corners or taxing the engine and gearbox too heavily. He had no reasonable chance of holding them so, as long as they lasted the distance, he decided to content himself with being an "also ran".

Reconciled to that, Black set out so relaxed that when he tried to wipe clean his goggles at the start, after being peppered by stones and dust by a fast-departing Hugh Hamilton, his chamois gloves encountered some Spearmint chewing gum on the lenses. He had stuck it there absent-mindedly!

Proof as to the wisdom of his tactics was not long in coming. It was provided by fellow motorcycle TT veteran Walter Handley. The latter's cream and brown MG Magnette had hurtled into the lead from the start, followed by Eyston, Hall and Black. Handley stirred up a cloud of dust behind him which lingered for upwards of 150 yards. Now he screamed down the Promenade at over 100mph to complete lap 1. He had been passed by Eyston but had regained the lead and built it up to seven seconds.

Embarking on lap 2 in a similar style, Handley took a tight line past the pits, scattering a cloud of dust over pit counters and mechanics. Then he skidded whilst trying to take the turn into Broadway too fast. His car slid broadside with both off-side wheels in the air and the rear near-side wheel hit the sandbagged base of the lamp standard in the centre of the road. With the fuel tank ruptured and the rear axle bent, his race was over.

That was the first of the contenders to fall by the wayside. More followed as Black held back and waited his chance. One by one they would drop out. The unfortunate Ron Gibson was left on the starting grid with a gearbox seizure. After a long time at his pit, he eventually retired. Other early visitors to the pits were Fairfield, Baird and Lewis, who retired with a warped valve.

Hall passed Dixon on lap 4, but Dixon soon regained second place.

Completing five laps, Eyston led at an average of 70.61mph. He was closely followed by Dixon, Hall, Hamilton and Black. Thirteen seconds covered the first five cars.

After a fierce battle Dixon took the lead on lap 10, pursued by Eyston, Hamilton, Black, Paul and Dodson. Hall had stopped at his pit on lap 8 and retired a lap later, with a burst fuel pipe.

At the end of lap 15, Dixon had increased his lead on Eyston from 8eight seconds to 28. The order remained unchanged except that Paul had dropped back, so that Dodson was fifth and Horton sixth.

On lap 18 Dixon had a bad skid on the tramlines approaching Broadway but continued. Fairfield had various incidents, including hitting the bags at Onchan and going on the pavement at Bray Hill.

Eyston's lead on Hamilton was only one second at the end of lap 20, with the first six unchanged. Dixon lapped at 73.57mph with a lead of 53 seconds on Eyston, who lapped slightly faster at 74.50mph.

On Lap 22 Hamilton, now in second place after Eyston

Turning into Broadway, Eddie Hall (MG Magnette K3) leads the similar cars of Ron Horton (1), P.L. Donkin (2), Charlie Martin (12), and the Rileys of Victor Gillow (18) and Cyril Paul (21). Martin finished fourth, Paul sixth and Horton seventh but Hall, Donkin and Gillow all retired. [R and L Kelly collection]

Leading going into Broadway at very high speed on lap 2, Walter Handley lost control of his MG Magnette K3. This photograph shows his unsuccessful effort to recover. [Stan Hughes collection]

had stopped to refuel, was descending Summer Hill when a front brake locked. This pulled the car sideways towards a brick wall. He damaged a Worthington advertisement, crashed into a telegraph pole (co-incidentally the same pole as had been struck the previous year by Lace in the Mannin Moar) and brought down the wires. As in 1933, the breakdown gang was super-efficient, clearing the road in 20 seconds.

Black was just 50 yards behind Hamilton when it happened. "Luckily," he recalled in *The Light Car* afterwards, "Hammy's car bounced back from the off side of the road to the near side and just left me room to scrape through."

Hamilton was forced to retire, with his front axle broken and his nearside front wheel buckled. Later, he remarked that he had come to rest beside an advertising sign "Hire a car and drive yourself"! He escaped serious injury on this occasion. Later that season, however, he would not be as fortunate, being killed instantly on the last lap of the Swiss Grand Prix at Bremgarten when his Maserati left the road, crashed into a tree and rebounded into another tree.

With Hamilton out of the race, Black quickly caught and passed Eyston to take second place. After 25 laps, the half-way point of the race, he was 1 minute 25 seconds

Freddie Dixon (Riley, 20) follows George Eyston (MG, 8) up Broadway. They shared the fastest lap at 74.40 mph with Eyston finishing third behind MG drivers Norman Black and Charlie Dodson but Dixon retiring out of fuel. Dodson also finished second in the Mannin Moar. [National Motor Museum]

behind Dixon and two seconds ahead of Eyston. Dodson, Horton and Donkin occupied the next three places.

At the end of lap 26 Eyston stopped for fuel and oil, taking 53 seconds.

Everitt's MG Midget lost first gear, making it difficult for him to accelerate out of the hairpin at the foot of Bray Hill. Several drivers had problems there as the surface began to break up. The Rileys often skidded, with Dixon

Hugh Hamilton in his streamlined MG Magnette K3 passes the sandbagged lamp standard where Walter Handley crashed on the second lap of the race. Later, Hamilton would also crash out, hitting a telegraph pole on Summerhill, descending to the Promenade from Onchan. [Magna Press]

and Fairfield almost colliding on one occasion. Baird also had trouble and *Motor Sport* said that "Gillow, of course, took an erratic line almost every time".

With 30 laps completed, Dixon had extended his lead over Black to 1 minute 47 seconds. Horton slowed, and later pitted, due to cooling system trouble. This let Donkin take fifth place, with Martin sixth. Dixon was now a lap ahead of third-placed Eyston, but had not stopped for fuel. Could he go to the finish without stopping?

The Morning Post reckoned this was a "race of narrow escapes." The narrowest of all was one witnessed by its correspondent on lap 37. It happened close to the junction of Victoria Road and Broadway. About twelve spectators were having tea on the steps of a boarding house when P.L. Donkin lost control of his MG Magnette whilst overtaking another competitor. The MG went on to the pavement on the far side of the road, swung round to face the boarding house and then made a charge at the spectators who were having tea. Donkin regained control only after the MG mounted the pavement. He swung the MG to the left and continued along the pavement for about fifty yards, making *The Morning Post*'s correspondent jump aside. Only then did it regain the road.

The correspondent wrote later, "The tea party proudly informed me that nobody had spilt a drop." Damage caused to the MG by the incident led to Donkin's retirement at the pits. This promoted Martin to fifth and Eccles to sixth.

Eventually Black realised he was lying in second place, with just Freddie Dixon in front. He decided then: "Right boy, let her go." Because of the bumpy condition of the road at Governor's Bridge he had curbed his speed here and this had kept down his average speed. Now, for the next two laps, he took the straight at Governor's Bridge flat out. He reckoned this to be about 110mph. In reality, however, it was too hectic, he decided. Most cars, and especially the Rileys, were being thrown about here. One observer reckoned that Black was airborne for 22 feet after hitting one bump!

This, combined with the effects of shock absorbers which were not quite tight enough, proved to be a bruising experience. At the end of the race Black said he had "a nice selection of bruises."

After two laps at a punishing pace, Black throttled back. What he had been doing, he decided, was putting at risk his already excellent position.

Even so, Black had a nasty moment when he decided to overtake Victor Gillow's Riley on the ascent of Bray Hill. Gillow accelerated. His Riley went into an acceleration skid on wet tar and Black only avoided a collision with the Riley's tail by coming almost to a stop with his off-side wheels touching the kerb. Even so, Gillow's offside rear wheel and Black's near side front wheel were reported to have touched.

Gillow excited the crowds with tail slides and slide slips. On another lap he hit the sandbags on Bray Hill. A couple of laps later he spun round in the road. Black-flagged by officials, he was told to bring his car into the pits for examination by scrutineers. When he did, they examined the front axle and wheels. The suspicion was that the car's brakes were not working correctly. Later, there were reports that a locking rear brake was the problem but this did not seem to concern the scrutineers. Gillow was told that he could continue. He retired instead, however, saying it was not worth continuing.

Meanwhile, Everitt went round the lamp standard at the foot of Broadway where Handley had crashed on lap 2. Various drivers had lurid skids there. They included Dixon, Paul and Fairfield, who had to change a wheel after hitting a wall. This led the *Mona's Herald* to comment that the lack of a grandstand was a lost opportunity, as "there was money going begging here".

Just five laps from the end, Black finally took the lead. Dixon had intended to gain a time advantage by not having to stop at the pits for refuelling. He had an auxiliary tank alongside him in the cockpit but this tank had been holed and his fuel had leaked away unnoticed. On lap 44 his engine was misfiring at the TT Grandstand. He completed lap 45 but on starting his 46th lap the car seemed to hesitate on the ascent of Broadway. Dixon made it up Bray Hill but just after the St Ninian's junction, virtually opposite St Ninian's Church, the engine sputtered and expired, only 17 miles from the finish and after Dixon had led the race for 35 laps.

Black realised what had happened when he passed Dixon and saw him looking disconsolately into his tank. "Thereafter," he would recall, "I enjoyed an exhilerating run to the finish."

One driver who did not was Charlie Dodson. A flying stone had hit his goggles, smashed a lens and driven some fragments into an eye. It pained him but he did not dare stop. On lap 43 he had passed Eyston to take second place. If he had stopped now, Eyston would have re-taken the position. So Dodson persevered to the finish with his injury. This meant that Eyston took third place, 37 seconds behind Dodson, followed by the Magnettes of Martin and Eccles, Paul's Riley, Horton's Magnette and Everitt's MG Midget.

Under the rule that competitors would be flagged off 15 minutes after the winner had crossed the line, three competitors were stopped. Pat Fairfield in his Riley had completed 49 laps, Henry Laird in his McEvoy Special, 46 laps, and Baird in his Riley, 35 laps. For Laird the flagging down was particularly upsetting. His little car was not really

Charlie Martin is pictured passing the café at the foot of Broadway. He finished fourth of the MG Magnette K3 drivers, behind the winner Norman Black, Charlie Dodson and George Eyston but ahead of Roy Eccles, the sixth placed Riley of Cyril Paul, the Magnette of Ron Horton and the MG Midget of Bill Everitt. [Stan Hughes collection]

Race winner Norman Black relaxes after the finish. He was first of eight finishers, all of which were MGs except for Cyril Paul who finished sixth in his Riley. [Peter Kelly collection]

a racer. It was for touring and trials. Yet, had it not been for clutch trouble, Laird reckoned he would have finished, which would have been a remarkable achievement considering what had happened to other competitors.

"It is probable", said the *Isle of Man Times* "that a more thrilling spectacle was never witnessed". The new course had proved to be much faster than the 1933 one. *The Light Car* suggested it had "much more the character of a road race". Norman Black had averaged 70.99mph, compared with Freddie Dixon's 1933 winning average of 54.41mph. The course had been a challenging one too. No team had finished intact.

For MG the race had been an emphatic victory, although overshadowed by Frank Tayler's death after Kaye Don's late evening testing crash. Not only did the company redeem its 1933 debacle by dominating the finishers' list with seven cars out of the eight which completed the course, but the individual performances compared incredibly well with the much more powerful

Roy Eccles and his mechanic are pictured with his MG Magnette K3 at the pits on Douglas Promenade. He finished fifth out of eight finishers of which all but Cyril Paul's Riley (which was sixth) were MGs. [Magna Press]

continental cars entered for the Mannin Moar.

Paul's Riley was the only non-MG finisher, in sixth place.

1934 Mannin Beg Race Results

Wednesday 30th May 1934. Start 10.00am. 50 laps of 3.650 miles circuit, total distance 182.9 miles. 19 starters, 8 finishers.

1. Norman Black (1,086cc MG Magnette), 2hrs 34mins 37secs (70.99mph)
2. Charlie Dodson (1,086cc MG Magnette), 2hrs 36mins 20secs (70.20mph)
3. George Eyston (1,086cc MG Magnette), 2hrs 36mins 57secs (69.93mph)
4. Charles Martin (1,086cc MG Magnette), 2hrs 41mins 5secs (68.11mph)
5. Roy Eccles (1,086cc MG Magnette), 2hrs 44mins 22secs (66.78mph)
6. Cyril Paul (1,486cc Riley), 2hrs 44mins 25secs (66.67mph)
7. R. T. Horton (1,086cc MG Magnette), 2hrs 44mins 54secs (65.58mph)
8. W. G. Everitt (746cc MG Midget), 2hrs 48mins 3secs (65.30mph)

Fastest lap, George Eyston (1,086cc MG Magnette) and Freddie Dixon (1,486cc Riley) 2mins 57secs (74.40mph)

Failed to complete required 50 laps:

Pat Fairfield (1,089cc Riley), completed 49 laps

Henry Laird (1,454cc McEvoy Special), completed 46 laps

Robert Baird (1,088cc Riley), completed 36 laps.

Retirements:

Lap 1:

R. Gibson (1,087cc MG Magnette), at the start with seized gear box

Walter Handley (1,086cc MG Magnette), hit lamp standard

Lap 4:

The Honourable Brian Lewis (1,493cc Singer), first

believed to be a blown gasket but later identified as a warped valve
Lap 8:
E. R. Hall (1,087cc MG Magnette), burst petrol tank
Lap 22:
Hugh Hamilton (1,087cc MG Magnette.), hit telegraph pole
Lap 37:
P. L. Donkin (1,087cc MG Magnette S.), hit kerb
Lap 40:
Victor Gillow (1,086cc Riley), retired at pits with brake problems
Lap 45:
Freddie Dixon (1,486cc Riley), out of fuel.

1934 Mannin Moar Race – Lewis Wins Again

Just ten starters lined up on Friday for the week's big race. It was a sunny morning with a heat haze over land and sea. There were four Alfa Romeos, four Bugattis and two Rileys.

It could have been fewer but for last-minute substitutions of drivers. As Kaye Don was still in hospital following his crash, A. P. Hamilton took over Don's black Alfa Romeo. John Cobb, meanwhile, had left the Island after Monday's practice to be at the bedside of his sick brother, Stanley, in London, who had died on the following morning. Charlie Dodson, however, took over John Cobb's grey two-seater Alfa Romeo, in which Lewis won the 1933 Mannin Moar. Thus, after coming second in his first-ever car road race, he now had an international champion's car.

The front row of the starting grid was shared by Brian Lewis in the Scuderia Ferrari Alfa Romeo and Freddie Dixon in his Riley. They were the joint practice leaders with laps of 2mins 44secs (80.30mph). Dixon had encountered problems after changing engines on the day between the races. The cylinder head gasket had broken, oil pressure had been unsatisfactory and there had been a rear axle problem. Finally, exhausted, he arrived on the grid 20 minutes before the start. The *Isle of Man Times* contrasted the Alfa Romeo "the most perfect product of the finest motor racing factory in the world" with the Riley and Freddie Dixon "working day and night to get his car fit to come to the Start".

The second row of the grid consisted of the Bugattis of Rose-Richards (2mins 47secs) and Staniland (2mins 49secs), with Sameiro's yellow Alfa Romeo (2mins 50secs). Behind them were Dodson's Alfa Romeo (2mins 51secs) and Shuttleworth's Bugatti (2mins 52secs), with the back row made up by Eccles' Bugatti (2mins 53secs), Paul's Riley and Hamilton's Bugatti (3mins 10secs).

Right from the start Brian Lewis delivered the expected. His lightweight Ferrari Alfa Romeo may have been difficult to handle on the bumpy Manx roads, leaping and shuddering at the slightest bump. Wheel-spin and a tendency to skid if accelerated too eagerly out of a corner may have been added complications. Even so, he delivered speeds that had never been seen before on the Island, travelling at an estimated 130mph along the Promenade. Audible gasps could be heard from spectators. Had it not been for the dangerous state of the loose surface on Summer Hill, *The Motor* reckoned that he would have averaged over 80mph. After the first lap *The Autocar* said he was "so far ahead that a presumably Manx cat atop the pillar of a boarding house gate yawned cavernously and retired certain of the result".

Rose-Richards in his Bugatti, Freddie Dixon in his Riley and Charlie Dodson in his Alfa Romeo chased Lewis hard. Actually, Rose-Richards held some power in reserve, sticking rigidly to a policy of not exceeding 5,000rpm. He wanted to last the distance; a policy Dixon well understood. There was always the prospect that the "unbeatable" might yet be beaten by the event itself and retire. Indeed, unbeknown to Rose-Richards, Lewis did have a problem. After a few laps, he lost third gear as the selector locking equipment stopped functioning. Ignorant of that, Dixon indulged in some uncharacteristic rashness. On lap 2 he passed Dodson at Governor's Bridge and reached the Onchan hairpin on Rose-Richards's tail, much too fast, brakes squealing and the car sliding from side to side. Rose-Richards slowed suddenly. Dixon shot past, realised he could not make the corner and disappeared up the slip road. That put him down from third to seventh place. To make things worse, whilst striving to regain lost ground, he overshot Broadway on lap 4 and dropped from fourth to sixth.

Meanwhile, Staniland had pitted and retired at the end of the second lap with a broken lay-shaft.

After five laps, Lewis still led, averaging 74.26mph and "practically touring", said *The Autocar*. The pursuers were Rose-Richards at eight seconds, Dodson at 30 seconds and then Sameiro, Eccles and Shuttleworth. The latter three, and Dixon, were observed in a fierce scrap at Broadway on lap 6, while Hamilton had a speed wobble while passing the Start.

Lewis' seventh lap, at 76.12mph, was the fastest to date. On the next lap he was a whole lap ahead of the last man, Cyril Paul. The fast-charging Dixon, meanwhile, was sixth on lap 6 and fourth on lap 7. On lap 8, Sameiro overshot the corner at Broadway, allowing Dixon to take third place, almost ramming Sameiro in the process. Dixon then speeded up still further, with a fastest lap of the race on lap 9 at 76.56mph.

By the end of lap 10, Lewis had increased his lead over

Freddie Dixon's Riley (7) leads Charlie Dodson's Alfa Romeo (9) and Richard Shuttleworth's Bugatti (11) off the Promenade into Broadway. Vasco Sameiro's Alfa Romeo (12) can be seen further up the hill. Dodson finished second to Lewis but the others all retired with mechanical problems. [National Motor Museum]

Rose-Richards to 15 seconds, with Dixon a further 27 seconds behind. Sameiro, Dodson and Eccles followed in a very close battle for fourth place. Dixon was observed to be driving hectically at Broadway, Bray Hill and Summer Hill, but the gap was now constant. Lewis was visibly mastering the Alfa with a more relaxed style. He was braking earlier, cornering carefully, accelerating smoothly and increasing his average speed.

Dixon slipped into second place when disaster hit Rose-Richards. Almost a Promenade-length behind Lewis, Rose-Richards arrived at the pits on lap 13 with steam rising from his Bugatti's radiator. Veteran TT car racer, Kensington Moir, who was in charge of the Bugatti pit, refilled the radiator but, when a mechanic tried to restart the engine with a swing of the handle, nothing happened. Repeated attempts failed. The engine finally fired only after an infuriating delay, when the carburettor was adjusted. By then Rose-Richards had spent five minutes at his pit and had dropped to ninth place - not that it particularly mattered. Soon afterwards the water came on the boil again and this time, when Rose-Richards arrived at the pits, after 14 laps, he retired. The cause of his problem was a broken water-pump spindle. "Who heard of a Bugatti water-pump spindle breaking?" wondered *The Motor*. Had such an unusual problem not occurred the story of the race could have been different.

Rose-Richards' retirement left Dixon in second place, 44 seconds behind Lewis, pursued by Dodson, 19 seconds back and still scrapping with Sameiro and Eccles. Hamilton was now sixth, but over a minute behind Eccles. Dodson lost third place to Sameiro by overshooting at Broadway on lap 16.

One of the most irritating retirements shortly afterwards was that of Hamilton in Kaye Don's black Alfa Romeo. The entire tail pipe collapsed whilst he was travelling at speed along the Promenade. He stopped to re-secure it but it dropped down again, this time becoming bent and mis-shapen by one of the rear wheels rolling over it. Technically the pipe was relatively unimportant. Hamilton could have continued. Race rules, however, required the presence of a tail pipe. This meant he had no alternative but to retire.

Lewis posted a new fastest lap on lap 20, at 77.01mph. He now led Dixon by 46 seconds. Following Hamilton's retirement, the new sixth man was Shuttleworth, but he was over a lap behind Eccles after spending a lap at the pits following an overshoot at Broadway on lap 11.

More vocal than most in his irritation was Freddie Dixon. On lap 21 he had roared under the wooden pedestrian footbridge after climbing Broadway, but then his engine had cut out. After a quick inspection, his audible comments were such that, according to *The Autocar*, mothers said "hush" and sent children to another place.

This was particularly significant as Dixon was one of the favourites among Manx children, probably because of his long and legendary association with the motorcycle TT. His popularity was reflected at the end of the race when he was mobbed by shouting boys and girls who wanted his autograph. *The Motor* thought it was "a fine sight."

Although stranded where he was, Dixon refused to accept automatic retirement. He walked back to the pits, collected some tools, returned to his car and investigated what was wrong. It was not until he had removed the sump that he conceded defeat. His problem lay with a centre roller bearing in the crankshaft. There was nothing he could do about it so he announced that "the shop was shutting for the day" and walked to the pits. From there he helped control the progress of Cyril Paul in the other Riley.

Meanwhile Lewis' majestic progress continued. Another fastest lap, at 77.46mph, increased his lead over Sameiro to 1 minute 27 seconds at half distance. Dodson, Eccles and Shuttleworth followed, with Paul sixth and last.

Shuttleworth was next to drop out. It happened on lap 30, with a broken conrod. This left only five runners. The order remained the same until lap 37, Lewis only slightly increasing his lead over Sameiro, who had a bad skid at Summer Hill. He recovered but later water poured from his radiator at Bray Hill and he stopped at his pit at the end of the lap. Dodson was now second but only 50 yards ahead of Eccles. Sameiro took on water, re-started, but retired after only one more lap. Later, he was seen at his pit, consuming Bass from a bottle – "an old Portugese custom" according to the *Isle of Man Examiner*.

Only four cars remained, but not for long. Eccles had been quietly gaining on Dodson, second by second, until, on lap 40, he came into the pits. With wheels locked, he overshot by about three pits. The rear of the car was jacked up and the rear wheels were spun. The pit crew looked relieved. Eccles re-started but after only a few yards, according to *The Motor*, "even in the grandstand opposite they could hear a very nasty clink! clink! clink! from the back axle". The crown wheel was broken. So now there were three.

With ten laps left, Lewis led Dodson by two minutes and one second. Paul was a further seven minutes behind. The latter visibly slowed at York Road but all was well. Dixon, however, remembering how his car had run out of fuel so close to home in the Mannin Beg, reckoned that Paul should not take a chance. Just finishing was all that mattered now. So Dixon borrowed one of Roy Eccles' circular pit signal boards, wrote on it "Plenty of time. Stop for fuel," and displayed it to Paul at the end of the pits. In fact, Paul had no need of it.

The remaining trio continued, with Lewis gaining a further minute on Dodson and Paul by the end of lap 45. Like Paul, neither Lewis nor Dodson had stopped to refuel, so there was anxiety that any of them might suffer the same fate as Dixon in the Mannin Beg.

Such fears were groundless. Brian Lewis completed the fifty laps at an average speed of 75.34mph. Four minutes later, Dodson repeated his second place in the Mannin Beg. There was time for Cyril Paul to finish third, just over 12 minutes in arrears. Paul was an unlikely finisher. He had been slowed by a misfire at the beginning of the race. Starting to turn into the pits, he had changed his mind, decided to try another lap and the misfire had cleared.

The Press verdict was polarised. "Great as were the thrills afforded by the Mannin Beg, the Mannin Moar beat them hollow", the *Isle of Man Weekly Times* commented. *The Light Car*, however, thought that after Dixon's retirement "the race lost much of its interest and compared poorly with the Mannin Beg". In fact, it was an interesting race, with Rose-Richards, Dixon, Sameiro and Dodson all chasing Lewis in turn and Dixon matching Lewis' speed for ten laps. Of course, Lewis had lost third gear early in the race, the Alfa Romeo had been a handful on the bumpy and slippery roads and it was impossible to know how much the driver had in hand. Was he simply looking after the car and ensuring a win at the slowest possible speed? There were two interesting post-race rumours. One alleged that Mussolini had

The Bugatti of Lindsay Eccles takes Onchan hairpin, known locally as "the lazy corner". Back axle trouble forced retirement after 39 laps of the 50 lap race when Eccles was pressing Dodson for second place. [R and L Kelly collection]

Brian Lewis enjoys a cigarette after his second Mannin Moar victory. His "works" Alfa Romeo ran faultlessly throughout and he beat Charlie Dodson, driving another Alfa Romeo, by more than three minutes. [Peter Kelly collection]

demanded to know why Dixon, with a car of only 1,800cc, had come so close to winning. The other claimed that both Lewis and Dixon had been approached to drive for Scuderia Ferrari. The first could not be confirmed; the second, if true, did not come to fruition.

As in the Mannin Beg, the circuit had proved to be much faster than its predecessor and, again, this had pleased the drivers. The winning average in the Mannin Moar had been 75.34mph, compared with 64.23mph in 1933. In the Mannin Beg, the corresponding figures had been 70.99mph in 1934 compared with 54.41mph in 1933. Interestingly, in the Mannin Beg, Black had been able to improve on Dixon's 1933 winning average by over 16mph. In the Mannin Moar Brian Lewis' average had improved by only 11mph, although he had a much faster car than in 1933.

Despite the faster speeds, there had been no incident in the entire race.

1934 Mannin Moar Race Results

Friday 1st June 1934. Start 10.00am. 50 laps of 3.658 miles circuit, total distance 182.9 miles. 10 starters, 3 finishers.

1. The Honourable Brian Lewis (2,655cc Alfa Romeo), 2hrs 25mins 41secs (75.34mph)
2. Charlie Dodson (2,336cc Alfa Romeo) 2hrs 29mins 5secs (73.61 mph)
3. Cyril Paul (1,808cc Riley) 2hrs 37mins 13secs (69.83mph)

Fastest lap: The Honourable Brian Lewis (2,655cc Alfa Romeo), on lap 21, 2mins 50secs (77.46mph)

Retirements:

Lap 2: Chris Staniland (2,263cc Bugatti), sheared layshaft

Lap 14:

Tim Rose-Richards (2,263cc Bugatti), broken water-pump spindle

Lap 16:

A. P. Hamilton (2,336cc Alfa Romeo), exhaust pipe fell off

Lap 20:

Freddie Dixon (1,808cc Riley), centre main bearing problem

Lap 29:

R. O. Shuttleworth (2,263cc Bugatti), connecting rod problem

Lap 38:

Vasco Sameiro (2,336cc Alfa Romeo), connecting rod problem

Lap 39:

Lindsay Eccles (2,263cc Bugatti), back axle problem.

Reaction

The 1934 Races provoked much less public criticism than 1933, largely due to the change of course which was well received by residents, visitors and competitors alike. The inconvenience and disruption experienced in 1933 by residents, particularly business people, was greatly reduced by moving the course away from the town centre. Visitors had unrestricted access to and use of the beach at all times, even during racing. Spectators were able to move and watch safely from better vantage points. Barriers were no longer needlessly far from the course. Drivers enjoyed the faster course, with the many sharp corners which imposed great stresses on cars by causing constant fierce acceleration followed by heavy braking.

At the Mannin Beg Presentation (attended by only three of the seven award winners) Colonel Lindsay Lloyd, a Steward of the Meeting and Chairman of the RAC Competitions Committee, said that, if persevered with, the Manx races would become a classic event in world motor racing.

Press comment also was favourable. Writing in *The Autocar*, Sammy Davis thought that, although the number of spectators was not great and the grandstands were not full, the results of the races were relatively satisfactory to the Manx authorities. It was more than probable, he said, that the races would be repeated in 1935, over a similar course but with the roads smoothed very considerably. *Motor Sport* praised the new course as "a great improvement in interest both to driver and spectator, the only criticism being that it was rough in places". Reporting on the Mannin Beg, *The Sydney Mail* praised the Island for closing roads for motor racing and expressed the wish that the day would come when a similar breadth of official outlook would be revealed in the State of New South Wales. The *Isle of Man Times* said that the races had passed off to everyone's gratification. There had been no serious accident in the official practices or in the races, a high tribute to the care and skill of the drivers who had regaled the public with a really fine exhibition of daring and of talent. The public had not been irritated by the vexatious restrictions of last year. In every way the second Mannin races excited more sympathy and appreciation than the first. The newspaper also commented on the enormous publicity generated for the Island and praised the organisation.

Despite its earlier positive tone, however, on 10th November 1934 the *Isle of Man Times* advocated the abandonment of the races. The reason for this surprising volte-face, apparently, was extreme concern about bad publicity for the Island arising from the Kaye Don incident and subsequent trial. There had been a critical article by Sammy Davis in *The Autocar* and a bitter attack on the Island in a biography of Kaye Don by the famous author J. Wentworth Day. There was a suggestion that drivers would give the races "an absolute cold shoulder". While the Times had replied vigourously to these attacks, there had been no reply from the lay or motor press or from the RAC, leading to the Times concluding that they agreed and approved Day's remarks.

This provoked a reaction. Only two weeks later the Times reported that Captain Phillips, in an interview with a Times representative, had disassociated both the RAC and himself from any criticism of the Island, particularly Day's book and Davis' article in *The Autocar*.

The Kaye Don Affair

Kaye Don

Kaye Earnest Donsky, known as Kaye Don, was born in Dublin in 1893. After education at Wolverhampton he took employment with the Avon Rubber Company. During the First World War he served in the Army, was discharged on medical grounds but later joined the Royal Flying Corps, serving in France until 1918. He worked for Avon until 1930, becoming Sales and Competitions Manager, and visited the Isle of Man for the motorcycle TT Races during the twenties.

Don started his motorsport career in motorcycle trials but soon graduated to cars. Well known at Brooklands, he was twice British Champion and the first driver to lap the Outer Circuit at 130mph. He also won the 1928 TT at Ards, driving a Lea-Francis. In 1930 he made a Land Speed Record attempt at Daytona driving a Sunbeam. Turning to speedboats, he followed Sir Henry Segrave in driving Lord Wakefield's boat Miss England II in four successful Water Speed Record attempts in 1931 and 1932, becoming the first man to exceed 120mph on water. He was, for his time, an unusually serious and professional competitor and achieved considerable fame especially from speedboat successes in the United States, racing against Gar Wood in the Harmsworth Trophy.

He married in September 1932. His wife Eileen, only 23 years old at the time of his trial, was the daughter of Leonard Martin of Greenwich, Connecticut, USA. Although generally believed to be American she was in fact English.

The 1934 crash ended Don's racing career. In 1947 he set up a company to manufacture Ambassador motor cycles and retired in 1963 when he sold the company to DMW. He died at Chobham, Surrey, in 1981.

Frank Tayler

Francis Leonard Cyril (known as "Frank" or "Frankie") Tayler was one of the first employees of the MG Car Company and worked in the Competitions Department from its outset in 1923. A very popular, hard-working and well-liked member of the MG racing team, he was the riding mechanic in Norman Black's victorious MG Midget in the 1931 Tourist Trophy at Ards. Chief Mechanic at the time of the 1934 Mannin Beg, he was aged 27 and had recently married. *Maintaining the Breed*, John Thornley's 1950 history of MG racing cars, contains clear evidence of the regard in which he was held, both in the dedication to Frank Tayler jointly with former MG Managing Director Cecil Kimber, and also in Thornley's comment "Time invariably softens the recollection of personal grief, but one does not easily forget the sight of grown men in tears."

The Crash

In the first practice session on Monday 28th May, Kaye Don completed four laps in his MG Magnette K3. Afterwards, he complained to the MG mechanics that the steering was "not very satisfactory". The car felt "heavy", tended to wander and was unsteady on the road. In the evening, after adjustments and after Don had asked Frank Tayler to check the steering and brakes, further work was done by Tayler and an Assistant Mechanic, Arthur Barrett. They road-tested the car and found it satisfactory. Don was informed and at about 10.15pm he and Tayler left the Douglas Bay Hotel, where the MG team was based, to test the car. Don drove up Royal Avenue to Onchan village, continued on the main road north towards Laxey and turned back towards Onchan near the Liverpool Arms public house. The car had no lights, although lighting-up time was 10.33pm. At about 10.30pm, on a bend near the junction with Begoade Road, the MG crossed the centre of the road and collided with the off-side of a Buick taxi travelling in the opposite direction. The MG knocked off the rear off-side wheel and tyre of the taxi before

This photograph shows the damage to the offside of the Buick taxi with which Kaye Don's MG Magnette K3 collided in the crash which resulted in the death of MG race mechanic Frankie Tayler. [Isle of Man Public Record Office]

Kaye Don's damaged MG Magnette K3 is pictured outside Faragher's garage in Richmond Grove, Douglas. The car was taken there after the crash in which MG race mechanic Frankie Tayler was fatally injured while accompanying Don in a late evening test on the main Laxey to Onchan road on 28th May 1934. [Isle of Man Public Record Office]

mounting the sod hedge on the right hand side of the road, continued along the hedge and landed in the road facing back towards Laxey. Tayler was thrown out of the MG and suffered a skull fracture and numerous injuries to his body. Don was pinned under the car and suffered cuts and bruises. Both were taken to hospital where Tayler died at 5.15am the next morning.

The Inquest

An Inquest into Frank Tayler's death was opened by the Coroner, with a Jury of eleven men, at Douglas on Tuesday 29th May. After Norman Black had given identification evidence, the Inquest was adjourned to the following Monday, 4th June, when the cause of death was stated to be shock following the multiple injuries suffered in the crash.

One of the passengers in the taxi said that the MG had "rounded the bend as if driven by a madman" and the taxi driver referred to "terrific speed".

As Kaye Don had been unable to examine the car since the crash his Counsel Edwyn Kneen asked leave to call technical evidence. First, he called Norman Black who said that the car was fitted with "soft" plugs which limited the engine speed to 3,000 to 3,500rpm, equivalent to a road speed of 64mph. He then called Vernon Brook, a Consultant Engineer, who said that in his opinion the crash had been caused by sudden application of the brakes, which had been maladjusted. The front brake had come on before the rear, he said, causing excessive strain which had broken the dumb iron. This had caused the steering failure. The bend could be taken safely at 60-70mph.

Percy Cowley, Counsel for Frank Tayler's widow and the MG Car Company, also called evidence. He said it had been suggested in the national Press that Tayler had been unhappy with the steering and yet had asked Don to test the car and also that Tayler had failed to adjust the brakes correctly. To rebut this, he called Arthur Barrett, who said that Tayler had tested the car with him and that they had found both the steering and brakes satisfactory. Hugh McConnell, RAC examiner, Brooklands scrutineer and MG Team Manager in Italy, disagreed with both Brook's and Black's evidence. He said that the plugs were half way between "soft" and "hot" and good for 5,000rpm (80mph). He said that Brook's theory that steering failure had caused the crash was impossible.

Kaye Don was brought to Court in a wheelchair, wearing a dressing gown. His head and right hand were swathed in bandages and he reportedly looked very ill and spoke almost inaudibly. He said that he saw the Buick and turned the steering wheel but the steering failed to respond, causing the collision. His speed was probably 50mph, normally a safe speed for the bend. He had tested the brakes very severely just before the collision and the front had come on before the back. He said that Tayler had been anxious that he should test the car before the Tuesday practice. He had thought it rather late but the mechanics had worked hard and late to prepare the car. He could have taken the bend at 90mph. He had not braked when he saw the Buick because there was no need. Cross-examined, Don said that he had taken the car out in the afternoon with a mechanic named Cook, to test the brakes. He had told Tayler to check the brakes and steering. He admitted that he had been driving on the crown of the road.

After the Coroner had summed up the evidence, the Jury retired at 5.30pm to consider its verdict. It returned after just over an hour with a verdict of "culpable negligent driving". The Coroner then committed Kaye Don for trial for manslaughter. Don was granted bail on his own bond of £500 and two sureties of £250 each, *Isle of Man Times* Editor George Brown and Chartered Accountant Harry Kneale.

Don was discharged from hospital on 14th June and returned to London. The *Isle of Man Times* said that he was still far from well and showing signs of his injuries. He issued a statement of thanks for messages of sympathy. Shortly afterwards, the Times reported that a civil claim had been issued against Don on behalf of Ralph Caine, the taxi driver, and that an application had been made to the Court for the arrest of Don's assets in the Isle of Man. This claim was settled out of Court in December 1934.

The Trial

The Trial opened on Thursday 12th July 1934 before Deemster Farrant, one of the Island's High Court Judges, and a twelve man jury. The venue was the Tynwald Court Chamber, the meeting place of the world's oldest parliament, as Douglas Court House was not large enough to accommodate the large number of Advocates, Press and agency representatives, witnesses and members of the public expected to attend. The public gallery was packed and many would-be spectators were unable to gain admittance. The *Isle of Man Times* said that the proceedings had attracted world-wide interest.

The prosecution was led by the Isle of Man Attorney General, Ramsey Moore. He was assisted by two junior Counsel, George Moore (son of the Attorney General) and Douglas Hanson (father of the author). Counsel for the Defence was Edwyn Kneen, one of the leading Manx Advocates of the time. He was assisted by junior Counsel Arthur Cain. Also present on Kaye Don's behalf, although not licensed to conduct cases in Manx Courts, were English Barrister Edward Terrell and English Solicitor H. Kenwright.

After an opening speech, the Attorney General called medical evidence. Then Arthur Barrett, the Assistant Mechanic who had given evidence at the Inquest confirmed that he and Frank Tayler had tested the car and had found that the steering and brakes were in good working order.

Ralph Caine, the taxi driver, described the crash and said that his speed at the time of impact was about 15mph. The MG was travelling very fast, in the middle of the road. Evidence was also given by his passengers, one of whom said that the MG's speed was "much too fast".

There was a wide difference in the opinions of the technical experts. For the prosecution, Hugh McConnell (a Brooklands scrutineer and an adviser to the MG Car Company), Hubert Charles (MG Car Company Chief Draughtsman) and Edward Bradley Christian (Motor Engineer and later the Island's Ford dealer) all maintained that Kaye Don's car had been in good order before the crash. The Attorney General asked McConnell whether violent braking would tend to break the dumb iron, allowing free movement of the axle which would upset the steering. McConnell said that this would not be possible due to torque reaction cables which would limit the strain caused to the front axle by heavy braking. He estimated the speed of the MG immediately before the accident at 60mph, while Christian's estimate was 90mph. Both Christian and Charles said that there was nothing wrong with the steering. The defence experts were Major Eugene Beaumont (a past President of the Institute of Automobile Engineers), Major Vernon Brook (RAC Engineer) and Donald Marendaz (a car designer and test pilot). They all adhered to the contrary opinion given by Brook at the Inquest that the heavy testing of the brakes had set up a strain which resulted in axle failure and fracture of the dumb iron.

Kaye Don, looking pale, gave his evidence in a low voice and had to be asked to speak louder. He said that Tayler had been very anxious that he should test the car but that the decision to do so was entirely his own. When he tested his brakes before the collision they appeared satisfactory. When he reached the bend he had turned the steering wheel to the left but with no response. His revolution counter had shown 2,700rpm which represented a speed of 50mph. There would be no difficulty, he said, in taking the corner at nearly 80mph, or at 60-65mph on his own side of the road.

Cross-examined by the Attorney General, Don admitted that he had made no enquiries about lighting-up time, sunset or traffic. The Attorney General then, very controversially, asked Don whether he had made any enquiries as to whether Tayler, while conscious, had exonerated him. Don replied that he had not. He agreed that he had heard that Tayler had made a statement to the Doctor but he did not know what Tayler had said and did not remember who had told him about the statement. Mr Kneen objected, pointing out that the statement of a dying man was admissible only if given under certain conditions. The Attorney General had not called evidence of any such statement. Deemster Farrant said that the statement could not be put to Don and the Attorney General said that he had not intended to put it to Don

Unusually, the local newspapers succeeded in obtaining and publishing photographs taken in the courtroom during Kaye Don's trial. This photograph shows Deemster Farrant (the Judge) and prosecuting and defence counsel. [Author's collection]

Kaye Don was admitted to Noble's Hospital Douglas for treatment of his injuries in the crash in which mechanic Frankie Tayler lost his life. On discharge, Don returned to London. This photograph shows him, heavily bandaged, on arrival at Euston Station. [Author's collection]

unless he knew about it. By then, the damage had been done. The line of questioning could have prejudiced Don by influencing the jury into thinking that Tayler had blamed Don and that Don knew, or suspected that he had. Thus Don's credibility could have been undermined.

In his closing speech, Kneen said that the evidence for the Crown had practically been given by the MG Car Company. Most of the Attorney General's instructions had come from the Company and he wished the jury to take this into account. The jury had to decide whether to believe experts who made their livings from the Company or experts called by the defence. He asked the jury to give Don the same consideration as they would give to the humblest working man. A poor working man or mechanic would get a verdict of not guilty and he asked for the same consideration for Don.

The Attorney General, in his closing speech, asked the jury to leave aside the theories and to rely on admitted facts. The Defendant's driving had constituted a grave peril on the road and had resulted in a death. Deemster Farrant then summed up and directed the jury on matters of law. The jury retired at 6.25pm to consider its verdict and returned at 8.00pm with a verdict of guilty.

In a plea for leniency, Edwyn Kneen referred to Don's injuries, the costs which he had incurred and the claims which he faced. The verdict might mean the end of his racing career. He asked the Deemster to impose a fine rather than imprisonment. The Deemster then said that he would consider matters and would pass sentence on Monday morning. Bail was continued with Times Editor George Brown as the sole surety for £500.

On Monday morning, with Kaye Don looking very pale and worried, Deemster Farrant passed sentence. He said the sentence he would normally impose was six months' imprisonment but, in all the circumstances, including the effect on the Defendant's career and reputation, he had decided on a sentence of four months.

Mr Kneen immediately gave notice of appeal against both conviction and sentence and the Deemster agreed that Don would be released on bail when leave to appeal was granted. At a hearing the same day, the Island's senior Judge, Deemster LaMothe, granted leave to appeal. Don was released on bail at 3.10pm and left the Island with his wife on the 4.00pm boat to Liverpool.

The Appeal

The Appeal hearing opened at Douglas on Wednesday 26th September 1934 before Deemster Harold Derbyshire, the Isle of Man Judge of Appeal, and Acting Deemster R. Kingsley Chappell, both English King's Counsel. There were sixteen grounds of appeal. The major ground concerned the Attorney General's cross-examination of Kaye Don about the statement alleged to have been made by Frank Tayler before his death. It was claimed that this line of cross-examination was inadmissible as no such statement had been put in evidence by the Crown and, as it was prejudicial to the Defendant, the Deemster ought to have stopped it and directed the jury to disregard it. Other grounds concerned evidence about lack of lights and a horn on the car, and that Don was driving without a licence and without insurance, all of which was said to be irrelevant to the charge of manslaughter but prejudicial to the Defendant. In addition, the Deemster's summing up was attacked because of alleged mis-directions and non-directions. The verdict was claimed to be unreasonable and against the weight of the evidence.

After three full days of legal argument, the two Appeal Judges gave their judgment on the morning of Saturday 29th September. The appeal against conviction was dismissed. The basis of this decision was that, although there had been "wrong decisions on questions of law which might amount to a miscarriage of justice" there had been no "substantial" miscarriage of justice. In other words, the jury would still have convicted Don on the evidence even if the irrelevant and prejudicial matters had not been introduced. Although Mr. Kneen again argued for a fine instead of imprisonment, the Court rejected this and ordered that the sentence of four months imprisonment would stand. The term would normally run from that day but the Judges ordered that it should run from the previous Wednesday, 26th September, when the Appeal hearing had started.

Don was then taken to the prison and his wife left the Island by boat on Saturday afternoon, to stay with friends at Sunningdale. On the following Wednesday, 3rd October, Don's Advocates informed the Court that there would be no appeal against the Appeal Court's decision and the Press was informed on the same day. The Court then released the car and parts, which were returned to England.

English Press Reaction

Writing in the *Daily Sketch*, "Candidus" said that no impartial reader of reports of the appeal hearing would doubt the fairness of the trial or sentence. While Don's eminence and injuries would advertise the sentence, this would be for the general good. English juries had been very slow to convict for clear offences and the fact that a Manx jury had done its duty and been supported on appeal could not fail to have a wholesome effect on public opinion and administration of the law in England. He thought, however, that laws prohibiting reckless driving and imposing speed limits were useless if roads and even streets were used as race tracks. In a reply in the *Isle of Man Examiner*, 1934 Mannin Beg competitor Henry Laird said roads had been very adequately fenced off during official practising and races, and the only criticism was of people testing cars on public highways when open to the public.

The *Sunday Observer* took a similar line to that of the *Daily Sketch*. Kaye Don, it said, was one of many who had indulged in grossly excessive speed with fatal consequences. He had had the misfortune to come before jury men who knew manslaughter when they saw it and judges who recognised no divinity hedging a motorist from prison. Justice in England might acquire a little more courage from the example set by Manx Courts.

While *The Motor* reported the dismissal of the appeal in a mere six lines of an issue of 199 pages, other magazines had rather more to say. Writing in *The Autocar*, Sammy Davis accepted that according to strict law the case was one of manslaughter and that the driver had to suffer the penalty. In his opinion, however, Don would have been charged with manslaughter in any other country. Davis went on to argue that this was a case of an accident to a racing mechanic caused by an error of judgment by a driver. The mechanic, he thought, shared any dangers and no mechanic would blame a driver. It would be different if a person other that a team member had been affected. Referring to the previous year's Mathieson case, Davis said that there had been "unusual unpleasantness" on both occasions when the Mannin races had been held and questioned the wisdom of racing in the Isle of Man. There was definite prejudice on the Island and it raised quite serious misgivings about racing there.

Similar comments appeared in other periodicals, including the *Border Cities Star* of Windsor, Ontario, Canada but, in the *Isle of Man Examiner* of 30th November 1934, a reader's letter from "Manxland" pointed out the flaw in Davis' argument. Having conceded that the death of the mechanic was manslaughter, Davis was suggesting that "racing drivers ought to be exempt from the penalties to which lesser folk are subject". In every year in England, drivers who drove in a criminally negligent manner resulting in the deaths of passengers were prosecuted for manslaughter. An accident in an official practice or a race was different. What if a mechanic were killed in a racing car being tested on a public road near to the Brooklands Track on the eve of a big race? He would surely be charged with manslaughter, he said. "Manxland" also pointed out that a sudden death meant an Inquest and the jury was under a sworn duty to give a true verdict according to the evidence. Once the jury had done this, the Coroner had been obliged by law to commit Kaye Don for trial. Although Davis suggested that a mechanic would not blame a driver, "Manxland" doubted whether being a passenger in a racing car being tested on a public road by a highly skilled driver should involve risk to life or even limb. The suggestion of the Isle of Man being prejudiced against racing drivers seemed to be based solely on Don's conviction and on a failed civil claim by an English visitor against a driver.

Writing in *The Motor Cycle*, "Ixion" said that in the Isle of Man at race times, although the normal laws applied except while the course was closed for practices and races, "considerable licence exists, winked at by the powers that be". High speed testing outside the set hours of practice and away from the course was normal. Don had done what every racing man did and his misfortune was that a calamity had occurred which had been handled by meticulous rigidities of law without the least reference to pre-race "atmosphere". "Ixion" thought that the moral was that competitors should keep within the law and that the organisers should forbid racing machines to go on the roads at all except on the actual course within official practices.

Manx Press Reaction

In the week after the appeal hearing the *Ramsey Courier* commented on the main impressions of the proceedings. These were the "wonderful and unrelenting fight" by Don's Counsel Edwyn Kneen, the "exclusively fair hearing" given by the Appeal Judges, and the "fairness and restraint" shown by the Attorney General. Don, it said, could not have had a fairer trial. The *Courier* also commented on the threatened boycott by drivers, despite which the RAC had announced that the Mannin races would be repeated in 1935, and the "rubbish" about the Isle of Man gaol which had appeared in the English Press.

In its issue of 6th October 1934, the *Isle of Man Times* commented at length on the trial, the appeal and the outcome. There was no deliberate unfairness to racing motorists. *The Times* felt that the Manx people "would take a not unfriendly attitude" to Kaye Don. His offence was not necessarily proof of wickedness and after punishment he could hold up his head again and face the world. *The Times* suggested that Don and Tayler were taking a common risk and that, following the problems in practice and in view of the limited amount of official practice time, it was "not unnatural" that both should have wanted to test the car and that Don should have felt some obligation to accede to Tayler's request to do so. *The Times* suggested that the Governor should show such leniency as was compatible with fairness to other prisoners, for example, by granting remission so as to allow Don to be at home with his wife for Christmas.

The Times went on to criticise the Attorney General for

asking prejudicial questions at the trial about the alleged statement made by Frank Tayler in hospital. It thought that the Attorney General's explanation was "ingenious but hopelessly unconvincing" and that many would say that he was guilty of a serious offence against the administration of justice.

Kaye Don's Counsel, Edwyn Kneen, was praised by the Times for fighting "a magnificent battle" at the trial and appeal. The Appeal Judges had "most justly" used the word "tenacious" it said.

"Kaye Don – the Man"

A biography entitled "Kaye Don – the Man" by well-known English author J. Wentworth Day was on sale by the beginning on November 1934. The book included a chapter dealing with Kaye Don's crash, trial, appeal and subsequent imprisonment. This chapter contained extracts from reports of the trial and the appeal hearing in the Times. It also contained abusive attacks on the Isle of Man and its people. Day said that the Manxman "is fully aware of the money-drawing capacities of a butcher's holiday. This is why, although road racing is prohibited in England, our best and finest motor drivers can legally kill themselves to the plaudits of the tourist crowd beneath the benignant eye of the Manx law". He continued in the same vein, describing the Island as "somewhat inter-bred", as "that insignificant little piece of goat-infested hill set in the Irish sea" and "this Isle-of-very-little-Man".

In a review of the book the *Isle of Man Examiner* wondered whether Kaye Don had seen a proof of the final chapter and, if not, what he would think when he read it. This question was answered by Don himself immediately following his release from prison. In a statement read to reporters, *Isle of Man Times* Editor George Brown said that Kaye Don had sent a message by his wife entirely dissociating himself from the scurrilous attack made upon the Manx people by Mr. Wentworth Day in his book. Personally he had no resentment against the people of the Island. On the contrary, he recognised that he had received from them the utmost consideration and kindness in the unfortunate circumstances in which he was placed.

Imprisonment

The English National Press lost no time in commenting on Kaye Don's imprisonment. The *Daily Mail* said that the Isle of Man prison looked like a country house but discounted stories of prisoners living in happy retirement with delightful privileges which allowed them to possess keys and to go out once a week on parole, as well as to visit a cinema. Harold Pemberton of the *Daily Express* said that stories of prisoners having their own bedrooms, enjoying bridge parties and visiting a cinema once a week were far from the truth. It was doubtful if Don would receive any visitors other than his legal advisers as he would not let his wife visit him in prison. But this was not what was worrying Don. He faced the hardships of prison life with equanimity but would be worried about how friends and the public would regard him after his release. Pemberton thought Don need have no anxiety. He had more friends now than in the height of his fame having received messages of sympathy and condolence from all over the world and especially from the United States.

On 5th October 1934, less than two weeks after Don had entered the prison, the *Isle of Man Examiner* reported that the Prison Regulations had been revised one month previously. One effect had been to class Kaye Don as a First Class prisoner. In order to be classed as "First Class" a prisoner had to have no previous convictions, his crime had to be one not involving "moral turpitude" and his sentence had to be without hard labour. This gave privileges normally reserved for civil prisoners. Don could wear his own clothes instead of normal prison clothing. He would not be compelled to have his hair cut and could follow a trade. He could have his own bedding and other necessaries but no extravagance or luxury. He could use the prison library but was not allowed newspapers. He was allowed "a reasonable quantity of cooked provisions and malt liquor not exceeding one pint in any one day of 24 hours". He could have one or two visitors for 15 minutes once a week and could send and receive one letter a week, subject to censorship. The number of visitors or the duration of visits could be increased by the visiting Magistrates. Instead of a cell, he had a fair-sized private room with a partial view of Falcon Cliff Glen. He was locked in his room except when taken out for exercise but was not exercised with the other prisoners and would not even see them.

The change to the Prison Regulations had come just in time for Kaye Don. If he had been imprisoned immediately following his conviction in July 1934, he would have been classed as a criminal prisoner. Although in the "star" rather than "ordinary" category, he would have had harsher conditions than under the new rules, including wearing prison clothes, being locked in a cell and being exercised with other prisoners. He would have had to rise at 7am, make his bed, wash and sweep his cell and work six to ten hours a day. For the first fourteen days he would have had to sleep on a plank bed before being allowed a mattress. He would have been allowed only one visit per month and to send and receive only one letter per month, subject to censorship.

It was stated, however, that the change in the Regulations had not been made for Don's benefit, but only to bring the Isle of Man prison into line with English prisons. Nevertheless the Regulation became known as "The Kaye Don Regulation".

Interesting details of Don's imprisonment emerged in articles by veteran Manx Journalist Terry Cringle in the *Isle of Man Examiner* in 1997. He was contacted by a lady whose mother had been the manageress of the nearby Falcon Cliff Hotel while Don was in prison. She had revealed that Don's meals were prepared at the hotel and taken to the prison on silver trays. Later, however, Don's wife had come to the Island and rented a house in Onchan. She had informed the manageress of the Falcon Cliff Hotel that she intended to take over the cooking of her husband's meals but wished the hotel to continue to provide his breakfast. She had been told flatly that the hotel would supply all Don's meals or none. There was no question of supplying breakfast only. However an *Isle of Man Times* article of 15th December 1934 states that Mrs Don prepared her husband's food in the small house which she had rented and delivered it to the prison daily at 7am, noon and 5pm. Although the Times article implies that this took place throughout Don's imprisonment an *Isle of Man Examiner* article written in the first week of his term confirmed that, then at any rate, all his meals were supplied by the Falcon Cliff Hotel.

A man who had been an inmate of the prison at the same time as Kaye Don gave an insight into the harsh conditions endured by the other 27 prisoners while Don lived in comparative luxury. Don never came near the other prisoners, he said. He would never look at them, never mind speak to them. He would turn away, covering his face in his hands. The prisoners thought Don was a snob who thought that they were nothing better than dogs. They thought he despised them and they despised him.

Release

On 26th October 1934, just four weeks after Don's imprisonment, the *Ramsey Courier* reported, under the heading "More Kaye Don Nonsense", a *News of the World* story that Don's health was causing anxiety and efforts were being made in London to obtain remission of the four months sentence. Well- known racing drivers had approached the Home Secretary and some had decided to boycott the Isle of Man. Don was depressed and his wife was very worried about the change in her husband. It was suggested that as he was the only first class prisoner he was in solitary confinement and therefore his sentence was more severe than it would have been in an English prison. Although Government Office in Douglas issued a statement that there was no cause for concern and no move for remission, the report was a foretaste of what was to come.

Rumours of Don's imminent release persisted until, on Monday 10th December, the news broke that he had walked free from the prison that morning and had left for Liverpool on the 9am steamer after completing less than eleven weeks of his four months sentence. The *Isle of Man Examiner* told how the Government Secretary had denied knowledge of any move to secure Don's release when an *Examiner* representative had spoken to him on the previous Friday and had even said that the Lieutenant Governor was away and nothing could be done until his return. Despite this, Mrs Don and her husband had been informed on Saturday that he would be released on Monday. The official Government statement said that the Lieutenant Governor had remitted the remainder of the sentence on medical advice.

It emerged that Mrs Don had gone to the prison in her husband's Sunbeam sports car at 7am on the Monday morning. Also there was *Isle of Man Times* Editor George Brown, a personal friend of Mr and Mrs Don. When Don emerged, looking much thinner and greyer than before and showing signs on mental strain, the party went to Brown's home. After what must have been a very hurried breakfast, they had gone to the pier at 7.30am to embark on the steamer, a private cabin having been booked on Saturday. Despite the concerns about his health, it did not go unnoticed that Don could jump from the pier to the deck of the ship without waiting for the gangway to be put in place. Don's car was loaded onto the steamer and the English Press later reported that, on arriving at Liverpool, he had been able to drive 200 miles to London, through fog.

Later in the day, George Brown held a press conference. He read a statement by Don thanking the Manx authorities, the Gaoler, the prison staff doctors and padre and the Manx people for the consideration and kindness shown to his wife and said that he hoped to take part in the next year's races. Brown said Don's health was

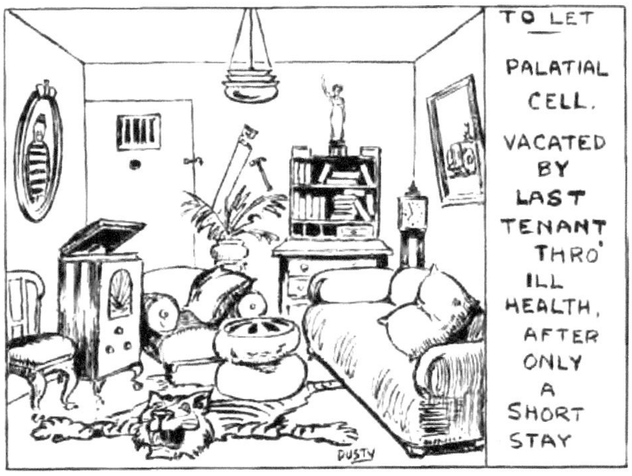

After Kaye Don's early release from imprisonment for the manslaughter of MG race mechanic Frankie Tayler this cartoon by Isle of Man Examiner cartoonist "Dusty" appeared in the 1935 Examiner *Annual. [Author's collection]*

in a very serious condition. It had been feared that he might suffer a complete breakdown. He had suffered insomnia and agony of mind. He had also suffered very severe pain in his head, caused by the accident. He had not been able to receive specialist treatment in prison and the doctor had advised against moving him to hospital because he would not receive even the amount of exercise which he had received in prison. Don's racing friends intended to give a come-back dinner in his honour and he and his wife hoped to take a holiday in Florida early in the New Year.

The Press was critical of the secrecy surrounding Don's release as well as the release itself. The *Ramsey Courier* reminded readers that it had forecast on 30th November that Don would be released in early December, only to be "pooh-poohed by a Douglas contemporary". The *Isle of Man Examiner* felt that medical opinion had to be accepted but that the mystery surrounding Don's discharge did not tend to encourage public confidence. During his captivity he had been given "almost regal privileges". Repeated assurances had been given that fears about his health were groundless. If he was ill, could he not have been treated in hospital? The Island's legal system had been applauded for the courage shown in the administration of justice but some of the lustre had fallen as a result of the Governor yielding to representations regarding Don's health. Influence had been used to secure his release on grounds which could apply to any prisoner. It had been a grave mistake to yield, the *Examiner* thought. It would have been better for all if the lenient sentence which had been confirmed on appeal had been allowed to stand – if the appeal judges saw no reason to reduce a sentence why should it be in the power of someone else to do so? In fact, with the normal one-sixth remission for good behaviour Don would have been released on 6th January. He received additional remission of four weeks, serving 75 days of a sentence of 123 days.

The *Isle of Man Times* suggested that Kaye Don had been unlucky because previously drivers had been convicted of manslaughter only where there had been excessive drinking or deliberate callousness. In cases where the lack of care or error of judgment had been as great as Don's the drivers had been acquitted. The leader criticised the English Press for the manner in which they had harassed Don and his wife, both on the Island and on their return to England.

Reportedly Don returned to work at his office in the week after his release. In early January Mr and Mrs Don went to Florida on holiday, returning in mid-March. The 1934 incident resulted in his retirement from active participation in motor racing.

1935 Mannin Beg & Mannin Moar – Wins For Fairfield & Lewis

Planning

Rumours that the future of the races might be affected by the Kaye Don case were quickly denied by the local Race Committee and by the RAC. In December 1934, Douglas Town Council voted in favour of organizing the Mannin Races in 1935, subject to a course alteration proposed by Captain Phillips. Instead of turning right from the Promenade into Broadway, the course would continue along the sea side of the Promenade past Broadway for some 200 yards to Greensill's corner (where the 1933 course had turned right into Church Road Marina) and loop round in a 180 degree turn, continuing back along the land side of the Promenade before turning left into Broadway. This avoided the lamp standard where Walter Handley had crashed in 1934 but the commercial explanation was that spectators on the Villa Marina grandstand would see much more action, as in 1933.

This alteration entailed moving the Start and Finish from opposite the Crescent Cinema to a point opposite the Villa Marina, with the pits again set well back from the roadway. The road would be divided into three strips separated by artificial barricades of evenly-spaced refuse bins linked by bunting. There would be a narrow access strip for the pits and two much wider ones for racing. The change lengthened the course from 3.66 miles to 4.035 miles and a 50-lap race from 183 miles to 201.750 miles. The race dates were to be Wednesday 29th and Friday 31st May, with early morning practices on Monday 27th and Tuesday 28th May from 5.00am to 7.00am.

A new wooden footbridge was erected across Broadway, at the junction with Victoria Road and Glen Falcon Road.

It was announced that the unloading of cars from Isle of Man Steam Packet Company ships at Douglas would be expedited. The Harbour Board had decided to place "Florenes" landing gear on the Victoria Pier. This was a Belgian invention which was already in use at Dover and at most Continental ports, claimed to be capable of handling one car every thirty seconds. Less than a year earlier, an *Isle of Man Times* photograph of a car being unloaded at Douglas had been accompanied by a caption claiming "how perfect and simple" the arrangements were!

After successfully broadcasting the 1934 Mannin Moar, the BBC had decided to broadcast both 1935 races, from 9.45am to 10.10am and from 12 noon to 12.45pm. Again, there would be two commentators, Alan C. Hess at the Start/Finish and Victor Smythe at the TT Grandstand. They would have telephone links to other points on the course and would provide eye-witness accounts of incidents at Bray Hill, Onchan and Summer Hill.

Mannin Beg Entries

Two rival teams of experimental small-capacity supercharged cars were entered for the Mannin Beg. They came from the MG Car Co. Ltd of Abingdon and the Austin Motor Company Ltd of Longbridge, Birmingham.

Although a side-valve supercharged Austin had been raced the previous year, this was claimed on the Island to be the first public appearance of the Austins. The nominated drivers were three motorcycle TT riders, L.P. Driscoll, Charlie Dodson and Stanley Woods. The side-valve cars were claimed to be extremely fast and remarkable for their acceleration but, as the race date approached, it would become questionable whether they would be ready in time.

The "R" type MG Midgets were technically very advanced. The first MGs to be designed and built for sale as single-seater racing cars, they were equipped with all-round independent torsion-bar suspension. An "official" team of three cars was entered by George Eyston with Eyston himself, Walter Handley and Norman Black as drivers. In addition, Bobby Baird and Ron Horton entered their own cars. The Eyston team and two other "R" types had been raced in the International Trophy at Brooklands on 6th May, when all had retired except one car driven by Malcolm Campbell. Strenuous experimental work continued right up to the Mannin race period.

While MG "works" interest concentrated on the new model, K3 Magnettes were entered by Eddie Hall (K3006), the Ford/Baumer duo (K3028) and "Jock" Manby-Colegrave (K3004).

After an inauspicious debut in 1934, ERA was beginning to achieve success. In the autumn of 1934 Raymond Mays had won the Nuffield Trophy at Donington Park as well as the famous Shelsey Walsh hill climb. In the spring of 1935, he had repeated his Shelsley victory, covering the course in less than 40 seconds for the first time. There were two 1,100cc ERA entries for the Mannin Beg, a "works" car for Raymond Mays and a "customer" car for Pat Fairfield. Mays' car was equipped with a Zoller vane supercharger which gave greater boost than the Jamieson supercharger which was fitted to Fairfield's car. The company had decided that "works" cars should be more powerful than the cars sold to their customers. *The Autocar* doubted whether the cars would be ready.

Freddie Dixon again entered his 1486cc unsupercharged Riley. P.L. Donkin entered a 1,086cc supercharged Maserati, and a 1,496cc Bugatti was to be driven by T. K. Humber.

In addition, two Altas were entered by Manxman Alfred Lace. One was to be driven by Lace himself, the other by D. Tennant with Lord Avebury as reserve driver.

Mannin Moar Entries

Two supercharged ERAs were the only British entries in the Mannin Moar. One was a 1,980cc version to be driven by Raymond Mays and the other a 1,488cc car to be driven by Humphrey Cook. There were high hopes of a British victory over the French and Italian opposition which consisted of five Alfa Romeos, two Maseratis and six Bugattis.

Richard Shuttleworth was to drive a 2.9 litre Alfa Romeo Monoposto which was an updated version of Brian Lewis' 1934 winning car. There were two 2.6 litre Alfa Romeos, one (ex Scuderia Ferrari) for Austin Dobson and the other for R.S. Wilkins. Luis Fontes, the Brazilian winner of the International Trophy, would drive the 2.3 litre Monza model in which Brian Lewis had won in 1933 and Charlie Dodson had been runner-up in 1934. The remaining Alfa was another Monza, entered by A.P. Hamilton.

The two Maseratis were three-litre cars to be driven by Tim Rose-Richards and the up-and-coming Richard Seaman, in his second season of racing. He had driven an MG Magnette K3 in 1934, with a victory at Berne, second place in the Nuffield Trophy at Donington and third places at Pescara in Italy and Brno in Czechoslovakia.

Tim Rose-Richards drove a Maserati but the car broke a universal joint at Onchan on the first lap, leaving him to tour to the pits and retire. [Peter Kelly collection]

Charlie Martin entered two Bugattis in the race, one driven by himself and the other by Charles Brackenbury. Martin finished second to Brian Lewis' Bugatti but Brackenbury failed to finish, completing only 48 laps of the 50 lap race. [Peter Kelly collection]

E.K. "Teddy" Rayson drove his Bugatti to fourth place behind the Bugattis of Brian Lewis and Charlie Martin and the Alfa Romeo of Luis Fontes. [Peter Kelly collection]

During a practice Eddie Hall's Mannin Beg MG Magnette K3 (11) and Lindsay Eccles' Mannin Moar Bugatti (9) round the Onchan hairpin from Governor's Road into Summerhill Road. Hall was unclassified in the Mannin Beg and Eccles retired from the Mannin Moar with a broken universal joint. [Author's collection]

Three of the six Bugattis were 3.3 litre Type 59 Grand Prix cars for Brian Lewis (whose car was entered by Earl Howe and Noel Rees and reputedly insured for £5,000), Lindsay Eccles and Charlie Martin. There were two 2.3 litre cars, to be driven by the Honourable Jock Leith (who was related to the Taubman family of The Nunnery, near Douglas) and Charles Brackenbury. The sixth Bugatti was a two-litre car entered by E.K. "Teddy" Rayson.

Practices

All the Mannin Moar entries arrived, with the exception of Richard Seaman's Maserati. Arrivals for the Mannin Beg suffered a far worse rate of attrition. Disappointingly, but as expected, the team of three Austins was not ready. This was particularly unfortunate for Charlie Dodson. Having given up motorcycle racing to concentrate on car racing, he had neither a motorcycle nor a car for the Island's major racing events. Also, the public were deprived of seeing motorcycle TT star Stanley Woods at the wheel of a racing car. Other Mannin Beg absentees were Donkin's supercharged 1,100cc Maserati and Horton's privately entered MG "R" type which was not ready. At least, despite *The Autocar*'s earlier doubts, the ERAs arrived.

Despite this, Captain Phillips (who had taken over as Clerk of the Course from Commander Armstrong) forecast in a pre-practice interview that the races would be "the best yet". The Mannin Moar, in particular, would be an excellent race. One basis for this seemed to be a belief that the acceleration of most cars had improved since the previous year. Phillips' optimism would not be reflected in final verdicts, however.

As in 1934, practices were held in the early mornings of Monday and Tuesday, between 5am and 7am. Conditions were very cold and this affected carburation. On Monday morning, according to the *Mona's Herald*, "a large number of spectators faced a bleak dawn with heroic fortitude". *The Autocar* thought spectators were "very few and far between, fewer than last year". Interest in the race appeared to be limited.

On both mornings, but particularly the first, almost all drivers did "short laps". They did so by following the 1934 circuit. This involved turning right off the Promenade into Broadway to cut out the Greensill's Corner loop. The reason for this was unclear. So, too, was the official attitude to this novel proceeding. While times for short laps were ignored for allocation of grid positions, there was apparently no physical barrier across the entry to Broadway and so nothing to prevent departures from the course. In fact the number of short laps which were completed suggested that this procedure had official blessing. The presumption must be that driving round the loop was regarded as a waste of valuable practice time for drivers who wanted to concentrate on learning the more difficult parts of the Course before setting qualifying times over the full Course. Nevertheless, there must have been a danger of collisions as short-cutting drivers entered Broadway from the right and faced the prospect of encountering drivers coming from the left as the latter attempted to set qualifying times on the full circuit. No incidents, however, were reported.

Richard Shuttleworth used a Bugatti for practice, instead of the Alfa Romeo which he would use in the race. According to the *Mona's Herald*, black cats which crossed the Course at York Road and Bray Hill had lucky escapes. A chicken was less lucky when Fontes collided with it and returned to the pits with his radiator smothered with feathers. The 3.3 litre Bugattis seemed good on acceleration and brakes but the new "R" type MGs had problems with universal joints.

Tyres generally lasted well despite the number of small stones on the course. In fact *The Autocar* would refer later to "the devastating effect of an impossible road surface..." Gear ratios, meanwhile, were a problem for most. They

Roy Eccles' Alta (2) leads the field on the Greensill's corner loop, followed by Walter Handley (MG "R", 17), Raymond Mays (E.R.A., 8), Norman Black (MG "R", 18), Ludovic Ford (MG K3, 12), George Eyston (MG "R", 16) and T.K. Humber (Bugatti, 6). [Stan Hughes collection]

Lindsay Eccles drove a Bugatti in all three Mannin Moar races but was unlucky each time. This early morning practice photograph shows him spinning at Greensill's corner at the south end of the loop which was added to the 1934 circuit to avoid the right turn into Broadway where Walter Handley crashed into a lamp standard in 1934. [Isle of Man Times]

made the Broadway to Bray Hill section difficult. The Greensill's loop reduced lap speeds considerably despite speeds at the braking point being even higher than at the Onchan braking point. The narrow pit road could be a problem if a car were to leave its pit while another came in. There was also a problem with signalling from the pits. This was solved by moving the signallers to the side of the road opposite to the pits. Summer Hill was still very rough and the bump at Governor's Bridge had not been removed.

In the first practice, the fastest Mannin Moar times were set by Fontes' Alfa Romeo and Lewis' Bugatti at 3mins 12secs. Martin's Bugatti was one second slower. In the Mannin Beg, Fairfield's ERA was fastest in 3mins 31secs. He was followed by Handley's MG in 3mins 32sesc and Dixon's Riley in 3mins 35secs.

In the second session, Martin set the fastest Mannin Moar time in 3mins 08secs. Shuttleworth equalled the first session times of Fontes and Lewis. Handley and Dixon both improved their earlier Mannin Beg times by one second.

1935 Mannin Beg Race – Fairfield's ERA Victory

The weather was fine for the Mannin Beg. A cool inshore breeze, however, would prove disconcerting for pit attendants. It was high tide and waves broke over the promenade wall into the rear of some of the pits; not a pleasant prospect for attendants who were based there. Not surprisingly, they criticised race organisers for fixing the time of the race to coincide with high tide.

As expected, thirteen cars lined up on the starting grid. On the front row were Pat Fairfield's ERA, Walter Handley's MG Midget (both 3mins 31secs) and Freddie Dixon's Riley (3mins 34secs). Behind them were Eddie Hall's MG Magnette (3mins 34secs) and Norman Black's MG Midget (3mins 37secs). The third row consisted of the MG Midgets of Bobby Baird (3mins 40secs) and George Eyston (3mins 44secs) alongside the Alta of Roy Eccles who had taken over Tennant's car (3mins 48secs). Behind them were "Jock" Manby-Colegrave's MG (3mins 49secs) and Humber's Bugatti (3mins 50secs). The final grid row consisted of Lace's Alta (3mins 40secs), Ford's MG (3mins 52secs) and Mays' ERA (4mins 01secs).

Actually, only 12 cars got away and three (Manby-Colegrave, Black and Humber) only after some hesitation. The engine of Humber's Bugatti actually cut out after the U-turn on the promenade and did not start again until the pack had departed.

The one that stayed behind was Lace's Alta. It refused to budge and had to be pushed back to the pits. There it stayed for what must have seemed like an eternity as other

During Tuesday morning's practice, Lord Avebury changes plugs in a desperate attempt to qualify his Alta, driven by D. Tennant. His Lordship was the reserve driver. The car did qualify but was driven in the race by Roy Eccles, whose wife is the lady in the photograph. [Peter Kelly collection]

At the foot of Broadway the winner, Pat Fairfield in his E.R.A. is followed by an MG Magnette K3. The K3 had been dominant in 1934 after serious reliability problems in 1933 but had been superseded by the "R" type which emulated the 1933 problems of the K3 with two cars retiring and two unclassified. [Isle of Man Times]

Walter Handley, winner of four motorcycle TT races, returned to the Mannin Beg in 1935 after crashing into retirement in the 1934 race. In his MG "R" type, he completed only three laps before rear axle failure forced another retirement. [Isle of Man Times]

competitors lapped the course repeatedly. Eventually, however, Lace emerged to the cheers of spectators after replacing the rocker arm shaft. That first lap was credited as having taken him one and a half hours!

Fairfield led into the hairpin. He was followed by Dixon but positions changed rapidly. Eddie Hall's Magnette led at the end of the lap, followed by Fairfield, Mays, Dixon, Handley and Ford. By the end of the second lap, however, Mays was the leader. Superior acceleration of his "official" ERA enabled him to pass first Fairfield and then Hall.

On lap 3, Fairfield had passed Hall to take second place. Then, two laps later, he took the lead when Mays stopped at his pit with his face covered with oil from a cracked high pressure pipe. He re-joined the race, but gradually slipped behind the leaders.

Early retirements were Handley (broken rear axle), Eccles (burst fuel tank), Manby-Colegrave (broken rear axle), Ford (fuel tank punctured by rear axle dip-stick) and Eyston (broken magneto drive).

Walter Handley lifts the nearside front wheel of his MG "R" type as he turns off the Promenade into Broadway, leaving the new loop added to the 1934 circuit to avoid the lamp standard in the background, where he crashed in 1934 when the circuit turned right off the Promenade into Broadway. [Isle of Man Times]

Fairfield increased his lead. His sixth lap was the fastest of the race at 71.21mph (3mins 24secs). By the end of the tenth lap he led Dixon by 48 seconds. Mays lay in third place but over five minutes behind Dixon. Humber, Black, Hall and Baird followed. Black then pitted to change plugs and to check his contact-breaker and brakes.

At the end of lap 14 Mays returned to the pits, smothered in oil. He had almost been blinded coming down Summer Hill and had nearly run into the sea. There was no option now but to retire.

One lap later, Norman Black was forced to retire with yet another broken rear axle. Fairfield, meanwhile, drove calmly and confidently but excited spectators at Onchan where he took "close shaves" with his cornering. The fastest way of taking the hairpin from Governor's Road into Hague Road, he had decided, was by driving over the pavement on the "elbow". He also took to the pavement at Governor's Bridge. At the Presentation of Awards, he would say that when he came from South Africa in 1933 he had seen Freddie Dixon win the Mannin Beg by slithering round corners. This had persuaded him that this was the game for him. His car was marvellous. "It was just like an armchair ride all the way through", he said, adding "if there were any bumps I didn't feel them". After twenty laps he led Dixon by 1min 42secs. Baird, meanwhile, had stopped on Bray Hill with a back axle problem which proved to be a jammed shock absorber arm.

At the end of lap 24, Fairfield stopped at the pits to take on 22 gallons of fuel and to replenish his radiator. This took 1min 30secs which reduced his lead over Freddie Dixon, who had no need of a fuel stop, to 37 seconds.

Fairfield remained that little bit faster than Dixon, however, so gradually expanded his lead. By the end of lap 35 it was more than a minute. During this time

After driving steadily while others retired, T.K. Humber held third place in his old 1.5 litre unsupercharged Bugatti from lap 17 until lap 30 when he was forced to retire with a broken connecting rod. A photographer captured the moment when the car expired in clouds of smoke near the foot of Broadway. [Ron Brew collection]

Humber retired his Bugatti with both a split fuel tank and a broken connecting rod. Now only four cars were left in the race.

After forty laps, Fairfield's lead was 1min 28secs. Meanwhile Lace, who had been struggling to fix his car since the start, finally retired. He had completed only one more lap after his very slow first lap.

Then, at last, it was settled. After 42 laps, Freddie Dixon made an unscheduled pit stop. Steam poured from the Riley's radiator. For six minutes his mechanics worked on the engine. There were reports of a faulty gasket. Dixon took on more water and then the Riley had to be push-started. The engine fired, but still sounded unhealthy. Fairfield, meanwhile, had roared by, a clear two laps ahead of his former tutor. With Dixon's radiator boiling and his speed reduced, Fairfield slowed but his lead still increased over the final laps so that he took the chequered flag 8mins 52secs before Dixon. They were the only two finishers, with Eddie Hall and Bobby Baird being flagged off. They had completed 49 laps and 41 laps respectively.

After the finish, there were frantic scenes at the ERA pit, during which photographers climbed onto the pit roof which collapsed under the strain. The winner meanwhile remained calm, smiling and modest.

The victory was hailed as the ERA's first big win. In *The Motor*'s opinion "ERA may be said to have arrived." *The Autocar* concluded that the firm responsible for the ERA "has now definitely come into its own as a serious challenger for racing honours." Fairfield, too, had arrived, with a well-deserved victory. He had led from the end of the fifth lap to the finish in a calm and consistent manner which belied his "Skidder" nickname. Throughout the race his average speed had varied only slightly until he had slowed as Dixon's challenge had faded. Fairfield later told Prince Chula that he had enjoyed his first win more than any other and Chula later wrote that "it was clear that 'Skidder' Fairfield had given place to a fast but cool and meticulous driver".

The ERA triumph was an MG disaster. It was as big a failure for the 'R' types as the 1933 failure had been for the K3 Magnettes. Again a problem which had been identified in practising had revealed itself in the race. Out of five cars, four had retired with the same fault while Baird's car had been delayed so much that he been unable to complete the race within the time limit.

The big, and initially puzzling, problem had been the breakage of the short propeller shafts between the differential and rear wheels. . The car designers had not been able to identify any unforeseen stresses and the drive shafts had been considered to be sufficiently strong. Interest had focussed on the climb up Bray Hill where there were points where other roads joined or crossed the

Pat Fairfield takes the chequered flag in his privately entered E.R.A. Out of 13 starters he and Freddie Dixon (Riley) were the only finishers and he beat Dixon by 8mins 52secs after the latter lost over six minutes with a late stop due to a gasket problem. It was E.R.A.'s first major victory. [Sport & General]

Eddie Hall drives through Onchan in his MG Magnette K3. He was running at the end of the race but was not classified as he was a lap behind. Only the winner Pat Fairfield (E.R.A.) and the runner-up Freddie Dixon (Riley) completed the full 50 laps. [Magna Press]

Pat Fairfield's victory was very significant for E.R.A. after their 1934 Isle of Man debacle when their car had to be withdrawn due to handling problems. In 1934 the MGs had dominated the race but in 1935 only two finished, with neither completing the full distance. [Peter Kelly collection]

course. At these points the gradient levelled and then rose again, causing the cars to become airborne briefly, before landing heavily. Having identified the problem, however, it had been decided that the bump stops were well within the maximum angle of movement of the universal joints of the drive shafts. Even so, the problem had continued. Only post-race investigations would establish that a rise in temperature in the hydraulic shock absorbers weakened their efficiency. This enabled the wish-bone springs to hit their stops harder than intended. This led to an excessive deflection of the drive shafts, causing fractures.

As with the K3 Magnette differential problem in 1933, the stresses of racing had revealed a weakness and the remedy was simple and obvious. Sadly, however, less than three months after the Mannin Beg, the MG factory would withdraw from racing. It was suggested that Lord Nuffield's decision to withdraw had been prompted by adverse publicity resulting from the death of Frankie Tayler in 1934 and the subsequent conviction and imprisonment of Kaye Don for manslaughter. The MG withdrawal would remove any chance of the "R" type returning in triumph in 1936, as the K3 had done in 1934.

1935 Mannin Beg Race Results

Wednesday 29th May 1935. Start 10.00am. 50 laps of 4.035 miles circuit, total distance 201.75 miles. 13 starters, 2 finishers.

1. Pat Fairfield (1,090cc ERA R4A), 2hrs 59mins 54secs (67.29 mph)
2. Freddie Dixon (1,486cc Riley, 3hrs 8mins 46secs (64.13 mph)

Fastest lap: Pat Fairfield (ERA) on lap 6, 3mins 24secs (71.21 mph)

Failed to complete required 50 laps:
Eddie Hall (1,087cc MG Magnette), 49 laps completed, 3hrs 18mins 20secs (58.60 mph)
W. R. Baird (746cc R-type MG Midget), 41 laps completed, 3hrs 12mins 25secs (51.60 mph)
Retirements:
Lap 2:
A. C. Lace (1,074 cc Alta), ignition problems
Lap 3:
Walter Handley (746cc R-type MG Midget), transmission trouble
Lap 4:
Roy Eccles (1,074cc Alta), split petrol tank
Lap 6:
G. F. Manby-Colegrave (1,087cc MG Magnette), broken rear axle
J. L. Ford (1,087cc MG Magnette), fuel tank punctured by back axle dipstick
Lap 8:
George Eyston (746cc R-type MG Midget), broken magneto drive
Lap 15:
Norman Black (746cc R-type MG Midget), broken rear axle shaft,
Raymond Mays (1,090cc E.R.A. R3A), supercharger oil pump fractured
Lap 30:
T. K. Humber (1,496cc Bugatti), broken conrod.

1935 Mannin Moar Race – Lewis' Hat-trick

There were 14 starters in the Mannin Moar – an increase of four on the previous year. Brian Lewis, with his Grand Prix Bugatti which had allegedly cost £3,500, was

This photograph of the start shows Lewis (7), Martin (10), Shuttleworth (3) and Eccles (9) (all Bugattis), Fontes (Alfa Romeo, 5), Mays (E.R.A., 15), Brackenbury (Bugatti, 11), Rose-Richards (Maserati, 6), Cook (E.R.A., 14), Rayson (Bugatti, 16), Hamilton (Alfa Romeo, 1), Wilkins (Alfa Romeo, 2), Dobson (Alfa Romeo, 4) and Leith (Bugatti, 8). [Stan Hughes collection]

R. S. Wilkins and the Hon. Jock Leith relax with their race cars, Alfa Romeo (2) and Bugatti (8) respectively at the Nursery Hotel, Onchan, where they were both based. On the second lap of the race, they collided on the left turn into Broadway. Both then pitted to check their cars and Wilkins was able to continue although Leith retired with a bent rear axle. [Stan Hughes collection]

the popular favourite. Charles Martin (Bugatti) and the Alfa Romeo drivers Richard Shuttleworth and Luis Fontes were also fancied. Raymond Mays in his ERA was regarded as a "dark horse".

The morning of race day was warm with a sea haze. Crowds were much larger than on Wednesday and more enthusiastic.

On the grid's front row were the Bugatti of Martin (3mins 08secs) with the Alfa Romeo of Shuttleworth and the Bugatti of Brian Lewis (both 3mins 12secs). Behind them were Fontes' Alfa Romeo (3mins 12secs) and Eccles' Bugatti (3mins 13secs). The third row comprised Tim Rose-Richards' Maserati (3mins 13secs), Raymond Mays' ERA (3mins 14secs) and Charles Brackenbury's Bugatti (3mins 19secs), and row 4 contained the Bugattis of Rayson and Leith (3mins 23secs and 3mins 24secs respectively). Humphrey Cook's E.R.A. (3mins 24secs) A.P. Hamilton's Alfa Romeo (3mins 26secs) and Wilkins' Alfa Romeo (3mins 29secs) were on row 6 with Austin Dobson in the rear in his Alfa Romeo (3mins 34secs).

Lewis led into the Greensill's hairpin, but Shuttleworth forced his way past almost immediately and led the field into Broadway. At the end of the first lap the order was Shuttleworth, Lewis, Martin, followed by Eccles and Mays. Then, on lap 2, Broadway provided the drama for the first but not the last time. The Honourable Jock Leith turned his Bugatti off the Promenade to find Wilkins confronting him, beginning to broadside his Alfa Romeo. Leith averted a major collision by skidding parallel with the Alfa and then striking it side-on. Both continued to the pits to check their cars. An unscathed Wilkins was able to continue but Leith's Bugatti had to retire with a bent rear axle.

Meanwhile, Rose-Richards toured back to the pits from Onchan to retire with a universal joint failure and Fontes hit the bags at Onchan but continued.

After five laps, Shuttleworth led Lewis by five seconds. His average speed was 73.96mph. Martin was third, ten seconds behind Lewis, followed by a close battle for fourth between Eccles, Mays and Fontes.

The brakes on Hamilton's Alfa Romeo made the car "waltz" about the road. At Onchan it hit the sandbags on the turn from Main Road into Hague Road. At Broadway it struck a kerb. At Greensill's hairpin it overshot on braking. After all three incidents Hamilton was able to continue. Then came one from which he could not. On lap 10 the Alfa Romeo skidded after hitting a bad bump about half way up Broadway whilst Hamilton was changing from second to third gear. The car struck a kerb, went out of control, passed sideways under the wooden pedestrian bridge, and only a short distance in front of Humphrey Cook in his E.R.A. The Alfa then mounted the pavement, swiped a garden wall with its tail, and somersaulted end-over-end up the road. It came to rest upturned with Hamilton pinned beneath it, still seated in the cockpit and held tight by his feet.

When marshals reached the wrecked car and righted it, Hamilton was found to have escaped relatively lightly. He had a broken nose, cuts and bruises and was badly shaken. Taken into a house, he was seen by a Doctor and then led through the house to an ambulance which awaited him in the back lane. After a visit to the hospital, he was back at the pits before the end of the race.

Lewis was also in the wars. Struck a stunning blow in the face by a stone thrown up by another car, he managed to keep control and pressed on with blood running down his face and a huge lump between his eyes.

After ten laps, Shuttleworth still led Lewis but only by three seconds. The order behind them was unchanged except that Mays had passed Eccles to take fourth place.

On the eleventh lap Lewis passed Shuttleworth at the foot of Summer Hill. By now Shuttleworth was slowing, with difficulty in changing gear. On lap 12 he lost second place to Martin and, at the end of lap 13, he retired at the pits with gearbox and rear axle problems.

Around this time, the tide reached its height. As during Wednesday's Mannin Beg, pit attendants were drenched by spray. The *Isle of Man Times* reported jocularly that Captain Phillips sent out a frenzied SOS for King Canute, but to no avail! *The Autocar* feared that octopus or cod might be found in the pits.

Despite his injury, Lewis increased the pace. On his fifteenth lap he did the fastest lap of the race in marginally over three minutes, an average of 78.10mph. This was slightly faster than his 1934 fastest lap of 77.46mph over the shorter course, driving the Ferrari Alfa Romeo. At the end of the lap, his average was 75.46mph and he led Charles Martin by nineteen seconds. Behind them, Mays was nearly one minute behind Martin, followed at a respectful distance by Eccles, Fontes and Brackenbury. Drivers said the road surface at Bray Hill was in a shocking state.

Lewis went faster. After twenty laps his average was up to 75.89mph, his lead over Martin 48 seconds. Humphrey Cook in the second ERA took sixth place from Brackenbury.

On lap 23 Mays stopped at the pits. He was away quickly but stopped again on the next lap to have his radiator cap wired in place. On the next lap Cook pitted for fuel.

At half-distance, Lewis' average was 76.03mph. He led Martin by one minute and one second. Following his stops, Mays was down to fifth, with Eccles now third and Fontes fourth. Brackenbury was back up to sixth, having passed Cook, who had two stops to change oiled plugs.

For Brackenbury, however, there was a nasty experience on lap 29. His seat collapsed beneath him as he approached the bottom of Bray Hill. The hefty Brackenbury was deposited on the prop-shaft. As a metal sheet touched the shaft he saw sparks emitted from it. These ignited the lagging round the spare fuel tank. Brackenbury brought his car to a halt in record time, said *The Autocar*. In fact, the car hit a hedge but the driver jumped out before the impact. The flames were quickly put out by an extinguisher and then Brackenbury went on his way again. He halted briefly at the pits for his seat to be re-secured and then continued.

At the end of lap 30, Lewis led Martin by 1min 18secs. His average was now faster than ever, at 76.41mph, and he could afford to slacken his pace. Eccles was 1min 54secs behind Martin and 1min 05secs in front of Fontes. Mays was fifth, a further 2mins 13secs behind Fontes. Rayson was now sixth, over six minutes behind Mays.

On lap 32 there was more action at Broadway. Eccles took the slip road to retire with a broken universal joint. Cook stopped for another plug change but soon afterwards toured in to retire with a scavenging pump failure. Lewis had noticeably reduced speed, using the brakes sparingly, but still increasing his lead over Martin. By the end of lap 35 the lead was up to 1min 33secs. Fontes was third, Mays fourth, Rayson fifth and Dobson sixth.

Martin stopped on lap 36 for 16 gallons of fuel, and water. This took just 39 seconds. Four laps later, Lewis stopped for fuel, oil, water and lemonade. His stop took only 33 seconds, which gained him six seconds on Martin. Fontes also stopped to take on eight gallons of fuel and change the offside rear tyre .He was away in 1min 27secs. Raymond Mays was now third. Wilkins, still going despite his collision on lap 2, hit the bags at Onchan but again was able to continue.

The pit stops left Lewis leading Martin by 1min 39secs with Mays third, four minutes behind Martin and 1min 21secs ahead of Fontes, who had a huge lead over Rayson.

Mays stopped again, for water and oil. He spent 30 seconds at his pit, but without losing his position. Fontes lost third gear temporarily, while Mays lost first.

With five laps left, Lewis' lead over Fontes was reduced by 23 seconds, to 1min 16secs. Raymond Mays was 38 seconds ahead of Fontes who had a brake problem. Martin continued to chase Lewis, reducing the deficit to just over one minute and then to 53 seconds. He lapped Fontes in a spectacular overtaking move on lap 49.

Lewis duly took the chequered flag, 51 seconds ahead of Martin. An unexpectedly long gap followed. As everyone wondered where Mays was, Fontes appeared, taking the finishing flagman completely by surprise, to claim third. Only then came disastrous news of Mays. He had stopped on Bray Hill on the last lap. Universal joint failure had cruelly deprived him, and ERA, of a well-

After two Mannin Moar wins in Alfa Romeos, the Hon. Brian Lewis (who was better known as a Bugatti driver and in fact nicknamed "Bug" Lewis) reverted to the French marque for 1935, but without giving up his winning habit. He beat Charlie Martin in another Bugatti by 51 seconds. [Stan Hughes collection]

deserved and creditable third place to add to Fairfield's Mannin Beg win.

Rayson finished fourth, exactly fifteen minutes after Lewis. Another second and he would have exceeded the deadline and would have been flagged off. Three other drivers, Dobson, Wilkins and Brackenbury (with his seat still loose) were still running and were flagged off as non-finishers, having completed 49 laps.

According to *The Autocar* the Mannin Moar was "not perhaps an intensely exciting but certainly a very interesting race". *The Motor*, rather more enthusiastically, said "what the Mannin Beg may have lacked in the more spectacular thrills the Mannin Moar made up. The race was dramatic from first to last".

1935 Mannin Moar Race Results

Friday 31st May 1935. Start10.00am. 50 laps of 4.035 miles circuit, total distance 201.75 miles. 14 starters, 4 finishers.

1. The Honourable Brian Lewis (3,255cc Bugatti) 2hrs 40mins 11secs) (75.57mph)
2. Charles Martin (3,255cc Bugatti) 2hrs 41mins 2secs (75.16mph)
3. Luis Fontes (2,336cc Alfa Romeo) 2hrs 48mins 14secs (71.94 mph)
4. E. K. "Teddy"Rayson (1,990cc Bugatti) 2hrs 55mins 11secs (69.10 mph)

Fastest lap: The Honourable Brian Lewis (Bugatti) 3mins 6secs (78.10mph)

Failed to complete required 50 laps:

Austin Dobson (2,600cc Alfa Romeo), R. S. Wilkins (2,600cc Alfa Romeo) and Charles Brackenbury (2,263cc Bugatti) - 48 laps

Retirements:

Lap 1:

T. E. Rose-Richards (2,992cc Maserati), broken universal joint

The Honourable Jock Leith (2,263cc Bugatti), collision at Broadway corner. Driver uninjured

Lap 9:

A. P. Hamilton (2,336cc. Alfa Romeo), crash into wall at Broadway, driver not seriously injured

Lap 13:

R. O. Shuttleworth (2,904cc Alfa Romeo), gear box problems

Lap 30:

Humphrey Cook (1,488cc ERA), scavenge pump

Lap 32:

Lindsay Eccles (3,255cc Bugatti G.P), broken universal joint

Lap 50:

Raymond Mays (1,980cc ERA), universal joint failure.

Reaction

The races had been a disappointment, again failing to attract the anticipated number of spectators; fewer in fact than in 1934.

The organisation by the RAC had been perfect, said *The Autocar*. It was difficult to see why the races had failed to attract interest. Questions arose as to whether the races had been too early in the year or whether the spectacle of cars racing in town streets was not acceptable. The car TT had attracted many more British spectators than the Mannin Races and had made them more welcome.

There did not seem to be much enthusiasm for the races even on the Island, an unfortunate comparison with the excitement generated by the motorcycle TT races. *The Autocar* wondered whether the Manx people as a whole liked the races. There was little evidence that they did.

The Motor thought that the races had not been a fiasco despite the large number of retirements. Neither had they been the success that they should have been. It was doubtful that there had been as many as 10,000 spectators, compared with an estimated 50,000 at the Monaco Grand Prix. The inference was that the quality of entries was responsible for the difference. If the Monaco Grand Prix entries could be attracted to Douglas, there could be 30,000 spectators. *The Motor* thought there should be two races: one on Friday, for the present cars in two classes, run concurrently; the other on Saturday, an "International Manx Grand Prix". This would be an invitation race for Mercedes-Benz, Auto-Union, Alfa Romeo, Bugatti and the best independent drivers together with some of the best British drivers. Inevitably start money, as well as substantial prizes, would be required.

British newspaper stories alleged heavy-handed policing involving traps for drivers but the RAC's Colonel Lindsay Lloyd said that the Police had helped in every possible way. Reports of Police strictness were dismissed by *The Autocar* as "Tommy nonsense". The Police were a help, not a hindrance. No driver had reported any problem.

Criticism of the condition of the road surface was general. *The Motor* described it as "appallingly bumpy". This was blamed for many of the troubles which eliminated five cars from the Mannin Beg with broken axles and burst tanks. The descent of Summer Hill was branded as the most dangerous part. *Motor Sport* said the course was "disturbingly rough". Speaking at the Mannin Moar Presentation, after congratulating Douglas Corporation and the RAC on the organisation, Brian Lewis joked that he hoped next year to be able to congratulate the "Road Mending Association", but there was a serious point. Tyres may have lasted well but, clearly, little had been done to improve the roads after the problems of 1934. The bump at Governor's Bridge had not been removed, Summer Hill had still been very rough and Bray Hill had broken up badly during both races.

In Tynwald, opinions were widely diverse on what should be done. Shortly after the races, when members voted £1,500 to pay for them, they voiced their concern about inadequate advertising and adoption of an inappropriate course. Ten thousand posters may have been distributed throughout Britain but it had not been enough. People in Birmingham and Coventry had not known the races were taking place. It was argued that the proper place to stage the races was not Douglas but the countryside where spectators could watch from hedgerows. New courses were suggested - one in the north and another with a start at Mount Murray. "Pathetically empty" grandstands, meanwhile, were explained by the charge of 10s 6d for a seat.

In a letter published in the *Isle of Man Examiner* of 7th June 1935, a reader's letter from "Mannin" (probably Tom Moore, 1933 Mannin Beg driver and Proprietor of *Motor Sport*) made the point that the Mannin races had been tried for only three years and yet they were being criticised and "set down as rank failures". "Mannin" thought that comparisons with the TT motorcycle races and the number of visitors which they attracted were unfair. He questioned how many visitors were attracted by the TT in 1910, when they were only three years old. The TT had been allowed to continue and was attracting 10,000 people to see the Senior Race alone. There was a long way to go for the Mannin races to reach perfection, he conceded, but other resorts would jump at the opportunity to have the event. Prize money should be substantially increased so as to attract Continental "aces". The question was not whether the Island could afford to have the races but whether it could afford not to have them.

1936 Rac International Light Car Race – Seaman's Delage Win

Planning

In October 1935, Manx newspapers reported that the fate of the races hung in the balance. Douglas Corporation's Finance Committee had decided to recommend to the Town Council that the races should be held in 1936. The Council, however, had a long and heated debate. Strong opponents denounced the races as "a dismal failure" and "a washout".

The main ground of opposition was that, although the races brought wonderful free publicity for the Island, they did not bring enough visitors. It was said that the TT and Manx Grand Prix motorcycle races brought between 8,000 and 10,000 people in a single day while the car races did not attract as many hundreds. The publicity value, the date and the amount of the prize fund were questioned. While there was a strong feeling that the races had had their chance, the Mayor reminded his colleagues that great efforts had been made to induce the RAC to bring car races back to the Island. After three years, because the races had not immediately been a tremendous success, there was strong criticism. If the races were rejected now, others would be glad to have them and it would be difficult ever to get them back. The Council voted by the narrowest possible margin, twelve votes to eleven, to give the event another trial.

The next announcement came in December. There were to be no more "Mannin" races. Instead there would be one important race, to be called the "British Road Race Championship", open to cars of up to 1,500cc. Prize money would be increased to attract Continental drivers. The proposed date was the Friday morning before the Whit weekend but a Thursday afternoon race was being considered, as Thursday was early closing day in Douglas which meant less disruption to business and more chance for workers to marshal or to watch the races. The RAC thought the Mannin races had not been a success. Overshadowed by the big cars in the Mannin Moar, the Mannin Beg had failed to attract the attention it deserved while the Mannin Moar had been dominated by foreign cars. The RAC thought it should do all in its power to encourage, develop and advertise British cars.

The RAC decision was a tacit, belated acceptance of Earl Howe's 1933 objection to the Mannin Beg limit to supercharged 1,100cc and supercharged 1,500cc cars. The supercharged 1,500cc cars (like Howe's Delage) which were excluded from the Mannin Beg had no alternative but to compete in the Mannin Moar against Alfa Romeos, Bugattis and other larger-engined cars. This had been a serious deterrent as, in three years, only four supercharged 1,500cc cars had entered for the Mannin Moar and only one had started a race. Now at last there would be an open race for all 1,500cc cars, including supercharged ones, as was usual on the Continent but there would now be no race for Grand Prix type machines.

At the same time, a new course was announced. Unusually, the direction was anti-clockwise. The Start/Finish would be at the TT Grandstand. The course would follow the TT course to the top of Bray Hill, turn left and descend to the Promenade via Ballaquayle Road and Broadway. Turning left again, the course would continue north along the Promenade, to the Douglas Bay Hotel. There, at Port Jack, a hairpin left, closely followed by a hairpin right, would take cars into Royal Avenue and thence to Onchan Village. A left turn into Main Road would be followed by an almost straight run along

Governor's Road and Glencrutchery Road to the Start. The lap distance would be approximately four miles.

According to the *Isle of Man Examiner*, the course had been chosen in conjunction with Captain Phillips of the RAC, influenced mainly by the improved road surface and the width of the roads. Parts of the Promenade, however, were unsuitable for racing and the RAC had asked for improvements to be made. There would be alterations at the TT Grandstand to enable pit stops to be made behind the pits, as it would be unsafe for cars to stop on the outside of the pits as in the motorcycle races.

Three weeks later, another new course was announced! Although parts of the promenade were unsuitable for racing, it would be impossible to re-surface it entirely in time for the race. The new course would abandon much of the "round the houses" character of the Mannin races. From the start at the TT Grandstand it would turn right at the top of Bray Hill, into Ballanard Road. Another right turn at Willaston cross roads would take cars via Johnny Watterson's Lane to Cronk-ny-Mona. After following the TT Course to Signpost Corner, cars would continue straight on via Hillberry Road and Avondale Road to Onchan Village. Turning right at the Manx Arms public house, the course would continue through the village and via Governor's Road and Glencrutchery Road to the TT Grandstand. The lap distance would be approximately four miles. The race would be at 2pm on Thursday 28th May, with early morning practices from 5am to 7am on Tuesday 26th and Wednesday 27th May.

The *Isle of Man Examiner* of 3rd January 1936 announced that the race would be called "The RAC International Light Car Race". The newspaper's leader attacked the choice of course. With its high hedges, it would abandon the unique character of the Mannin courses and become a poor imitation of many other courses. The efforts of three years would have been wasted. The race would be "an absolute flop", the *Examiner* thought, and it would have been better to have abandoned it altogether if the RAC was not prepared to continue with a "round the houses" course.

The *Isle of Man Weekly Times* attacked the course as "quite featureless" and "quite unsatisfactory". Overtaking would be impossible on most of the course, said the Times, and the race deserved something better. The solution was to use the Promenade, as the short length which could not be improved in time was "quite good enough for any racing car". Alternatively, part of the 1935 circuit should be used in reverse, starting at the TT Grandstand and turning left at the top of Bray Hill to descend to the Promenade. The suggested course would turn left onto the Promenade, proceed up Summer Hill to Onchan hairpin and return to the Grandstand. *The Times* added that constant changes of course were no good. The TT course had remained unchanged and its famous corners had become household names the world over. The car races needed similar continuity.

A week later, on 11th January, the Times back-pedalled, explaining that its criticism was of the course and not of the race itself. If racing were to be abandoned in 1936, it would be for all time and all the time, trouble and money spent to regain car racing would have been in vain. The car TT had been lost to the Island "through our own colossal stupidity". It had gone to Belfast, where it would stay, the Island having tried and failed to get it back. That must not be allowed to happen again, said the Times.

The *Isle of Man Examiner* of 17th January reported that the Race Committee would meet that day to discuss what amounted to a "Take it or leave it" ultimatum from the RAC. The 1936 race would be run on the new country course or not at all. The RAC would not consider a course which used the part of the Promenade which was under reconstruction. The *Examiner* said that the RAC was perturbed at, and greatly resented, the attitude of the Manx Press which, the RAC said, had caused considerable indignation. The RAC even suggested that the local attitude to the races had not been too friendly all along. The *Examiner* maintained that it had correctly reported public opinion, and if the RAC insisted on the country course the *Examiner*'s view was that the Committee would interpret public opinion correctly if it decided to drop the race. Nevertheless a footnote to the report, timed at 12 noon, stated that the Committee had unanimously agreed to accept the RAC ultimatum.

The *Weekly Times* had not given up. In a lengthy article on the day after the decision, it reported that Freddie Dixon supported its views. He had said that the Promenade was "quite OK to race over". Captain Phillips had said that, if the race were to be abandoned, responsibility would rest with the Manx Press. *The Times* refuted this, blaming the RAC for trying to foist on the public a course quite unworthy of the amount of money which would have to be spent on it. On a more positive note, the Times said that people on the Promenade were in favour of racing being given a fair trial. They believed that the international race, with more prize money, would give the race a bigger appeal and that it could grow into an event of as great importance as the motorcycle TT. *Mona's Herald* later commented that the new country course was the only one which could be prepared with a suitably even surface in time and within budget. No new Grandstands or bridges would be needed and only one race would mean more prize money.

The total prize money on offer was £1,550, to be divided between the first six finishers, with the winner taking £500. In addition, there was to be £30 for any finisher outside the top six. This compared with a total fund of £650 per race for the 1935 Mannin races, with each winner taking £300. Prince Chula of Thailand, cousin, guardian and sponsor of Prince Birabongse Bhanutej Bhanubandh (known as "Bira") who would compete on the Isle of Man in 1936 for the first time, reckoned that as the prize money was the highest for any race in the British Isles, the race could be safely regarded as the most important road race of the year for racing cars.

Extensive road works were undertaken by the Highway Board and Douglas Corporation to meet RAC requirements. Almost all the roadway was resurfaced. Gullies and gutters were filled in and dangerous corners were sandbagged. Also, two corners were widened at Birchley Terrace, Onchan.

Particular attention was paid to the grandstand and pits area. To keep the fast stretch past the Grandstand completely clear during pit stops, a pit lane was created between the pits and the grandstand. As well as being safer, spectators on the Grandstand would have a better view of pit stops. The side of the pits facing the road was restricted to signalling.

The Highway Board agreed to an extension of practice times - starting at 4.30am instead of 5am and finishing fifteen minutes later at 7.15am. Road closures for the racing were fixed at between 1.15pm and no later than 6.15pm.

The BBC again arranged to provide live radio commentary on the race, by the usual team of Alan Hess at the Grandstand and Victor Smythe at Cronk-ny-Mona

Entries

In the interests of safety the race was restricted to no more than 30 cars. The RAC believed this to be the absolute maximum that could be accommodated on the course in safety.

In view of the numbers entered for the Mannin series (20 for the 1935 Mannin Beg) and the fact that an entry of 15 cars for a classic Grand Prix was reckoned to be "better than first class," this number may have seemed ambitious. In fact, it came close to being equalled, with 26 entries received. Only 20 actually reached the Island but their quality prompted the organisers to describe the line-up as magnificent and the best received for any Isle of Man car race since the Great War.

It was a vindication of the decision to run an "open" 1,500cc race for both supercharged and unsupercharged cars in place of the Mannin Beg formula, with which the RAC had persevered in the face of annual criticism. The increased prize fund may also have played a part.

Entries included no less than ten ERAs. According to the Official Programme, three of these were works entries, for Raymond Mays, Earl Howe and Marcel Lehoux. 1935 winner Pat Fairfield, although entered by Arthur Dobson, would drive a car in the ERA colour of apple green and may also have been one of the works team. Private ERA entries were Cyril Paul, (entered by Arthur Dobson), Bill Everitt, Reggie Tongue, Tommy Wisdom, "Jock" Manby-Colegrave and Prince Birabongse of Siam (known as "Bira" or "B. Bira"). This was an abbreviation for Prince Birabongse Bhanutej Bhanubandh, a grandson of King Mongkut, the character made famous in the stage and film musical "The King and I."

Bira had started racing in March the previous year with a Riley Imp. Later he had graduated to an MG K3 Magnette (K3030). Then he had been given a 1,500cc ERA, R2B, as a 21st birthday present. These cars were supplied to private customers by ERA Ltd at a cost of £1,700. It was in this car that Bira had achieved his early successes. In 1936, when he had acquired a second ERA, R5B, and had called it "Remus", he had named his first supercharged racer as "Romulus". Bira chose "Romulus" for the Manx race because of its reliability and because, although "Remus" was the faster car, it was needed for the Nurburgring on 14th June. "Romulus", painted in what had become known as "Bira blue" with a little white mouse mascot painted on a wing mirror, was entered by "Bira's" older first cousin once removed, guardian, race sponsor and pit attendant, Prince Chula Chakrabongse of Siam. Some thought the white mouse was the Disney cartoon character Mickey Mouse but, in fact, it was just an ordinary mouse. It was there because Bira's entrant, Prince Chula, had a Siamese nickname of "Nou" which meant "Mouse." Bira came to the Island fresh from wins in the Coupe Rainier at Monaco (only a week after a race at Donington when a flying stone had broken his goggles and left glass splinters in an eye) and in the International Trophy at Brooklands. "Romulus", like each of the works cars, had an electric starter fitted to the nose of the car.

The two foreign ERA drivers gave the entry an international flavour which the Mannin races had lacked. Lehoux was born in Algeria of French parents. He won several races in North Africa between 1924 and 1929 and a number of Grands Prix in Europe since then. He drove for the Ferrari Alfa Romeo team in 1934 before an unsuccessful 1935 season with a private Maserati. For 1936, Lehoux joined the ERA team where his experience was a great asset, but he was killed in the Deauville Grand Prix, in a collision with Farina's Alfa Romeo. His car, R3B, was destroyed in the crash – the only ERA not to survive. After his death the "works" ERAs were painted black.

Other entries included a three-car team from the Austin Company. These brand-new all-white overhead camshaft 744cc cars had been designed by Murray

Jamieson on the instructions of Sir Herbert Austin with the intention of dominating the 750cc racing class. In so doing, it was hoped to promote the sales of the already-famous Austin Seven. The supercharged four-cylinder engines were capable of 90bhp at 7,600rpm and there were development plans to raise this to 14,000rpm. Regarded as being probably the most interesting in the race, they were "beautiful little jobs", according to the writer of the official programme. If they got over the teething problems which beset cars of an entirely new design, he wrote, they could be reckoned to give a remarkably good account of themselves. The lightweight 454kg Austins had experienced problems over their fuel. Now, however, they were on dope and this seemed to have transformed their performance. The nominated drivers were Charlie Dodson, L.P. Driscoll and C.L. Goodacre with Bert Hadley as the team's reserve driver.

Freddie Dixon entered his Riley, which was supercharged for the first time.

Two Maseratis were regarded as "mystery cars." One was to be driven by the Swiss driver, Christian Kautz, who had finished fourth in the Coupe Rainier race for light cars at Monaco that year, which Bira had won. In fact, Kautz did not make it to the Island. The other Maserati was to be driven by E.K. "Teddy" Rayson who had earned a reputation in the 1935 Mannin Moar for driving his Bugatti "like a man possessed."

The entry by Richard Seaman of an all-black but silver-wheeled ten-year-old Delage previously owned by Earl Howe was regarded as exciting. In November 1935 the racing world had been astonished by Seaman's decision to sell his ERA and buy the 1927 1,500cc straight-eight supercharged Grand Prix Delage. He had been persuaded to do so by the former team manager of Alfa Romeo, Giulio Ramponi, who had been preparing Seaman's ERA. Ramponi, it was said, had believed that the Delage could be improved considerably. Seaman had decided to give him the chance and had bought it with a spare engine and many other parts. Ramponi had lightened it by 250lbs. This had been achieved by fitting new duralumin wheels, a new radiator and a new combined fuel tank and tail with lighter alloy material. The heavy ENV gearbox fitted by Earl Howe was replaced by a five-speed 1925 Delage gearbox as originally fitted to the 1925 cars. Lockheed hydraulic brakes replaced mechanically operated ones, high compression pistons were fitted and the supercharger pressure was increased. The timing gears had been found to have been incorrectly marked by Earl Howe's mechanics. Correcting this alone had resulted in a significant increase in power. The modifications resulted in a power output of 195bhp, making the car competitive with the ERAs. Now the Delage was viewed with new respect. In its younger days when it, and others like it, had swept to repeated triumphs in Continental Grand Prix, it had been capable of 130mph. Now modernised, it was speculated that it might even be faster, although some were sceptical. The Manx race was to be Seaman's first long-distance race in the car, following two wins in a club meeting at Donington. Shortly before coming to the Island, Seaman also won the British Empire Trophy Race at Donington in a Maserati.

There were four Altas, as yet relatively unknown quantities, to be driven by J.H. Bartlett, A.J. Cormack, J.P. Wakefield and the Irish driver P.M. Dwyer. Philip Jucker entered his Frazer Nash, Roy Eccles had a

The runner-up Bira (left) Earl Howe, who retired with a split fuel tank, (centre) and winner Richard Seaman (right) pose in the pit lane. [Stan Hughes collection]

1,084cc Rapier Special and there were two MG K3 Magnettes entered by L.R. Briggs (K3020) and H. Williams. The only unsupercharged car in the entry was the old Bugatti of Humber.

Practices

Only 20 entries actually arrived for practice. The six absentees were, disappointingly, the Maserati of Christian Kautz together with the Austins of Driscoll and Goodacre, the Altas of Bartlett and Dwyer, and Tommy Wisdom's ERA.

Competitors were disturbed by what they found.

Immediately on his arrival on the Island, even before checking into the Majestic Hotel in Onchan, Bira drove round the course several times in the Rolls-Royce in which he, his cousin Prince Chula, and his pet dog, the wire-haired fox terrier, Joannie, had motored from London. Prince Chula thought the race distance of 200 miles was wrong for 1,500cc cars. It would allow some cars to be driven non-stop without refuelling whilst others would be penalised by having to refuel. That was unfair, he thought. He believed that the correct race distance was one in which either all competing cars had to stop once for fuel or one in which none had to stop.

Prince Chula also considered the changes at the pits, whilst excellent for safety, to be a further handicap for competitors who had to stop. Drivers would have to be slower in their approach so that they could negotiate the bend into the loop road behind the pits. On emerging, meanwhile, they could be delayed. Thus fast work by mechanics at the pits could be negated. Here was a further advantage for a car which did not have to stop.

Bira was more interested in the course itself and this he found to be "difficult." Charlie Dodson, who spent the week prior to practising in learning the course, described it as "interesting but difficult". He predicted lap speeds of 72-73mph. Reggie Tongue, winner of the previous weekend's race at Cork, had made an early visit to the Island. He disliked the grass banks which obstructed the sight lines through the corners.

On the eve of practising, fourteen drivers, led by the ERA works team, wrote a letter (later described as a "petition") to the RAC. One of their concerns was flag marshalling. There had been problems at Monaco and now they wanted an assurance that the flag marshalling on the Island was adequate. One of their fears was coming round a blind corner and encountering a car across the road. According to *Motor Sport* the narrow, twisty and high-hedged section between Willaston and Cronk-ny-Mona presented a particular hazard. Even with a well organised system of flag marshals, it said, it would be difficult to avoid a collision if someone went broadside round one of the blind corners. The Daily Mirror said that drivers were calling the stretch "Suicide Switchback." The RAC was able to satisfy the petitioners with the assurance that there were 33 flagmen planned.

The RAC was also able to satisfy the petitioners on two other points, although not so quickly. Competitors disliked the small, square card number boards which they were required to fix to car fronts. They proposed the replacement of the boards by larger, more visible numbers painted on radiator grills or immediately above the grills. After a trial next day at the first practice session, the RAC accepted that the painted numbers were legible and could be used. A few, notably Dick Seaman (Delage) and Charles Dodson (Austin), omitted the board numbers altogether. Other competitors carried both. Cramped accommodation at the pits was a more difficult problem to overcome. It was resolved, however, by re-arranging the car and accessory pits.

Prince Chula observed later that RAC officials and the Clerk of the Course, Captain Phillips, were willing to do everything they could to improve things, while *The Autocar* said that in the end, though nobody liked the circuit, everyone agreed that any race was better than none and the RAC had done all it could to help.

As pre-race tensions mounted, Bira reacted by playing with realistic toys. As an avid collector of toys which were miniature representations of the real thing, he toured local toy shops until he was a well-known and popular visitor. There was not one toy shop on the Island that he did not know, he said afterwards. He flew a model aircraft in the spacious grounds of the Majestic Hotel until his terrier destroyed it after a forced landing. Then, to the delight of local youngsters, Bira arrived at a boating pool with a toy submarine. This was his way of keeping calm and reserving his strength for racing, he said later. If he became anxious in any way then he always did badly.

The ERAs dominated the first early morning practice, held on Tuesday 26th May in excellent weather. Bira's "Romulus" had had an overhaul, including removal of the cylinder head, prior to being brought to the Island. Now, after 13 cautious laps in which he learnt the course, Bira delivered the joint-fastest lap of the day - a time of 3 minutes 23 seconds. He shared the honours with another ERA driver, Cyril Paul. Bill Everitt (ERA) and Freddie Dixon (Riley) were next, tied on 3mins 26secs. They were followed by Marcel Lehoux (ERA) on 3mins 27secs with Charlie Dodson's impressive little Austin and Pat Fairfield's "official" ERA a further second behind. There were "narrow squeaks" but no incidents except that Bill Everitt dented his tail near the Nursery. Dick Seaman caused some anxiety when he failed to complete a lap. Later he was located, having stopped on St. Ninian's straight with gearbox trouble. It was noted that the front end of the Delage was lively under braking.

Some drivers considered the course hazardous and *The Light Car* commented that the course demanded a readjustment of normal discretion to valour ratios.

Wednesday morning's second practice was cloudy but dry. Bira was slower than usual. Prince Chula reckoned that if he was to get a position on the front row at the start he would have to do better and called him into the pits. There he was told to do better. This was necessary sometimes with Bira, said Chula later. He was so consistent that he would deliver repeatedly the same lap time unless he was told that it was not fast enough. This, apparently, had the desired effect. Bira delivered a lap time of 3 minutes 19 seconds. Later, Chula reckoned it was this which inspired French Algerian Marcel Lehoux. Getting into Earl Howe's car instead of his own, he went three seconds faster than Bira, averaging 73.47mph. It was not realised at the time that, as the grid positions were allocated by reference to car rather than driver, this would put Earl Howe in pole position while the unfortunate Lehoux was relegated to eighth position, based on his fastest time in his own car! Seaman was third fastest in 3mins 20secs, followed by Dodson, Mays and Fairfield, all separated by gaps of one second.

On Wednesday evening, the eve of race day, Dick Seaman was the guest of Princes Chula and Bira for dinner at the Majestic Hotel. Prince Chula asked him if it was true that the Delage would be able to complete the race without refuelling. Seaman, however, was non-committal. He hoped so, he said, but he wasn't sure.

After dinner, Seaman and Bira played a game of ping pong. Someone joked that the loser of this match would win the following day's race.

Bira lost but Prince Chula still did not fancy Bira's chances next day. He thought that as long as Seaman could keep going in his Delage, he would win. Bira's best hope then was to come second.

This belief inspired Prince Chula's race tactics for his cousin. Chula believed that carefully prepared tactics were essential when running against the formidable ERA works team of four cars and strong privateers such as Seaman and Paul. Therefore Bira was instructed to stay close to Seaman but not push his ERA too hard in the hope of trying to take a lead which he could not hold when he stopped to refuel. He must not bid for the lead, he was told, unless he received a pit signal to go faster. The principal target was to be most careful and above all to keep the car on the road. A "good third" position for the first half of the race and then a second place would be acceptable for this. Perhaps Lehoux, starting from the front row, would push Seaman so hard that the old Delage would not be able to stand the pace. At this time Chula was still unaware that Lehoux would not be starting from the front row after all, because his fastest time had been set in Howe's car. When the true position was confirmed it was nevertheless stated that the time set by Lehoux would be recognised as a record.

1936 RAC International Light Car Race

As drivers assembled for the start, on a bright sunny afternoon with a light breeze, Freddie Dixon was missing. Just before the start news came that he had left his hotel ten minutes previously. On arrival at the pits, wearing a neat suit, he told the *Isle of Man Examiner* reporter that he had decided to go fishing. The official reason for his withdrawal was that he thought that his car was unsuitable for the course. During the race, however, an *Isle of Man Times* reporter found Freddie at the Manx Arms corner in Onchan, "a very interested but disappointed spectator". He was characteristically forthright in his condemnation of the course as "quite unsuitable for a serious race". He did not feel justified in starting and perhaps meeting with serious trouble, he said. It was better to keep out. Having given the course a fair trial during practice he was forced to the conclusion that it was worse than useless. He added that there was no reason why the 1935 course had been abandoned in favour of a totally unsuited circuit. Prince Chula said afterwards that he believed that Dixon's wife had influenced his decision but it was also suggested that there was a problem with his supercharger. Significantly, he had driven much slower in practice than the other principal drivers, his fastest lap being 3min 41sec, surprisingly 25 seconds slower than Lehoux.

The start was delayed for a short time while spectators at the Nursery Hotel bends were moved from an unsafe area. With many spectators all around the course and the Grandstand almost full, it was generally agreed that the crowd was the largest ever at a Manx car race. Visitors, apparently, were not numerous – according to the *Mona's Herald*, the "immense crowd was practically all natives". The *Isle of Man Times* claimed credit for encouraging locals to support the race but the fact that the race took place on early closing day must also have had some effect.

Nineteen cars lined up for the start in two-one-two formation instead of the normal three-two-three. This was because of the narrowness of the road. The front row consisted of the ERAs of Earl Howe (benefiting from the time of 3mins 16secs (73.47mph) set by his car while driven by Lehoux) and Bira (3mins 19secs). Dick Seaman in his Delage, alone on the second row with a time of 3mins 20secs, was the favourite. Perceived by some as probably his greatest challenger was Marcel Lehoux but, despite his meteoric lap in Howe's car, his performance in

This photograph of the start shows Howe (E.R.A., 16), Bira (E.R.A., 17), Seaman (Delage, 9), Mays (14, E.R.A., behind Bira), Dodson (Austin, 6), Fairfield (E.R.A., 10), Everitt (E.R.A., 12), Paul (E.R.A., 11), Wakefield, Alta, 4), Manby-Colegrave (E.R.A., 20), and Lehoux (E.R.A., 15). [R and L Kelly collection]

his own car relegated him to row six. Behind Seaman were Mays' ERA (3mins 21secs) and Dodson's Austin (3mins 22secs), followed by the ERAs of Pat Fairfield on row four (3mins 23secs), Cyril Paul and Bill Everitt on row five and Lehoux alone on row six.

Howe led the field into the first corner at St. Ninians followed by Bira, who was passed by Seaman after Willaston. Bira then lost third place to Paul, who had already passed Fairfield, Mays and Dodson. This was the order at the end of the lap. There were two retirements on the first lap – Humber's Bugatti with big end trouble and Rayson's Maserati with the supercharger drive sheared.

At the end of lap 4, Seaman, conscious that Lehoux was moving up the field, passed Howe in front of the pits to take the lead, which he would keep until the chequered flag. Shortly afterwards, Howe pitted with excessive air pressure in his fuel tank, promoting Dodson's Austin to fourth behind Bira. Lehoux had been hit by a flying stone and stopped to change goggles.

After ten laps, Seaman averaged 69.78mph and led Paul by eight seconds, with Bira a further four seconds behind. Fairfield was 25 seconds behind Bira closely followed by Mays with Dodson sixth, after a pit stop due to carburettor flooding. At this point, Chula decided that there was no point in speeding up Bira as he was practically convinced that Seaman would not stop for fuel. Even if Bira had speeded up, he would be unable to gain a large enough lead over Seaman to cover the time which he would lose in his pit stop. Incidentally, Chula's pit signals were novel. They were composed of Siamese characters on a coloured background.

Retirements were already numerous. Philip Jucker managed only three laps in his Frazer Nash (rod through crankcase). Reggie Tongue, whose troubled practice had included a smashed windscreen, retired his ERA after five pit stops in six laps, with ignition trouble. After eight laps Williams retired his MG Magnette with a broken shock-absorber. He had been lucky to start as a shock-absorber mounting bracket had broken as he drove to the start. Cormack (Alta) suffered oil pump failure after eight laps while Roy Eccles, having spun and stalled his Rapier Special at Manx Arms corner in Onchan, retired after ten laps with supercharger trouble. Only twelve were now running.

On lap 11, Lehoux lapped in 3mins 22secs, 71.29mph,

The winner, Richard Seaman (Delage) is followed past the Manx Arms in Onchan Village by L.R. Briggs (MG Magnette K3) whom presumably he had lapped on the descent to the corner. Briggs was still running at the finish but he was seven laps behind, having completed only 43 laps. [Stan Hughes collection]

With the road surface covered by loose stones, Pat Fairfield swings his "official" E.R.A. into Main Road and the long straight leading to the start/finish. Hampered by a misfire at high speed, the 1935 Mannin Beg winner had to settle for fourth. [R and L Kelly collection]

Roy Eccles spins his Lagonda Rapier engined special at the Manx Arms corner. He retired after nine laps with a broken valve rocker. [R and L Kelly collection]

the fastest lap of the race so far.

At the end of lap 13, Dodson stopped again. He had hit the bank at Willaston while trying to make up time after his earlier stop. After his car had been checked he re-joined the race but had to stop for a plug change when flying stones entered his front cowling and smashed the insulation on a spark plug.

After lap 18, Wakefield retired his Alta with a broken valve spring.

At 20 laps the order was unchanged except that Lehoux had replaced Dodson in sixth place. Seaman had increased his average to 69.99mph and his lead to 15 seconds, with Bira only two seconds behind Paul. On the next lap, Bira passed Paul to take second place, and pulled away. Fairfield was a further 23 seconds back. Meanwhile, at the end of lap 20 Howe stopped for petrol and bananas. He retired after two more laps, with a burst fuel tank. This had been caused by excessive air pressure which had sprung the tank, causing it to come into contact with the rear axle on the bumpier parts of the course.

Bira stopped for fuel at the end of lap 26. He was only 35 seconds at his pit, losing second place to Paul. Soon Mays, Lehoux and Fairfield all stopped for fuel. Due to a misunderstanding, Fairfield came in at the same time as Mays and had to be sent away while Mays was refuelled.

Seaman speeded up, completing lap 26 in 3mins 21secs (71.64mph) and lap 27 in 3mins 20secs (72.00mph). This was the fastest lap of the race. It was after this that he experienced a nasty moment which encouraged him to ease back. He heard a loud crunching noise from the rear axle. Thinking that was the end of the race for him, Seaman decided to pull off the course. Because he did not have sufficient momentum to do so, he pressed the accelerator and, to his surprise, the car responded as if nothing was wrong. As a result, Seaman continued but, more carefully. It was not until Seaman and his car were back in London that it was established what that noise had been. When the back axle was stripped it was found that the crown wheel had three broken teeth and the pinion

Photographed from the Nursery Hotel grounds, Cyril Paul's white E.R.A passes Birchleigh Terrace on the long descent into Onchan. He finished third, 1min 44secs behind Bira. [R and L Kelly collection]

Despite a nasty facial cut from a flying stone, Cyril Paul finished third in his E.R.A. Seen here in Onchan Village, he was running second to Richard Seaman at quarter distance but later lost the place to Bira. [The late Alf Caley, Onchan]

had two broken teeth. Seaman reckoned that only sheer luck had kept him in the race.

On completion of 30 laps, Seaman, despite his alarming experience, was averaging 70.27mph and led Paul by 1min 26secs. Bira was chasing Paul, only 12 seconds ahead of him, and had a lead of 30 seconds over Mays. Lehoux was fifth, 21 seconds behind Mays with Fairfield a further 36 seconds back.

On lap 31 Bira caught and passed Paul on the straight before the pits to re-take second place, whereupon Paul stopped to refuel. It had been rumoured that the Paul's large tank would enable him to go the full distance without a fuel stop. He lost two places, so that Mays and Lehoux were now chasing Bira.

Mays now began to threaten Bira. On lap 30, the gap between them had been 30 seconds. On lap 32 the gap was 21 seconds, on lap 33 it was 20 seconds and on lap 34, 18 seconds. During lap 35, however, the unfortunate Mays retired on the far side of the circuit with a broken rear axle. Lehoux was now third of the nine remaining runners.

At almost the same time, there was a near miss at Cronk-ny-Mona hairpin, where Bill Everitt had spent about 17 minutes in the escape road fixing a leaking carburettor. He finally succeeded, managed to restart, and was about to rejoin the course when Pat Fairfield arrived in the escape road, braking hard after having to avoid another car which had hit a lamp-post. According to *The Autocar* the drivers avoided a head-on smash by coolness and a miracle. Fairfield said later that his thoughts on seeing Everitt directly in front had been "poor fellow, what a pity", while Everitt said that he had turned up his overall collar, crouched down and prayed hard.

After 40 laps, Seaman had reduced speed slightly, averaging 70.03mph and leading Bira by 1min 21secs. Lehoux was 1min 40secs behind Bira, and six seconds in front of Paul. Fairfield was fifth.

The amazing Dodson then hit the sandbags at the Manx Arms corner at Onchan, followed soon afterwards on lap 41 by Lehoux, whose efforts to pass so many slower cars in front of him had been a feature of the race. This damaged the front axle and stopped the engine. It took him a little while to get restarted, despite at least eight marshals giving him a push from the rear and on either side of the car, and more time was lost at the pits when he stopped there for the tie rod to be freed from a bent radius rod. He managed to keep going but was overtaken by both Paul and Fairfield and with damaged steering he could not improve his fifth place.

Seaman continued at slightly reduced speed, to complete the 50 lap race at an average of 69.76mph, beating Bira by 1min 17secs. Paul was third, 1min 44secs behind Bira and 21 seconds ahead of Fairfield who had been sitting in a puddle of petrol and experiencing a misfire at high speeds. Lehoux, no doubt reflecting on

Winner of two motorcycle TT races Charlie Dodson is pictured at the Manx Arms in the 746cc Austin. Sixth fastest in practice and fifth during the early laps of the race, his fastest race lap was 3mins 24secs, only 4 seconds slower than Seaman's winning Delage. Delayed by carburettor and fuel pump trouble, as well as plugs broken by flying stones, he was running at the end but was not classified. [Onchan District Commissioners]

Richard Seaman takes the chequered flag in his 1927 Delage. He drove a dominant race, taking the lead from Earl Howe's E.R.A. on lap five and, without having to stop to re-fuel, stayed ahead throughout. His fastest lap was 3mins 20secs (72.00 mph) and he finished 1min 17secs ahead of the runner up, Bira. [Stan Hughes collection]

what might have been, finished fifth, only 24 seconds behind Fairfield. The only other finisher was the ERA shared by "Jock" Manby-Colegrave and "Buddy" Featherstonhaugh, a distant sixth, 9 minutes 10 seconds behind Lehoux.

Three drivers were still running at the finish but were flagged off 15 minutes after the winner finished. They were Everitt (47 laps), Dodson (44 laps) and Briggs (43 laps). Dodson's fastest lap in the tiny Austin had been a very creditable 3 minutes 24 seconds.

Although Everitt did not complete the full race distance, the Team Prize was awarded to the ERA team of Paul, Fairfield and Everitt.

Despite concerns about the safety of the course, there had been no incidents during either of the practice sessions and only minor incidents during the race. The only serious injury during the race was to a spectator, Robert Shimmin of Richmond Grove, Douglas, who fell backwards off the hedge at Cronk-y-Berry and suffered a fractured arm.

However, a problem with the course not mentioned in the drivers' "petition" but of considerable irritation was its surface of compressed granite chippings. This had worked loose in places. The numbers of loose stones were particularly abundant at sharp corners. As competing cars had no fixed mudguards, the tyres constantly projected the stones into the air, making them dangerous missiles. These flew about in "unpleasantly large quantities," said *The Autocar*. Cyril Paul sustained a nasty gash on the cheek from one whilst in second place and Lehoux had his goggles smashed by a stone on Lap 4 whilst he was fourth. His stop at the pits for a replacement cost him two places.

The winner and runner-up receive congratulations behind the grandstand after the race. Richard Seaman stands alongside Bira and his E.R.A. "Romulus". [R and L Kelly collection]

Bill Everitt accelerates his E.R.A. in Main Road, Onchan, after exiting the right turn from the Avondale Road descent (invisible between the Manx Arms and the Manx Co-operative). He was still running at the end but was unclassified after being delayed by a leaking carburettor. He completed 47 laps of the 50 lap race. [The late Alf Caley, Onchan]

Dick Seaman, who had no protection in his low-slung Delage, sustained several cuts on the lip and cheek from other stones.

In addition to injuries to drivers, all cars suffered "starred" or broken windscreens, according to *Motor Sport*. The bodywork of Dodson's Austin, meanwhile, was "practically riddled," said *The Autocar*. Because the Austin lacked a wire grill on its nose like the other cars, showers of stones thrown up by cars immediately ahead of it penetrated the radiator block and caused havoc with the engine. The stones splintered at least one plug, got into the air intake and generally handicapped Dodson's fine drive.

Prince Chula's prediction had been fulfilled. There was no catching Seaman's Delage. Bira said later that until he stopped to refuel he could "just about" keep up with him but was unable to gain a yard. He was just able to keep the Delage in sight, seeing it bounce from side to side with the familiar figure of a big man at the wheel. "It reminded me," he wrote later in his reminiscences *Bits and Pieces*, "of some over-grown child pedalling his toy car." He doubted if anyone else could have driven the Delage so fast on such narrow roads.

Seaman's ability to complete the race without a pit stop had given him a considerable advantage. At his "pit counter" petrol churns were piled high as if in readiness but he had no need to call upon them. His light alloy tank gave him extra capacity and the Delage delivered more than seven miles to the gallon, which appeared to be better than most cars in the race. He finished with seven gallons left. According to *The Motor* the lightness of the Delage in front had been accentuated by the provision of powerful new hydraulic brakes but although this made the car a "handful" over the bumpy roads it did not seem to perturb Seaman. Although he led from the fourth lap, for most of the time, particularly in the latter half of the race, observers reckoned that he never extended his car despite his fastest laps of 71.64mph and 72mph.

At the end of the race, Seaman told Bira in the winner's enclosure that he had been worried about Bira's proximity behind him. However, Bira felt that, had he wished to, Seaman could have got away from him at any time. The fact was, he could have let Bira overtake him and still emerged victorious by regaining the lead when Bira was forced to stop for fuel.

At the Presentation of Awards, Col. Lindsay Lloyd commented that the RAC had "found a course equal to any to be found anywhere in Europe (applause) – but – wait a minute (laughter) it is not quite good enough to be used again, although it only wants the surface to be put right". He stressed the need to continue with the races so as not to lose the date on the international racing calendar. Prince Bira, no doubt relieved that there had been no serious accidents despite the drivers' concerns, thanked the flag marshals, and Captain Phillips said that the absence of accidents was due to the superlative skill of the drivers.

1936 RAC International Light Car Race Results

Thursday 28th May 1936. Start 2.00pm. 50 laps of 4 miles circuit, total distance 200 miles. 19 starters, 6 finishers.

1. Richard Seaman (1,460cc Delage), 2hrs 52mins 1sec (69.76mph)
2. B. Bira 1,488cc ERA R2B), 2hrs 53mins 18secs (69.23mph)
3. Cyril Paul (1,486cc ERA R7B), 2hrs 55mins 2secs (68.57mph)
4. Pat Fairfield (1486cc ERA R4A), 2hrs 55mins 23secs (68.40mph)
5. Marcel Lehoux 1,488cc ERA R3B), 2hrs 55mins 47secs (68.27mph)
6. G. F. A. Manby-Colegrave/R. E. L. Featherstonhaugh (1,488cc ERA R1B), 3hrs 4mins 57secs (64.90mph)

Fastest lap:
Richard Seaman (Delage), on lap 27, 3mins 20secs, (72.00mph)
Failed to complete the required 50 laps:
Bill Everitt (1,486cc ERA R6B), 47 laps
Charles Dodson (744cc Austin), 44 laps
L. R. Briggs (1,087cc MG Magnette), 43 laps
Team prize: E.R.A. (Cyril Paul, Pat Fairfield and Bill Everitt). No other team finished.
Retirements:
Lap 1:
T. K. Humber (1,496cc Bugatti), big end
E. K. "Teddy" Rayson (1,496cc Maserati), sheared supercharger drive
Lap 3:
Philip Jucker (1,496cc Frazer Nash), connecting-rod through sump
Lap 6:
Reggie Tongue (1,488cc ERA R11B), ignition
Lap 8:
A. J. Cormack (1.496cc Alta), oil pump
H. Williams (1,087cc MG Magnette), broken shock absorber
Lap 10:
Roy Eccles (1,084cc Rapier Special), broken valve rocker
Lap 18:
J. P. Wakefield (1,496cc Alta), broken valve spring
Lap 23: Earl Howe (1,488cc ERA R8B), split fuel tank
Lap 35: Raymond Mays (1,488cc ERA R4C), broken half-shaft.

Reaction

The Autocar said the race was easily the best held on the Island for some time. It had character, coherence and much of the atmosphere which made racing so fascinating on the Continent but which the preceding events had most notably lacked.

The *Isle of Man Times*, however, was not so sure. It was difficult, it said, to decide whether the race was the success which could reasonably have been anticipated. There had been a better attendance than at any car race for many years, but almost entirely locals. While the Times was glad that locals had responded to its appeal to support the races, the Island did need visitors – the race could not be kept going without them. There had been much publicity but a good deal of it concerned defects of the course, which the Times had described as "dangerous and devoid of interest". The paper thought that the time and venue of the race should be changed – it should be held at the end of June or in July and on a better course. Many drivers would not have entered if they had realised the state of the course. The Promenade needed resurfacing and a better course would start at the TT Grandstand, descend to the Promenade and continue beyond the north end of the Promenade along the coast past Groudle to the Liverpool Arms Hotel and from there through Onchan back to the TT Grandstand.

The *Isle of Man Times* proposals ignored three realities. Firstly, in 1933 the races had been held in July and had then been moved to May because of public opposition to the closure of the Promenade and other parts of the Town at the height of the tourist season. Secondly, an International race needed a vacant date on the International calendar if it were to attract the famous drivers needed to draw visiting crowds and dates in June and July had already been found to be unsuitable for this reason. Thirdly, the 1936 course was not ideal and had been used only because the Promenade resurfacing could not be completed in time and it had been a case of using that course or not having a race.

The story of the victory of the 1927 Delage over a very strong field, including nine ERAs, attracted a great deal of publicity in the UK National Press. Much was on the lines of a heap of scrap being tuned and raced by a poor young man who was still a Cambridge undergraduate. Prince Chula, apparently thinking that this was unfair to the ERA company, pointed out that the Delage had cost one million francs (approximately £10,000 in 1936) while ERAs could be bought for £1,800. At this time a production MG sports car cost £222.

The *Isle of Man Times* reported an unfortunate dispute. The Stewards of the RAC (the RAC's appeal body) had been convened to hear an appeal by the entrants of the five cars which finished the race behind the winner. All appealed against the RAC decision to pay prize money of the amounts stated in the Supplementary Regulations rather than the increased amounts set out later in the Official Programme, although the Regulations had stated that additional awards might be offered. These higher amounts would have meant £100 more to second third and fourth finishers Bira, Paul and Fairfield (£400, £300 and £200 instead of £300, £200 and £100 respectively), £50 more to fifth finisher Lehoux (£100 instead of £50) and £20 to sixth finisher Manby-Colegrave (£50 instead of £30). The Stewards upheld the appeal and ordered payment of the increased amounts. The *Isle of Man Times* asked who would pay the additional £400 (actually £370) – the RAC or the Island authorities. The Programme stated that all the prize money had been generously provided by the Isle of Man Government and the Corporation of Douglas and they provided the additional amount.

At a Douglas Town Council meeting in September 1936 it was revealed that the races had been run within the budget of £3,000, at a total cost of £2,775. Later, the Mayor said that the cost would have been £370 less but for a printing error in the Programme and Regulations. This suggests that the amount included in the budget for prize money had been the lower figure and that the RAC had deliberately or accidentally increased it!

1937 – The RAC Tourist Trophy

The future of the RAC TT was in crisis following the deaths of eight spectators in a crash in Newtownards during the 1936 race. While Northern Ireland Prime Minister Lord Craigavon still supported the race, Down County Council voted by 17 votes to 3 to refuse to close roads through Newtownards and Comber. The days of the Ards circuit were over. Inevitably, there was renewed speculation, both inside and outside the Isle of Man, about a possible return of the TT to the land of its birth.

The Island had campaigned for return of the TT. The RAC had refused. Now, needing to relocate the race and having failed to make the "Round the Houses" races a success, the RAC thought that a return of the TT to the Island seemed a logical step. In response to Manx Press enquiries, Captain Phillips of the RAC said that there were three alternatives. First, the RAC would ask the Northern Ireland authorities whether they wanted the TT to be transferred to another course in the Province. If not, then the RAC would ask the Isle of Man. If the Isle of Man said "no", the third choice was an English short circuit – Donington Park, Brooklands or Crystal Palace. The *Isle of Man Times* promptly declared that the TT was "ours if we ask for it" and "we let it slip once and must not again". It was suggested that if the TT returned, part of the cost could be raised by dropping the June race.

After rejecting proposed courses in Northern Ireland, the RAC announced that the 1937 TT would not take place there and asked whether the Isle of Man Government would be interested in staging the race on 4th September. "Now is the Isle of Man's chance", said the *Isle of Man Times*, but the Island's reaction was not what the RAC expected. The Highway Board was hesitant. In difficult times financially, the cost of making a course satisfactory to the RAC could be enormous. Members deferred consideration pending the RAC providing details of the course it wanted and the likely cost of making it fit for racing. Major capital investment in road works was not ruled out but the cost had to be regarded as an investment, it was decided. That would mean off-setting the cost against measurable benefits over a period of years. The RAC was talking of one race. The Isle of Man needed a guarantee of continuity, in the absence of which the Board recommended to the Lieutenant Governor that the RAC proposal be rejected.

The Governor then reported to Tynwald. He said that he felt, after consulting widely, that there was substantial agreement that the RAC's date in the middle of the Manx Grand Prix race period was unacceptable for tourism reasons, further road closures during the tourist season were unacceptable, visitors were unlikely to be attracted and publicity would be more effective before the tourist season. The Island could not afford two car races and there was no guarantee of continuity. The Governor decided that he could not give the RAC any expectation that Tynwald would vote the money required. He proposed therefore to tell the RAC that the Island could not stage the race in 1937, but would be prepared to discuss the question for 1938, if the RAC wished. This was agreed.

The *Isle of Man Times*, while regretting the decision, thought that few could disagree. It agreed that a guarantee of continuity was essential – the point which had concerned the Northern Ireland Government when they were offered the TT.

Left without a traditional road circuit, the RAC switched the TT to Donington on an experimental basis but the general opinion was that it was not a success.

1937 Rac International Light Car Race – Bira Sings In The Rain

Planning

Douglas Town Council met in October 1936 to consider a majority Finance Committee recommendation that a race should be held in 1937. There was "strenuous opposition" with opponents maintaining that Douglas did not get value for money, that there was too much racing on the Island and that car races kept visitors away at a quiet time of the season. Supporters said that the races had put the Island in the national news at the right time of the year and that the publicity could not be bought for the amount spent. Lifting of sanctions could result in Italian entries, and Germany was "deeply interested". After a "spirited debate" the Council resolved, by a 2/3 majority, to support a race in 1937. As in 1936, a guarantee of £1,500 was agreed subject to the Government matching it. This was thought to be good value but, despite optimism about German interest, there would be no Mercedes-Benz or Auto-Union entries.

Yet another new course was chosen for 1937. This was the course originally proposed for 1936 but rejected by the RAC because of the need for Promenade resurfacing. The new course, the only anti-clockwise circuit ever used for a Manx car race, returned part of the action to the heart of Douglas and its Promenade. It started at the TT Grandstand on Glencrutchery Road, where the 1936 pit lane was retained, turned left at St Ninian's and plunged down Ballaquayle Road and Broadway to the Promenade. This long, steep descent with room for overtaking was expected to be the most thrilling part of the course for spectators. An extremely fast straight of nearly a mile along Central and Queen's Promenades was followed by a

This re-creation of a contemporary advertisement for Services watches gives a very accurate image of the motorcycle TT Grandstand and start/finish area used for the 1936 and 1937 R.A.C. races and for the BRDC British Empire Trophy Races from 1947 to 1953. [Author's collection]

climb into Onchan via King Edward Road and the two hairpin bends at Port Jack, leading into Royal Avenue. After climbing to Onchan Village, the course continued along Main Road to Governor's Bridge and Glencrutchery Road. The distance was 3 miles 1,586 yards, giving a total race distance over 50 laps of 195 miles 100 yards. Access to the shore would be available during racing and a footbridge at the junction of Victoria Road and Glen Falcon Road would allow pedestrian access into the town, as in 1935. After Captain Phillips' inspection, the main requirement was completion of the Promenade resurfacing from Palace Terrace past Summer Hill to the tramway terminus, unfinished in 1936.

The Motor thought the course was a 100 percent improvement on 1936. In distance and contour it was "as good as many circuits in Europe used for Grand Prix racing. It combines the thrills of street racing with really high speed stretches". It was bumpy in places, particularly Onchan, but the most alarming section was the dip down on the curve at Governor's Bridge. Only the best drivers could take this bend flat out, it said. Cars swayed and leapt in the air when they hit bumps at full speed. The same problem had been found in 1934 and 1935 when the course had gone in the opposite direction, but the 1936 course had used the same direction as the new course, apparently without complaint.

The race was to be held on Thursday 3rd June at 2pm with early morning practices from 5am to 7am on Tuesday and Wednesday 1st and 2nd June. Previously, cash awards had been unclaimed because of retirements or failure to complete the full number of laps, Now it was decided that the prize fund of £1,330, funded jointly by Tynwald and Douglas Corporation (reduced from the £1,550 paid, after dispute, in 1936), should go to competitors irrespective of whether or not they completed the full race distance. The only obligation to qualify for an award was to cover at least 25 laps (half the race distance). The ten cash prizes ranging from £400 to £30 would be awarded on the basis of the greatest number of laps completed in the shortest time.

Entries

The 1937 RAC International Light Car Race attracted an entry of 22. This was slightly fewer than in 1936 but the quality was considered to be outstanding. With eight British ERAs and six Italian Maseratis, particular attention was focussed on this British-Italian confrontation. Such a massed challenge, reckoned the official programme, should provide "an epoch-making struggle". Prince Chula thought that the entry list was "impressive and worthy of a race of this importance – being really the premier 1,500cc event of the year".

There was also a family confrontation. One of the Maseratis was to be driven by Austin Dobson. His brother, Arthur, was the entrant and driver of one of the "independent" ERAs. Unlike the works cars, which were in green livery, his was painted white.

Unfortunately, Earl Howe would be prevented by an accident at Brooklands from taking his place in the ERA team but Raymond Mays and Pat Fairfield (the only previous Isle of Man winner in the field) still made a formidable team. A possibility, at the wheel of his "unofficial" ERA known as "Romulus", was the 1936 runner-up, the colourful and accomplished racer known simply as "B. Bira." The previous year, whilst in conversation with Prince Chula, Earl Howe had placed Bira third in order of top British racing drivers, with only Mays and Bill Everitt ahead of him. It would be interesting, he had added, to see how a major crash would affect Bira's driving. In common with the saying that one could not become a real horseman until after many falls, it was said by racing drivers that one could not be a real racing driver without a crash. How can one drive fearlessly without ever having experienced a crash? Now, on the Isle of Man, everyone would get the chance to see Bira's reaction. Prior to coming to the Isle of Man he had crashed a Maserati badly at Cork after losing control at a corner. The previous night he had been ill and at the start of the race he had still felt the same. After knocking down a signpost he had crashed into a stone wall. The Maserati had been wrecked but his only injury had been a sprained thumb. What effect would that have on his driving now?

However, there was a possibility also that instead of the ERA he might drive the Delage in which Richard Seaman won the 1936 race on the Island. When Seaman had been given a place in Germany's Mercedes-Benz team, Chula had bought the Delage along with a spare engine and the only other Delage in Britain (owned by Captain Davis), thereby removing the possibility of someone else having a car which could last long distances without refuelling. The idea was to modernise both cars by equipping them with new frames and independent front suspension. The work had been undertaken at Hammersmith but had taken so much longer than expected that the Delages had not received much testing. Chula had submitted two entries for Bira, giving him the option of driving either an ERA or a Delage and, if one of the Delages was ready in time for the Manx race and Bira decided to drive it, then it was felt that this could "run away with it."

Three other private ERAs entries were submitted by Ian Connell, Reggie Tongue and Peter Whitehead (with Peter Walker as reserve driver).

Another intriguing entry was a 1,486cc Dixon Special, built by Freddie Dixon and to be driven by Charlie

Dodson. Such a combination was reckoned to provide one of the greatest potential dangers for other competitors.

The only "unblown" car was a Riley driven by Percy Maclure. He was known as the "Champion of Donington" because he had won more races there than anyone else.

Three newcomers to British racing were included in the Maserati challenge. Two were Scuderia Helvetia drivers, the Swiss-American John du Puy, and the young Swiss Baron Emanuel "Toulo" de Graffenried. Du Puy was originally resident in Switzerland and later in the United States, before returning to Switzerland. As well as driving Maseratis himself he entered various drivers, including Bob Gerard at Silverstone in 1956. Baron de Graffenried was at the start of a distinguished career which would take him to the Alfa Romeo Grand Prix Team in 1950, as team-mate to Fangio. The third newcomer, the Italian Luigi Villoresi, was entered by Count Giovanni Lurani on behalf of the Scuderia Ambrosiana. He was to drive the latest 1937 Maserati model 6CM, whereas du Puy had a late 1936 six-cylinder model, and the Baron was entered at the wheel of an early 1936-type four-cylinder 4CM Maserati. He was an unusually colourful character. One of his idiosyncracies was the sucking of a cigarette holder whilst driving. This was only his third race. In it, however, he would display such skills that *The Autocar* would observe later that he looked like "being really good." In fact, he would become the Italian champion and a Ferrari Grand Prix driver from 1949 to 1953. Du Puy's car had an aluminium body and blue chassis.

The two other Maserati entries were Robin Hanson, with a late 1936 car, and the Hon. Peter Aitken (son of Lord Beaverbrook).

A new British car entered privately was one of only three four-cylinder cars in the race. Geoffrey Taylor's Alta Car and Engineering Co. of Tolworth in Surrey had been producing reasonably-priced hand-built sports cars since 1929 but they had failed to make any impression in major races. Now, only weeks before the Isle of Man race, Taylor had produced a new model which featured a new chassis, all round independent suspension, and an improved 1,496cc engine which delivered 180bhp. When tested at Brooklands this reached 144 m.p.h. The first car was bought by the irrepressible Philip Jucker whose cryptic remarks had earned the name of "Juckerisms." During the previous season he had unsuccessfully raced a Frazer Nash in which he had competed in many events including the Manx race, in which he had retired on lap 3. He had changed to the Alta for 1937 in the hope of reversing his run of bad luck. Painted gold, the car had been referred to jokingly within the racing fraternity as "Jucker's Gold Standard." Technical problems had still beset him, however. Prince Chula reckoned that he was the unluckiest racing driver he knew. Now Jucker hoped that the new Alta would reverse this image. In fact the opposite occurred.

The remainder of the entry consisted of the Martin J.A.P. of Charlie Martin, remembered for his epic battle with Brian Lewis in the 1935 Mannin Moar, the Talbot of Anthony Powys-Lybbe and the MG K3 Magnettes of Reg Parnell and Bill Hughes. Parnell's ex Hugh Hamilton single-seater car (K3008) now had an enlarged engine of 1,486cc.

The two Scuderia Helvetia Maseratis of Swiss driver Emanuel "Toulo" de Graffenried and American driver John Du Puy are pictured on the Isle of Man Steam Packet Co ferry en route to the Island. De Graffenried finished sixth in the race but Du Puy was the first retirement, on lap 1, with loss of oil pressure. [Stan Hughes collection]

Practice

Out of 22 entries, Earl Howe (injury), Charlie Martin, Peter Aitken and Anthony Powys-Lybbe (cars not ready) all failed to arrive. Missing for the first practice session were the Maseratis of du Puy and de Graffenreid (delayed by Customs at Dover) and also Villoresi (arrived but not ready). Thus 15 cars practised in the first session on Tuesday 1st June, with the three missing Maseratis arriving in time for the second session on Wednesday morning.

A shadow was cast over the event when tragedy struck early in the first practice session, at 5.33am.

Philip Jucker was on his fourth practice lap in his Alta. Approaching Port Jack corner at very high speed and apparently too far to the right side of the road, he appeared to brake too late to take the left-hand hairpin. He hit the kerb, began to skid and so tried to take the escape road, making no attempt to take the corner. In doing so, he went into a broadside skid (possibly due to camber, thought *The Autocar*), and crashed into one of the Manx Electric Railway's overhead electricity supply poles. The car was, in effect, wrapped round the pole which was wedged between the left hand rear wheel and the car body, and the cockpit was crushed. Jucker was extricated from the wreckage with difficulty, due to distortion of the car body and leaking fuel. He was taken to Noble's hospital by ambulance but died there about ten minutes after admission.

During the first early morning practice, Philip Jucker lost control of his Alta as he approached the sharp left hand corner at Port Jack, at the northern end of Douglas Promenade. After spinning, the car crashed into a tramway pole. [Peter Kelly collection]

Philip Jucker's Alta is pictured after the crash at Port Jack. The driver was extricated from the car and taken to hospital but sadly he died later. It was his second Isle of Man race – he had competed in 1936, in a Frazer Nash. [Peter Kelly collection]

An Inquest was held at Douglas on the following day by Coroner of Inquests H. Percy Kelly, sitting with an eleven man jury. RAC engineer Maurice Hudlass, who had examined the car after the crash, said that there was a tendency for the accelerator to stick in the full-throttle position, but he was unable to say whether had been a cause or a result of the crash. The verdict was accidental death.

The Alta was rebuilt and raced in 1938 by George Abecassis but, although fast, lacked reliability.

A total of 152 laps were completed in the first practice. Fastest was Pat Fairfield's ERA with a lap of 3min 02ses, 77.17mph. Peter Walker, reserve driver for Peter Whitehead, was only one second slower. Bira's Delage and Whitehead tied on 3min 07sec with Bira one second slower in his ERA. Raymond Mays' best lap was 3min 11sec.

For Bira and his cousin, Prince Chula, the first practice left them undecided on which car to use. Although the Delage had lapped in one second faster than the ERA, that was only after favouring the Delage with 13 laps and "Romulus" with only five.

In the second practice session Bira, using low gears more on the twists and turns, improved his time in the Delage to 3min 06sec, only one second faster that on Tuesday, while Raymond Mays lapped in 3mins 03sec and then shocked everyone with an amazing lap of 2 minutes 59 seconds, an average of 78.45 mph. As the speed conversion table in the official programme did not provide for lap times less than three minutes, it was reckoned that even the RAC had been surprised. It was the first time that Chula had seen a car deliver a lap time that had not been anticipated by the official programme. Meanwhile Fairfield improved his time to 3mins dead and Villoresi equalled Bira's Delage time, only one second faster that Whitehead's 3min 07secs in Tuesday's session.

The Delage's performance was clearly not good enough to challenge the latest works ERAs, even with the benefit of having no need to stop for fuel because, over 50 laps, a deficit of a few seconds a lap added up to considerably more than the time gained by the Delage not having to be refuelled.

Near the end of the practice, Bira took out "Romulus" and tried to do better. His first lap was 3 minutes 3 seconds. Every lap thereafter was fractionally faster until he finally equalled that recorded by Mays. That settled it. If "Romulus" could at least match the leading works ERA then its potential overall race performance was better than that of the Delage. Although observers reported that the Delage was the more stable of the two cars on the bumpier sections of the course, Bira felt that the faster ERA also gave the easier ride. It was this car, therefore, that he decided to race, expecting to finish third at best. He did not expect to beat the latest "works" ERAs of Mays and Fairfield as "Romulus" (the first "customer" ERA) was still in its original 1935 specification. The other "unofficial" ERAs had been built to 1936 specification.

Charlie Dodson, driving the Dixon Special, completed only three of the five laps required to qualify for the race due to a sheared supercharger drive and would not be allowed to start.

1937 RAC International Light Car Race

Fifteen cars lined up for the start. The weather was miserable. Indeed, it was so bad that some drivers actually suggested that the race should be abandoned. There had been a bright and sunny dawn but now it was raining heavily and only a handful of spectators braved the elements on the badly exposed, uncovered grandstand. On the course also there was little sign of spectators. People sheltered in doorways and other less exposed places, emerging only at the finish to acknowledge the winner, and it seemed as if the race was being staged in a deserted town. Official uniforms for the day for race organisers were thick oilskins. The Press accommodation was deplorable, said the *Isle of Man Times*, with the seats and desks not even wiped down. Some coverings for the pits were borrowed from a local farmer. *Motor Sport* quoted a comment that the rain was so heavy that the Antifyre tenders were quite unnecessary.

The conditions were what Bira called "sticky-wicky." They were, he said, the kinds that prompted him to wear a cork crash-hat with vizor and imagine himself in a submarine, peering through a periscope! Until immediately prior to the start he wore a bright blue mackintosh and sou'wester, while Raymond Mays sported an umbrella as he sat in his car.

Bira had almost become a non-starter because the previous day his mechanics had discovered that a front ball race had been damaged. Although the more modern works ERAs had slightly different hubs from those fitted to Bira's 1935 model, by chance, the ERA team had brought a complete hub with them and supplied it to Bira's team.

As in 1936, a 2 – 1 – 2 starting grid formation was used, due to the narrowness of the road. On the front row were the two ERAs of Mays and Bira (both 2mins 59secs), with the ERA of Pat Fairfield (3mins 0secs) behind them. The third row consisted of Villoresi's Maserati (3mins 6secs) and Whitehead's ERA (3mins 7sces), followed by Arthur Dobson's ERA (3mins 11secs). Row 5 contained the de Graffenried Maserati (3mins 11secs) and Reggie Tongue's ERA (3mins 12secs). Connell's ERA (3mins 16secs) was alone on row 6, followed by Parnell's MG (3mins 25secs) and Austin Dobson's Maserati (3mins 26secs). Hanson's Maserati was next (3mins 26secs) with Maclure's Riley (3mins 27secs), du Puy's Maserati and Hughes' MG (3mins 40secs) bringing up the rear.

The ERA team tactics were for Mays to "go all out" from the start and rely on a fast fuel stop while Fairfield would conserve fuel and complete the race non-stop. Hence Mays led from the start, from Bira, Villoresi, Fairfield and Tongue. Only a car's length behind Mays after the descent to the Promenade, Bira found that the sheet of blinding spray raised by the car ahead blurred his vision badly and he had to use one of his hands repeatedly to wipe his vizor. It was a tricky undertaking for really both hands and all his concentration were needed for his driving. In anticipation of this sort of problem, Reggie Tongue had had a sponge tied to his overalls and used his to wipe his visor. He had bought it on the way to the start.

Heavy rain made the smooth tarmac surface of Douglas Promenade particularly hazardous. Bira found it "quite impossible" to control his car. "When my wheels went over the tram lines," he wrote later, "it was just like driving on glass." Later he would marvel at how he and others managed to complete the first lap intact. Now, Bira kept up the pressure. It nearly resulted in a nasty incident at the turn at the end of the Promenade, for Mays appeared to brake earlier than Bira expected him to do so. To Bira's surprise, he found himself level with Mays and capable of overtaking him. With a contented pat on the side of "Romulus", Bira took the lead and kept it, except for a brief interlude after his refuelling stop. Usually he did not like to take the lead in a race too soon, especially when it was from someone who was capable of driving as fast as he was. In this case, however, there was a positive advantage. He would escape the screen of spray emitted from Mays' car and Mays would have that disadvantage.

In 1937, for the first time, the course ran down, instead of up Broadway. Bira is pictured at the foot of Broadway, turning left onto the Central Promenade, en route to a dominant win. [Stan Hughes collection]

Bira led by 100 yards at the end of the lap, from Mays, Fairfield, Tongue, Connell and Villoresi. After only one lap Walker pitted for a plug change and du Puy retired with oil pressure pump trouble.

By the end of lap 4 Mays was already suffering brake problems, as his team-mate Fairfield would soon do, and had dropped back to fourth, passed by Fairfield and Tongue, ruining the ERA tactics. Although the ERAs' experimental brake drums had been changed after practising, the brakes were beginning to fail again; a problem which had occurred in other races. This made Mays, in particular, ease back. Later, getting accustomed to a virtually brakeless system and using the gearbox to brake, he began to regain some of his lost time. If only he had learnt the technique much earlier, he told *The Autocar* later, he might have delivered a better performance. "I braked largely on the engine the latter part of the race," he said, "taking it up to appalling revs".

Meanwhile Reg Parnell stopped at the end of laps 3 and 4 to change oiled plugs – a common problem with the K3

Magnettes. He also had magneto trouble later in the race.

Villoresi was on a charge. By the end of lap 8 he was third, having passed Connell, Mays and Tongue, whose time of 3min 15sec on lap 9 was the fastest of the race at that point. Villoresi then had a titanic battle with Fairfield. Completing lap 10, he was only two seconds behind Fairfield and 41 seconds behind Bira. On lap 11 he passed Fairfield on the Promenade, only to be re-passed on lap 12 despite Fairfield suffering brake problems. The fight continued, with both lapping in 3min 13secs (72.77mph), until lap 15 when Villoresi slowed at the north end of the Promenade. He continued to Port Jack, where he finally stopped and began the long wet walk back to the pits. The cause of his retirement was variously reported as a choked fuel pipe and a fault in the oil feed which had filled the supercharger with oil. Tongue was now third again.

Another man on a charge was Peter Walker, making up time after his early pit stop. Amid reports of skids at St. Ninians on every lap and also at Port Jack, he went from twelfth to fifth in six laps, matching the speed of Fairfield and Villoresi. On lap 16, he passed Mays to gain fourth briefly and was gaining two seconds a lap on Bira. This was not enough to be a serious threat to Bira but, on lap 22, Walker gained four seconds and was only 1min 35sec behind Bira.

In Bira's pit it was suggested that a lead of 48 seconds was enough and that he ought to be slowed to reduce the risk of a bad skid, they thought. However, Chula resisted the advice. Firstly, he remembered that in 1936 the works ERAs had been beaten by Seaman's Delage because Seaman did not have to refuel, so they were likely to try to run non-stop. Secondly, he remembered that, on the evening of the first practice, when he had dined at the Majestic Hotel with Raymond Mays and Peter Berthon of the ERA team, Mays and Berthon were anxious to know if a decision had been reached as to which car Bira would drive. Chula had not committed himself. Everything would rest on the refill question, he had said. Although the Delage was slower than the new ERA, if it showed that it

The 1,496cc Maserati 4CM of Baron Emanuel "Toulo" de Graffenried (16) follows the Peter Walker/Peter Whitehead 1,498cc E.R.A. (11) through the second hairpin at Port Jack. The E.R.A. finished fifth, with the Maserati sixth, one lap behind. [Manx National Heritage]

Next to the Mobiloil pit, Ian Connell's E.R.A. is pictured in the flooded pit lane. Note the fuel funnel, churns and very basic weather protection for the pit crew. Connell finished eleventh, five laps behind the winner, Bira. [Simon Lewis Transport Books]

The winner, Bira, made his pit stop on lap 31, taking on 20 gallons in 45 seconds. He excelled in the heavy rain, leading for most of the race. He was overtaken by Raymond Mays and Pat Fairfield while at his pit but quickly regained the lead after refuelling and beat Mays by 42 seconds, with Fairfield third. [Simon Lewis Transport Books]

could save sufficient time by running non-stop without fuelling then Bira would drive the Delage. Chula had emphasized his view that, apart from the Delage, all cars would have to stop. Nobody had replied, but Chula had detected a strange light in the eyes of Peter Berthon. Chula's deduction was that, as the new C-type ERAs had larger fuel tanks, there was a plan for Mays and Fairfield to complete the race without refuelling. Therefore he calculated that Bira needed a lead of at least a minute to compensate for the fact that he would have to stop for fuel. On lap 23, therefore, Chula gave Bira a signal indicating a lead of 43 seconds but refused to slow him down.

This puzzled Bira, who thought that he ought to have been instructed to slow down. Nevertheless, with complete faith in Chula, he continued to increase his lead but decided to question Chula at the pit stop.

By half way, the first five had lapped all the others. Bira was 45 seconds ahead of a rain-hating Pat Fairfield, averaging 70.81mph despite the rain-drenched road surfaces. Reggie Tongue was 1 min 22secs behind. Mays came one second behind him and then, ten seconds later, came the gum-chewing Walker.

On lap 27, Hughes retired his MG Magnette with a blown cylinder head gasket. On lap 28, Mays, having earlier raised the record to 3mins 12secs (73.15mph), established the record race lap of 3mins 10secs (73.92mph) which, although much slower than the fastest practice laps of 2mins 59secs, was an excellent time in appalling conditions and with a chronic brake problem. His charge took him past Tongue and into third place. At the end of lap 30, Bira had extended his lead over Fairfield from 47 seconds on lap 20 to 55 seconds with Mays 1min 6secs behind the leader, compared with 1min 38secs ten laps earlier. Tongue was 32 seconds behind Mays and seven seconds ahead of Walker.

It was now time for refuelling which, in the conditions, was a hazardous business. So many officials were standing about in the pit access road that Bira said later that it was a miracle that he did not kill anyone. Tongue and Walker stopped at the end of lap 30, stopping for 23 seconds and 35 seconds respectively, with Walker handing over to Whitehead. Bira stopped on lap 31, taking on 20 gallons of fuel and a gun of lubricant in 45seconds. When he arrived at his pit, a thick tarpaulin was thrown over his shoulders, to prevent "dope" fuel splashing onto his clothes and eventually burning his skin. The tarpaulin made communication difficult but Chula managed to shout to Bira that he should keep going as he was and that he might just stay ahead. Although the refuelling was quick, the 55 seconds lead proved insufficient and Bira lost two places as Raymond Mays and Pat Fairfield, who had not stopped for refuelling and did not appear to need to, went through into first and second places just before Bira left the pit. With a shout from Chula that he was now third, Bira re-joined the race. Although Chula then feared that Bira would have to settle for third behind the two works ERAs, their lead was short-lived. Bira had the cars in his sight, despite the rain and spray, and gave chase.

Pat Fairfield was caught at Broadway on lap 33 when he braked to take the sharp corner onto the Promenade, Bira delayed doing so and gained upon him rapidly. Very quickly they were level, accelerating along the Promenade side by side for about a hundred yards until finally Bira pulled ahead.

The chase was now on for Raymond Mays. Soon his lead was down to just 20 yards. Both were travelling very fast for the conditions. Bira said later that he did not dare look at his rev counter. His hands, meanwhile, were quite numb. They managed to grip the steering wheel only through "sheer determination." For several laps the gap between them was narrowed only marginally, then, on lap 36 Bira got the chance to repeat his act at Broadway corner. Mays throttled back to avoid the risk of losing grip on the wet road surface. Bira maintained his speed a little longer and went past. Immediately after this, on lap 37, Mays went into the pits to refuel letting Fairfield (who was able to continue without refuelling) into second place, which Mays quickly regained. Incredibly, Bira had rebuilt his lead over Mays to 45 seconds by the end of lap 40, proving to be so much more capable than the others at coping with the wet conditions that Chula and the mechanics actually prayed for the rain to get heavier. Fairfield was a further 13 seconds in arrears. Tongue, Whitehead and de Graffenried followed at intervals of 1min 10secs, 1min 16secs and 4mins 54secs respectively.

In briefly improving conditions towards the end of the race the E.R.A.s of Raymond Mays, Pat Fairfield and Reggie Tongue approach the foot of Broadway before the left turn onto the Promenade. They finished second, third and fourth respectively. [Stan Hughes collection]

The result was now virtually settled. Barring accidents or mechanical problems, Bira was unbeatable and Fairfield with his failing brakes could not catch Mays and could possibly be caught by Tongue. In the final laps Bira slightly increased his lead over Mays until on the last lap he had a nasty moment when, worried about an uncontrollable slide, he almost stalled his car at Broadway corner. By now he had eased back sufficiently to notice the half-concealed spectators around the course applauding him as he passed by. He had managed a glance at his favourite toy shop on the Promenade and had been gratified to see the shop assistants on the pavement to give him a wave.

Now, at Broadway, the revs of his ERA dropped and the engine began to misfire. For some moments Bira thought he had wet the plugs and he would have to cruise to the finish. In so doing he would lose his lead. The thought of that nearly gave him a heart attack, he said later. Then, after coaxing "Romulus" "like an old friend," the engine responded with some puffs of smoke from the exhaust and the car accelerated away again.

So Bira won the race, 42 seconds ahead of Mays with Fairfield third. They, together with Tongue and Whitehead/Walker were the only drivers who completed 50 laps. Seven other drivers were still running at the finish: de Graffenried (49 laps), Arthur Dobson, Austin Dobson, Hanson, Maclure (all 48 laps), Connell (45 laps) and Parnell (35 laps). There were only three retirements – Hughes (20 laps), Villoresi (15 laps) and du Puy (1 lap). The small number of retirements, in marked contrast to the four previous years, may have been due to the atrocious conditions resulting in the cars being less stressed. There were no incidents except that Robin Hanson touched the bags at Onchan and the pavement at St. Ninian's but continued on each occasion.

At the finish, a thoroughly drenched and partially deafened Bira, anxious for a quick bath, paid particular tribute to Mays'driving. Later he would recall his achievement as the best race of his career, in conditions like a fast motor-boat regatta. Although his blue overalls were supposed to be waterproof, the cold rain soaked him underneath, especially down his neck, he said. What struck him at the time as he sat on "Romulus" was the lack of fizz in the glass of champagne that was thrust into his hand. It was half full of rain water!

Bira takes the chequered flag at the end of a heroic drive during one of the wettest of the Isle of Man races. He led from lap 1 until his refuelling stop on lap 31. After re-joining the race behind Mays and Fairfield he passed Fairfield on lap 33 and Mays on lap 36 and then led until the flag. [Stan Hughes collection]

The death of Philip Jucker in the first practice and the bad weather of race day were two features which depressed everyone, but more was to come after the race. Firstly, Humphrey Cook of ERA, as entrant of Raymond Mays, was called before the race Stewards and fined £2 for allowing three mechanics to refuel Mays' car although the regulations stipulated a limit of two. Allegedly, Cook was wrongly informed by a minor official. Secondly, BBC listeners tuning in to hear commentary on the finish of the race were disappointed to find that the race had finished earlier than the BBC expected and the result was not announced until much later in the day.

Now the prize presentation at the Villa Marina created yet more ill-feeling. The Island's Lieutenant-Governor, Sir Montagu Butler, and the Mayor of Douglas were among the VIPs who attended but, in what the *Isle of Man Times* described as "a shocking display of bad manners and lack of courtesy to the Governor and the Mayor of Douglas", only three of the ten prize winners did so - Bira, Raymond Mays and Pat Fairfield. The latter two were late but arrived in time to join Bira to receive the Team Award on behalf of ERA. Bira, who said he was happy to have won but wished that the weather had been dry so that more people could have seen the race, left the Island by boat later that night with "Romulus" as deck cargo.

The *Isle of Man Daily Times* was particularly critical. His Excellency seemed to feel the indignity inflicted upon him, it said. In his speech he said that it would have been "much nicer if there had been anybody to present the prizes to". The newspaper described the BBC coverage of the presentation as "a poor affair", complaining that the Governor's speech was omitted and Bira's speech was barely audible.

In a letter of apology, Captain Phillips explained that the drivers' absence had been caused by a combination of problems. The presentation had been brought forward to accommodate the BBC broadcast, making some drivers late. Announcements from the stage had not been audible at the back of the hall and some drivers had been unable to reach the stage due to the aisles being congested. He added that all drivers had been present and that many had apologised to the Governor at the reception after the presentation.

After the race, an ingenious propaganda move on the safety of Manx roads was the removal of a piece of the surface of a major road in Douglas and its despatch to London as an exhibit at an exhibition. It was an example of a road surface on which cars had raced in torrential rain at 120mph without skidding!

1937 RAC International Light Car Race Results

Thursday 3rd June 1937. Start 2.00pm. 50 laps of 3.9 miles circuit, total distance 195 miles. 15 starters, 12 finishers.

1. B. Bira (1,488cc ERA R2B) 2hrs 45mins 34secs (70.69 mph)
2. Raymond Mays (1,488cc ERA R4B) 2hrs 46mins 16secs (70.39 mph)
3. Pat Fairfield (1,488cc ERA R12C) 2hrs 46mins 53secs (70.04 mph)
4. Reggie Tongue (1,488cc. ERA R11B) 2hrs 48mins 5secs (69.63mph)
5. Peter Whitehead/Peter Walker (1,488cc ERA R10B) 2hrs 50mins 30secs (68.64 mph)

Failed to complete the required 50 laps:

6. Emanuel de Graffenried (1,496cc Maserati 4CM), 49 laps, 2hrs 51mins 23secs (66.73 mph)
7. Arthur Dobson (1,486cc ERA R7B), 48 laps, 2hrs 51mins 2secs (65.50 mph)
8. Austin Dobson (1,500cc Maserati 6CM), 48 laps, 2hrs 52mins 42secs (64.87 mph)
9. Robin Hanson (1,490cc Maserati 6CM), 48 laps, 2hrs 53mins 16secs (64.66 mph)
10. Peter Maclure (1,487cc Riley), 48 laps, 2hrs 53mins 56secs (64.41 mph)
11. Ian Connell (1,488cc ERA R6B), 45 laps, 2hrs 51mins 57secs (61.08 mph)
12. Reg Parnell (1,486cc MG Magnette K3), 35 laps, 2hrs 51mins 35secs (47.61 mph)

Fastest lap: Raymond Mays (1,488cc E.R.A.) 3mins 10secs (73.92mph)

Team Prize: ERA, B. Bira, Raymond Mays and Pat Fairfield

Retirements:

LAP 1:

John Du Puy (1,490cc Maserati 6CM), no oil pressure

LAP 15:

Luigi Villoresi (1,500cc Maserati 6CM), supercharger oil leak

LAP 26:

Bill Hughes (1,087cc MG Magnette K3), blown gasket.

Reaction

The race was described by *The Autocar* as "a really first class event" and by *Motor Sport* as "Britain's most important road race". It took place on a circuit which, despite the rain, seemed to have found more favour with drivers that the different circuits used in each of the previous four years. Thanks to introduction in 1936 of the "open" 1,500cc formula used for Continental races, several foreign drivers had been attracted. At last, progress was apparent. Nevertheless, on the Island the 1937 race was regarded as a failure.

At a sitting of Tynwald on 9th July when members were asked to vote funds for racing in 1938, serious doubts were expressed about the race being worth the investment. The races were not fulfilling expectations either in publicity for the Island or the number of people attracted to the Island and were a failure, it was suggested, and the £1,500 grant could be better spent. When the Attorney General agreed, the issue was referred to a Committee of five, charged with considering the funding of road racing on the Island, both on two wheels and four.

Douglas Town Councillors were united in their opposition to the car races. When the Car Race Committee asked whether the Town Council wished the Committee to organise a car race in 1938 the Council, accepting a Finance Committee recommendation, agreed in a matter of three seconds, without comment, that it did not. The races had been "dogged with misfortune," said the *Isle of Man Examiner* afterwards. A change of course each year had never given the races a chance to establish themselves.

The *Isle of Man Times* agreed, saying that the car races had "passed away unwept, unhonoured and unsung". There had been unforeseen misfortunes from the start and the crowning misfortune had been the behaviour of the winners in not attending the presentation. This contrasted with the Manx Grand Prix motorcycle races presentation, where every replica winner had been present to receive his award.

No one was opposed to other forms of car racing - just the type that had failed. Regaining the TT still appealed. The *Isle of Man Examiner* thought that there would not be many regrets at the loss of the "Round-the-Houses" races and that this placed the Island in a better position to talk business with the RAC over the possibility of the TT being returned to the Island.

1933 – 1937 WINNERS.

Hon. Brian Lewis, Alfa Romeo – 1933, 1934 and 1935 Mannin Moar

Brian Lewis, later Lord Essendon, son of a shipping magnate, was an aeroplane dealer who had a long and varied racing career. He started racing with an AV monocar before moving on to Frazer Nashes and he then became so involved with Bugattis that he acquired the nickname of "Bug" Lewis. He became a Talbot works driver and also drove Alfa Romeos, Delage, Riley, Maserati, Singer, Lagonda and ERA. He won British Racing Drivers' Club gold stars in 1931 and 1934. His hat-trick of Mannin Moar wins were arguably his major successes but he was a consistent finisher with eight second or third places at Brooklands in 1931, three third places at Le Mans, (1930, 1932 and 1933) and two fourth places in the RAC TT at Ards (1931 and 1934).

Freddie Dixon, Riley – 1933 Mannin Beg

Even before the 1933 Mannin Beg, Middlesborough motor engineer Freddie Dixon was a celebrity on the Isle of Man due to his motorcycle TT successes. In 17 TT races between 1912 and 1928 he rode Cleveland, Douglas, H.R.D. and Indian machines. He won twice (the 1921 Sidecar TT on his famous "banking" Douglas outfit and the 1927 Junior TT on an H.R.D.) and also had one second and two third places.

He took up car racing in 1932 with a modified Riley Nine, in which he lapped the Brooklands Outer Circuit at over 115mph and led the Ards TT until going over a hedge. He was a genius at modifying lightening and tuning his Rileys and was very secretive about his methods.Wins in the 1935 and 1936 Ards TT Races (in a car shared with Charlie Dodson in 1936) made him the only man ever to win TT Races on two, three and four wheels. He won two 500-mile races at Brooklands and two British Racing Drivers' Club Gold Stars. His Riley successes ended with the advent of the ERAs. He was a tough, hard-driving and sometimes wild competitor, with a personality off the track which matched his driving exploits

Norman Black, MG Magnette K3 – 1934 Mannin Beg

Norman Black was a sports car dealer in London and, until turning to car racing in 1931, a successful motorcycle racer. He took part in eleven Isle of Man TT races between 1920 and 1928 with varied results, the best being 5th in the 1923 Lightweight TT riding a Cedos.

In cars, he was immediately successful, winning the 1931 car TT at Ards in a 750cc MG Midget, the Irish Grand Prix at Phoenix Park and the British Racing Drivers' Club Gold Star. He was a successful hillclimb driver, with wins at Mont des Mules in 1931 and 1932 and at Shelsley Walsh. In 1934, in addition to his Mannin Beg success, he won the light car class at the Le Mans 24 hour race, in which he drove annually from 1932 to 1937 in MG s and Singers. He also drove annually in the Monte Carlo Rally from 1931 to 1936 and continued rally driving after the War.

Pat Fairfield, ERA – 1935 Mannin Beg

Although he was born in England, Pat Fairfield spent much of his early life in South Africa, where his father was a fruit grower. After returning to England he became a protege of Freddie Dixon and drove a Riley in British events, earning the reputation of an erratic driver and the nickname of "Skidder". In 1935 he acquired the first "customer" ERA, which had a 1,100cc engine and his Mannin Beg victory was the company's first major race success. He also won the Dieppe Grand Prix despite competing against cars with 1,500cc engines. These wins overcame the "Skidder" image but his 1936 season was less successful due to reliability problems, and a mid-season change from private entrant to official ERA works driver produced no improvement. In 1937, ERA reliability improved and Fairfield won the Coronation Trophy at Crystal Palace and the Nuffield Trophy at Donington and finished third in the rain at Douglas, behind Bira and Mays. Sadly, only a week after his Donington victory, while driving a works B.M.W. in the Le Mans 24 hour race he was involved in a multiple crash at White House and died of his injuries two days later.

Richard Seaman, Delage – 1936

Dick Seaman's career began with an MG Magna which he used in trials. He began racing in 1933 in a Bugatti but his career took off when, while he was an undergraduate at Cambridge University, he became friendly with the American Whitney Straight from whom he acquired a K3 MG Magnette which Straight had raced in 1933. Seaman raced this car during the 1934 season, winning at Berne and achieving second and third places at Donington and Pescara respectively.

For 1935, Seaman acquired an ERA in which he gained victories at Pescara, Berne and Brno and a fourth place at Nurburgring. Then, looking for greater performance and reliability, he acquired the 1927 Grand Prix Delage for the 1936 season. In addition to his Isle of Man win, he finished first at Pescara, Berne and Donington (twice). He also won the British Empire Trophy at Donington in a Maserati, before the Delage was ready, and the end of season Donington Grand Prix with Hans Ruesch in an Alfa Romeo. He was runner-up to Bira for the British Racing Drivers' Club Gold Star.

His 1936 successes established Seaman as the top 1,500cc driver in Europe and brought him to the notice of the Mercedes-Benz racing manager, Neubauer, who invited him to join their Grand Prix team for 1937. His best result was second in the Vanderbilt Cup race in America, with fourth places in the Italian Grand Prix and in the Masaryk Grand Prix in Czechoslovakia. In 1938 he won the German Grand Prix, finished second in the Swiss Grand Prix and third at Donington. He remained with the team for 1939 but in only the second race of the season, the Belgian Grand Prix at Spa, while leading in wet conditions, he crashed into a tree and later died in hospital.

"B. Bira", ERA – 1937.

Prince Birabongse Bhanubandh (known as "B. Bira" or simply "Bira") was a Siamese prince, grandson of King Mongkut who was the inspiration for the main character in the musical "The King and I". Educated at Eton College and Cambridge under the watchful eye of his first cousin once removed, guardian and mentor Prince Chula Chakrabongse (known as "Chula"), Bira became a successful athlete and sculptor.

Bira's racing career started at Brooklands in March 1935 in a tuned Riley Imp. After six races, he quickly progressed to an MG K3 Magnette in which he contested four races.In July 1935, as a 21st birthday present, Chula bought him the 1,500cc supercharged ERA known as "Romulus" which was the first of three ERAs to join their "White Mouse stable". As well as contesting light car races in Europe, with wins at Monte Carlo, Peronne and Albi in 1936, Bira won three British Racing Drivers' Club Road Racing Gold Stars in 1936, 1937 and 1938. In the reduced 1939 season he managed three wins in England and retired in the Le Mans 24 hour race in which he shared an Alfa Romeo with Raymond Sommer. Chula later calculated that the five pre-war seasons had cost over £16,000 in capital expenditure and over £10,000 in running expenses.

After spending the war years in Cornwall, Bira returned to racing, winning the 1946 Ulster Trophy at Ballyclare in the ERA "Hanuman" and the 1947 Manx Cup in a Simca-Gordini. The latter victory meant that he was the only driver to win pre-war and post-war Isle of Man Races. He had other successes in Simca-Gordinis, including wins in Switzerland and France, and also acquired a Maserati 4CL, which he campaigned with less success. His partnership with Chula ended in 1948 and his career tailed off after a successful 1949 season but continued intermittently until 1955. His last major victory was in the 1955 New Zealand Grand Prix in a Maserati 250F. After retirement from motor racing, he took up yacht racing and ran an airline in Thailand. He died in London in 1985.

1938 – The RAC Tourist Trophy

The fact that the 1937 Donington TT had not been a success ("a dreadful flop", said the *Isle of Man Times*) strengthened the Isle of Man's hand when the RAC made an approach to stage the 1938 TT in the Isle of Man on Saturday 3rd September 1938. "It's ours for the taking", said the *Isle of Man Examiner*, and "it should be taken up without delay". The cost of making a course suitable for the TT could be justified if the RAC guaranteed to hold the TT on the Island for at least five years.

The Government Secretary arranged a conference to discuss a new race for 1938. This conference was presided over by Deemster Percy Cowley and was attended by Captain Phillips of the RAC and other interested parties, including representatives of the Highway Board and the Manx Motor Cycle Club. The fact that the RAC wanted to stage the TT on the Saturday of Manx Grand Prix practice week and that TT practices would clash with MGP practices was a complication. It was suggested, however, that car practising could be in the mornings and motorcycle practising in the evenings or that the Manx Grand Prix could be held a week later. The outcome of the conference was inconclusive. It was decided to leave a decision to the Tynwald committee which was considering the future of races on the Island.

On 19th November, the *Examiner* reported an article in *The Autocar* stating that there had been a proposal for a TT race over the full TT Mountain Course with an interval start, but that there was little or no hope of the TT returning to the Island. A similar indication appeared in *Speed* which said "If the I.O.M. Press can be taken as a criterion, then it would appear that the Islanders do not want the race in September, and if they are to have it at all, they only want it on their own terms. And we cannot see that the RAC will stand for this sort of attitude".

In early December the Tynwald Committee presented its report. It revealed that it had met Captain Phillips who had suggested that the 1938 TT could be held on September 17th to avoid the Manx Grand Prix. The Committee had rejected this date as too late in the season for publicity value and also too close to the Manx Grand Prix in terms of public inconvenience in country areas. Then Captain Phillips had suggested Thursday 28th May (which was what the Island had wanted all along). However the RAC still wanted £1,500 prize money and a guarantee against loss of at least £1,000, which the Committee thought could reach as much as £3,000, still with no guarantee of continuity. The Committee's recommendation was that the present grant of £1,500 for the RAC International Light Car Race could not be justified and nor could a grant of £2,500 for the proposed TT race. This meant the end of Manx car racing, and of the RAC TT, for the foreseeable future.

On 4th December 1937 the *Isle of Man Times* reported that Captain Phillips had inspected two more proposed Northern Ireland courses and found both too narrow. The paper commented that "the poor RAC, wealthy beyond dreams, is finding it difficult to persuade any place to pay for the privilege of running these races, which at one time were the leading races in the world".

Early in 1938, yet another Northern Ireland course was proposed. Antrim County Council was prepared to close a ten miles circuit but would require a new by-pass for Templepatrick and the omission of certain crossroads near Belfast. Road repairs would cost £10,000 and a three year guarantee would be required. The TT would stay at Donington for 1938.

In April 1938 the Secretary of the Highway Board commented at a local motor-cycle club dinner that, in the early days of the TT, the RAC had given a donation towards the upkeep of roads, offered the Board a steam roller and paid £200 a year for three years. Now the RAC wanted roads prepared, prize money and administrative expenses.

The *Isle of Man Times* reported that the 1938 TT at Donington attracted only 12,000 spectators. Spoilt by rain, the race had been a poor spectacle. *The Times* said that it should have been run on the Island on a proper course and would have been but for the obstinacy of certain RAC officials.

In 1939 the RAC planned again to run the TT at Donington, on 2nd September but the race was cancelled in the rapidly deteriorating international situation which led to the declaration of the Second World War on 3rd September.

Prince Bira returned to the Island in 1947 with high hopes after winning the last pre-war race in 1937. Favourite for both races, he won the Manx Cup in his Simca-Gordini but in the Empire Trophy his Maserati, pictured at Cronk-ny-Mona, had handling problems and he finished fifth. [Onchan District Commissioners]

1947 – Bob Gerard's First Manx Victory – Bira's Second

Post-war Revival

Motor racing was slow to restart in Europe after the Second World War, due to lack of available circuits and shortages of cars, fuel, tyres and spare parts. The first post-war race took place in the Bois de Bologne in Paris on 9th September 1945 and the first official Grand Prix was the Grand Prix des Nations at Geneva on 21st July 1946, followed by races at Nice, Marseilles and Albi.

In the British Isles, the first airfield race was held at Gransden Lodge in June 1946 and the first road race was the Ulster Trophy at Ballyclare, Northern Ireland, on 10th August 1946. The winner was Bira in an ERA.

On the Isle of Man, motorcycle racing re-started with the Manx Grand Prix in September 1946 with the first post-war motorcycle TT following in June 1947. On the UK mainland there was a dire shortage of circuits with Brooklands, Donington and Crystal Palace all unavailable and it was natural that race organisers should again turn to the Island and that the Island should welcome all opportunities to resume the tourist industry. In March 1947 the *Isle of Man Examiner* reported an approach from the British Racing Drivers' Club. Wishing to revive the British Empire Trophy series on a genuine road circuit, BRDC Secretary Desmond Scannell had visited Douglas, met the Tynwald Race Committee and inspected likely courses. Surprisingly, the newspaper had forgotten that there had been a race in Douglas in 1937 – it stated that the last race had been in 1936, the last of a series of four, an error repeated in the Official Programme for the 1947 event!

The *Isle of Man Times* announced that the Tynwald Race Committee intended to propose revival of the 1936 course despite the RAC's view after the 1936 race that it was "not fit to be used again". *The Times* thought the course was "dangerous and devoid of interest" and recalled that Freddie Dixon had withdrawn after practice, saying "the course is hopeless and quite unsuitable for a serious motor race. Better to keep out as I do not feel justified in starting and perhaps meeting with serious trouble". The Committee, however, said very little work would be necessary to make the course suitable. Hedges might have to be cut back between Willaston and Cronk-ny-Mona and opposite the Nursery Hotel in Onchan, where the road was barely 15 feet wide.

Tynwald Recommendation

Tynwald accepted a Race Committee recommendation of a grant of £2,000 to stage a 50 lap (200 miles) race in August for the British Empire Trophy for which an entry of 15 was anticipated. The Manx Government would pay travel expenses for drivers and cars and for two mechanics per car. The winner would receive £250 and every starter who completed at least one lap would receive a refund of £15 of the £20 entry fee. There would be a second race, "The Manx Cup", with the winner receiving the Dunlop Trophy and £50. Starters would have £7.10s of their £10 entry fee refunded.

The course was inspected by Earl Howe, Chairman of the RAC Competitions Committee and President of the BRDC. While he had found it "very difficult and very dangerous" as a driver in 1936, Earl Howe said "it is now a very different course, the surface is very much better and the road seems wider". The *Isle of Man Examiner* reported that the British Empire Trophy (40 laps, 155 miles) would be for cars of the current Grand Prix formula – supercharged cars up to 1,500cc and unsupercharged up to 4,500cc. The Manx Cup (12 laps, 46.5 miles) would be for supercharged cars up to 1,100cc and unsupercharged up to two litres.

The Autocar announced that Desmond Scannell was arranging to obtain racing fuel. There was also the possibility of free shipment of cars direct from Belfast after the Ulster Trophy race on Saturday 9th August. The *Isle of Man Examiner* announced that a new silver and niello trophy for the fastest lap had been presented by Siamese silversmiths to commemorate the hospitality shown to Prince Bira by the British motor racing community. At the

In preparation for the Island's first post-war races, extensive road widening was needed, particularly at Cronk-y-Berry and Onchan. On the uphill approach to Cronk-y-Berry, illustrated, the road was widened from 18 feet to 45 feet for a distance of approximately 240 yards. [Peter Kelly collection]

same time it was revealed that practices were to take place on the evenings of Tuesday and Wednesday 19th and 20th August between 6pm and 8pm, with the Manx Cup Race to start at 2pm on Thursday 21st August, followed by the British Empire Trophy Race at 3pm.

The Autocar expressed concern about the crude way in which the Isle of Man Steam Packet Company handled vehicles. It said that an "Autocarrier", as used on Channel routes, was needed. Conditions which caused scratches, marks and bent bumpers should not be continued longer than absolutely necessary.

Meanwhile, extensive road widening took place. Douglas Corporation gave land for widening between Willaston Corner and Cronk-y-Berry, from 18 feet to 45 feet for a distance of 240 yards. At Onchan, the Nursery Hotel bends were widened and the kerb outside the Isle of Man Bank was chamfered and the pavement re-surfaced with a slight camber so that cars could run on the pavement on the exit of the sharp right hand Manx Arms corner. On Ballanard Road a channel near to Willaston Corner was filled in and "mattresses" were placed at danger points. Nevertheless the roads were still bumpy, the surface of granite chippings was still inclined to rut and break up and there were still narrow sections between high hedges. Whether due to road widening or more accurate measurement, the official course distance was reduced from 4 miles in 1936 to 3.87 miles in 1947. Recalling that Dick Seaman's 1936 winning average in the Delage had been 69mph, *The Autocar* expected that the race average would exceed 70mph and that the fastest cars could lap at over 80mph. These forecasts would prove to be optimistic.

A round-the-course commentary was arranged although the BBC was not prepared to provide a live radio commentary but only a brief report during the evening of the day after the races.

The Autocar published a useful guide for spectators, pointing out "It is quite simple and comparatively inexpensive to get to the Isle of Man, even at short notice and for the day only". Steamers would leave Fleetwood for Douglas on race day at 9.30am and 10.30am, returning at 6pm after the race, which was expected to finish by about 5.15pm. A first class day return at excursion rate would cost 16s (80p) compared with the ordinary first class return at 35s (£1.75). For air travellers, Air Enterprises Ltd of Gatwick was quoting £10 17s 6d (£10.75) for the return flight, leaving Gatwick at 9am and returning after the race. Flight time was 2hrs 40mins.

British Empire Trophy Entries

The British Empire Trophy attracted a strong entry of 23 cars, considerably exceeding early expectations. No less than eleven were ERAs. George Abecassis (a war-time R.A.F. Squadron-Leader and Stirling bomber pilot who had been awarded the D.S.O. and had started the HW Motors company with John Heath) had an "A" type, R2A, with large capacity fuel tank with which he expected to complete the race without stopping. Ulster Trophy winner Bob Gerard, a 33 years old engineer from Leicester who had also finished fourth in the European Grand Prix at Spa and third at Reims, entered a "B" type, R14B, which had been sold to Johnnie Wakefield in 1938. Following Wakefield's death in the Fleet Air Arm during the war, Gerard had acquired the car (his third ERA) and had made various modifications. This, too, had a large capacity tank of nearly 50 gallons which would enable him also to complete the race non-stop. Other "B" types were entered by Peter Whitehead (fifth finisher in the 1937 Manx race in the same car, R10B), George Bainbridge/Brian Shawe-Taylor (R9B) and the Sheffield motor engineer T.C. ("Cuth") Harrison (R8B), while Leslie Brooke and Reg Parnell (a 1937 veteran) entered streamlined "E" types. Further ERAs were entered by John Bolster, Raymond Mays (runner-up to Bira in the 1937 Isle of Man race), Joe Ashmore (who was in his first season of racing and yet had finished third at Jersey behind Reg Parnell and Louis Chiron) and Bira (who had the alternative of a Maserati which he would decide to race in preference to the ERA). Other Maserati entries were the burly Birmingham brewer Bob Ansell, Guy Jason-Henry and Fred Ashmore (brother of Joe and also in his first season). Scuderia Milan entries of two further Maseratis did not appear.

There were three Altas, to be driven by Geoff Crossley, John Williams and Gordon Watson/ Bob Cowell. Captain Barry Woodall, runner-up to Gerard in the Ulster Trophy, entered his Delage, which was similar to the car in which Richard Seaman had won the 1936 Isle of Man race and which was said to be fitted with the same engine as in 1936. Mrs Sheila Darbishire (ERA engined Riley Special) was the only lady driver ever to compete in an Isle of Man car race on closed public roads – Dorothy Levitt had been entered to drive a Mors in the first RAC TT in 1905 but had withdrawn due to illness. David Hampshire had the Challenger, a special designed by Reg Parnell and fitted with a 1927 Grand Prix Delage engine, Wilson gearbox and pneumatic front suspension without shock absorbers. Rear suspension was by torsion bars and de Dion layout. The remainder of the field consisted of single examples of Bugatti (Michael Chorlton), Alfa Romeo (Tony Rolt) and Darracq (Leslie Johnson). The Alfa Romeo (fitted with eight S.U. carburettors by Freddie Dixon) and the Darracq were the only unsupercharged cars in the entry.

Manx Cup Entries

There were 26 entries for the Manx Cup. While the field consisted mainly of resurrected pre-war racing cars, three new models attracted particular interest. Two were "works" Simcas, entered by Bira's White Mouse Stable for Equipe Simca Gordini and to be driven by Bira and by Amedee Gordini himself. These were tubular chassis 7cwt single-seater cars powered by 1,100cc four-cylinder Fiat engines producing some 65bhp. The cars had not previously raced in the British Isles but Bira's was the actual car which had won the Cup of the Little Cylinders at Reims. Also of great interest was the Emeryson to be driven by Eric Winterbottom. This was a "special" with a twin overhead camshaft four-cylinder 1,100cc Lagonda Rapier engine fitted with Marshall superchargers giving two stages of induction pressure. It had a tubular chassis, self-change Armstrong gearbox with alternative final drive ratios giving six forward speeds, independent front suspension and de Dion rear suspension. Said to have reached 130mph on test, it had been built since December 1946 by civil servant Paul Emery and his son, allegedly from parts of seven different makes, some of which were over 25 years old. The car had appeared previously at Gransden and at Great Auclum hill-climb, in an unfinished state. In appearance the low streamlined single-seater resembled the E-type ERA. entered by Leslie Brooke in the Empire Trophy Race.

There were five pre-war MG entries. Four were K3 Magnettes. Bobby Baird (a Northern Ireland driver who had raced on the Isle of Man in 1934 and 1935) had K3028, Hector Graham/D.H. Kyle entered K3006 (raced by Eddie Hall in the 1933 and 1934 Mannin Beg), Frank Kennington entered K3752 (the ex-Earl Howe/Count Lurani Mille Miglia car later driven by Ronald Yallop in the 1933 Mannin Beg) and Ian Nickols had K3009 (driven by Robin Mere in the 1933 Mannin Beg). Ronald "Curly" Dryden entered a Q- type MG Midget. Five FrazerNash B.M.W.s were entered by Tony Crook (who later became the owner of the Bristol car company), Hugh Carrington, T.M. Gay, Oscar Moore and Gilbert Tyrer. Rileys were entered by George Burton, Cuth Harrison (whose 2 litre car was fancied as a possible winner), C.C.D. Miller/Guy Jason-Henry and Francis Penn. Three H.R.G s were to be driven by Peter Clark, G.H. Robins and John Wyer. Reg Parnell entered an ERA. The 17 stone Owen Finch entered an Amilcar. In addition there were single entries of Alvis (C.G.H. Dunham), Aston Martin (Geoff Ansell, cousin of Bob), Rapier (Ian Metcalfe) and Bugatti (Mrs Sheila Darbishire/Edward Pool).

Practice

Practice took place during the evenings of Tuesday and Wednesday 19th and 20th August in perfect conditions. *The Autocar* commented on the large number of new faces and new names among the drivers which, it thought, proved how the races offered a fine opportunity to British racing drivers in the absence of tracks at home.

There were notable non-arrivals for the Empire Trophy. Reg Parnell's "E" type ERA had suffered rear suspension problems in the Ulster Trophy only ten days previously; his Maserati had been crashed by Joe Ashmore at Comminges and his "B" type ERA had also been crashed at the same circuit by Fred Ashmore, so that both Ashmore brothers were also withdrawals.

Parnell's withdrawal was a great disappointment not only for the man himself but also for the many Manx and visiting spectators. Reg was a major star, having won the Jersey International Race (beating Chiron and Mays) and finished third in the Nimes Grand Prix in his Maserati. He maintained his Manx interest by helping Mrs Darbishire when repeated losses of oil pressure led to a seized camshaft in her Riley special during Wednesday's

Prince Bira started as the firm favourite for both the 1947 Isle of Man races. He won the Manx Cup in this Fiat 1,100cc engined works Simca Gordini but although he started from pole in the British Empire Trophy his Maserati had handling problems in the race and he could finish only fifth. [Stan Hughes collection]

Eric Winterbottom finished third in the Emeryson, pictured at the Manx Arms. This special was home-built by Paul Emery and his son. It had a tubular chassis with independent front suspension, De Dion rear suspension and a Lagonda Rapier engine with two stage supercharger. [Stan Hughes collection]

In the first practice Michael Chorlton over-braked and lost control of his Bugatti in Avondale Road on the descent into Onchan Village and the car overturned after hitting a wall. Chorlton was lucky to suffer no more than cuts and bruises to the head and back. This photograph shows the front end of the car after the crash. [Peter Kelly collection]

practice. Her problems were overcome only by extensive overnight repair work. Reg seemed to love losing sleep and getting really dirty for other people's sake, observed the BRDC Yearbook later. He also drove Cuth Harrison's ERA during practice.

Raymond Mays' ERA was another Ulster Trophy casualty, having suffered a broken connecting rod and damaged block, for which he had no replacement. Gordon Watson's Alta was unfit after the Ulster race while the Alta of John Williams was not ready and John Bolster's ERA was also absent.

The Manx Cup was also affected by non-arrivals. Sadly, there was only one Simca Gordini, as Amedee Gordini was racing elsewhere and the car he was to have driven had crashed. Again, Parnell had no car. Dryden (MG), Burton (Riley), Gay (Frazer Nash B.M.W.) and the Miller/Jason-Henry Riley were also missing.

There were several driver changes, with John Panks driving C.G.H. Dunham's Alvis and the H.R.G.s of Robins and Wyer being taken over by Jack Scott and A.C. Molyneux respectively.

Michael Chorlton's Bugatti is recovered after its crash on the approach to the Manx Arms in Onchan. [Peter Kelly collection]

The first practice session saw the only serious accident of the meeting. It happened in Avondale Road on the downhill approach to the 90 degree right hand corner at the Manx Arms public house in Onchan Village when Michael Chorlton, a cameraman in his early thirties, over-braked, locked up and lost control of his Bugatti which crashed into a shop wall and overturned. The driver was extricated and taken to hospital with cuts and bruises to his head and back.

In the second practice, Barry Woodall's Delage broke a connecting rod and he thought that he was out of the race. In the event, he decided to race with seven sparking plugs, eight cylinders and nine pistons, using two spare pistons to block up the inoperative cylinder!

Leslie Brooke changed the Zoller supercharger of his "E" type ERA for a Jamieson Roots type replacement. He detuned the engine by reducing the boost to only 6 lb., intending to run an experimental race. David Hampshire found the pneumatic front suspension of his Challenger rather too flexible, with a rise-fall distance of seven inches.

By the end of practice, Bira had set fastest time for both races and was fancied to win both. In the absence of both Parnell and Mays, the main opposition in the Empire Trophy was expected to be the ERA's of Abecassis and Gerard with their extra-large fuel tanks, and Whitehead. In the Manx Cup, Cuth Harrison's Riley, Nickols' MG and the new Emeryson of Eric Winterbottom were likely to be competitive.

1947 Manx Cup Race – Bira Wins Again

A crowd estimated at 50,000 thronged the course, with the grandstand full. If this estimate was correct, it was one of the largest crowds ever seen at a motor race in the British Isles. The largest, attracted to the 1938 Donington Grand Prix by the Auto Union and Mercedes-Benz teams, had been 60,000. Blue skies and warm sunshine were as much an attraction as the promise of the first car race on the Island for ten years.

There were 18 starters. Ian Metcalfe's Rapier was withdrawn after breaking a piston in the final practice and Finch's Amilcar was also withdrawn after practice. Bira's Simca was on pole with a time of 3mins 29secs (66.81mph) which was five seconds faster than anyone else and would have been good enough for the third row of the Empire Trophy starting grid. Cuth Harrison's Riley was second (3mins 34secs) and Ian Nickols' MG (3mins 36secs) completed the front row. The second row consisted of Hector Graham's MG (3mins 39secs) and Gillie Tyrer's Frazer Nash B.M.W. (3mins 45secs). On the third row were Eric Winterbottom's Emeryson (3mins 47secs), John

Cuth Harrison in his two litre six cylinder Riley, seen at the Manx Arms corner, almost kept pace with Bira in the early stages of the race but fell back when lapping slower cars. He finished second, 31 seconds behind Bira and 3mins 29secs ahead of third placed Eric Winterbottom's Emeryson. [The late Alf Caley, Onchan]

Panks' Alvis (3mins 48secs) and Oscar Moore's Frazer Nash B.M.W. (3mins 50secs). They were followed by the MG of Frank Kennington, alone on the fourth row (3mins 54secs). The fifth row consisted of the Riley of Francis Penn (4mins 2secs), the H.R.G. of Peter Clark (4mins 03 secs) and the MG of Bobby Baird (4mins 4secs). On row six were Edward Pool's Bugatti and the H.R.G. of Molyneux (both 4mins 11secs). The seventh row was occupied by the Frazer Nash BMWs of Tony Crook (4mins 16secs) and Hugh Carrington (4mins 23secs) while the last row consisted of Jack Scott's H.R.G. (4mins 25secs) and Geoff Ansell's Aston Martin (4mins 26secs).

Bira made a slightly slow start and both Harrison and Nickols got away in front, although Bira led at Parkfield. When the flag fell, Panks' Alvis hit the back of Winterbottom's Emeryson and pushed it into the front of the scoreboard. The collision put out the tracking of the Emeryson's front wheels but Winterbottom continued in the race.

The Emeryson of Eric Winterbottom and the MG Magnette K3 shared by Hector Graham and Henry Kyle approach Willaston corner. Winterbottom finished third behind Bira's Simca-Gordini and Harrison's Riley but the MG retired on the tenth lap with a brake seizure. [Ray Stanfield collection]

At the end of the first lap Bira led with a time of 3mins 40secs (63.47mph), followed by Harrison and Graham, although the latter had skidded off the road at Cronk-ny-Mona. The possibility of a serious challenge from Ian Nickols in his twin-cam M.G. Magnette disappeared as a switch which controlled the fuel tank pressure had not been switched on, causing fuel starvation which led to piston damage. At the end of the lap he coasted into his pit to retire. For the rest of the race he chewed on Jamaican cigars and philosophized, according to *The Autocar*. Kennington and Baird also retired and Penn stopped at the pits.

On lap 2, Harrison passed Graham and presented Bira with a serious challenge. They were reportedly nose to tail at Cronk-ny-Mona during lap 5, before Bira speeded up and shook off his pursuer, who lost time while lapping back-markers. Meanwhile Panks took the escape road at Parkfield where Molyneux skidded and nearly collided with Graham.

After five laps, Bira led Harrison by nine seconds, averaging 65.56mph. Graham was now 29secs behind Harrison, followed by Winterbottom (who had just passed Tyrer). After Tyrer came Moore, Panks and Clark. Pool retired his Bugatti. Two laps later Bira led by 16secs and continued to extend his lead by 3secs a lap. On lap 7 he did the fastest lap of the race – 3mins 27secs (67,45mph). At the end of the tenth lap, the lead was 26secs and

Harrison led Graham by 2mins 30secs. Clark overshot at Parkfield and hit the bags, while Panks followed the TT Course for some distance down Bray Hill.

On lap 11, Graham toured in to retire, promoting Winterbottom to third. Oscar Moore stopped at the same time, with low oil pressure. This was a mistake – if he had continued for a further lap, he would have been classified as a finisher.

Bira took the chequered flag 31 seconds in front of Harrison, at an average speed of 66.05mph which would have been good enough for third place in the Empire Trophy race. Winterbottom's third place in the Emeryson, 2mins 58secs behind Harrison, was rewarded with a sale of the car immediately afterwards. According to *The Motor* the car was sold to Robert Baird of Belfast. The first three finishers completed the full 12 laps distance. The next three, Tyrer, Panks and Penn completed 11 laps with Scott, Crook, Ansell, Carrington and Clark completing 10 laps. The final (twelfth) finisher, Molyneux, completed nine laps.

During the race there was an unpleasant incident in the pits. Princess Chula, wife of Bira's Team Manager, stood on Bira's pit counter, which was contrary to race regulations. She refused to move when officials asked her to do so, clinging to an upright post. The Police had to be called and P.C. (later Superintendent) Robert Kermeen pulled the Princess down. She was then taken to the first aid post.

The race had been an exciting spectacle. Bira's victory in perfect conditions revived memories of his victory in the torrential rain of the previous Manx race, ten years earlier and increased the expectation of a third win later in the day.

1947 Manx Cup Race Results

Thursday 21st August 1947. Start 2.00pm. 12 laps of 3.8789 miles circuit, total distance 46.55 miles. 18 starters, 12 finishers.

1. B. Bira (1,100cc Simca-Gordini), 42mins 17secs (66.05mph)
2. T. C. ("Cuth") Harrison (1,986cc Riley), 42mins 48secs (65.25 mph)
3. Eric Winterbottom (1,100cc Emeryson Special), 45mins 46secs (61.02mph)

Did not complete required 12 laps:

4. Gilbert Tyrer (2 litre Frazer Nash B.M.W.), 11 laps, 42mins 48secs (59.81mph)
5. John Panks (1,842cc Alvis), 11 laps, 43mins 11secs (59.28mph)
6. Francis Penn (1,986cc Riley), 11 laps, 44mins 35secs (57.42mph)
7. Jack Scott (1.5 litre H.R.G.), 10 laps, 42mins 35secs (54.65mph)
8. Anthony Crook (2 litre Frazer Nash B.M.W.), 10 laps, 42mins 54secs (54.25mph)
9. Geoffrey Ansell (2 litre Aston Martin), 10 laps, 43mins 15secs (53.76mph)
10. Hugh Carrington (2 litre Frazer Nash B.M.W.), 10 laps, 43mins 36secs (53.38mph)
11. Peter Clark (1.5 litre H.R.G.), 10 laps, 45mins 44secs 50.89mph)
12. A.C. Molyneux (1.5 litre H.R.G.), 9 laps, 45mins 54secs (45.64mph)

Fastest lap: B. Bira (1,100cc Simca-Gordini), 3mins 27secs (67.45mph)

Team Prize: H.R.G. (Jack Scott, Peter Clark and A.C. Molyneux), only team to finish

Retirements:

Lap 1:

Frank Kennington (MG)

W. R. Baird (MG)

Ian Nickols (MG) piston problem

Lap 5:

E. G. Pool (Bugatti).

Lap 6:

Oscar Moore (Frazer Nash B.M.W.)

Lap 10:

Hector Graham (MG), seized brake.

1947 British Empire Trophy Race – Bob Gerard's First Manx Victory

Fifteen starters out of the original 23 entries lined up on the starting grid. In addition to the seven who had not practised, Michael Chorlton was a non-starter following his practice crash. For Bob Gerard, there was last minute panic. Early in the race-day morning, after stripping the supercharger drive and fitting replacement gears, he found that the engine was running extremely hot. It seemed that he would have to withdraw. Indeed, at 11.45am he decided to do so but at 12.30pm it was noticed that the ignition had been accidentally set to full retard. When this was corrected the car was tested and at 1.20pm was found to be fit to race. It was brought to the paddock at 1.50pm, out of time according to the regulations, but was accepted for the start even so.

Bira occupied pole position by virtue of his qualifying time of 3mins 16secs (71.24mph) in his Maserati. After his Manx Cup victory, there was keen speculation that he might achieve his second victory of the day and his third Manx win overall. He shared the front row of the grid with the ERAs of Peter Whitehead (3mins 18secs) and George Abecassis (3mins 20secs). The second row consisted of Tony Rolt's Alfa Romeo (3mins 26secs) and Bob Gerard's ERA (3mins 28secs). Cuth Harrison's ERA (3min 31secs) was on the third row with Bob Ansell's Maserati (3mins 32secs) and Brian Shawe-Taylor's ERA (3mins 33secs).

Leslie Brooke's "E" type ERA (3mins 33secs) and Leslie Johnson's Darracq (3mins 39secs) formed the fourth row. On the fifth row were Barry Woodall's Delage (3mins 41secs) with Geoff Crossley's Alta and David Hampshire's Challenger (both 3mins 45secs), while Sheila Darbishire (Riley – 3mins 54secs) and Guy Jason-Henry (Maserati – 4mins 29secs) brought up the rear.

The start was spectacular. Abecassis shot ahead of Bira and Whitehead to lead the pack towards the right hand corner at Parkfield, but it was Bira who led out of the corner into Ballanard Road. Bira was still in the lead at Cronk-ny-Mona, harried by Abecassis, Whitehead and Gerard and struggling with handling problems. At the end of the lap, Abecassis led the field with Whitehead four seconds behind and Gerard, Harrison, Ansell, Brook and Shawe-Taylor all in hot pursuit. Bira coasted into the pits to report his problem. The dampers were slackened but the problem persisted. He returned to the pits on the second, fourth and sixth laps. Reduced air pressure in the tyres on one visit failed to achieve anything so a wheel change was tried. Eventually it was discovered that the shock-absorbers had broken. Bira continued to race but at a slower speed. That and the accumulated lost time meant that his chances of achieving the double had evaporated.

On lap 1 there was drama at Onchan. The engine of Leslie Johnson's Darracq caught fire whilst he was lying in sixth place and he stopped outside the Manx Arms. The fire was extinguished, not with "Red Label" as a local reporter suggested, but by "over-enthusiastic attentions of the local fire party," which were blamed for his retirement. They directed every available extinguisher on the engine, filling the air intakes and rendering the car impossible to restart. Also in trouble on the first lap was Guy Jason-Henry's Maserati, with fuel starvation which would force his retirement on lap 8.

After five laps, Abecassis led Whitehead by 13 seconds with Whitehead four seconds back. Gerard, with a heavy fuel load, bided his time 11 seconds behind Whitehead. Harrison was fourth and Brooke fifth. Abecassis was now increasing his lead lap by lap – 20 seconds on lap 6, 25 seconds on lap 7 and 28 seconds on lap 8. Gerard was now 14 seconds behind Whitehead. Harrison dropped back and then stopped at Cronk-ny-Mona with fuel starvation and lost five laps, letting Brooke into fourth place. Guy Jason-Henry retired with fuel starvation on lap 8.

Abecassis was the next driver in trouble. At the end of lap 10, with his lead down to 23 seconds after several skids caused by leaking oil on his rear tyres, he stopped at his pit for about two minutes. Whitehead took the lead with Gerard 18 seconds behind him and 11 seconds ahead of Brooke's ERA. Abecassis re-joined in fourth place. While this was happening, Crossley made a second stop to change plugs in his Alta, Hampshire did likewise and Harrison reached his pit after re-starting from Cronk-ny-Mona.

George Abecassis took the lead when Bira pitted after the first lap but stopped with leaking oil on his back tyres. He continued but touched a kerb at high speed at Governor's Bridge and then, with oil on his goggles and pedals, crashed into the sand bags at the Isle of Man Bank in Onchan. [The late Alf Caley, Onchan]

The Manx Arms corner was always well staffed with marshals, who quickly crossed the road to extract George Abecassis' E.R.A. from the sand bags in front of the Isle of Man Bank. His pit stop had dropped him to third after leading for the first ten laps. Bent front suspension meant that his race was over. [The late Alf Caley, Onchan]

Whitehead, knowing that Gerard would not need to stop for fuel, did his utmost to build a lead sufficient to cover the time that he would lose when he had to stop to refuel. His lead reached 30 seconds before Gerard responded, reducing the lead to 23 seconds by the end of lap 15. Meanwhile Brooke and Ansell changed places and Abecassis moved up to third despite his continuing oil leakage, which caused him to snake luridly at Governor's Bridge dip at over 100mph. He bounced off the kerb and snaked again before recovering control. Now he was only seven seconds behind Gerard and 12 seconds ahead of Bob Ansell, with Brooke fifth and Rolt sixth.

At the front, Whitehead and Gerard continued their titanic battle, with Gerard gaining a second on lap 17 and losing it on lap 18 but gaining two seconds on lap 20.

David Hampshire rounds Parkfield in the technically interesting Challenger. The straight eight Delage engined car had a tubular chassis, pneumatic independent front suspension with no shock absorbers and rear suspension with torsion bars and De Dion layout. The front suspension proved much too flexible but magneto trouble forced retirement. [Stan Hughes collection]

Sheila Darbishire approaches Parkfield on her way to eighth place in her troublesome Riley. The number of spectators clinging to the high wall surrounding Parkfield House reflects the size of the race day crowd, estimated at 50,000. [Ray Stanfield collection]

Passing the Manx Arms in Onchan Village, the winner Bob Gerard (E.R.A., 22) pursues Bob Ansell (Maserati, 36). Ansell finished third, one lap behind the winner and second-placed Peter Whitehead, driving another E.R.A. [The late Alf Caley, Onchan]

Sheila Darbishire was the only lady to drive in a Manx road race. Pictured in her Riley at the Manx Arms corner, she completed the race eighth out of nine finishers but was eight laps behind the winner after being delayed by oil on her pedals and later by a clutch failure. [The late Alf Caley, Onchan]

Meanwhile Crossley stopped for another plug change and Sheila Darbishire stopped at the pits to clean oil off her pedals. When she was lapped by Bira, the commentator at Nursery Bends caused mirth by announcing "Prince Bira is chasing Mrs Darbishire round the Nursery". Tony Rolt pitted to investigate falling oil pressure.

At half distance, Whitehead led Gerard by 21 seconds, with Abecassis still third but now 1min 32secs behind Gerard and only two seconds ahead of Ansell. Brooke was fifth, Shawe-Taylor sixth, Bira progressing steadily in seventh place and Rolt down to eighth after his pit stop. Whitehead's lap times had not varied by more than four seconds over the first 20 laps, but he still did not have the lead he needed for his fuel stop.

On lap 21, Shawe-Taylor pitted to refuel and to hand over the car to George Bainbridge. On the next lap Whitehead was reported as "well up the bank" at Cronk-ny-Mona where Harrison stopped for the second time, but again managed to continue.

Lap 22 brought more drama. On the descent of Avondale Road into Onchan Village, Abecassis braked hard and was showered with oil which covered both his goggles and his pedals. Temporarily blinded, unable to brake fully and off line for the 90 degree right turn, he crashed into the bags in front of the Isle of Man Bank. His Technauto front suspension bent, he had no option but to to retire. Fortunately he was unhurt. He had led for ten laps, building a lead of 28 seconds until his oil leak problems. Brooke, seeing the crash, slowed and shouted to check that Abecassis was all right before continuing.

Whitehead dived into the pits at the end of lap 25. In a well-organised stop, he took on 15 gallons of fuel and was away to loud cheers from the grandstand,in 42 seconds. While he was at his pit, Gerard went past to lead by 16 seconds. Could Whitehead catch him in the remaining 15 laps?

Meanwhile, Crossley continued to change plugs before retiring on lap 18, David Hampshire retired the Challenger on lap 19 with magneto trouble, Rolt's oil pressure problems forced him to retire on lap 24 and Abecassis walked in from Onchan. Harrison still struggled with carburation problems and Mrs Darbishire stopped with clutch slip. By now she was thought to be practically furious and was reported to have exclaimed a most unlady-like "Oh, bother!"

By the end of 26 laps, Gerard led by 26 seconds which had increased to 30 seconds two laps later. Bira refuelled, now fifth behind Brooke. Gerard and Whitehead continued to trade seconds until, on lap 30, Gerard did the fastest lap so far in 3mins 20secs (69.82mph) to increase his lead to 33 seconds. Ansell was third, 2mins 59secs behind Gerard and 3mins 24secs ahead of Brooke, who led Bira by 48secs. Bainbridge was sixth, a further 17 seconds back.

It was now obvious that despite his heroic efforts, Whitehead could not catch Gerard. He lost further time with another encounter with the bank at Cronk-ny-Mona but, on lap 33 he did a new fastest lap at 3mins 19secs (70.17mph). On lap 35, while Gerard responded with the final fastest lap of 3mins 18secs (70.53mph), Whitehead spun completely on the right hand corner at the foot of the descent into Onchan. At the end of the lap, Gerard led by 53 seconds and Whitehead's great effort was over. Slowed by a broken shock absorber, he settled for second, with a secure lead over Ansell of 2mins 55secs. Brooke, Bira and Bainbridge still occupied the next three places.

Gerard continued to the chequered flag and a well-deserved victory by a margin of 1min 43secs. Whitehead finished second after a precautionary second fuel stop and took the Lucas award for the best all-British car, while Ansell was a steady third. Leslie Brooke finished fourth in his E-Type ERA. In so doing, although he had entered only to gain some race experience with the car in de-tuned form, he became the first driver of an E-Type to finish in an international race. He had complaints about the handling of the car, with rear suspension and steering problems making him feel "airborne" most of the time. Bira was fifth after his early handling problems, followed by Bainbridge, Woodall, Mrs Darbishire and Harrison. The unfortunate Crossley retired with a broken piston when, had he managed another lap, he would have been classified as a finisher. As well as the British Empire Trophy, Bob Gerard won the Bangkok Cup for the fastest race lap and the Pat Fairfield Memorial Trophy for the best performance by a BRDC Member.

It had been a particularly fast and spectacular race for the 50,000 spectators. Gerard's fastest lap of 3mins 18secs had beaten Richard Seaman's 1936 record of 3mins 20secs. The 1947 course, however, was allegedly shorter by 213 yards than the 1936 course. This meant that Gerard's 1947 fastest lap speed was officially 70.53mph, compared with Seaman's 1936 official fastest lap speed of 72.00mph. Nevertheless, one can only speculate how much faster and more exciting the race might have been if Parnell and Mays had been able to join in the battle and if Bira had not had handling problems from the start!

1947 British Empire Trophy Race Results

Thursday 21st August 1947. Start 3.00pm. 40 laps of 3.8789 miles circuit, total distance 155.16 miles. 15 starters, 9 finishers.

1. Bob Gerard (1,488cc ERA R14B), 2hrs 16mins 52secs (68.02mph)
2. Peter Whitehead (1,486cc ERA R10B), 2hrs 18mins 35secs (67.17mph)

Did not complete required 40 laps:

3. Robert (Bob) Ansell (1.5 litre Maserati 4CL), 39 laps, 2hrs 17mins 38secs (66.06mph)
4. Leslie Brooke (1,486cc E-Type ERA GP2), 38 laps, 2hrs 18mins 48secs (63.71mph)
5. B. Bira (1.5 litre Maserati 4CL), 38 laps, 2hrs 19mins 49secs (63.25mph)
6. George H. Bainbridge/ Brian Shawe-Taylor (1,486cc ERA R9B), 38 laps, 2hrs 20mins 24secs (62.90mph)
7. Barry Woodall (1,494cc Delage), 36 laps, 2hrs 19mins 38secs (60.00mph)
8. Mrs Sheila Darbishire (1,486cc Riley), 32 laps, 2hrs 19mins 21secs (53.45mph)
9. T. C. ("Cuth")Harrison (1,486cc ERA R8B), 25 laps, 2hrs 17mins 24secs (42.34mph)

Fastest lap: Bob Gerard (ERA), 3mins 18secs (70.53mph). Established lap record.

Retirements:

Lap 1:
Leslie Johnson (4 litre Darracq), fire at Onchan

Lap 8:
Guy Jason-Henry (Maserati 6CM), fuel starvation

Lap 18:
Geoff Crossley (Alta), broken piston

Lap 19:
David Hampshire (Challenger), magneto trouble

Lap 21:
George Abecassis (ERA R2A), broken oil pipe and crash at Onchan

Lap 24:
Tony Rolt (2.9 litre Alfa Romeo), loss of oil pressure.

Reaction

Local media reaction was, as usual, mixed. In a leader, the *Mona's Herald* commented on the importance of the races. Firstly, this was an initial post-war attempt to stage a British road race of real magnitude. Secondly, it showed the readiness of the motor industry to return to the Isle of Man and gave the Island the chance to become the mecca of motor racing again.

The *Isle of Man Examiner* commented on the ideal weather and the large crowds of holiday-makers who had enjoyed a unique attraction. Races of this kind were well worth cultivating, the *Examiner* said, but there must be an appreciation by those concerned of the high standards of organisation to which the Island was accustomed and rightly expected. Slick presentation and efficient attention to minor detail were necessary. The BRDC were newcomers, so allowances had to be made but the paper thought they would be well advised to take full advantage of expert advice available from very experienced Manx people. The *Examiner* thought that the circuit was not ideal but that consistency was needed. It hoped that the BRDC would return and would appreciate that the criticism was with no other motive than a desire to make the events the blue riband of the British motor racing world.

The *Isle of Man Times* described the Isle of Man as the mecca of racing for cars, motorcycles and bicycles, and welcomed the fact that all the leading hotels were booked-up for the forthcoming Manx Grand Prix motorcycle races. It thought that the 1948 races should be held in the week before Whit, on the TT Course. It reported that motoring journalist Tom Wisdom in The *Sporting Life* had advocated the return of the RAC TT to its original home and urged the RAC to act accordingly.

The Green Final said the races had lacked the showmanship of the TT and Manx Grand Prix races and criticised the Press arrangements, as the local media had done in 1937 but, in marked contrast to the pre-war races, the local Press reported no complaints from local authorities or individuals.

At the prize presentation, the BRDC President Earl Howe announced "If possible next year we shall be back to do our best". He paid tribute to Manxman Tom Moore, former Proprietor of *Motor Sport* and a 1933 Mannin Beg driver, for his efforts in making the races possible and for making them such a success.

The motoring Press was generally supportive, praising the organisation and commenting favourably on the large number of spectators, in contrast to the previous Isle of Man races. *The Autocar* published a letter from C.G.H. Dunham, entrant of fifth Empire Trophy finisher John Panks, recording his appreciation of the efforts of Clerk of the Course Desmond Scannell. *Motor Sport* regarded the races as an unqualified success and hoped that they would be repeated in 1948. The Manx Cup had been an effective curtain-raiser and the Empire Trophy had been "a first-class race in which driving and organisation were well up to Continental standard".

It was later announced that the event had made a net profit of £824, shared between the Club and the Isle of Man Government. The Tynwald Race Committee, in its 1948 report, stated that the races had been financially successful and most successful in every way.

1948 – Geoff Ansell's Win – Reg Parnell's Loss

Planning

Early in 1948, the race date was announced as Tuesday 25th May, with practices from 6pm to 9pm in the evenings of Saturday 22nd and Monday 24th May.

The British Racing Drivers Club decided to run three races – the British Empire Trophy, the Manx Cup and a new event, the Castletown Trophy Race, for a trophy presented by the Castletown Brewery. The British Empire Trophy, as in 1947, would be for Grand Prix type cars of up to 1,500cc supercharged or 4,500cc unsupercharged. The Manx Cup would be for supercharged cars of up to 1,100cc as in 1947, but with the limit for unsupercharged cars raised from 2 litres to 2.5 litres. Nobody took advantage of the increase. The Castletown Trophy, to be run simultaneously with the Manx Cup and over the same distance, would be for supercharged and unsupercharged cars of unlimited capacity, catering for large pre-war cars such as the Bugattis and Alfa Romeos which were ineligible for the other two races and ineligible for Continental races which restricted supercharged cars to only 500cc and unsupercharged cars to 2 litres. *The Autocar* thought that such cars were a little too big for real speed on the Manx course. Running small and big cars together was not considered suitable. The bigger cars would be handicapped by the smaller ones which would be difficult to pass. The course did not provide the best of chances for speed between corners. Race distances were changed with the British Empire Trophy reduced from 40 laps (155 miles) to 36 laps (140 miles) and the Manx Cup lengthened from 12 laps (45 miles) to 18 laps (70 miles).

Following the success of the 1947 meeting, the Isle of Man Government again agreed to give a guarantee not exceeding £2,000. Although petrol was still rationed, Clerk of the Course Desmond Scannell hoped to obtain an allowance but most cars would use 90% methanol (which was un-rationed) and racing cars could run on 100% methanol if necessary.

Again there would be no live broadcast by the BBC.

For the first time on the Island, race starts were to be controlled electronically instead of by dropping the National flag. Joseph Lucas Ltd of Birmingham provided a red, amber and green traffic light system. The red light was to be displayed at five minutes before the start. Countdown boards would then be shown with the light changing to amber at one minute to go. The start would signalled by a change to green. The new system was expected to avoid false starts. The guest starter was to be John Cobb, holder of the World Land Speed Record and the first man to travel at over 400mph on land.

There were further course improvements. Resurfacing took place on Glencrutchery Road adjacent to the cemetery and on Main Road in Onchan, from the Manx Arms corner to the Summer Hill Road junction. Also there was further widening of the Nursery Hotel bends.

British Empire Trophy Entries

There were 29 entries for the British Empire Trophy Race. They were mainly British cars, with no less than 12 ERAs. These were entered by Peter Walker, Sheila Darbishire (who was to share Edward Pool's car with the owner), Raymond Mays (with a "D" type which he had crashed in the Jersey race), Cuth Harrison, the 1947 winner Bob Gerard, Geoff Ansell (cousin of Bob Ansell) in the second race of his career with an old "B" type, Leslie Johnson, Reg Parnell, John Bolster, Joe Ashmore, Charles Mortimer and Leslie Brooke. Johnson and Parnell both had the new "E" types with Johnson driving a "works" car with Zoller supercharger, having acquired a controlling interest in the ERA company. George Abecassis entered a brand new Grand Prix Alta, with a second Alta entered by Gordon Watson. An ERA Riley was entered by Geoff Richardson and an Emeryson by Bobby Baird with Paul Emery as reserve driver. The Emeryson now had a 4.5 litre Duesenberg engine in place of the 1,100cc supercharged Lagonda Rapier engine used in 1947.

Maserati was the most numerous foreign marque, with seven cars entered by Anthony Baring, Duncan Hamilton (with the car in which George Abecassis finished second in the Jersey race), Roy Salvadori, Bob Ansell, John Gordon, Fred Ashmore and Lance Seyd. Michael Chorlton, who had crashed his Bugatti in practice in 1947, entered again, David Hampshire entered his Delage and Tony Rolt had his 3.4 litre Alfa Romeo, greatly modified and much faster than in 1947. Guy Jason-Henry entered a Delahaye and Leslie Brooke hoped to have a Ferrari as an alternative to his ERA. Finally, an interesting entry which was withdrawn at an early stage was the Talbot of the French driver Gianfranco Comotti, the 1937 Donington RAC TT Winner.

A missing, and much-missed driver was "Bira", well known and popular on the Isle of Man as winner of the last pre-war and first post-war Isle of Man races. His racing partnership with his cousin Chula had ended at the end of the 1946 season and *Motor Sport* made the cryptic comment that "not everyone was surprised that Chula did not enter him".

Manx Cup Entries

The Manx Cup also attracted 29 entries, of 11 different makes. MG was the most numerous, with ten of varying types. There were five K3 supercharged models, including the Parnell Special entered by Ian Nickols, two cars entered by Frank Kennington for himself and John Marshall and other examples entered by Bobby Baird and Hector Graham. Other MGs were the Lund Special PB model of Ted Lund, the "R" type Midget of Leonard Gill and E.C. Spero, the J4 Midget of D.A. Wilcocks, the 746cc Midget of David Murray and H.G. Dudley and the unsupercharged 1,250cc T.C. Midget of George Phillips. Five Rileys were entered by Francis Penn, Cuth Harrison, George Nixon, George Burton, and Horace Ripley (reserve driver M.E. Matthias). Peter Clark entered four H.R.Gs for himself, Dudley Folland, Bill Holt and Jack Scott. There were two

This practice photograph at the Manx Arms corner shows two very different MGs. Frank Kennington's Magnette K3 was a non-starter in the race due to supercharger trouble in practice while George Phillips' 1,250cc TC engined special finished fifth. [Manx National Heritage]

In practice, John Marshall rounds the Manx Arms corner in his supercharged 1.087cc MG Magnette K3 entered by fellow Magnette driver Frank Kennington. Marshall was the more fortunate of the two drivers, finishing tenth in the race, while Kennington non-started with supercharger trouble. [Manx National Heritage]

interesting Cooper entries. American dirt-track driver Spike Rhiando entered a 996cc J.A.P. engined car while Dorchester-on-Thames inn-keeper R.M. "Curly" Dryden had a 496cc Norton engine. Gilbert Tyrer and Ken Watkins entered Frazer Nash B.M.W.s. There were single entries of Appleton Special (John Appleton), Alvis (C.G.H. Dunham), Aston Martin (John Rowley and N.I. Bond-Williams), Buckler (a Ford 10 engined tubular chassis special built by the driver Derek Buckler), a Monnier Special (with a two litre Bristol engine, tubular chassis and swing-axle independent front suspension) entered by French driver Maurice Monnier and O.B.M. (a Frazer Nash BMW based "special" entered by Oscar Moore).

Castletown Trophy Entries

The entry of only five cars for the "unlimited" race was very disappointing for the organizers, as they had arranged the race due to complaints from drivers of the larger cars that there were no "proper races" in which they could drive, but only sprints and hill-climbs. Two Alfa Romeos were entered by Dennis Poore (3.8 litres) and Roy Salvadori (2.9 litres). Poore's car was 50013, the ex Tazio Nuvolari car with which Richard Seaman and Hans Ruesch won the 1936 Donington Grand Prix while Salvadori had another ex Nuvolari car, with which the maestro had won the 1935 German Grand Prix. Noel Carr entered a two litre supercharged Alta, and Jack Fairman and Kenneth Bear entered Bugattis. Fairman's was a two litre car and Bear's was a 3.3 litre 1933 Grand Prix car. Despite the poor entry for this new race, the *Isle of Man Times* commented that the races were the best supported Isle of Man car races since the 1914 Tourist Trophy.

Practice

With the event moved from August to May, race day was changed from Thursday to Tuesday, with practices arranged for the evenings of Saturday 21st and Monday 23rd May. Non-arrivals for the British Empire Trophy were Joe Ashmore and Charles Mortimer (both ERA), G.N. Richardson, (ERA Riley) who had mumps, and the Maserati of Lance Seyd. Absent Manx Cup drivers were David Murray and H.G. Dudley (MG), George Burton who had been injured in a crash at home (Riley) and Oscar Moore whose O.B.M. was not ready. All Castletown Trophy entries arrived.

There were also changes of drivers and cars in the Empire Trophy race, Reg Parnell decided to drive his Maserati (entered for Fred Ashmore to drive) and entrusted his "E" type ERA to his Chief Mechanic "Wilkie" Wilkinson. Leslie Brooke's Ferrari was not ready and he drove his old ERA which he had entered for Willie Couper to drive. Leslie Johnson's "works" ERA "E" type would not be ready until the morning of race day, so he practised in C.G.H. Dunham's Alvis which Dunham had entered for both to drive in the Manx Cup. David Hampshire acquired the Parnell-Ashmore ERA "A" type on the eve of the race. Basil de Mattos took over Bobby Baird's MG K3 in the Manx Cup.

An interesting technological first for the Isle of Man marked an expansion of racing in 1948. Two-way continuous radio communication between pits and cars was introduced into the Manx Cup Race by Peter Clark and Jack Scott of the H.R.G. team. Cambridge-based Pye Telecommunications Ltd, which installed it, said that the equipment was light (although, reportedly, it added 40lb extra weight to the cars), neat, compact, yet strong and very reliable. It was claimed on behalf of H.R.G. that it was the first time anywhere that this had been done and Pye announced boldly: "For the first time in racing history." *Motor Sport*, however, questioned whether it was the first time that a racing driver had used radio equipment. It had been tried 26 years earlier, it said. However, it accepted that this was "probably the first race in which radio contact was established between cars and pit." During practice, Clark reported that the system worked well. He had a 40-ft aerial above the radio station

Peter Clark entered an H.R.G team of four cars for himself, Dudley Folland, Bill Holt and Jack Scott. Two, with aerodynamic bodies, were driven by Scott (43) and Clark (37), seen here at Governor's Bridge. The cars had radio communication with the pits, the aerial on Scott's car being clearly visible. [Stan Hughes collection]

which he set up in his Bentley parked in the paddock. There, according to *Motor Sport*, H.R.G. Competitions Manager Marcus Chambers (later to become B.M.C. Competitions Manager) "issued orders to the H.R.G. drivers and received appropriate replies". *The Autocar* commented that the system "amply justified itself" enabling genuine comments to be heard from drivers at various points on the course. The magazine mentioned an

H.R.G. and Pye were quick to advertise their pioneering use of radio between the H.R.G. team cars and the pits during the 1948 race. [Author's collection]

amusing incident during practice when a friend telephoned for information about a particular driver just in time to be told that the driver in question had just "broken his blinking gearbox"! Clark and Scott had cars with aerodynamic bodies, while the other team cars of Folland and Holt had standard bodies.

The weather for both sessions was cool and dry and speeds were high. Saturday's session was relatively uneventful, but Derek Buckler hit the kerb at The Nursery and damaged his steering while Castletown Trophy driver Noel Carr's Alta broke a drive shaft and Sheila Darbishire's ERA ran its big ends. Fastest of the British Empire Trophy contenders were Bob Gerard (ERA) and Tony Rolt (Alfa Romeo) in 3mins 20secs (69.82mph), followed by Reg Parnell's Maserati (3mins 21secs). Leslie Brooke (E.R.A.) and Bob Ansell (Maserati) both lapped in 3mins 24secs. In the Manx Cup practice, the Rileys of Francis Penn and Cuth Harrison led with laps of 3mins 33secs (65.56mph) and 3mins 38secs (64.06mph) respectively. Leslie Johnson (Alvis) was third fastest in 3mins 43secs. Fastest by far of the Castletown Trophy drivers was Dennis Poore with a lap of 3mins 21secs (69.47mph) followed by Roy Salvadori in the other Alfa Romeo (3mins 33secs). Manx Cup drivers Maurice Monnier and John Appleton had problems with their cars which necessitated frantic weekend work.

Monday evening's session was much more eventful. In the British Empire Trophy practice Duncan Hamilton crashed his Maserati into the bags at Onchan, splayed the front wheels and retired to the Manx Arms for a consolatory beer. Earlier, he had been in difficulty with front end damping and a locking rear brake. Plug problems were also prevalent, with Walker, Baring and Emery all affected and Reg Parnell complaining that all

Edward Pool entered his E.R.A. with the intention of sharing the driving with Sheila Darbishire. Pictured at the Manx Arms during practice with Sheila Darbishire at the wheel, the car later ran its big ends and was a non-starter in the race. [Manx National Heritage]

his cars were in trouble. In the combined Manx Cup and Castletown Trophy session, on the left hand bend between Willaston and Cronk-ny-Mona, "Curly" Dryden slid and overturned his Cooper-Norton. He was pinned under the car and extricated by spectators who righted the car! He was lucky to escape with a cut nose and bruises. *The Light Car* thought he was "rather too enthusiastic with the loud pedal". The other Cooper was also in trouble. After delay due to a broken carburettor needle, "Spike" Rhiando's engine seized as he approached the right hand corner at Parkfield at over 100mph. In a heart-stopping moment, the car was all over the road. A crash was averted but the engine was unlikely to be repaired in time for the race. Despite plug problems, Reg Parnell managed the second fastest time of 3mins 12secs (71.61mph) two seconds behind Bob Gerard's pole time of 3mins 10secs (73.49mph). The fastest Manx Cup driver was Cuth Harrison who lapped in 3mins 27secs (67.45mph), four seconds faster than Leslie Johnson. Francis Penn, who had been fastest on Saturday, was not seen on Monday. In the Castletown Trophy, Dennis Poore was again fastest with a lap of 3mins 17secs (70.88mph) with Noel Carr four seconds slower.

This starting grid photograph shows the following cars (or parts of them): 51 Francis Penn (Riley), 35 Spike Rhiando (Cooper), 1 R.J.W. Appleton (Appleton Special), 55 George Nixon (Riley), 47 Maurice Monnier (Monnier Special), 39 Dudley Folland (H.R.G.), 41 Bill Holt (H.R.G.), 15 Henry Kyle (MG), 37 Peter Clark (H.R.G.), 43 Jack Scott (H.R.G.) [Brian Mylchreest collection]

1948 Manx Cup and Castletown Trophy Races – Wins for Nixon and Bear

After heavy overnight rain, which necessitated the use of sand on the Douglas Promenade horse tram tracks, the weather improved during the morning and the sun was shining as the combined grid of 23 Manx Cup and 5 Castletown Trophy cars lined up for the start. Out of the 26 Manx Cup drivers who had practised, the non-starters were "Curly" Dryden (practice crash), Frank Kennington (supercharger trouble) and Leonard Gill, whose MG "R" type had failed scrutineering due to a steering problem. All five of the Castletown Trophy drivers were on the grid.

In pole position was Castletown Trophy driver Dennis Poore whose Alfa Romeo had lapped in 3mins 17secs (70.88mph) in Monday's practice. He shared the front row with the Castletown Trophy Alta of Noel Carr and the fastest Manx Cup driver, Cuth Harrison (Riley), who had lapped in 3mins 27secs ((67.45mph). The second row contained the Castletown Trophy cars of Kenneth Bear (Bugatti) and Roy Salvadori (Alfa Romeo). The latter said later that he had found the circuit very difficult. On row three were the Manx Cup cars of Francis Penn (Riley), Leslie Johnson (Alvis) and Gillie Tyrer (B.M.W.). Spike Rhiando (Cooper J.A.P.) shared the fourth row with the remaining Castletown Trophy driver, Jack Fairman (Bugatti). Row 5 consisted of John Appleton (Appleton Special), George Nixon (Riley) and John Rowley (Aston Martin). They were followed by Maurice Monnier (Monnier Special) and Ted Lund (Lund Special). On row 7 were Dudley Folland (H.R.G.) and George Phillips (MG). Bill Holt (H.R.G.) had row 8 to himself, ahead of the all MG ninth row of Henry Kyle, John Marshall and Basil de Mattos and the all H.R.G tenth row of Peter Clark and Jack Scott. Ken Watkins (B.M.W.), Wilcocks (MG) and Matthias (Riley) formed row 11, with Derek Buckler (Buckler Special) and Ian Nickols (Parnell Special) bringing up the rear.

Cuth Harrison made a good start and led the charge towards the first corner at Parkfield. Before the corner, he was passed by Dennis Poore who immediately had a major problem when his radiator cap opened. Showered with hot water and steam, he was temporarily blinded and swerved off line whereupon Harrison, forced to take avoiding action, hit the bags, quickly followed by Francis Penn. More drivers became involved in the melee, while others found a way past. Poore and Harrison were both able to continue, in eleventh and fourteenth places respectively, and started to carve their ways through the field.

Noel Carr had managed to avoid the Parkfield melee and led the Castletown Trophy for the first two laps, from Kenneth Bear's Bugatti and Francis Penn's Riley. Meanwhile Dennis Poore, taking full advantage of the power of his 3.8 litre Alfa Romeo, charged through the field and was back at the front by the end of the third lap, setting the fastest race lap of 3mins 17secs (70.88mph). By the end of lap 5, he led Bear by 12 seconds. Carr's Alta retired with engine trouble after a pit stop, Jack Fairman's

Bugatti was delayed in the pits and Roy Salvadori's Alfa Romeo made several stops for plug changes before retiring with broken valve springs. Poore's lead, however, was short-lived. He stopped at Parkfield with brake problems and was unable to restart for some three minutes. This delay let Bear into a safe lead of 35 seconds. Poore then stopped at his pit with a retarded magneto in addition to his brake problem. He resumed, but his stops had left him with no chance of catching Bear whose pit crew gave him a "slow down" signal. Further back still, Fairman, still circulating slowly, pushed his car to his pit but managed to continue. Thus Kenneth Bear's pre-war Bugatti, after a trouble-free run, won the Castletown Trophy at an average speed of 62.90mph, with Dennis Poore five laps behind and Jack Fairman a further three laps behind Poore.

In the Manx Cup, Harrison, like Poore, charged through the field after the first lap delay at Parkfield. After five laps at an average of 62.90mph, he led Leslie Johnson by 47 seconds. John Rowley was third, 54 seconds behind Harrison, pursued by Nixon, Phillips and Lund who were respectively 1min 17secs, 1min 24secs and 1min 51secs behind the leader. On only the second lap, Monnier crashed his Special into the bank at Willaston Corner, bending the front axle. Other early retirements were Ian Nickols with gearbox trouble and "Spike" Rhiando with a broken piston, both at three laps.

After five laps, Harrison led Johnson's Alvis by 47 seconds, with Rowley's Aston Martin third, a further nine seconds back.

Although Harrison had made up lost ground and was happier in his Riley than he would be later in his ERA in

Four Riley specials took part in the race. Frank Penn, pictured on Glencrutchery Road, retired after 8 laps with a sticking throttle and brake trouble, while leading the race. [Stan Hughes collection]

the main race, his brakes had been damaged in his first lap crash and locked up during a fast approach to Parkfield on lap 6. Another crash into the bags meant his retirement and a big surprise when he was told that he had been leading the race. His pit crew had not given him a signal and he had been pushing harder than necessary! He had done the fastest lap of the race, 3min 28secs (67.13mph). On the same lap Dudley Folland, who had made an early pit stop, retired with engine trouble after an oil pipe had fractured, and a lap later De Mattos retired with engine trouble. There was more action at Parkfield with both Wilcocks and Kyle spinning their MGs there and Nixon hitting the bags. All were able to continue.

After eight laps Frank Penn's Riley retired with a sticking throttle and brake trouble and Ted Lund retired his MG Special with engine trouble a lap later.

The Hector Graham/Henry Kyle MG Magnette K3 passes through Onchan Village. Driven by Kyle, the car retired on lap 16, out of fuel due to a leaking tank. [The late Alf Caley, Onchan]

This rear view shows George Nixon's winning Riley about to pass the packed grandstand at Governor's Bridge in the middle of the long Governor's Road/Glencrutchery Road straight from Onchan Village past the start/finish to the right hand corner at Parkfield. [Stan Hughes collection]

The winner, George Nixon is congratulated at the finish. He averaged 61.07 mph, finishing 18 seconds ahead of Gillie Tyrer's Frazer Nash B.M.W. 328 and 36 seconds ahead of Leslie Johnson's Alvis. [Onchan District Commissioners]

Wilcocks' MG J4 also retired at nine laps with lubrication trouble. After ten laps, Leslie Johnson, having inherited the lead from Harrison, averaged 60.79mph and led Rowley by 18 seconds and Nixon by 30 seconds. The next three were Tyrer, making good progress in his Frazer Nash BMW, Phillips and Holt, 54secs, 1min 4secs and 2min 51secs respectively behind Johnson. Rowley's Aston Martin was soon overtaken by both Nixon and Tyrer. The latter had an "off" at Willaston, as did Matthias in his Riley, but both were able to continue. Appleton retired his Special at 14 laps with gearbox trouble.

With fifteen laps completed, Johnson's brakes were fading rapidly and his lead over second-placed Nixon was down to only four seconds, with Tyrer also a threat, 23 seconds behind the leader. Rowley was now well back, 56 seconds behind Johnson with Phillips fifth, 14 seconds behind Rowley. Holt was still a distant sixth, three minutes behind Phillips. On lap 16 the Graham/Kyle MG retired, out of fuel due to a leaking tank, and Jack Scott overshot at Cronk-ny-Mona.

Leslie Johnson, pictured in Main Road, Onchan, drove C.G.H. Dunham's Alvis 12/70 to third place, only 36 seconds behind the winner, George Nixon. This pre-war car won the 1951 Manx Cup, driven by Dunham's son, Gerry. [The late Alf Caley, Onchan]

The Buckler Special of Derek Buckler passes the Grandstand pursued by Kenneth Bear in the 3,255cc Bugatti (70) in which he won the Castletown Trophy and the 1,496cc H.R.G. (41) of Bill Holt in which he finished sixth in the Manx Cup. [Malcolm Buckler collection]

Despite a loose exhaust pipe shield, which fell off, Nixon passed Johnson to take the lead on lap 16 and Tyrer took second place from Johnson on lap 17. Nixon went on to take the chequered flag in his first major race with a race average of 61.07mph (5mph less than Bira's 1947 winning average), with Gillie Tyrer 18 seconds behind and the third-placed Leslie Johnson a further 18 seconds back. Rowley was fourth, 1min 24secs behind the winner, and George Phillips fifth at 1min 34secs. The remaining finishers were Holt, Clark, Watkins, Scott, Marshall, Matthias and Buckler, all of whom were one lap behind. Commenting on the performance of the last finisher, Derek Buckler, *The Light Car* said that to finish a gruelling 18 lap road race in what was virtually a home-made trials "special" with a standard Ford Ten engine was deserving of anyone's applause.

1948 Manx Cup Race Results

Tuesday 25th May 1948. Start 2.00pm. 18 laps of 3.8789 miles circuit, total distance 69.82 miles. 23 starters, 12 finishers.

1. George Nixon (1,749cc Riley Special), 1hr 8mins 36secs (61.07mph)
2. Gilbert Tyrer (1,971cc Frazer Nash B.M.W.), 1hr 8mims 54secs (60.80mph)
3. Leslie Johnson (1,844cc Alvis), 1hr 9mins 12secs, (60.53mph)
4. John Rowley (1,950cc Speed Model Aston Martin), 1hr 10mins 0sec (59.84mph)
5. George Phillips (1,250cc MG TC), 1hr 10mins 10secs (59.70mph)

Did not complete the required 18 laps:

6. Bill Holt (1,496cc H.R.G.), 17 laps, 1hr 9mins 51secs, (56.64 mph)
7. Peter Clark (1,496cc H.R.G. Aerodynamic),17 laps, 1hr 10mins 18secs, (56.27mph)

Derek Buckler makes a pit stop in his 1,228cc standard Ford 10 engined tubular chassis Buckler trials special. He damaged his steering when he hit the kerb at the Nursery Hotel bends on the descent into Onchan Village, but still managed to press on to a very creditable finish. [Malcolm Buckler collection]

8. Ken Watkins (1,971cc type 328 Frazer Nash B.M.W.), 17 laps, 1hr 10mins 29secs, (56.13mph)
9. Jack Scott (1,496cc H.R.G. Aerodynamic), 17 laps, 1hr 10mins 31secs, (56.11mph)
10. John Marshall (1,087cc MG K3), 17 laps, 1hr 10mins 36secs, (56.04mph)
11. M. E. Matthias (1,496cc Riley), 16 laps, 1hr 12mins 08secs, (51.62mph)
12. C. D. F. Buckler (1,228cc Buckler Special), 16 laps, 1hr 13mins 23secs, (50.74mph)

Fastest lap: T. C. Harrison (1,986cc Riley), 3mins 28secs (67.13mph)

Retirements:

Lap 2:

Maurice Monnier (Monnier Special) bent front axle at Willaston Corner

Lap 3:

Ian Nickols (1,100cc MG), gearbox trouble

Spike Rhiando (996cc Cooper J.A.P.), piston problems

Lap 5:

Dudley Folland (1,496cc H.R.G. Le Mans Model), broken oil pipe

Cuth Harrison (1,986cc Riley), crash due to damaged brakes

Lap 6:

Basil De Mattos (1,100cc MG), engine trouble

Lap 8:

Frank Penn (1,986cc Riley), brake failure when leading

Lap 9:

Ted Lund (972cc MG PB), engine trouble

D. A. Wilcocks (747cc MG J4), lubrication problems
Lap 14:
John Appleton (1,100cc Appleton Special), gearbox problems
Lap 16:
Hector Graham (1,100cc MG K3), out of fuel.

1948 Castletown Trophy Race Results

Tuesday 25th May 1948. 18 laps of 3.8789 miles circuit, total distance 69.82 miles. 5 starters, 3 finishers.

1. Kenneth Bear (3,255cc Bugatti), 1hr 6mins 36secs (62.90mph)

Did not complete required 18 laps:

2. Dennis Poore (3,800cc Alfa Romeo), 13 laps, 1hr 11mins 51secs (42.11mph)
3. J. E. G. Fairman (1,955cc Bugatti), 10 laps, 1hr 10mins 53secs (32.83mph)

Fastest lap: Dennis Poore (3,800 c.c. Alfa Romeo), 3mins 17secs (70.88mph)
Retirements: Roy Salvadori (2,900cc Alfa Romeo), broken valve springs)
Noel Carr (1,998cc Alta), engine trouble.

1948 British Empire Trophy Race – Geoff Ansell's Win – Reg Parnell's Loss

There were 21 starters for the main race, with Sheila Darbishire a non-starter, having run her big-ends in practice leaving owner Edward Pool without a drive. The Maserati of John Gordon was also a non-starter. Bob Gerard (ERA "B-C" type), was in pole position with a time of 3mins 10secs and had chosen to start from the left (pits) side of the road. He shared the front row with Reg Parnell (Maserati 4CL16 valve) (3mins 12secs) and Tony Rolt (Alfa Romeo 3.4 litre) (3mins 15secs). They were followed by Bob Ansell (Maserati 4CL 16 valve) and Raymond Mays

George Abecassis lines up his Grand Prix Alta on the starting grid. He qualified on the fifth row and had a very short race, hitting the sandbags at Parkfield and then retiring on the second lap with gearbox trouble. [Brian Mylchreest collection]

(ERA "D" type) who had lapped in 3mins 16secs and 3mins 18secs respectively. On the third row were Geoff Ansell and Leslie Brooke (both 3mins 20secs and both driving ERA"B" types), with the Emeryson 4.5 litre of Paul Emery (3mins 21secs). John Bolster (3mins 22secs) and Duncan Hamilton (3mins 23secs), driving ERA "B" type and Maserati 6CM respectively, occupied row 4 ahead of David Hampshire (ERA "A" type) and George Abecassis (G.P. Alta), both having lapped in 3mins 25secs, and "Wilkie" Wilkinson (ERA "E" type) who was four seconds slower. Cuth Harrison was alone on row 6 in his ERA"B" type (3mins 31secs). Anthony Baring (Maserati 6CM) (3mins 35secs), Peter Walker (ERA"B" type) (3mins 42secs) and Guy Jason-Henry (Delahaye 3.6 litre) (3mins 37secs) were on row 7. Gordon Watson's Alta 1.5 litre (3mins 51secs) and Roy Salvadori's old Maserati 4CM (3mins 49secs) made up row 8 with Michael Chorlton (Bugatti Type 51A 1.5 litre) (3mins 51secs) and Leslie Johnson (ERA"E" type) completing the field on the back row.

The race started at almost 4pm, 35 minutes behind schedule. Lady Bromet, wife of the Lieutenant-Governor, had the honour of starting the race. She was deputising for John Cobb who was unable to be present due to the death of his wife. Rolt and Parnell led from the green light, closely followed by Gerard, Bob Ansell and Mays and the rest of the field, with the Emeryson having to be pushed away last. At the end of the lap it was Parnell who led, by two seconds from Rolt, and then Gerard, Bob Ansell, Wilkinson, Geoff Ansell and Brooke. Walker made an early stop for a plug change. Abecassis, who had hit the bags at Parkfield, retired on lap 2 with gearbox trouble, as did Mays (sheared supercharger drive). By the end of lap 2, Rolt was back to fourth. Watson pitted and asked for beer, Bob Ansell overshot at Parkfield and Walker retired with engine trouble on lap 4.

At the end of lap 5, Parnell still led, averaging 69.27mph. Gerard was only two seconds behind, Bob Ansell four seconds behind him and Rolt, Brooke and Geoff Ansell in pursuit. At this stage the fastest laps had been done by Gerard and Bob Ansell, in 3mins 18secs. Then Gerard caused alarm by stopping at the pits with oil loss, which was reported to be from the breather and not causing concern. Wilkinson, after an earlier plug change, retired the "E" type ERA with magneto trouble and the Maseratis of Salvadori and Baring both stopped to change plugs. Peter Walker also retired, after five laps, with a cylinder head problem.

After nine laps Gerard retired at the pits with his off-side rear brake torque plate cracked. The fuel tank was also reported to be suspect. While Parnell increased his average to 69.58mph at the end of the tenth lap, Bob Ansell replaced Bob Gerard as the main challenger, only four seconds in arrears, having lapped at 69.82mph on

Bob Gerard, 1947 winner, rounds Cronk-ny-Mona in his E.R.A. He retired early in the race when a rear brake back plate fractured and the surprise winner, after Reg Parnell's Maserati stopped on the last lap with a fuel feed problem, was novice Geoff Ansell in another E.R.A. [Stenlake Publishing]

laps 8, 9 and 10. Brooke was a further 55 seconds back, followed by Geoff Ansell, Hampshire and Rolt. The latter was slowing after hitting the bags at Parkfield and would retire after twelve laps with the rear axle casing cracked. After ten laps, Salvadori over-revved his engine and retired with valve trouble, Tony Rolt was out with a broken rear axle casing and Paul Emery with transmission trouble.

On lap 13, Bob Ansell's consistently fast driving paid off as he took the lead from Reg Parnell with a lap of 3min 15secs, prompting Parnell to speed up with successive laps of 3mins 18secs, 3mins 16secs and 3mins 14secs. While this battle raged, others continued to have problems. Watson changed plugs, Johnson hit the bank at Cronk-ny-Mona but continued, the Emeryson had both oil and radiator trouble before retiring at Cronk-ny-Mona on lap 12 with broken transmission and Hamilton spun at Parkfield.

After 15 laps Ansell led, averaging 69.92mph. Parnell bided his time, six seconds behind. There was then a huge gap to Brooke, 83 seconds behind Parnell, with Geoff Ansell, Hampshire and Bolster in the next three positions. Five laps later, Ansell had increased his average to 70.19mph, with Parnell (70.15mph) only two seconds behind. Hampshire had taken fourth place from Geoff Ansell.

On lap 21, Parnell regained the lead from Bob Ansell and promptly set the fastest lap of the race in 3mins 13secs (72.35mph). He opened a seven seconds gap, which he had doubled by the end of lap 25. By then Geoff Ansell had passed both Hampshire and Brooke (who had brake problems) but was 2mins 53secs behind the leader. Harrison was now sixth following Bolster's retirement at Willaston with a broken half-shaft. Meanwhile, melting tar at Parkfield caused Jason-Henry to spin the Delahaye and stop round the corner. Quick work by the marshals created a narrow gap which enabled Parnell to squeeze through. Chorlton, in clouds of steam, pitted his Bugatti for fuel and water, Hamilton retired on lap 22 with engine trouble and Baring had a blow-off valve problem.

On Lap 29 Bob Ansell's fine drive ended. The brakes of his green Maserati failed on the descent into Onchan Village as he caught Leslie Brooke, who was shown the blue flag to warn him that he was about to be overtaken. Seeing the flag, Brooke went wide and slowed, whereupon the Maserati bumped the ERA in the rear and pushed it into the sandbags. Ansell engaged first gear, over-revved and, although this got him under way again, by Governor's Bridge he was brought to a halt in a cloud of a smoke with a conrod through the side of the engine. His retirement left Parnell with a lead of 3mins 34secs over Geoff Ansell who led third man Hampshire by 33 seconds. Brooke was fourth, Harrison fifth.

By now Leslie Johnson had caused a sensation in his "E" type ERA. Although he owned the controlling interest in the company, he had received strict orders not to exceed 5,500rpm during the race. The engine allegedly could go up to 8,000rpm. Despite this limitation, his lack of practice, the fact that he had never driven the car before, and the car's tendency to weave due to excessive wear in the steering and his earlier bump at Cronk-ny-

The Maseratis of Duncan Hamilton (36) and Reg Parnell (40) take the hairpin at Cronk-ny-Mona in close company. Parnell retired on the last lap with a fuel feed problem while Hamilton retired on lap 36 with engine trouble. [Stenlake Publishing]

Mona, he was sixth at the end of lap 30 and equalled Reg Parnell's fastest lap of the race at 72.35mph. This new record was faster in average speed, as well as in time, than Seaman's 1936 record average of 72.00mph, resolving the anomaly caused by the 1936 course being allegedly 213 yards longer than the post-war course.

When Jason-Henry's Delahaye stalled at the Nursery bends, he jumped out and threw his helmet (leather, fortunately) at the engine. This had no effect but, calming down, he repaired his broken throttle cable and continued. Brooke, slowing with brake problems, overshot twice at Willaston and was soon down to sixth. Chorlton's gear lever broke and, after giving it to his pit crew, he continued, grasping the stump of the lever between finger and thumb.

Reg Parnell pressed on, leading by more than a lap. His fuel was running low but this did not concern him. As at the race in Jersey the previous month, he had a spare

The winning E.R.A. of Geoff Ansell passes the Isle of Man Bank in Main Road, Onchan. Although he was lucky to inherit Reg Parnell's apparently certain victory when the latter stopped with a fuel feed problem on the last lap he nevertheless drove very creditably in only his second major road race. [Manx National Heritage]

five-gallon tank strapped to the side of the car. Only on starting the last lap, on his way to what seemed such a certain victory that the finishing marshal had his race number out ready to greet him at the finish, did he discover a problem. When he switched over to the spare tank on his approach to Parkfield Corner the Maserati spluttered to a halt round the corner in Ballanard Road. When Parnell failed to appear, his pit crew took a can of fuel and ran in the wrong direction, back up the course towards Governor's Bridge. Meanwhile Geoff Ansell, in his blue B-type ERA, passed Parnell to unlap himself and completed another lap to seize the lead as Parnell desperately tried to overcome his predicament. No fuel was getting through from the spare tank. He was "like the starving man on the raft with a tin of food and no opener," reported *The Motor* later. Not knowing what the problem was, but presuming that it might be an air-lock, Parnell tried to free it by hammering the spare tank until he dented it. He even punctured it and finally tore the fuel pipe away but achieved nothing. Only later was it discovered that the main tank had been split and a lack of air pressure in both tanks had prevented the flow of fuel. "Seldom has a race been so nearly won only to be lost," reported *Motor Sport* later.

Thus Geoff Ansell took his first victory in only his second major road race, at an average of 67.71mph. David Hampshire took a creditable, if surprising, second place in his Delage, 43 seconds back. Leslie Brooke was third, 1min 34secs behind Ansell. Cuth Harrison, Leslie Johnson and Gordon Watson occupied the next three places, respectively one, two and three laps behind the winner. After their troubles Guy Jason-Henry (four laps behind) and Michael Chorlton (six laps behind) finished seventh and eighth, while Anthony Baring was classified as the ninth and last finisher despite completing only 24 laps.

Back at the pits a dispirited Reg Parnell waved away the autograph hunters while commiserating with Bob Ansell on his earlier retirement. Fellow competitors offered their sympathy but it appeared to take a lot of persuading by Parnell's wife to convince him that it was not his fault that the Maserati had failed. His excellent driving was much admired, particularly by Alf Francis (later to become mechanic to Stirling Moss) who described Parnell as the Moss of his day and commented on the way in which his wheels passed over exactly the same spot at the pits on every lap of the race.

1948 British Empire Trophy Race Results

Tuesday 25th May 1948. Start 4.00pm. 36 laps of 3.8789 miles circuit, total distance 139.64 miles. 21 starters, 9 finishers.

1. Geoffrey Ansell (1,488cc ERA R9B), 2hrs 3mins 45secs (67.71mph)
2. David Hampshire (1,494cc ERA R1A), 2hrs 4mins 28secs (67.32mph)
3. Leslie Brooke (1,488cc ERA R7B), 2hrs 5mins 19secs (66.86mph).

Did not complete the required 36 laps:

4. T. C. Harrison (1,488cc ERA R1B), 35 laps, 2hrs 3mins 46secs (65.82mph).
5. Leslie Johnson (1,488cc "E" type ERA GP2), 34 laps, 2hrs 4mins 00secs (63.82mph).
6. G. M. Watson (1,490cc Alta), 33 laps, 2hrs 6mins 2secs (60.94mph)
7. G. Jason-Henry (3,557cc Delahaye), 32 laps, 2hrs 9mins 20secs (57.58mph)
8. M. C. Chorlton (1,498cc Bugatti), 30 laps, 2hrs 5mins 17secs (55.73mph)
9. A. A. Baring (1,496cc Maserati 6CM), 24 laps, 2hrs 6mins 17secs (44.23mph).

Fastest lap: Reg Parnell (1,496cc Maserati 4CL) and Leslie Johnson (1,488cc "E" type E.R.A.) 3mins 13secs, (72.35mph). New lap record.

Retirements:

Lap 2:
Raymond Mays (1,488cc ERA R4B), sheared supercharger drive
George Abecassis (1,490cc Alta), gear box problem.

Lap 5:
W. E. Wilkinson ("E" type ERA GP1), ignition timing fault.
P. D. C. Walker (1,488cc ERA R10B), cylinder head problem

Lap 9:
Bob Gerard (1,488cc ERA R14B), cracked brake backplate

Lap 10:
Roy Salvadori (1,496cc Maserati 4CM), valve problems.

Lap 12:
Paul Emery/Robert Baird (4,470cc Emeryson), transmission failure
Tony Rolt (3,442cc Alfa Romeo), cracked back axle casing

Lap 22:
Duncan Hamilton (1,496cc Maserati 6CM), engine trouble.

Lap 25:
John Bolster (1,488cc ERA R5B), broken half-shaft

Lap 28:
Bob Ansell (1,496cc Maserati 4CL), broken connecting rod.

Lap 35:
Reg Parnell (1,496cc Maserati 4CL), failure of auxiliary fuel tank feed.

Reaction

At the presentation, Earl Howe said that there was no track in England where cars could be tuned up. He appreciated what the Island had done in providing the opportunity to stage events in the best traditions of British sportsmanship and commented that the results had shown that British built cars were still in the forefront. In reply, the Lieutenant Governor said that he hoped that the races would be a permanent feature of the Manx season. They were a splendid test for cars, drivers and manufacturers.

The motoring Press was complimentary. *The Light Car* praised "a pretty slick piece of organisation" and described the Press arrangements (much criticised in 1947) as "top of the class". *The Autocar* found the Press facilities and scoreboard "the best in British racing since the War" and said that valuable lessons in car preparation and race organisation had been learned. *Motor Sport* said that the race organisation was really first class and that Rodney Walkerley (Sports Editor of *The Motor*) gave an excellent commentary. The Press were "allowed commendable freedom and were very well served indeed with information, not forgetting refreshments". *Motor Sport*'s Editor William Boddy commented that "the IOM really is a delightful place" and mentioned racing cars being driven around Douglas before and after the race with no restrictions, well-built policemen who were friendly to all, plentiful food and the keenness of nearly all the inhabitants. He said that he was sorry to leave this island of comic firemen, horse-drawn trams and "free-and-easydom".

Motor Sport also devoted considerable space to details of drivers' clothing, even to the colours of individuals' overalls. Headgear was woefully inadequate by modern standards, with the majority wearing leather or cloth helmets. Some had "crash-hats", one wore a cap back to front, and two were bare-headed! Helmets did not become compulsory until 1952.

The Isle of Man Press made no criticisms and reported none. The local newspapers reported that Ronaldsway Airport had been very busy on race day, with 165 aircraft operations. A total of 71 charter aircraft ranging in size from Austers carrying one passenger to 24 seat Douglas Dakotas had brought 310 passengers from England, Scotland and Northern Ireland, with British European Airways scheduled flights bringing a further 128, making a total of 438 passengers in all. The normal schedule was 12 aircraft per day in and out.

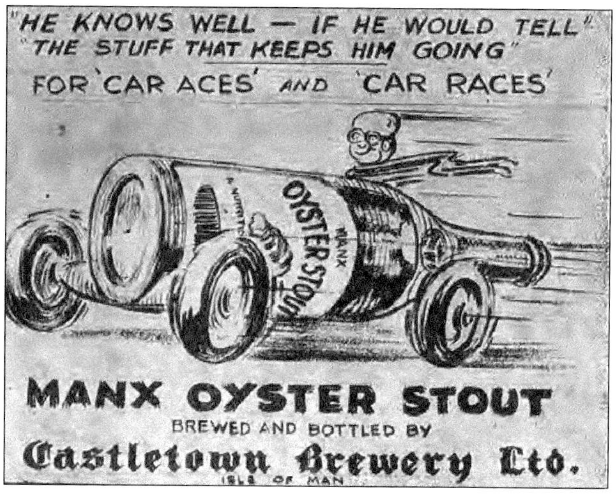

This Castletown Brewery advertisement in the Official Programme reflects an amazingly relaxed attitude to drinking and driving in the early post-war years. [British Racing Drivers' Club]

1949 – Gerard's Second Manx Victory – Heath's Manx Cup

Planning

In December 1948, the announcement that the 1949 race day would be Thursday 26th May caused controversy. The 1948 date (Tuesday 25th May) had been chosen because it was after the Whit holiday weekend, when the Isle of Man Steam Packet Company's summer sailing schedule would be in force, with double daily sailings between Liverpool and Douglas. Although the 1949 date was in the same week as in 1948, the Whit holiday of 1949 was to be 6th June, two weeks later than in 1948. This meant that summer sailings schedule would not start until 3rd June. The *Isle of Man Examiner* commented that the season would not begin until Saturday 4th June, people could not be induced to come to the Island in May, and that the Steam Packet Company could not be blamed for declining to operate services before traffic expectations justified it.

On the recommendation of its Race Committee, Tynwald approved a grant of £1,000 for the 1949 races, with an additional £400 guarantee against loss, plus the cost of haulage, police, fire and ambulance services, half the cost of telephones (approximately £200), a £700 guarantee against loss in shipping costs for competing cars and £500 to attract star foreign drivers. The Committee reported that the 1948 races had been "reasonably successful", with grandstand receipts and programme sales considerably down on 1947 (£878 compared with £1,233 in 1947). As the Steam Packet Company would not operate double sailings and would find it difficult to carry race cars in addition to normal traffic, the BRDC arranged to charter a Tank Landing Craft which could carry 130 cars. This would make two trips at a cost of £500 per trip and there was a demand for non-race bookings to take up spare space. Therefore the £700 guarantee against loss was thought to be justified, as the Steam Packet Company had been paid £643 for transporting race cars in 1948. However the *Isle of Man Times* reported on 16th April that the Tank Landing Craft had proved too expensive and that the Steam Packet Company had been asked, and agreed, to do what they could to bring competitors' cars to the Island in time. This would mean the closest co-operation between the company and the race competitors, many of whom would have to travel earlier than would have been necessary if daily double sailings had been in force.

The Autocar announced in March that the British Empire Trophy and Manx Cup were to be run to the same formulae and over the same distances (40 laps and 36 laps respectively) as in 1948 but that the Castletown Trophy Race had been dropped.

The BBC arranged to broadcast a commentary on the last half hour of the Empire Trophy race from 5.30pm on the Light Programme. The commentators were to be Raymond Glendenning and Murray Walker at the Grandstand with Alan Clarke and Leslie Adams at Cronk-ny-Mona. Arrangements were made for the newsreel filming by Gaumont, British Movietone and Pathe.

British Empire Trophy Entries

The race attracted 25 entries. Despite announcements in January and April, confirmed in *The Autocar* after entries closed, that Bira would drive a Scuderia Ambrosiana Maserati, his name did not appear in the Official Programme. There were, however, eight Maseratis in the entry list. Three were from Scuderia Ambrosiana, the drivers being Reg Parnell, Luigi Villoresi and Fred Ashmore, while Ecurie Geneve entered the Swiss hill-climb driver Ernst Ramseyer. Also there were four private Maserati entries – David Murray (in Parnell's 1948 car), Bob Ansell, Roy Salvadori and Anthony Baring. Eight ERAs were entered. The 1947 winner, Bob Gerard, had recently won the Jersey race and was a pre-race favourite, while there were two 1948 winners over the course – Empire Trophy winner Geoff Ansell and Manx Cup winner George Nixon. Other ERA drivers were 1948 runner-up David Hampshire, Cuth Harrison, Peter Walker, John Bolster (entrant Peter Bell) and Leslie Johnson ("E" type entered by T.A.S.O. Mathieson, who had crashed his Bugatti in Marina Road during the 1933 Mannin Moar). Johnson's car was reckoned to be as fast as the fastest Maserati. Altas were entered by George Abecassis (shared with John Heath) and Gordon Watson. There was a single twelve-cylinder 1.5 litre supercharged Ferrari Grand Prix car entered by Scuderia Ferrari for Peter Whitehead, who was back after a year recovering from air crash injuries. The Ferrari had run in the Jersey race when it was handicapped by wet roads, but was expected to be faster that the Maseratis and Johnson's ERA if the roads were dry. Film Director Michael Chorlton had replaced his Bugatti with a C.D.L. (with Bugatti engine) which he intended to share with J. Boothby. Geoff Richardson entered his R.R.A. and Archie Butterworth had his Steyr powered A.J.B. Rob Walker entered two cars, a 3.6 litre Delahaye and a 3.4 litre Alfa Romeo, for both of which he nominated two drivers, Guy Jason-Henry and Tony Rolt. Finally, Ecurie Belge entered a 4.5 litre Talbot for Johnny Claes. Son of a Scottish mother and a Belgian father, he was well known in the world of jazz for his band "Johnny Claes and his Clay Pigeons" in which fellow racing driver Les Leston played. Twice winner of the Liege-Rome-Liege Rally (once with a clean sheet), he was named 1953 Driver of the Year by the Guild of Motoring Writers.

Manx Cup Entries

There were 30 entries for the Manx Cup. Six were Coopers with "Curly" Dryden again entering his 499cc Norton engined model, and five other drivers entering 996cc models. They were John Cooper, Spike Rhiando, George Abecassis/John Heath, Eric Winterbottom and the 19 years old Stirling Moss looking forward to his first race outside England in the dry-sump 1,000cc J.A.P. engined car in which he had won the Goodwood Easter Handicap (beating the similar car of George Abecassis by 25 seconds). Supercharged MGs were entered by Basil de Lissa, George Phillips, Hector Graham (reserve D.H. Kyle) and Dick Jacobs. Among the more interesting cars, John Wyer entered a two litre Ferrari 166 for Dudley Folland, which was the most modern and fastest car in the entry. Wyer and Folland were both directors of Monaco Motor and Engineering Co. Ltd of Watford. Frank Kennington had a 1,100cc Cisitalia, Ken Hutchinson entered a B.M.W. engined Veritas and Major Guy Gale entered what must have been a very early example of a Connaught, powered by a 1,767cc pushrod Lea-Francis engine. Rileys were the choice of Ken Downing (entered by George Nixon, the 1948 winner), Gordon Shillito (entrant Cuth Harrison), Neville Gee and Jack Fairman. There were three examples of H.R.G. to be driven by Peter Clark/Jack Scott, Bill Holt (entrant Dudley Folland) and Hugh Clapp. There were also single examples of Aston Martin (St. John Horsfall), H.W.-Alta (John Heath/George Abecassis), R.D.L. Lea Francis (Kenneth Rose/Gilbert Baird), I.R.A. (Irish Racing Automobiles), the car was formerly known as the H.G. Dobbs offset Riley, and the driver was Joe Kelly), Baird Meteorite (Bobby Baird), B.M.W. (Ken Watkins), Spikins Special (Basil de Mattos – entrant Bob Spikins), Lund Special (Ted Lund – entrant N.S. Utley) and Alvis (Gerry Dunham).

Practice

With race day reverting to Thursday, the two practice sessions reverted to Tuesday and Wednesday, from 6pm to 9pm. The *Isle of Man Times* reported that only six race cars had made the ferry crossing on the preceding Friday, although 18 had been booked, and wondered how the remainder would reach the Island. Part of the reason for the absences may have been the withdrawal of no less than nine of the British Empire Trophy competitors. *The Motor* reported that there had not been sufficient time to repair cars which had suffered crash or mechanical damage during the British Grand Prix meeting at Silverstone on 14th May, only a week before the cars needed to be brought to the Island, and said that "workshop lights had been glowing through many nights and into the pale dawn". The problem must have been exacerbated by lack of flexibility in late ferry bookings due to the limited winter schedule still being in force. The non-arrivals were Leslie Johnson's "E" type ERA (reportedly to be out of action for some time), Peter Whitehead's "works" Ferrari, the Maseratis of Bob Ansell, Luigi Villoresi, Roy Salvadori, Anthony Baring and Ernst Ramseyer, Archie Butterworth's A.J.B. and Gordon Watson's Alta. One driver, John Bolster, had been injured in a crash at Silverstone and was replaced at the wheel of Peter Bell's ERA (fitted with two stage supercharged engine from R5B) by St. John ("Jock") Horsfall who had been a British secret agent during the war. Bob Gerard had changed engines after Silverstone but had to make a last minute change of cylinder head, reverting to the head used at Silverstone, which Cuth Harrison changed to an older engine from R1B. The Manx Cup entry was much less reduced, the only missing competitors being Bill Holt (H.R.G.), Ken Hutchinson (Veritas), and Guy Gale (Connaught).

The fastest driver in British Empire Trophy practice was Reg Parnell, lapping at 3mins 06secs (75.08mph) in his Maserati. This time was three seconds faster that Peter Walker in his ERA and was a new unofficial lap record. George Abecassis set the third fastest lap of 3mins 13secs in the Alta which he was sharing with John Heath, but the lap was discounted when Abecassis became a non-starter due to his Manx Cup practice crash. John Heath had not set a time in the car and therefore, although he could drive in the race, the car was relegated to the back of the grid. The next fastest, sharing the second row, were the ERA drivers Bob Gerard and St. John Horsfall (the latter deputising for the injured John Bolster) with times of 3mins 14secs and 3mins 15secs respectively.

There were two sensations in Manx Cup practice. One was the incredible speed of 19 years old Stirling Moss. After George Abecassis had taken his Vincent-H.R.D engined Cooper round in a creditable 3mins 18secs (70.53mph) Moss lapped his Cooper-J.A.P. in 3mins 13secs (72.35mph) which gave him pole position. This superb lap matched Reg Parnell's British Empire Trophy fastest lap in 1948 and also equalled the time which would have put Abecassis' Alta in third place on the British Empire Trophy grid! It was an apt reply to the doubters who thought that young Moss was driving beyond his ability. The other sensation was provided by the unfortunate Abecassis, also in a Cooper, shared, like his Alta, with John Heath. Trying to beat Moss' time, he lost control at an estimated 100mph at Governor's Bridge when the throttle stuck wide open. He had attached a piece of wood to brace himself and this had moved, jamming the pedal. He careered from pavement to pavement before crashing into a tree. According to *The Motor* the car was "smashed to pieces." Amazingly, Abecassis emerged from the wreckage with just a violent shaking and bruises all over, torn muscles and abrasions to his legs. He was "a very fortunate young man" reckoned *The Motor*. "Lucky to be alive," said *The Autocar*. It was the end of his racing for a while and he watched the races from the Grandstand, "stiff as a poker and wobbly on his legs" according to *The Motor*, using two mops as improvised crutches.

1949 Manx Cup Race – Heath the Victor – Moss the Phenomenon

The weather was sunny, with a strong breeze. The spectator attendance was described as "good" although, typical of Manx reluctance to pay to see what could be watched elsewhere for free, the grandstand was not well filled. Control of it was found wanting too. Non-Press people managed to get into Press seats and disturb reporters with their idle chatter, while *Motor Sport* reported that ragged boys displayed great ability in climbing into the stand from the back and were joined later in the afternoon by children on their way home from school.

In addition to the injured George Abecassis, Spike Rhiando (Cooper) Hector Graham (MG) and Bobby Baird (Meteorite) were non-starters, so that 23 cars assembled on the starting grid, with engines ranging from 500cc single-cylinder (Dryden's Cooper) to 2,000cc twelve-cylinders (Folland's Ferrari). Although unsupercharged cars up to 2.5 litres were allowed, none of those entered exceeded 2 litres. Stirling Moss (1,000cc Coooper J.A.P.), "full of hope and chewing gum" as he told the *Isle of Man Times* reporter before the race, was in pole position due to his 3mins 13secs (72.35mph) practice lap. He shared the front row with Eric Winterbottom (1,000cc Cooper Vincent) who had been third in practice with a lap of 3mins 31secs. Second place on the grid was vacant, due to Abecassis' crash in practice, but the loan of Abecassis' clutch enabled Winterbottom to start the race, despite stopping at Cronk-ny-Mona on the parade lap. The second row consisted of "Jock" Horsfall who did not start (3mins 32secs) and Dudley Folland's Ferrari, (3mins 33secs) with Gordon Shillito's Riley (3mins 35secs) John Heath's H.W. Alta (3mins 36secs) and Basil de Mattos' Spikins (3mins 38secs) on the third row. Joe Kelly (IRA, 3mins 38secs) and Frank Kennington (Cisitalia, 3mins 40secs) shared the fourth row. Behind them were John Cooper (3mins 40secs) Jack Fairman with his Riley (3mins 41secs) and Basil de Lissa (MG, 3mins 42secs). Ken Downing's Riley and Dick Jacons' MG made up the sixth row (both 3mins 43secs) ahead of Gerry Dunham's Alvis (3mins 45secs), Norman Gee's Riley (3mins 49secs) and Peter Clark's H.R.G. (3mins 50secs). Kenneth Rose (R.D.L) and Ted Lund (Lund Special) shared row seven with times of 3mins 55secs and 4mins 01secs respectively and the final row consisted of Hugh Clapp's H.R.G. (4mins 03secs), Ken Watkins' BMW (4mins 06secs) and George Phillips (4mins 09secs).

From the green light, Moss shot into the lead, where he was to stay until three laps from the end. At the end of the lap, Basil de Mattos (Spikins Special) was second, followed by Winterbottom, Kelly and Heath but George Phillips had already retired his MG with engine trouble.

Moss quickly established a 30 seconds lead and was signalled to slow down. He had almost lapped Watkins' B.M.W.. By the end of lap 5, however, Folland's Ferrari was up to second, averaging 64.89mph compared with

The Coopers of Stirling Moss (7) and Eric Winterbottom (11) on Ballanard Road. Moss was the sensation of both practice and race, starting from pole and leading until magneto failure forced his retirement. Winterbottom retired with a cylinder head problem. [Stan Hughes collection]

1949 saw the Manx debut of six of the rear-engined cars manufactured by John Cooper and his father, Charles. John drove a 996cc JAP engine model, seen here at the Manx Arms in Onchan. He finished fifth, a lap behind the winner John Heath. Ten years later, Jack Brabham would win the World Championship in a Cooper. [Manx National Heritage]

Moss' 66.69mph. John Heath (64.00mph) was third in his Alta, de Mattos (63.59mph) was down to fourth and Gordon Shillito (63.53mph) was fifth in Cuth Harrison's Riley. Shillito, who was the same age as Moss, had been lectured by Harrison about wild driving in practice and appeared to have settled down. Frank Kennington's Cisitalia was sixth, averaging 62.78mph. "Curly" Dryden stopped his Cooper Norton at Cronk-ny-Mona, restarted, but retired later.

On lap 6, Moss, Folland and Heath all had the same lap time – 3mins 29secs (66.81mph) but Folland soon retired at the pits with clutch failure. Soon de Mattos also retired with brake failure after going up the escape road at Cronk-ny-Mona and Winterbottom slowed due to one cylinder intermittently failing to fire. By the end of lap 10, Moss was averaging 66.24mph and had again been signalled to slow. He led Heath (65.19mph) by 34 seconds. Shillito (64.20mph) was 33 seconds further back, followed by Kennington, Winterbottom, John Cooper (also on one cylinder, due to an oiled plug) and Neville Gee (Riley).

Winterbottom soon retired. Jack Fairman's Riley put a conrod through the side of the engine after lapping in 3mins 28secs. This was only two seconds slower than the fastest lap of the race set by Moss, which was a new Manx Cup record, one second faster than Bira's fastest lap in 1947. Ted Lund's MG special had fuel feed problems, Ken Watkins' B.M.W. had gearbox failure after earlier taking to an escape road, and Kenneth Rose retired his R.D.L. with no oil pressure, having earlier had a spin at Parkfield. Basil de Lissa hit the bags at Onchan (twice, on consecutive laps) and the hedge at Cronk-ny-Mona, before retiring at the pits with big-end failure, nearly collecting people walking in the pit road. Dick Jacobs' MG developed clutch slip when he was challenging for fifth place but he persevered to the finish. Other drivers with problems were Gerry Dunham who spun his Alvis through 180 degrees at Nursery Bends, Peter Clark who had transmission problems, and Joe Kelly (third in the early laps until slowed by a plug change) who stopped at the pits with oil line trouble. All three reached the finish.

Meanwhile, with a 33 seconds lead over second-placed John Heath and heading for an apparently certain victory, Stirling Moss was approaching the pits at the end of his 15th lap when disaster struck. According to *The Light Car*, the previously crisp-sounding engine of his Cooper J.A.P. went "strangely flat." *The Motor* said it "spluttered and slowed." *The Autocar* said the engine cut out. Moss sped into the pit road, jumped out of the car, removed his helmet and joined his father and the mechanics in a huddle under the bonnet. Precious seconds ticked away. The action in replacing a plug was "frenzied," according to *The Autocar*. Even so, it was not fast enough. The delay was too long. The car refused to restart quickly – despite a push. Eventually it got going but by now Moss had been reduced to fourth place. Worse was to befall him, however. As he came to Parkfield Corner, just a few hundred yards away from the pits, the engine died. The magneto drive had sheared. With a sympathetic wave of the hand, John Heath passed Moss and went on to a

John Heath (1,960cc H.W.-Alta), seen here at the Manx Arms, won the Manx Cup after inheriting the lead when Stirling Moss retired his 996cc Cooper with magneto drive failure. Moss had a sensational drive and, with a 33 seconds lead, had looked certain to win until bad luck intervened. [Manx National Heritage]

Seen passing the Manx Arms, Frank Kennington drove this unusual 1,090cc Fiat engined Cisitalia to third place behind John Heath's 1,960cc H.W.-Alta and Gordon Shillito's 1,986cc Riley. [Manx National Heritage]

comfortable win, more than a minute ahead of Shillito on the last lap.

When he crossed the line, however, no one bothered to give him the chequered flag or display his number. Jubilant mechanics in his pit waved aloft an open golf umbrella but, in the absence of any official signal, Heath wisely continued on his way. His H.W. Alta did a further lap before he was flagged down! Gordon Shillito came home second, 1min 8secs in arrears with Frank Kennington third, a further 1min 32secs behind Shillito. Fourth finisher Neville Gee had gained on Kennington late in the race and finished a further 46 seconds back, the last driver to complete the full 18 laps. The remaining finishers were John Cooper (Cooper), Gerry Dunham (Alvis), Dick Jacobs (MG), all completing 17 laps with Joe Kelly (IRA) and Hugh Clapp (H.R.G.) completing 16 laps and Peter Clark (H.R.G.) completing 12 laps. The fastest lap was set by Stirling Moss – 3mins 26secs (67.78mph) and John Heath's winning average of 65.32mph was 4.25mph faster than George Nixon's 1948 winning average.

The Motor commented that the general impression was that "these Cooper 1000s are a phenomenon and Moss phenomenal".

1949 Manx Cup Race Results

Thursday 26th May 1949. Start 2.00pm. 18 laps of 3.8789 miles circuit, total distance 69.82 miles. 23 starters, 10 finishers.

1. John Heath (1,960cc H.W. Alta), 1hr 4mins 8secs (65.32 mph)
2. Gordon Shillito (1,986cc Riley), 1hr 5mins 16secs (64.18 mph)
3. Frank Kennington (1.090cc Cisitalia D46), 1hr 6mins 48secs (62.71 mph)
4. Neville Gee (1,496cc Riley), 1hr 7mins 30secs (62.06mph).

The following failed to complete the required 18 laps:

5. John Cooper (996cc Cooper-J.A.P.), 17 laps, 1hr 5mins 12secs (60.67 mph).
6. Gerry Dunham Jnr (1,844cc Alvis), 17 laps, 1hr 5mins 20secs (60.56 mph).
7. R. W. "Dick" Jacobs (1,087cc MG T-type), 17 laps, 1hr 8mins 18secs (57.92 mph).
8. Joe Kelly (1,726cc IRA), 16 laps, 1hr 5mins 09secs (57.16 mph).
9. Hugh Clapp (1,047cc H.R.G.), 12 laps, 1hr 6mins 4secs (56.36 mph)
10. Peter Clark (1,047cc H.R.G.), 12 laps, 1hr 14mins 20secs (37.57 mph)

Fastest lap: Stirling Moss (996cc Cooper-J.A.P.), 3mins 26secs (67.78 mph).

Retirements:

Lap 2: George Phillips (MG), engine

Lap 5: "Curly" Dryden (Cooper-Norton).

Lap 6: Basil de Mattos (Volkswagen-suspended, Lea-Francis powered Spikins), failed brakes

Lap 7: Basil de Lissa (MG), big end failure.

Ken Downing (Riley)

Ted Lund (Lund Special), carburettor problems

Lap 8: Jack Fairman (Riley), broken con rod.

Lap 9: Dudley Folland (Ferrari 166C), clutch failure

Lap 10: Ken Watkins (B.M.W. 328), gearbox

Kenneth Rose (R.D.L.), failed oil pressure

Lap 14: Eric Winterbottom (Cooper-Vincent-H.R.D.), cylinder head

Lap 15: Stirling Moss (Cooper-J.A.P.), slipped magneto drive.

1949 British Empire Trophy Race – Bob Gerard's Second Manx Victory

Although the nine non-arrivals had reduced the entry to 16 cars, they all lined up on the grid, with John Heath at the wheel of the Alta which the injured George Abecassis had entered for both of them to drive. Heath was relegated to the back row of the grid because the practice time which would have placed the car on the front row had been set by

This photograph of the start shows Reg Parnell (Maserati, 30), Peter Walker (E.R.A., 20), Bob Gerard (E.R.A., 14), and St. John Horsfall (E.R.A., 6). Gerard and Horsfall finished first and second respectively, with Parnell and Walker both retiring. [Brian Mylchreest collection]

Abecassis before he crashed his Cooper.

Reg Parnell's Maserati was on pole. His practice time of 3mins 06secs (75.08mph) was an unofficial course record – a full four seconds faster than the previous fastest time. The only other car on the front row, due to the absence of Abecassis, was the ERA of Peter Walker with a time of 3mins 09secs. Behind them were the ERAs of Bob Gerard (3mins 14secs) and Jock Horsfall, one second slower. The third row contained the Alfa Romeo of Tony Rolt (3mins 16secs) and the ERAs of Cuth Harrison (3mins 17secs) and David Hampshire (3mins 19secs), while row 4 consisted of the Maseratis of David Murray (3mins 19secs) and Fred Ashmore (3mins 20secs). Geoff Ansell (ERA, 3mins 26secs), Jonnny Claes (Ecurie Belge Talbot, 3mins 29secs) and Michael Chorlton (C.D.L., 3mins 30secs) formed row 5, followed by Geoff Richardson's R.R.A. (3mins 36secs) and George Nixon's ERA (3mins 40secs). Guy Jason-Henry in his Delahaye (3mins 57secs) was on the back row alongside John Heath in his Alta, who had not set a time.

From the start, Parnell established a clear lead in his Maserati. He lapped at 3mins 18secs from a standing start, seven seconds faster that his Scuderia Ambrosiana team-mate Fred Ashmore. They were followed at the end of the first lap by Gerard (12 seconds off the lead), Walker, Horsfall, Rolt, Murray and Hampshire. Walker passed Gerard on lap 2. Meanwhile Parnell extended his lead, lapping in 3mins 11secs on lap 2, 3mins 15secs on lap 3 and 3mins 16secs on lap 4, building a lead of almost 30 seconds. Then, as in 1948, disaster struck while he was leading the race. It happened on lap 5 at the Manx Arms in Onchan. His supercharger drive sheared, forcing him to retire and he walked in to the grandstand area to help in Ashmore's pit. On the same lap, Murray stopped for a plug change.

With five laps completed, Ashmore, averaging 68.65mph, led Walker by four seconds. Gerard was a further second behind Walker and led Horsfall by a second. Rolt was a further 20 seconds back. Ashmore was reported to have circled a lamp-post in the mouth of the escape road at Parkfield but continued without losing the lead.

On lap 7 Walker's brakes began to fail and Gerard passed him. Two laps later, Walker stopped for adjustments, losing third place to Horsfall. At the same time Nixon pitted to change a front wheel which had been bent in an impact with bags at the Manx Arms corner in Onchan.

After ten laps, Ashmore's average was 69.75mph and his lead over Gerard was 13 seconds. Gerard led Horsfall by two seconds. Fourth man Walker was 24 seconds off the lead but over a minute ahead of Rolt, who was passed by Harrison on lap 11. The order was the same at the end of lap 15, with Ashmore averaging 70.31mph and leading Gerard by 19 seconds. Horsfall, falling back, was now 11 seconds behind Gerard. Walker was 23 seconds behind Horsfall and 59 seconds ahead of Harrison. The order remained identical with 20 laps completed but Ashmore had increased his average to 70.64 mph with his lead virtually unchanged at 18 seconds. The leaders obviously had problems in lapping slower cars, as, on lap 20 Ashmore could manage only 3mins 20secs while Gerard did the same lap in 3mins 13secs. Horsfall was now 21 seconds behind Gerard and 50 seconds ahead of Walker with Harrison a further 31 seconds back. They were followed by Rolt, Hampshire, Claes, Murray, Heath and Ansell.

On lap 21, after leading for 16 laps, Ashmore began to lose oil. His 29 second pit stop for oil and fuel during which some of the fuel, which Reg Parnell poured from a churn, was spilled on to the driver's seat, cost him a total of about 50 seconds and he lost the lead to Bob Gerard by about 20 seconds. He then set about reducing the deficit, which he did by two seconds per lap. Meanwhile, on lap 24, Walker stopped for brake adjustments and lost fourth place to Harrison.

After 25 laps, Gerard's average was 70.55mph and his lead over Ashmore had been reduced to 13 seconds. Horsfall was 25 seconds behind Ashmore and over a minute ahead of Harrison, while Walker, after his stop, trailed Harrison by 1min 40secs. Gerard had lapped the rest of the field. On lap 26 Murray retired with gearbox trouble. Gerard then speeded up with a new lap record of 3mins 09secs (73.88mph) on both laps 27 and 28, beating Parnell's 1948 record by four seconds.

Meanwhile other dramas were taking place, according to *The Autocar*. At Governor's Bridge, John Heath ran wide in his Alta, hit a kerb and shot across the road with six inches of daylight visible under his offside wheels, but survived. The marshals and spectators had barely had time to recover before Jock Horsfall, flailing his elbows and spraying the marshals with gravel, passed Guy Jason-Henry's Delahaye on the outside at over 100mph with only inches to spare. George Nixon was "sliding his turns with abandon and biting big divots out of banks wherever they encroached on his somewhat unpredictable itinerary."

Perhaps Ashmore would have overtaken Gerard eventually for the latter, true to past practice, was avoiding pushing his ERA too hard, anxious to avoid technical problems. An incident, however, intervened; exactly the sort of thing Gerard was relying upon. On lap 29 at Nursery Bends on the descent into Onchan, whilst intent on reducing Gerard's lead, the frustrated Ashmore tried to lap George Nixon's ERA which was hindering his progress. Nixon however, apparently still unpredictable, bounced across his path. There was no time in which to brake, so Ashmore tried to scrape through a narrow opening between the car ahead and a stone wall. He did not quite make it. A brush with the wall and a kerb burst the off-side front tyre and the wheel developed a nasty wobble. Gerard immediately speeded up, lapping twice in 3mins 9secs (73.88mph), the fastest laps of the race.

Back at the pits, Ashmore's team, led by Reg Parnell, did a wonderful job in changing the wheel in 31 seconds but the affair had cost him too much time. At the end of lap 30, Gerard's average was 70.91mph and he led Horsfall by 1min 9 secs and Ashmore by 1min 24secs. Barring Gerard experiencing technical problems, Ashmore did not have the capability of eliminating so great a lead. In fact, Gerard was drawing further ahead to avoid being caught by Horsfall and the best Ashmore could realistically hope for now was to take second place from Horsfall. In trying to do so, he grazed the hedge at Willaston allegedly in a second encounter with George Nixon and, in fact, Gerard increased his lead over Horsfall by 18 seconds in the last six laps and the latter increased his lead over Ashmore by 19 seconds.

Bob Gerard passes the Manx Arms on his way to his second Manx win in his E.R.A. When early leader Reg Parnell retired with a sheared supercharger drive Fred Ashmore took over the lead but pitted with oil loss. He might have caught Gerard later but for a tangle with George Nixon on the descent into Onchan. [Manx National Heritage]

On the final lap everyone expected to see Ashmore's Maserati ahead of Horsfall's ERA but, although Ashmore's final lap effort equalled Gerard's time of 3mins 16secs, it was the ERA and not the Maserati which followed Gerard to the chequered flag. Thus Bob Gerard won in 1 hour 57mins 54secs (average 71.06mph) with Jock Horsfall second, 1min 27secs in arrears and Fred Ashmore only four seconds behind Horsfall. Cuth Harrison was the fourth finisher, one minute behind Ashmore, these four being the only drivers to complete 36 laps. Peter Walker and Tony Rolt finished one lap behind – for the latter it was his first finish in three starts on the Douglas circuit – while David Hampshire, Johnny Claes, Geoff Ansell and John Heath were two laps down. Geoff Richardson and Guy Jason-Henry completed only 32 laps and the final finisher was George Nixon, with 31 laps completed.

In addition to winning the British Empire Trophy and £250, Bob Gerard received the Lucas award of £100 for the first all-British car to finish, the Fairfield Memorial Trophy for the first BRDC member to finish, and the Siam Trophy for the fastest lap.

Just over two months after the race, Jock Horsfall lost his life in the *Daily Express* International Trophy Race at Silverstone when the ERA which he had driven on the Isle of Man overturned at a fast corner.

1949 British Empire Trophy Race Results

Thursday 26th May 1949. Start 4.10pm. 36 laps of 3.8789 miles circuit, total distance 139.64 miles. 16 starters, 13 finishers.

1. Bob Gerard (1,488cc ERA R14B), 1hr 57mins 54secs (71.06 mph).
2. St. John (Jock) Horsfall (1,488cc ERA R11B), 1hr 59mins 21secs (70.20 mph).
3. Fred Ashmore (1,496cc Maserati 4CLT/48), 1hr 59mins 55secs (70.16 mph)
4. Cuthbert Harrison (1,488cc ERA. R8B), 2hrs 0mins 55secs (69.29 mph)

The following failed to complete the required 36 laps:

5. Peter Walker (1,488cc ERA R10B), 35 laps, 1hr 59mins 15secs (68.31 mph).
6. Tony Rolt (3,440cc Alfa Romeo B), 35 laps, 2hrs 1min 27secs (67.07 mph)
7. David Hampshire (1,488cc ERA R12C), 34 laps, 1hr 58mins 27secs (66.80 mph)
8. Johnny Claes (4,480cc Talbot 26C), 34 laps, 1hr 58mins 48secs (66.61 mph)
9. Geoffrey Ansell (1,488cc ERA R9B), 34 laps, 2hrs 0mins 58secs (65.41 mph)
10. John Heath (1,496cc G.P. Alta), 34 laps, 2hrs 1min 47secs (64.98 mph)
11. Geoff. Richardson (1,488cc R.R.A.), 32 laps, 1hr 59mins 13secs (62.47 mph)
12. Guy Jason-Henry (3,600cc Delahaye 135), 32 laps 2hrs 0mins 10secs (61.98 mph)
13. George Nixon (1,488cc ERA R2A), 31 laps, 1hr 59mins 34secs (60.34 mph)

Fastest lap: Bob Gerard (ERA.), 3mins 09secs, (73.88 mph). New lap record.

Retirements:

Lap 5: Michael Chorlton (C.D.L.), split fuel tank

Reg Parnell (Maserati 4CLT/48), supercharger drive sheared.

Lap 26: David Murray (Maserati 4CL), gearbox problem.

Reaction

At the Presentation of Awards, Bob Gerard praised the organisation as "second to none" and referred to the magnificent course and facilities. The Deputy Governor, Deemster Cowley, who presented the awards, welcomed the BRDC and hoped that the races would be repeated.

There was virtually no Press comment, although *Motor Sport* said that, compared with the previous year, the Press bulletins during the races were not quite so informative and the tea and cakes provided in the Press area of the grandstand had been missed. The magazine conceded however, "but there, we always grumble and on the whole the arrangements were good".

Grandstand receipts were again reduced but this was thought to be due to the races being held in May, before the start of the summer ferry schedule.

After the comments in the 1948 *Motor Sport* race report about the variations in drivers' headgear, *The Autocar* interestingly referred to the course having a normal highway's imperfections and hazards and said that it was not surprising that all but one of the drivers in the Empire Trophy race donned crash hats. Nevertheless a post-race photograph of Manx Cup winner John Heath shows him wearing a leather helmet!

1950 – Gerard's Third Manx Victory – Moore's Manx Cup

Planning

After chaos over the choice of dates for the motorcycle TT, the International Bicycle Races and the British Empire Trophy, the BRDC confirmed its 1950 date as Thursday 15th June. As in 1949, there were to be two races – the British Empire Trophy and the Manx Cup, over 36 laps (140 miles) and 18 laps (70 miles) respectively, with official practices to be held on the Tuesday and Wednesday evenings. Meanwhile, Tynwald announced that the financial arrangements were to be as in 1949. There was to be a Grant of £1,000 with a further guarantee against loss of £400, a contribution towards transportation costs of £600 and £500 start money for star continental drivers, a total of £2,500.

Later it was announced that, for the first time, there were to be cash awards to mechanics of the cars finishing first and second in each race – £10 and £5 for the British Empire Trophy Race and £6 and £4 for the Manx Cup.

The finish of the Empire Trophy Race was to be broadcast on the BBC Light Programme, the commentators being Philip Robinson, Raymond Baxter, Alan Clarke and Leslie Adams.

British Empire Trophy Entries

Only 18 entries were received for the British Empire Trophy compared with 25 in 1949, 29 in 1948 and 23 in 1947. Again ERA and Maserati were the predominant marques, with five of the former and seven of the latter. Bob Gerard headed the field, looking for his third series victory, with other ERA entries from Peter Walker, Graham Whitehead (brother of Peter), Cuth Harrison and Brian

Shawe-Taylor. The Maserati challenge consisted of three Scuderia Ambrosiana entries of Reg Parnell, David Hampshire and David Murray. Private entrants were Colin Murray (a newcomer to the course) and Joe Kelly and two well-known foreign drivers making welcome returns – Prince Bira (entered by the Italian driver/team owner Enrico Plate) and Baron Emanuel ("Toulo" or "Barney") de Graffenried. The Prince had made his Isle of Man debut in 1936 and had won in 1937 and 1947 (Manx Cup), while the Baron had also competed in 1937. Rob Walker entered his 1927 Grand Prix Delage which was partly the car in which Richard Seaman had won on the same Douglas circuit in 1936. The car had been rebuilt by Jack Playford, formerly Brian Lewis' mechanic, and tuned by Freddie Dixon. Tony Rolt was named as driver of this car, while a similar Delage was entered by John Rowley. Anthony Baring entered a 1,960cc H.W.M. This was an evolution of the H.W.-Alta and, as a similar car driven by Johnny Claes had won the Grand Prix des Frontieres, could be regarded as a serious contender. The field was completed by the Alta of Gordon Watson, the 4,480cc Tornado 1 of Bobby Baird and the 4,425cc A.J.B. of Archie Butterworth.

Tom Meyer, a newcomer to motor racing, entered an ex-John Heath streamlined 1,961cc H.W.-Alta, pictured in the pit lane. Meyer finished tenth in the race, four laps behind the winner. [Manx National Heritage]

Manx Cup Entries

The Manx Cup attracted 26 entries. There were seven Coopers, all with 1,100cc or 1,000cc engines, They consisted of the works entry of John Cooper, Eric Winterbottom, Hector Graham/Henry Kyle, Michael Christie, Eric Brandon, Joe Potts and Bill Merrick. Former Cooper driver Spike Rhiando entered his 998cc Rhiando-Trimax. Supercharged MGs were entered by Bobby Baird, Dick Jacobs and Basil de Lissa, with an unsupercharged 1.5 litre Lester MG entered by Harry Lester for the up-and-coming Jim Mayers. There were three H.R.G. entries. One, to be driven by Peter Clark/R. Lord, had a Lea-Francis engine. The other drivers were Hugh Clapp and W.H. ("Bill") Murray. The latter was an Isle of Man resident, aged 29, who was the Manager of the Manx Brick Company of Milntown and lived with his wife and child at Glen Auldyn near Ramsey. He was the son of J.H. Murray of Dunluce, near Ramsey. A relative newcomer to racing, he had finished 8th at Goodwood and 4th at Blandford. He was helped greatly with preparation of his car by Edgar Hamill, the proprietor of Hamill's Garage in Derby Square, Douglas.

A Le Mans Frazer Nash was entered by Norman Culpan. No stranger to Isle of Man racing, he had ridden in the 1928 and 1929 Amateur motorcycle TT Races on a Rudge and had returned to the Manx Grand Prix in 1947 and 1948, racing under the nom de course of "Anno Domini". An accomplished rider, he had finished 8th in both the 1947 Senior and 1948 Junior races and had finished his motor-cycle racing career with second place in the 1948 Senior race. Moving on to car racing, he had finished third overall in the 1949 Le Mans 24 hour race in his Frazer Nash, co-driving with Fraser Nash company owner H.J. Aldington. He intended to travel immediately from Douglas to Le Mans for the 1950 race.

Two H.W.-Alta cars were entered, designed by George Abecassis and John Heath of Hersham and Walton Motors and as entered by them in the 1949 Manx Cup. The ex-John Heath car was entered by Tom Meyer, a newcomer to motor racing, and the other was entered by J.H. Walton for Peter Bolton to drive. A well-known racing driver, Peter Bolton, later drove a works Triumph in the Mille Miglia, led the AC Cobra team at Le Mans with Ninian Sanderson and Jack Sears, and drove in twenty Monte Carlo Rallies and ten times at Le Mans. Later still he became an Isle of Man resident and co-founder, with the Earl of Northesk, of the Manx Motor Racing Club.

Rileys were entered by Peter Reece and Gordon Shillito, Gillie Tyrer entered his Frazer Nash B.M.W., Ted Lund had forsaken MGs to drive a Lea-Francis in which he

Ted Lund sits in his Lea Francis in the pit lane while Billy Skelly looks for something under the car. In the race, Lund finished seventh, two laps behind the winner, Oscar Moore. [Billy Skelly collection/Keig collection]

The Hector Graham/Henry Kyle 1,100cc Cooper is pictured on Ballanard Road, approaching Willaston corner during a sunny evening practice. In the race the car retired on lap 2 with hydraulic failure. [Manx National Heritage]

had won the Blandford Trophy Race, Gerry Dunham again had his father's Alvis and Joe Kelly entered his IRA. Basil de Mattos was entered by Bob Spikins but the Spikins Special was replaced by the Lea-Francis engined Cromard Special. Finally Oscar Moore returned with his B.M.W. based O.B.M., an evolution of the Frazer Nash B.M.W. which he had raced in 1947. He had entered the O.B.M. in 1948 but had withdrawn, and had not entered in 1949.

Practice

Three Empire Trophy drivers failed to arrive due to their cars not being ready. They were Anthony Baring (H.W.M), Robert Baird (Tornado1) and (for the second year running) Archie Butterworth (A.J.B.). The sole Manx Cup absentee was Joe Kelly, as his IRA was not ready.

The weather on both evenings was cool and sunny, with a stiff and gusty wind.

Tuesday evening practice was relatively uneventful, although Dick Jacobs put his supercharged MG in a ditch on the back part of the circuit, rupturing the fuel tank. He admitted to being "carried away by it all" after finding that the car was pulling 7,000rpm in top gear on the long straight. The fastest Empire Trophy time was set by Cuth Harrison (ERA) with a lap of 3mins 11secs (73.11mph). Brian Shawe-Taylor (ERA) managed 3mins 18secs, one second faster than Bob Gerard's ERA and Reg Parnell's Maserati. In the Manx Cup practice, the Coopers of Hector Graham, John Cooper and Eric Brandon were fastest with times of 3mins 23secs (69.78mph), 3mins 24secs and 3mins 26secs respectively, the first two unofficially breaking the class lap record of 3mins 26secs set by Stirling Moss in 1949 but coming nowhere near Moss' incredible practice lap of 3mins 13secs. The Prince and the Baron (Bira and de Graffenried) both missed Tuesday's practice due to their late arrival after racing in the Swiss Grand Prix at Bremgarten nine days earlier. Bira arrived on Tuesday evening, having flown direct from Rennes to the Isle of Man in his Miles Gemini. He drove his Maserati in a lounge suit. The Baron arrived on Wednesday in a Fiat saloon with many badges including an RAC badge and an Isle of Man flag on the seat. The cars had been transported across Europe in a three-ton lorry.

There was high drama for Peter Walker and his E-type ERA GP1 in Wednesday evening's second practice session. He had taken the car out for just one fast lap. As he approached Cronk-y-Berry the car "threw yet another rod" (according to *The Autocar*), or "broke a drive-shaft" (according to *Motor Sport*). Whichever it was, the fuel tank burst and the car burst into flames. Walker jumped out before the car stopped, landed on his feet, turned somersaults and landed in a hedge, sustaining several

Peter Walker crashed his E.R.A. at Cronk-y-Berry during the second evening practice after a mechanical problem variously reported as a broken driveshaft or a thrown con-rod. The driver was thrown out and the car quickly caught fire. [Manx National Heritage]

Marshals attempt to extinguish the fire after Peter Walker's crash. They were unsuccessful and a fire engine was sent along the course from the start. Meanwhile Walker was taken to hospital by ambulance. [Manx National Heritage]

fractured ribs and a sprained wrist. Meanwhile, burning fiercely, the ERA ran up the hedge very close to where its unconscious driver lay. The hedgerow caught fire and a nearby house was at risk. Walker was attended by a St. John Ambulance officer, who, worried about the risk of an explosion and as flames were scorching the paint on his first aid box, quickly arranged for Walker to be moved. He was then taken to hospital by ambulance.

Meanwhile, as the ERA had approached the hedge the flagman, Douglas Accountant and Manx Grand Prix Race Secretary Cyril Ducker had jumped for his life into the garden of the adjoining house. His flags lay abandoned on the hedge, where they were destroyed when the blazing ERA landed on top of them. Happily, Ducker escaped with no more than a shaking and his hair full of soil.

Race Control sent a fire engine along the course from the pits, among the race cars. Meanwhile at Parkfield, Race Steward Douglas Hanson telephoned the Clerk of the Course to obtain permission for off-duty Fire Chief F. Courtie, who was spectating there, to be driven to the scene of the crash in an MG owned by another spectator, Mr J.E. Scott. The fire engine ran out of extinguisher fluid during unsuccessful attempts to put out the fire, and returned to the pits for more, at a speed almost as quick as many of the cars, according to spectators. Arriving at the crash scene on their second lap, the fire crew still could not extinguish the fire and the ERA was completely destroyed. Fortunately, it was insured.

Peter Walker suffered fractured ribs and a sprained wrist. After treatment, he was moved from hospital to Queenscliffe Nursing Home in Douglas, where he was reported as "quite comfortable" but had said "This is the dreaded end!" This was taken to imply that, although insured and one of only two of its type made, the car might not be restored. Because of its past record of poor reliability *The Autocar* questioned whether it would be rebuilt. "Its unfortunate record," it said, "has certainly caused many of us to wonder whether such a process would be worth the expense and effort involved."

The fastest Empire Trophy time was set jointly by Cuth Harrison (ERA) and Reg Parnell (Maserati). Their time of 3mins 10secs (73.49mph) was one second faster than Harrison's Tuesday time and one second outside the record. Parnell, however, had set his time in Hampshire's car and would therefore be relegated to row 4 of the starting grid based on the time he set in his own car (3mins 19secs). As Bira's Maserati was not ready for Wednesday's practice, he shared de Graffenried's car and would therefore start the race from the back of the grid, not having set a time in his own car. The fastest Manx Cup time was Oscar Moore's 3mins 33secs (65.56mph), a full ten seconds slower than the three Coopers.

1950 Manx Cup Race – Oscar Moore Outlasts the Coopers

Rain had been forecast but conditions remained dry throughout the Manx Cup race, although gathering clouds caused worries that rain would affect the Empire Trophy event.

The Cromard Special of Basil de Mattos had a broken rear axle and Eric Winterbottom's Cooper had a broken crankshaft, reducing the field to 23 starters. The three Coopers of Hector Graham, John Cooper and Eric Brandon locked out the front row of the grid with practice times of 3mins 23secs, 3mins 24secs and 3mins 26secs respectively. Dick Jacobs (3mins 33secs) had row 2 to himself due to the absence of Eric Winterbottom who

*This starting grid photograph shows Ted Lund (black overalls) beside his Lea Francis (22). Next to Lund is Jim Mayers (helmet) and beyond him, seated in his Frazer Nash (8), is Norman Culpan. Behind Lund's car is Billy Skelly (wearing natty pullover). Further back are the H.R.G.s of Bill Murray (7) and Hugh Clapp (6). On the far left Paul Emery stands in the middle of the group behind Bobby Baird's MG K3 (1). [*The Motor*/Billy Skelly collection]*

had lapped in 3mins 32secs before his crankshaft broke. Row 3 consisted of the Frazer Nash B.M.W. of Gillie Tyrer and the O.B.M. of Oscar Moore (both 3mins 33secs) together with Bill Merrick's Cooper (3mins 34secs).

The start was ragged. Tyrer had to be pushed to the pavement, Shillito's Riley and Potts' Cooper both stalled and Peter Bolton's Alta was left behind, having had trouble on the warm-up lap. All got away, but Potts retired after two laps and Bolton, who had lost a complete lap before getting away, completed only three laps.

At the end of the first lap, Brandon, Cooper and Graham led, followed by Moore, Jacobs, Norman Culpan (Frazer Nash), Gerry Dunham (Alvis), Ted Lund (Lea-Francis), Potts, Hugh Clapp (H.R.G.), Tom Meyer (H.W.-Alta) and Peter Clark (mis-firing H.R.G.). Bobby Baird retired his MG K3, despite two all-night sessions by his mechanics. Merrick's Cooper and Spike Rhiando's Trimax also retired.

On lap 2, Brandon set the fastest lap of the race in 3mins 23secs (68.78mph), which was three seconds faster than Stirling Moss' 1949 record. At the end of the lap Graham, who had overshot at Parkfield, pitted with loss of brake fluid. He continued, losing second place to Moore, but soon retired. Basil de Lissa also retired his MG with back axle failure, and Joe Potts retired his Cooper. Lap 3 brought two more retirements – Peter Reece (Riley) and Bill Murray (H.R.G). Murray was initially reported as having retired at Willaston but it later transpired that he had taken a wrong line at Parkfield and crashed into the bags, bending his front axle and buckling a wheel. He said he had been watching the car in front and not the road. He had been 11th.

With five laps completed, Brandon still led, averaging 67.79mph, followed by Cooper (67.07mph) and Moore (65.50mph). On lap 6 Shillito, pushing hard after his poor start, passed Dunham and on lap 7 he passed

Basil de Lissa in his MG special collides with the sandbags at Parkfield. He continued, only to retire shortly afterwards with rear axle failure. [Manx National Heritage]

Isle of Man resident Bill Murray crashed his H.R.G. at Parkfield on lap 3, bending his front axle and buckling a wheel. The inset photograph shows the driver with the Manx three legs emblem on his helmet. [Ramsey Courier]

Culpan. Dunham hit the hedge at Cronk-y-Berry but was able to continue. At the end of lap 9, Cooper drove slowly to his pit with a piston failure, which had also happened in practice. Moore was now second.

At the end of lap 10, Brandon had slowed to 67.10mph, with Moore second and Shillito third. A lap later, Brandon stopped at his pit for a plug change but the engine would not restart. The magneto drive had sheared. With the last of the Coopers out, Moore now led from the charging Shillito. However, Shillito's challenge to Moore was fading with his brakes and Culpan, whom he had passed on lap 7, was catching him, despite a spin at Cronk-ny-Mona on lap 14.

During the race, wet tar and a bad pothole at Onchan caused problems for several drivers, including some impacts with the bags, but no serious incidents were reported.

After fifteen laps, with three laps left, Moore's lead looked secure. His average was 66.58mph, with Shillito at 66.44mph and Culpan close behind at 65.15mph. On lap 17 the gap was down to five seconds. Moore took the chequered flag, but who would be second? It was Shillito, by less than a car's length from Culpan, who must have rued his spin at Cronk-ny-Mona.

Moore's time for the race was 1 hour 2mins 51secs, an average of 66.66mph. Shillito, as in 1949, was runner-up, 1min 12secs in arrears with Culpan just one second behind. Gerry Dunham was fourth, a further 1min 19secs behind Culpan. Tyrer, almost without brakes, came in fifth by a further 35secs. Only the first five completed the full distance. Two laps behind at the finish were Jim Mayers (Lester MG), Ted Lund (Lea Francis), Hugh Clapp (H.R.G.) and Dick Jacobs (MG). Jacobs had lost time when he over-revved his engine trying to keep up with Moore and had to stop at his pit where the ever-helpful Reg Parnell helped to refit one of the blower belts. There were two more finishers, Meyer's H.W.-Alta and Clarke's H.R.G., four and five laps behind respectively.

Oscar Moore's reliability had seen off the challenge of the fast but unreliable Coopers but, although he had been well off the pace of the Coopers, his race average of 66.66mph was 1mph faster that John Heath's 1949 winning average. Dick Jacobs wrote later that John Cooper had told him on the starting grid that the Coopers would not last and *The Autocar* commented that the J.A.P. engine fitted to five of the seven Coopers had obviously not overcome its teething troubles and that "a concentrated effort must now be made to achieve reliability with these machines, which have every other virtue necessary for success".

1950 Manx Cup Race Results

Thursday 15th June 1950. Start 2.00pm. 18 laps of 3.8789 miles circuit, total distance 69.82 miles. 23 starters, 11 finishers.

1. Oscar Moore (1,971cc O.B.M.), 1hr 2mins 51secs (66.66mph)
2. Gordon Shillito (1,980cc Riley) 1hr 4mins 3secs (65.41mph)
3. Norman Culpan (1.971cc Frazer Nash), 1hr 4mins 4secs (65.39mph)
4. Gerry Dunham (1,842cc Alvis), 1hr 5mins 23secs (64.07mph)
5. Gilbert Tyrer (1,996cc Frazer Nash - B.M.W.), 1hr 5mins 58secs (63.51mph)

Failed to complete the required 18 laps:

6. Jim Mayers (1,474cc Lester MG), 16 laps
7. Ted Lund (1,670cc Lea-Francis), 16 laps
8. Hugh Clapp (1,496cc H.R.G.), 16 laps
9. Dick Jacobs (1,086cc MG), 16 laps
10. Tom Meyer (1,961cc H.W.-Alta), 14 laps.
11. Peter Clark (1,674cc H.R.G.), 13 laps

Fastest lap: Eric Brandon (1,097cc Cooper), 3mins 23secs (68.78mph).

Retirements:

Lap 1: Bobby Baird (MG), Bill Merrick (1,097cc Cooper), Spike Rhiando (Trimax)

Lap 2: Basil de Lissa (MG), rear axle failure

Hector Graham (1,100cc Cooper), hydraulic failure

Joe Potts (998cc Cooper).

Lap 3: Peter Bolton (H.W.-Alta)

Bill Murray (H.R.G.), crash

Peter Reece (Riley).

Lap 9: John Cooper (1,088cc Cooper), broken piston

Lap 11: Eric Brandon (1,098cc Cooper), sheared magneto drive.

Also retired: Michael Christie (1,096cc Cooper) – no details available.

1950 British Empire Trophy Race – Bob Gerard's Third Manx Victory

There were two non-starters – Peter Walker, due to his practice crash, and John Rowley, whose camshaft drive gear had failed. The remaining thirteen cars lined up under dark skies and a light drizzle. Cuth Harrison's ERA had pole position by virtue of his 3mins 10secs practice time. Next to him were Tony Rolt's Delage (3mins 12secs) and Bob Gerard's ERA (3mins 13secs). Row 2 consisted of David Murray, who had changed to a "C" type ERA after blowing up his Maserati, and Brian Shawe-Taylor ("B" type ERA), both of whom had recorded 3mins 17secs. Behind them were the Maseratis of David Hampshire (3mins 17secs), Baron de Graffenried (3mins 19secs) and Reg Parnell (3mins 19secs, although he had done 3mins 10secs in Hampshire's car). Row 4 was shared by the "B" type ERA of Graham Whitehead (3mins 25secs) and Joe Kelly's Maserati (3mins 27secs). Gordon Watson's Alta, the pre-selector gearbox of which had lost first gear on the eve of the race (3mins 36secs) and Colin Murray's Maserati (3mins 38secs) was on the back row with Bira, who had not set a time in his race car.

Harrison led from the start, followed by Gerard, de Graffenried and David Murray. Rolt faltered and Watson, without bottom gear, made a slow start. At the first corner, Parkfield, Harrison over-braked and overshot, handing the lead to Gerard who was first to complete the lap, in 3mins 27secs, followed by Parnell (who had passed six cars), Bira (who had passed ten), de Graffenried, Shawe-Taylor, David Murray, Rolt, Hampshire, Kelly, Whitehead, Harrison, Colin Murray and Watson. On lap 2 Parnell passed Gerard and de Graffenried made a pit stop to adjust shock-absorbers and/or brakes, dropping to ninth.

By now, although the far side if the course was dry, the rain had become heavier on Glencrutchery Road in the start/finish area. As usual when rain follows a dry spell, the road surface was covered with a treacherous slime of oil and rubber. Approaching Parkfield on lap 3, Bira hit a particularly slippery patch of road, slid wildly, held his car broadside for some distance, spun and was rammed by David Murray. Kelly, avoiding them, hit the wall on the apex of the corner head-on. Nobody was hurt, but Bira had two buckled wheels and a damaged axle, Murray a broken frame and Kelly a buckled wheel. All three were out of the race. Meanwhile, at Cronk-ny-Mona, Parnell slid and lost time.

At the end of lap 3, with only ten cars still running, Gerard led from Shawe-Taylor (up from fourth), Parnell (whose clutch has started to slip), Rolt (whose troublesome shock absorbers were giving him a rough and erratic ride), Harrison, Hampshire and de

Graffenried. Soon, the rain stopped, the roads dried and speeds rose.

After five laps, Gerard was averaging 66.43mph and led Shawe-Taylor by 17seconds. Parnell was third, a further 17 seconds back, followed by de Graffenried. Colin Murray's Maserati had wheel judder under braking.

David Hampshire, whose Maserati seemed to lack performance, was passed by Harrison, who was up to fifth and passed Rolt on lap 7, to take fourth and de Graffenried on lap 9, to take third. Meanwhile Gerard, driving superbly with his car sounding grand according to *Motor Sport*, began to lap the back-markers on lap 8. He had lapped at 3mins 26secs in the rain and 3mins 13secs, 3mins 11secs and then 3mins 9secs in the dry.

With ten laps completed, Gerard had increased his average to 66.62mph and led Shawe-Taylor by 29 seconds. Parnell was still third, Harrison fourth, de Graffenried fifth, Rolt sixth and Hampshire seventh. On lap 11, Hampshire passed Rolt and Parnell passed Shawe-Taylor and on lap 12 Watson retired at Parkfield in a huge cloud of smoke, with a broken piston.

At the end of lap 15, Gerard had speeded up to an average of 67.85mph and led Parnell, averaging 67.31mph, by 25 seconds. Shawe-Taylor was still third and Harrison fourth. Parnell gained four seconds on lap 16 but Gerard immediately recovered two seconds. On lap 18, Colin Murray crashed his Maserati at Nursery Bends without injury, having earlier hit the sandbags at Parkfield. Now there were only eight.

On lap 19, Gerard made his only error of the race, but an error which could have cost him the race. He overshot at Parkfield, losing 20 seconds and leaving him only one second ahead of Parnell at the end of the lap. On lap 20, Parnell took the lead, lapping in 3mins 10secs, and led Gerard by one second at the end of the lap. Shawe-Taylor was still third, Harrison fourth, de Graffenried fifth and Hampshire sixth. On lap 24 de Graffenried stopped to refuel, losing 22 seconds. He was the only driver to do so.

Colin Murray looks bemused after crashing his Maserati into the sandbags at Parkfield. He was unable to continue. [Still Time Collection]

Parnell's lead was short-lived. His clutch started to slip so seriously that Gerard had fully recovered his previous lead by the end of lap 21. Parnell was 23 seconds back and was soon caught and passed by Shawe-Taylor. Harrison, on a charge, passed both of them on lap 22, to take second place. For Parnell, things got worse before they got better. Hampshire passed him on lap 25, when he had the indignity of being lapped by Gerard, who then had a comfortable lead of 1min 32secs.

On lap 26, there was an alarming incident at the Manx Arms corner in Onchan. Observers saw a wheel rolling down the hill, followed at a distance by Graham Whitehead in a three-wheeled ERA. There was a suggestion that Whitehead's hub cap had nudged Colin Murray's crashed car at Nursery Bends, further up the hill. Fortunately the driver was unhurt and walked to the finish. The field was now reduced to seven.

After being passed by Rolt on lap 27, Parnell speeded up on lap 28, with his clutch working normally again. By the end of the lap he was fifth, behind Gerard, Harrison, Shawe-Taylor and de Graffenried. The latter had made his second pit stop at the end of lap 24, to take on fuel.

By the end of lap 30 Gerard's average was 69.70mph. Parnell was still charging. On lap 32 he re-passed Rolt and on lap 33 he lapped in 3mins 8secs (74.28mph), a new lap record. Then his clutch again ceased to grip and again he slowed.

There was a final surprise when a mistake gave third place to de Graffenried. Reduced to fourth place because of his 22 seconds fuel stop, he regained his third place from Shawe-Taylor on the last lap. A white flag was being shown to warn drivers that a service car was on the course. When Shawe-Taylor saw it he thought it signified the end of the race, raised his goggles and began touring. This gave de Graffenried his chance. He shot past. Shawe-Taylor accelerated hard when he realised his mistake but had to content himself with hanging on the Baron's tail for the remainder of the race.

Gerard finished first in a time of 1 hour 59mins 36.8secs (70.05mph). Harrison was 1min 32.4secs behind, with de Graffenried third, a further 1min 14.8secs back. Shawe-Taylor came in fourth, only 11.6 seconds after the Baron following his last lap mistake. The final three finishers, Hampshire, Parnell and Rolt, were all a lap behind.

For Gerard, his third win in four Isle of Man races was a testimony to his consistently fast and calm driving style, and to the reliability of his pre-war ERA. It was also the end of an era, for the 1950 event would be the last of the Empire Trophy Races for Grand Prix racing cars.

1950 British Empire Trophy Race Results

Thursday 15th June 1950. Start 3.45pm.36 laps of 3.8789 miles circuit, total distance 139.64 miles. 13 starters, 7 finishers.

1. Bob Gerard (1,488cc ERA R14B), 1hr 59mins 36.8secs (70.05mph)
2. Cuth Harrison (1,488cc ERA R8B), 2hrs 1min 9.2secs (69.17mph)
3. Baron Emanuel de Graffenried (1,490cc Maserati 4CLT/48), 2hrs 2mins 24.9secs (68.45mph)
4. Brian Shawe-Taylor (1,488cc ERA R9B), 2hrs 2mins 35.6secs (68.34mph)

Failed to complete the required 36 laps:

5. David Hampshire (1,490cc Maserati 4CLT/48), 35 laps, 2hrs 0 mins 58 secs (67.33mph)
6. Reg Parnell (1,490cc Maserati 4CLT/48), 35 laps, 2hrs 1min 54secs (66.82 mph)
7. Tony Rolt (1,498cc Delage 1558), 35 laps, 2hrs 2mins 41secs (66.40mph)

Fastest lap: Reg Parnell (Maserati 4CLT/48), 3mins 08secs (74.28mph). New lap record and permanent lap record for racing cars.

Retirements:

Lap 3: J. Kelly (Maserati 6CM), David Murray (ERA R12B) and B. Bira (Maserati 4CLT/48), multiple collision at Parkfield corner

Lap 12: Gordon Watson (Alta), broken piston

Lap 18: Colin Murray (Maserati 4CL), crash

Lap 26: Graham Whitehead (ERA R10B), lost wheel due to broken hub

Reaction

The local Press was unusually quiet but there was positive comment in the English motoring Press.

The Motor commented that the Manx Cup had been an interesting race. The field was "extremely assorted", including real racing cars like the Coopers, real sports cars like Gillie Tyrer's B.M.W. and various "refangled" pre-war cars. This mixture made the race extremely popular with BRDC members who rarely had the chance of taking part in real road racing with these types of cars.

Writing in his column in *The Autocar*, Sammy Davis said that the meeting had been as pleasant and friendly as ever. He thought that, while the circuit admittedly had its disadvantages, it was interesting and varied in character and, as a genuine road circuit it was of far greater value than the English aerodrome circuits. Mentioning that the event always seemed to produce more trouble and concentrated work in the days before the race than other circuits, Davis praised Douglas garage owner Alf Kelly, whose premises were always full of competitors' cars needing attention. He said that the garage never closed its doors for the 48 hours before the start and that, despite the disruption of his business, Alf was always cheerful and helpful and his wife always had the kettle boiling and the teapot working overtime.

Alf Kelly's garage in Green Lane, behind Derby Square in Douglas, was always in demand by car and motorcycle race competitors alike because Alf went to no end of trouble to help with problems and the kettle was always on. This 1947 photograph shows Eric Winterbottom's Emeryson in the lane outside the garage. [Stan Hughes collection]

1951 – Moss Wins, Griffith Unlucky – Dunham's Manx Cup

Planning

A major change was announced in February 1951. Returning to the principles which had made the early RAC TT races on the Island so popular, the Race Committee of Tynwald agreed with the BRDC that the 1951 British Empire Trophy Race would be for sports cars which could be sold to the general public. The Manx Cup, however, would now be a Formule Libre event, open to Grand Prix type cars which had raced in the Empire Trophy, as the previous engine capacity limits for this race were removed. There would, however, be special awards in the Manx Cup for smaller cars of up to 2,500cc unsupercharged or 1,100cc supercharged, the previous capacity limits for the race.

There were two reasons for the radical change to the Empire Trophy Race. Firstly, it was becoming difficult to get entries for pure racing cars, due to the shortage of Grand Prix type cars, proved by the decline in entries over the four years since 1947 with entries down to 18 and starters down to 13 in 1950. This had caused the Tynwald Race Committee to voice its concern about the future viability of the race in its previous form. Secondly, there was increasing interest in races for the new types of British sports cars which were providing a welcome boost for exports in the early post-war years. The theory was that the public were more interested in the performance of cars which they could buy themselves than Grand Prix cars. This had been proved by the popularity of the production car race during the 1949 *Daily Express* International Trophy meeting at Silverstone, in which Manx driver Brian Mylchreest had driven in a team of Rileys, and the successful 1950 revival of the RAC Tourist Trophy at Dundrod in which the new Jaguar XK 120 models driven by Stirling Moss and Peter Whitehead had finished first and second. Works entries, of course, would be faster than standard showroom models, but the chances were that racing developments would be incorporated in future standard cars.

There was one serious miscalculation. The date announced in August 1950 was 14th June but, now that the Manx race was to be for sports cars, staging it just a week before the 24 hours sports car classic of Le Mans would mean that cars intended for that event would be unable make it to the Isle of Man.

More details were announced in April. The Empire Trophy Race would be run over 35 laps while the Manx Cup Race would again be run over 18 laps. The Manx Cup, however, was not to be a Formule Libre race as previously announced but would retain its previous formula for racing cars of up to 2.500cc unsupercharged and 1,100cc supercharged. The larger engined racing cars, such as ERAs, Alfa Romeos, Bugattis and the larger engined Maseratis, would still be catered for by the revival of the Castletown Trophy, previously run in 1948.

Rodney Walkerley, Sports Editor of *The Motor*, conceded that the definition of a sports car had been the subject of heated argument for years and no satisfactory definition had yet been discovered. A rough description, however, was that a sports car was a touring car designed and built for at least two passengers, with equipment suitable for normal use on roads, but which was designed to be much faster.

For a sports car to qualify for the Empire Trophy Race, it had to satisfy one of the fundamental rules of the Le Mans race, that "at least 10 models identical in every other respect to the car entered, including any optional extras, must have been catalogued and sold by 1st May 1951". Details which did not appear in a catalogue, such as the compression ratio and the weight, shape and material of con-rods and pistons, could be modified and any type of fuel could be used. In the interests of safety closed cars had to be fitted with laminated glass, perspex or some similar plastic material which would not become opaque if hit by a stone. Open cars were permitted to lower their windscreens or even fit small aero screens.

Because the race was open to all ranges of cars – from the 745cc Dyna Panhard to the 5.4 litre Allard with its Cadillac engine, with their maximum speeds ranging from 75-80mph to approximately 130mph – a handicap system had to be introduced. This had to be one that was easily understood by spectators because a confusing system could depress enthusiasm. The solution for the Manx event was the introduction of three capacity classes, with "credit laps". Cars up to 1,500cc would receive four "credit laps" in the 35 lap race, so that they would have to do only 31 laps. Cars up to 3,000cc would get one "credit lap", so that they would have to do only 34 laps and cars over 3,000cc with no credit at all would have to do 35 laps. There would be the usual massed start, with grid positions being allocated according to practice times. The theory was that by the end of the race all cars, regardless of their power, should be capable of finishing in a dead heat.

The prize fund was increased to £900 with the entrant of the Empire Trophy winner receiving £100 presented by the *Daily Express*, the entrant of the highest placed British car receiving £100 presented by Joseph Lucas Ltd. and the entrant of the fastest finisher receiving £50 presented by Dunlop. Tynwald agreed an increase of the grant for the races from £2,300 to £2,500 after the Chairman of its Race Committee said that sponsorship by a U.K. national newspaper would be of great value to the Island.

The *Mona's Herald* arranged a race day excursion. A train from Manchester Victoria station would call at various east Lancashire towns and connect with the 10.30 steamer from Fleetwood to Douglas. Special buses would take passengers direct from Douglas pier to the course in time for the start of racing and the steamer would return at 6.30pm, arriving at Fleetwood at 9.30pm to connect with the train back to Manchester.

British Empire Trophy Entries

The new formula attracted an excellent total of 31 entries, one more than the course limit. They were almost equally divided between the three classes, with 10 in the up to 1.5 litres class, 13 in the up to 3 litres class and 8 in the over 3 litres class.

An unusual entry in the 1.5 litres class was a French 745cc front wheel drive air-cooled Dyna Panhard saloon entered by an American driver using the nom de course of "Dave". This was the only foreign entry. Apart from a Jowett Jupiter with closed bodywork entered by William Robinson, the remainder of the class consisted of MG engined cars. Harry Lester entered two of his Lester MGs with 1,467cc bored-out MG TC 1,250cc engines in light tubular frames, to be driven by Jim Mayers and Pat Griffith. There were two Cooper MGs of Lionel Leonard and Jack Reece (the former fitted with a particularly attractive body in the style of a miniature Ferrari) and four of the new MG TD series Midgets to be driven by Dick Jacobs, Ted Lund, Mike Pople and Trevor Line.

In the 3 litres class Rob Walker entered his 2.6 litres DB2 Aston Martin, nominating Peter Walker or Guy Gale as drivers and Ben Whitehouse entered a 2 litre DB1 model. John Lyons entered his 1,767cc Connaught, Bobby Baird entered his 2 litre Ferrari and John Buncombe and S. Hill/ G. Cooper entered 2.5 litres Healey Silverstones. The latter was a reserve because of the course limit of 30 cars. There were also seven 1,971cc Frazer Nash Le Mans Replica entries – Rodney Peacock, Norman Culpan, David Clarke, Donald Pitt, Isle of Man resident Bill Murray, Bob Gerard and Stirling Moss, the latter driving the Gilby Engineering car entered by Squadron-Leader Sydney Greene.

Interesting entries in the over 3 litres class were two examples of the world's fastest car in quantity production – the 3.4 litres Jaguar XK 120. These were entered by Peter Binns and 1950 Manx Cup winner Oscar Moore. Rob Walker entered his 1936 3.5 litres Delahaye with the same alternative drivers as for his Aston Martin. Reg Parnell had a 3.8 litres works entered Nash Healey which finished sixth at Le Mans, driven by Tony Rolt and Duncan Hamilton. There were four Allards: Kidderminster Ford dealer Peter Collins and Sydney Allard had 5.4 litres Cadillac engined cars while D.F. Annable entered a 3.9 litres Ardun-Mercury engined car to be driven by himself and Peter Scott-Russell and Frank Curtis entered a similar car.

Manx Cup Entries

The Manx Cup attracted 20 entries. Four were 1.1 litre Coopers, entered by Bill Aston, Bill Merrick, Eric Brandon and London meat trader John Barber. Stirling Moss was entered in a works H.W.M. while Oscar Moore and Tom Meyer had 1950 team cars. Gerry Dunham was again entered in his father's pre-war Alvis while E.C.W. Stapleton entered an Aston Martin and Bobby Baird had his tubular chassis de Dion axle twin supercharged 1,100cc Baird Griffin. Lionel Leonard entered the Cooper MG which he also entered in the Empire Trophy race, while Dick Jacobs also had entries in both races but would drive his normal supercharged K3 engined MG special in the Manx Cup. There were two Rileys, entered by Gordon Shillito and Horace Richards. Peter Clark entered only one H.R.G. instead of his usual team of three, nominating Gerry Ruddock as driver. Joe Kelly entered his usual IRA, Tom Simpson entered a Healey Silverstone to be driven by Peter Simpson, Scottish Ford dealer Billy Skelly entered a Lea-Francis for Ted Lund and himself, J.H. Webb entered a Turner Special which had a twin o.h.c. MG Magnette engine once owned by Reg Parnell and R.C. Willis entered a Frazer Nash B.M.W.

Castletown Trophy Entries

The BRDC decision to revive the Castletown Trophy Race to provide a race for larger engined racing cars displaced from the Empire Trophy received a disappointing response of only seven entries. David Murray, Reg Parnell, David Hampshire and Miles Martin entered Maseratis, Joe Ashmore and John Green each entered an ERA and Rob Walker again entered his Grand Prix Delage, to be driven by Peter Walker.

Practice

There were non-arrivals for all three races. In the British Empire Trophy, all the cars in the 1.5 litres class arrived and practised. There were three non-arrivals in the 3 litres class – the Connaught of John Lyons, the Ferrari of Bobby Baird and the Healey of John Buncombe – while the XK120 Jaguars of Peter Binns and the 1950 Manx Cup winner Oscar Moore were disappointing absentees from the over 3 litres class. Rob Walker arranged for George Abecassis to replace the nominated driver, Peter Walker, in his Aston Martin. In the Manx Cup, the works H.W.M. entered for Stirling Moss was not ready and the Frazer Nash- B.M.W. of R.C. Willis was also absent. Castletown Trophy entries, already woeful, were reduced from seven to four by the absence of Peter Walker (Delage) and David Hampshire (Maserati), and by Miles Martin lending his Maserati to John Green to drive in place of Martin's ERA which Green had entered.

Lionel Leonard, who had entered his new Cooper-MG for both the Manx Cup and the Empire Trophy, experienced superb after-sales service. The car was barely finished in time and, on its first time out, Leonard took it to the Cooper works for some last-minute adjustments on his way to Liverpool for the ferry crossing to the Island. The firm's senior partner Charlie Cooper (John's father, who had been Kaye Don's mechanic and manager during Don's racing career) immediately volunteered to go to the Island with Leonard, grabbed a toothbrush, told his wife where he was going, and they were off!

The weather for the first (Tuesday evening) session was fair but the Wednesday session was extremely cold with some rain and mist on the highest part of the course between Cronk-ny-Mona and the descent to Onchan. On Tuesday Reg Parnell did very few laps in his Maserati, the best being 3mins 11secs (73.11mph), three seconds outside his record but fastest of the Castletown Trophy cars. The fastest Manx Cup driver was Bill Aston (Cooper) who lapped in 3mins 22secs. On Wednesday, despite the poor conditions, David Clarke went round in 3mins 26secs (67.78mph), one second faster than Stirling Moss,

The change to production sports cars attracted a varied field in which the most unusual entry was the Dyna-Panhard saloon driven by "Dave" from the U.S.A., pictured at Governor's Bridge. After practice problems and many pit stops during the race, the car was still running at the end, but was unclassified. [R and L Kelly collection]

At Parkfield, Ted Lund corners the 1,670cc Lea Francis special entered by Billy Skelly. Both drivers practised the car but Lund drove it in the race, retiring with a burst water hose. [Guy Griffiths/Billy Skelly collection]

to claim pole position on the Empire Trophy starting grid.

Practice problems included Bobby Baird's Griffin (sheared primary blower drive shaft), "Dave's" Dyna-Panhard (valve gear trouble, requiring parts which arrived by aeroplane from Paris a few hours before the start of the race) and Eric Brandon's Cooper (unspecified engine trouble). Sydney Allard lost a wheel but managed to hold the car and Guy Gale luckily squeezed his Delahaye through an extremely narrow gateway when he went astray in the mist. Both Ted Lund and entrant Billy Skelly had practised their Lea-Francis but it was decided that Lund should drive the entire race. Interviewed 62 years later, Billy Skelly, then an Isle of Man resident for 26 years, still remembered the bumps on Ballanard Road and elsewhere on the course. Nevertheless he said that the races were well organised and that the circuit was "an excellent circuit to race on" and "like a billiard table compared with Irish circuits".

1951 Manx Cup and Castletown Trophy Races – wins for Dunham and Parnell

The combined grid assembled in dry and sunny conditions, with big holiday crowds lining the course well before the 2pm start. In addition to Bobby Baird's Baird Griffin, there were two last-minute non-starters for the Manx Cup – Lionel Leonard had decided to save his Cooper MG for the Empire Trophy while Oscar Moore was absent due to the timing chain of his H.W.M. breaking when the engine was started in the garage to drive up to the start. Also Bill Merrick (Cooper) was a non-starter. This left 14 Manx Cup and 4 Castletown Trophy cars on the grid.

Reg Parnell's Maserati was on pole by virtue of his 3mins 11secs lap on Tuesday evening. Alongside him were the Maserati of David Murray, who was driving in short sleeves, (3mins 18secs) and the Cooper of Bill Aston (3mins 22secs). Behind them, having lapped in 3mins 29secs, were Eric Brandon (Cooper) and John Green (Maserati). Row 3 comprised Gerry Dunham's Alvis (3mins 30secs) with the ERA of Joe Ashmore and the H.W.M. of Tom Meyer (both 3mins 34secs). Ted Lund (Lea-Francis) had row 4 to himself due to the absence of Oscar Moore. Row 5 consisted of Gordon Shillito (Riley), John Barber (Cooper) and Dick Jacobs (MG special). Gerry Ruddock (H.R.G.) and J. Webb (Turner) were on row 6 in front of Horace Richards (Riley) and Peter Simpson (Healey Silverstone). E.C.W. Stapleton (Aston Martin) and Joe Kelly (IRA) brought up the rear.

There was immediate drama when Castletown Trophy driver David Murray misread the traffic light signals at the start. His goggles had dark lenses so, when the lights showed amber 20 seconds from the start, he thought they showed green. He roared away from the start in his 4CLT Maserati and realised his mistake only when past the pits. He braked violently, slewed across the road and, thinking that the start must have been delayed, turned round in the road with the intention of returning to the grid. He was promptly confronted by the pack tearing down upon him at an estimated 95 mph, led by Bill Aston, Eric Brandon and Reg Parnell.

"It had all the makings of a multiple crash," said *The Light Car*. Only superlative driving by everybody saved the situation. As Murray sat tight in his Maserati, cars flashed past by him on both sides. According to *The Motor* there were only inches to spare. Nobody knew how they all scraped past.

In addition to the delay caused by having to let everyone else get away before he could resume racing, Murray was penalised one lap. This meant that Parnell was almost certain to win the Castletown Trophy but he was unaware of the penalty.

At the end of the first lap Parnell led by 10 seconds, having lapped in 3mins 21secs (69.47mph). He was followed by Aston's Cooper (the Manx Cup leader), Dunham's Alvis, Green's Maserati, Barber's Cooper and Meyer's H.W.M. Eric Brandon (Cooper) and Joe Ashmore (ERA) both retired at the pits, with a broken gear lever and a broken piston respectively. Dick Jacobs made a quick stop for a plug change. Later, while catching the back of the main field, his supercharger seized, breaking both drive belts and forcing his retirement.

On lap 2 Parnell increased his speed to 3mins 15secs (71.61mph) with Aston second and Murray back up to third. On his second lap, Aston matched Parnell's standing start lap of 3mins 21secs, the fastest Manx Cup lap. Ruddock's H.R.G., Green's Maserati, Lund's Lea-Francis and Kelly's IRA all stopped briefly. By the end of lap 3, Parnell led Aston by 17 seconds.

After five laps, Parnell led Murray by 23 seconds, averaging 70.38mph, while Aston still led the Manx Cup, averaging 68.64mph and 46 seconds ahead of Dunham's Alvis. Meyer (H.W.M.) was third, 20 seconds back and

On Ballanard Road, approaching Willaston corner, Ted Lund driving the 1,670cc Lea Francis entered by Billy Skelly (17) leads the 2,500cc Alvis of Gerry Dunham (1), the race winner. Lund retired with a burst water hose. [Guy Griffiths/Billy Skelly collection]

leading Shillito's Riley by only two seconds. Webb's Turner was fifth, 54 seconds behind Shillito. Green retired his Maserati with a broken piston, leaving Parnell and Murray as the only Castletown Trophy runners. Richards made a pit stop in his Riley but continued, while Lund retired his Lea-Francis with a burst water hose.

By virtue of lurid cornering, Murray was now gaining steadily on Parnell. With laps of 3mins 13secs (72.35mph) and 3mins 12secs (72.73mph – the fastest lap of the race), he was within 3 seconds of the leader (whose average was 70.26mph) after the tenth lap and they circulated in close company for several laps.

In the Manx Cup, Aston led until he retired at Willaston on lap 9 with little end trouble. He was only 38 seconds behind the Maseratis. Dunham then inherited the lead, whereupon, with remarkable consistency, he recorded the same time of 3mins 30secs (66.50mph) for each of the next eight laps.

After ten laps, Dunham's average was 56.02mph and he led Meyer's H.W.M. by 27 seconds. Webb was now up to third, 1min 43secs behind, having passed Shillito who had been delayed by two pit stops. Stapleton (Aston Martin) was a further 30 seconds back. Barber (Cooper) and Ruddock (H.R.G.) both retired, the latter with a gear selector problem.

On lap 15, Murray managed to pass Parnell between Willaston and Cronk-ny-Mona although, due to his penalty, he was actually a lap behind. His lead on the road was short-lived, however, for he lost some 50 seconds with a spin and a collision with the hedge at The Nursery, letting Parnell slip past.

The remaining three laps were uneventful with the two winners, Parnell and Dunham crossing the line abreast, albeit Dunham still had to complete his last lap.

So, in the Castletown Trophy, Reg Parnell and David Murray finished first and second with Parnell's winning average 70.04mph. His time for the race was 59mins 49secs, 1min 26secs ahead of Murray, but with Murray's penalty putting him a lap behind. In the Manx Cup, Gerry Dunham's winning time was 1 hour 3mins 19secs (66.16mph), just 28 seconds slower than Oscar Moore's 1950 time. He finished 1min 16secs ahead of Tom Meyer. They were the only drivers to complete 18 laps. Webb, Gordon Shillito and Peter Simpson all completed 17 laps, while Stapleton completed 16 laps, Horace Richards 15 laps and the seventh and final finisher, Joe Kelly, 14 laps.

Reg Parnell's win was perhaps devalued by the lack of opposition but it was a win nevertheless, and a welcome change in his unlucky record of mechanical problems when leading the Empire Trophy in each of the previous three years. Asked by an *Isle of Man Times* reporter for a post-race comment, Parnell replied "Your roads are – rough". In contrast to Parnell, Gerry Dunham was an unlikely winner. His Alvis was an old-timer; a special 12/70 raced at Brooklands in the 1930s by his father, now fitted with a 1933 Speed Twenty engine and a consistent finisher in all four previous Manx Cup Races, placed fifth, third, sixth and fourth.

Even so, by lap 10 Dunham had been well in front and both he and his car had been smooth, consistent and reliable throughout the race. *The Light Car* said that it was "as nice a bit of driving as one has seen for a long time. His papa is proud of him".

1951 Manx Cup Race Results

Thursday 14th June 1951. Start 2.00pm. 18 laps of 3.8789 miles circuit, total distance 69.82 miles. 14 starters, 8 finishers.

1. Gerry Dunham (2,500cc Alvis), 1hr 3mins 19secs (66.16mph)
2. Tom Meyer (1,960cc H.W.M. two-seater), 1hr 4mins 35secs (64.87mph)

Failed to complete the required 18 laps:

3. J. H. Webb (1,087cc Turner), 17 laps, 1hr 3mins 36secs (62.21mph)
4. Gordon Shillito (1,988cc Riley), 17 laps, 1 hr 3 mins 44 secs (62.08mph)
5. Peter Simpson (2,443cc Healey), 17 laps, 1hr 5mins 27secs (60.45mph)
6. E.C.W. Stapleton (1,984cc Aston Martin), 16 laps 1hr 5mins 59secs (56.44mph).
7. Horace Richards (1,087cc Riley),15 laps, 1hr 9mins 31secs (50.22mph)
8. Joe Kelly (1,500cc IRA), 14 laps, 1hr 5mins 50secs (49.49mph)

Fastest lap: Bill Aston (1,098cc Cooper), 3mins 21secs (69.47mph).

Retirements:

Lap: 2 Eric Brandon (1,098cc Cooper) broken gear lever

Lap: 10 Bill Aston (1,098cc Cooper) little end trouble

Also: John Barber (994cc Cooper).

Dick Jacobs (1,087cc MG), seized supercharger.

Geoff Ruddock (1,750cc H.R.G.) gear selector problem.

Ted Lund (1,670cc Lea-Francis) burst water hose.

1951 Castletown Trophy Race Results

Thursday 14th June 1951.18 laps of 3.8789 miles circuit, total distance 69.82 miles. 4 starters, 2 finishers.

1. Reg Parnell (1,490cc Maserati 4CLT), 59mins 49secs (70.04mph)

Failed to complete the required 18 laps:

2. David Murray (1,490cc Maserati 4CLT), 17 laps, 1hr 1min 15secs (64.60mph)

Fastest lap: David Murray (1,490cc Maserati 4 CLT), 3mins 12secs 72.73 mph.

Retirements:

Lap 2: Joe Ashmore (1,488cc ERA) broken brake cam lever

Lap 5: John Green (1,490cc Maserati 4CL) broken piston.

1951 British Empire Trophy Race – Moss Wins After Griffith's Bad Luck

Although the start was brought forward by ten minutes to 3.35pm due to a forecast of rain, conditions remained dry. All 26 cars which had practised were on the grid, although there was one change of driver, with George Abecassis taking over Rob Walker's DB2 Aston Martin for which Peter Walker was the nominated driver.

Grid positions were based on practice times, irrespective of class. The front row was a Frazer Nash monopoly by David Clarke (3mins 26secs, 67.78mph), Stirling Moss (3mins 27secs) and Bob Gerard (3mins 29secs). Sydney Allard in his Cadillac engined Allard (3mins 31secs) was the fastest of the over 3 litres class and shared the second row with Donald Pitt in another Frazer Nash (3mins 32secs). They were followed by two more Frazer Nash drivers, Manx resident Bill Murray (3mins 36secs) and Norman Culpan (3mins 37secs) together with Peter Collins in another Allard Cadillac (3mins 37secs). Row 4 contained the first of the 1.5 litres class, Pat Griffith (Lester MG) and Rodney Peacock in the seventh Frazer Nash. Row 5 consisted of Frank Curtis (3.9 litre Allard), Jack Reece (Cooper MG) and Reg Parnell (Nash Healey). Behind them were Jim Mayers (Lester MG) and Guy Gale in Rob Walker's Delahaye. The seventh row consisted of S. Hill (Nash Healey), Peter Scott-Russell (3.9 litre Allard) and Lionel Leonard (Cooper MG) while row 8 comprised Ben Whitehouse (Aston Martin DB1) and Ted Lund in the fastest of the new MG TD models. Two more MG TD drivers, Dick Jacobs (whose 9 year old daughter presented a bouquet to the Douglas Mayoress Mrs T. Radcliffe before the race) and Mike Pople made up row 9 with George Abecassis (Aston Martin DB2). Row 10 comprised William Robinson (Jowett Jupiter) and Trevor Line (MG TD) and the Dyna-Panhard of "Dave" brought up the rear.

The practice performance of the Lester MGs meant that, with three laps' start over the Frazer Nashes they were expected to challenge for outright victory. Stirling Moss did not think that he had much chance. In effect, he was giving the Lesters a 12 miles start and in practice his Frazer Nash, although handling well, was under-geared, the engine felt feeble between 3,500 and 4,300 rpm and he did not know its braking capabilities. He even doubted his chances against the other Frazer Nashes but the car felt much better in the race than in practice.

Two dramatic first lap accidents dictated much of the outcome of the race.

The first happened at the first corner at Parkfield, shortly after the start by the Lieutenant Governor, Air Vice-Marshal Sir Geoffrey Bromet. Gerard had led through the corner, followed by Moss, Pitt and Culpan. Further back in the tightly packed field, Guy Gale's 3.5-

Rob Walker entered two cars – his 3,557cc Delahaye (25) for Guy Gale in the over 3,000cc class and his 2,580cc Aston Martin DB2 (12) for George Abecassis in the up to 3,000cc class. Pictured at Governor's Bridge, Abecassis finished eleventh overall and fifth in class while Gale was thirteenth overall and third in class after a first lap collision at Parkfield. [R and L Kelly collection]

litre Delahaye was hit in the rear by S. Hill's Healey Silverstone. The blue Delahaye spun in the road and then its radiator cowl smashed into a sandbagged gate pillar of Parkfield House on the apex of the corner. While other competitors squeezed past, Gale jumped out and, with help from marshals, pushed the Delahaye off the course. The battered rear wing was jammed against the tyre and would not yield to kicking and levering with various implements. Gale then seized a grappling hook, applied the end to the wing and pulled. This was successful, so he then dashed round to attend to the front end of the car. He then drove round to the pits and, after further work, was able to re-join the race although inadequate brakes, loss of oil pressure and furiously boiling water meant that he was unable to make up the lost time. Hill's Healey reached the pits but was unable to re-join the race.

The second, and more significant, accident happened on the "S" bend known as Grange Corner on the approach to the double bend at Onchan's Nursery Hotel. Moss had taken the lead from Gerard and Sydney Allard had passed both Clarke and Pitt. Allard, "rather over-enthusiastic" said *The Autocar* slid his big Cadillac-Allard which touched a bank and swung round to hit the opposite hedge, puncturing the fuel tank. The Frazer Nash of David Clarke ploughed into Allard and the two cars virtually blocked the road. Next along was Donald Pitt in his Frazer Nash, slowed by a flat tyre. On seeing a gap, he aimed for it but just then Bill Murray's Frazer Nash arrived at a much faster pace, became airborne on hitting the other cars and literally flew over the cars of Pitt and Clarke before landing heavily and hitting a telegraph pole. One of Murray's tyres actually ran along Pitt's back, leaving the outline of its tread. It tore Pitt's shirt and dented his helmet but Pitt sustained only a bruise on the back of his head. He saved his life, it was reckoned, by ducking just in time. Before the flagman had a chance to stop the following competitors, the Allard driven by Peter Collins piled into the wreckage, breaking its front axle.

All other competitors managed to get through but, although the incident removed five cars from the race, incredibly only Clarke was injured sufficiently to warrant hospital treatment. He was admitted with concussion, bruising to the head and a suspected fractured skull. The other drivers suffered only bruises and shock.

According to the *Isle of Man Times*, the flagman was the only witness to the crash and he was unsure what had happened after the initial collision of Clarke and Allard. Interviewed later by the Times reporter, Bill Murray said "I came round the bend at about 80mph and saw Allard in the ditch, with another car. I jammed everything on, but couldn't escape them. My car shot into the air over both the others and landed on top of David Clarke's model. Then my car hit a telegraph pole". His Frazer Nash had been purchased only on the previous Friday at a cost of £3,000 – the list price of the competition MG TD mark. II at the time was £630 – and since then he had been running it in, mainly at the former R.A.F. airfield at Andreas. It appeared after the crash to be a total wreck. Donald Pitt said that he had "an unpleasant moment" when he saw the car hurtle over his head.

As they crossed the line at the end of the lap, with six cars already out of the race, the order on the road was Moss (with a big lead over Gerard), Culpan, Griffith (first of the 1,500cc cars and already going very fast), Peacock, Parnell and Curtis. Mayers' Lester MG was the second "1,500", followed by the Cooper MG models of Leonard and Reece.

It was soon clear that Griffith would be difficult to catch on handicap. Moss was gaining several seconds a lap on Gerard, completing lap 3 in 3mins 30secs (66.50mph). Griffith, however, lapped at 61mph and of course had to do three laps less than the Frazer Nashes. Parnell was having trouble with the Nash Healey's gear changing and soon lost the lead in the over 3 litres class to Curtis' Allard.

Autosport described Moss' cornering as "magnificent, never wavering, never varying, always extremely fast yet safe". Gerard was "every bit as confident", Culpan "more spectacular, braking hard for each corner and slamming the throttle hard open coming out" while Curtis was "somewhat lurid at times, and on one occasion he overshot Parkfield and headed straight for the sandbags, pulling up in the nick of time stopped just short of the bags with a squeal of brakes and tyres". Robinson on the Jupiter was "cornering well, seemingly trying each lap to see how close he could go to the wall without touching it!"

By the end of lap 5 Moss was already catching the tail-enders in the 1.5 litres class. At this point, Griffith's Lester MG led on handicap from the Cooper MGs of Leonard

Reg Parnell drove a 3.8 litres works entered Nash Healey which later finished 6th at Le Mans, driven by Tony Rolt and Duncan Hamilton. Pictured in Onchan Village, the car lasted only 14 laps before the gear lever broke. [Norman Caley collection]

and Reece with the MG TDs of Lund and Jacobs fourth and fifth. The circuit was proving to be hard on brakes, particularly at Parkfield, where Jacobs, Abecassis, Whitehouse, and Curtis all had "moments".

After ten laps Moss had increased his average to 67mph. Griffith still led on handicap, with a time of 22mins 41secs (61.56mph). Leonard was 1min 24secs behind (57.98mph) with Reece third, only four seconds behind Leonard. Lund was a further 11 seconds back with Jacobs 26 seconds behind him. Griffith completed laps 10, 11 and 12 all in the same time: 3mins 42secs (62.90mph).

Culpan was catching Gerard. On lap 12 he drew level at the Manx Arms in Onchan where both passed Parnell's Nash Healey and, at Parkfield on lap 13, Culpan led by a car's length. By Cronk-ny-Mona the gap was five lengths but Gerard then closed the gap and re-passed. Abecassis hit the bank at the Nursery and damaged the front end of his car and, after 14 laps, Parnell retired on Ballanard Road with his gear lever broken, and walked back to the pits. Robinson retired a lap later, when his Jowett Jupiter's engine seized.

At the end of lap 15 Griffith had extended his lead on handicap over Reece to 2mins 35secs with a time of 41mins 14secs (62.09mph). Lund was now third, 17secs behind Reece, with Leonard down to fourth, a further 40secs back. Jacobs was still fifth, 17secs behind Leonard. He retired after 18 laps with piston trouble.

The pits were busy with Abecassis making several stops with brake and cooling problems with his Aston Martin. Scott-Russells' Allard had body damage at the nearside rear and the Dyna-Panhard saloon of "Dave" made frequent stops but one of the most incredible race incidents concerned Lionel Leonard's Cooper-MG which some called "the baby Ferrari". On his arriving in the pits with a fractured carburettor float chamber, it seemed that he might be out of the race. His mechanics did not have a spare. Then they remembered seeing an MG in the grandstand car park. It would have precisely the part they needed. Who and where the owner was they did not know. Presumably he was somewhere on the grandstand. There was no time to hunt for him or make an appeal for his help over the public address system so they simply did what the emergency required of them. They went to the parked MG, removed the vital component and left a message to that effect on the car's windscreen. After the race, when the mechanics returned the float chamber to the MG they found that its owner was "very nice about it." The incident was reminiscent of 1933, when Kaye Don's chief mechanic Donald Finlayson had successfully scoured

On the descent to the Manx Arms corner in Onchan, George Abecassis in Rob Walker's Aston Martin DB2 leads a Le Mans Replica Frazer Nash. After several pit stops, Abecassis finished eleventh overall and fifth in the up to 3,000cc class. [Stan Hughes collection]

Douglas to find an MG Magnette road car from which to borrow a rear axle for Don's K3 race car. In 1933, however, the owner gave permission before the parts were removed!

After 20 laps the picture became clearer with the appearance of Moss on the handicap leader board. Griffith still led with a time of 59mins 40secs (62.27mph). Reece was still second, four minutes back and two seconds ahead of Lund. Jim Mayers in the second Lester MG was now fourth, 2mins 19secs behind Lund but Moss was now fifth, having lapped at 67.45mph and then 68.12mph. He was only 13secs behind Mayers, averaging 66.75mph and ¾ of a lap ahead of Gerard. Ben Whitehouse retired with clutch failure after 22 laps and several stops.

Ted Lund made a fuel stop and Norman Culpan was slowed by brake trouble, causing him to hit something somewhere on the course although he was able to keep going, despite a buckled wheel.

On lap 24 Moss did the fastest lap of the race in 3mins 23secs (68.78mph). At the end of lap 25, Griffith was averaging 62.30mph, with a race time of 1hr 18mins 27secs. His lead over Reece was now 4mins 51secs. Moss was up to third on handicap, averaging 67.00mph and only 4secs behind Reece but still almost 5mins and over a lap behind Griffith and facing a seemingly impossible task even for him. Lund was fourth, 51secs behind Moss with Gerard sixth, a further 1min 46secs back and averaging 64.96mph. Mayers had been in trouble with a constant misfire, caused by an unpinned magneto lead. His exhaust pipe was also off and, after 28 laps, he was forced to retire at Willaston, where he was picked up by "Dave" and dropped off at the pits during one of Dave's many stops there!

On lap 30, Moss caught and passed Jack Reece to take second place, increasing his average to 67.19mph. At the end of the lap, Griffith's time was 1hr 36mins 45secs (average 62.55mph). Moss had four laps still to do and

Race winner Stirling Moss rounds the hairpin at Cronk-ny-Mona in Syd Green's Gilby Engineering Frazer Nash Le Mans Replica. He won the race after a brilliant drive with a handicap of three credit laps to the 1,500cc class. The similar car of three times winner Bob Gerard finished second. [Stan Hughes collection]

3mins 42secs to make up on Griffith. Reece was 2mins 28secs behind Moss and 45secs ahead of Gerard, who was 18secs ahead of Lund.

Then, with only two laps still to run, Griffith was overdue! A whole minute passed before the announcement that he had stopped at Governor's Bridge with his engine seized due to complete lack of oil. Moss came through in the lead and his father signalled him to slow down. At the same time Gerard passed Reece and the two Frazer Nashes went on to finish first and second. Moss completed the race in 1hr 57mins 38secs (67.27mph) despite slowing after Griffith's retirement. His average compared well with Bob Gerard's ERA winning average of 70.05mph in the previous year. Gerard was 3mins 24secs behind Moss (average 65.38mph) with Reece third in his Cooper MG, the first of the small car class, a lap behind and averaging 58.84mph. Next was Ted Lund's MG TD, 59secs behind Reece and averaging 58.36mph. Rodney

On the Manx Arms Corner in Onchan Jim Mayers' Lester MG (2) is about to be passed by race winner Stirling Moss in his Frazer Nash (22) while Mike Pople follows in his MG Midget TD. Mayers retired with engine failure but Pople finished seventh overall and third in class. [Stan Hughes collection]

The new production sports car formula which replaced out-and-out racing machines was emphasised by entries of four virtually standard MG TD models. Mike Pople's example, seen here at Governor's Bridge, finished third in class and seventh overall. [R and L Kelly collection]

Peacock was fifth in his Frazer Nash, completing 33 laps at an average of 62.50mph while the first of the over 3 litres class was Frank Curtis' Allard, completing 32 laps at 63.03mph. The relatively standard MG TD models of Mike Pople and Trevor Line both completed 32 laps, finishing seventh and ninth respectively, with Pople only two seconds behind Curtis. They were punctuated by Norman Culpan's Frazer Nash, which had slowed towards the end of the race. Peter Scott-Russell finished tenth in Annable's Allard, and George Abecassis was eleventh in Rob Walker's Aston Martin, both completing 31 laps. The twelfth finisher was Lionel Leonard in the second Cooper MG with the "borrowed" float chamber (30 laps) and Guy Gale was the last classified finisher in Rob Walker's Delahaye, damaged in the first lap Parkfield collision. He did 28 laps. The Dyna-Panhard of 'Dave' was still running at the finish, but he was not classified, despite having persevered doggedly to complete 18 laps with many pit stops.

Driving superbly in his first major race – his previous experience being limited to one meeting at Goodwood and a few laps at Castle Combe – Pat Griffith had shown consistency and maturity only to suffer the sort of bad luck which had dogged Reg Parnell in Manx races. At the prize presentation, Stirling Moss, after another fine drive, said with characteristic modesty "The only thing I can say is how sorry I am for Pat Griffith, for I could never have caught him had he not had trouble".

1951 British Empire Trophy Race Results

Thursday 14th June 1951. Start 2.00pm. 35 laps of 3.8789 miles circuit, total distance 135.76 miles. 26 starters, 13 finishers.

1. Stirling Moss (1,971cc Frazer Nash), 1hr 57mins 38secs (67.27mph). 1 credit lap
2. Bob Gerard (1,971cc Frazer Nash), 2hrs 1min 2secs (65.38mph). 1 credit lap
3. Jack Reece (1,250cc Cooper MG), 34 laps, 1hr 58mins 40secs (58.84mph) 4 credit laps
4. Ted Lund (1,250cc MG), 34 laps, 1hr 59mins 39secs (58.36mph) 4 credit laps
5. Robin Peacock (1,971cc Frazer Nash), 33 laps, 1hr 59mins 10secs (62.50mph) 1 credit lap
6. Frank Curtis (3,925cc Allard), 32 laps, 1hr 58mins 10secs (63.03mph). Scratch.
7. Mike Pople (1,250cc MG), 32 laps, 1hr 59mins 12secs (54.67mph) 4 credit laps
8. Norman Culpan (1,971cc Frazer Nash), 32 laps, 2hrs 1min 3secs (53.83mph) 1 credit lap
9. Trevor Line (1,250cc MG), 32 laps, 2hrs 1min 15secs (53.75mph) 4 credit laps
10. Peter Scott-Russell (3,917cc Allard), 31 laps, 1hr 58mins 46secs (60.75mph) Scratch.
11. George Abecassis (2,580cc Aston Martin DB2), 31 laps, 2hrs 1min 4secs (57.59mph), 1 credit lap
12. Lionel Leonard (1,250cc Cooper MG), 30 laps, 1hr 59mins 05secs (50.81mph). 4 credit laps.
13. Guy Gale (3,557cc Delahaye), 28 laps, 1hr 59mins 31secs (54.53mph). Scratch

Unclassified: 'Dave' (745cc Dyna Panhard) 18 laps completed. 4 credit laps

Fastest lap: Stirling Moss (1,971cc Frazer Nash), Lap 24, 3mins 23secs (68.78mph). Established lap record for production sports cars.

Class winners:

Up to 1,500cc
- 1st Jack Reece (Cooper MG)
- 2nd Ted Lund (MG)
- 3rd Mike Pople (MG)

Up to 3,000cc
- 1st Stirling Moss (Frazer Nash)
- 2nd Bob Gerard (Frazer Nash)
- 3rd Robin Peacock (Frazer Nash)

Over 3,000cc
- 1st Frank Curtis (Allard)
- 2nd Peter Scott-Russell (Allard)
- 3rd Guy Gale (Delahaye)

Retirements:

Lap 1: S. Hill (2,443cc Healey Silverstone), at pits following a collision with sandbags at Parkfield Corner, Sidney Allard (5,420cc Allard Cadillac), David Clarke (1,971cc Frazer Nash), Donald Pitt (1,971cc Frazer Nash), Bill Murray (1,971cc Frazer Nash), Peter Collins (5,420cc Allard Cadillac), all in multiple crash on "S" bend known as Grange Corner near Nursery Hotel, Onchan.

Lap 14: Reg Parnell 3,848cc (Nash Healey), broken gear lever

Lap 15: William Robinson (1,485cc Jowett Jupiter), engine seizure

Lap 18: Dick Jacobs (1,250cc MG TD Mk II), piston problem

Lap 22: Ben Whitehouse (1,970cc Aston Martin DB1), clutch problem

Lap 28: Jim Mayers (1,467cc Lester-MG), engine problem

Lap 31: Pat Griffith (1,467cc Lester-MG), seized engine.

Reaction

The races continued to receive favourable comment in the motoring Press. Writing in *The Autocar*, Sammy Davis said "The Isle of Man meeting was as much fun as it always is; there is something in the atmosphere of Mona's Isle that is especially conducive to good motor racing. Much of it, of course, must be put down to tradition and the long connection of the Island with motor racing; but I think that it must be more than that alone". *The Motor*, too, was

1951 motorcycle TT Senior and Junior winner and World Champion in the 500cc and 350cc classes, Geoff Duke was on duty as a flag marshal between Cronk-y-Berry and Edge's and this experience aroused his interest in car racing. Next year he would return, driving a works Aston Martin DB3. [Manx Motor Racing Club]

generous in its praise: "As always, this is a meeting run by the club for club members, many of whom race motorcars which are not entirely suited to the requirements of modern Grand Prix racing, but who race for the fun of it and as such it is unique in the crowded calendar and is imbued with something of the air of a garden party. There is always a pleasantly informal atmosphere which does nothing to detract from the extremely efficient organization and running of the meeting, and this is one of the most enjoyable motor racing events of the entire calendar graced by the presence of His Excellency the Lieutenant Governor of the Island, Air Vice-Marshal Sir Geoffrey Bromet and the Mayor of Douglas, Mr Radcliffe.

The Light Car also praised the organization, saying it was "excellent – as always" and that Secretary Desmond Scannell had "gathered a fine crew round him"

Motor Sport described the Island as "rather a remarkable place", commenting that "Apart from its police with sticks, horse trams and racing cars allowed to mingle with the traffic on the prom, it closes its roads by Act of Parliament and can fine anyone who trespasses thereon up to £20".

Both *The Autocar* and *Motor Sport* remarked on the fact that Geoff Duke, who won his first two motorcycle road racing World Championships later in the year, had been on duty as a flag marshal near Cronk-ny-Mona. He had told *The Autocar* that it had been a long time to stand up but worth it if only to see Moss taking the Frazer Nash through the tricky left and right hand bends at that point. Next year, Geoff would be able to sit down and enjoy a different view of Moss, from behind the wheel of a works Aston Martin!

1952 British Empire Trophy Race – Griffith's Luck Changes

Planning

In April, Tynwald considered the estimates for the 1952 car, motorcycle and bicycle races. In a debate which probably marked the beginning of the end for car racing on the Island it was admitted that the car races did not bring many visitors but did have publicity value in the early season. The Tynwald Race Committee therefore thought that the event should be continued but one member of the Committee regarded it as being "on trial" in 1952. Mr Teare, the Committee Chairman, revealed that he had been advised that the great expense of owning and maintaining a racing car made it increasingly difficult to organise a race for this type of vehicle without offering larger prizes and big "starting money" for competitors. The production car races were less expensive and increasing in popularity. Tynwald had voted £2,500 for the two races held in 1951 (of which £2,371 had been spent) but for 1952 there would be one race only, for production cars, on 29th May. This was the May date, before the TT motorcycle races, used in 1948 and 1949 rather than the post-TT date used in 1950 and 1951. The race was to be sponsored by the *Daily Dispatch* and a vote of £2,250 was recommended but a member of the Tynwald Race Committee said that the future of the event would be determined very largely by what happened in 1952.

Considerable road widening took place at Nursery Bends where the sod hedge was removed and the road width increased to 24 feet, at the corner before Nursery Bends where the 1951 pile-up had taken place and at Willaston Corner. The course was expected to be much faster after the improvements.

In April, Silver City Airways announced a new car ferry service from Liverpool Speke Airport. This was to be available for four days before the car, motorcycle and bicycle races, using one of the Bristol Freighter aircraft used on the airline's cross-channel services to France. The aircraft could carry two cars or nine motorcycles together with up to twelve passengers, at a cost of £13 per car and £4.5s (£4.25) per passenger.

The abandonment of the Manx Cup race and the concurrent Castletown Trophy meant a reduction of 27 entries compared with 1951 but the BRDC announced that the British Empire Trophy race would be run over 52 laps (201.71miles) compared with 18 laps (69.82 miles) in 1951. The classes and class handicaps were to be identical to those of 1951.

The BBC arranged to film the race for a television newsreel. Stirling Moss agreed to take the films with him by air to London immediately after the race, so that they could be screened in a five minutes slot in the 3pm news broadcast on Friday, which was to be repeated on Saturday and Sunday.

Entries

As in 1951, the BRDC accepted 31 entries for the 30 available places. The 1.5 litres class again consisted mainly of MG and MG engined cars. There were three examples of the current TD model, privately entered by Mike Llewellyn, Ted Lund and Trevor Line, together with the older TC model of Peter Jackson. The Monkey Stable entered three Lester MGs which were to be driven by Pat Griffith, Jim Mayers and Gerry Ruddock while Cooper MG models were entered by Cliff Davis and Lionel Leonard. The only other marque represented in the class was Jowett with five Jupiters, to be driven by Joe Kelly (reserve H. Sullivan), J.A. Cowap, E.W. Cuff Miller (reserve F. Dudley), Billy Skelly, and William Robinson. Competitors in this class would again receive four credit laps but the extended length of the race meant that the larger cars would have more laps in which to catch them.

In the 3 litres class Geoff Duke, the popular motorcycle TT winner and 1951 500cc and 350cc motorcycle road racing world champion attracted great interest. Following the tradition established by other stars by switching from two wheels to four, the Southport-based star, destined to make his home on the Isle of Man four years later, was to make his car-racing debut at the wheel of a privately entered but works prepared 2.6 litres Aston Martin DB3.

During the previous year's British Empire Trophy meeting Duke had acted as a flag marshal near Cronk-ny-Mona. It had been a long time to stand up, he had said later, but it had been worth it to see how Stirling Moss had taken his Frazer Nash through the difficult left and right-hand bends. Now he had a chance to apply that knowledge.

In the autumn of 1951, when he had been presented in London with the Sportsman of the Year Trophy, he had been approached on behalf of Aston Martin by veteran TT car racer, Lord Brabazon. The latter had asked him to consider a trial drive of an Aston Martin DB2 on a test track at the Motor Industry Research Association's circuit in Nuneaton. Duke had agreed and had performed so well, driving the DB2 faster than it had been driven on the track before, that a works drive with a prototype DB3 at Goodwood at Easter 1952 had been arranged soon afterwards. He had finished second, beating Stirling Moss (Jaguar C type) who had finished fourth. In his next race, at Silverstone, Geoff crashed due to oil dropped by another car but in a fantastic drive in the Swiss Grand Prix at Berne in an Aston Martin DB2 (which suited his driving style better than the DB3) he finished fourth behind three works Mercedes after losing nearly a lap when he was held up after the fourth Mercedes demolished a tree. This drive led to his being offered a place in the Mercedes sports car team for 1953.

The Manx race was to be Duke's fourth and last drive in 1952 for Aston Martin.

Lined up against the lone Aston Martin were six Frazer Nash entries, five of which were Le Mans replica cars. Stirling Moss was again entered by Sid Green to drive the Gilby Engineering car in which he had won the 1951 race after Pat Griffith's retirement. Moss would have a busy week, racing at Nurburgring on the previous Sunday in a Formula 2 H.W.M. and flying from the Island to the south of France straight after the Empire Trophy in time for Friday morning practice for the Monaco Grand Prix. Roy Salvadori was entered by Tony Crook, Jack Walton entered himself and Peter Bolton and two other cars were entered by H.A. Mitchell and Jack Reece. Mike Hawthorn, the winner of the 1951 *Motor Sport* Brooklands Memorial Trophy, was entered by Leonard Potter to drive the latter's streamlined Mille Miglia car which arrived with front wing damage sustained when the car was being loaded onto the ferry at Liverpool. According to Roy Salvadori, this car was generally reckoned to be slower than the Le Mans type cars. The only other car in the class was John Buncombe's Healey. This class again received one credit lap.

The over 3 litres scratch class was almost a Jaguar monopoly with seven of the XK120 sports models which were now more readily available than in 1951. Three of these were the "exquisitely turned-out" (according to *Autosport*) Ecurie Ecosse team cars of team founder David Murray (standing in for Bill Dobson), Ian Stewart and Sir James Scott Douglas, while the remaining four were cars entered privately by Bill Holt (reserve Graham Whitehead), Stanley Boshier, John Swift, and W. Belfrage Black. In addition, Duncan Hamilton entered his Jaguar C-type (XKC 004) which, according to *The Motor*, was the only privately owned car of this type in the country. The only other car in the class was the 5.4 litres Cadillac engined Allard of Alfred Hitchings.

Practice

Practice took place in the evenings of Tuesday 27th and Wednesday 28th May. On Tuesday the roads were damp and there were two incidents – Cuff Miller's reserve driver, F. Dudley, crashed the former's Jowett Jupiter into the wall at Parkfield and Alfred Hitchings hit the bank at Cronk-y-Berry. Miller's car was too severely damaged to be repaired in time for the race but neither driver was hurt.

In Tuesday's damp conditions, Duncan Hamilton managed a very quick lap in 3mins 16secs (71.24mph), seven seconds faster than Stirling Moss and eight seconds faster than Geoff Duke. Hamilton found after the practice that there was a problem with the steering of his Jaguar

XK120C and did not take part in Wednesday's session. He did not need to. Despite the damp roads his Tuesday time was good enough for pole position, with Duke and Moss lapping in the dry conditions on Wednesday in 3mins 17secs and 3mins 18secs respectively. Duke later said that he found the course bumpy, quite difficult and "a bit narrow" for the larger cars like the Aston Martin and the Jaguars, making overtaking difficult. The fastest 1,500cc car was Jim Mayers' Lester MG with a time of 3mins 29secs (66.81mph).

There was speculation after practice as to how the handicapping would work out over the extended race distance. The Lester MG drivers reportedly thought that they could stay ahead of their larger pursuers. If Mayers could complete each of his 48 laps in 3min 29secs and if Duke lapped in 3mins 17secs on each of his 51 laps, then Mayers would beat Duke by 15 seconds. On the other hand, if Hamilton could improve his lap time to 3mins 13secs and maintain this for 52 laps he would finish only four seconds after Mayers. Of course, what could be achieved in practice and what could be achieved in the race would be entirely different.

1952 British Empire Trophy Race

Race day was dry and breezy, with occasional sunshine. There were 27 starters out of 31 entries, the absentees being Cuff Miller's Jowett Jupiter which could not be repaired after its practice crash, Cowap's Jupiter and the Frazer Nash entries of Walton/Bolton and Jackie Reece. All the cars were of British manufacture.

On pole position was Duncan Hamilton's C-type Jaguar, whose practice lap of 3mins 16secs (71.24mph) was an unofficial sports car record. He shared the front row with Geoff Duke's Aston Martin (3mins 17secs) and Stirling Moss' Frazer Nash (3mins 18secs). Behind them were Mike Hawthorn's Mille Miglia Frazer Nash and Mitchell's Le Mans Replica. Jim Mayers' Lester MG was the fastest 1,500cc car in practice and he shared row 3 with Roy Salvadori's Frazer Nash and Ian Stewart who was in the first of the Jaguar XK120 models and over 3mph faster than the next XK120. Salvadori had changed his rear axle ratio after finding the car over-geared in practice. Pat Griffith in the second Lester MG and John Swift's XK 120 made up the fourth row ahead of the all-Jaguar fifth row of Stanley Boshier, Sir James Scott Douglas and David Murray. Behind them were Lionel Leonard (Cooper MG) and Gerry Ruddock (Lester MG), followed by Belfrage Black (Jaguar XK120), Alfred Hitchings (Allard) and Cliff Davis (Cooper MG). Row 8 consisted of John Buncombe's Healey and Bill Holt's Jaguar XK120 while on row 9 were the Jowett Jupiters of William Robinson and Joe Kelly with the MG TD of Michael Llewellyn. Row 10 contained two more MG TD models of Ted Lund and Trevor Line with Billy Skelly (Jowett Jupiter) and Peter Jackson (MG TC) bringing up the rear.

Duncan Hamilton led the field into Parkfield, followed by Hawthorn, Salvadori, Duke, Mitchell and Moss, but, by the time they reached Onchan, Moss had passed both Salvadori and Hawthorn and was close behind Hamilton at the end of the lap. At the end of lap 2, dramatically and to loud cheers from his many supporters, Duke passed Hamilton in front of the Grandstand. Moss was up to fourth behind Hawthorn and Jim Mayers made the first pit stop, due to trouble with an oil pressure relief valve. By now Pat Griffith, lapping at 61mph, led the 1,500cc class from Mayers, Ruddock, Leonard and Davis.

At the end of lap 3, Duke had stretched his lead over Hamilton to 200 yards and, on lap 4, he set a new sports car lap record of 3mins 18secs (70.53mph), which he was to repeat on laps 6, 7 and 13, beating Moss' 1951 record by 5 seconds. He now led Hamilton by 14 seconds but, dropping back on the next lap, Hamilton retired after Onchan Village after the combination of a full fuel load and the bumpy section at Governor's Bridge caused failure of the 'A' bracket. This became a regular fault on C-type Jaguars. Moss was now Duke's nearest challenger but Duke steadily increased his lead: 25 seconds on lap 6, 29 seconds on lap 7, 33 seconds on lap 8, 36 seconds on lap 9, 39 seconds on lap 10 and 44 seconds on lap 11. On handicap, he was already only two laps behind Griffith and Ruddock. Meanwhile Hitchings' Cadillac Allard retired with gearbox failure after 8 laps and Lund retired his MG with big end failure at the end of lap 11.

On lap 13, Moss stopped for a plug change, losing almost two minutes. Two laps later he was back for a coil

Alfred Hitchings powers his Cadillac-Allard out of Cronk-ny-Mona hairpin. His was the only non-Jaguar in the scratch class for cars of over 3,000cc. He retired with gearbox trouble. [Manx National Heritage]

Stirling Moss, seen at Willaston corner driving the Gilby Engineering Frazer Nash in which he won in 1951, led his class for a time until after many pit stops he was forced to retire with misfiring, over-heating and fuel pump problems. [Manx National Heritage]

change, losing over seven minutes. Duke now led Hawthorn by 1min 13secs, the latter having shed his exhaust. The leaders on handicap were Griffith, Ruddock, Leonard, Davis and Kelly, but Davis soon suffered a bearing failure. Holt pitted with a broken throttle return spring, Swift retired with clutch trouble and Murray's brakes failed due to a total loss of hydraulic fluid. First he overshot at Parkfield and then he spun at Onchan and nearly went backwards through a shop window. This incident was of benefit to the regular Ecurie Ecosse drivers who had complained to Murray about the XK120 brakes, only to have their comments brushed aside, but, said Ian Stewart "after that we never had any trouble with David when we complained about the brakes because he suddenly understood the problem".

On lap 19 Duke caught Joe Kelly to take fourth place on handicap, behind Griffith, Ruddock, and Leonard and was barely a lap behind Griffith, whom he had every chance of catching. Then it all went wrong. Suddenly, on Lap 22, the Aston Martin's engine cut out at the Manx Arms in Onchan. The lead between the ammeter and the coil had become detached at the ammeter end and was causing the car's engine to misfire. This had happened during practising so Duke was familiar with the difficulty. He tinkered with the problem area, managed to get the engine started and limped in to the pits. To put things right was a frustratingly major operation. The loose terminal could not be reached without substantial dismantling of the instrument panel. That took seven critical minutes. Finally, however, Duke was on his way again only to encounter further problems. Again, disaster struck at the Manx Arms corner. This time the crankshaft broke. With the help of a police sergeant and two constables, Duke pushed the car off the course, watched some of the race there and then ambled nonchalantly along the course to the pits. He smiled when a fellow driver roaring into the pits made him jump to one side. "It was not, perhaps, really a 'near thing,' but it looked as though it was going to be," recorded the *Isle of Man Daily Times*. What was particularly galling for Duke was a subsequent apology he received from the owner of Aston Martin, David Brown. "He told that if they had realised how well I was going to do," said Duke, "they would have given me a decent engine". The engine that had been fitted in Duke's car had spent hundreds of hours on a test bench. "That was why the crankshaft broke," said Duke later. "It was fatigued." Later that year, after several successful

The Cooper MG of Cliff Davis, at Willaston, was running fourth on handicap until forced to retire when an engine bearing failed. A similar problem had occurred during practice. [Manx National Heritage]

drives for Aston Martin, Duke became a contracted works driver for 1953. By then, having experienced a bad motorcycle accident at the Schottten circuit in Germany, he was inclined to give up two-wheeled racing altogether. He discovered later, however, that he could not bring himself to do that so negotiated a release from his car racing contract to join the Gilera team.

Moss stopped for a new fan belt, losing a further 5mins 37secs. Jim Mayers retired at the Pits with a broken steering box mounting while the action continued at Onchan's Manx Arms corner when the handicap leader, Pat Griffith, collided with an errant dog. The impact broke a front wing stay but the dog survived and ran off

Among the seven near-standard Jaguar XK120 entries in the over 3,000cc class was one driven by John Swift, pictured at Willaston corner. His was the second fastest XK120 in practice, faster than two of the Ecurie Ecosse cars, but he retired from the race with clutch trouble. [Manx National Heritage]

Geoff Duke passes the Isle of Man Bank on Main Road Onchan in the works Aston Martin DB3. He had two stops in Onchan, the first to re-connect a loose wire behind the dashboard and the second when his crankshaft broke, bringing a fine drive to a premature end. [Stan Hughes collection]

Mike Hawthorn rounds Cronk-ny-Mona in the smart cream-painted Frazer Nash Mille Miglia replica entered by Len Potter, in which he finished third and won the class for cars up to 3,000cc. [Manx National Heritage]

Five Jowett Jupiters contested the 1,500cc class, reflecting the popularity of the production car format introduced to the British Empire Trophy in 1951. Scottish motor trader Billy Skelly, who later became an Isle of Man resident, is pictured at Willaston. He retired with vibration caused by a broken fan blade. [Manx National Heritage]

"showing spectators what speed really is", according to the *Isle of Man Times*. The car, however, was more damaged than the dog for Griffith had to make a brief pit stop to have the loose wing torn off. At about this time, near the Grandstand, another errant dog was arrested by a Police Sergeant.

At half-distance (26 laps completed) the order on handicap was Griffith, Ruddock, Leonard, Hawthorn and Salvadori, with Griffith and Ruddock looking increasingly unlikely to be caught. Moss made his fourth pit stop - this time for a new condenser. A lap later, he had to stop again, for a change of fuel pump, losing over six minutes.

With 30 laps completed, the order was unchanged, with Hawthorn leading Salvadori and Mitchell comfortably but still four minutes behind Griffith. The Jaguar class (all-Jaguar since the retirement of the Allard) was led by Ian Stewart and Sir James Scott Douglas. Stanley Boshier had hit the bags at Parkfield and now pitted for brakes and fuel.

Lionel Leonard retired his Cooper MG on lap 37 with a blown gasket. Hawthorn was now third but with little chance of catching the Lesters. Stewart retired with a broken fuel pipe and loss of oil, giving the class lead to Scott Douglas who was well ahead of Black and Holt, while Black was struggling with his dynamo loose and no belt to his water pump. Skelly retired his Jupiter with severe vibration which was initially thought to be a valve problem but was eventually traced to a broken blade of his four-bladed fan, and Moss finally retired after a wretched race. Hawthorn made a quick pit stop, taking on five gallons of fuel in 19 seconds and making his pursuit of Griffith and Ruddock even more futile.

The race was now effectively over. With only four laps left, Jackson's MG was the last of 14 retirements, and Pat Griffith was the first of only 13 finishers. Gerry Ruddock finished only 21 seconds back, with Mike Hawthorn 31 seconds behind Ruddock, winning the up to three litres class. Roy Salvadori came fourth and was happy to be "well in the money" (£50) and enjoyed combining the race with a good holiday. Mitchell was the third Frazer Nash driver to finish with Sir James Scott Douglas sixth and the winner of the over three litres class. Robinson finished in seventh place in his Jupiter, followed by the MG TD models of Line and Llewellyn who finished only three seconds apart. Joe Kelly was tenth in his Jupiter, followed by the Jaguars of Stanley Boshier, Belfrage Black and Bill Holt.

Pat Griffith was a deserving winner after his last-minute retirement while leading in 1951. This time it was the pursuer who suffered the disappointment, for Geoff Duke had mounted a realistic challenge in the early laps when his incredible pace had made him the likely winner until he was let down by an unreliable car. He had the compensation of the Siam Trophy for the fastest lap and a new sports car lap record.

1952 British Empire Trophy Race Results

Thursday 29th May 1952. Start 2.30pm. 52 laps of 3.8789 miles circuit, total distance 201.70 miles. 27 starters, 13 finishers.

1. Pat Griffith (1,467cc Lester-MG), 2hrs 54mins (64.20mph) 4 credit laps
2. Gerry Ruddock (1,467cc Lester-MG), 2hrs 54mins 21secs (64.07mph). 4 credit laps
3. Mike Hawthorn (1,971cc Frazer Nash), 2hrs 54mins 52secs (67.88mph) 1 credit lap
4. Roy Salvadori (1,971cc Frazer Nash), 2hrs 56mins 20secs (67.31 mph) 1 credit lap
5. H. A. Mitchell (1,971cc Frazer Nash), 2hrs 57mins 42secs (66.79 mph). 1 credit lap
6. Sir James Scott Douglas (3,442cc Jaguar XK120), 2hrs 54mins 52secs (65.22mph) Scratch.
7. William Robinson (1,486cc Jowett Jupiter), 48 laps, 2hrs 56mins 12secs (58.12 mph) 4 credit laps.
8. Trevor Line (1,250cc MG TD.), 47 laps, 2hrs 56mins 47secs (56.61mph) 4 credit laps
9. Michael Llewellyn (1,250cc MG TD.), 2hrs 56mins 50secs (56.59mph) 4 credit laps
10. Joe Kelly (1,486cc Jowett Jupiter), 2hrs 57mins 45secs (56.30mph). 4 credit laps.
11. Stanley Boshier (3,442cc Jaguar XK120), 2hrs 57mins 02secs (57.84mph) Scratch.
12. Belfrage Black (3,442cc Jaguar XK120), 2hrs 55mins 21secs (57.07mph) Scratch.
13. Bill Holt (3,442cc Jaguar XK120), 2hrs 56mins 38secs (51.39mph) Scratch.

Fastest lap: Geoff Duke (Aston-Martin), 3mins 18secs (70.53mph). New lap record for production sports cars.

Class Results:

Up to 1,500cc

1. Pat Griffith (Lester MG).
2. Gerry Ruddock (Lester MG).
3. W. H. Robinson (Jowett Jupiter).

Fastest lap: Jim Mayers (Lester MG), 3mins 29secs (66.81mph).

1,501cc to 3,000cc

1. Mike Hawthorn (Frazer Nash).
2. Roy Salvadori (Frazer Nash).
3. H. A. Mitchell (Frazer Nash).

Fastest lap: Geoff Duke (Aston Martin), 3mins 18secs (70.53mph).

Over 3,000cc

1. Sir James Scott Douglas (Jaguar XK120).
2. Stanley Boshier (Jaguar XK120).
3. W. Belfrage Black (Jaguar XK120).

Fastest lap: Duncan Hamilton (Jaguar C-type), 3mins 22secs (69.13mph).
Retirements:
Duncan Hamilton (3,442cc Jaguar C-type) 'A' bracket
Alfred Hitchings (5,420cc Cadillac Allard) Gearbox
Ted Lund (1,250cc MG TD) Big end
Cliff Davis (1,496cc Cooper MG) Bearing
John Swift (3,442cc Jaguar XK120) Clutch
David Murray (3,442cc Jaguar XK120) Brakes
Geoff Duke (2,580cc Aston Martin) Crankshaft
Jim Mayers (1,467cc Lester MG) Steering
Lionel Leonard (1,496cc Cooper MG) Blown gasket
Ian Stewart (3,442cc Jaguar XK120) Fuel pipe and oil loss
Billy Skelly (1,486cc Jowett Jupiter) Vibration caused by broken fan blade
Stirling Moss (1,971cc Frazer Nash) Electrics and fuel feed
Peter Jackson (1,250cc MG TC) Big end
John Buncombe (2,443cc Healey).

Reaction

The race was an undoubted success, thanks largely to Geoff Duke's record-breaking pursuit of Pat Griffith and the other 1,500cc cars and its dramatic conclusion. At the Presentation the Governor commented that, as a sporting spectacle, the race was the best staged on the Island in the post-war years and was probably the best type of event for the tricky little Douglas course. Sir Algernon Lee Guinness, the Chief Steward of the race, added that it was 47 years since he had first driven in the Island – he had driven a Darracq in the 1905 TT – and that he had never ceased to love the place.

Two weeks after the race, the *Isle of Man Examiner* reported that the recently published Tynwald Race Committee Annual Report stated that the car races provided valuable publicity in the national Press and brought visitors to the Island but that it was clear that they were not a notable attraction for visitors. On 15th August 1952, the *Examiner* reported a Douglas Town Council debate which had resulted in the Council informing the Tynwald Race Committee that, in the Council's opinion, the races were not sufficiently attractive to warrant road closures in and around Douglas and expenditure of public moneys. It was said that the Grandstand revenue from the 1952 race was £256 compared with £579 in 1951. Although the cost of course preparation, Grandstand administration, printing, advertising and other expenses incurred by the Council had fallen from £229 in 1951 to £131 in 1952 the surplus had been only £124 compared with £350 in 1951. The Council had spent £256 on hospitality and entertainment in 1952, compared with £233 in 1951. Although he referred to inconvenience and noise caused by repeated road closures, Alderman Skillicorn nevertheless suggested that a sidecar race would be a greater attraction! Councillor Stephen, however, thought that Douglas was not so flush with holiday attractions that they could afford to give one away, even a small one like the car races.

In October, the *Isle of Man Examiner* reported a change of heart. The Tynwald Race Committee had decided that the race might continue, on 18th June or alternatively in August, as the Committee felt that it should be continued as an attraction for visitors and as a means of publicity for the Island. The race should be for "sports or production cars". The Clerk of Tynwald had informed the Town Council of this decision and had asked whether the Council would support a race on either date. The Finance Committee had agreed to recommend to the full Council that it should support a race on 18th June provided it was "confined to production cars as distinct from the races held previously". As the Empire Trophy had been a production car race in both 1951 and 1952, it was not clear what kind of race the Council wanted but it seems that they had in mind a race which would have full manufacturer support and not, as Aldermen Cowell rather dismissively described the 1952 race, "a run around for the boys". Councillor Stephen suggested that a sidecar race, as proposed by Alderman Skillicorn, should be organised by the Manx Motor Cycle Club as a support race.

The *Examiner* returned to the subject in a leader in the next week's issue. The criticism had been that the races had failed to produce a big following compared with other events. Car races in England were attracting huge crowds who went to watch famous drivers. The Isle of Man was the birthplace of car racing but had only a minor role. No effort had been spared to build the motorcycle races but the Island had never considered car racing seriously and so the car racing fraternity had never regarded seriously the Island's efforts to attract them. The *Examiner* thought that the car races should be undertaken on a big scale with serious intent – it was no use dabbling in minor events of no significance. Big events meant big money – the TT was not run on a pittance.

In December the *Mona's Herald* reported that the Douglas Town Council had received a letter from the Clerk to Tynwald confirming that Thursday June 18th had now been officially allocated to the BRDC as the date for the 1953 British Empire Trophy Race. Apparently still confused, the Council instructed the Town Clerk to enquire whether the race would be for production cars or whether it would be "in all respects a race similar to the one held last year".

Geoff Duke's Car Racing Career

While Geoff Duke's interest in car racing was sparked by his spell as a Flag Marshal during the 1951 British Empire Trophy it may have come to nothing but for an approach by Lord Brabazon to Aston Martin owner David Brown. Team Manager John Wyer then arranged a secret test drive of a lightweight Aston Martin DB2 when Wyer was surprised to find that Geoff immediately lapped only one second off the best time ever recorded at the track by an Aston Martin. Later, he was faster than any other Aston Martin driver and a contract was soon signed.

Duke's first race for Aston Martin was at the British Automobile Racing Club's Easter meeting at Goodwood. Driving the second prototype DB3 in a six lap handicap race for sports cars he finished third behind two Jaguar XK120s and ten seconds ahead of the Jaguar C-type of Stirling Moss. The next race, at Silverstone, ended with a collision with an MG which deposited oil when Geoff was about to lap it, and later steering failure.

The Swiss Grand Prix meeting on the Bremgarten circuit at Berne combined both car and motorcycle races and Geoff drove an Aston Martin DB2 in the sports car race as well as riding Nortons in the motorcycle Grand Prix, winning the 350cc race but retiring in the 500cc. He knew the circuit very well from motorcycle races and had the advantage of driving a lightweight DB2 which he preferred to the DB3 as the precise handling of the DB2 resembled that of a motorcycle. In the first practice Duke found his car's handling poor, so John Wyer suggested that he should try team-mate Reg Parnell's car in the second session. Geoff then set the fifth best time behind four works Mercedes Benz 300 SL models. This put Parnell on the second row of the grid, while Geoff languished at the back. To add insult to injury, Norton boss Joe Craig had been watching the second practice out on the course and said that Geoff had been very good but that Parnell was really flying in the second session. (Craig had failed to notice that Duke was driving Parnell's car!). In the race, despite his poor grid position, Geoff passed a works Lancia and fought his way through the field until Caracciola's Mercedes crashed and brought down a tree. This delayed all but the three leading Mercedes drivers who were ahead of the crash, but Geoff eventually finished fourth behind the three Mercedes, and had the satisfaction of finishing ahead of Reg Parnell. Geoff said in 2011 that he remembered this event as the highlight of his car racing career.

The Berne result greatly impressed legendary Mercedes Team Manager Alfred Neubauer. Soon, Geoff was at Hockenheim testing a 300 SL and received an offer to drive for the Mercedes sports car team in 1953. Although this could have led to a full Grand Prix drive in 1954, Geoff declined the offer, deciding to stay with Aston Martin for 1953 despite a rather strained atmosphere, particularly with Peter Collins.

The next 1952 outing was the British Empire Trophy, which Duke found frustrating to say the least. He was stopped temporarily by the wiring fault which should have been eradicated before the race, then forced into retirement by crankshaft failure and finally, incredibly, told by David Brown that the engine had been well-worn in bench testing and that he would have been given a better car had they realised how well he would drive!

For 1953, Duke accepted Wyer's offer of a full contract, which meant no motorcycle racing. In the first event, the 12 hours race at Sebring, Florida, he shared a DB3 with Peter Collins. Driving the first stint, Collins built up a substantial lead before handing over to Duke. He kept the lead until he caused a collision on a medium speed right hand bend by diving inside a much slower MG which he was lapping. The MG driver held his line but the DB3 drifted, collided with the MG, spun and hit a concrete-filled oil drum course marker, causing rear suspension failure and forcing retirement. Collins then made comments about his competence as a driver which changed the atmosphere from poor to unbearable.

After the Sebring race Geoff became depressed and disillusioned with car racing. He tried a standard production 350cc Manx Norton at Silverstone, finished 7th in the race and enjoyed it so much that he felt motorcycle racing was the life for him. After his Aston Martin's clutch failed in the sports car race, Geoff went home thinking very deeply about his future. There was clearly no opportunity of returning to Norton and after testing a Gilera at Monza, he contacted David Brown who agreed to release him from the Aston Martin contract. Then he joined Gilera where he remained for five years, until they withdrew from racing at the end of 1957, winning three 500cc World Championships with the team.

Interviewed in 2011, Geoff said that it was the atmosphere in the Aston Martin team which made him give up. Otherwise he would have completed his contract. It was clear that John Wyer thought highly of him but, apart from persuading the team to change successfully to Avon tyres which had proved excellent on Norton motorcycles, he did not get what he wanted with the cars. Development was very limited in 1952 but improved in 1953, after Geoff had left, with the DB3S. All in all, it was not a pleasant interlude. The car racing world was quite different from motorcycles, and he was not at ease. Even the Mercedes offer had not been tempting, despite the possibility of Grand Prix as well as sports car racing.

John Wyer thought that Duke had difficulty settling in the Aston Martin team and that the other drivers, resentful of the greater publicity which he attracted, did nothing to make it easier for him. Wyer regarded his early retirement as a loss to motor racing.

Roy Salvadori, who replaced Duke in the Aston Martin team, thought that Geoff "never had a chance". While team-mates had said that he had the talent to become a World

Championship contender, he had not had the chance to gain experience in minor races before graduating to international events. Also, most of the team were against him. Salvadori mentioned Peter Collins in particular, saying that Collins himself never looked for publicity but resented the star publicity which Duke attracted. Salvadori described Geoff's Berne drive as "absolutely sensational" and reflected that it was a pity that he had missed out on the DB3S which was a much better car.

There was, however, a possibility of Geoff returning to car racing in 1955. Towards the end of 1954 he was one of several drivers invited by Jaguar Team Manager "Lofty" England to test a D-type Jaguar. England said that he drove "very sensibly but not very quickly" and nothing came of the test as far as Duke was concerned.

In 1960, after final retirement from motorcycle racing, Geoff accepted an offer from Graham Warner of The Chequered Flag, a garage business in Chiswick, West London, to drive a Formula Junior Gemini. At Monaco, after a spin, he was hit from behind by Tim Parnell (son of Reg) and forced to retire with broken suspension. At Silverstone, he aquaplaned off in torrential rain while in second place. At the end of the season Warner withdrew from racing which Duke found sad as the car had shown promise and the team was very enthusiastic.

An unexpected opportunity came in June 1961 with a telephone call from Fred Tuck, a former speedway rider who had a Formula 1 Cooper which he invited Geoff to drive at the Nurburgring and also at Karlskoga, Sweden. Tuck abandoned the Nurburgring entry due to insufficient funds, much to Geoff's disappointment. At Karlskoga he was making progress until the gearbox locked up on the fifth lap. The car spun, hit a grass bank and shot up in the air, rolled over and crashed down on top of the driver. Geoff's injuries included ribs torn from the sternum, collapsed left lung, damage to heart muscles, fractured collar-bone, cracked pelvis and haematoma on the left hip. After a few days in hospital when his condition caused great worry to Roy Salvadori and John Surtees, he was discharged but, after a very difficult journey home to the Isle of Man, he was again hospitalised. After recovery, he was told by the specialist who had been treating him to remember that he had been very near death. This was the end of his driving career.

1953 British Empire Trophy Race – Reg Parnell Wins At Last.

Planning

In April 1953 the Tynwald Race Committee proposed a grant of £3,250 for the 1953 Race, compared with £2,250 in 1952. The Committee was not enamoured with the contribution made by the races but the Tourist Board had called a conference of delegates of Douglas Corporation and bodies closely connected with the visiting season and the unanimous conclusion had been that it would not be wise to abandon the race immediately while no alternative had been found. BRDC Secretary and Clerk of the Course Desmond Scannell had visited the Island and made suggestions for different forms of races. The proposal favoured by the Committee involved two heats and a final, which might avoid the lack of interest caused by large numbers of retirements but which would cost more due to more cars in separate heats and more prize money. The Committee thought this was worth trying but made it clear that if it was not successful the Committee would not consider a continuance for another year. The report also recommended Tynwald to support a Sidecar race in 1954, either on the car race circuit or on a variation of that circuit.

An amendment to delete the race from the list of grants was moved by opponents. It was said that although the race attracted little publicity it was costing £1,000 more than the Manx Grand Prix. The car races had not brought the enthusiasts that the TT Races brought but only a few drivers who departed within 48 hours. One of the problems, a member said, was that the races had never been held in the same week – the date was changed every year. The amendment to delete the grant was defeated heavily but an amendment calling for an early report from the Tynwald Race Committee with proposals for 1954 was passed unanimously. The race had survived but it was highly likely that the 1953 event would be the last.

In its issue of 15th May, *The Autocar* commented that it was unfortunate that the only road circuits in the British Isles were in Douglas and at Dundrod, Northern Ireland. Many who would like to see the British Empire Trophy Race were unable to do so which meant that, although the Douglas course was a fine venue, it was a sad

This cartoon by "Dusty" in the Isle of Man Times illustrates the artist's view of the Isle of Man Government's attitude to the cost and value to the Island of the British Empire Trophy Races. [Isle of Man Times]

possibility that the 1953 event would be the last, due to lack of public support. The magazine went on to confirm that there would be two or more heats of eight laps each and a final of sixteen laps. The event, previously restricted to production sports cars, would now be open to any sports cars including prototypes and individually built sports cars which should stimulate a varied and interesting entry and keener competition in each class. Cars of up to 1,500cc would receive three minutes' start, cars from 1,500cc to 2,600 cc would be given one minute's start and those over 2,600cc would start on scratch. The first seven in each heat and the next nine fastest in the heats would contest the final, which would be limited to 30 cars. There would be cash prizes of £50 each for the winner and for the fastest finisher, £100 for the entrant of the first all-British car and £75, £50 and £40 for the first three finishers in each class.

On 5th June, *The Autocar* reported good entries and hoped that there would be a good crowd of spectators as otherwise it was doubtful that the event would be held again. Later, the magazine commented that the entry was so good that there would be three heats and a final with the first seven in each heat and the next nine fastest in the heats eligible for the final. Also there would be a high speed demonstration lap by the V-16 BRM Grand Prix car. A special race day excursion from Fleetwood was available, priced at 15 shillings (75p).

Entries

The new format, with each of the three classes having its own heat, enabled the organisers to attract more entries. Previously, with only one race and no heats, entries had been restricted to the course limit of 30 cars. Now 48 entries were accepted (16 in each class) and the Press reported that the total might have been 60 but for the limit.

In the 1,500cc class, The Monkey Stable had replaced their Lester MG cars with three Kiefts. The 1952 team drivers, Jim Mayers and Pat Griffith, were joined by Mike Keen. A rumoured entry for Trevor Line did not materialize. Gerry Ruddock, who had driven in the team in 1952, entered his own Lester MG and similar cars were entered by Peter Jackson and by Alfred Hitchings, who would use the car in which Pat Griffith had won the 1952 race. Cliff Davis entered his Cooper MG, with Peter Reece and Horace Gould entering similar cars. Lionel Leonard would drive his Leonard MG (having originally intended to drive a Tojeiro) and other MG drivers were John Haesendonck (entered by T.W. Dargue), Ernest Cooper Harewood and Ted Lund. John Riseley Pritchard was entered by Cornhill Racing Team to drive a Cooper Riley, John Goldschmidt entered a Performance Special and Chris Threlfall had a Tojeiro.

The upper limit for the over 1,500cc class was now 2,600cc (previously 3,000cc). No less than six Le Mans Replica Frazer Nashes were entered. Syd Green's Gilby Engineering car, which had taken Stirling Moss to victory in 1951 but had given him no end of trouble in 1952, was to be driven by 1951 Manx Cup winner Gerry Dunham. Another interesting Frazer Nash driver was Ken Wharton who had raced a wide range of cars and had been British hill-climb champion in the previous two years. He had the latest version of the car, with a de Dion rear axle and knock-on wire wheels. Other drivers with similar cars were Peter Scott-Russell (entered by H.A. Mitchell), Bill Belfrage Black and course newcomers and friends Peter Kenneth and James Neilson, both of whom were in the fish trade in Scotland. Aston Martin DB2 models were entered by Peter Clark and Nigel Mann while Gray Mickel, Peter Simpson and A.C. Westwood entered Healeys. John Barber entered his ultra-streamlined Golding Cooper which resembled a flying saucer and R.J. Chase entered a Cooper Bristol to be driven by Alan Brown. M.C. Kearon entered a Connaught for A.R. Huxley to drive, P.A.B. Stewart entered an H.W.M. Alta and Cliff Davis' Tojeiro was to be driven by Peter Gammon.

The over 2,600cc class had seven Jaguar entries five of which were C-types. Stirling Moss (who had recently taken up flying and flew himself direct to the Island from Le Mans where he had been runner-up in a works C-type shared with Peter Walker) had a works car. A rumour that Walker would drive a second works car on the Island came to nothing. Ecurie Ecosse entered three cars for Ian Stewart (XKC006), Ninian Sanderson (XKC042) and Jimmy Stewart (elder brother of Jackie who would win 27 Grands Prix and 3 World Championships) in XKC041. John Swift entered his own C-type while David Boston and H. Kemp Place entered XK120 models. There were two Allards – Desmond Titterington had a 3.9 litre car while Ken Watkins had a 5.4 litre Cadillac-engined model.

Reg Parnell was to drive a works Aston Martin DB3S (a much developed, lighter and faster 2.9 litre version of the DB3 driven by Geoff Duke in 1952). Parnell was anxious to make amends after a disastrous Le Mans where he went off the road in the first hour in the DB3S which he was sharing with Peter Collins. Asked by Team Manager John Wyer what had happened, Reg had replied that he had lost concentration and had been thinking about his pigs! He therefore asked Wyer if he could drive YMY 307, the prototype DB3S (which Wyer treated as a "travelling parts department"), on the Island. Aston Martin owner David Brown told Wyer "Yes, if you think you can win, have a go" so, very early on the Monday morning after the Le Mans race, Parnell set off alone from Le Mans in the race car for the ferry crossing to England and then drove to Liverpool via the Aston Martin factory at Feltham and his farm near Derby, arriving in Douglas after the crossing from Liverpool in time for the first practice on Tuesday.

Private Aston Martins were entered by Ken Downing and Bob Dickson. Veteran Swiss driver Hans Ruesch made a one event return to racing with a red 4.1 litre Ferrari 340 MM with Superleggera Touring bodywork. He had been active, and successful, between 1933 and 1939, driving an ex-Scuderia Ferrari 3.8 litre eight-cylinder Alfa Romeo (in which he won the Donington G.P. in 1936 with Richard Seaman) and a 1.5 litre Maserati. Joe Goodhew entered a 3,996cc Darracq, Dan Margulies entered a 3,557cc Delahaye and 1950 Manx Cup winner Oscar Moore entered a 3.4 litre Jaguar-engined H.W.M.

Practice

All cars entered in the 1,500cc class arrived and practised. The 2,600cc class was reduced by four absentees – the Aston Martins of Peter Clark and Nigel Mann, the Healey of Peter Simpson and the H.W.M-Alta of P.A.B. Stewart. In the over 2,600cc class Joe Goodhew's Darracq, Dan Margulies' Delahaye and Oscar Moore's H.W.M. were absent. This left 41 cars of which 37 turned out for the first practice on the evening of Tuesday 16th June, in "high wind, rain and a general atmosphere of extreme discomfort" according to *Autosport*.

The session was free of serious incidents. Parkfield saw most of the action. Gerry Dunham skidded and spun his Frazer Nash, left enough room for Alan Brown to squeeze past in his Cooper Bristol, and then continued. John Goldschmidt stopped when his engine seized and Ken Downing overshot and went some distance down Bray Hill before turning his Aston Martin and re-joining the course. Mike Keen spun his Kieft at Cronk-y-Berry and lost a wheel, and Bill Belfrage Black had a slide at Willaston. Despite the poor conditions, Reg Parnell took the works DB3S Aston Martin round in 3mins 17secs (70.88mph). This was one second inside Geoff Duke's 1952 record, although Duke had managed 3mins 17secs in practice. The next fastest in the over 2,600 class were newcomer Hans Ruesch who lapped in his Ferrari in 3mins 20secs (69.82mph) and Stirling Moss in the works Jaguar C-type (3mins 21secs, 69.47mph). In the 2,600cc class Alan Brown set the pace in his Cooper Bristol in 3mins 19secs (70.17mph), followed by Gerry Dunham's Frazer Nash and Cliff Davis' Tojeiro who were tied on 3mins 22secs (69.13mph). Fastest 1,500 was Peter Gammon in Cliff Davis' Cooper MG (3mins 27secs, 67.45mph), with Pat Griffith's Kieft two seconds slower (66.81mph) and Ted Lund's MG a further two seconds back (66.18mph).

In vastly improved conditions on Wednesday evening, Reg Parnell set fastest lap and came in saying he could go faster any time he needed to. Then, according to John Wyer, he went gossiping in the paddock. Meanwhile both Moss and Ruesch went faster, displacing Parnell from the front row. Wyer then went looking for Parnell, eventually found him and reminded him that he could go faster any time he needed to! Parnell was reluctant, saying he could win from the second row. After much pushing, Parnell eventually got in the car, broke the lap record on his first flying lap and again on the second lap, produced an incredible time – 3mins 5secs (75.48mph). This was 13 seconds inside Geoff Duke's sports car lap record and one second inside Reg's 1950 outright record, set in his Formula 1 Maserati and was so incredible that the commentator did not announce the time of the first lap as he did not believe it! Ruesch and Moss both managed laps in 3mins 10secs (73.49mph) with Ian Stewart only one second slower in his Ecurie Ecosse C-type Jaguar. In the 2,600cc class Ken Wharton in his Frazer Nash looked very competitive and consistent with three laps of 3mins 11secs, five seconds faster that Alan Brown. In the 1,500 class, Cliff Davis took over his Cooper MG from Peter Gammon and was fastest in 3mins 22secs, with Jim Mayers one second behind. A.C. Westwood's Healey hit a wall and was too badly damaged to race and Peter Gammon, now driving Cliff Davis' Tojeiro, broke a universal joint.

Reg Parnell's car also suffered a broken universal joint on the way back to the garage, almost putting him out of the race, as the Aston Martin team had no spares because this car was the spares! In the late evening it was impossible to contact anyone at the factory. Fortunately, John Wyer received a telephone call from his wife and arranged for her to rouse racing mechanic Dickie Green who went to the factory at midnight with another mechanic, removed a universal joint from one of the Le Mans cars, drove through the night to Liverpool and caught the first flight to the Island. Green then worked with the other mechanics to fit the part and the car was ready for the heat on Thursday afternoon.

Heat 1 – Up to 1,600cc

In cool, dry, overcast conditions, 14 cars came to the line. John Riseley Pritchard's Cooper Riley had engine problems and Peter Reece's Cooper MG had no oil pressure. Cliff Davis led from the lights, followed by Jim Mayers, Ernest Harewood, Pat Griffith, Gerry Ruddock, Lionel Leonard and John Haesendonck. The race immediately became a battle between Davis' Cooper MG and Mayers' Kieft, with Davis leading by three seconds at the end of lap 1, with Griffith third and Harewood fourth. Further back, Ted Lund's MG TD lacked acceleration and

At Cronk-ny-Mona Corner, in the heat for cars up to 1,500cc, the Cooper MG of Cliff Davis (6) leads the Kieft MG of Jim Mayers (1). They finished first and second in the heat but Mayers' clutch disintegrated on the last lap putting him out of the final, in which Davis retired with half-shaft failure. [Ron Brew collection]

Threfall's Tojeiro stopped briefly for a plug change. At Cronk-ny-Mona the engine of Mike Keen's Kieft blew up on lap 2 leaving a trail of oil, to which the marshals were slow to react, and later Horace Gould's Cooper suffered engine failure. Ruddock managed to pass Harewood on lap 2 but could not get past Griffith. Gerry Ruddock retired his Lester MG on lap 5 with engine problems, Goldschmidt's Performance Special retired after over-heating and Alfred Hitchings' shock absorbers had failed so that the progress of his Lester MG resembled a yo-yo. Meanwhile, at the front the procession continued. Mayers was unable to pass Davis, although he came close on laps 3 and 7, while Griffith stayed third throughout. At the flag, Davis won by three seconds from Mayers with Griffith 1min 20secs behind. Harewood was fourth, followed by Leonard, Haesendonck, Jackson, Hitchings and Threlfall, with Lund a lap behind.

Heat 2 – 1,600cc – 2,600cc

The sun came out as 11 starters assembled on the grid, Westwood's Healey being unfit to race after its practice crash. This heat was another procession in which Ken Wharton's Frazer Nash led Alan Brown's Cooper Bristol and Peter Kenneth's Frazer Nash. On lap 2 Brown broke the sports car lap record for the course with a time of 3mins 16secs (71.24mph) but, on lap 3, Wharton did 3mins 13secs (72.35mph) which he repeated and Brown matched on the last lap. Behind the leaders, Peter Scott-Russell and Gerry Dunham fought for fourth all the way but the former, having passed the latter on lap 3, managed to stay ahead. Peter Gammon had a nasty incident on lap 4 when the bonnet of his Tojeiro flew open depriving him of vision. Shaken, Gammon came to a halt with a broken screen and a damaged wing. Huxley retired his Connaught with gearbox trouble on lap 6. At the finish, Wharton led Brown by four seconds with Kenneth trailing 44 seconds behind Brown. Scott-Russell took fourth by one second from Dunham and they were followed to the flag by James Neilson, John Barber, Bill Belfrage Black and Gray Mickel.

Heat 3 – over 2,600cc

In yet another procession, Reg Parnell led the 13 starters, followed by the Jaguar C-types of Stirling Moss and Ian Stewart, followed by the Ferrari of Hans Ruesch. On lap 1 Parnell matched Geoff Duke's 1952 record of 3mins 17secs (70.88mph). On lap 2, he smashed the record with a lap of 3mins 9secs (73.88mph) and led Moss by six seconds, with Ian Stewart, Ruesch, Ninian Sanderson, John Swift and Jimmy Stewart in their wake. Ken Downing's Aston Martin overshot at Parkfield and twice scraped the bank at Cronk-ny-Mona. On lap 3 Parnell led by eight seconds, lapping in 3mins 8secs. Moss, Stewart and Ruesch all lapped in 3mins 10secs and Moss and Ruesch got down to 3mins 9secs on lap 4. Ruesch was trying to pass Ian Stewart, blowing his horn and shaking his fist until Stewart pitted at the end of lap 7 to retire with clutch slip, letting Ruesch into third. On the rise from Cronk-ny-Mona, Ruesch tried the same tactics with Moss who waved him past, but Ruesch did not have the speed to make the pass. Parnell took the flag ten seconds ahead of Moss, who beat Ruesch by two seconds. They were followed by the three Jaguars of Sanderson, Jimmy Stewart and Swift, the Aston Martins of Dickson and Downing and the XK120 Jaguars of Kemp Place and Boston. Watkins' Allard retired on lap 5.

Results of Heats

Thursday 18th June 1953. Start 1.55pm, 2.55pm and 3.50pm. Each heat over 8 laps of 3.8789 miles, total distance 31.03 miles.

Heat 1

(Cars up to 1,500cc)

1. Cliff Davis (1,467cc Cooper MG), 27mins 16secs (68.28 mph)
2. Jim Mayers (1,467cc Kieft M.G.), 27mins 19secs (68.16 mph)
3. Pat Griffith (1,467cc Kieft M.G.), 28mins 39secs (64.99mph)
4. Ernest Harewood (1,467cc MG), 29mins 4secs (64.05mph)
5. Lionel Leonard (1,467cc Leonard MG), 29mins 27secs (63.25mph)
6. John Haesendonck (1,467cc MG), 29mins 31secs (63.08mph)
7. Peter Jackson (1,467cc Lester MG) 30mins 0secs (62.06mph)
8. Alfred Hitchings (1,467cc Lester MG) 30mins 4secs (61.93mph)

9. Chris Threlfall (1,467cc Tojeiro), 7 laps, 28mins 28secs (57.23mph)
10. Ted Lund (1,466cc MG), 7 laps, 30mins 29secs (53.44mph)

Fastest lap: Cliff Davis and Jim Mayers, 3mins 22secs (69.13mph).

Retirements:
John Goldschmidt (1,467cc Performance Special), overheating
Lap 2: Mike Keen (1,467cc Kieft), engine, at Cronk-ny-Mona
Lap 4: Horace Gould (1,467cc Cooper MG), engine, at Cronk-ny-Mona
Lap 5: Gerry Ruddock (1,467cc Lester MG), engine.

Heat 2
(Cars over 1,500cc and up to 2,600cc)

1. Ken Wharton (1,971cc Frazer Nash), 26mins 7secs (71.29mph)
2. Alan Brown (1,971cc.Cooper Bristol), 26mins 11secs (71.11mph)
3. Peter Kenneth (1,971cc Frazer Nash), 26mins 55secs (69.17 mph)
4. Peter Scott-Russell (1,971cc Frazer Nash), 27mins 3secs (68.83mph)
5. Gerry Dunham (1,971cc Frazer Nash) 27mins 4secs (68.79mph)
6. James Neilson (1,971cc Frazer Nash), 27mins 23secs (67.99mph)
7. John Barber (1,971cc Cooper Bristol), 28mins 15secs (65.90mph)
8. Bill Belfrage Black (1,971cc Frazer Nash), 28mins 51secs (64.53mph)
9. Gray Mickel (2,443cc Healey), 29mins 27secs (63.22mph)

Fastest lap: Ken Wharton and Alan Brown, 3mins 13secs (72.35mph).

Retirements:
Lap 4: Peter Gammon (1,971cc Tojeiro), accident
Lap 6: A.R. Huxley (1,767cc Connaught), gearbox, at Pits.

Heat 3
(Cars over 2,600cc)

1. Reg Parnell (2,922cc Aston Martin DB3S), 25mins 23secs (73.35mph)
2. Stirling Moss (3,442cc Jaguar C-type), 25mins 33secs (72.87mph)
3. Hans Ruesch (4,100 c.c. Ferrari 340), 25mins 35secs (72.78mph)
4. Ninian Sanderson (3,442 c.c. Jaguar C-type), 26mins 12secs (71.06mph)
5. Jimmy Stewart (3,442cc Jaguar C-type, 26mins 13secs (71.62mph)
6. John Swift (3,442 c.c. Jaguar XK120), 26mins 47secs (69.52 mph)
7. Bob Dickson (2,922cc Aston Martin), 27mins 7secs (68.66mph)
8. Ken Downing (2,922cc Aston Martin), 27mins 29secs (67.75mph)
9. Desmond Titterington (3,917cc Allard), 28mins 27secs (65.44mph)
10. H. Kemp Place (3,442cc Jaguar XK120), 7 laps, 25mins 44secs (63.31mph)
11. David Boston (3,442cc Jaguar XK120), 7 laps, 26mins 35secs (61.28mph)

Fastest lap: Reg Parnell, 3mins 8secs (74.28mph).

Retirements:
Ken Watkins (5,420cc Allard),
Lap 7: Ian Stewart (3,442cc Jaguar C-type), clutch trouble at Pits.

Note: As there were only 30 finishers in the heats, all had the opportunity to compete in the final. Jim Mayers (Kieft) and Ken Downing (Aston Martin) were unable to do so, due to clutch and brake failures respectively.

The B.R.M. Demonstration

Raymond Mays and Peter Berthon, the men behind the ERA which had proved so successful in voiturette racing in the mid to late 1930s, started work immediately after the Second World War on producing a Grand Prix car. The B.R.M. had a V-16 engine of 1.5 litres with two stage centrifugal supercharger and a five-speed gearbox. The car first appeared at Silverstone in 1950, to be driven by Raymond Sommer, but broke a drive-shaft on the start line. Reg Parnell had two wins at Goodwood in 1950 but he and Peter Walker both retired at Barcelona. They finished fifth and seventh respectively in the 1951 British Grand Prix and 1952 brought one win for Parnell and two for Froilan

This Isle of Man Examiner cartoon dated May 1952 captures the public frustration at the poor reliability record of the BRM V16 Grand Prix car. [Isle of Man Examiner]

The race organisers, the British Racing Drivers' Club, arranged a race day high speed demonstration of the 1.5 litre V16 supercharged BRM Grand Prix car. The car had a very poor reliability record but Reg Parnell, seen here at the Manx Arms corner, completed five practice and three race day laps without problems. [Peter Kelly collection]

Gonzalez and two podium places each for Parnell and Ken Wharton, but 11 retirements. The car's persistent problems were making it a by-word for unreliability.

The Autocar revealed on 5th June that a high speed demonstration of the car would be a feature of the British Empire Trophy meeting. This was obviously an attempt to increase spectator interest and contemporary reports suggest that it was highly successful. There was, however, a disagreement as to whether Parnell or Wharton would drive the car and after what Aston Martin mechanic Eric Hind described as "a terrible row which almost came to fisticuffs between the two". The question was resolved in Parnell's favour. Parnell then showed that he meant business when he took the car onto the course at the end of the Wednesday evening practice. According to the *Isle of Man Examiner*, he completed five laps and "his flat-out runs on the Glencrutchery straight were particularly exciting for the large crowds who filled the grandstand and lined the hedges". Parnell's lap times were impressive: 3mins 7.8secs, 3mins 7.6secs and 3mins 7.4secs on his third, fourth and fifth laps.

On race day, the demonstration was scheduled to take place in the gap between the heats and the final, while the starting grid for the final was sorted out. After

Douglas Hanson, one of the Race Stewards, prepares to flag in the BRM. As the car was ill-suited to the bumpy roads of the Douglas circuit, Reg Parnell's fastest lap of 3mins 7secs compared very well with his outright lap record of 3mins 5secs, set later in the Aston Martin DB3S. [Author's collection]

winning his heat Parnell jumped out of his Aston Martin and into the B.R.M., which had been warmed up in the pit lane. He left two long tyre marks as he took off with "a joyous howl of revs", said *The Motor*, whereupon he completed three fast laps to the obvious delight of the crowd, with the car "in fine voice and fettle". His best lap was 3mins 7secs (74.67mph), two seconds slower than the new lap record which he later set in the Aston Martin during the final but "highly satisfying", thought *The Motor*, as the circuit, with its short straights, scarcely suited the car.

As Parnell howled past the grandstand to start his last lap, Clerk of the Course Desmond Scannell handed the chequered flag to race Steward Douglas Hanson with the words "Here, Douglas, you can flag in the B.R.M. – not many have had the chance!" While this comment accurately reflected the car's unfortunate reputation, this time it went all the way.

1953 British Empire Trophy Final

Although 38 drivers had contested the heats for one of the 30 available places in the final, eight retirements meant that nobody had to be eliminated and two drivers who had qualified for the final could not take part. The Kieft of Jim Mayers, runner-up in his heat, had terminal clutch failure and the Aston Martin of Ken Downing, eighth in his heat, had brake failure. Thus, only 28 cars assembled on the starting grid.

The handicap meant that the smaller cars, which received three minutes' start, were at the front, in heat finishing order. In pole position, therefore, was Cliff Davis' Cooper MG, sharing the front row with Pat Griffith's Kieft, with Jim Mayers' space unoccupied. The second row consisted of Harewood's MG and Leonard's Leonard MG. They were followed by Haesendonck's MG and the Lesters of Jackson and Hitchings with the fourth row consisting of Threlfall's Tojeiro and Lund's MG. Row five was the front row of the intermediate class, receiving one minute's start. The first three of this class were the Frazer Nashes of Ken Wharton and Peter Kenneth on either side of the Cooper of Alan Brown. Behind them were the Frazer Nashes of Scott-Russell and Dunham, followed on row seven by Neilson (Frazer Nash), Barber (Cooper) and Black (Frazer Nash). In the "scratch" class of cars of over 2,600cc, there was a formidable front row of Parnell (Aston Martin), Moss (Jaguar C-type) and Ruesch (Ferrari). The C-type Jaguars of Sanderson and Jimmy Stewart were on the next row, followed by the first Jaguar XK120 of Swift and the Aston Martin of Dickson, with Downing's empty space. Titterington's Allard and Kemp Place's Jaguar XK 120 came next, with Boston's XK120 alone at the rear.

Although Cliff Davis and Pat Griffith made quick starts, Harewood stormed through from the second row to provide the incredible spectacle of his old MG, dubbed the "beam axle bombshell" by *Autosport*, leading the field into the first corner at Parkfield. By the end of the lap, however, he had been passed by both Davis and Griffith with the former leading by eight seconds.

In the second group, Brown led on the first lap from Wharton, followed by Kenneth and Barber while in the scratch group, Moss took an initial but short-lived lead, being quickly overtaken by Parnell whose faster car enabled him to gain 150 yards on Moss on the hill past Willaston.

Meanwhile, on the first lap, tragedy struck at Cronk-y-Berry which had been the scene of Peter Walker's fiery crash during practice in 1951. Approaching the left hand corner on a different line and faster than other drivers, James Neilson appeared to make no attempt to take the corner. His Frazer Nash slid sideways, hit the offside hedge, ran sideways up the hedge and then landed in the road with the back of the car against the hedge. The unfortunate driver was thrown out of the car and landed in the road on the racing line. Several following cars were already close to the corner and the leader of this group, John Barber, had no chance of avoiding Neilson. Barber continued to the pits, where he reported the incident and retired immediately. Neilson was taken to hospital by ambulance but sadly died of his injuries in the early hours of Friday morning. He was 40 years old, married with three children and lived in Largs, Ayrshire, where he worked as a fishmonger. Later that day, an Inquest was held by Coroner Howard Lay, who recorded a verdict of accidental death, commenting that it seemed that Neilson had approached the corner too fast and off the racing line – an error of judgment which was only too easy in a dangerous sport like car racing. The Coroner added that John Barber had no possible chance of avoiding the collision, was in no way to blame and had nothing to reproach himself for. It was a very fine sport and all the more attractive to young men with an adventurous spirit.

By the end of lap 2 Davis had extended his lead over Harewood and Griffith to 19 seconds. Wharton passed Brown on lap 2 to lead the 2,600cc class and Parnell was already well ahead of all the other cars in his class.

On lap 3, Parnell set a new outright lap record in 3mins 5secs (75.48mph) which he was to repeat on laps 8 and 9. Clearly he would catch the 1,500cc cars within about five laps and would catch the Wharton group several laps before the end of the race. Scott-Russell and Dunham were scrapping in their evenly-matched Frazer Nashes as they had in the heat but this time Dunham was ahead and intent on staying there.

John Swift's Jaguar C-type (53) Hans Ruesch's Ferrari 340 (46) and Bob Dickson's Aston Martin DB3 (43) are pictured in Onchan Village. Ruesch finished third and Dickson twelfth but Swift retired on lap 5 after a minor accident. [The late Alf Caley, Onchan]

At Cronk-ny-Mona on lap 4, Cliff Davis was forced into retirement when his Cooper MG lost a half-shaft and wheel. This let Harewood into the lead, four seconds ahead of Griffith and ten seconds ahead of Leonard. Wharton was rapidly catching Harewood and Parnell was working his way through the 2,600cc class. Hans Ruesch, who nearly hit the bags at Parkfield on lap 4, was also on a charge, fourth in his class and chasing Sanderson and Moss. On the next lap Harewood still clung on to a lead of two seconds but was quickly relegated to third when he was passed by Wharton and Brown at Parkfield on lap 6. By this time, Parnell was fourth, only 27 seconds off the lead with 12 laps to go, and taking five or six seconds a lap out of Wharton's lead. Swift retired after a minor crash caused bodywork damage and Ruesch found a way past Sanderson and set about chasing Moss.

By the end of lap 7 Parnell was up to third and only 21 seconds behind Wharton, despite having to dodge an errant dog at Parkfield. Brown was still second while Griffith passed Harewood to lead the 1,500cc class. Harewood was now in trouble, dropping back with gear selection problems, and retired at the Manx Arms in Onchan Village on lap 9. Now, at half distance, Wharton led Brown by three seconds, with Parnell third and only 17 seconds off the lead. Moss was fourth but under threat from Ruesch and Griffith was sixth and led the 1,500cc class.

The Moss/Ruesch battle was now taking the same form as in the heat, with Moss repeatedly waving Ruesch past but with Ruesch prevented from passing by severe wheel-spin. He eventually made the pass on lap 11.

Parnell took the lead from Wharton between the Grandstand and Parkfield on lap 12, having passed Brown on lap 10 after two quick laps of 3mins 5secs on laps 8 and 9, equalling his own newly-set record. Brown had developed a mis-fire and retired with a blown cylinder head gasket on lap 11. The race had now settled down. Parnell had only to keep going and in fact drew away from

On Glencrutchery Road with headlights blazing, Hans Ruesch in his Ferrari 340 Mille Miglia chases Stirling Moss' Jaguar C-type. Their battle lasted for many laps, with Moss repeatedly waving Ruesch past but with Ruesch lacking the necessary power. Eventually he succeeded and Moss could not re-pass. [Stan Hughes collection]

Wharton with another 3mins 5secs lap. After 15 laps, he was averaging 74.18mph. Ruesch was catching Wharton by 2 seconds per lap and drawing away from Moss, while Sanderson had his hands full to keep ahead of Jimmy Stewart. The Dunham/Scott-Russell battle was still on while Griffith and Leonard still led their class from Haesendonck and Lund. The yo-yo Lester of Alfred Hitchings was still running and, according to *Autosport*, breaking the height record over the bumps at Governor's Bridge.

Reg Parnell in the works Aston Martin took the chequered flag amid enthusiastic cheers. His decisive victory and the change of his previous bad luck on the Douglas circuit were both well-deserved and must have gone some way to make up for his uncharacteristic lapse at Le Mans. The fact that his winning average of 73.96mph was 3.43mph faster than Geoff Duke's lap record of the previous year was an eloquent testimony to the quality of both driver and car. Second placed Ken Wharton won his class, finishing five places, one lap and 4.14mph ahead of the class runner-up Gerry Dunham in a similar car. Hans Ruesch was an impressive third in his come-back drive in the Ferrari, 25 seconds ahead of Stirling Moss in the works Jaguar C-type. After second place at Le Mans, it must have been surprising that Moss could manage only fourth at Douglas, and that he finished only 33 seconds ahead of Ninian Sanderson's Ecurie Ecosse C-type. The explanation was that the car was not the 1953 Le Mans car but the very different 1952 car which Moss had used in the Mille Miglia. This old car did not have the latest brakes and carburettors, which had been vital at Le Mans. Jimmy Stewart in the second of the Ecurie Ecosse C-types was sixth, the last driver to complete the full distance of 16 laps. The seventh to fourteenth finishers completed 15 laps and the rest of the 21 finishers completed 14 laps. The seventh, eighth and ninth finishers were the Frazer Nash trio of Gerry Dunham, Peter Scott-Russell and Peter Kenneth. Pat Griffith (who had the distraction of his passenger door swinging open on several occasions as he rounded Parkfield) and Lionel Leonard were the first 1500s to finish (10th and 11th respectively). They finished ahead of Bob Dickson's Aston Martin and the remaining 1,500cc cars of John Haesendonck, Ted Lund, Peter Jackson and Alfred Hitchings. Gray Mickel's Healey was 17th, followed by Desmond Titterington's Allard, Bill Belfrage Black's Frazer Nash and the two XK120 Jaguars of Kemp Place and David Boston. The latter had the distinction of being the last driver to take the chequered flag in a Manx car race on closed public roads.

Reg Parnell presses on through Onchan Village to a well-deserved win in the works Aston Martin DB3S. After reliability problems in previous Isle of Man races, he had the best car in the 1953 race and made the most of it, beating Ken Wharton by 18 seconds. [The late Alf Caley, Onchan]

1953 British Empire Trophy Race Results.

Thursday 18th June 1953. Start 5.00pm. 16 laps of 3.8789 miles circuit, total distance 62.06 miles. 28 starters, 21 finishers.

1. Reg Parnell (2,922cc DB3S Aston Martin), scratch; 53mins 21secs (73.96mph)
2. Ken Wharton (1,971cc Frazer Nash), 1min; 53mins 39secs (72.10mph)
3. Hans Ruesch (4,200cc Ferrari 340), scratch; 54mins 16secs (72.64mph)
4. Stirling Moss (3,442cc Jaguar C-type), scratch; 54mins 41secs (72.05mph)
5. Ninian Sanderson (3,442cc Jaguar C-type), scratch; 55mins 14secs (71.29mph)
6. James (Jimmy) Stewart (3,442cc Jaguar C-type), scratch; 55mins 19secs (71.18mph).

Failed to complete required 16 laps:

7. Gerry Dunham (1,971cc Frazer Nash), 1min; 15 laps, 53mins 22secs (67.96mph)
8. Peter Scott-Russell (1,971 Frazer Nash),1min; 15 laps, 53mins 24secs (67.92mph)
9. Peter Kenneth (1,971cc Frazer Nash), 1min; 15 laps, 53mins 54secs (67.26mph).
10. Pat Griffith (1,467cc Kieft MG), 3mins; 54mins 43secs (63.80mph)
11. Lionel Leonard (1,467cc Leonard MG), 3mins; 15 laps, 54mins 55secs (63.57mph)
12. Bob Dickson (Aston Martin DB3) 15 laps, scratch; 55 minutes 06secs (67.01mph)
13. John Haesendonck (1,467cc MG), 15 laps, 3mins; 55mins 50secs (62.53mph)
14. Ted Lund (1,466cc MG), 15 laps, 3mins; 56mins 04secs (62.27mph)
15. Peter Jackson (1,467cc Lester MG), 3mins; 14 laps, 53mins 49secs (60.55mph)
16. Alfred Hitchings (1,467cc Lester MG), 3mins; 14 laps, 53mins 51secs (60.51mph)
17. Gray Mickel (2,443cc Healey Silverstone), 1min; 14 laps, 54mins 29secs (62.08mph)
18. Desmond Titterington (3,917cc Allard), scratch; 14 laps, 54mins 45secs (61.96mph)
19. Bill Belfrage Black (1,971cc Frazer Nash), 1min; 14 laps, 55mins 40secs (60.71mph)
20. H. Kemp Place (3,442cc Jaguar XK120), scratch; 14 laps, 56mins 0secs (61.48mph)
21. David Boston (3,442cc Jaguar XK120), scratch; 14 laps, 56mins 26secs (60.98mph)

Fastest lap: Reg Parnell, 3mins 5secs (75.48mph), on laps 3, 8 and 9, new outright circuit record.

Class results

Up to 1,500cc

1. Pat Griffith (Kieft MG)
2. Lionel Leonard (Leonard MG)
3. John Haesendonck (MG).

Up to 2,600cc

1. Ken Wharton (Frazer Nash)
2. Gerry Dunham (Frazer Nash)
3. Peter Scott-Russell (Frazer Nash).

Over 2,600cc

1. Reg Parnell (Aston Martin DB3S)
2. Hans Ruesch (Ferrari 340)
3. Stirling Moss (Jaguar C-type).

Retirements:

Lap 1: James Neilson (1,971cc Frazer Nash), fatal accident at Cronk-y-Berry

John Barber (1,976cc Cooper), accident at Cronk-y-Berry

Lap 3: Chris Threlfall (1,467cc Tojeiro) at Pits

Lap 4: Cliff Davis (1,467cc Cooper MG) broken half shaft at Cronk-ny-Mona

Lap 5: John Swift (3,442cc Jaguar XK120), minor accident

Lap 9: Ernest Harewood (1,467cc MG), engine trouble at Onchan

Lap 12: Alan Brown (1,971cc Cooper-Bristol), blown gasket at Pits.

Reaction

At the prize presentation, the recently appointed Lieutenant Governor, Sir Ambrose Dundas, said that he had found his first race most exhilarating and thrilling. He had been proud to garland Reg Parnell, who had done so much for British motor racing. He congratulated the drivers for their skill and sportsmanship and expressed sympathy for James Neilson, who had been seriously injured and who had died early the following morning. Reg Parnell thanked the Aston Martin team for their support in driving through the night to Liverpool with a replacement universal joint, without which he would have been unable to take part in the heat and final. The credit for his win, he said, belonged to his helpers and to the wonderful car. He hoped that the race was a financial success and that they could return next year.

The motoring Press was generous. *Autosport* said that the event had aroused considerably more interest among the general public than it did in 1952. *The Autocar* thought that road racing on the Isle of Man was tottering for lack of support and said that the 1953 race threatened to be the last, which would be a great pity as the circuit was a first-class proving ground. *The Light Car* remarked that the fate of the event was still in the balance but for popular appeal the race on 18th June could hardly have been surpassed. The spectacle of Reg Parnell setting a new lap record in the Aston Martin faster than his own 1950 Maserati record of 3mins 6secs had been well worth the journey from the mainland, it said. The Manx authorities had always been helpful to motor racing but it did not have the same spectator appeal as the motorcycle TT. The heats for each class with a handicap final had been an excellent idea, although the three minutes start was not enough for the 1,500cc cars and something like six minutes would have been needed to provide a close finish. Having said that, nobody could have anticipated that Parnell could take 13 seconds off Duke's 1952 lap record, or that Ken Wharton would have shown such speed in his Frazer Nash. The writer echoed the thoughts of many in saying that the tragic death of James Neilson was deeply regretted by everybody connected with the sport.

On the day before the race, Tynwald had debated a vote on expenses for 1953 races. Although the Tynwald Race Committee wanted to abandon the races a suggestion was made that a sidecar race proposed for 1954 should be an addition and not as replacement. Mr Moore suggested saving the £3,250 cost of the car race as it was "no good to the Isle of Man" but Mr Nivison said that the car races were more valuable than a sidecar TT which would attract only six international experts and should be made more attractive and successful by the allocation of a fixed date in the calendar.

The *Isle of Man Times* repeated its customary support for the races. They had been continued for 1953 only as an experiment as some members of Tynwald and the public felt that they did not attract many visitors and were not worth a government grant but this year from many points of view they had been thoroughly successful. The Press had taken notice, there had been a BBC commentary, a petrol company had sent three cameramen to make a film and the grandstand and other vantage points had been crowded. If there were not many visitors, there was a great deal of publicity and the races had "won through". The cost was not large and the event should be recognised as an early season attraction and given a better date and more publicity.

At the end of September, however, the Times reported than the Tynwald Race Committee had decided not to recommend that a car race should be held in 1954 as it had been on trial in 1953 and did not justify the expenditure of public money. *The Times* felt that Tynwald should give much thought before agreeing. The Island needed every attraction. Numbers could be increased but were limited by safety. A different course was needed as the Willaston circuit was not big enough for a production car race and the short straights were not long enough. This had been proved when Reg Parnell's B.R.M. demonstration was baulked by corners and bends. If the races were to be abandoned there had to be certainty that they had no future. Car racing, once lost, would be difficult to recover. Perhaps the Island would still have the TT if a suitable circuit had been found.

In October, the Town Council changed its mind, deciding that the car races should not be lost without another attraction to replace them. Councillor Stephen thought that the races had been more successful as an attraction in 1953. Then both the *Isle of Man Examiner* and the Green Final called for a re-think, urged the Tynwald Race Committee to issue a factual statement giving reasons for its decision and suggested a review of the matter in Tynwald or at a public meeting.

Between September 1953 and January 1954 the *Ramsey Courier* regularly published a list of provisional dates for 1954 attractions, including a car race on 1st July. Sadly, this was a false dawn.

In May 1954, apparently without any review in Tynwald or public meeting as called for in the Press, the Tynwald Race Committee presented its annual report which did not recommend support for the car race. The report mentioned, however, that the Committee was investigating the possibility of running a race for production cars on the TT Course. There were many difficulties to be overcome but if such a race became a possibility, a further Report would be made before the end of the year. The Report went on to say that it appreciated that there was some controversy about the desirability of running a sidecar race and using the Clypse Circuit (the new 10.79 miles circuit on which it was proposed to run the 125cc TT Race), but the Committee felt that if there was no car race in 1954, a sidecar race should be given a trial, and should be given as much support as possible.

With no members questioning the decision to abandon car racing, there was no further discussion and the Committee's recommendations, including a contribution of £1,500 towards the cost of an international sidecar race, were accepted. There was also a contribution of an additional £400 to the international bicycle race (making £1,300 in total) and the balance of the £3,250 cost of the 1953 British Empire Trophy was saved.

A Sidecar TT Race was held on the new TT Clypse Circuit in June 1954. There were 24 entries (including 7 from abroad), 20 starters and 15 finishers. With Isle of Man Government support the sidecar race achieved the continuity which the car races had never been given the opportunity to achieve, becoming an established and popular part of the TT Races.

WINNERS 1947-1953

Bob Gerard, ERA – 1947, 1949, 1950 British Empire Trophy.

One of the more successful amateur drivers of the post-war era despite the handicap of wearing spectacles, Bob Gerard started in trials in 1933 and competed in sprints and races up to 1939. After the war he turned to racing ERAs, owning three, of different specifications, which he prepared and modified with great skill. In road racing, he won the 1947 Ulster Trophy at Ballyclare and the 1949 Jersey Road Race and was runner-up to de Graffenried in the 1949 British Grand Prix. He was also successful in hill-climbs, particularly at Shelsley Walsh and Prescott, in which he shared a car with his wife Joan who was a very capable driver both in hill-climbs and in circuit racing. His three Manx victories added considerably to his fame. It could have been four because, in the 1948 race, he retired when he was running a close second to Reg Parnell whose late retirement handed a lucky victory to Geoff Ansell. From the inauguration of the British Empire Trophy at Brooklands in 1932, Gerard was the only driver to win it more than once until Stirling Moss in 1956 at Oulton Park. After 1950 Gerard turned to driving a Frazer Nash, in which he was runner-up to Moss in the 1951 British Empire Trophy, and a Cooper-Bristol. Later, he raced a Turner sports car, before finally retiring in 1960. He then became an entrant of various drivers. Gerard's Bend at the Mallory Park Circuit was named after him.

Geoff Ansell, ERA – 1948 British Empire Trophy.

Geoff Ansell and his better-known cousin Bob were members of the Ansell's brewery family. A newcomer to the sport after the war, Geoff finished 9th in the 1947 Manx Cup, driving an Aston Martin. Before his 1948 victory he had raced his ERA only once, in the April 1948 Jersey race in which he finished eighth. He campaigned the car at Zandvoort, Silverstone and Goodwood during the 1948 season and finished ninth in the 1949 Empire Trophy race.

Stirling Moss, Frazer Nash – 1951 British Empire Trophy.

Isle of Man spectators were fortunate to be able to watch Stirling Moss early in his career. In his first two seasons of racing, 1948 and 1949, he drove 500cc and 1,000cc Cooper-J.A.P.s, and the 1949 Manx Cup was his first race outside England. His speed astonished the experts and mechanical failure deprived him of what should have been an easy win. After winning the 1950 Dundrod TT in a Jaguar XK120, he returned to the Island in 1951 to win the Empire Trophy at the wheel of a Frazer Nash but said that he could not have caught Pat Griffith if the latter had not retired. He drove the same Frazer Nash in the 1952 race but retired with mechanical problems. In 1953 he drove a works Jaguar C-type in the final Isle of Man race but his car could not match the speed and handling of Reg Parnell's Aston Martin DB3S, and he finished second in his heat and fourth in the final. He drove a Maserati in 1954 before joining the Mercedes-Benz Grand Prix and Sports Car Championship team in 1955. He was an incredibly versatile driver, scoring over 100 victories in races of all types, in his 14 year career. He was never World Champion but he won 16 Grands Prix and did the fastest lap in 14 World Championship races. He retired after a serious crash at Goodwood in 1962.

Pat Griffith, Lester MG – 1952 British Empire Trophy.

Later to become Chairman of G.K.N., Pat Griffith started his racing career in 1951 when he and Jim Mayers bought Lester MG sports cars. At the time of the British Empire Trophy, Pat had done only one race meeting at Goodwood and a few laps at Castle Combe. Nevertheless, with the benefit of a generous handicap but driving with great skill, he led the Empire Trophy race until retiring two laps from the end when his engine seized due to loss of oil. This handed the win to Stirling Moss who admitted that he could not have caught Griffith. In 1952, Griffith and Mayers joined forces with Gerry Ruddock to form The Monkey Stable. In the British Empire Trophy, their main opposition was Geoff Duke's Aston Martin. Mayers retired with piston failure but Griffith and Ruddock survived to finish first and second, reversing the order at Jersey several weeks later. These successes earned Griffith a place in the Aston Martin works team and he won the Goodwood nine-hours race with Peter Collins. In 1953 The Monkey Stable changed to Kiefts and Griffith won his class in the 1953 British Empire Trophy. He won the Tourist Trophy at Dundrod for Aston Martin, again sharing a car with Peter Collins, and they finished second in the Goodwood nine-hours. The following year was less successful for Griffith. Badly injured at Hyeres, he missed Le Mans and retired in the Tourist Trophy due to mechanical failure. Accepting that he was less fast following his accident at Hyeres, Pat Griffith retired at the end of the 1954 season.

Reg Parnell, Aston Martin – 1953 British Empire Trophy.

After starting racing in 1935, Reg Parnell made his Isle of Man debut in 1937 when he finished 12th after making many pit stops in an uncompetitive MG Magnette K3. He then lost his racing licence following a serious accident at Brooklands but remained involved in the sport. He bought a number of racing cars before and during the war and sold some of them after the war to help the revival of the sport at a time when few cars were available. Resuming his racing career with ERAs and

Maseratis, he also drove works cars for Alfa Romeo, B.R.M and Aston Martin. On the Isle of Man he was unlucky, retiring in 1948 and 1949 and finishing 6th in 1950 before gaining the consolation of an easy win in the Castletown Trophy of 1951 in a Maserati. He drove a Nash Healey in 1952 but retired. He finally won the Empire Trophy in 1953 in a works DB3S Aston Martin. On retirement from racing in 1957 he became Team Manager of Aston Martin and later managed the Yeoman Credit and Bowmaker teams in Formula One. He died in 1964, following an operation, at the age of 53.

"B. Bira", Simca – 1947 Manx Cup.

See Winners 1933 – 1937.

George Nixon, Riley – 1948 Manx Cup.

George Nixon was the owner of a Ford dealership in Newcastle-under-Lyme, Staffordshire. The Manx Cup was his first road race in which he took part, having watched the Jersey race in the previous month. His car was a special with a Riley engine owned by Freddie Dixon. During the first practice the car burned two pistons, necessitating an 18 hour rebuild and careful running-in during the second practice and the early part of the race. After driving in two Formula One events at Silverstone and in the 1949 Jersey race he returned to the Island for the 1949 meeting, finishing 13th in the Empire Trophy in an ERA but retiring in the Manx Cup. He drove again at Silverstone in August 1949, after which he appears to have retired from racing.

Kenneth Bear, Bugatti – 1948 Castletown Trophy.

The owner of an insurance business in Chesham, Buckinghamshire, Kenneth Bear was a Bugatti expert and a founder of the Bugatti Owners' Club. He started his motorsport career in 1931, competing in rallies and hill-climbs. He also played rugby, was a first class tennis player and owned his own aeroplane. The 1948 Castletown Trophy was his first road race and was to be his only race on the Isle of Man. He lost his life in practice for the 1949 Jersey Road Race, in a crash which also killed a Doctor and a Police Sergeant and injured four marshals. Litigation, in which the Doctor's widow unsuccessfully sued Bear's estate and the race organisers, continued until 1951. His 1933 Type 59 Bugatti was the car which finished second in the 1935 Mannin Moar, driven by Charlie Martin. Martin had sold the car to the Duke of Grafton who lost his life while driving it in the 1936 Limerick road race.

John Heath, H.W.-Alta – 1949 Manx Cup

John Heath was in partnership with George Abecassis in the H.W. Motors business at Walton-on-Thames and collaborated with Abecassis in the H.W.M Formula Two project. He took up racing in 1946 with a sports Alta and finished second in the 1947 Grand Prix des Frontieres at Chimay, Belgium. In 1948 he drove the H.W.-Alta in which, with a replacement body, he won the Manx Cup in 1949. After a long absence from racing due to pressure of business, he decided to drive the H.W.M.-Jaguar, which he and Abecassis had developed, in the 1956 Mille Miglia. He lost control of the car in heavy rain and crashed fatally near Ravenna.

Oscar Moore, O.B.M. – 1950 Manx Cup.

London night-club owner Oscar Moore's racing career started in 1947, when he competed in a Frazer Nash-BMW in various Continental events and in the Manx Cup, in which he retired. He returned in 1950 with the O.B.M., a B.M.W. based special which he had raced in 1949 at many Formula Two non-championship events on the Continent and also at Blandford where he had a win.

Gerry Dunham, Alvis – 1951 Manx Cup

A regular campaigner of his father's pre-war Alvis, Gerry Dunham finished sixth and fourth in the Manx Cup races of 1949 and 1950 before his victory in the 1951 race. Following the abandonment of the Manx Cup, he returned in 1953 with a Frazer Nash in which he finished seventh in his British Empire Trophy heat and fifth in the final. He was a regular competitor in the Alvis at Goodwood and other U.K. circuits.

Reg Parnell, Maserati – 1951 Castletown Trophy

See above.

Bids For TT Return 1949 – 1966

After the war the Isle of Man renewed its efforts to persuade the RAC to return the TT to the land, and preferably to the course, of its birth.

In May 1949 the *Isle of Man Times* suggested an approach to the RAC. The TT Mountain Course, said the Times, presented a unique challenge and the Ulster TT Races had done nothing to "improve the breed". The Island authorities should offer suitable inducements to the RAC as an Isle of Man TT would help to maintain and expand the export trade in cars by propaganda and by making the product more competitive. In October 1949, when the RAC announced that, subject to finding a suitable circuit, it intended to revive the TT in 1950, the Times suggested that the RAC should be invited to the Island but the RAC soon announced its acceptance of an invitation from Antrim County Council to hold the 1950 TT on the 7.4 miles Dundrod circuit near Belfast.

The Manx Automobile Club then formed a Race Committee to investigate the possibility of organising a production car race on the TT Course in 1951, in the same week as the British Empire Trophy race. This resulted in a meeting at Silverstone between Club and RAC representatives and a revelation by Club Race Committee Secretary Brian Mylchreest that Government support would be forthcoming provided sufficient competitors could be attracted to ensure a first class race. The Club deputation received an encouraging response from the RAC. The proposal then went to the Tynwald Race Committee which agreed to present a favourable report to Tynwald. The Club also met the Highway Board, the June Effort and Season Extension Committee and the Isle of Man Steam Packet Company and obtained the support of Douglas Town Council. Later, however, the Tynwald Race Committee "reluctantly" turned down the proposal. The reasons given were opposition to road closures, lack of expectation of large receipts in early season, the requirement for a Government guarantee of £5,350 and the need for course improvements estimated to cost £20,000. It was revealed that the RAC Course Inspector, Earl Howe, required the removal of four street lamps at Quarterbridge, kerbs to be filled in, drainage to be improved, removal of bumps at Highlander, Ballagarraghyn and Milntown, removal of electricity poles at Ramsey, a complete ban on spectators on the two miles stretch from Kate's Cottage to Hillberry and road widening from Signpost Corner to Governor's Bridge or alternatively the course to follow the British Empire Trophy course from Signpost via Onchan Village to Governor's Bridge. The Chief Constable was concerned about lack of legal powers to restrict spectators on private land. Both the Manx Automobile Club and the June Effort Committee announced that they did not regard this as the end of the idea and vowed to overcome the difficulties.

The next scheme was for a "Coronation Cup Race" in 1953. This idea, first mentioned in January 1953, was obviously too late but attracted controversy nonetheless, with former motorcycle racer Bertie Rowell saying that "rubberisation" of the TT Course by racing cars would make it unsafe for the motorcycle races. Geoff Duke dismissed these fears as "exaggerated", pointing to the Swiss Grand Prix, where cars and motorcycles raced during the same weekend. He was supported in this by 1950 Manx Grand Prix winner Don Crossley. It became clear that there was no change in the views of the RAC.

When it became clear that there would be no British Empire Trophy Race on the Island in 1954, thoughts again turned to the TT Course. Firstly, Douglas Town Council expressed its support for a production car race in 1954. Then the June Effort and Season Extension Committee decided to make a fresh approach to the Tynwald Race Committee. While it was too late to arrange a race in 1954, the Race Committee Chairman announced that the Committee intended to meet Dean Delamont, Director of the RAC. *Motor Sport* Division, to discuss a production car race on the TT Course. There was also a suggestion by the Manx Automobile Club that Stirling Moss, Peter Collins, Reg Parnell and Tony Rolt might participate in a trial with sports cars on the TT Course during the Manx Grand Prix. However, while Delamont considered the course "probably suitable for car racing" provided modifications were made and proper safety precautions taken, he said that houses in Kirk Michael and other parts of the course might have to be evacuated during racing, pointing out that a car travelling at 150mph could go in on one side of a house and come out on the other side! There would need to be a large number of prohibited areas. Gardens, hedges and existing grandstands would have to be cleared and new legislation would probably be needed. Faced with this, the Tynwald Race Committee described Delamont as "very pessimistic" and announced that the chances of car racing on the TT Course in the current year, the following year or ten years in the future were "grossly exaggerated". The Committee also thought that unless the proposed race were a "Classic" (presumably meaning the TT) people would not come to the Island to watch it, and even if it were a Classic they would not come in sufficient numbers to justify the required expenditure because the event would take years to establish, as the motorcycle TT had done. The proposed trial during the Manx Grand Prix was cancelled, but the Manx Automobile Club said that it would continue its efforts.

The deaths of three drivers in crashes during the 1955 Golden Jubilee TT at Dundrod led to an RAC announcement that the circuit would no longer be used for car racing and that there would be no TT in 1956. Again the TT was homeless and again the Isle of Man Government approached the RAC with a proposal to return to the Island. Tourist Board Secretary Leonard Bond met Dean Delamont in London for discussions and the *Isle of Man Examiner* reported that the financial guarantee required by the RAC, allegedly amounting to £8,000, would not be an obstacle to the running of the race on the Island. The *Examiner* pointed out that, as a round of the World Sports Car Championship, the TT would attract the world's leading drivers. This meeting resulted in confirmation that it was too late for the TT to be held in 1956 but that it was hoped that it could be held on the Island in 1957. The need for an early decision had been stressed by the Island authorities and an RAC deputation was to visit the Island to attempt to find a circuit capable of meeting the stringent safety criteria. It was suggested that a circuit of about 5 miles would be appropriate, which appeared to rule out the TT Mountain Course. The race, if held, would be 1,000 kilometres (621 miles) in length with an entry of about 50 cars. However, when Dean Delamont visited the Island with Earl Howe, nothing had changed except that the RAC requirements had increased and the cost of meeting them would have been prohibitive. In 1958 the TT was revived at Goodwood, where it remained until 1964, with the original TT lap distance of 52 miles reduced to a mere 2.4 miles.

In 1961 the Tourist Board adopted a new approach with a proposal for a new short circuit. This idea attracted little enthusiasm but the Tourist Board persisted and sports car racing driver David Piper visited the Island in 1964 to inspect possible sites. One, proposed by Geoff Duke, was in the southern hills near Round Table cross roads but this was ruled out on the grounds of expense and also likely problems with mist and rain. While Piper's preference was for the TT Course, he felt that it would be unsuitable without extensive road alterations and widening.

When closure of Goodwood became imminent, the RAC again became interested in the Island, expressing the thought that a return of the TT in 1966 might be appropriate. A planned visit never took place but in 1965 Dean Delamont visited the Island with two colleagues to inspect the Tholt-y-Will hill-climb course. While on the Island, they asked to inspect the TT Course and both parties became quite enthusiastic about the idea of a TT Course race in 1968. Basil Tye, Dean Delamont's deputy, carried out a full course inspection in 1966. Applying the same safety standards to the TT Course as those used for the United Kingdom short circuits, Tye's report required one breakdown vehicle and one ambulance per mile, 1,300 marshals, 417 two-gallon fire extinguishers, 200 fire blankets, 200 pairs of asbestos gloves and 199 sets of grappling irons, 199 radio or telephone points and 15 miles of Armco barrier. The RAC Competitions Committee then decided that there could be no racing on the TT Course because they were not prepared to accept a lower standard of safety and protection than that required for short circuits. Commenting on the report in December 1966, *Motor Sport* pointed out that long road circuits in Europe were running successful races at that time and suggested that "vested interests" had influenced the report and that Tye had merely been "going through the motions". In January 1967 *Motor Sport* published a detailed reply from Dean Delamont whereupon the magazine's Continental Correspondent, Denis Jenkinson, returned to the controversy in February with an article containing comments about the RAC and Basil Tye for which *Motor Sport* apologised in its June issue, allegedly under threat of a libel action. After considering the Tye report, the Tourist Board asked the RAC whether it was prepared to guarantee continuity of the TT for a period of years to give the Island a chance of a realistic return on the capital investment which would be required. When this proved impossible, the negotiations ended.

Geoff Duke suggested another idea in 1969. This was a 5.75 miles road circuit in the north of the Island, on sparsely populated roads encircling the former R.A.F airfield at Jurby. A test was arranged early one morning, when FordSport arranged for four Formula Ford racing cars to be flown to Jurby in a British Air Ferries Carvair aircraft, the largest aircraft ever to land there. The cars were driven by Tony Brooks, Olivier Gendebien, Stirling Moss and Maurice Trintignant. There was no official road closing order and the circuit was closed only by the presence of marshals and police on the road junctions, despite which the local milkman managed to join in! Nevertheless, the drivers averaged 67 mph and were enthusiastic about the circuit but, even for this short circuit the cost of safety precautions was prohibitive. A shortened version of this circuit (the 4.43 miles Jurby South course) was used for motorcycle racing from 1970 to 2010, after which the Island's Department of Infrastructure found it uneconomical to maintain the roads to the required standard.

Duke had not given up, however. In 1982-83 he revived his earlier plan for a 4.35 miles "Nurburgring" circuit in the southern hills but, again, without success. Undaunted, Geoff's next idea was for a 4.25 miles circuit based on the former Second World War R.A.F. airfield at Andreas in the north of the island. This site, close to sea level, would eliminate weather problems and also avoid the need for costly adaptation of public roads. Finance was available for the acquisition of the 500 acres site, refurbishment of parts of the runways and the building of a 400 bedroom hotel. The circuit could have been used virtually all the year round, including winter testing but particularly for the RAC TT. The abandonment of the project, when negotiations for the acquisition of 80 acres of the site proved unsuccessful, meant the death of the Island's sixty years' dream for the return of the TT to its birthplace.

APPENDICES

1 INDEX OF DRIVERS, GORDON BENNETT TRIALS 1904 AND 1905

Abbreviations: R = retired, NF = non-finisher.

BIANCHI, Cecil
1905 2 Wolseley

EARP, Clifford
1904 1 Napier
1905 1 Napier

EDGE, Cecil
1905 R Napier

EDGE, Selwyn F.
1904 3 Napier

EDMOND
1904 R Darracq

GIRLING, Sidney
1904 2 Wolseley
1905 R Siddeley

GOODWIN, F.R.
1905 R Star

GOODWIN, H.G.
1905 R Star

GUINNESS, Algernon Lee
1905 R Darracq

HARGREAVES, John
1904 NF Napier
1905 R Napier

HEMERY, Victor
1904 R Darracq

JARROTT, Charles
1904 5 Wolseley

MacDONALD, Arthur E.
1905 R Napier

MAYHEW, Mark
1904 R Napier

MUIR, Campbell
1904 R Wolseley

RAWLINSON, A. ("Toby")
1904 R Darracq

ROLLS, Hon, Charles S
1905 R Wolseley

STOCKS, J.W. ("Jack")
1904 4 Napier

2 INDEX OF DRIVERS, RAC TOURIST TROPHY RACES, 1905-1922.

Abbreviations: T = Touring Cars, HT = Heavy Touring Cars, Fuel = out of fuel, 1,500 = 1,500cc Trophy, NF = Non-Finisher, D = Disqualified, R = Retired

ARNOTT, E.H
1905 R Minerva
1907 HT R Arrol-Johnston

ASTELL, W.H.
1905 7 Orleans

BABLOT, Paul.
1906 2 Berliet

BATE, H.A.
1906 R Fuel S.C.A.R.

BAXENDALE, Guy
1905 R Thornycroft

BEDFORD, G.
1922 1,500 R Hillman

BEIREIZ, Karl
1905 R Fuel Dixi

BELL, R.A.
1906 R Deasy

BENNETT, F.S.
1905 R Cadillac

BENTLEY, Walter O
1914 6 D.F.P.
1922 4 Bentley

BERGER, R.
1914 R S.A.V.A.

BERTELLI, A.C.
1922 1,500 5 Enfield-Allday

BIANCHI, Cecil
1914 13 Crossley

BRAUD, Georges
1906 4 Clement
1907 T R Fuel Clement

BROWN, G.W.A.
1908 R Coventry-Humber

BROWNING, H.R.
1908 NF Rover

BUCKLEY, H.S.
1908 R. S.C.A.T.

BURGESS, F.T.
1914 R Humber

CATELL, C.L.
1905 R Fuel James & Browne
1906 R Fuel James & Browne

CHASSAGNE, Jean
1922 1 Sunbeam

CLAY, Arthur J.
1905 14 Ryknield

CLEMENT, Frank
1914 R Straker-Squire
1922 2 Bentley

CLENCH, Claude
1905 R Whitlock-Aster

COATALEN, Louis.
1906 6 Coventry-Humber
1907 T R Hillman-Coatalen
1908 9 Hillman-Coatalen

COLEMAN, Frederic
1905 R White Steam Car

COLLIER, R.H
1907 T R West-Aster

COOPER, C.H.
1907 HT R Beeston-Humber

COURTIS, Ernest
1905 5 Rover
1907 T 1 Rover

COX, W.H.
1903 R Fuel Maudslay

du CROS, Harvey
1905 6 Swift

CROSSMAN, Robert
1914 R Star

CROWDY, A.E.
1906 8 Siddeley

CUNDY, Frank G.
1905 15 Napier

CUPPER, Oscar
1907 T R Fuel Metallurgique
1908 R Metallurgique

DEAN, Percy
1905 R Fuel Scout
1906 9 Scout
1907 T R Scout

DEBUISSEY, Andre
1908 R Piccard-Pictet

DENNIS, John
1905 16 Dennis

DEW, A.J.
1905 R Speedwell

DIVO, Albert
1922 1,500 2 Talbot-Darracq

DOWNIE, John
1905 R Fuel Argyll

DOWNING, Robert
1905 18 Dennis

EARP, Clifford
1905 10 Napier

EVERY, R.
1906 R Swift

FENTON, Grahame
1907 HT 2 Gladiator

FOLKER, E.R.
1907 T NF Rover

FRISWELL, Charles
1905 13 Peugeot

GALL, J.
1908 R Westinghouse

GEORGE, A.E.
1906 D Argyll
1908 3 Darracq

GIRLING, Sidney
1905 R Siddeley
1906 R Fuel Darracq

GOEBEL, Otto
1914 R Adler

GOODWIN, H
1907 T NF Star

GRAHAM, Philip
1908 R Deasy

GUINNESS, Algernon Lee
1905 R Darracq
1906 3 Darracq
1907 T R Fuel Darracq
1908 2 Darracq
1914 R Sunbeam
1922 1,500 1 Talbot- Darracq

GUINNESS, Kenelm Lee
1907 T R Darracq
1908 R Hillman-Coatalen
1914 1 Sunbeam

HADLEY, James
1905 NF Wolseley

HANCOCK, A.J.
1905 11 Vauxhall
1914 R Vauxhall

HARDMAN, W.L.
1906 R Fuel Hardman

HARPER, R.O.
1908 R S.C.A.T.

HARRISON A.E.
1907 HT R Fuel Argyll

HARTRIDGE, A.
1908 R Westinghouse

HAWKES, W. Douglas
1922 5 Bentley

HIGGINSON, J
1914 R Vauxhall

HODGE, D.S.
1908 10 Thornycroft

HOLLOWAY, W.C.
1905 R Minerva

HUTTON, Ernest
1906 R Fuel Berliet
1907 T R Berliet
1908 R Hutton

JENNER, Thomas
1905 9 Orleans

KENT, A.C.
1905 R White Steam Car

LAMB, P.R.
1907 R West-Aster

LANCASTER, E.H.
1905 R Fuel Clement

LASCELLES, Richard
1905 17 New Simms- Welbeck
1906 R Vici

LEWIS, Edmund W.
1905 12 Rover
1908 R Deasy

LISLE, Joseph
1906 R Fuel Star

LISLE, Richard
1914 R Star

LITTLEJOHN, Norman
1905 3 Vinot-Deguingand
1907 T R Fuel Vinot

MARSHALL, Bertram
1922 1,500 6 Bugatti

MAUDSLAY, R.W.
1905 11 Standard

MAURY, Mones
1922 1,500 3 Bugatti

MILLS, George P.
1907 HT 1 Beeston-Humber

MOIR, H. Kensington
1922 1,500 R Aston Martin

MOLON, Leon
1908 NF Vinot
1914 3 Minerva

MOORE-BRABAZON, J.T.C.
1908 R Metallurgique

MORICEAU, Jean
1922 1,500 R Talbot-Darracq

MOSS, Geoffrey
1908 R Arrol-Johnston

McCONNELL, Hugh
1906 R Fuel Bianchi

NAPIER, John S.
1905 1 Arrol-Johnston
1906 7 Arrol-Johnston
1907 T R Fuel Arrol-Johnston

NIBLETT, H
1907 HT R Fuel Gladiator

NORTHEY, Percy
1905 2 Rolls-Royce
1906 R Rolls-Royce

OUTHWAITE, Roland
1908 NF Vinot

PARK, Matthew
1922 R Vauxhall

PAYNE, Oswald
1922 3 Vauxhall

PORPORATO, Jean
1907 NF Berliet
1914 5 Minerva

PORTER, Leslie
1908 4 Calthorpe

PREW, G.F.
1906 R Fuel Star
1907 T R Star

PULLINGER, Thomas
1906 5 Beeston-Humber

RAWLINSON, A. ("Toby")
1905 R Darracq
1908 7 Darracq

REID, James
1905 R Fuel Beeston-Humber
1907 T 2 Beeston-Humber
1908 R Beeston-Humber

RESTA, Dario
1908 R Arrol-Johnston
1914 R Sunbeam

RIECKEN, C.
1914 2 Minerva

RIMMER, T.
1907 T NF Vulcan
1908 8 Vulcan

ROBERTS, Cyril
1905 4 Arrol-Johnston
1907 T R Arrol-Johnston
1908 NF Arrol-Johnston

ROBINSON, J.
1908 R Calthorpe

ROLLS, Hon. Charles S
1905 R Rolls-Royce
1906 1 Rolls-Royce

ROSS BROWNE, M.
1906 R Minerva
1907 T NF Gladiator
1908 6 Vinot

RUTSCH, Joseph
1914 R Adler

SANGSTER, Charles
1907 HT R Fuel Ariel

SEGRAVE, H.O.D.
1922 R Sunbeam

SMITH, Turberville
1906 R Fuel Academy

SQUIRE, L.
1907 HT R Fuel Straker-Squire

STAPP, P.
1914 R Adler

STIRLING, P.D.
1908 R Hutton

STOCKS, Jack
1908 R de Dion

SWAIN, Ernest
1922 R Vauxhall

THOMAS, W. Parker
1906 8 Argyll

THORNYCROFT, Tom
1905 R Thornycroft
1906 R Fuel Thornycroft
1907 T R Fuel Thornycroft
1908 5 Thornycroft

TUCK, W.G.
1907 T R Beeston-Humber
1908 R Beeston-Humber
1914 R Humber

USMAR, Gordon
1906 R Fuel Vinot

de VIZCAYA, Pierre
1922 1,500 4 Bugatti

WARD, F.
1908 R S.C.A.T.

WARREN, W.J.
1905 R Speedwell

WATSON, T
1906 R Climax

WATSON, W.
1907 HT R Fuel Berliet
1908 1 Hutton
1914 R Vauxhall

WITCHELL, R.S.
1914 4 Straker-Squire

WRIGHT, Grahame
1906 R Siddeley

WRIGHT, Sam
1914 R Humber

WRIGHT, Warwick
1906 R Minerva
1908 R Metallurgique

3. INDEX OF DRIVERS, "ROUND THE HOUSES" RACES 1933 – 1937

Abbreviations: MB = Mannin Beg MM = Mannin Moar NF = Non-finisher R = Retired

*Denotes driver who also drove in 1947-1953.

***B. BIRA"**
1936 2 E.R.A.
1937 1 E.R.A.

***BAIRD, Robert "Bobby"**
1934 MB NF Riley
1935 MB NF MG Midget 'R'

BAUMER Maurice/FORD, J Ludovic
1933 MB 3 MG Midget
1935 MB R MG Magnette K3

BLACK, Norman
1934 MB 1 MG Magnette K3
1935 MB R MG Midget 'R'

BRACKENBURY, Charles
1935 MM NF Bugatti

BRIGGS, L.R.
1936 NF MG Magnette K3

CONNELL, Ian
1937 11 E.R.A.

COOK, Humphrey W.
1935 MM R E.R.A.

CORMACK, A.J.
1936 R Alta

CRABTREE Sydney A.
1933 MB R MG Midget

DIXON, Freddie W.
1933 MB 1 Riley
1934 MB R Riley
1935 MB 2 Riley

DOBSON, Arthur
1937 7 E.R.A.

DOBSON, Austin
1935 MM NF Alfa Romeo
1937 8 Maserati

DODSON, Charlie
1934 MB 2 MG Magnette K3
1934 MM 2 Alfa Romeo
1936 NF Austin

DON, Kaye
1933 MB R MG Magnette K3
1933 MM R Alfa Romeo

DONKIN, P.L.
1934 MB R MG Magnette K3

ECCLES, A.H. Lindsay
1933 MM R Bugatti
1934 MM R Bugatti
1935 MM R Bugatti

ECCLES, Roy
1934 MB 5 MG Magnette K3
1935 MB R Alta
1936 R Rapier Special

EVERITT, Bill
1934 MB 8 MG Midget
1936 NF E.R.A.

EYSTON, George E.T.
1933 MB R MG Magnette K3
1933 MM R Alfa Romeo
1934 MB 3 MG Magnette K3
1935 MB R MG Midget 'R'

FAIRFIELD, Pat
1934 MB NF Riley
1935 MB 1 E.R.A.
1936 4 E.R.A.
1937 3 E.R.A.

FEATHERSTONHAUGH, Buddy
1936 6 E.R.A.

FONTES, Luis
1935 MM 3 Alfa Romeo

FORD, J. Ludovic
(see BAUMER, Maurice)

FOTHRINGHAM,T.S.
1933 MM R Bugatti

GARDNER, E.L.
1933 MB R MG Midget

GIBSON, Ron
1934 MB R MGMidget

GILLOW, Victor
1933 MB R Riley
1934 MB R Riley

***de GRAFFENRIED, E.**
1937 6 Maserati

HALL, Eddie R.
1933 MB R MG Magnette K3
1934 MB R MG Magnette K3
1935 MB NF Magnette K3

HAMILTON A.P.
1934 MM R Alfa Romeo
1935 MM R Alfa Romeo

HAMILTON, Hugh
1933 MB R MG Magnette K3
1934 MB R MG Magnette K3

HANDLEY, Walter
1934 MB R MG Magnette K3
1935 MB R MG Midget R

HANSON, Robin
1937 9 Maserati

HORTON, R.T.
1934 MB 6 MG Magnette K3

HOWE, Earl
1936, R E.R.A.

HUGHES, W.
1937 R MG Magnette K3

HUMBER, T.K.
1935 MB R Bugatti
1936 MM R Bugatti

JUCKER, Philip F
1936 R Frazer Nash

LACE, Alfred C.
1933 MM R Invicta
1935 MM R Alta

LAIRD, Henry
1934 MB NF Mc Evoy Special

LEHOUX, Marcel
1936 5 E.R.A.

LEITH, The Hon. Jock
1935 MM R Bugatti

LEWIS, The Hon. Brian E.
1933 MM 1 Alfa Romeo
1934 MB R Singer
1934 MM 1 Alfa Romeo
1935 MM 1 Bugatti

MACLURE, Percy
1937 10 Riley

MANBY-COLEGRAVE, G.F.A.
1935 MB R MG Magnette K3
1936 6 E.R.A.

MANSELL, Dennis
1933 MB 2 MG Midget

MARTIN, Charlie
1934 MB 4 MG Magnette K3
1935 MM 2 Bugatti

MATHIESON T.A.S.O
1933 MM R Bugatti

***MAYS, Raymond**
1935 MB R E.R.A.
1935 MM R E.R.A.
1936 R E.R.A.
1937 2 E.R.A.

MERE, R.M.
1933 MB R MG Magnette K3

MOORE, T.G.H.M. ("Tom")
1933 MB R Frazer Nash

***PARNELL, Reg**
1937 12 MG Magnette K3

PAUL, Cyril
1934 MB 6 Riley
1934 MM 3 Riley
1935 3 E.R.A.

du PUY, John
1937 R Maserati

RAYSON, E.K. "Teddy"
1935 MM R Bugatti
1936 R Maserati

ROSE-RICHARDS, Tim
1933 MM 2 Bugatti
1934 MM R Bugatti

SAMEIRO, Vasco
1934 MM R Alfa Romeo

SEAMAN, Richard J.B.
1936 1 Delage

SHUTTLEWORTH, Richard
1933 MM R Bugatti
1934 MM R Bugatti
1935 MM R Alfa Romeo

STANILAND, Chris
1934 MM R Bugatti

SULLIVAN, W.
1933 MB R Morris Minor Sp.

TONGUE, Reggie E.
1936 R E.R.A.
1937 4 E.R.A.

VILLORESI, Luigi
1937 R Maserati

WAKEFIELD, J.P.
1936 R Alta

***WALKER, Peter/**
***WHITEHEAD, Peter**
1937 5 E.R.A.

WILKINS, R.S.
1935 MM NF Alfa Romeo

WILLIAMS, H.
1936 R MG Magnette K3

YALLOP, R.A.
1933 MB R MG Magnette K3

4 INDEX OF DRIVERS, BRITISH EMPIRE TROPHY RACE MEETINGS 1947-1953

Abbreviations:-

BET = British Empire Trophy MC = Manx Cup CT = Castletown Trophy H = Heat F = Final

NF = Non-Finisher R = Retired

* Denotes driver who also drove in 1933-1937

ABECASSIS, George
1947 BET R E.R.A. "B" type
1948 BET R Alta
1951 BET 11 Aston Martin DB2

ALLARD, Sydney
1951 BET R Allard Cadillac

ANSELL, Geoffrey
1947 MC 9 Aston Martin
1948 BET 1 E.R.A.
1949 BET 9 E.R.A. "B" type

ANSELL, R. E. ("Bob")
1947 BET 3 Maserati
1948 BET R Maserati

APPLETON, R.J.
1948 MC R Appleton Special

ASHMORE, Fred
1949 BET 3 Maserati

ASHMORE, Joe
1951 CT R E.R.A

ASTON, Bill
1951 MC R Cooper

BAINBRIDGE, George
1947 BET 6 E.R.A. "B" type
(with Brian Shawe-Taylor)

***BAIRD, W.R. ("Bobby")**
1947 MC R MG
1948 BET R Emeryson (with P Emery)
1950 MC R MG

BARBER, John
1951 MC R Cooper
1953 BET H7, FR Cooper

BARING, Anthony A
1948 BET 9 Maserati

BEAR, Kenneth
1948 CT 1 Bugatti

***"B BIRA"**
1947 MC 1 Simca-Gordini
BET 5 Maserati
1950 BET R Maserati

BLACK, Bill Befrage
1952 BET 12 Jaguar XK120
1953 BET H8, F19 Frazer Nash

BOLSTER, John V
1948 BET R E.R.A. "B" type

BOLTON, Peter R
1950 MC R H.W.-Alta

BOSHIER, Stanley J
1952 BET 11 Jaguar XK120

BOSTON, David S
1953 BET H11, F21 Jaguar XK120

BRANDON, Eric
1950 MC R Cooper
1951 MC R Cooper

BROOKE, H. Leslie
1947 BET 4 E.R.A. "E" type
1948 BET 3 E.R.A.

BROWN, Alan
1953 BET H2, FR Cooper Bristol

BUCKLER C. Derek F
1948 MC 12 Buckler Sp

BUNCOMBE, John
1952 BET R Healey

CARR, Noel
1947 CT R Alta

CARRINGTON, Hugh
1947 MC 10 Frazer Nash BMW

CHORLTON, Michael
1948 BET 8 Bugatti
1949 BET R C.D.L.

CHRISTIE, Michael
1950 MC R Cooper

CLAES, Johnny
1949 BET 8 Talbot Lago

CLAPP, Hugh
1949 MC 9 H.R.G.
1950 MC 8 H.R.G.

CLARK, Peter C.T.
1947 MC 11 H.R.G
1948 MC 7 H.R.G
1949 MC 10 H.R.G
1950 MC 11 H.R.G

CLARKE, David
1951 BET R Frazer Nash

COLLINS, Peter
1951 BET R Allard Cadillac

COOPER, John
1949 MC 5 Cooper-J.A.P.
1950 MC R Cooper

CROOK, Anthony
1947 MC 8 Frazer Nash B.M.W

CROSSLEY, Geoff
1947 BET R Alta

CULPAN, Noel
1950 MC 3 Frazer Nash
1951 BET 8 Frazer Nash

CURTIS, Frank
1951 BET 6 Allard

DARBISHIRE, Sheila
1947 BET 8 Riley

"DAVE"
1951 BET NF Dyna- Panhard

DAVIS, Cliff
1952 BET R Cooper MG
1953 BET H1, FR Cooper MG

DICKSON, Bob
1953 BET H7, F12 Aston Martin

DOWNING, Ken
1953 BET H8 Aston Martin

DRYDEN, R.M. ("Curly")
1949 MC R Cooper-Norton

DUKE, Geoffrey E.
1952 BET R Aston-Martin

DUNHAM, Gerry
1949 MC 6 Alvis
1950 MC 4 Alvis
1951 MC 1 Alvis
1953 BET H5, F7 Frazer Nash

EMERY, Paul
1948 BET R Emeryson
(with R. Baird)

FAIRMAN, Jack
1948 CT 3 Bugatti
1949 MC R Riley

FOLLAND, Dudley
1948 MC R HRG
1949 MC R Ferrari

GALE, Guy
1951 BET 13 Delahaye

GAMMON, Peter
1953 BET H R Tojeiro

GEE, Neville
1949 MC 4 Riley

GERARD, F.R. ("Bob")
1947 BET 1 E.R.A. "B" type
1948 BET R E.R.A. "B-C" type
1949 BET 1 E.R.A. "B-C" type
1950 BET 1 E.R.A. "B-C" type
1951 BET 2 Frazer Nash

GOLDSCHMIDT, John
1953 BET H R Performance Sp.

GOULD, Horace
1953 BET H R Cooper MG

***de GRAFFENRIED, Emanuel**
1950 BET 3 Maserati

GRAHAM, Hector
1947 MC R MG
1948 MC R MG
(with D.H. Kyle)
1949 MC R Cooper

GREEN, John
1951 CT R Maserati

GRIFFITH, Pat
1951 BET R Lester MG
1952 BET 1 Lester MG
1953 BET H3, F10 Kieft MG

HAESENDONCK, John
1953 BET H6, F13 MG

HAMILTON, Duncan
1948 BET R Maserati
1952 BET R Jaguar C-type

HAMPSHIRE, David
1947 BET 2 E.R.A.
1949 BET 7 E.R.A. "C" type
1950 BET 5 Maserati

HAREWOOD, Ernest C
1953 BET H4, FR MG

HARRISON, T.C. ("Cuth")
1947 MC 2 Riley
BET 9 E.R.A. "B" type
1948 MC R Riley
BET 4 E.R.A.
1949 BET 4 E.R.A. "B-C" type
1950 BET 2 E.R.A. "B-C" type

HAWTHORN, Mike
1952 BET 3 Frazer Nash

HEATH, John
1949 MC 1 H.W.-Alta
1949 BET 10 G.P. Alta

HILL, S
1951 BET R Healey

HITCHINGS, Alfred
1952 BET R Cadillac Allard
1953 BET H8, F16 Lester MG

HOLT E.W. ("Bill")
1948 MC 6 H.R.G.
1952 BET 13 Jaguar XK 120

HORSFALL, St. John
1949 MC R Aston Martin
BET 2 E.R.A. "B"

HUXLEY, A.R
1953 BET HR Connaught

JACKSON, Peter
1952 BET R MG TC
1953 BET H7 F15 Lester MG

JACOBS. R.W. ("Dick")
1949 MC 7 MG
1950 MC 9 MG
1951 MC R MG
1951 BET R MG TD Mk.2

JASON-HENRY, GUY
1947 BET R Maserati
1948 BET 7 Delahaye
1949 BET 12 Delahaye

JOHNSON, Leslie
1947 BET R Darracq
1948 MC 3 Alta
1948 BET 5 E.R.A. "E"

KEEN, Mike
1953 BET H R Kieft

KELLY, Joe
1949 MC 8 I.R.A
1950 BET R Maserati
1951 MC 8 I.R.A
1952 BET 10 Jowett Jupiter

KEMP PLACE, H.
1953 BET H10, F20 Jaguar XK120

KENNETH, Peter
1953 BET H3, F9 Frazer Nash

KENNINGTON, Frank W.
1947 MC R MG
1949 MC 3 Cisitalia

KYLE, D.H.
1948 BET R MG
(with H. Graham)

LEONARD, Lionel
1951 BET 12 Cooper MG
1952 BET R Cooper MG
1953 BET H5, F11 Leonard MG

LINE, Trevor
1951 BET 9 MG TD
1952 BET 8 MG TD

De LISSA, Basil
1949 MC R MG
1950 MC R MG

LLEWELLYN, Michael,
1952 BET 9 MG TD

LUND, Ted
1948 MC R MG PB
1949 MC R Lund Special
1950 MC 7 Lea Francis C-type
1951 MC R Lea Francis
BET 4 MG TD Mk2
1952 BET R MG TD
1953 BET H10, F14 MG

MARSHALL, John
1948 MC 10 MG K3

MATTHIAS M.E.
1948 MC 11 Riley Sprite

de MATTOS, Basil
1948 MC R MG
1949 MC R Spikins

MAYERS, J.C.C. ("Jim")
1950 MC 6 Lester MG
1951 BET R Lester MG
1952 BET R Lester MG
1953 BET H2 Lester MG

***MAYS, Raymond**
1948 BET R E.R.A. "D" type

MERRICK, R.W. ("Bill")
1950 MC R Cooper

MEYER T.M. ("Tom")
1950 MC 10 H.W.-Alta
1951 MC 2 H.W.M

MICKEL, R. Gray
1953 BET H9, F17 Healey

MITCHELL H.A.
1952 BET 5 Frazer Nash

MOLYNEUX A.C.
1947 MC 12 H.R.G

MONNIER Maurice
1948 MC R Monnier Sp

MOORE, Oscar B
1947 MC R Frazer Nash
1950 MC 1 O.B.M

MOSS, Stirling
1949 MC R Cooper-JAP
1951 BET 1 Frazer Nash
1952 BET R Frazer Nash
1953 BET H2, F4 Jaguar

MURRAY, Colin
1950 BET R Maserati

MURRAY, David
1949 BET R Maserati
1950 BET R E.R.A. "B" Type
1951 CT 2 Maserati
1952 BET R Jaguar XK120

MURRAY, W.H. ("Bill")
1950 MC R H.R.G
1951 BET R Frazer Nash

NEILSON, James
1953 BET H6 Frazer Nash
Fatal crash in final

NICKOLS, Ian H
1947 MC R MG
1948 MC R MG

NIXON, George
1948 MC 1 Riley Sp
1949 BET 13 E.R.A. "A"

PANKS, John
1947 MC 5 Alvis

***PARNELL, Reg**
1948 BET R Maserati
1949 BET R Maserati
1950 BET 6 Maserati
1951 CT 1 Maserati
1951 BET R Nash Healey
1953 BET H1, F1 Aston Martin DB3S

PEACOCK, Robin
1951 BET 5 Frazer Nash

PENN, Francis
1947 MC 6 Riley
1948 MC R Riley

PHILLIPS, George
1948 MC 5 MG TC
1949 MC R MG TC

PITT, Donald
1951 BET R Frazer Nash

POOL, Edward
1947 MC R Bugatti

POORE, Dennis
1948 CT 2 Alfa Romeo

POPLE, Mike
1951 BET 7 MG TD

POTTS, Joe
1950 MC R Cooper

REECE, Jack
1951 BET 3 Cooper MG

REECE, Peter
1950 MC R Riley

RHIANDO, "Spike"
1948 MC R Cooper J.A.P.
1950 MC R Trimax

RICHARDS, Horace
1951 MC 7 Riley

RICHARDSON, Geoff M
1949 BET 11 R.R.A

ROBINSON, William
1951 BET R Jowett Jupiter
1952 BET 7 Jowett Jupiter

ROLT, A.P.R. ("Tony")
1947 BET R Alfa Romeo
1948 BET R Alfa Romeo
1949 BET 6 Alfa Romeo
1950 BET 7 Delage

ROSE, Kenneth
1949 MC R R.D.L

ROWLEY, A. John W
1948 MC R Aston Martin

RUDDOCK, Gerry
1951 MC R H.R.G
1952 BET 2 Lester MG
1953 BET HR Lester MG

RUESCH, Hans
1953 BET H3, F3 Ferrari 340

SALVADORI, Roy
1948 CT R Alfa Romeo
1948 BET R Maserati
1952 BET 4 Frazer Nash

SANDERSON, Ninian
1953 BET H4, F5 Jaguar C-type

SCOTT, Jack
1947 MC 7 H.R.G
1948 MC 9 H.R.G

SCOTT DOUGLAS, Sir James
1952 BET 6 Jaguar XK120

SCOTT-RUSSELL, Peter
1951 BET 10 Allard
1953 BET H4, F8 Frazer Nash

SHAWE-TAYLOR, Brian
1947 BET 6 E.R.A. "B" type
(with G.H. Bainbridge)
1950 BET 4 E.R.A. "B" type

SHILLITO, Gordon
1949 MC 2 Riley
1949 MC 2 Riley
1951 MC 4 Riley

SIMPSON, Peter
1951 MC 5 Healey

SKELLY, Bill
1952 BET R Jowett Jupiter

STAPLETON, E.C.W.
1951 MC 6 Aston Martin

STEWART, Ian
1952 BET R Jaguar XK 120
1953 BET HR Jaguar C-type

STEWART, Jimmy
1953 BET H5, F6 Jaguar C-type

SWIFT, John
1952 BET R Jaguar XK120
1953 BET H6, FR Jaguar XK 120

THRELFALL, Chris
1953 BET H9, FR Tojeiro

TITTERINGTON, Desmond
1953 BET H9, F18 Allard

TYRER, Gilbert
1947 MC 4 Frazer Nash BMW
1948 MC 2 Frazer Nash BMW
1949 MC 5 Frazer Nash BMW

***WALKER, Peter D.C**
1948 BET R E.R.A. "B"
1949 BET 5 E.R.A. "B"

WATKINS, Ken
1948 MC 8 Frazer Nash BMW
1949 MC R BMW
1953 BET HR Allard

WATSON, Gordon M
1948 BET 6 Alta
1950 BET R Alta

WEBB, J.H
1951 MC 3 Turner

WHARTON, Ken
1953 BET H1, F2 Frazer Nash

WHITEHEAD, Graham
1950 BET R E.R.A. "B"

***WHITEHEAD Peter N**
1947 BET 2 E.R.A. "B"

WHITEHOUSE, Ben
1951 BET R Aston Martin DB1

WILCOCKS, D.A
1948 MC R MG J4

WILKINSON, W.E
1948 BET R E.R.A "E"

WINTERBOTTOM, Eric
1947 MC 3 Emeryson
1949 MC R Cooper-Vincent HRD

WOODALL, Barry
1947 BET 7 Delage

5. BIBLIOGRAPHY

Allison, Mike and Browning, Peter, The Works MGs (second edition published 2011 by Haynes Publishing, Sparkford).

Appleton, John, The Jaguar C-type, Classic Car Profile No.36 (published 1966 by Profile Publications Ltd., Leatherhead).

Barker J.R.W, E.R.A. – A Concise History (published 1992 by Transport Bookman Publications, Isleworth).

Beighton, Peter and Douglas, Andrew, You Couldn't Do It Now (published 1993 by Mannin Printing Ltd., Douglas).

Berthon, Darrell, A Racing History of the Bentley (published 1962 by Autobooks Ltd., Brighton).

Birabongse of Siam, Prince, *Bits and Pieces* (published 1942 by G. T. Foulis and Co. Ltd., Henley-on-Thames).

Bradford, Paul, Isle of Man TT & MGP Memorial 1907 – 2007 (published 2008 by Author, Douglas).

Brendon, Piers, The Motoring Century (published 1997 by Bloomsbury Publishing Plc, London).

Brown, Norman, History of the Manx Grand Prix (published 1960 by Shell, London).

Chula Chakrabongse of Siam, Prince, Dick Seaman - Racing Motorist (published 1941 by G. T. Foulis and Co. Ltd).

Chula Chakrabongse of Siam, Prince, Road Racing 1936 (published 1946 by G. T. Foulis and Co. Ltd, London).

Chula Chakrabongse of Siam, Prince, Road Star Hat Trick (published 1939 by G. T. Foulis and Co Ltd London).

Davey, Keith and Pritchard, Anthony, The Ferrari Tipo 340 & 375 Sports Cars, Classic Car Profile No. 84 (published 1966 by Profile Publications Ltd., Leatherhead).

Demaus, A.B. and Tarring, J.C., The Humber Story 1868-1932 (published 1989 by Alan Sutton Publishing Ltd., Stroud).

Dixon, Alan, The TT Riders (published 1967 by Stanley Paul and Co Ltd, London).

Duke, Geoffrey E., Geoff Duke – In Pursuit of Perfection (published 1988 by Osprey Publishing Limited, London).

Edge, Selwyn F., *My Motoring Reminiscences* (published 1972 by EP Publishing Limited, Wakefield).

Edwards, Robert, Stirling Moss The Authorised Biography (published 2002 by Weidenfeld & Nicholson, London).

Gauld, Graham, Ecurie Ecosse (published 1992 by Graham Gauld Public Relations Ltd., Edinburgh).

Gauld, Graham, Reg Parnell (published 1996 by Patrick Stephens Limited, Sparkford).

Gauld, Graham, and others, Mr. Bob The Life and Times of Bob Gerard (published 2013 by Porter Press International Ltd., Tenbury Wells).

Georgano, G.N. (ed.), The Encyclopaedia of *Motor Sport* (published 1971 by Ebury Press and Michael Joseph Ltd, London).

Georgano, G.N., The Complete Encyclopaedia of Motorcars 1885 to the Present (published 1982 by Ebury Press, London).

Handley, John, *None More Brave* (published 2012 by Aspect Design, Malvern).

Harding, Anthony (ed.), The Guinness Book of Car Facts and Figures (published 1971 by Guinness Superlatives Ltd, Enfield).

Hay, Neville, Rolt and Bira The Forgotten Stars (published 2008 by Transport Bookman Publications, Hook, Hampshire).

Higgins, L.R., Tourist Trophy Races Isle of Man 1907-1953 (published 1954 by Shell & BP, London)

Hodges, David and Mundy, Harry, The V-16 B.R.M., Classic Car Profile No.96 (published 1966 by Profile Publications Ltd., Leatherhead).

Holliday, Bob, Racing Round the Island (published 1976 by David & Charles, Newton Abbot).

Hough, Richard, Tourist Trophy (published 1957 by Hutchinson & Co., London).

Hull, Peter, Alfa Romeo Monoposto Type B P3, Cars in Profile No. 6 (published 1973 by Profile Publications Ltd., Windsor).

Jacobs, Dick, An MG Experience (published 1976 by Transport Bookman Publications, London).

Jarrott, Charles, Ten Years of Motors and Motor Racing (published 1956 by G.T. Foulis & Co. Limited, London).

Jenkinson, Denis, The Le Mans Replica Frazer Nash, Classic Car Profile No.20 (published 1966 by Profile Publications Ltd., Leatherhead).

Kelly, Robert, How the TT Started (published by Island Development Co. Ltd, Douglas).

Kelly, Robert, TT Pioneers (published 1996 by The Manx Experience, Douglas).

Lyndon, Barre, Circuit Dust (published 1934 by John Miles Ltd, London).

Lyndon, Barre, Grand Prix (published 1935 by John Miles Ltd, London).

Mason, David, Freddie Dixon the Man with the Heart of a Lion (published 2008 by Haynes Publishing, Sparkford).

McComb, F. Wilson, The M.G. Magnette K3. Classic Car Profile No. 15 (published 1966 by Profile Publications Ltd., Leatherhead).

Meynell, Laurence, Rolls: Man of Speed (published 1953 by The Bodley Head, London).

Monkhouse, George, Grand Prix Racing Facts and Figures (published 1950 by G.T Foulis & Co Ltd, London).

Montagu of Beaulieu, Lord, *The Gordon Bennett Races* (published 1963 by Cassell & Company Ltd., London).
Montagu of Beaulieu, Lord, Rolls of Rolls-Royce (published 1966 by Cassell & Company Ltd., London)
Moss, Sir Stirling O.B.E. with Henry, Alan, All My Races (published 2009 by Haynes Publishing, Sparkford).
Moss, Sir Stirling with Nye, Doug, Stirling Moss My Cars, My Career (published 1988 by Guild Publishing, London).
Nixon, Chris, Racing with the David Brown Aston Martins volume 2 (published 1980 by Transport Bookman Publications Ltd., Middlesex).
Nockolds, Harold, The Magic of a Name (published 1945 by G.T. Foulis & Co. Ltd., London).
Pearson, F.K., Isle of Man Tramways (published 1970 by David & Charles (Publishers) Limited, Newton Abbot).
Pomeroy, Laurence, The 1914 Grand Prix Vauxhall, Classic Car Profile No. 21 (published 1966 by Profile Publications Ltd., Leatherhead).
Posthumus, Cyril, The 1926-27 1 ½-Litre Delage, Classic Car Profile No. 18 (published 1966 by Profile Publications Ltd., Leatherhead).
Salvadori, Roy and Pritchard, Anthony, Roy Salvadori Racing Driver (published 1985 by Patrick Stephens, Wellingborough).
Sheldon, Paul with Rabagliati, Duncan, A Record of Grand Prix and Voiturette Racing Volume 3, 1932-1936, Volume 4, 1937-1949 and Volume 5, 1950-1953 (published 1988).
Spicer, John, West Cars of Coventry 1904-1915 (published 2005).
Thornley, J.W., *Maintaining the Breed* (published 1950 by Motor Racing Publications Limited, London).
Twelvetrees, Richard and Squire, Pepys, Why Dennis – and How (1945)
Venables, David, Bentley A Racing History (published 2011 by Haynes Publishing, Sparkford)
Venables, David, The Racing Fifteen-Hundreds (published 1984 by Transport Bookman Publications, Isleworth).
Weguelin, David, The History of English Racing Automobiles Limited (published 1980 by White Mouse Editions Ltd., London).
Wentworth Day, J., Kaye Don the Man (published 1934 by Hutchinson, London).
Wyer, John with Nixon, Chris, Racing with the David Brown Aston Martins Volume 1 (published 1980 by Transport Bookman Publications Ltd., Middlesex).

PERIODICALS

Reference has been made to contemporary reports and later articles in *Aston – The Journal of the Aston Martin Heritage Trust, Automobile Club Journal, Autosport, Car, Daily Express, Daily Post, Manx Life, MG Magazine, Mona's Herald, Motoring Illustrated, Motor Sport, News Chronicle, Ramsey Courier, Speed, Sydney Mail, The Autocar, The Automobile, The Automotor Journal, The Car Illustrated, The Daily Telegraph, The Graphic, The Isle of Man Daily Times,* The *Isle of Man Examiner, The Isle of Man Weekly Times, The Light Car & Cyclecar, The Manx Sun, The Motor, The Motor Year Books, The Peel City Guardian, TT Special, The Veteran and Vintage Magazine* and two New Zealand newspapers – *Ellesmere Guardian* and *Evening Post.*

Assistance was obtained from the Official Programmes published by the Royal Automobile Club and the British Racing Drivers' Club in connection with the Isle of Man races, the 1947 and 1948-1949 B.R.D.C Yearbooks, Minutes of the Isle of Man Highway and Transport Board and the daily Journal of the Chief Constable of the Isle of Man.

6. CIRCUIT MAPS

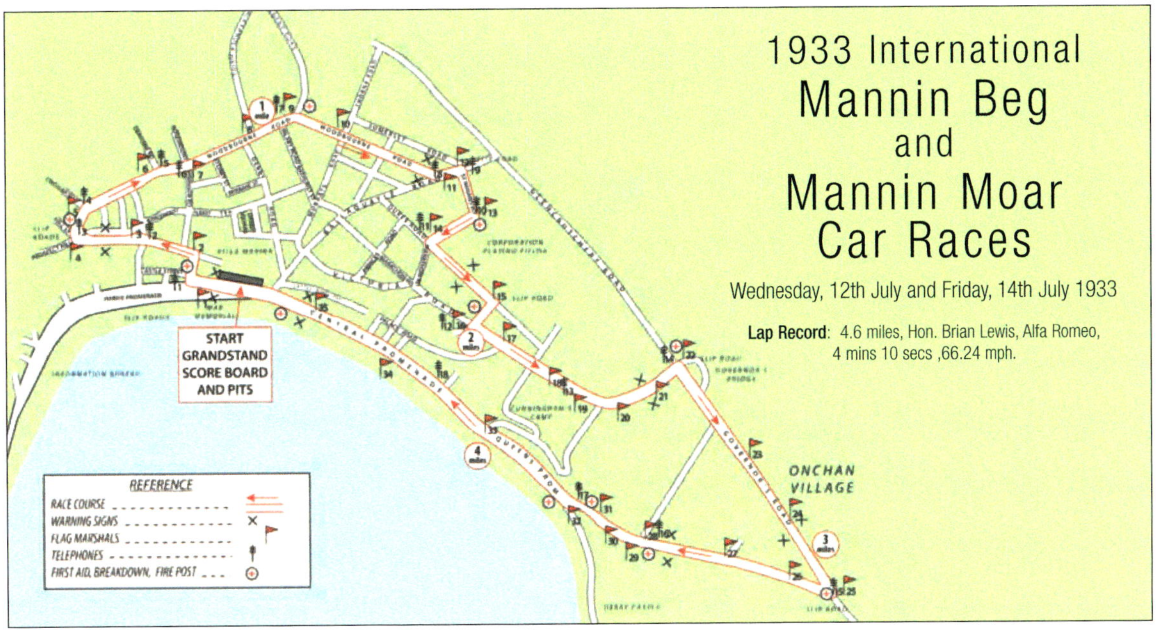
1933 International
Mannin Beg
and
Mannin Moar
Car Races
Wednesday, 12th July and Friday, 14th July 1933
Lap Record: 4.6 miles, Hon. Brian Lewis, Alfa Romeo,
4 mins 10 secs ,66.24 mph.
START
GRANDSTAND
SCORE BOARD
AND PITS
ONCHAN
VILLAGE
REFERENCE
RACE COURSE
WARNING SIGNS
FLAG MARSHALS
TELEPHONES
FIRST AID, BREAKDOWN, FIRE POST

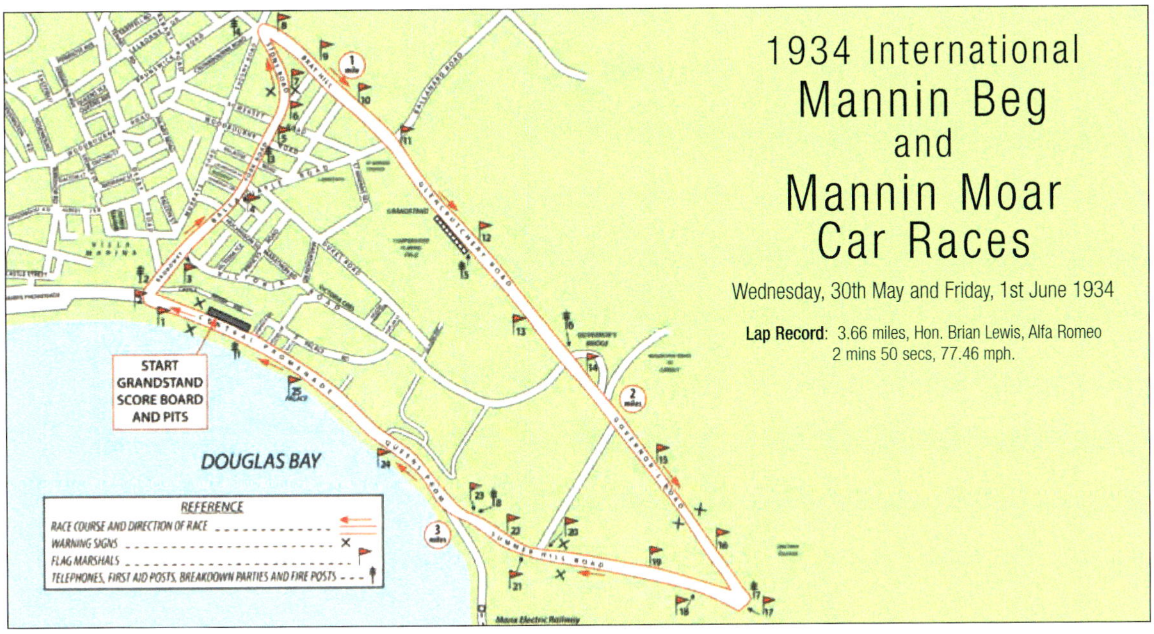
1934 International
Mannin Beg
and
Mannin Moar
Car Races
Wednesday, 30th May and Friday, 1st June 1934
Lap Record: 3.66 miles, Hon. Brian Lewis, Alfa Romeo
2 mins 50 secs, 77.46 mph.
START
GRANDSTAND
SCORE BOARD
AND PITS
DOUGLAS BAY
REFERENCE
RACE COURSE AND DIRECTION OF RACE
WARNING SIGNS
FLAG MARSHALS
TELEPHONES, FIRST AID POSTS, BREAKDOWN PARTIES AND FIRE POSTS

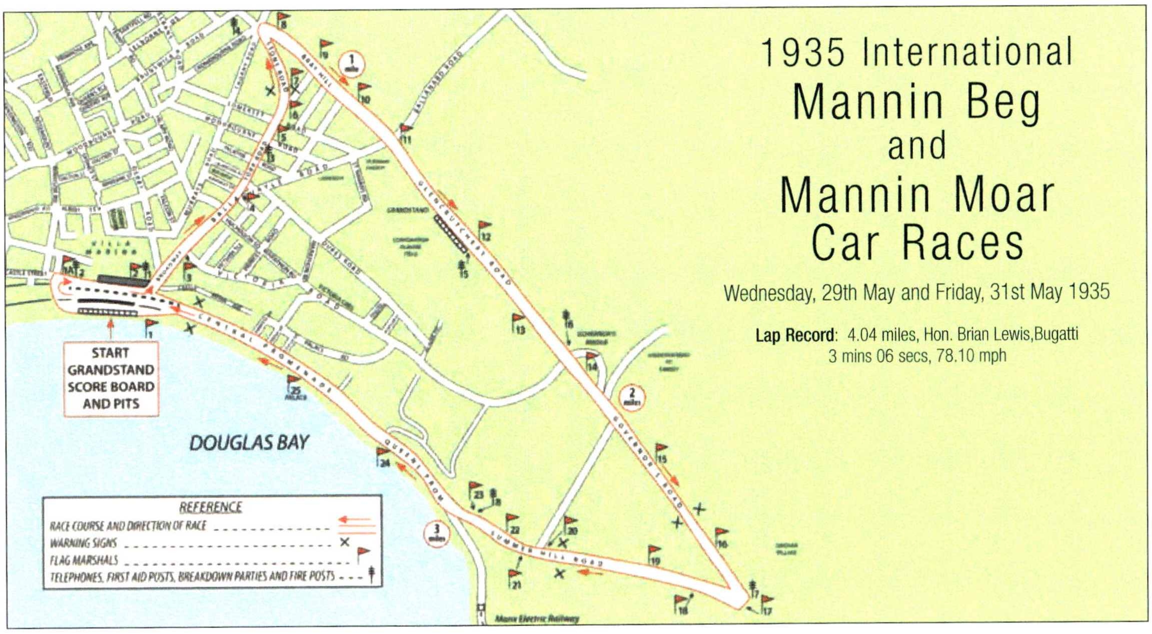
1935 International
Mannin Beg
and
Mannin Moar
Car Races
Wednesday, 29th May and Friday, 31st May 1935
Lap Record: 4.04 miles, Hon. Brian Lewis,Bugatti
3 mins 06 secs, 78.10 mph
START
GRANDSTAND
SCORE BOARD
AND PITS
DOUGLAS BAY
REFERENCE
RACE COURSE AND DIRECTION OF RACE
WARNING SIGNS
FLAG MARSHALS
TELEPHONES, FIRST AID POSTS, BREAKDOWN PARTIES AND FIRE POSTS

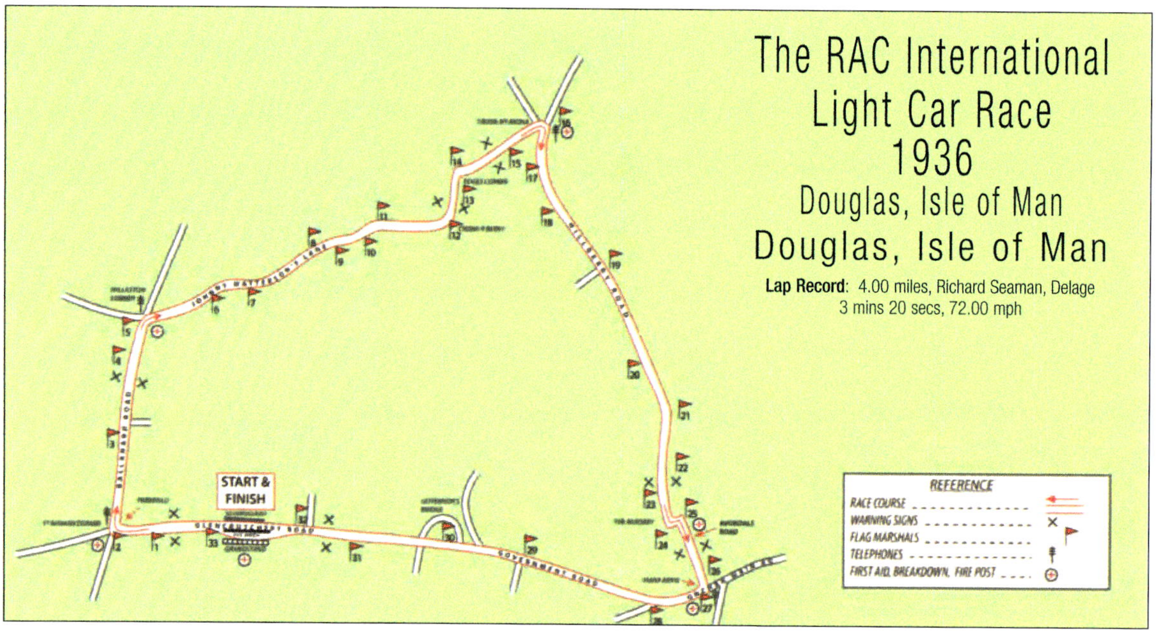
The RAC International
Light Car Race
1936
Douglas, Isle of Man
Douglas, Isle of Man
Lap Record: 4.00 miles, Richard Seaman, Delage
3 mins 20 secs, 72.00 mph
START &
FINISH
REFERENCE
RACE COURSE
WARNING SIGNS
FLAG MARSHALS
TELEPHONES
FIRST AID, BREAKDOWN, FIRE POST

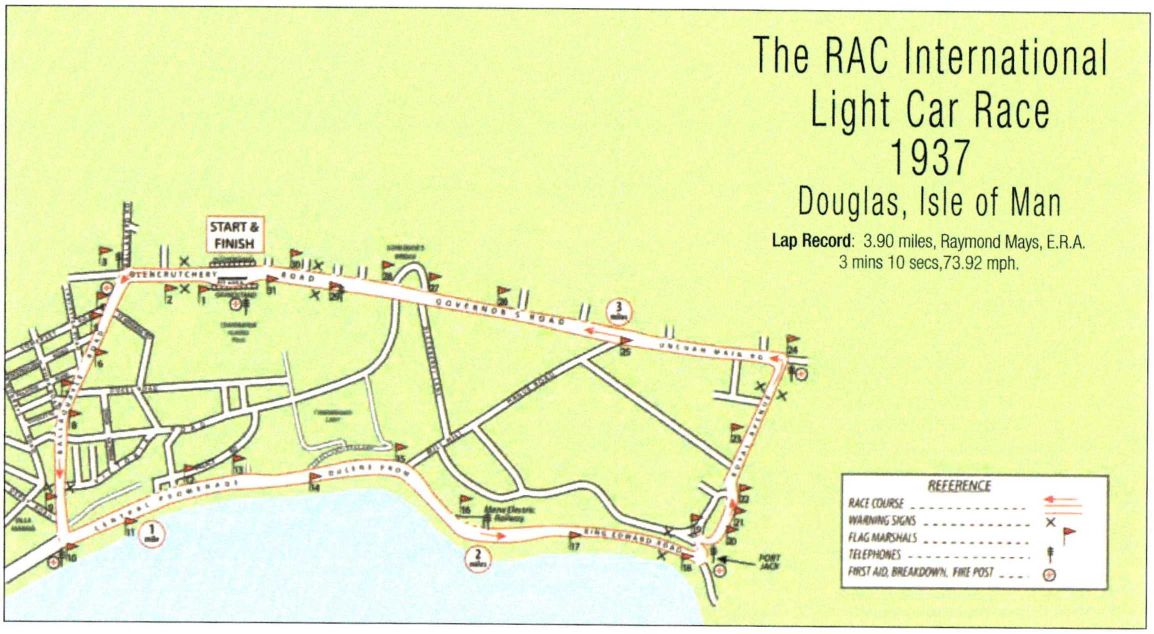
The RAC International
Light Car Race
1937
Douglas, Isle of Man
Lap Record: 3.90 miles, Raymond Mays, E.R.A.
3 mins 10 secs,73.92 mph.
START &
FINISH
REFERENCE
RACE COURSE
WARNING SIGNS
FLAG MARSHALS
TELEPHONES
FIRST AID, BREAKDOWN, FIRE POST

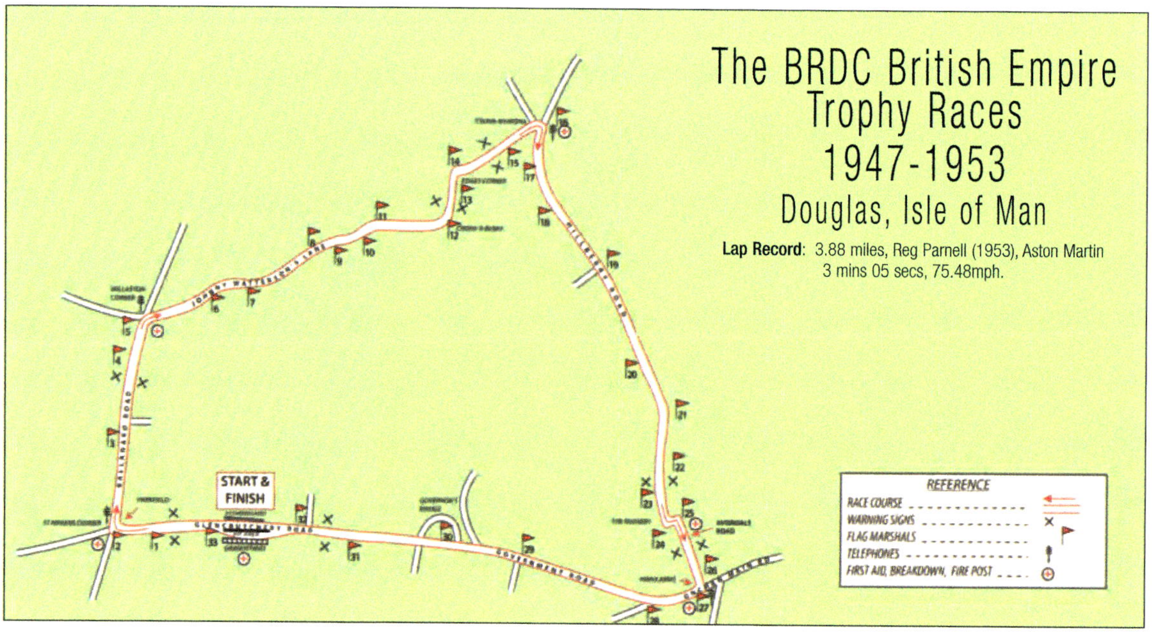
The BRDC British Empire
Trophy Races
1947-1953
Douglas, Isle of Man
Lap Record: 3.88 miles, Reg Parnell (1953), Aston Martin
3 mins 05 secs, 75.48mph.
START &
FINISH
REFERENCE
RACE COURSE
WARNING SIGNS
FLAG MARSHALS
TELEPHONES
FIRST AID, BREAKDOWN, FIRE POST

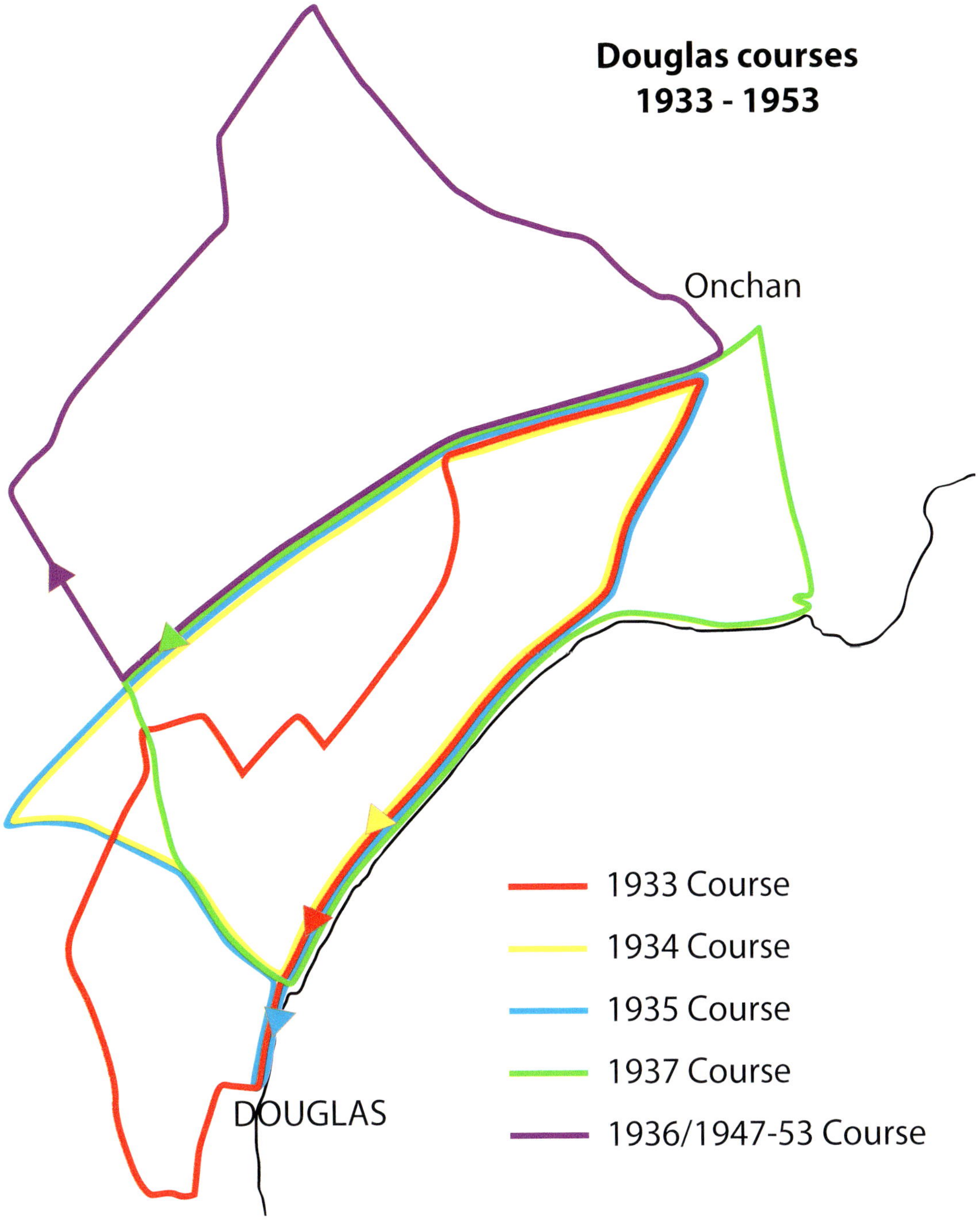
Douglas courses
1933 - 1953
Onchan
DOUGLAS
1933 Course
1934 Course
1935 Course
1937 Course
1936/1947-53 Course

7 ENTRY LISTS

1904 GORDON BENNETT ELIMINATING TRIAL ENTRY LIST

Tuesday 10th May 1904. Start 9.00am. 5 laps of 51.1 miles course, total distance 255.5 miles. 11 starters – 5 finishers.

1	J.W. Stocks	Napier
2	Edmond	Darracq
3	John Hargreaves	Napier
4	Victor Hemery	Darracq
6	W. Clifford Earp	Napier
7	E. Campbell Muir	Wolseley
9	Selwyn F. Edge	Napier
10	Sidney Girling	Wolseley
11	A. Rawlinson	Darracq
12	Charles Jarrott	Wolseley
14	Mark Mayhew	Napier

Numbers 5,8 and 13 were allocated to Huttons which were non-arrivals.

1905 GORDON BENNETT ELIMINATING TRIAL ENTRY LIST

Tuesday 30th May 1905. Start 9.00am. 6 laps of 51.1 miles circuit, total distance 306.6 miles. 10 starters – 3 finishers.

1	H.G. Goodwin	Star 70hp
2	F.R. Goodwin	Star 70hp
3	Hon Algernon Lee Guinness	Darracq 100hp
4	Cecil Bianchi	Wolseley 96hp
6	Cecil Edge	Napier 80hp
7	W. Clifford Earp	Napier 80hp
9	John Hargreaves	Napier 80hp
10	Sidney Girling	Siddeley 100hp
11	Hon. Charles S. Rolls	Wolseley 96hp
12	Arthur E. Macdonald	Napier 90hp

1905 TOURIST TROPHY RACE ENTRY LIST

Thursday 14th September 1905. Start 9.00am. 4 laps of 52 miles circuit, total distance 208 miles. 42 starters – 18 finishers.

1	Hon Charles S. Rolls	Rolls-Royce 20hp.
2	W. Clifford Earp	Napier 18hp
3	Frank G. Cundy	Napier 18hp
6	W.J. Warren	Speedwell 12hp
7	A.J. Dew	Speedwell 14hp
8	W.H. Astill	Orleans 15hp
9	Thomas Jenner	Orleans 15hp
10	James Hadley	Wolseley 14hp
11	Sidney Girling	Siddeley 18hp
12	Tom Thornycroft	Thornycroft 14hp
14	R. Lascelles	New Simms-Welbeck 20hp
17	John Downie	Argyll 14hp
18	W. Parker Thomas	Argyll 14hp
19	C.L. Cattell	James and Browne 14hp
20	F.S. Bennett	Cadillac 9hp
21	W.H. Cox	Maudslay 20hp
22	Percy W. Northey	Rolls-Royce 20hp
23	A.J. Hancock	Vauxhall 12hp
24	C.H. Cooper	Beeston Humber 16hp
25	Harvey du Cros Jnr	Swift 16hp
27	Arthur J. Clay	Ryknield 15hp
28	A.C. Kent	White steam
29	Frederic Coleman	White steam
30	James Reid	Beeston Humber 16hp
31	E.H. Lancaster	Clement 14hp
32	R.W. Maudslay	Standard 16hp
34	Charles Clench	Whitlock-Aster 15hp
35	R. Downing	Dennis 14hp
36	John C. Dennis	Dennis 14hp
37	E. H. Arnot	Minerva 16hp
39	J. Percy Dean	Scout 14hp
40	Hon Algernon Lee Guinness	Darracq 10hp
41	A. Rawlinson	Darracq 10hp
42	Karl Beireiz	Dixi 14hp
45	W.C. Holloway	Minerva 16hp
46	Charles Friswell	Peugeot 10hp
47	Guy V. Baxendale	Thornycroft 14hp
48	Edmund W. Lewis	Rover 16hp
49	Ernest Courtis	Rover 16hp
52	Norman Littlejohn	Vinot et Deguingand 14hp
53	John S. Napier	Arrol-Johnston 18hp
54	E.J.Cyril Roberts	Arrol-Johnston 18hp

1906 TOURIST TROPHY RACE ENTRY LIST

Thursday 26th September 1906. Start 9.00am. 4 laps of 40.25 miles circuit, total distance 161 miles. 29 starters – 9 finishers.

1	John S. Napier	New Arrol-Johnston 18hp
2	Hon Algernon Lee Guinness	Darracq 15hp
3	Sidney Girling	Darracq 15hp
4	Hon Charles Rolls	Rolls-Royce 20hp
5	Percy W. Northey	Rolls-Royce 20hp
6	Warwick J. Wright	Minerva 22hp
8	C.L. Cattell	James and Browne 20hp
9	Norman Littlejohn	Vinot 16hp
10	E. Campbell Muir	New Arrol Johnston 18hp

11	W. Parker Thomas	Argyll 16hp
12	A.E. George	Argyll 16hp
13	Ernest Courtis	Rover 16hp
14	Albert Brown	Brown 20hp
15	Georges Braud	Clement 20hp
16	Georges Dumont	Pipe 28hp
17	T.C. Pullinger	Beeston Humber 16hp
18	Louis Coatalen	Coventry Humber 20hp
21	J.K. Starley	Rover 16hp
22	Charles Friswell	Peugeot 10hp
23	J. Ernest Hutton	Berliet 22hp
24	Montagu Grahame-White	Siddeley 18hp
25	A.E. Crowdy	Siddeley 18hp
26	Paul Bablot	Berliet 22hp
27	Tom Thornycroft	Thornycroft 14hp
28	G.F. Prew	Star 18hp
29	R.A. Bell	Deasy 24hp
30	J.W.F. Crouch	Deasy 24hp
31	Gordon Usmar	Vinot 16hp
32	J. Percy Dean	Scout 17hp
33	J. Lisle	Scout 18hp
34	M.L. Braithwaite	Speedwell 18hp
35	E.W. Leather	Climax 14hp
36	R. Every	Swift 16hp
37	W.L. Hardman	Hardman 25hp
38	H.P. McConnell	Bianchi 16hp
39	Arthur McCormack	Gladiator 20hp
40	Sidney Straker	Straker-Squire 12hp
41	L.R.L. Squire	Straker-Squire 12hp
42	Thomas Watson	Climax 16hp
43	Oscar Cupper	Metallurgique 24hp
44	W.G. Batchelor	Armadale 16hp
45	G.W. Roberts	Rapid 20hp
46	Turberville Smith	Academy 14hp
47	H.A. Bate	S.C.A.R. 18hp
48	Richard Lascelles	Vici 12hp
49	Lieut. J. Lesmoir Gordon	Florentia 18hp

1906 "GRAPHIC" TROPHY ENTRY LIST

Friday 27th September 1906. Start 10.30 am. 4.25 miles hill climb on Douglas to Castletown Road from Quarterbridge to Santon.

1	C.H. Cooper	Beeston-Humber 60hp
2	H.A. Bate	S.C.A.R. 18hp
3	J. Ernest Hutton	Berliet 40hp
4	George S. Barwick	Daimler 30-40hp
5	William Watson	Berliet 24-40hp
6	C.A. Glentworth	Napier 50hp
7	H.O. Hall	Isotta-Fraschini 28-35hp
8	J. Ernest Hutton	Ariel-Simplex 50hp
9	G.A. Roberts	Rapid 20hp
10	H.A. Bate	Sorex 30-35hp
11	Albert Farnell	Daimler 30hp

1907 TOURIST TROPHY RACE ENTRY LIST

Thursday 30th May 1907. Start 9.11am. 6 laps of 40.25miles circuit, total distance 241.50 miles. 22 starters – 2 finishers.

2	Hon Algernon Lee Guinness	Darracq 18hp
3	Kenelm Lee Guinness	Darracq 18hp
4	Jean Porporato	Berliet 22hp
5	J. Ernest Hutton	Berliet 22hp
7	E.J.C. Roberts	Arrol-Johnston 25hp
8	John S. Napier	Arrol-Johnston 25hp
9	Oscar Cupper	Metallurgique 24-28hp
10	Tom Thornycroft	Thornycroft 14hp
11	J. Percy Dean	Scout 17-20hp
12	W.G. Tuck	Coventry Humber 16-20hp
13	T.C. Pullinger	Beeston Humber 16-20hp
14	Harry G. Goodwin	Star 18hp
15	G. Prew	Star 18hp
16	D.S. Hodges	West-Aster 16-20hp
19	Thomas Rimmer	Vulcan 20hp
20	Georges Braud	Clement 18hp
21	M. Ross-Browne	Gladiator 18hp
22	Ernest Courtis	Rover 20hp
23	P. Nevers	West-Aster 16-20hp
24	Louis Coatalen	Hillman-Coatalen 20hp
25	Edgar R. Folker	Rover 20hp
27	R. Goodenough	Leader 10-12hp
28	Norman Littlejohn	Vinot 24hp

1907 HEAVY TOURING CAR RACE ENTRY LIST

Thursday 30th May 1907. 5 laps of 40.25 miles circuit, total distance 201.25 miles. 9 starters – 2 finishers.

1	L.R.L. Squire	Straker-Squire 25-30hp
2	Willliam Watson	Berliet 40hp
4	H. Niblett	Thornycroft 30hp
5	Graeme Fenton	Gladiator 25hp
6	Charles Sangster	Ariel-Simplex 30hp
8	E.H. Arnot	Arrol-Johnston 40hp
9	Baron Petiet	Aries
10	C.H. Cooper	Beeston Humber 20-30hp
12	A.E. Harrison	Ariel-Simplex
14	George P. Mills	Beeston-Humber 30hp

1907 "GRAPHIC" TROPHY ENTRY LIST

Friday 31st May 1907. 2,550 yards hill climb on Ramsey to Douglas coast road, from Ballure Bridge, Ramsey to Rest and be Thankful Inn. 9 starters – 7 finishers.

1	F. W. Baily	Napier 50hp
2	J. Ernest Hutton	Berliet 60hp
3	J. Ernest Hutton	Berliet 40hp
4	George S.Barwick	Daimler 35hp
5	William Hillman	Hillman-Coatalen 20hp
6	John S.Napier	Arrol-Johnston 38-45hp

7	Capt. W.E.D. Owen	Junior 40hp
8	Francis A. Bolton	Daimler 35hp
9	Selwyn F. Edge	Napier 45hp
10	Thomas Henshaw	Daimler 35hp
11	C.H. Saunders	Gracile 40hp
12	William Watson	Berliet 24-40hp
13	Charles Sangster	Ariel-Simplex 35hp
14	Charles Sangster	Ariel-Simplex 35hp

1908 TOURIST TROPHY RACE ENTRY LIST

Thursday 24th September 1908. Start 9.00am. 9 laps of 37.5 miles circuit, total distance 337.5 miles. 35 starters – 10 finishers.

1	H.B. Browning	Rover
2	William Watson	Hutton
3	E.J. Cyril Roberts	Arrol-Johnston
4	A. Rawlinson	Darracq
5	G.W.A. Brown	Coventry Humber
6	Louis Coatalen	Hillman Coatalen
7	Oscar Cupper	Metallurgique
9	Tom Thornycroft	Thornycroft
10	M. Ross-Browne	Vinot
11	Leslie Porter	Calthorpe
12	Philip Graham	Deasy
13	J. Gaal	Westinghouse
14	R. Harper	S.C.A.T.
15	J. Ernest Hutton	Hutton
16	Dario Resta	Arrol-Johnston
17	Hon Algernon Lee Guinness	Darracq
18	James Reid	Beeston Humber
19	Kenelm Lee Guinness	Hillman Coatalen
20	J.T.C. Moore-Brabazon	Metallurgique
22	D.S. Hodge	Thornycroft
23	T. Rowland Outhwaite	Vinot
24	M. Robinson	Calthorpe
25	E.W.Lewis	Deasy
26	A.L. Hartridge	Westinghouse
27	F. Ward	S.C.A.T.
28	P.D. Stirling	Hutton
29	Geoffrey Moss	Arrol-Johnston
30	A.E. George	Darracq
31	W.G. Tuck	Beeston-Humber
32	J.W. Stocks	De Dion Bouton
33	Warwick Wright	Metallurgique
34	Andre Debuissey	Piccard
36	M.L.Molon	Vinot
37	T. Rimmer	Vulcan
38	Harold S. Buckley	S.C.A.T.

1914 TOURIST TROPHY RACE ENTRY LIST

Wednesday/Thursday 10th/11th June 1914. Start 9.00am.16 laps of 37.5 miles circuit, total distance 600 miles. 22 starters – 6 finishers.

1	Jean Porporato	Minerva I	3,308cc
2	F.T.Burgess	Humber I	3,295cc
3	R.S. "Dick" Witchell	Straker-Squire I	3,260cc
4	Kenelm Lee Guinness	Sunbeam I	3,297cc
5	Richard Lisle	Star I	3,295cc
6	A. J. Hancock	Vauxhall I	3,308cc
7	Philip Stapp	Adler I	3,308cc
8	W.O. Bentley	D.F.P.	2,001cc
9	Rene Berger	S.A.V.A	3,252cc
10	Alfred Rawlinson	Hudson	3,309cc
11	Cecil Bianchi	Crossley	3,273cc
12	Leon Molon	Minerva II	3,308cc
13	W.G. Tuck	Humber II	3,295cc
14	Frank C. Clement	Straker-Squire II	3,260cc
15	Dario Resta	Sunbeam II	3,297cc
16	Robert F.L. Crossman	Star II	3,295cc
17	William Watson	Vauxhall II	3,308cc
18	Otto Goebel	Adler II	3,308cc
19	C. Riecken	Minerva III	3,308cc
20	S. Wright	Humber III	3,295cc
21	Hon Algernon Lee Guinness	Sunbeam III	3,297cc
22	J.Higginson	Vauxhall III	3,308cc
23	J. Rutsch	Adler III	3,308cc

1922 TOURIST TROPHY RACE ENTRY LIST

Thursday 22nd June 1922. Start 9.30am. 8 laps of 37.75 miles circuit, total distance 302 miles. 8 starters – 5 finishers.

1	Kenelm Lee Guinness	Sunbeam I	2,973cc
2	Matthew C. Park	Vauxhall I	2,985cc
3	Frank C. Clement	Bentley I	2,996cc
4	Henry O.D. Segrave	Sunbeam II	2,973cc
5	Oswald Payne	Vauxhall II	2,985cc
6	W. Douglas Hawkes	Bentley II	2,996cc
7	Jean Chassagne	Sunbeam III	2,973cc
8	Ernest Swain	Vauxhall III	2,985cc
9	W.O. Bentley	Bentley III	2,996cc

1922 INTERNATIONAL 1,500cc TROPHY RACE ENTRY LIST

Thursday 22nd June 1922. 6 laps of 37.75 miles circuit, total distance 226.5 miles. 9 starters – 6 finishers.

22	Pierre de Vizcaya	Bugatti I	1,452cc
23	G. Bedford	Hillman	1,496cc
24	Sir Algernon Lee Guinness	Talbot-Darracq I	1,486cc
25	A.C. Bertelli	Enfield-Allday	1,496cc
26	H. Kensington Moir	Aston Martin	1,487cc
27	Mones Maury	Bugatti II	1,452cc
28	Jean Moriceau	Talbot-Darracq II	1,486cc
30	Bertram S. Marshall	Bugatti III	1,452cc
31	Albert Divo	Talbot-Darracq III	1,486cc

1933 INTERNATIONAL MANNIN BEG RACE ENTRY LIST

Wednesday 12th July 1933. Start 9.30am. 50 laps of 4.6 miles circuit, total distance 230 miles. 14 starters – 3 finishers.

No.	Driver	Reserve Driver	Entrant	Car
1	Robin M. Mere			MG Magnette 1,087cc
2	Eddie R. Hall			MG Magnette 1,087cc
3	W. Sullivan			Morris Minor Sullivan Special 732cc
4	Dennis K.Mansell			MG Midget 746 cc
5	Raymond Mays			Riley 1,486cc
6	Humphrey W. Cook			Riley 1,487cc
7	Freddie W. Dixon	Cyril Paul		Riley 1,089cc
8	C.M.Needham	N.A.Berry		Frazer Nash 1,496cc
9	Thomas G. Moore	N.A. Berry		Frazer Nash 1,496cc
10	Earl Howe			MG Magnette 1,100cc
11	Victor Gillow	P.W. Charles		Riley 1,086cc
12	J. Ludovic Ford	Maurice H. Baumer		MG Midget 745cc
14	Ronald A. Yallop	E. Fronteras		MG Magnette 1,087cc
15	George E.T. Eyston	A. Denly		MG Magnette 1,086cc
16	Hugh C. Hamilton			MG Magnette 1,086cc
17	J.H. Bartlett		Jimmy Nervo	Salmson 1,087cc
18	Kaye Don		Bernard Rubin	MG Magnette 1,086cc
19	Sydney A. Crabtree	W.L. Handley		MG Midget 746cc
20	Whitney Straight			MG Magnette 1,086cc
21	E. L. Gardner	C.W.G. Lacey		MG Midget 747cc

1933 INTERNATIONAL MANNIN MOAR RACE ENTRY LIST

Friday 14th July 1933. Start 9.30am. 50 laps of 4.6 miles circuit, total distance 230 miles. 9 starters – 4 finishers.

No.	Driver	Reserve Driver	Entrant	Car
1	Alfred C. Lace			Invicta 4,467cc
2	Whitney W. Straight			Maserati 2,514cc
3	Richard O. Shuttleworth	C. Brackenbury		Bugatti 2,300cc
4	Raymond Mays			Riley 1,486cc
5	T.S. Fothringham			Bugatti 2,263cc
6	Hon. Brian Lewis		N. Rees and A.W.Fox	Alfa Romeo 2,336cc
7	C.M.Needham	N.A. Berry		Frazer Nash 1,657cc
8	W.E. Harker			Harker Special 1,496cc
9	Tim Rose-Richards			Bugatti 2,263cc
10	T.A.S.O. Mathieson			Bugatti 1,998cc
11	George E.T. Eyston			Alfa Romeo 2,336cc
12	A.H. Lindsay Eccles			Bugatti 2,263cc
14	Kaye Don			Alfa Romeo 2,336cc
15	Walter L.Handley	S.A. Crabtree		Alfa Romeo 2,336cc
16			Bernard Rubin	Alfa Romeo 2,336cc

1934 INTERNATIONAL MANNIN BEG RACE ENTRY LIST

Wednesday 30th May 1934. Start10.00am.50 laps of 3.658 miles circuit, total distance 182.9 miles.
19 starters – 8 finishers.

No.	Driver	Reserve Driver	Entrant	Car
1	Ron T. Horton			MG Magnette 1,086cc
2	P.L. Donkin			MG Magnette 1,087cc
3	Eddie R.Hall			MG Magnette 1,087cc
4	Hugh C. Hamilton			MG Magnette 1,087cc
6	Humphrey W. Cook	Raymond Mays		E.R.A. 1,091cc
7	Henry Laird	M.A. McEvoy		McEvoy Special 1454cc
8	George E.T. Eyston			MG Magnette 1,086cc
9	Walter L.Handley		G.E.T. Eyston	MG Magnette 1,086cc
10	Charlie J.P. Dodson		G.E.T. Eyston	MG Magnette 1,086cc
11	Roy Eccles			MG Magnette 1,086cc
12	Charlie E.C. Martin		Roy Eccles	MG Magnette 1,086cc
14	E.K. Rayson			Riley 1,089cc
15	W.G. "Bill" Everitt			MG Midget 746cc
16	Hon. Brian Lewis		A.W. Fox	Singer 1,493cc
17	F. Allen			MG Midget 750cc
18	Victor Gillow			Riley 1,086cc
19	Pat Fairfield		Freddie Dixon	Riley 1,089cc
20	Freddie Dixon			Riley 1,486cc
21	Cyril Paul		Freddie Dixon	Riley 1,486cc
22	Norman Black			MG Magnette 1,086cc
23	Kaye Don		Norman Black	MG Magnette 1,086cc
24	A.P. Hamilton		Norman Black	MG Magnette 1,086cc
25	W.R. "Bobby" Baird			Riley 1,088cc
26	Dudley Froy			Jamieson Special 996cc
27	G.Manby-Colegrave			MG Magnette 1,087cc

1934 INTERNATIONAL MANNIN MOAR RACE ENTRY LIST

Friday 1st June 1934. Start 10.00am. 50 laps of 3.658 miles circuit, total distance 182.9 miles.
10 starters – 3 finishers.

No.	Driver	Reserve Driver	Entrant	Car
1	T.A.S.O. Mathieson			Bugatti 2,300cc
2	Tim Rose-Richards			Bugatti 2,300cc
3	A.H. Lindsay Eccles			Bugatti 2,300cc
4	Hon. Brian Lewis		N. Rees and A.W.Fox	Alfa Romeo 2,655cc
6	R. Featherstonhaugh		Whitney W.Straight	Maserati 2,991cc
7	Freddie Dixon			Riley 1,808cc
8	Cyril Paul		Freddie Dixon	Riley 1,808cc
9	John Cobb			Alfa Romeo 2,336cc
10	Kaye Don			Alfa Romeo 2,336cc
11	Richard O. Shuttleworth			Bugatti 2,296cc
12	Vasco Sameiro		E.F.Abecassis	Alfa Romeo 2,336cc
14	Raymond Mays	H.W. Cook	H.W.Cook	E.R.A. 1,488cc

1935 INTERNATIONAL MANNIN BEG RACE ENTRY LIST

Wednesday 29th May 1935. Start10.00am. 50 laps of 4.035 miles circuit, total distance 201.75 miles.
13 starters –
2 finishers.

No.	Driver	Reserve Driver	Entrant	Car
1	Alfred C. Lace			Alta 1,074cc
2	D. Tennant	Lord Avebury	A.C. Lace	Alta 1,074cc
3	L.P. Driscoll		Sir Herbert Austin	Austin 747.5cc
4	Charlie J.P. Dodson		Sir Herbert Austin	Austin 747.5cc
5	Stanley Woods		Sir Herbert Austin	Austin 747.5cc
6	T.K. Humber			Bugatti 1,496cc
8	Raymond Mays		H. W. Cook	E.R.A. 1,090cc
9	Pat Fairfield			E.R.A. 1,090cc
10	P.L.Donkin			Maserati 1,086cc
11	Eddie R. Hall			MG Magnette 1,087cc
12	J. Ludovic Ford	Maurice H. Baumer		MG Magnette 1,087cc
14	G.F.Manby-Colegrave			MG Magnette 1,087cc
15	R.T. Horton			MG Midget 746cc
16	George E.T. Eyston			MG Midget 746cc
17	Walter L. Handley		G.E.T. Eyston	MG Midget 746cc
18	Norman Black		G.E.T. Eyston	MG Midget 746cc
19	W.R. "Bobby"Baird			MG Midget 746cc
20	Freddie Dixon			Riley 1,486cc

1935 INTERNATIONAL MANNIN MOAR RACE ENTRY LIST

Friday 31st May 1935. Start10.00am.50 laps of 4.035 miles circuit, total distance 201.75 miles.
14 starters – 4 finishers.

No.	Driver	Reserve Driver	Entrant	Car
1	A.P. Hamilton			Alfa Romeo 2,336cc
2	R.S. Wilkins			Alfa Romeo 2,600cc
3	Richard O. Shuttleworth			Alfa Romeo 2,904cc
4	Austin Dobson	A.C. Dobson		Alfa Romeo 2,600cc
5	Luis Fontes			Alfa Romeo 2,336cc
6	Tim Rose-Richards			Maserati 2,992cc
7	Hon. Brian Lewis		Earl Howe & N. Rees	Bugatti 3,300cc
8	Hon. Jock Leith			Bugatti 2,263cc
9	A.H. Lindsay Eccles			Bugatti 3,255cc
10	Charlie E.C.Martin			Bugatti 3,255cc
11	Charles Brackenbury		C.E.C. Martin	Bugatti 2,263cc
12	Richard Seaman			Maserati 2,992cc
14	Humphrey W. Cook			E.R.A. 1,488cc
15	Raymond Mays		H.W. Cook	E.R.A. 1,980cc
16	E.K.Rayson			Bugatti 1,990cc

1936 RAC INTERNATIONAL LIGHT CAR RACE ENTRY LIST
Thursday 28th May 1936. Start 2.00pm. 50 laps of 4 miles circuit, total distance 200 miles.
19 starters – 6 finishers.

No.	Driver	Reserve Driver	Entrant	Car
1	J.H. Bartlett			Alta 1,485cc
2	P.M. Dwyer			Alta 1,485cc
3	A.J Cormack			Alta 1,496cc
4	J.P. Wakefield			Alta 1,496cc
5	L.P. Driscoll	H.L. Hadley	Sir Herbert Austin	Austin 744cc
6	Charlie J.P. Dodson	H.L. Hadley	Sir Herbert Austin	Austin 744cc
7	C.L. Goodacre	H.L. Hadley	Sir Herbert Austin	Austin 744cc
8	T.K. Humber			Bugatti 1,496cc
9	Richard Seaman			Delage 1,460cc
10	Pat Fairfield		A.C. Dobson	E.R.A. 1,486cc
11	Cyril Paul		A.C. Dobson	E.R.A. 1,486cc
12	W.G. "Bill" Everitt			E.R.A. 1,486cc
14	Raymond Mays		H.W. Cook	E.R.A. 1,488cc
15	Marcell Lehoux	H.W. Cook	H.W. Cook	E.R.A. 1,488cc
16	Lord Howe	H.W. Cook	H.W. Cook	E.R.A. 1,488cc
17	"B. Bira"			E.R.A. 1,488cc
18	Reggie Tongue			E.R.A. 1.488cc
19	T.H. Wisdom		N. Black & T.H. Wisdom	E.R.A. 1.488cc
20	G.F.A. Manby-Colegrave	R.E.L. Featherstonhaugh		E.R.A. 1,488cc
21	P.F. Jucker			Frazer Nash 1,496cc
22	E.K.Rayson			Maserati 1,496cc
23	Christian Kautz			Maserati 1,498cc
24	L.R. Briggs			MG Magnette 1,087cc
25	H. Williams			MG Magnette 1,087cc
26	Roy H. Eccles			Rapier Special 1,084cc
27	Freddie Dixon			Riley 1,486cc

1937 RAC INTERNATIONAL LIGHT CAR RACE ENTRY LIST
Thursday 3rd June 1937. Start 2.00pm. 50 laps of 3.9 miles circuit, total distance 195 miles.
15 starters – 12 finishers.

No.	Driver	Reserve Driver	Entrant	Car
1	P.F. Jucker			Alta 1,496cc
2	"B. Bira"		H.R.H Prince Chula of Siam	Delage 1,486cc
3	Charlie Dodson		F.W. Dixon	Dixon Special
4	Arthur Dobson			E.R.A. 1,486cc
5	"B. Bira"		H.R.H. Prince Chula of Siam	E.R.A. 1,488cc
6	Ian P. Connell			E.R.A. 1,488cc
7	Raymond Mays		H.W. Cook	E.R.A. 1,488cc
8	Earl Howe		H.W. Cook	E.R.A. 1,488cc
9	Pat Fairfield		H.W. Cook	E.R.A. 1,488cc
10	Reggie Tongue			E.R.A. 1,488cc
11	Peter Whitehead	Peter Walker	P.N. Whitehead	E.R.A. 1,488cc
12	Charlie E.C. Martin			Martin J.A.P. 1,500cc
14	Robin Hanson		Mrs. M.E. Hall-Smith	Maserati 1,490cc
15	John Du Puy			Maserati 1,490cc
16	E. de Graffenried		John du Puy	Maserati 1,496cc
17	Hon. P. Aitken			Maserati 1,500cc

18	Austin Dobson	Hon. P. Aitken	Maserati 1,500cc
19	Luigi Villoresi	Count Lurani	Maserati 1,500cc
20	Reg Parnell		MG Magnette 1,486cc
21	W.Hughes		MG Magnette 1,087cc
22	Peter Maclure		Riley 1,487cc
23	A. Powys-Lybbe		Talbot 1,496cc

1947 MANX CUP RACE ENTRY LIST

Thursday 21st August 1947. Start 2.00pm. 12 laps of 3.3789 miles circuit, total distance 46.55 miles. 18 starters – 12 finishers.

No.	Driver(s)	Entrant	Car
1	Owen Finch		Amilcar
3	Eric Winterbottom		Emeryson
5	Reg Parnell		E.R.A.
7	W. Robert "Bobby" Baird		MG
9	R.M. "Curly" Dryden		MG
11	Hector Graham & D.H. Kyle	Hector Graham	MG
15	Frank W. Kennington		MG
17	Ian H. Nickols		MG
19	Ian Metcalfe		Rapier
21	George H.G. Burton		Riley
23	C.G.H. Dunham		Alvis
25	G.E. "Geoff" Ansell		Aston Martin
31	Sheila Darbishire & Edward G. Pool	E.G. Pool	Bugatti
33	Anthony "Tony" Crook		Frazer Nash B.M.W
35	Hugh M.F. Carrington		Frazer Nash B.M.W
37	T.M. Gay		Frazer Nash B.M.W
39	Oscar Moore		Frazer Nash B.M.W
41	Gilbert Tyrer		Frazer Nash B.M.W
43	Peter C.T. Clark		H.R.G.
45	G.H. Robins	Peter C.T. Clark	H.R.G.
47	John Wyer	Peter C.T. Clark	H.R.G.
49	T.C. "Cuth" Harrison		Riley
51	C.C.D. Miller & Guy Jason-Henry	C.C.D. Miller	Riley
53	Francis N. Penn	S.B. Reece	Riley
55	"B. Bira"	White Mouse Stable for Equipe Simca Gordini	Simca
57	Amedee Gordini	White Mouse Stable for Equipe Simca Gordini	Simca

1947 BRITISH EMPIRE TROPHY RACE ENTRY LIST

Thursday 21st August 1947. Start 3.00pm.40 laps of 3.8789 miles circuit, total distance 155.16 miles. 15 starters – 9 finishers.

No.	Driver(s)	Entrant	Car
2	Geoff. Crossley		Alta
4	Gordon. M. Watson & R.M. Cowell	G.M. Watson	Alta
6	John H. Williams		Alta
8	Michael C. Chorlton		Bugatti
10	David A. Hampshire		Challenger
12	Capt. Barry Woodall		Delage
14	George E. Abecassis		E.R.A.
16	George H. Bainbridge & Brian N. Shawe-Taylor	R. E. Ansell	E.R.A.

No.	Driver(s)	Entrant	Car
18	John V. Bolster	P.H. Bell	E.R.A.
20	H. Leslie Brooke		E.R.A.
22	F. R. "Bob" Gerard		E.R.A.
24	T.C. "Cuth" Harrison		E.R.A.
26	Raymond Mays		E.R.A.
28	Reg Parnell		E.R.A.
30	Joe Ashmore	R. Parnell	E.R.A.
32	Peter N. Whitehead		E.R.A.
34	"B. Bira"	White Mouse Stable	E.R.A. or Maserati
36	Robert E. "Bob" Ansell		E.R.A.
38	Guy Jason-Henry	J.S. Gordon	Maserati
44	Fred Ashmore	R. Parnell	Maserati
46	Sheila Darbishire	S.B. Reece	Riley
48	A.P.R. "Tony" Rolt		Alfa Romeo
50	Leslie Johnson		Darracq

1948 MANX CUP AND CASTLETOWN TROPHY RACES ENTRY LIST

Tuesday 25th May 1948. Start 2.00pm. Races run concurrently over 18 laps of 3.3789 miles circuit, total distance 69.82 miles. Manx Cup: 23 starters – 12 finishers, Castletown Trophy: 5 starters – 3 finishers.

No.	Driver(s)	Entrant	Car
Manx Cup Race			
1	R. John W. Appleton		Appleton Special 1,089cc
3	David Murray & H.G. Dudley	Brian Finglass	MG 746cc
5	Leonard D. Gill & E.C. Spero	L.D. Gill	MG 746cc
7	D.A. Wilcocks		MG 747cc
9	Ted Lund		Lund Special 972cc
11	Robert "Bobby" Baird & Paul Emery	Robert Baird	MG 1,087cc
15	Hector Graham & D.H. Kyle	Hector Graham	MG 1,087cc
17	Frank W. Kennington		MG 1,087cc
19	John Marshall	F.W. Kennington	MG 1,087cc
21	Ian H. Nickols		Parnell Special 1,087cc
23	George H.G. Burton		Riley 1,087cc
25	Leslie G. Johnson & C.G.H. Dunham	C.G.H. Dunham	Alvis 1,844cc
27	John W. Rowley & H.I. Bond-Williams	H.I. Bond-Williams	Aston Martin 1,950cc
29	Ken Watkins		Frazer Nash B.M.W. 1,971cc
31	C. Derek F. Buckler		Buckler 1,228cc
33	R.M. "Curly" Dryden		Cooper 496cc
35	Spike Rhiando		Cooper 996cc
37	Peter C.T. Clark		H.R.G. 1,496cc
39	Dudley Folland	Peter C.T. Clark	H.R.G. 1,496cc
41	E.W. "Bill" Holt	Peter C.T. Clark	H.R.G. 1,496cc
43	Jack Scott	Peter C.T. Clark	H.R.G. 1,496cc
45	George E. Phillips		MG 1,250cc
47	Maurice Monnier		Monnier Special 1,971cc
49	Oscar Moore		O.B.M 1,971cc
51	Francis N. Penn	S.B. Reece	Riley 1,986cc
53	T.C. "Cuth" Harrison		Riley 1,986cc
55	George Nixon		Riley 1,749cc
57	Horace J.C. Ripley & M.E.Matthias	H.J.C. Ripley	Riley 1,496cc
59	Gilbert Tyrer		Frazer Nash 1,971cc

Castletown Trophy Race

60	R. Dennis Poore	Alfa Romeo 3,800cc
62	Roy F. Salvadori	Alfa Romeo 2,900cc
64	Noel Carr	Alta 1,998cc
66	Jack E.G. Fairman	Bugatti 1,955cc
70	Kenneth W. Bear	Bugatti 3,255cc

1948 BRITISH EMPIRE TROPHY RACE ENTRY LIST

Tuesday 25th May 1948. Start 4.00pm. 36 laps of 3.8789 miles circuit, total distance 139.64 miles.
21 starters – 9 finishers.

No.	Driver(s)	Entrant	Car
2	George E. Abecassis		Alta 1,490cc
4	Gordon. M. Watson		Alta 1,490cc
6	Michael C. Chorlton		Bugatti 1,498cc
8	David A. Hampshire		Delage 1,494cc
10	Geoff Ansell		E.R.A. 1,488cc
12	Joe Ashmore		E.R.A. 1,488cc
14	John V. Bolster	P.H. Bell	E.R.A. 1,488cc
16	W. M. Couper	H.L. Brooke	E.R.A. 1,488cc
18	Sheila Darbishire & Edward G. Pool	E.G. Pool	E.R.A. 1,488cc
20	F. R. "Bob" Gerard		E.R.A. 1,488cc
22	T.C. "Cuth" Harrison		E.R.A. 1,488cc
24	Leslie G. Johnson		E.R.A. 1,488cc
26	Raymond Mays		E.R.A. 1,488cc
28	Charles K. Mortimer	R.C. Rowland Motors	E.R.A. 1,488cc
30	Reg Parnell		E.R.A. 1,488cc
32	Peter D.C. Walker		E.R.A. 1,488cc
34	Geoffrey N. Richardson		E.R.A. Riley 1,488cc
36	Duncan Hamilton	George E. Abecassis	Maserati 1,496cc
38	Robert E. "Bob" Ansell		Maserati 1,496cc
40	Fred Ashmore		Maserati 1,496cc
42	Anthony Baring		Maserati 1,496cc
44	John. S. Gordon	Gordon & Macklin	Maserati 1,496cc
46	Lance Seyd	R.C. Rowland Motors	Maserati 1,496cc
48	Roy F. Salvadori		Maserati 1,496cc
50	A.P.R. "Tony" Rolt		Alfa Romeo 3,442cc
52	Guy Jason-Henry	Selborne (Mayfair) Ltd.	Delahaye 3,557cc
54	R. "Bobby" Baird & Paul Emery	R. "Bobby" Baird	Emeryson 4,470cc
56	H. Leslie Brooke		Ferrari 1,992cc
58	Gianfranco Comotti		Talbot 4,480cc

1949 MANX CUP RACE ENTRY LIST

Thursday 26th May 1949. Start 2.00pm. 18 laps of 3.3789 miles circuit, total distance 69.82 miles.
23 starters – 10 finishers.

No.	Driver(s)	Entrant	Car
1	R.M. "Curly" Dryden		Cooper 496cc
3	John N. Cooper		Cooper 996cc
5	Spike Rhiando		Cooper 996cc
7	Stirling Moss		Cooper 996cc
9	George Abecassis & John Heath	John Heath	Cooper 990cc
11	Eric Winterbottom & V. Davison	Eric Winterbottom	Cooper 996cc

No.	Driver(s)	Entrant	Car
15	Basil de Lissa		MG 1,086cc
17	Ken Downing	George Nixon	Riley 1,749cc
19	Dudley Folland	J. Wyer Ltd.	Ferrari 1,995cc
21	Frank W. Kennington		Cisitalia 1,090cc
23	E.W. "Bill" Holt	Dudley Folland	H.R.G. 1,496cc
25	St. John Horsfall		Aston Martin 1,986cc
27	Ken Hutchinson		Veritas 1,946cc
29	John Heath & George E. Abecassis	John Heath	H.W. Alta 1,960cc
31	George E. Phillips		MG 1,086cc
33	Hector Graham & D.H. Kyle	Hector Graham	MG 1,087cc
35	Kenneth H.F. Rose & Gilbert Baird	K.H.F. Rose	R.D.L. 1,767cc
37	Joe Kelly		I.R.A. 1,726cc
39	R.W. "Dick" Jacobs		MG 1,087cc
41	Gordon S. Shillito	T.C. "Cuth" Harrison	Riley 1,986cc
43	Peter C.T. Clark & Jack Scott	Peter C.T. Clark	H.R.G. 1,496cc
45	G. Neville Gee		Riley 1,496cc
47	Robert "Bobby" Baird		Baird Meteorite 1,087cc
49	Jack E.G. Fairman		Riley 1,954cc
51	Ken Watkins		B.M.W. 1,971cc
53	Basil de Mattos	F.R.G. Spikins	Spikins Special 1,496cc
55	Major Guy F.A. Gale		Connaught 1,767cc
57	Ted Lund	N.S. Utley	Lund Special II 972cc
59	C.G.H.F. "Gerry" Dunham	C.G.H. Dunham	Alvis 1,844cc
61	Hugh Clapp		H.R.G. 1,047cc

1949 BRITISH EMPIRE TROPHY RACE ENTRY LIST

Thursday 26th May 1949. Start 4.10pm. 36 laps of 3.8789 miles circuit, total distance 139.64 miles.
16 starters – 13 finishers.

No.	Driver(s)	Entrant	Car
2	George E. Abecassis & John Heath	G.E.Abecassis	Alta 1,490cc
4	Michael C. Chorlton & J. Boothby	M.C. Chorlton	Bugatti 1,498cc
6	John V. Bolster	P.H. Bell	E.R.A. 1,488cc
8	George Nixon		E.R.A. 1,488cc
10	David A. Hampshire		E.R.A. 1,488cc
12	Geoff Ansell		E.R.A. 1,488cc
14	F. R. "Bob" Gerard		E.R.A. 1,488cc
16	T.C. "Cuth" Harrison		E.R.A. 1,488cc
18	T.A.S.O. Mathieson & Leslie G. Johnson	T.A.S.O. Mathieson	E.R.A. 1,487cc
20	Peter D.C. Walker		E.R.A. 1,488cc
22	Peter N. Whitehead	Scuderia Ferrari	Ferrari 1,496cc
24	David Murray		Maserati 1,496cc
26	Robert E. "Bob" Ansell		Maserati 1,496cc
28	Fred Ashmore	Scuderia Ambrosiana	Maserati 1,496cc
30	Reg Parnell	Scuderia Ambrosiana	Maserati 1,496cc
32	Luigi Villoresi	Scuderia Ambrosiana	Maserati 1,496cc
34	Roy F. Salvadori		Maserati 1,496cc
36	Anthony Baring		Maserati 1,496cc
38	R. Ramseyer	Ecurie Geneve	Maserati 1,496cc
40	Geoffrey N. Richardson		R.R.A. 1,488cc
42	Archie J. Butterworth		A.J.B. 4,425cc
44	Guy Jason-Henry & A.P.R. "Tony" Rolt	R.R.C. Walker	Delahaye 3,600cc

46	Gordon. M. Watson		Alta 1,490cc
48	Johnny Claes	Ecurie Belge	Talbot 4,480cc
50	A.P.R. "Tony" Rolt & Guy Jason-Henry	R.R.C. Walker	Alfa Romeo 3,440cc

1950 MANX CUP RACE ENTRY LIST

Thursday15th June 1950. Start 2.00pm. 18 laps of 3.3789 miles circuit, total distance 69.82 miles.
23 starters – 11 finishers.

No.	Driver(s)	Entrant	Car
1	Robert "Bobby" Baird		MG 1,096cc
2	R.W. "Dick" Jacobs		MG 1,086cc
3	Basil de Lissa		MG 1,086cc
4	J.C.C. "Jim" Mayers	Harry Lester	Lester MG 1,474cc
5	Peter C.T. Clark &R. Lord	Peter C.T. Clark	H.R.G. 1,674cc
6	Hugh Clapp		H.R.G. 1,496cc
7	W.H. "Bill" Murray		H.R.G. 1,496cc
8	Norman R. Culpan		Frazer Nash 1,971cc
9	Gilbert Tyrer		Frazer Nash-B.M.W. 1,996cc
10	Basil de Mattos	F.R.G. Spikins	Cromard Special 1,167cc
11	Tom M. Meyer		H.W.-Alta 1,961cc
12	Peter R. Bolton	J.H. Walton	H.W.-Alta 1,961cc
14	Oscar B. Moore		O.B.M. 1,971cc
15	C.G. H.F. "Gerry" Dunham	C.G.H. Dunham	Alvis 1,844cc
16	Joe Kelly		I.R.A. 1,726cc
17	Michael A.H. Christie		Cooper 1,096cc
18	Eric Winterbottom		Cooper 996cc
19	Hector Graham & D.H. Kyle	Hector Graham	Cooper 1,100cc
20	Spike Rhiando		Rhiando-Trimax 998cc
21	John N. Cooper	Cooper Car Co. Ltd.	Cooper 1,088cc
22	Ted Lund		Lea-Francis 1,670cc
23	Peter B. Reece		Riley 1,980cc
24	Gordon S. Shillito		Riley 1,988cc
25	Eric Brandon		Cooper 1,098cc
26	Joe Potts		Cooper 998cc
27	R.W. "Bill" Merrick		Cooper 1,097cc

1950 BRITISH EMPIRE TROPHY RACE ENTRY LIST

Thursday 15th June 1950. Start 3.45 pm. 36 laps of 3.8789 miles circuit, total distance 139.64 miles.
13 starters – 7 finishers.

No.	Driver(s)	Entrant	Car
1	F. R. "Bob" Gerard		E.R.A. 1,488cc
2	Reg Parnell	Scuderia Ambrosiana	Maserati 1,490cc
3	David A. Hampshire	Scuderia Ambrosiana	Maserati 1,490cc
4	David Murray	Scuderia Ambrosiana	Maserati 1,490cc
5	Baron de Graffenried		Maserati 1,490cc
6	"B.Bira"	Enrico Plate	Maserati 1,490cc
7	A.P.R. "Tony" Rolt	R.R.C. Walker	Delage 1,498cc
8	John.W. Rowley		Delage 1,484cc
9	Gordon. M. Watson		Alta 1,491cc
10	Peter D.C. Walker		E.R.A. 1,490cc
11	A.Graham Whitehead		E.R.A. 1,488cc

No.	Driver(s)	Entrant	Car
12	T.C. "Cuth" Harrison		E.R.A. 1,488cc
14	Colin Murray		Maserati 1,490cc
15	Brian N. Shawe-Taylor		E.R.A. 1,488cc
16	Joe Kelly		Maserati 1,490cc
17	Anthony Baring		H.W.M. 1,960cc
18	Robert "Bobby" Baird		Tornado 4,480cc
19	Archie J. Butterworth		A.J.B. 4,425cc

1951 MANX CUP AND CASTLETOWN TROPHY RACES ENTRY LIST

Thursday 14th June 1951. Start 2.00pm. Races run concurrently over 18 laps of 3.3789 miles circuit, total distance 69.82 miles. Manx Cup: 14 starters – 8 finishers, Castletown Trophy: 4 starters – 2 finishers.

No.	Driver(s)	Entrant	Car
Manx Cup Race			
1	C.G.H.F. "Gerry" Dunham	C.G.H. Dunham	Alvis 2,500cc
2	E.C.W. Stapleton		Aston Martin 1,984cc
3	Robert "Bobby" Baird		Baird Griffin 1,096cc
4	W.S. "Bill" Aston		Cooper 1,098cc
5	R.W. "Bill" Merrick		Cooper 1,132cc
6	Eric Brandon	R.G. Brandon	Cooper 1,098cc
7	John D. Barber		Cooper 994cc
8	Lionel Leonard		Cooper MG 1,467cc
9	R.C. Willis		Frazer Nash B.M.W. 1,996cc
10	Stirling Moss	HW Motors Ltd	H.W.M. 1,960cc
11	Oscar B. Moore		H.W.M. 1,960cc
12	Tom M. Meyer		H.W.M. 1,960cc
14	Joe Kelly		I.R.A. 1,500cc
15	Gerry A. Ruddock	Peter C.T. Clark	H.R.G. 1,750cc
16	Peter J. Simpson	Tom H.Simpson	Healey 2,443cc
17	W.J. "Billy" Skelly & Ted Lund	W.J. Skelly	Lea Francis 1,670cc
18	Horace A. Richards		Riley 1,087cc
19	Gordon S. Shillito		Riley 1,988cc
20	R.W. "Dick" Jacobs		MG 1,087cc
21	John H. Webb & J.H. Turner	John H. Webb	Turner 1,087cc
Castletown Trophy Race			
23	Peter D.C. Walker	R.R.C. Walker	Delage 1,490cc
24	David Murray		Maserati 1,490cc
25	Reg Parnell		Maserati 1,490cc
26	David Hampshire		Maserati 1,490cc
27	Miles Martin		Maserati 1,490cc
28	John V. Green		E.R.A. 1,488cc
29	Joe Ashmore		E.R.A. 1,488cc

1951 BRITISH EMPIRE TROPHY RACE ENTRY LIST

Thursday14th June 1951. Start 3.45 pm. 35 laps of 3.8789 miles circuit, total distance 135.76 miles. 26 starters – 13 finishers.

No.	Driver(s)	Entrant	Car
Up to 1,500cc (4 credit laps)			
1	"Dave"		Dyna-Panhard 745cc
2	J.C.C."Jim" Mayers	H. Lester (Cars) Ltd.	Lester MG 1,467cc

3	Harry Lester & P.W.C. "Pat" Griffith	H. Lester (Cars) Ltd.	Lester MG 1,467cc
4	William H. Robinson		Jowett Jupiter 1,485cc
5	R.W. "Dick" Jacobs		MG 1,250cc
6	Ted Lund		MG 1,250cc
7	Mike J. Pople & M. Holt	M.J. Pople	MG 1,250cc
8	Trevor Line & M. Holt	J.T.K. Line	MG 1,250cc
9	Lionel Leonard		Cooper MG 1,250cc
10	J.G. "Jack" Reece		Cooper MG 1,250cc
Up to 3,000cc (1 credit lap)			
11	Ben Whitehouse		Aston Martin 1,970cc
12	Peter D.C. Walker or Guy Gale	R.R.C. Walker	Aston Martin 2,580cc
14	John B. Lyons		Connaught 1,767cc
15	Robert "Bobby" Baird		Ferrari 1,982cc
16	Robin F. Peacock		Frazer Nash 1,971cc
17	Norman R. Culpan		Frazer Nash 1,971cc
18	David A. Clarke		Frazer Nash 1,971cc
19	Donald C. Pitt	E.J. Newton	Frazer Nash 1,971cc
20	W.H. "Bill" Murray		Frazer Nash 1,971cc
21	F. R. "Bob" Gerard		Frazer Nash 1,971cc
22	Stirling Moss	S.G. Greene	Frazer Nash 1,971cc
23	John Buncombe		Healey 2,433cc
24	*S. Hill & G. Cooper	S. Hill	Healey 2,433cc
Over 3,000cc (scratch)			
25	Guy Gale or Peter D.C. Walker	R.R.C. Walker	Delahaye 3,557cc
26	Reg Parnell	Donald Healey	Nash Healey 3,848cc
27	Peter J. Binns		Jaguar XK 120 3,442cc
28	Oscar B. Moore		Jaguar XK 120 3,442cc
29	Peter Scott Russell & D.F. Annable	D.F. Annable	Allard 3,917cc
30	Peter J. Collins		Allard 5,420cc
31	Sidney H.Allard		Allard 5,420cc
32	Frank G. Curtis		Allard 3,925cc

1952 BRITISH EMPIRE TROPHY RACE ENTRY LIST

Thursday29th May 1952. Start 2.30pm. 52 laps of 3.8789 miles circuit, total distance 201.70 miles.
27 starters – 13 finishers.

No.	Driver(s)	Entrant	Car
Up to 1,500cc (4 credit laps)			
1	Mike R.G. Llewellyn		MG 1,250cc
2	Ted Lund		MG 1,250cc
3	J. Trevor.K. Line		MG 1,250cc
4	Peter Jackson		MG 1,250cc
5	Gerry A. Ruddock	The Monkey Stable	Lester MG 1,467cc
6	J.C.C."Jim" Mayers	The Monkey Stable	Lester MG 1,467cc
7	P.W.C. "Pat" Griffith	The Monkey Stable	Lester MG 1,467cc
8	Joe Kelly		
	Reserve: H. Sullivan	J. Kelly	Jowett Jupiter 1,486cc
9	J.A. Cowap		Jowett Jupiter 1,486cc
10	E.W. Cuff Miller		
	Reserve: F. Dudley	E.W. Cuff Miller	Jowett Jupiter 1,486cc
11	W.J. "Billy" Skelly		Jowett Jupiter 1,486cc
12	William H. Robinson		Jowett Jupiter 1,486cc

No.	Driver(s)	Entrant	Car
14	F. C. "Cliff" Davis		Cooper MG 1,496cc
15	Lionel Leonard		Cooper MG 1,250cc

No.	Driver(s)	Entrant	Car
Up to 3,000cc (1 credit lap)			
20	Stirling Moss	S.G. Greene	Frazer Nash 1,971cc
21	J.M. "Mike" Hawthorn		
	Reserve: Leonard Potter	L. Potter	Frazer Nash 1,971cc
22	Roy Salvadori	T.A.D. "Tony" Crook	Frazer Nash 1,971cc
23	J.H. "Jack" Walton & Peter R. Bolton	J.H. Walton	Frazer Nash 1,971cc
24	H.A. Mitchell		Frazer Nash 1,971cc
25	J.G. "Jack" Reece		Frazer Nash 1,971cc
26	John Buncombe		Healey 2,433cc
27	Geoffrey E. "Geoff" Duke		Aston Martin 2,580cc
Over 3,000cc (scratch)			
30	E.W. "Bill" Holt		
	Reserve: A. G. Whitehead	E.W. Holt	Jaguar XK120 3,442cc
31	Stanley Boshier		Jaguar XK120 3,442cc
32	John B. Swift		Jaguar XK120 3,442cc
33	W. Belfrage Black		Jaguar XK120 3,442cc
34	Sir James Scott Douglas	Ecurie Ecosse	JaguarXK120 3,442cc
35	David Murray	Ecurie Ecosse	JaguarXK120 3,442cc
36	Ian Stewart	Ecurie Ecosse	JaguarXK120 3,442cc
37	J. Duncan Hamilton		Jaguar "C" type 3,442cc
38	Alfred P. Hitchings		Allard 5,420cc

1953 BRITISH EMPIRE TROPHY RACE ENTRY LIST

Thursday 18th June 1953. 3 heats over 8 laps of 3.8789 miles circuit, total distance 31.03 miles, starting at 1.55pm, 2.55pm and 3.50pm. Final over 16 laps of 3.8789, total distance 62.06 miles. 28 starters in the Final, 11 finishers

No.	Driver(s)	Entrant	Car
Heat 1 – Up to 1,500cc. 14 starters, 10 finishers.			
1	J.C.C."Jim" Mayers	The Monkey Stable	Kieft 1,467cc
2	P.W.C. "Pat" Griffith	The Monkey Stable	Kieft1, 467cc
3	M.J.C. "Mike" Keen	The Monkey Stable	Kieft 1,467cc
4	H. John Goldschmidt		Performance Special 1,467cc
5	John Riseley-Pritchard	Cornhill Racing Team	Cooper-Riley 1,496cc
6	F. C. "Cliff" Davis		Cooper MG 1,467cc
7	Peter Reece		Cooper MG 1,467cc
8	Alfred P. Hitchings		Lester MG 1,467cc
9	Peter Jackson		Lester MG 1,467cc
10	Gerry A. Ruddock		Lester MG 1,467cc
11	E. John Haesendonck	T.W. Dargue	MG 1,467cc
12	Ernest Cooper Harewood		MG 1,467cc
14	Chris H. Threlfall		Tojeiro 1,467cc
15	Lionel Leonard		Leonard MG 1,467cc
16	Horace H. Gould		Cooper MG 1,467cc
17	Ted Lund		MG 1,466cc
Heat 2 – over 1,500cc and up to 2,600cc. 11 starters, 9 finishers.			
20	H.A. Mitchell & Peter Scott-Russell	H.A. Mitchell	Frazer Nash 1,971cc
21	Peter Kenneth		Frazer Nash 1,971cc
22	Ken Wharton		Frazer Nash 1,971cc

23	James Neilson		Frazer Nash 1,971cc
24	W. Belfrage Black		Frazer Nash 1,971cc
25	C.G.H.F. "Gerry" Dunham	S.G. Greene	Frazer Nash 1,971cc
26	Peter Clark		Aston Martin 2,580cc
27	Nigel Mann		Aston Martin 2,580cc
28	R. Gray Mickel		Healey 2,443cc
29	Peter J. Simpson		Healey 2,443cc
30	A.C. Westwood		Healey 2,443cc
31	John D. Barber		Cooper 1,976cc
32	Alan Brown	R.J. Chase	Cooper-Bristol 1,971cc
33	A.R. Huxley	M.C. Kearon	Connaught 1,767cc
34	P.A.B. Stewart		H.W.M.-Alta 1,960cc
35	Peter C. Gammon	Cliff Davis	Tojeiro 1,971cc

Heat 3 – over 2,600cc. 13 starters, 11 finishers.

40	J. Desmond Titterington		Allard 3,917cc
41	Ken Watkins		Allard 5,420cc
42	Ken H. Downing		Aston Martin 2,922cc
43	R. "Bob" Dickson		Aston Martin 2,922cc
44	Reg Parnell	David Brown	Aston Martin 2,922cc
45	Joe Goodhew		Darracq 3,996cc
46	Hans Ruesch		Ferrari 4,100cc
47	Dan Marguelis		Delahaye 3,557cc
48	Oscar Moore		H.W.M. 3,442cc
49	Ian Stewart	Ecurie Ecosse	Jaguar "C" type 3,442cc
50	Ninian Sanderson	Ecurie Ecosse	Jaguar "C" type 3,442cc
51	Jimmy Stewart	Ecurie Ecosse	Jaguar "C" type 3,442cc
52	Stirling Moss	William Lyons	Jaguar "C" type 3,442cc
53	John B. Swift		Jaguar "C" type 3,442cc
54	David S. Boston		JaguarXK120 3,442cc
55	H.Kemp Place		JaguarXK120 3,442cc

8 START LISTS

1904 GORDON BENNETT ELIMINATING TRIAL START LIST

Tuesday 10th May 1904. Start 9.00am. 5 laps of 51.1 miles course, total distance 255.5 miles. 11 starters – 5 finishers.

1	J.W. Stocks	Napier
2	Edmond	Darracq
3	John Hargreaves	Napier
4	Victor Hemery	Darracq
6	W. Clifford Earp	Napier
7	E. Campbell Muir	Wolseley
9	Selwyn F. Edge	Napier
10	Sidney Girling	Wolseley
11	A. Rawlinson	Darracq
12	Charles Jarrott	Wolseley
14	Mark Mayhew	Napier

Numbers 5,8 and 13 were allocated to Huttons which were non-arrivals.

1905 GORDON BENNETT ELIMINATING TRIAL START LIST

Tuesday 30th May 1905. Start 9.00am. 6 laps of 51.1 miles circuit, total distance 306.6 miles. 10 starters – 3 finishers.

1	H.G. Goodwin	Star 70hp
2	F.R. Goodwin	Star 70hp
3	Hon Algernon Lee Guinness	Darracq 100hp
4	Cecil Bianchi	Wolseley 96hp
6	Cecil Edge	Napier 80hp
7	W. Clifford Earp	Napier 80hp
9	John Hargreaves	Napier 80hp
10	Sidney Girling	Siddeley 100hp
11	Hon. Charles S. Rolls	Wolseley 96hp
12	Arthur E. Macdonald	Napier 90hp

1905 TOURIST TROPHY RACE START LIST

Thursday 14th September 1905. Start 9.00am. 4 laps of 52 miles circuit, total distance 208 miles. 42 starters – 18 finishers.

1	Hon Charles S. Rolls	Rolls-Royce 20hp.
2	W. Clifford Earp	Napier 18hp
3	Frank G. Cundy	Napier 18hp
6	W.J. Warren	Speedwell 12hp
7	A.J. Dew	Speedwell 14hp
8	W.H. Astill	Orleans 15hp
9	Thomas Jenner	Orleans 15hp
10	James Hadley	Wolseley 14hp
11	Sidney Girling	Siddeley 18hp
12	Tom Thornycroft	Thornycroft 14hp
14	R. Lascelles	New Simms-Welbeck 20hp
17	John Downie	Argyll 14hp
18	W. Parker Thomas	Argyll 14hp
19	C.L. Cattell	James and Browne 14hp
20	F.S. Bennett	Cadillac 9hp
21	W.H. Cox	Maudslay 20hp
22	Percy W. Northey	Rolls-Royce 20hp
23	A.J. Hancock	Vauxhall 12hp
24	C.H. Cooper	Beeston Humber 16hp
25	Harvey du Cros Jnr	Swift 16hp
27	Arthur J. Clay	Ryknield 15hp
28	A.C. Kent	White steam
29	Frederic Coleman	White steam
30	James Reid	Beeston Humber 16hp
31	E.H. Lancaster	Clement 14hp
32	R.W. Maudslay	Standard 16hp
34	Charles Clench	Whitlock-Aster 15hp
35	R. Downing	Dennis 14hp
36	John C. Dennis	Dennis 14hp
37	E. H. Arnott	Minerva 16hp
39	J. Percy Dean	Scout 14hp
40	Hon Algernon Lee Guinness	Darracq 10hp
41	A. Rawlinson	Darracq 10hp
42	Karl Beireiz	Dixi 14hp
45	W.C. Holloway	Minerva 16hp
46	Charles Friswell	Peugeot 10hp
47	Guy V. Baxendale	Thornycroft 14hp
48	Edmund W. Lewis	Rover 16hp
49	Ernest Courtis	Rover 16hp
52	Norman Littlejohn	Vinot et Deguingand 14hp
53	John S. Napier	Arrol-Johnston 18hp
54	E.J.Cyril Roberts	Arrol-Johnston 18hp

1906 TOURIST TROPHY RACE START LIST

Thursday 26th September 1906. Start 9.00am. 4 laps of 40.25 miles circuit, total distance 161 miles. 29 starters – 9 finishers.

1	John S. Napier	New Arrol-Johnston 18hp
2	Hon Algernon Lee Guinness	Darracq 15hp
3	Sidney Girling	Darracq 15hp
4	Hon Charles Rolls	Rolls-Royce 20hp
5	Percy W. Northey	Rolls-Royce 20hp
6	Warwick J. Wright	Minerva 22hp
8	C.L. Cattell	James and Browne 20hp
9	Norman Littlejohn	Vinot 16hp
10	E. Campbell Muir	New Arrol Johnston 18hp

11	W. Parker Thomas	Argyll 16hp
12	A.E. George	Argyll 16hp
13	Ernest Courtis	Rover 16hp
14	Albert Brown	Brown 20hp
15	Georges Braud	Clement 20hp
16	Georges Dumont	Pipe 28hp
17	T.C. Pullinger	Beeston Humber 16hp
18	Louis Coatalen	Coventry Humber 20hp
21	J.K. Starley	Rover 16hp
22	Charles Friswell	Peugeot 10hp
23	J. Ernest Hutton	Berliet 22hp
24	Montagu Grahame-White	Siddeley 18hp
25	A.E. Crowdy	Siddeley 18hp
26	Paul Bablot	Berliet 22hp
27	Tom Thornycroft	Thornycroft 14hp
28	G.F. Prew	Star 18hp
29	R.A. Bell	Deasy 24hp
30	J.W.F. Crouch	Deasy 24hp
31	Gordon Usmar	Vinot 16hp
32	J. Percy Dean	Scout 17hp
33	J. Lisle	Scout 18hp
34	M.L. Braithwaite	Speedwell 18hp
35	E.W. Leather	Climax 14hp
36	R. Every	Swift 16hp
37	W.L. Hardman	Hardman 25hp
38	H.P. McConnell	Bianchi 16hp
39	Arthur McCormack	Gladiator 20hp
40	Sidney Straker	Straker-Squire 12hp
41	L.R.L. Squire	Straker-Squire 12hp
42	Thomas Watson	Climax 16hp
43	Oscar Cupper	Metallurgique 24hp
44	W.G. Batchelor	Armadale 16hp
45	G.W. Roberts	Rapid 20hp
46	Turberville Smith	Academy 14hp
47	H.A. Bate	S.C.A.R. 18hp
48	Richard Lascelles	Vici 12hp
49	Lieut. J. Lesmoir Gordon	Florentia 18hp

1906 "GRAPHIC" TROPHY START LIST

Friday 27th September 1906. Start 10.30 am. 4.25 miles hill climb on Douglas to Castletown Road from Quarterbridge to Santon.

1	C.H. Cooper	Beeston-Humber 60hp
2	H.A. Bate	S.C.A.R. 18hp
3	Paul Bablot	Berliet 40hp
4	George S. Barwick	Daimler 30-40hp
5	William Watson	Berliet 24-40hp
6	C.A. Glentworth	Napier 50hp
7	H.O. Hall	Isotta-Fraschini 28-35hp
8	J. Ernest Hutton	Ariel-Simplex 50hp
9	G.A. Roberts	Rapid 20hp
10	Mr Anthony	Sorex 30-35hp
11	Albert Farnell	Daimler 30hp

1907 TOURIST TROPHY RACE START LIST

Thursday 30th May 1907. Start 9.11am. 6 laps of 40.25miles circuit, total distance 241.50 miles. 22 starters – 2 finishers.

2	Hon Algernon Lee Guinness	Darracq 18hp
3	Kenelm Lee Guinness	Darracq 18hp
4	Jean Porporato	Berliet 22hp
5	J. Ernest Hutton	Berliet 22hp
7	E.J.C. Roberts	Arrol-Johnston 25hp
8	John S. Napier	Arrol-Johnston 25hp
9	Oscar Cupper	Metallurgique 24-28hp
10	Tom Thornycroft	Thornycroft 14hp
11	J. Percy Dean	Scout 17-20hp
12	W.G. Tuck	Coventry Humber 16-20hp
13	T.C. Pullinger	Beeston Humber 16-20hp
14	Harry G. Goodwin	Star 18hp
15	G. Prew	Star 18hp
16	D.S. Hodges	West-Aster 16-20hp
19	Thomas Rimmer	Vulcan 20hp
20	Georges Braud	Clement 18hp
21	M. Ross-Browne	Gladiator 18hp
22	Ernest Courtis	Rover 20hp
23	P. Nevers	West-Aster 16-20hp
24	Louis Coatalen	Hillman-Coatalen 20hp
25	Edgar R. Folker	Rover 20hp
28	Norman Littlejohn	Vinot 24hp

1907 HEAVY TOURING CAR RACE START LIST

Thursday 30th May 1907. 5 laps of 40.25 miles circuit, total distance 201.25 miles. 9 starters – 2 finishers.

1	L.R.L. Squire	Straker-Squire 25-30hp
2	Willliam Watson	Berliet 40hp
4	H. Niblett	Thornycroft 30hp
5	Graeme Fenton	Gladiator 25hp
6	Charles Sangster	Ariel-Simplex 30hp
8	E.H. Arnott	Arrol-Johnston 40hp
10	C.H. Cooper	Beeston Humber 20-30hp
12	A.E. Harrison	Ariel-Simplex
14	George P. Mills	Beeston-Humber 30hp

1907 "GRAPHIC" TROPHY START LIST

Friday 31st May 1907. 2,550 yards hill climb on Ramsey to Douglas coast road, from Ballure Bridge, Ramsey to Rest and be Thankful Inn. 9 starters – 7 finishers

2	J. Ernest Hutton	Berliet 60hp
3	J. Porporato	Berliet 40hp
5	Louis Coatalen	Hillman-Coatalen 20hp
7	Capt. W.E.D. Owen	Junior 40hp
8	Francis A. Bolton	Daimler 35hp
10	Thomas Henshaw	Daimler 35hp
12	William Watson	Berliet 24-40hp
13	Charles Sangster	Ariel-Simplex 35hp
14	A.E. Harrison	Ariel-Simplex 35hp

1908 TOURIST TROPHY RACE START LIST

Thursday 24th September 1908. Start 9.00am. 9 laps of 37.5 miles circuit, total distance 337.5 miles. 35 starters – 10 finishers.

1	H.B. Browning	Rover
2	William Watson	Hutton
3	E.J. Cyril Roberts	Arrol-Johnston
4	Hon Algernon Lee Guinness	Darracq
5	G.W.A. Brown	Coventry Humber
6	Louis Coatalen	Hillman Coatalen
7	Oscar Cupper	Metallurgique
9	Tom Thornycroft	Thornycroft
10	M Ross-Browne	Vinot
11	Leslie Porter	Calthorpe
12	Philip Graham	Deasy
12A	A.L.Hartridge	Westinghouse
14	R. Harper	S.C.A.T.
15	J. Ernest Hutton	Hutton
16	Dario Resta	Arrol-Johnston
17	A.E. George	Darracq
18	James Reid	Beeston Humber
19	Kenelm Lee Guinness	Hillman Coatalen
20	J.T. C. Moore-Brabazon	Metallurgique
22	D.S. Hodge	Thornycroft
23	T. Rowland Outhwaite	Vinot
24	M. Robinson	Calthorpe
25	E.W.Lewis	Deasy
26	J. Gall	Westinghouse
27	F. Ward	S.C.A.T.
28	P.D. Stirling	Hutton
29	Geoffrey Moss	Arrol-Johnston
30	A. Rawlinson	Darracq
31	W.G. Tuck	Beeston-Humber
32	J.W. Stocks	De Dion Bouton
33	Warwick Wright	Metallurgique
34	Andre Debuissey	Piccard
36	M.L.Molon	Vinot
37	T. Rimmer	Vulcan
38	Harold S. Buckley	S.C.A.T.

1914 TOURIST TROPHY RACE START LIST

Wednesday/Thursday 10th/11th June 1914. Start 9.00am. 16 laps of 37.5 miles circuit, total distance 600 miles. 22 starters – 6 finishers.

1	Jean Porporato	Minerva I	3,308cc
2	F.T.Burgess	Humber I	3,295cc
3	R.S. "Dick" Witchell	Straker-Squire I	3,260cc
4	Kenelm Lee Guinness	Sunbeam I	3,297cc
5	Richard Lisle	Star I	3,295cc
6	A. J. Hancock	Vauxhall I	3,308cc
7	Philip Stapp	Adler I	3,308cc
8	W.O. Bentley	D.F.P.	2,001cc
9	Rene Berger	S.A.V.A.	3,252cc
11	Cecil Bianchi	Crossley	3,273cc
12	Leon Molon	Minerva II	3,308cc
13	W.G. Tuck	Humber II	3,295cc
14	Frank C. Clement	Straker-Squire II	3,260cc
15	Dario Resta	Sunbeam II	3,297cc
16	Robert F.L. Crossman	Star II	3,295cc
17	William Watson	Vauxhall II	3,308cc
18	Otto Goebel	Adler II	3,308cc
19	C. Riecken	Minerva III	3,308cc
20	S. Wright	Humber III	3,295cc
21	Hon Algernon Lee Guinness	Sunbeam III	3,297cc
22	J.Higginson	Vauxhall III	3,308cc
23	J. Rutsch	Adler III	3,308cc

1922 TOURIST TROPHY RACE START LIST

Thursday 22nd June 1922. Start 9.30am. 8 laps of 37.75 miles circuit, total distance 302 miles. 8 starters – 5 finishers.

2	Matthew C. Park	Vauxhall I	2,985cc
3	Frank C. Clement	Bentley I	2,996cc
4	Henry O.D. Segrave	Sunbeam II	2,973cc
5	Oswald Payne	Vauxhall II	2,985cc
6	W. Douglas Hawkes	Bentley II	2,996cc
7	Jean Chassagne	Sunbeam III	2,973cc
8	Ernest Swain	Vauxhall III	2,985cc
9	W.O. Bentley	Bentley III	2,996cc

1922 INTERNATIONAL 1,500cc TROPHY RACE START LIST

Thursday 22nd June 1922. 6 laps of 37.75 miles circuit, total distance 226.5 miles. 9 starters – 6 finishers.

22	Pierre de Vizcaya	Bugatti I	1,452cc
23	G. Bedford	Hillman	1,496cc
24	Sir Algernon Lee Guinness	Talbot-Darracq I	1,486cc
25	A.C. Bertelli	Enfield-Allday	1,496cc
26	H. Kensington Moir	Aston Martin	1,487cc
27	Mones Maury	Bugatti II	1,452cc
28	Jean Moriceau	Talbot-Darracq II	1,486cc
30	Bertram S. Marshall	Bugatti III	1,452cc
31	Albert Divo	Talbot-Darracq III	1,486cc

1933 INTERNATIONAL MANNIN BEG RACE START LIST

Wednesday 12th July 1933. Start 9.30am. 50 laps of 4.6 miles circuit, total distance 230 miles.
14 starters – 3 finishers.

No.	Driver	Reserve Driver	Entrant	Car
1	Robin M. Mere			MG Magnette 1,087cc
2	Eddie R. Hall			MG Magnette 1,087cc
3	W. Sullivan			Morris Minor Sullivan Special 732cc
4	Dennis K.Mansell			MG Midget 746 cc
7	Freddie W. Dixon	Cyril Paul		Riley 1,089cc
9	Thomas G. Moore	N.A. Berry		Frazer Nash 1,496cc
11	Victor Gillow	P.W. Charles		Riley 1,086cc
12	J. Ludovic Ford	Maurice H. Baumer		MG Midget 745cc
14	Ronald A. Yallop	E. Fronteras		MG Magnette 1,087cc
15	George E.T. Eyston	A. Denly		MG Magnette 1,086cc
16	Hugh C. Hamilton			MG Magnette 1,086cc
18	Kaye Don		Bernard Rubin	MG Magnette 1,086cc
19	Sydney A. Crabtree	W.L. Handley		MG Midget 746cc
21	E. L. Gardner	C.W.G. Lacey		MG Midget 747cc

1933 INTERNATIONAL MANNIN MOAR RACE START LIST

Friday 14th July 1933. Start 9.30am. 50 laps of 4.6 miles circuit, total distance 230 miles.
9 starters – 4 finishers.

No.	Driver	Reserve Driver	Entrant	Car
1	Alfred C. Lace			Invicta 4,467cc
3	Richard O. Shuttleworth	C. Brackenbury		Bugatti 2,300cc
5	T.S. Fothringham			Bugatti 2,263cc
6	Hon. Brian Lewis		N. Rees and A.W.Fox	Alfa Romeo 2,336cc
9	Tim Rose-Richards			Bugatti 2,263cc
10	T.A.S.O. Mathieson			Bugatti 1,998cc
11	George E.T. Eyston			Alfa Romeo 2,336cc
12	A.H. Lindsay Eccles			Bugatti 2,263cc
14	Kaye Don			Alfa Romeo 2,336cc

1934 INTERNATIONAL MANNIN BEG RACE START LIST

Wednesday 30th May 1934. Start10.00am.50 laps of 3.658 miles circuit, total distance 182.9 miles.
19 starters – 8 finishers.

No.	Driver	Reserve Driver	Entrant	Car
1	Ron T. Horton			MG Magnette 1,086cc
2	P.L. Donkin			MG Magnette 1,087cc
3	Eddie R.Hall			MG Magnette 1,087cc
4	Hugh C. Hamilton			MG Magnette 1,087cc
7	Henry Laird	M.A. McEvoy		McEvoy Special 1454cc
8	George E.T. Eyston			MG Magnette 1,086cc
9	Walter L.Handley		G.E.T. Eyston	MG Magnette 1,086cc
10	Charlie J.P. Dodson		G.E.T. Eyston	MG Magnette 1,086cc
11	Roy Eccles			MG Magnette 1,086cc
12	Charlie E.C. Martin		Roy Eccles	MG Magnette 1,086cc
15	W.G. "Bill" Everitt			MG Midget 746cc
16	Hon. Brian Lewis		A.W. Fox	Singer 1,493cc

No.	Driver	Reserve Driver	Entrant	Car
18	Victor Gillow			Riley 1,086cc
19	Pat Fairfield		Freddie Dixon	Riley 1,089cc
20	Freddie Dixon			Riley 1,486cc
21	Cyril Paul		Freddie Dixon	Riley 1,486cc
22	Norman Black			MG Magnette 1,086cc
24	Ron Gibson		Norman Black	MG Magnette 1,086cc
25	W.R. "Bobby" Baird			Riley 1,088cc

1934 INTERNATIONAL MANNIN MOAR RACE START LIST

Friday 1st June 1934. Start 10.00am. 50 laps of 3.658 miles circuit, total distance 182.9 miles.
10 starters – 3 finishers.

No.	Driver	Reserve Driver	Entrant	Car
1	T.A.S.O. Mathieson			Bugatti 2,300cc
2	Tim Rose-Richards			Bugatti 2,300cc
3	A.H. Lindsay Eccles			Bugatti 2,300cc
4	Hon. Brian Lewis		N. Rees and A.W.Fox	Alfa Romeo 2,655cc
7	Freddie Dixon			Riley 1,808cc
8	Cyril Paul		Freddie Dixon	Riley 1,808cc
9	Charlie Dodson			Alfa Romeo 2,336cc
10	A.P. Hamilton			Alfa Romeo 2,336cc
11	Richard O. Shuttleworth			Bugatti 2,296cc
12	Vasco Sameiro		E.F.Abecassis	Alfa Romeo 2,336cc

1935 INTERNATIONAL MANNIN BEG RACE START LIST

Wednesday 29th May 1935. Start10.00am.50 laps of 4.035 miles circuit, total distance 201.75 miles.
13 starters – 2 finishers.

No.	Driver	Reserve Driver	Entrant	Car
1	Alfred C. Lace			Alta 1,074cc
2	D. Tennant	Lord Avebury	A.C. Lace	Alta 1,074cc
6	T.K. Humber			Bugatti 1,496cc
8	Raymond Mays		H. W. Cook	E.R.A. 1,090cc
9	Pat Fairfield			E.R.A. 1,090cc
11	Eddie R. Hall			MG Magnette 1,087cc
12	J. Ludovic Ford	Maurice H. Baumer		MG Magnette 1,087cc
14	G.F.Manby-Colegrave			MG Magnette 1,087cc
16	George E.T. Eyston			MG Midget 746cc
17	Walter L. Handley		G.E.T. Eyston	MG Midget 746cc
18	Norman Black		G.E.T. Eyston	MG Midget 746cc
19	W.R. "Bobby"Baird			MG Midget 746cc
20	Freddie Dixon			Riley 1,486cc

1935 INTERNATIONAL MANNIN MOAR RACE START LIST

Friday 31st May 1935. Start10.00am.50 laps of 4.035 miles circuit, total distance 201.75 miles.
14 starters – 4 finishers.

No.	Driver	Reserve Driver	Entrant	Car
1	A.P. Hamilton			Alfa Romeo 2,336cc
2	R.S. Wilkins			Alfa Romeo 2,600cc
3	Richard O. Shuttleworth			Alfa Romeo 2,904cc

4	Austin Dobson	A.C. Dobson		Alfa Romeo 2,600cc
5	Luis Fontes			Alfa Romeo 2,336cc
6	Tim Rose-Richards			Maserati 2,992cc
7	Hon. Brian Lewis		Earl Howe & N. Rees	Bugatti 3,300cc
8	Hon. Jock Leith			Bugatti 2,263cc
9	A.H. Lindsay Eccles			Bugatti 3,255cc
10	Charlie E.C.Martin			Bugatti 3,255cc
11	Charles Brackenbury		C.E.C. Martin	Bugatti 2,263cc
14	Humphrey W. Cook			E.R.A. 1,488cc
15	Raymond Mays		H.W. Cook	E.R.A. 1,980cc
16	E.K.Rayson			Bugatti 1,990cc

1936 RAC INTERNATIONAL LIGHT CAR RACE START LIST

Thursday 28th May 1936. Start 2.00pm. 50 laps of 4 miles circuit, total distance 200 miles.
19 starters – 6 finishers.

No.	Driver	Reserve Driver	Entrant	Car
3	A.J Cormack			Alta 1,496cc
4	J.P. Wakefield			Alta 1,496cc
6	Charlie J.P. Dodson	H.L. Hadley	Sir Herbert Austin	Austin 744cc
8	T.K. Humber			Bugatti 1,496cc
9	Richard Seaman			Delage 1,460cc
10	Pat Fairfield		A.C. Dobson	E.R.A. 1,486cc
11	Cyril Paul		A.C. Dobson	E.R.A. 1,486cc
12	W.G. "Bill" Everitt			E.R.A. 1,486cc
14	Raymond Mays		H.W. Cook	E.R.A. 1,488cc
15	Marcell Lehoux	H.W. Cook	H.W. Cook	E.R.A. 1,488cc
16	Lord Howe	H.W. Cook	H.W. Cook	E.R.A. 1,488cc
17	"B. Bira"			E.R.A. 1,488cc
18	Reggie Tongue			E.R.A. 1.488cc
20	G.F.A. Manby-Colegrave	R.E.L. Featherstonhaugh		E.R.A. 1,488cc
21	P.F. Jucker			Frazer Nash 1,496cc
22	E.K.Rayson			Maserati 1,496cc
24	L.R. Briggs			MG Magnette 1,087cc
25	H. Williams			MG Magnette 1,087cc
26	Roy H. Eccles			Rapier Special 1,084cc

1937 RAC INTERNATIONAL LIGHT CAR RACE START LIST

Thursday 3rd June 1937. Start 2.00pm. 50 laps of 3.9 miles circuit, total distance 195 miles.
15 starters – 12 finishers.

No.	Driver	Reserve Driver	Entrant	Car
4	Arthur Dobson			E.R.A. 1,486cc
5	"B. Bira"		H.R.H. Prince Chula of Siam	E.R.A. 1,488cc
6	Ian P. Connell			E.R.A. 1,488cc
7	Raymond Mays		H.W. Cook	E.R.A. 1,488cc
9	Pat Fairfield		H.W. Cook	E.R.A. 1,488cc
10	Reggie Tongue			E.R.A. 1,488cc
11	Peter Whitehead	Peter Walker	P.N. Whitehead	E.R.A. 1,488cc
14	Robin Hanson		Mrs. M.F. Hall-Smith	Maserati 1,490cc
15	John Du Puy			Maserati 1,490cc

No.	Driver	Reserve Driver	Entrant	Car
16	E. de Graffenried		John du Puy	Maserati 1,496cc
18	Austin Dobson		Hon. P. Aitken	Maserati 1,500cc
19	Luigi Villoresi		Count Lurani	Maserati 1,500cc
20	Reg Parnell			MG Magnette 1,486cc
21	W.Hughes			MG Magnette 1,087cc
22	Peter Maclure			Riley 1,487cc

1947 MANX CUP RACE START LIST

Thursday 21st August 1947. Start 2.00pm. 12 laps of 3.3789 miles circuit, total distance 46.55 miles. 18 starters – 12 finishers.

No.	Driver	Entrant	Car
3	Eric Winterbottom		Emeryson
7	W. Robert "Bobby" Baird		MG
11	Hector Graham & D.H. Kyle	Hector Graham	MG
15	Frank W. Kennington		MG
17	Ian H. Nickols		MG
23	John Panks		Alvis
25	G.E. "Geoff" Ansell		Aston Martin
31	Sheila Darbishire & Edward G. Pool	E.G. Pool	Bugatti
33	Anthony "Tony" Crook		Frazer Nash B.M.W
35	Hugh M.F. Carrington		Frazer Nash B.M.W
39	Oscar Moore		Frazer Nash B.M.W
41	Gilbert Tyrer		Frazer Nash B.M.W
43	Peter C.T. Clark		H.R.G.
45	Jack Scott	Peter C.T. Clark	H.R.G.
47	A.C. Molyneux	Peter C.T. Clark	H.R.G.
49	T.C. "Cuth" Harrison		Riley
53	Francis N. Penn	S.B. Reece	Riley
55	"B. Bira"	White Mouse Stable for Equipe Simca Gordini	Simca

1947 BRITISH EMPIRE TROPHY RACE START LIST

Thursday 21st August 1947. Start 3.00pm.40 laps of 3.8789 miles circuit, total distance 155.16 miles. 15 starters – 9 finishers.

No.	Driver	Entrant	Car
2	Geoff. Crossley		Alta
10	David A. Hampshire		Challenger
12	Capt. Barry Woodall		Delage
14	George E. Abecassis		E.R.A.
16	George H. Bainbridge Brian N. Shawe-Taylor	R. E. Ansell	E.R.A.
20	H. Leslie Brooke		E.R.A.
22	F. R. "Bob" Gerard		E.R.A.
24	T.C. "Cuth" Harrison		E.R.A.
32	Peter N. Whitehead		E.R.A.
34	"B. Bira"	White Mouse Stable	Maserati
36	Robert E. "Bob" Ansell		E.R.A.
38	Guy Jason-Henry	J.S. Gordon	Maserati
46	Sheila Darbishire	S.B. Reece	Riley
48	A.P.R. "Tony" Rolt		Alfa Romeo
50	Leslie Johnson		Darracq

1948 MANX CUP AND CASTLETOWN TROPHY RACES START LIST

Tuesday 25th May 1948. Start 2.00pm. Races run concurrently over 18 laps of 3.3789 miles circuit, total distance 69.82 miles. Manx Cup: 23 starters – 12 finishers, Castletown Trophy: 5 starters – 3 finishers.

No.	Driver	Entrant	Car
Manx Cup Race			
1	R. John W. Appleton		Appleton Special 1,089cc
7	D.A. Wilcocks		MG 747cc
9	Ted Lund		Lund Special 972cc
11	Basil de Mattos		MG 1,087cc
15	Hector Graham & D.H. Kyle	Hector Graham	MG 1,087cc
19	John Marshall	F.W. Kennington	MG 1,087cc
21	Ian H. Nickols		Parnell Special 1,087cc
25	Leslie G. Johnson & C.G.H. Dunham	C.G.H. Dunham	Alvis 1,844cc
27	John W. Rowley & H.I. Bond-Williams	H.I. Bond-Williams	Aston Martin 1,950cc
29	Ken Watkins		Frazer Nash B.M.W. 1,971cc
31	C. Derek F. Buckler		Buckler 1,228cc
35	Spike Rhiando		Cooper 996cc
37	Peter C.T. Clark		H.R.G. 1,496cc
39	Dudley Folland	Peter C.T. Clark	H.R.G. 1,496cc
41	E.W. "Bill" Holt	Peter C.T. Clark	H.R.G. 1,496cc
43	Jack Scott	Peter C.T. Clark	H.R.G. 1,496cc
45	George E. Phillips		MG 1,250cc
47	Maurice Monnier		Monnier Special 1,971cc
51	Francis N. Penn	S.B. Reece	Riley 1,986cc
53	T.C. "Cuth" Harrison		Riley 1,986cc
55	George Nixon		Riley 1,749cc
57	Horace J.C. Ripley & M.E.Matthias	H.J.C. Ripley	Riley 1,496cc
59	Gilbert Tyrer		Frazer Nash 1,971cc
Castletown Trophy Race			
60	R. Dennis Poore		Alfa Romeo 3,800cc
62	Roy F. Salvadori		Alfa Romeo 2,900cc
64	Noel Carr		Alta 1,998cc
66	Jack E.G. Fairman		Bugatti 1,955cc
70	Kenneth W. Bear		Bugatti 3,255cc

1948 BRITISH EMPIRE TROPHY RACE START LIST

Tuesday 25th May 1948. Start 4.00pm. 36 laps of 3.8789 miles circuit, total distance 139.64 miles. 21 starters – 9 finishers.

No.	Driver	Entrant	Car
2	George E. Abecassis		Alta 1,490cc
4	Gordon. M. Watson		Alta 1,490cc
6	Michael C. Chorlton		Bugatti 1,498cc
10	Geoff Ansell		E.R.A. 1,488cc
12	David A. Hampshire		E.R.A. 1,488cc
14	John V. Bolster	P.H. Bell	E.R.A. 1,488cc
16	H. Leslie Brooke		E.R.A. 1,488cc
20	F. R. "Bob" Gerard		E.R.A. 1,488cc
22	T.C. "Cuth" Harrison		E.R.A. 1,488cc
24	Leslie G. Johnson		E.R.A. 1,488cc
26	Raymond Mays		E.R.A. 1,488cc

No.	Driver	Entrant	Car
30	W.E. Wilkinson		E.R.A. 1,488cc
32	Peter D.C. Walker		E.R.A. 1,488cc
36	Duncan Hamilton	George E. Abecassis	Maserati 1,496cc
38	Robert E. "Bob" Ansell		Maserati 1,496cc
40	Reg Parnell		Maserati 1,496cc
42	Anthony Baring		Maserati 1,496cc
48	Roy F. Salvadori		Maserati 1,496cc
50	A.P.R. "Tony" Rolt		Alfa Romeo 3,442cc
52	Guy Jason-Henry	Selborne (Mayfair) Ltd.	Delahaye 3,557cc
54	R. "Bobby"Baird & Paul Emery	R. "Bobby" Baird	Emeryson 4,470cc

1949 MANX CUP RACE START LIST

Thursday 26th May 1949. Start 2.00pm. 18 laps of 3.3789 miles circuit, total distance 69.82 miles. 23 starters – 10 finishers.

No.	Driver	Entrant	Car
1	R.M. "Curly" Dryden		Cooper 496cc
3	John N. Cooper		Cooper 996cc
7	Stirling Moss		Cooper 996cc
11	Eric Winterbottom & V. Davison	Eric Winterbottom	Cooper 996cc
15	Basil de Lissa		MG 1,086cc
17	Ken Downing	George Nixon	Riley 1,749cc
19	Dudley Folland	J. Wyer Ltd.	Ferrari 1,995cc
21	Frank W. Kennington		Cisitalia 1,090cc
25	St. John Horsfall		Aston Martin 1,986cc
29	John Heath & George E. Abecassis	John Heath	H.W. Alta 1960cc
31	George E. Phillips		MG 1,086cc
35	Kenneth H.F. Rose & Gilbert Baird	K.H.F. Rose	R.D.L. 1,767cc
37	Joe Kelly		I.R.A. 1,726cc
39	R.W. "Dick" Jacobs		MG 1,087cc
41	Gordon S. Shillito	T.C. "Cuth" Harrison	Riley 1,986cc
43	Peter C.T. Clark & Jack Scott	Peter C.T. Clark	H.R.G. 1,496cc
45	G. Neville Gee		Riley 1,496cc
49	Jack E.G. Fairman		Riley 1,954cc
51	Ken Watkins		B.M.W. 1,971cc
53	Basil de Mattos	F.R.G. Spikins	Spikins Special 1,496cc
57	Ted Lund	N.S. Utley	Lund Special II 972cc
59	C.G.H.F. "Gerry" Dunham	C.G.H. Dunham	Alvis 1,844cc
61	Hugh Clapp		H.R.G. 1,047cc

1949 BRITISH EMPIRE TROPHY RACE START LIST

Thursday 26th May 1949. Start 4.10pm. 36 laps of 3.8789 miles circuit, total distance 139.64 miles. 16 starters – 13 finishers.

No.	Driver	Entrant	Car
2	George E. Abecassis & John Heath	G.E.Abecassis	Alta 1,490cc
4	Michael C. Chorlton & J. Boothby	M.C. Chorlton	Bugatti 1,498cc
6	St.John Horsfall	P.H. Bell	E.R.A. 1,488cc
8	George Nixon		E.R.A. 1,488cc
10	David A. Hampshire		E.R.A. 1,488cc
12	Geoff Ansell		E.R.A. 1,488cc
14	F. R. "Bob" Gerard		E.R.A. 1,488cc

16	T.C. "Cuth" Harrison		E.R.A. 1,488cc
20	Peter D.C. Walker		E.R.A. 1,488cc
24	David Murray		Maserati 1,496cc
28	Fred Ashmore	Scuderia Ambrosiana	Maserati 1,496cc
30	Reg Parnell	Scuderia Ambrosiana	Maserati 1,496cc
40	Geoffrey N. Richardson		R.R.A. 1,488cc
44	Guy Jason-Henry & A.P.R. "Tony" Rolt	R.R.C. Walker	Delahaye 3,600cc
48	Johnny Claes	Ecurie Belge	Talbot 4,480cc
50	A.P.R. "Tony" Rolt & Guy Jason-Henry	R.R.C. Walker	Alfa Romeo 3,440cc

1950 MANX CUP RACE START LIST

Thursday15th June 1950. Start 2.00pm. 18 laps of 3.3789 miles circuit, total distance 69.82 miles.
23 starters – 11 finishers.

No.	Driver	Entrant	Car
1	Robert "Bobby" Baird		MG 1,096cc
2	R.W. "Dick" Jacobs		MG 1,086cc
3	Basil de Lissa		MG 1,086cc
4	J.C.C. "Jim" Mayers	Harry Lester	Lester MG 1,474cc
5	Peter C.T. Clark & R. Lord	Peter C.T. Clark	H.R.G. 1,674cc
6	Hugh Clapp		H.R.G. 1,496cc
7	W.H. "Bill" Murray		H.R.G. 1,496cc
8	Norman R. Culpan		Frazer Nash 1,971cc
9	Gilbert Tyrer		Frazer Nash-B.M.W. 1,996cc
11	Tom M. Meyer		H.W.-Alta 1,961cc
12	Peter R. Bolton	J.H. Walton	H.W.-Alta 1,961cc
14	Oscar B. Moore		O.B.M. 1,971cc
15	C.G. H.F. "Gerry" Dunham	C.G.H. Dunham	Alvis 1,844cc
17	Michael A.H. Christie		Cooper 1,096cc
19	Hector Graham & D.H. Kyle	Hector Graham	Cooper 1,100cc
20	Spike Rhiando		Rhiando-Trimax 998cc
21	John N. Cooper	Cooper Car Co. Ltd.	Cooper 1,088cc
22	Ted Lund		Lea-Francis 1,670cc
23	Peter B. Reece		Riley 1,980cc
24	Gordon S. Shillito		Riley 1,988cc
25	Eric Brandon		Cooper 1,098cc
26	Joe Potts		Cooper 998cc
27	R.W. "Bill" Merrick		Cooper 1,097cc

1950 BRITISH EMPIRE TROPHY RACE START LIST

Thursday15th June 1950. Start 3.45 pm. 36 laps of 3.8789 miles circuit, total distance 139.64 miles.
13 starters – 7 finishers.

No.	Driver	Entrant	Car
1	F. R. "Bob" Gerard		E.R.A. 1,488cc
2	Reg Parnell	Scuderia Ambrosiana	Maserati 1,490cc
3	David A. Hampshire	Scuderia Ambrosiana	Maserati 1,490cc
4	David Murray	Scuderia Ambrosiana	Maserati 1,490cc
5	Baron de Graffenried		Maserati 1,490cc
6	"B.Bira"	Enrico Plate	Maserati 1,490cc
7	A.P.R. "Tony" Rolt	R.R.C. Walker	Delage 1,498cc
9	Gordon. M. Watson		Alta 1,491cc
11	A.Graham Whitehead		E.R.A. 1,488cc

No.	Driver	Entrant	Car
12	T.C. "Cuth" Harrison		E.R.A. 1,488cc
14	Colin Murray		Maserati 1,490cc
15	Brian N. Shawe-Taylor		E.R.A. 1,488cc
16	Joe Kelly		Maserati 1,490cc

1951 MANX CUP AND CASTLETOWN TROPHY RACES START LIST

Thursday 14th June 1951. Start 2.00pm. Races run concurrently over 18 laps of 3.3789 miles circuit, total distance 69.82 miles. Manx Cup: 14 starters – 8 finishers, Castletown Trophy: 4 starters – 2 finishers.

No.	Driver	Entrant	Car
Manx Cup Race			
1	C.G. H.F. "Gerry" Dunham	C.G.H. Dunham	Alvis 2,500cc
2	E.C.W. Stapleton		Aston Martin 1,984cc
4	W.S. "Bill Aston		Cooper 1,098cc
6	Eric Brandon	R.G. Brandon	Cooper 1,098cc
7	John D. Barber		Cooper 994cc
12	Tom M. Meyer		H.W.M. 1,960cc
14	Joe Kelly		I.R.A. 1,500cc
15	Gerry A. Ruddock	Peter C.T. Clark	H.R.G. 1,750cc
16	Peter J. Simpson	Tom H.Simpson	Healey 2,443cc
17	W.J. "Billy" Skelly & Ted Lund	W.J. Skelly	Lea Francis 1,670cc
18	Horace A. Richards		Riley 1,087cc
19	Gordon S. Shillito		Riley 1,988cc
20	R.W. "Dick" Jacobs		MG 1,087cc
21	John H. Webb & J.H. Turner	John H. Webb	Turner 1,087cc
Castletown Trophy Race			
24	David Murray		Maserati 1,490cc
25	Reg Parnell		Maserati 1,490cc
27	John V. Green		Maserati 1,490cc
29	Joe Ashmore		E.R.A. 1,488cc

1951 BRITISH EMPIRE TROPHY RACE START LIST

Thursday14th June 1951. Start 3.45 pm. 35 laps of 3.8789 miles circuit, total distance 135.76 miles. 26 starters – 13 finishers.

No.	Driver	Entrant	Car
Up to 1,500cc (4 credit laps)			
1	"Dave"		Dyna-Panhard 745cc
2	J.C.C."Jim" Mayers	H. Lester (Cars) Ltd.	Lester MG 1,467cc
3	Harry Lester & P.W.C. "Pat" Griffith	H. Lester (Cars) Ltd.	Lester MG 1,467cc
4	William H. Robinson		Jowett Jupiter 1,485cc
5	R.W. "Dick" Jacobs		MG 1,250cc
6	Ted Lund		MG 1,250cc
7	Mike J. Pople & M. Holt	M.J. Pople	MG 1,250cc
8	Trevor Line & M. Holt	J.T.K. Line	MG 1,250cc
9	Lionel Leonard		Cooper MG 1,250cc
10	J.G. "Jack" Reece		Cooper MG 1,250cc
Up to 3,000cc (1 credit lap)			
11	Ben Whitehouse		Aston Martin 1,970cc
12	George Abecassis	R.R.C. Walker	Aston Martin 2,580cc
16	Robin F. Peacock		Frazer Nash 1,971cc
17	Norman R. Culpan		Frazer Nash 1,971cc

18	David A. Clarke		Frazer Nash 1,971cc
19	Donald C. Pitt	E.J. Newton	Frazer Nash 1,971cc
20	W.H. "Bill" Murray		Frazer Nash 1,971cc
21	F. R. "Bob" Gerard		Frazer Nash 1,971cc
22	Stirling Moss	S.G. Greene	Frazer Nash 1,971cc
24	*S. Hill & G. Cooper	S. Hill	Healey 2,433cc
Over 3,000cc (scratch)			
25	Guy Gale or Peter D.C. Walker	R.R.C. Walker	Delahaye 3,557cc
26	Reg Parnell	Donald Healey	Nash Healey 3,848cc
29	Peter Scott Russell & D.F. Annable	D.F. Annable	Allard 3,917cc
30	Peter J. Collins		Allard 5,420cc
31	Sidney H.Allard		Allard 5,420cc
32	Frank G. Curtis		Allard 3,925cc

* Reserve entry

1952 BRITISH EMPIRE TROPHY RACE START LIST

Thursday29th May 1952. Start 2.30pm. 52 laps of 3.8789 miles circuit, total distance 201.70 miles. 27 starters – 13 finishers.

No.	Driver	Entrant	Car
Up to 1,500cc (4 credit laps)			
1	Mike R.G. Llewellyn		MG 1,250cc
2	Ted Lund		MG 1,250cc
3	J. Trevor.K. Line		MG 1,250cc
4	Peter Jackson		MG 1,250cc
5	Gerry A. Ruddock	The Monkey Stable	Lester MG 1,467cc
6	J.C.C."Jim" Mayers	The Monkey Stable	Lester MG 1,467cc
7	P.W.C. "Pat" Griffith	The Monkey Stable	Lester MG 1,467cc
8	Joe Kelly		
	Reserve: H. Sullivan	J. Kelly	Jowett Jupiter 1,486cc
11	W.J. "Billy" Skelly		Jowett Jupiter 1,486cc
12	William H. Robinson		Jowett Jupiter 1,486cc
14	F. C. "Cliff" Davis		Cooper MG 1,496cc
15	Lionel Leonard		Cooper MG 1,250cc
Up to 3,000cc (1 credit lap)			
20	Stirling Moss	S.G. Greene	Frazer Nash 1,971cc
21	J.M. "Mike" Hawthorn	L. Potter	Frazer Nash 1,971cc
	Reserve: Leonard Potter		
22	Roy Salvadori	T.A.D. "Tony" Crook	Frazer Nash 1,971cc
24	H.A. Mitchell		Frazer Nash 1,971cc
26	John Buncombe		Healey 2,433cc
27	Geoffrey E. "Geoff" Duke		Aston Martin 2,580cc
Over 3,000cc (scratch)			
30	E.W. "Bill" Holt	E.W. Holt	Jaguar XK120 3,442cc
	Reserve: A. G. Whitehead		
31	Stanley Boshier		Jaguar XK120 3,442cc
32	John B. Swift		Jaguar XK120 3,442cc
33	W. Belfrage Black		Jaguar XK120 3,442cc
34	Sir James Scott Douglas	Ecurie Ecosse	JaguarXK120 3,442cc
35	David Murray	Ecurie Ecosse	JaguarXK120 3,442cc
36	Ian Stewart	Ecurie Ecosse	JaguarXK120 3,442cc
37	J. Duncan Hamilton		Jaguar "C" type 3,442cc
38	Alfred P. Hitchings		Allard 5,420cc

1953 BRITISH EMPIRE TROPHY RACE START LISTS FOR HEATS

Thursday 18th June 1953. 3 heats over 8 laps of 3.8789 miles circuit, total distance 31.03 miles, starting at 1.55pm, 2.55pm and 3.50pm. Final over 16 laps of 3.8789 miles, total distance 62.06 miles. 28 starters in the Final, 11 finishers.

No.	Driver	Entrant	Car
Heat 1 – Up to 1,500cc. 14 starters, 10 finishers.			
1	J.C.C."Jim" Mayers	The Monkey Stable	Kieft 1,467cc
2	P.W.C. "Pat" Griffith	The Monkey Stable	Kieft 1,467cc
3	M.J.C. "Mike" Keen	The Monkey Stable	Kieft 1,467cc
4	H. John Goldschmidt		Performance Special 1,467cc
6	F. C. "Cliff" Davis		Cooper MG 1,467cc
8	Alfred P. Hitchings		Lester MG 1,467cc
9	Peter Jackson		Lester MG 1,467cc
10	Gerry A. Ruddock		Lester MG 1,467cc
11	E. John Haesendonck	T.W. Dargue	MG 1,467cc
12	Ernest Cooper Harewood		MG 1,467cc
14	Chris H. Threlfall		Tojeiro 1,467cc
15	Lionel Leonard		Leonard MG 1,467cc
16	Horace H. Gould		Cooper MG 1,467cc
17	Ted Lund		MG 1,466cc
Heat 2 – over 1,500cc and up to 2,600cc. 11 starters, 9 finishers.			
20	H.A. Mitchell & Peter Scott-Russell	H.A. Mitchell	Frazer Nash 1,971cc
21	Peter Kenneth		Frazer Nash 1,971cc
22	Ken Wharton		Frazer Nash 1,971cc
23	James Neilson		Frazer Nash 1,971cc
24	W. Belfrage Black		Frazer Nash 1,971cc
25	C.G.H.F. "Gerry" Dunham	S.G. Greene	Frazer Nash 1,971cc
28	R. Gray Mickel		Healey 2,443cc
31	John D. Barber		Cooper 1,976cc
32	Alan Brown	R.J. Chase	Cooper-Bristol 1,971cc
33	A.R. Huxley	M.C. Kearon	Connaught 1,767cc
35	Peter C. Gammon	Cliff Davis	Tojeiro 1,971cc
Heat 3 – over 2,600cc. 13 starters, 11 finishers.			
40	J. Desmond Titterington		Allard 3,917cc
41	Ken Watkins		Allard 5,420cc
42	Ken H. Downing		Aston Martin 2,922cc
43	R. "Bob" Dickson		Aston Martin 2,922cc
44	Reg Parnell	David Brown	Aston Martin 2,922cc
46	Hans Ruesch		Ferrari 4,100cc
49	Ian Stewart	Ecurie Ecosse	Jaguar "C" type 3,442cc
50	Ninian Sanderson	Ecurie Ecosse	Jaguar "C" type 3,442cc
51	Jimmy Stewart	Ecurie Ecosse	Jaguar "C" type 3,442cc
52	Stirling Moss	William Lyons	Jaguar "C" type 3,442cc
53	John B. Swift		Jaguar "C" type 3,442cc
54	David S. Boston		JaguarXK120 3,442cc
55	H.Kemp Place		JaguarXK120 3,442cc

1953 BRITISH EMPIRE TROPHY RACE START LIST FOR FINAL

Thursday 18th June 1953. Final over 16 laps of 3.8789 circuit, total distance 62.06 miles, start at 5.00 pm. 28 starters, 11 finishers. Handicap race starting in 3 groups from grid positions allocated in accordance with finishing order in respective heats.

No.	Driver	Entrant	Car
Group 1 – 3 minutes' start.			
2	P.W.C. "Pat" Griffith	The Monkey Stable	Kieft1 467cc
6	F. C. "Cliff" Davis		Cooper MG 1,467cc
8	Alfred P. Hitchings		Lester MG 1,467cc
9	Peter Jackson		Lester MG 1,467cc
11	E. John Haesendonck	T.W. Dargue	MG 1,467cc
12	Ernest Cooper Harewood		MG 1,467cc
14	Chris H. Threlfall		Tojeiro 1,467cc
15	Lionel Leonard		Leonard MG 1,467cc
17	Ted Lund		MG 1,466cc
Group 2 – 1 minute's start			
20	H.A. Mitchell & Peter Scott-Russell	H.A. Mitchell	Frazer Nash 1,971cc
21	Peter Kenneth		Frazer Nash 1,971cc
22	Ken Wharton		Frazer Nash 1,971cc
23	James Neilson		Frazer Nash 1,971cc
24	W. Belfrage Black		Frazer Nash 1,971cc
25	C.G.H.F. "Gerry" Dunham	S.G. Greene	Frazer Nash 1,971cc
28	R. Gray Mickel		Healey 2,443cc
31	John D. Barber		Cooper 1,976cc
32	Alan Brown	R.J. Chase	Cooper-Bristol 1,971cc
Group 3 - scratch			
40	J. Desmond Titterington		Allard 3,917cc
43	R. "Bob" Dickson		Aston Martin 2,922cc
44	Reg Parnell	David Brown	Aston Martin 2,922cc
46	Hans Ruesch		Ferrari 4,100cc
50	Ninian Sanderson	Ecurie Ecosse	Jaguar "C" type 3,442cc
51	Jimmy Stewart	Ecurie Ecosse	Jaguar "C" type 3,442cc
52	Stirling Moss	William Lyons	Jaguar "C" type 3,442cc
53	John B. Swift		Jaguar "C" type 3,442cc
54	David S. Boston		JaguarXK120 3,442cc
55	H.Kemp Place		JaguarXK120 3,442cc

DRIVERS' INDEX

Bold type denotes photographs.